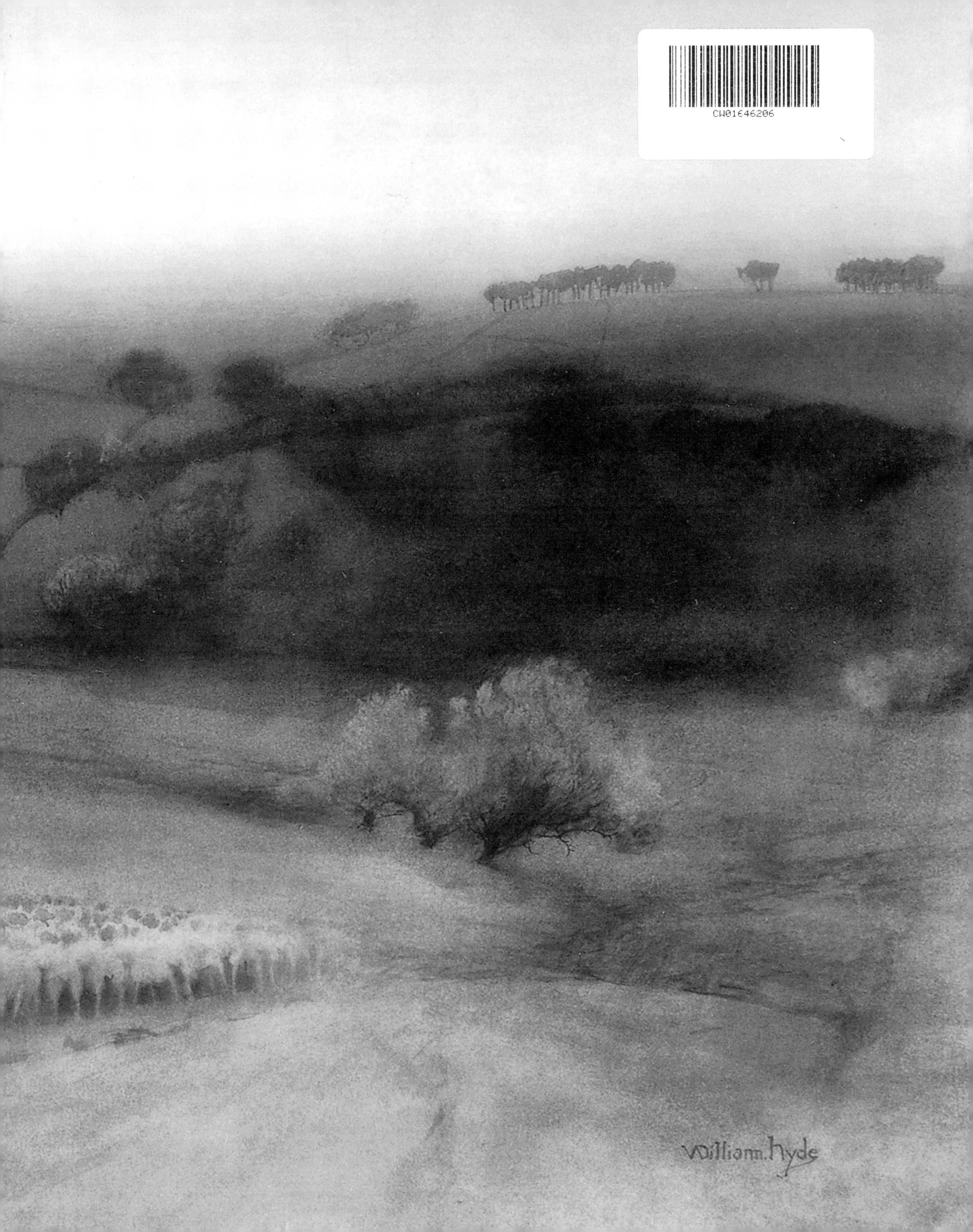
William Hyde

The Green Fuse

Pastoral Vision in English Art

1820-2000

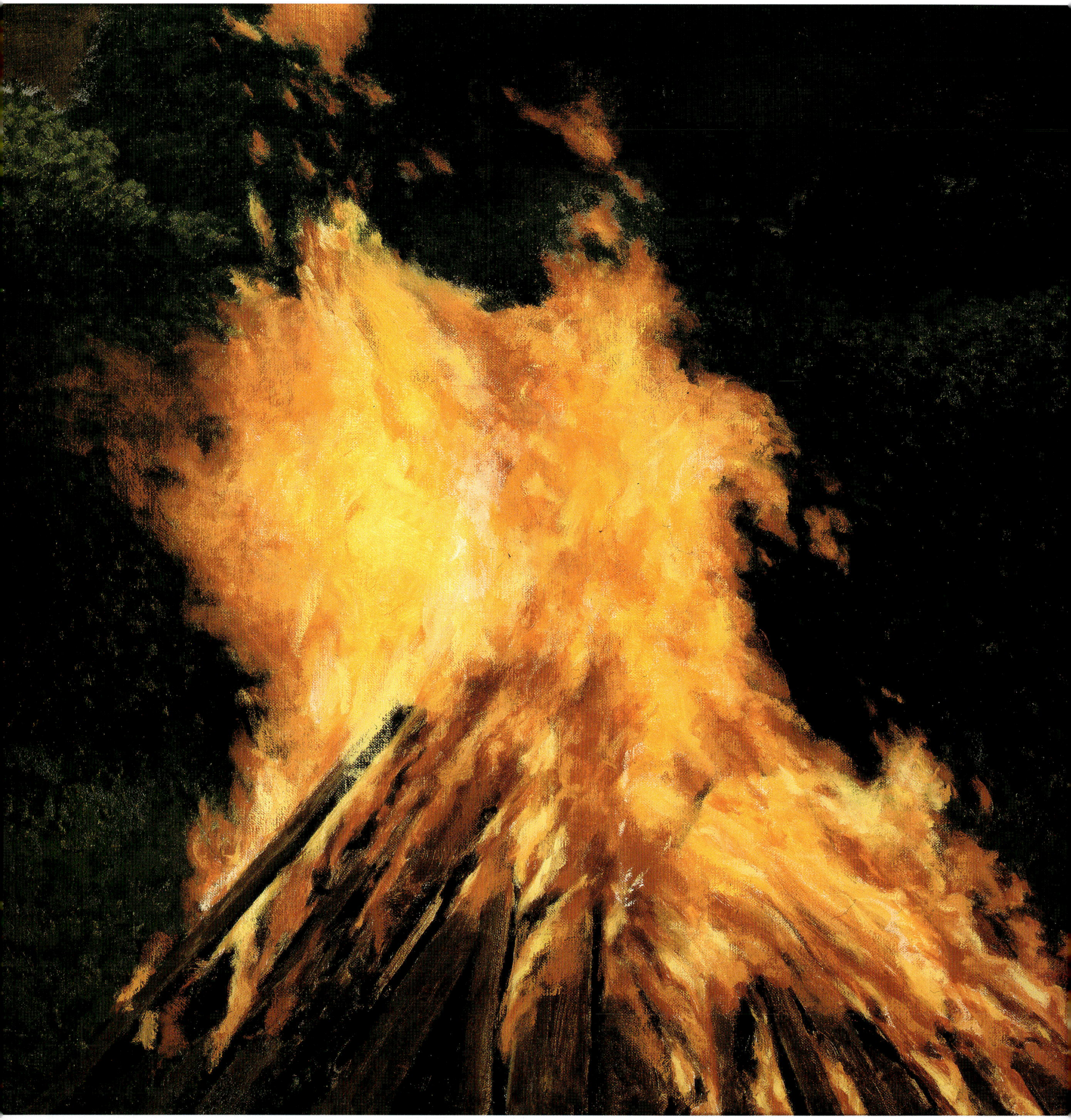

Above:
David Inshaw: *Bonfire,* 2000. Oil

Opposite:
Edward Gordon Craig: A pastoral poet, 1907. Wood engraving The Provost and Fellows of Eton College

The Green Fuse

Pastoral Vision in English Art 1820-2000

'The force that through the green fuse drives the flower
Drives my green age; that blasts the roots of trees is my destroyer.'
Dylan Thomas, *18 Poems* (1934)

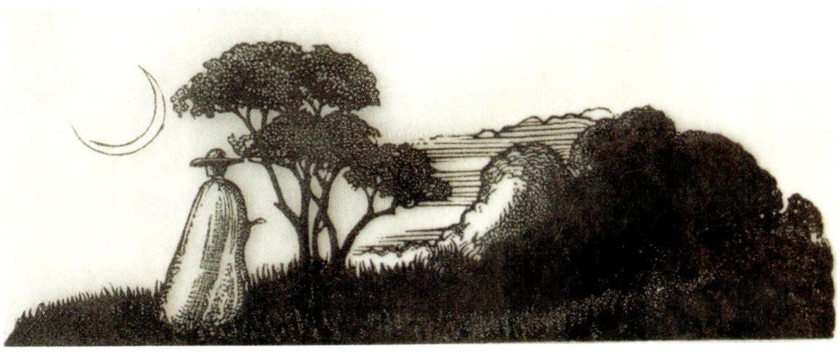

Jerrold Northrop Moore

Jerrold Northrop Moore
Cheltenham 9. x. 07

Antique Collectors' Club

ISBN-10: 1-85149-532-0
ISBN-13: 978-1-85149-532-0

British Library Cataloguing-in-Publication Data
A catalogue record for this book is available from the British Library

Printed in China
for the Antique Collectors' Club Ltd., Woodbridge, Suffolk

Contents

Acknowledgements and Dedication		6
Prologue		7
Epigraphs		7
Introduction		8
Chapter 1.	Samuel Palmer	20
Chapter 2.	William Hyde	74
Chapter 3.	F. L. Griggs	98
Chapter 4	Edward Gordon Craig	122
Chapter 5.	Paul Nash	140
Chapter 6.	Graham Sutherland	160
Chapter 7.	John Piper	178
Chapter 8.	John Minton and the Neo-Romantics	194
Chapter 9.	The Ruralists	210
Epilogue		251
Select Bibliography		252
Index		253

Acknowledgements and Dedication

This book has occupied nearly a decade – in drafting, writing, and pursuing emergent implications. To the extent that it draws on the experience of a lifetime, specific acknowledgements sometimes survey its outer bastions: some penetrate deeper. Yet all the people named below have given vital help. Without them the book would not have emerged in its present form – if it emerged at all.

For counsel through every degree of friendship over much of the writing, I thank Jonathan Cadman, Colin Harrison, Richard Osborne, David Haycock, Dr and Mrs Martin Butlin, Hilary Gerrish, Michael Campbell, Peyton Skipwith, Gordon Cooke, The Fine Art Society, Nial and Margaret Devitt, Sir Ian and Lady Wallace, Geoffrey and Margot Gilbert, and Michael Bennett/Fine Art Catalogues.

For the Palmer chapter: Graham Ovenden for creative and technical insights; David Linnell; Peter Nahum at the Leicester Galleries; the late Dr Raymond Lister, who read and commented helpfully on an early draft.

For the Hyde chapter: the late Joseph Cooper, Joan Hamilton, Mr and Mrs Eric Earle, Kenneth Chard, Barry Johnson, Nicholas and Frances McDowall, Christian Dettlaff at the Guildford House Gallery, Elizabeth Rich at Shere Museum, Messrs Archibald Constable Ltd, Cornell University Library (USA), Archibald Constable archives.

For the Griggs chapter: the artist's daughters Millicent Perron, Hilda Gray, Barbara van der Zee; Andrew McIntosh Patrick and his father, the late James McIntosh Patrick; Mrs P. Haines. Images © Estate of F. L. Griggs.

For the Craig chapter: Tom Craig, Michael Meredith, Nick Baker, the Provost and Fellows of Eton College. Images © Estate of Gordon Craig.

For the Paul Nash chapter: the late Audrey Withers, Prof Andrew Causey, Peter Nahum, Tate London, 2006. Images © Estate of Paul Nash; Tate, London 2006.

For the Sutherland chapter: Dr. Robert Karrer (Baer & Karrer, Zurich); The Lutterworth Press; Crane-Kalman Gallery. Images © Estate of Graham Sutherland.

For the Piper chapter: The Royal Collection, Windsor Castle; the artist's daughter Clarissa Lewis; and most especially Hugh Fowler-Wright. Images © Estate of John Piper.

For the Neo-Romantics chapter: John Craxton, Frances Spalding, the Royal College of Art. Images © Estates of the late artists; works of John Minton © Royal College of Art.

For the Ruralists chapter: the artists themselves, for generous interviews providing material for a first account of creative origins individual and collective; to Graham Ovenden especially for his skill at scanning. Images © the artists.

To the Museums and Galleries who conserve works herein credited to them. Should any due thanks have been omitted, a note to the publishers will secure acknowledgment in future editions.

Finally a few words of heartfelt thanks to my publishers. Diana Steel has assembled a team each of whom has comprehensive practical knowledge of the work entrusted, and provides most helpful answers and assistance: in particular Primrose Elliott for editing with a masterly light hand; Lynn Taylor, for realisation of all the layouts; Richard Weale, Tom Conway, and Stephen Mackinlay for fine scanning of many, many images; Mark Eastment for help with a maze of things; Pam Henderson for vital patient help with permissions and so much else; James Smith for his faith in the book and all that followed.

To all these I quote again the introductory words of Robert Louis Stevenson in his *Travels with a Donkey*:

> ... We are all travellers in what John Bunyan calls the wilderness of this world – all, too, travellers with a donkey; and the best that we find in our travels is an honest friend. He is a fortunate voyager who finds many. We travel, indeed, to find them. ...
>
> Every book is, in an intimate sense, a circular letter to the friends of him who writes it. ... The public is but a generous patron who defrays the postage. Yet though the letter is directed to all, we have an old and kindly custom of addressing it on the outside to one.'

Accordingly I inscribe this book to Andrew Neill, who through a friendship of thirty-five years has shown me so much of the best of England.

Jerrold Northrop Moore

Broadway, in Summer 2006

Prologue

This book traces for the first time a length of green heritage in English art. During the past two centuries especially, English artists have envisioned the pastoral mode. Their art uses landscapes of home – often quite specific localities – to shape vision.

The history begins with Samuel Palmer, who transplanted the act of vision from William Blake's heroic figures into the soil of English landscape art. Palmer's landscape vision was more influential than has yet been recognised. His tradition has enriched artists of every subsequent generation. One of them, Gordon Craig, is only now recognised as a pastoral visionary.

It is a history of constant challenge and renewing response – a continuing story of intensely private men and women seeking and finding materials and sustenance for their visions in the nature and climates of their country. The end of the book shows fresh renewal against internationalist odds.

In a country whose art has seldom been reckoned to show any continuity at all, this history may be definitive. It reveals English art drawing visionary nourishment – even as the writings of Shakespeare and the music of Elgar – from the land.

Epigraphs

'Nature never did betray
The heart that loved her... Therefore let the moon
Shine on thee in thy solitary walk;
And let the misty mountain-winds be free
To blow against thee: and, in after years...
Thy memory be as a dwelling place
For all sweet sounds and harmonies.'

Wordsworth, 'Tintern Abbey', 13 July 1798

'I respected and loved the English psyche, and the primacy there of the physical and moral nature over the intellectual. It is the safer order of things... Man was not made to understand the world, but to live in it.'

George Santayana, *Persons and Places* II, 40

'As art becomes more abstract, so the nuances of national distinction become more subtle and, consequently, more interesting to trace... But it requires a keener penetration to discover the essential spirit which seems to identify... the English spirit. ...

'A research of that kind has never, I believe, been seriously undertaken: for the simple reason that, in the plastic arts, an English genius has never been allowed. That it does exist... becomes obvious upon any study of the subject beyond surface appearances...

'English art has always shown particular tendencies which recur throughout its history:
a pronounced linear method in design...
a peculiar bright delicacy in choice of colours – somewhat cold but radiant and sharp in key;
a concentration in the practice of portraiture; as though everything must be a likeness rather than an equivalent; not only eligible persons and parts of the countryside, but the very dew, the light, the wind as it passed. ...

'There seems to exist, behind the frank expressions of portrait and scene, an imprisoned spirit... of the land; *genius loci* is indeed almost its conception. If its expression could be designated, I would say it is almost entirely lyrical.'

Paul Nash, 'Personal statement' for *Unit One* (1934)

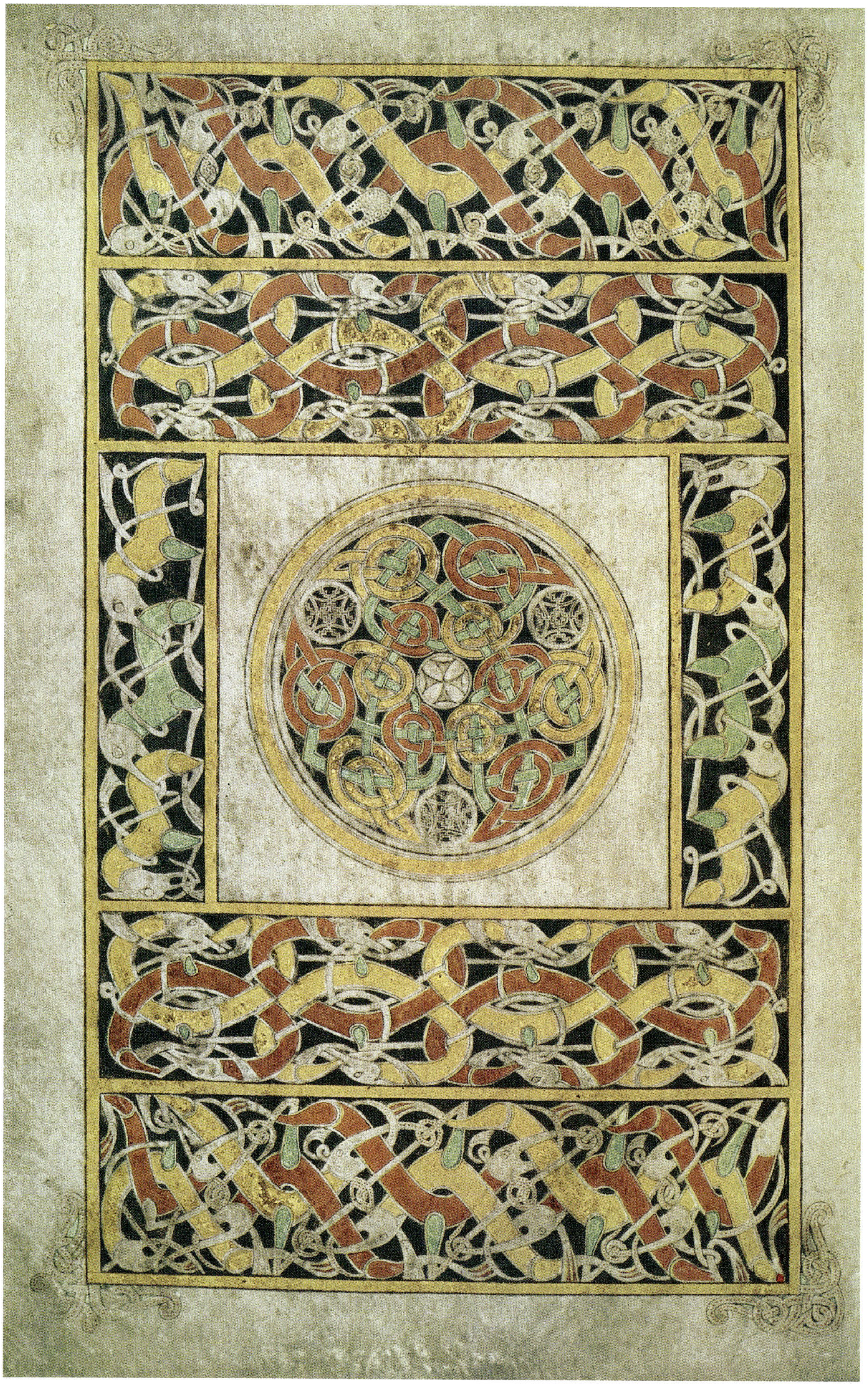

The first British landscape?
(see pages 10–11)

Plate 1. *Book of Durrow:* Gospels. Illuminated, perhaps Iona or Lindisfarne, *c.*650–675. fol. 192 v. The Board of Trinity College, Dublin

INTRODUCTION

The Landscape of English Art

England is a country of comfortable size. It is small enough to offer a unifying focus for its civilisation, yet large enough to hold a constant place in world affairs. From this paradox the country has drawn characteristic strengths.

England fills a major portion of the British island. Most of its boundaries are wide waters. So it has no border-quarrels (except where men have drawn internal boundaries). And the island kingdom, because an island, has a climate unique among powerful nations. It rains more than in many continental places; winds blow, and whole seasons can be damp. But the temperature seldom falls in winter or rises in summer to the discomforts encountered on the European land mass far from the sea.

The security of national borders and a steadier climate might seem to show English spirits more of nature's comforts than many of the European neighbours look for. The English have often seen themselves as fog-bound muddlers. Their national works, in this view, can take on the appearance of slow inevitability.[1]

The outlook is pragmatic – valuing facts of the here-and-now before many hypothetical notions of life hereafter. The pragmatic outlook has given English artists a vision of their own places to link to the inheritance of pastoral. Practically every English artist has produced some pastoral image or reference. But no continuous history of this green thread has yet been traced.

It has often been claimed that there is no continuity in English art – only the odd wood-note piped against successive invasions of foreign influence. In the seventeenth century, influence came from the Dutch inheritance of Flemish painting. In the eighteenth century, Italy renewed its Renaissance power through the popularity of the Grand Tour. At the turn of the nineteenth century, the compass needle did swing for a moment to England with Turner and Constable. Then it moved to the German provinces, whose revivalist Nazarene painters pointed a way for English Pre-Raphaelites.

The outside influences came mostly from small states. Each of them had been shaped, like England, by a sense of geographic identity, and was allied only loosely (if at all) to its neighbours. Then the loose confederations which had made Germany and Italy were shattered by the onslaughts of Napoleon. Napoleon launched his conquests from France – the ideal base, since France was the only large western European country already unified. The influence of France came inexorably forward.

France is both large and diverse. It is the only country in western Europe with territory on both sides of the mountain chain that divides north from south. A picture painted in one corner of France might meet with less understanding in other corners. Such disengagements could prove dangerous along France's many land-borders with other nations – borders traditionally guarded, worried over, maintained or expanded for the sake of the nation's identity.

Perhaps for these reasons France evolved as essentially absolutist. The thing to hold France together was just the abstract idea of France. Germany, after its unification in 1871, began to show the same traits. Italy followed. In response to the new absolutisms on her borders, France redoubled her own. These concentrations of size and mystic insistence on national identities opened the way towards the 'Great' European War of 1914-1918.

England, filling much of the British island, had remained somewhat outside the frame of continental nationalisms. The water that defined most English borders put those borders beyond dispute. The sea coasts made England more difficult to attack, more difficult to expand; and its remotely scattered Empire held no such explosive power.

1. Tom Fort, *Under the Weather: Us and the Elements* (Century, 2006), 8-14

From almost the dawn of recorded history, the national differences were there. One difference emerged in the contrasting developments of early Christianity in England and France following the conversion of the Roman Emperor Constantine in AD312. France remained with southern Europe attached to Roman Catholicism and its priests – needed for absolution from sins in this world, for the sake of another life to come.

In Britain, Christianity tended to follow the political patterns of Roman domination. Where Rome failed to establish lasting domination – in Ireland and the farther parts of Scotland and Wales – side by side with Christian incursions the old Celtic beliefs survived.

When Rome withdrew its imperial interest from Britain in 410, as if in response there appeared the first British man of whom any individual knowledge remains. He was the Christian monk Pelagius (*c*.360–*c*.420), born on the Welsh borders and educated probably in an early Christian school at Bangor in north-eastern Ireland. Pelagius went to Rome to challenge the Church's doctrine of original sin. He preached that man, made in God's image, remains individually able to choose his own good and evil in this life. It became known in Catholic Europe as 'the British heresy'.

Plate 2. *Cathach of St Columba:* Psalter. Illuminated, probably Ireland, *c*.625. Folio 48 recto

By permission of the Royal Irish Academy ©RIA

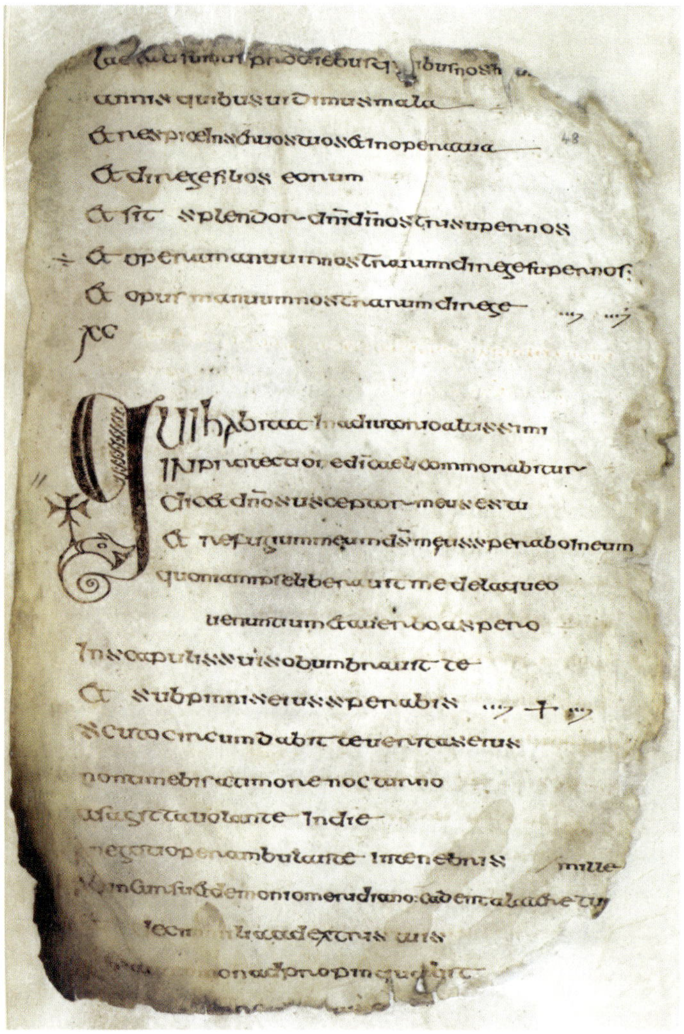

Almost two centuries after Pelagius, in 597 Pope Gregory the Great sent St Augustine to re-christianise Britain on Roman lines. Christianity was always the religion of the book: and St Augustine was described as wading ashore in Kent, holding before him an open book showing paintings of Christ and the Evangelists. The human figure had been constantly at the centre of classical and Mediterranean art, and it remained central to Roman Catholicism.

As if in reaction again, Christian monks in Ireland and Scotland began to fill their own books with very different figures. These derived from the old Celtic arts. They centred less on the human form than on vines and beasts.[2] Northern climates, cooler and cloudier than those of the south, had clearly imposed themselves on northern imaginations. Yet the Celts had been almost letterless: this paradoxic revival of their art in Christian books showed a remarkable power of survival.

Scottish and Irish book art was dominated from its beginning by vines, interlacing over and under each other to evoke depths. Such interlace had been used by worshippers of the old gods of earth and forest right across Europe. In Christian books of the British islands, interlace was claimed as a symbol of Christ 'the true vine'. But these vines hinted at wildness closer to home.

The earliest known Insular manuscript to show any decoration is a Psalter known by the old Irish word Cathach ('battler'), written perhaps around 625 (Plate 2). The inside of a large initial Q is interlaced with vine-like twists repeating in parallel, but the Q's tail morphs from vegetable to a serpent's head. The snake was one of the symbols of Odin, father of pagan gods. In this early Christian manuscript, the snake's head is almost collared by a Greek cross above it.

Within half a century, interlace was dominating entire pages in the *Book of Durrow*. This was written by monks of Irish origin, perhaps at St Columba's monastery on the Scottish isle of Iona, or at Iona's missionary monastery on the Northumbrian island of Lindisfarne.[3] Interlace patterns, grandly enlarged, embellish the opening words of each Gospel text. These would be known as incipit-pages.

Each *Durrow* Gospel is also announced with a separate frontispiece page of pure interlace. Its wholly linear impulse is a world away from contemporaneous Mediterranean painted illustrations of humans in stories. The *Book*

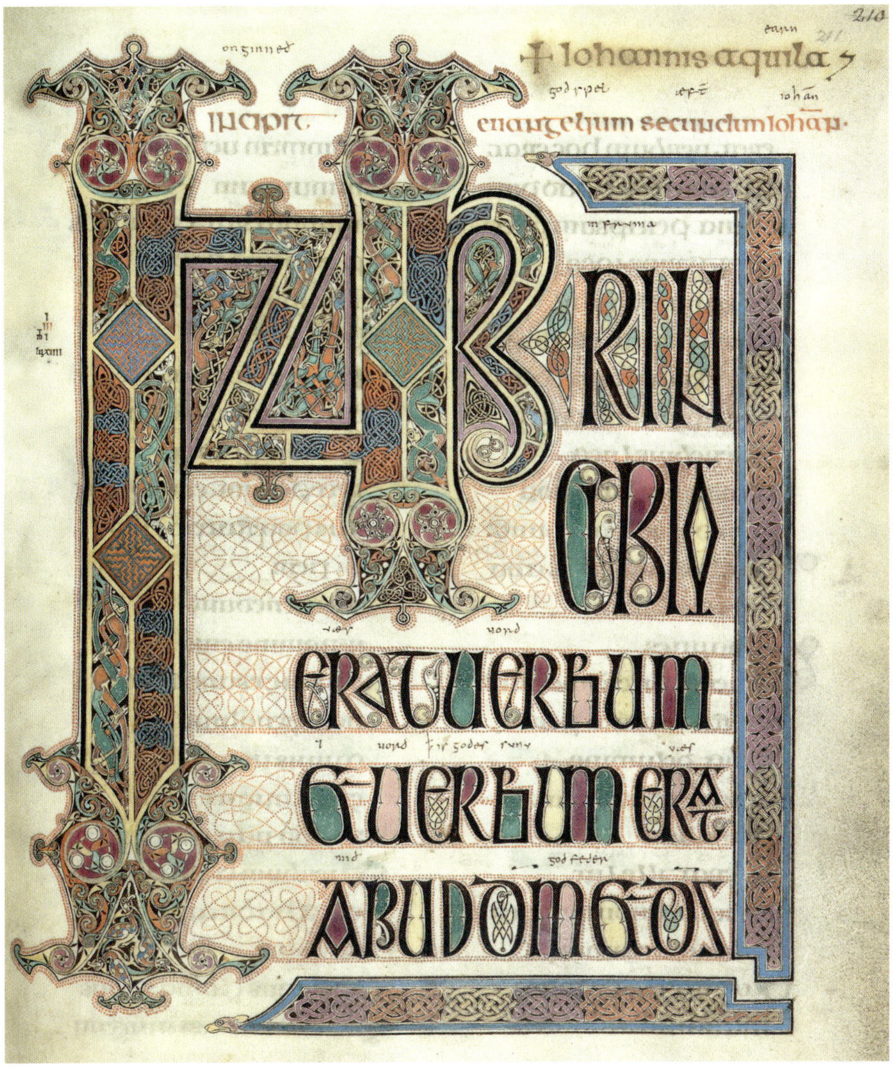

Plate 3. *Lindisfarne Gospels.* Illuminated, Lindisfarne, *c.*698. fol. 211 r.

Permission British Library
(shelfmark Cotton Nero D.IV fol. 211)

of Durrow shows a single human figure facing the reader from its own page. Elsewhere linearity takes the vines to new complexities.

The *Durrow* interlace fattens to suggest the bodies of snakes. In the frontispiece to St John's Gospel the snakes appear (Plate 1, page 8). Twisting red and yellow through thin vines and their own thick lengths, these snakes are headed with eyes and beaks of carrion birds. The beaked serpents bite each other through deep double borders top and bottom, to fill more than half their page. In single borders left and right, the beaked heads attach to boar-like beasts, each biting the vitals of him in front. All these creatures are symbols of Odin.[4] Yet the implications today appear almost proto-Darwinian.

Here is an opening page of British art – the earliest expression of its landscape. In a tiny circle at the centre stands a small Greek cross: Christianity a small presence amid ravening nature. (Landscapes of moor and mere, haunting Insular Christianity in the next century, forged a beginning for English literature in *Beowulf*.)

Perhaps fifty years after the *Book of Durrow*, in the late seventh or early eighth century, the Northumbrian island monks produced the *Lindisfarne Gospels* (Plate 3). Here the decoration pulls opposite ways. Interlace of the most complex refinement fills large frontispieces with whole-page crosses. Yet the *Lindisfarne* incipit-pages show their late classical uncial letters lengthening towards the magic rods of northern runes. Meanwhile, St John's opening 'In principio' reveals a new presence in the interlace: between the 'principio' second i and p, the decoration generates a human face in profile. Each *Lindisfarne* Gospel-opening is also marked by a whole-page 'portrait' of its Evangelist author, modelled on painted figures in Mediterranean books. But they make no difference to the persistent interlace.

2. Venceslas Kruta, *Celts* (Hachette Illustrated UK, 2004)

3. For evidence of *Durrow*'s Northumbrian production, see Walter Oakeshott, *The Sequence of English Medieval Art* (Faber, 1950), 8-12, Appendix I.

4. Lloyd and Jennifer Laing, *Early English Art and Architecture* (Stroud, Glos.: Sutton, 1996), 28.

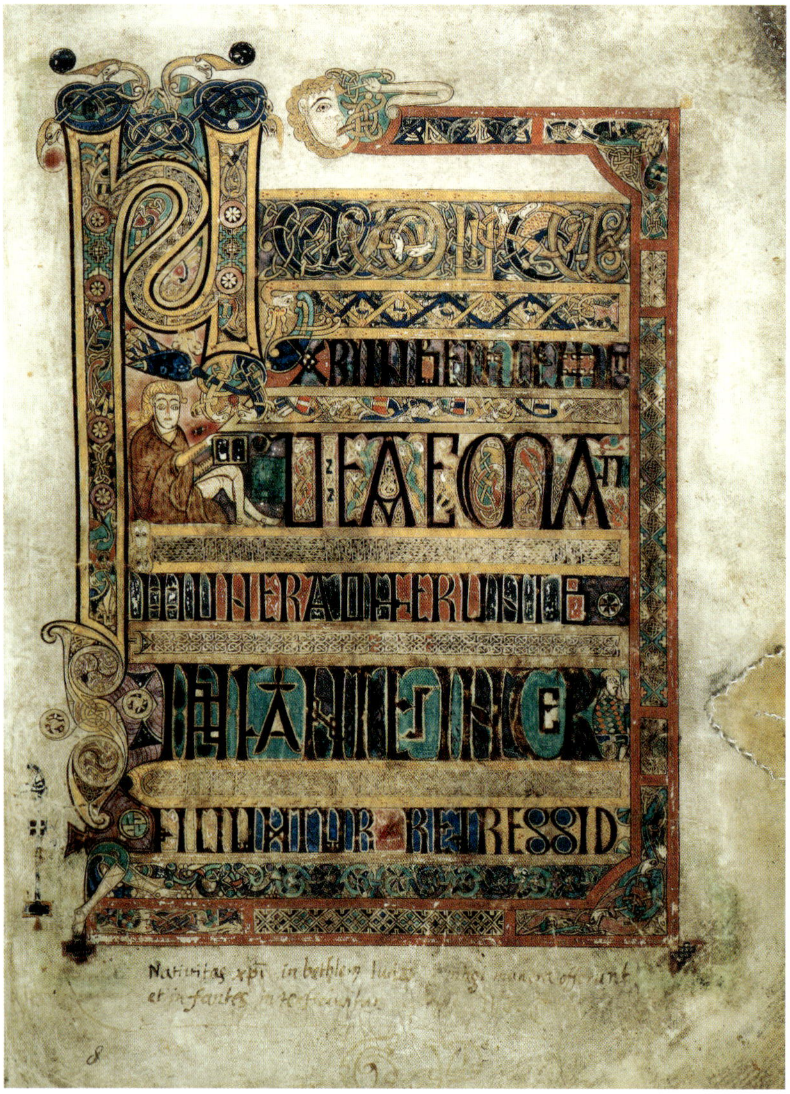

Plate 4. *Book of Kells:* Gospels. Illuminated, perhaps Iona, *c.*800. fol. 8 r.
The Board of Trinity College, Dublin

A century after the *Lindisfarne Gospels*, Insular art found its climax in the *Book of Kells* (perhaps largely written and decorated at Iona, before the book was taken to Ireland[5]). Odd individual pages are dominated by formalised human figures: two illustrations of actions and five frontal 'portraits'. Even a pagan Green Man appears, now as a figure of fun, atop one text incipit-page (Plate 4). Still the profuse *Kells* decoration is pervaded by interlace. It twines through a new welter of bird, animal, and human life – as through entire lines of Gospel text.

The interlace of Northumbria and Iona for a time spread south, to frame Romanesque and Carolingian human figures in illuminations made at Canterbury and Winchester. In purer form interlace spread eastwards across northern Europe. Monasteries in France, at Bobbio in northern Italy, in the Netherlands, Luxembourg, Germany, Switzerland, and Austria all produced books illuminated with Insular interlace. It was to remain Britain's greatest influence on the art of continental Europe for a thousand years, until the day of Turner and Constable. The spirit of the land pervades this art in a way which had no real parallel in early Christian painting from the Mediterranean south.

The entwining of interlace with Christian words, as it shaped the *Book of Kells*, testified to a high civilisation sheltered within the monasteries of northern Britain. In such places in such times, it was too good to last. Vikings in serpent-boats raided Lindisfarne in 793. At Iona in 806 they killed sixty-eight monks. Many of the survivors fled to Ireland, taking refuge at Kells – which gave its name to the great book they had perhaps brought with them. (The *Book of Durrow* may have gained its Irish name in a similar way, though the Irish themselves later produced interlace books of great quality.)

The Vikings adapted interlace to their own arts. Their influence was heaviest across the water when they raided the Frankish descendants of Charlemagne. To save Paris, the Franks were forced in the early tenth century to cede to the Norsemen the whole of their north-west province – which thenceforth became Normandy. And thus the Norman conquest of England – still using serpent-boats a century and a half later – was essentially the last and most successful Viking raid. French influence followed in the spread of great cathedral and monastery churches throughout England.

Less than a century after the Norman Conquest, architecture produced its own hint of earthly nature. The old Romanesque arch had juxtaposed straight line with half-circle. But then in twelfth-century northern France, line and circle-section were combined to shape an ever increasing curve – approaching much closer to the forms of nature. This new 'gothic' arch cast its influence wide and deep in England.

In the late 1530s Henry VIII (still wearing, in at least one portrait, the ancient interlace decoration) made the English Church independent of Rome. Through ensuing centuries of 'Renaissance' and classical revival, Gothic never wholly disappeared from English building. It persisted mostly in country and vernacular structures. They provided a spring for the 'Gothick Revival' in the eighteenth century. Two or three generations later, images of architectural relics of the old faith started boyhood dreams in the first visionary of this book.

Samuel Palmer (1805-1881) was being raised on a different side of English 'dissent', as a Baptist. His family home was in south London. London was necessarily the centre of the state Church. Dissent, whether Baptist or Catholic, kept the air of the shires. So it was that Palmer's boyish attraction to the old faith's remains would open his path to pastoral art.

The Baptist faith had begun to define itself in the 1640s. In those years the English civil war was fought partly over a perceived threat to reimpose Roman religion on the nation. The reigning king was beheaded. Dictatorship followed.

Yet after a dozen years of Cromwell, the English reasserted the more comfortable side of their pragmatism: they returned loyalty to its old lines by restoring the monarchy. The restoration was celebrated in London with a maypole. There in city streets, rooting back to Druid worship of indigenous nature, was the English character: ready to celebrate the experience of this life, pragmatic with uncertainty of any other.

The Restoration of English monarchy left standing the new chapel of Baptist 'dissent'. It found a focus in John Bunyan's *Pilgrim's Progress* (1678). Bunyan's pilgrim dissents from much organised religion as an impediment to private vision. His 'Progress' is 'from this world to that which is to come'. Yet the dreamer gets only a single glimpse of the Celestial City at the end – after more than two hundred pages about this life.

The bad landscapes through which Bunyan's pilgrim passes are horrid but survivable. (Thus they anticipate the romantic taste for 'the Picturesque' a century later.) After the Slough of Despond, the Pilgrim enters the House of the Interpreter – who bids him go forward on his quest.

The book's penultimate setting, much more fully described than the final glimpse of the Celestial City, is on the Delectable Mountains. Here gardens and orchards and vineyards frame the pastoral dialogue of man with nature – of form with earthly content. On the Mountain top, the Pilgrim is welcomed by shepherds feeding their flocks. Here the Baptist faith finds roots in a pastoral tradition reaching back to antiquity.

Bunyan's shepherds offer the Pilgrim prospects both backward and forward. For these they lend a 'perspective glass'. The Pilgrim sings:

> Thus, by the Shepherds, secrets are reveal'd,
> Which from all other men are kept conceal'd.
> Come to the Shepherds, then, if you would see
> Things deep, things hid, and that mysterious be.

Here again, after more than a thousand years, is the Pelagian doctrine of perfectability in this life.

Pilgrim's Progress established itself as the quintessential English vision. For three centuries it has stood on English bookshelves next to the Bible itself. Directly or indirectly, it touched the formative years of every artist in this book.

A century after Bunyan, in the shadow of the Industrial Revolution, Dissent found a more radical voice in William Blake (1757-1827). Blake demanded man's release from every organisation of religion or politics. For him the only power worth having was the power to envision. In his quest for that, Blake came to regard nature as the Devil's work. 'Imagination', he wrote, 'has nothing to do with Memory.'[6] No pastoral visionary could ever think that. When Blake himself invoked the pastoral note, it was almost always in aid of childish innocence.

Thus the pendulum-swing away from Roman Catholicism had continued its arc to reach the notion of every man his own pastor – almost, with Blake, every man his own god. Again the English sought moderation. The majority kept their faith in the middle ground now clearly defined: the Church of England.

Anglican worship was seen at its most effective by the Spanish-American philosopher George Santayana, at a late Victorian evensong in Winchester College Chapel:

> From my corner I drank in the memorable spectacle, more memorable for being something usual and the crown of every school day. …
>
> That everything external was perfunctory rather helped something internal to become dominant. … These reticent prayers, with their diplomatic dignity and courtesy, leave it for the heart to say the last word.
>
> It is all make-believe, as sports are: but in both those dramatic exercises there is excellent

5. Recent opinions on the origins of the *Book of Kells* are summarised in Françoise Henry, *The Book of Kells* (Thames and Hudson, 1974), 149-150; and Bernard Meehan, *The Book of Kells* (Thames and Hudson, 1994), 10, 90-92.

6. Noting his own disagreement in his copy of Wordsworth's *Lyrical Ballads* (2nd ed., 1815). Quoted in Alexander Gilchrist, *Life of William Blake* [hereinafter cited as Gilchrist: 'Everyman' rev ed: Dent, 1945], 340.

> discipline, and the art of life is half learned when they have been practiced and outgrown.
> What has been learned is the right manner, the just sentiments. It remains to discover the real occasions and the real risks.[7]

More recently, it has been wittily suggested that the practical function of the Church of England is to prevent religion being taken too seriously. Go far enough beyond the bounds of reason, and religion can become a notorious disturber of the peace. The same might be said of the English monarchy as it has evolved, in relation to the other great disturber of the peace and prosperity, politics.

How smoothly the English Church and State can still work together was shown by two events of 2002, both meticulously organised over several days for huge numbers of people with no disruption whatever. At the Queen Mother's funeral, a BBC roving microphone reached one of thousands lining the cortège route, who observed: 'I feel we have had our country given back to us again.' A few weeks later at the Queen's Golden Jubilee, a television camera showed the entire Mall from Buckingham Palace to Admiralty Arch filled with more than a million people, all happy. Many waved the Union Jack, but still more the English Cross of St George. No other country of substantial freedom in the twenty-first century could show such total spontaneous loyalty to one ideal. Yet the ideal is so deeply rooted that few English men or women would care to reduce it to any simplification of deft words.

These moderating acknowledgements of the irrational, in the interest of earthly contentment, link to English cautions over other offers to transcend the present world. The arts can be used to shape forms and textures more insistent than those usually seen in nature. If looking at nature is usefully instructive, looking too closely at anything unnatural or supernatural might be the reverse – and thus calculated to sow dissatisfaction with the earthly lot.

Hence perhaps has grown up an element of English suspicion of arts other than literature. Pictorial art and music both touch the sensory organs. Writing is different. Its materials are words: and words are mostly quite arbitrary signs for the things they represent. That fact digs a mental ha-ha, to keep at distance the dangerous or distressing parts – things all too easy to bring up to the foreground in drawings and paintings of the objects themselves. Words are also, of course, of prime use for practical communication.

English pragmatism also influenced the choices of materials in the nation's pictorial art. Oil painting is most vivid – and therefore most likely to foment dangerous illusions. So painting may be less useful than drawing: for drawing, like words, can assist practicalities. In this spectrum, monochrome wash may be more English than coloured washes; and pale colours (reflecting home climates of light through much of the year) more English than brilliant ones. Watercolour painting, with its clearer element of drawing, could be safer than oils.

The special patrons of English oil painting from the Industrial Revolution were the new rich. They wanted size to cover the large walls of their newly built mansions – and brightly painted morals to justify them. The older aristocracy tried to ignore such vulgarity, preferring drawings by English artists (if need be), but paintings from abroad.

Portraits were the favoured exception. A portrait in oils can preserve the image of its subject beyond the life. Therein younger generations can learn useful hints of their heritage. Portrait artists have always earned good livings in England.[8] The requirement of a fair likeness in most portraiture tends to control any over-insistence on pure form and design.

The same is true in landscape art. Form and design are best lit by the recognisable climates of home. Here English literature came first. The soft rains of April opened Chaucer's *Canterbury Tales*. Shakespeare raised countless unforgettable images of earth and sky. The visionary innocence and nostalgia in these perceptions was then caught – still a century and a half before Wordsworth's 'Intimations' Ode – by Henry Vaughan:

Happy those early dayes, when I
Shin'd in my Angell-infancy! …
When on some *gilded Cloud* or *flowre*
My gazing soul would dwell an houre.
('The Retreate', from *Silex Scintillans*, 1650)

Thus English faith as well as art could find expression through home landscapes, ever renewing their seasons. The island light itself offers transfiguration. The visitor Santayana saw this:

> … With colour and aerial quality the English weather plays unending tricks; what you see once you may never see again, yet you may count on soon seeing something new and in some way lovely.

The actual lights of English nature, Santayana found, support even the painterly extremities of Turner:

> It is not true… that the aerial effects in Turner's landscapes are exaggerated and melodramatic. Nature in England (and elsewhere – for instance in Venice) is often like that, or even more emphatic; and the delicacy with which Turner preserves the special character and melody of the parts in the midst of that violent ensemble, shows a sincere love of nature and life and a devout imagination.[9]

In France, despite their own revolution and dictatorship, everything was different. The absolutism holding a large geographic diversity together had a profound effect on French pictorial art. There the politics – indeed the religion – of the national imperative began to pare away at every specific subject, to serve the demands of form. That insistence moved through Impressionism and Cubism towards an ideal of total abstraction from any subject but pure form. So the French paradox shaped French art: the greatest patriotism in the greatest revolution. To the barricades then.

The highest emotional force is generated by oil colours. Compared to oil paintings, the French tend to regard watercolours and drawings more as preparation than as ends in themselves. Literal accuracy is only a sketch for the ideal.

It comes to this difference: to emphasise the subject, as the English like to do – and so in some sense celebrate the world as it is; or, with the French, to emphasise form and design – suggesting a perfection beyond this life's experience. The latter is the Roman Catholic view of the world, the former is the 'Protestant' view. (Both those traditional names lend a primacy to Rome: yet the English outlook roots back at least to the Druids, before Christianity existed.)

Here is a fundamental difference of character, sprung from the contrasting geographies. So it has come about that many transplantings from French art into English soil sooner or later tended to wither. When the French saw that, they said that England lacked the soil and climate and genes for art.

There have been British critics, and some artists, ready to agree with the French. Pragmatism can invite self-criticism: and that trait has been especially prominent in English estimates of their own non-literary arts. Absolutist France would never countenance such betrayals of national ideals from within. Accordingly, French art and artists have flourished with smoother continuity than the English.

A century ago the English Quaker critic and minor artist Roger Fry conceived an extreme admiration for French formalism, particularly as practised by the post-impressionist Cézanne. The extremity of Fry's *obeisance* then led him to dismiss most English art. Ready agreement came from Fry's friends at Cambridge and in London's Bloomsbury district. Fry's 'Bloomsbury' became a powerful cell of mutual admiration and promotion. His proscriptions gained the ears of intellectuals and snobs in sufficient numbers to challenge and nearly obfuscate the English tradition.

7. Santayana, *Persons and Places* (New York: Charles Scribner's Sons, 1963), II, 65.

8. The English love of portraits can take many forms. One of the Ruralist painters (see Chapter 9) tells me that he found trouble in obtaining car insurance cover, despite a clean driving record, on the ground of his stated profession of 'artist'. A friendly agent advised him to change his job-description to 'portrait painter' (since he had painted the odd portrait). The insurance cover was instantly forthcoming.

9. Santayana, *Persons and Places:* III, 20; I, 235-236.

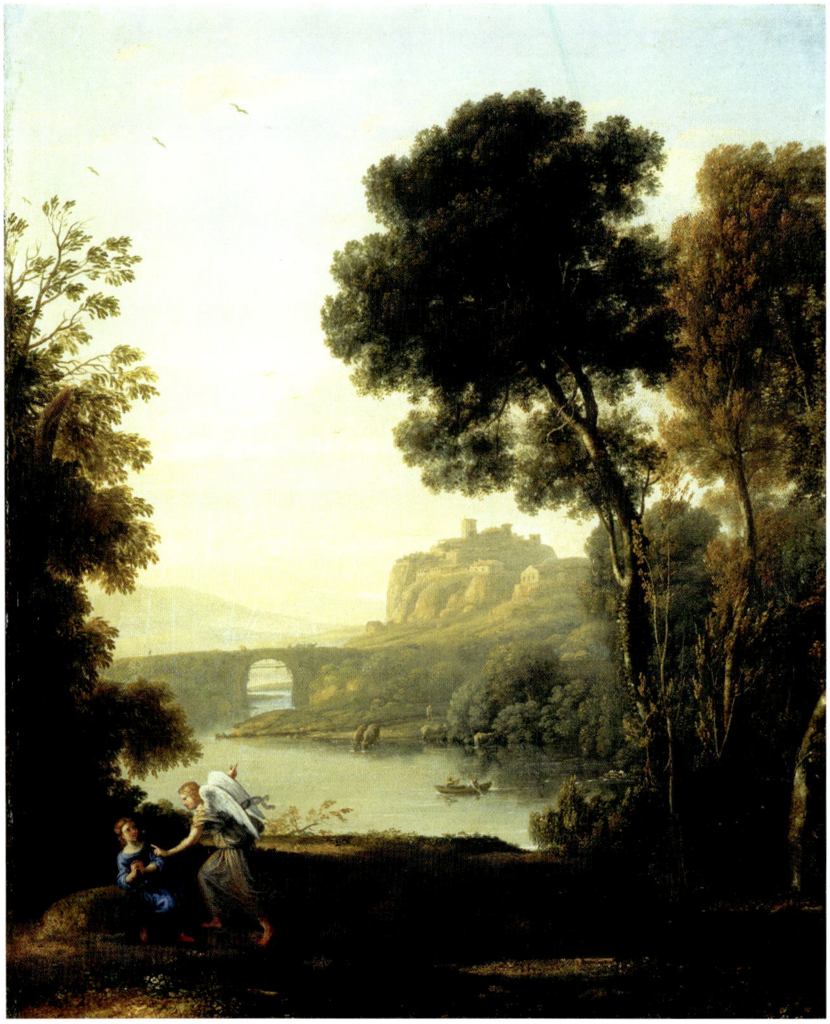

Plate 5. Claude Lorrain: *Landscape of Hagar and Angel,* 1646. Oil on canvas
© National Gallery, London

The English tradition, at its centre, is the envisioning of local land and light as an essence of character. This tradition differs from all later importations in its age and durability. Once brought from Flanders and the Italy of Claude Lorrain, it has rooted so deeply in England as to become a hardy perennial, self-renewing in each generation. This book seeks to connect, for the first time, defining points in its mature history.

⋆ ⋆ ⋆

If portraits and figures are about social things and human power structures, landscape painting is ultimately about solitude and self-forgetfulness. Landscape painting began in backgrounds behind human figures. In the early fourteenth century, such landscapes found new vividness about the Italian town of Siena. A century later landscapes appeared north of the Alps, in Germany and Flanders – with natural shapes clarified and colours often gilded in the lights of a lower sun. The northern intensities soon replanted their inspiration in Italy. But then Renaissance artists there solved the last problems of perspective; and the achievement was celebrated in Italian painting with perspective boxes drawn to replace the landscape function of enclosing figures.

Northern Europe, however, continued to develop its landscape tradition. In the last decade of the fifteenth century the German Albrecht Dürer drew the first pure landscapes, with few small figures or none. Within a few years Gérard David, in Bruges, painted a pure double landscape on the outer doors of an altarpiece whose inside showed the Nativity. So the forests of Flanders became the doors to vision.

Another source for English landscape painting came in the art of Claude Lorrain (1600-1682). Born near Flemish and German borders, Claude spent his mature life in Rome. But the transalpine artist did not paint the brilliant noonday lights so clear to native Italians. Instead, Claude's paintings sought the ambiguities of dawn, late afternoon and dusk – fugitive lights and atmospheres on the change. The humanised mythic figures which suggested Claude's titles receded through distances engulfed in romance (Plate 5).

Claude's paintings and drawings appealed as no others to English artists and collectors. Englishmen visiting Italy purchased so many Claudes that an actual preponderance of his work found its way to Britain. It seemed that Claude's art touched the English vision of their own misty island – perhaps the one vision their pragmatism allowed them.

Practically every British landscape artist of the eighteenth century referred his work to Claude. From the later eighteenth century, English artists were recommended to look at their landscape subjects through a 'Claude glass' – a darkening lens which 'gathers every scene reflected in it into a tiny picture and, by reducing the colours into a lower ratio, accentuates the tonal values'.[10] It offered to remake the 'perspective glass' lent by the Shepherds to aid the Pilgrim's prospects from the Delectable Mountains.

The Claude-glass vision suited the mood of later eighteenth century English art. The flush of enthusiasm which had greeted Burke's Essay on 'The Sublime' (1756) was giving way to reflection and analysis. What remained was an interest in 'the Picturesque'.

This moderating taste was named and framed by the Rev William Gilpin (1724-1804). A kindly, energetic Church of England vicar and headmaster, Gilpin had grown up in a family of amateur artists in Cumberland. From his parish in the south of England, Gilpin made summer excursions to places of greater landscape drama – the Wye Valley, the English Lakes, the Scottish Highlands. On each tour he kept a journal, illustrated with his own sketches.

Gilpin's writing explored the paradox of his generation. One part of him peered into romantic abysses. The other part went home to devise classical formulas and receipts for landscape ingredients to produce the romantic sentiments. It is easy to see this attempt to use academic means to secure romantic results as a muddle. But was Gilpin's search for mechanisms of the unconscious so different from Freud's search a century later?

Gilpin's illustrated Tours circulated in manuscript among influential friends. They all urged publication. So Gilpin revised his texts, and employed professional artists to convert his sketches to aquatint plates. The books proved so popular that new editions were called for every few years. As the plates wore, Gilpin had them redrawn – or substituted new subjects as his ideas clarified.

The words 'Picturesque Beauty' figured in every title. At first Gilpin was content to define 'Picturesque' as 'that kind of beauty which would look well in a picture'. But he was a clergyman: and that fact reshaped his ideas when he began to find that few actual landscapes were without some drawback or other. So he concluded that Nature, 'always great in design', could appear imperfect only to the limited purview of men:

> The case is, the immensity of nature is beyond human comprehension. She works on a *vast scale*: and, no doubt, harmoniously, if her scheme could be comprehended.[11]

And so, to suggest the greater perfection of nature, it became possible for Gilpin and his artists to alter certain details of what actually met their eyes in any one place. He instructed the artists not to aim at exact topography: there were already numbers of artists making what he called 'portraits' of 'picturesque' places. Gilpin's object was to use each of the views in his books as a sort of Claude glass to suggest nature's grander designs.

He set his artists limits as to what was permissible to alter. Anything man might move, or nature herself change overnight, that they might alter: move a tree, take away a cottage, shift slightly the line of a road or river to improve the 'design', even reshape a hill if not too large.[12] Still the general nature of a place must guide the picture. It was a new application of the English formula: accept the world as it is generally, but leave some little surrounding air for individual imagination and emotion to escape into (Plate 6).[13]

10. Christopher Hussey, *The Picturesque* (Putnam, 1927, rpr Frank Cass, 1967), 107. The Claude glass persisted in English art instruction as late as the 1950s: see below, Chapter 9, page 222.

11. *Observations on the River Wye, and several parts of South Wales, &c. relative to Picturesque Beauty made in the Summer of 1770* (R Blamire, 1782*ff*), 18.

12. *Observations, relative chiefly to Picturesque Beauty... in... the Mountains, and Lakes of Cumberland, and Westmoreland* (hereinafter cited as 'Tour of the Lakes') (3rd ed, Blamire, 1792, xxvii).

13. One early mark of Gilpin's influence was the use made of his Tours of the Wye and the Lakes by Wordsworth (1770-1850) in writing some of his earliest characteristic poems, notably 'An Evening Walk' and 'Tintern Abbey'. See Mary Jacobus, *Tradition and Experiment in Wordsworth's 'Lyrical Ballads'* (Oxford University Press, 1976), 110-111 n 2; Kenneth R. Johnston, *The Hidden Wordsworth* (Norton, 1998), 590-593; Mary Moorman, *William Wordsworth... The Early Years* (Oxford University Press, 1968), 116 n 1, 145, 402, 408.

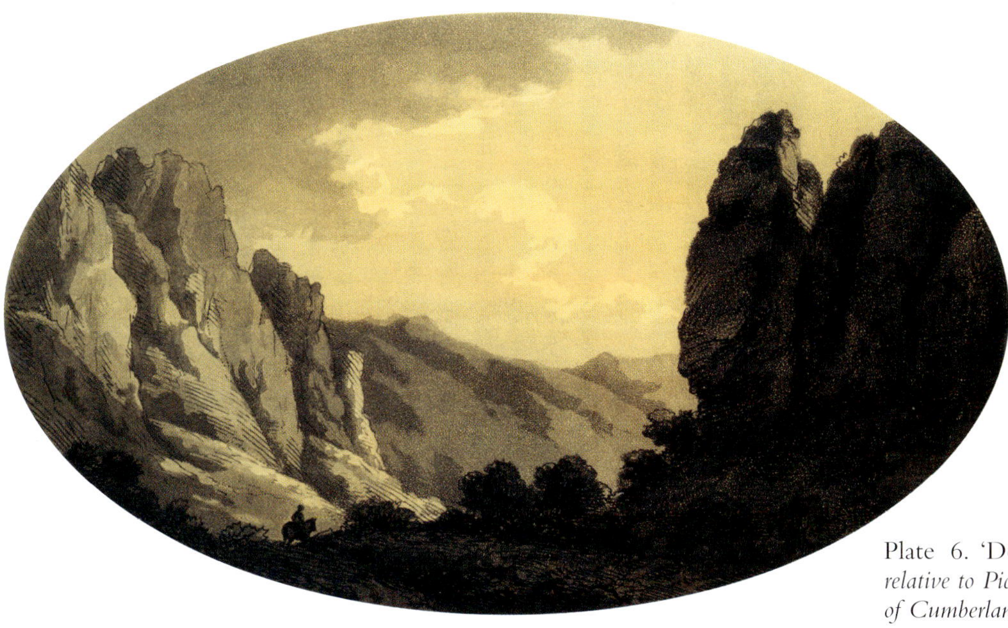

Plate 6. 'Dovedale'. Aquatint from Gilpin's *Observations relative to Picturesque Beauty... on... the Mountains and Lakes of Cumberland, and Westmoreland* (3rd ed., R. Blamire, 1792)

Gilpin's formulas did not extend anywhere so far as vision (unless to imply the hand of the Creator Himself). Yet by altering details so as to cater for human ideas of perfection, Gilpin's 'Picturesque' opened a door to further developments.

In the next generation, Gilpin's guidelines were converted into precepts for the physical altering of actual landscapes. The man who did this was 'Capability' Brown's follower Humphrey Repton (1752-1818). Repton invented the term 'landscape gardening', which often included new-built 'gothic ruins'. He practised his art in country house parks with great success.

Once 'the Picturesque' had been converted to actuality, it was time for imagination to make a further leap. It proved a giant one – made first, as so often in England, in literature. In the generation after Repton, Samuel Taylor Coleridge (1772-1834) pursued a landscape vision whose power would rise through the metaphor of human creativity. Already at twenty, in 1792, Coleridge had openly addressed

Imagination! Mistress of my Love!
Where shall mine Eye thy elfin haunt explore?

Six years later his answer came in 'Kubla Khan: or, A Vision in a Dream. Fragment.'

A prefatory prose note retails the vision's origin. It rose through the poet's opium-induced dream in a remote farmhouse on Exmoor. The dream's immediate source lay in his recent reading of an old book of exotic travels. *Purchas his Pilgrimage* (1626) had preceded Bunyan's *Pilgrim's Progress* by fifty years – but concentrated on ostensibly earthly places.

Coleridge's dream raised Kubla Khan's 'pleasure dome' with verse to evoke it in 'not less than from two to three hundred lines'. Waking he began to write them (drawing also on several further sources of recent reading). Coleridge's pleasure dome is surrounded with gardens and 'enfolding forests'; and the whole domain of ten miles' circumference is 'girdled round' with 'walls and towers'.

The pleasure dome's gardens and forests hold within them a 'deep romantic cavern'. It is 'a savage place', where 'a mighty fountain' of nature erupts with 'huge fragments' – which the poem's creative metaphor acutely compares to 'chaffy grain beneath the thresher's flail'. This volcanic energy feeds 'the sacred river' Alph (probably from the first letter in the Greek alphabet) flowing 'with mazy motion Through wood and dale' – until it reaches 'caverns measureless to man'. Only the tranquil middle is visible to human understanding:

It was a miracle of rare device
A sunny pleasure-dome with caves of ice!

At this point, thirty-odd lines into his creative landscape evocation, the poet was interrupted by 'a person on business from Porlock' (the nearest village), and detained for more than an hour. When at last he could return to his poem, he found that the lines still to be written had largely vanished. The interruption from Porlock stands for all the casual threats of daily things to creative vision.

In the circumstances, Coleridge could add only an *envoi* – addressed to a dark muse-figure singing to her dulcimer of 'Mount Abora'. What comes in her wake is a twisted echo of Milton's prayer 'At a Solemn Music' ('Oh, may we soon again renew that song, And keep in tune with Heaven'). Coleridge turns the other way – to claim his own creation, however fragmentary:

Could I revive within me
Her symphony and song,
To such a deep delight 'twould win me,
That with music loud and long,
I would build that dome in air,
That sunny dome! those caves of ice!

Then 'all who heard should see them there' – and would cry 'Beware!' of the artist:

> For he on honey-dew hath fed
> And drunk the milk of Paradise.

'Kubla Khan', risen out of shards of the Picturesque, opened a new prospect for vision seven years before the birth of Samuel Palmer. The chasm between Gilpin and Coleridge could be bridged with an inheritance known to every English schoolboy then. The 'pastoral' mode of expression originated in the keeping and keepers of sheep. Keeping sheep marks a stage in civilisation, since it affords a way to clothe the human body without killing. So 'pastoral' shows the land on one side, gentleness and generous care on the other.

The classical evocation of the shepherds' world had been greatly extended by writers from Virgil onwards. The most recent enlargements of it in English had been in the poetry of Milton (1608-1674), and then in *The Seasons* by the Scot James Thomson (1700-1748). All these poets and their works were in young Palmer's inheritance.

If Palmer's 'pastoral' was a common heritage, what did he understand of 'vision'? Perhaps his best definition of vision came in old age, as he recalled his young attraction to the art of Claude Lorrain:

> When I was setting out for Italy, I expected to see Claude's magical combinations. Miles apart I found the disjointed members, some of them most lovely, which he had suited to the desires of his mind. There were the beauties; but the Beautiful... was his own.

The parts of beauty – the means to it – are always more accessible than the whole version. Why is that whole vision so secret, so hard to reach? It may be owing to a quality we find nearly always involved in it – innocence. To recover that clarity, Coleridge had used drug and dream. Palmer used the sustaining vividness of remembered youth. He concluded:

> The sense of this ideal is so lost and forgotten by a materialistic age that Claude himself is considered rather as an accomplished master of aerial perspective – or what not – than as the genius, equally tender and sublime, who re-opened upon canvas the vistas of Eden.[14]

The vistas of Eden – innocence – reopened: the glimpsing of a lost whole, renewed (it may be) from still-familiar parts. Tenderness, then, linked to sublimity. This is, I think, a large part of 'vision' as the visionaries of English art have understood it.

Any idea of Eden, and innocence, inevitably carries the memory of its loss. So there gathers about innocence an atmosphere of retrospect. It is as if innocence is always in the past – a 'Golden Age'. Yet a drawing or etching or painting can bring it before our present eyes.

Palmer's art held a strong and continuing element of this paradox. It was brought to sharp focus a century later by the etcher F. L. Griggs (1876-1938), in the snow that covers the dissolving planes of his vast Gothic church in *The Almonry.* Not long after Griggs etched his *Almonry*, the young Graham Sutherland (1903-1980) wrote: 'I did not feel that my imagination was in conflict with the real, but that reality was a dispersed and disintegrated form of imagination.' Coleridge might have written that. The words reflect an English determination to keep some hold on the subject matter of this world, as the best material for an artist's journey.

14. Feb 1874 to P.G. Hamerton, in *The Letters of Samuel Palmer*, ed Raymond Lister (Oxford: Clarendon Press, 1974), 894.

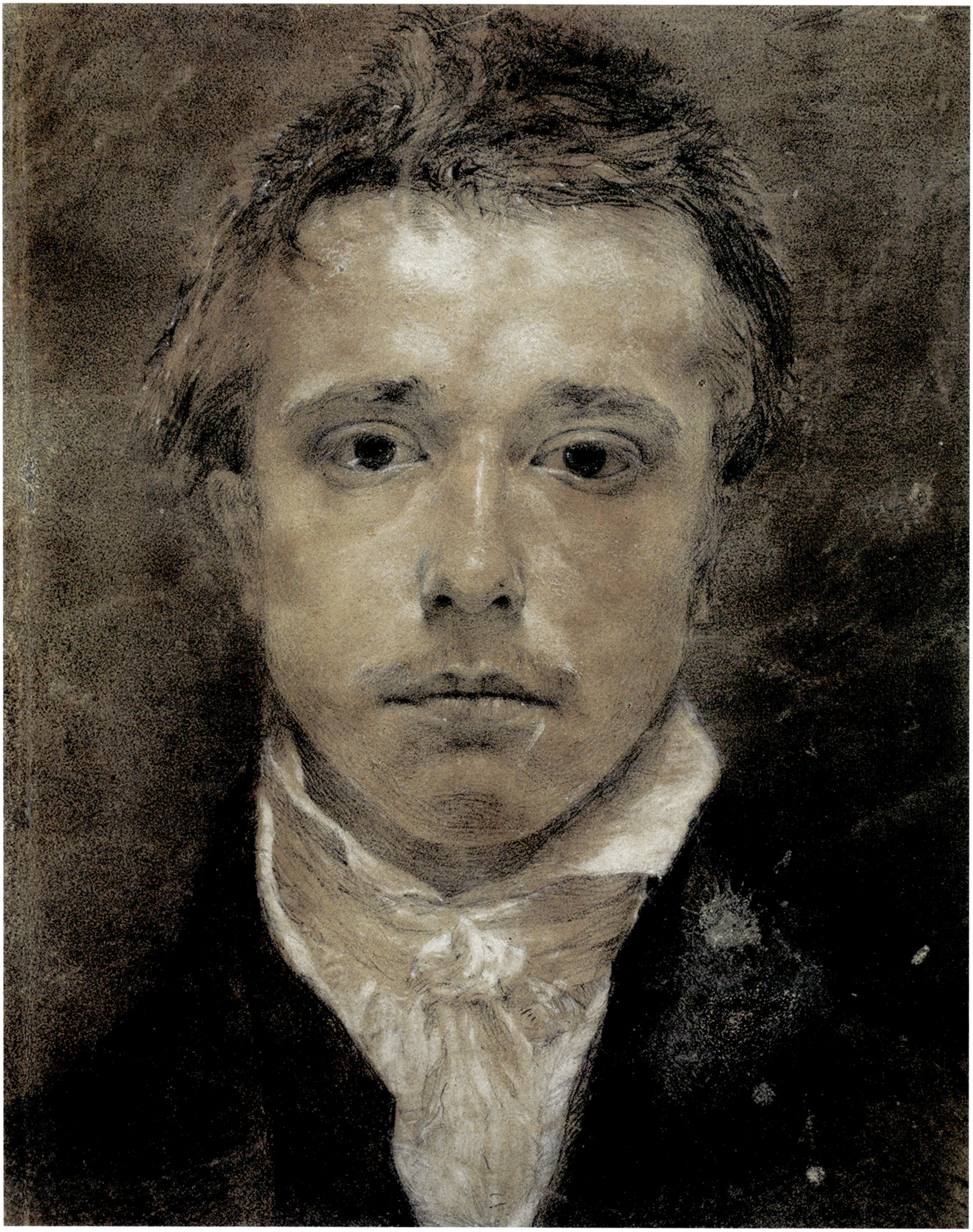

CHAPTER 1
Samuel Palmer (1805-1881)
'The force of local retrospection'

Opposite:
Plate 7. Self-portrait at about twenty years old, *c.*1825. Pencil, wash and chalk
Ashmolean Museum, Oxford

The word 'palmer' once designated 'a pilgrim wearing two crossed palms in token of having visited the Holy Land'. A cross of religious loyalties marked Samuel Palmer's family. His father's grandfather and great-grandfather had been Church of England vicars, but his mother's grandmother was immersed as a Baptist, and converted all her progeny. When her granddaughter Martha Giles came to marry, the husband Samuel Palmer (the elder) turned Baptist – but did not forget his Anglican heritage.

This family antithesis – of tradition *v* revelation – would be yoked by the younger Samuel Palmer to plough a field for his art. Like Bunyan's Pilgrim, the seed-bed he sought was some actual place – some field of earthly reality to root and fertilise his vision. He was later to describe what he was looking for as 'the force of local retrospection'.[1]

Palmer traced his 'first movement of poetic impulse' to a sight of shadows on a wall in his childhood home. It was a comfortable house in Surrey Square, off the Old Kent Road – now deep in south-east London, then on the borders of the country. Memory kept the picture of his child self there with his nurse Mary Ward, 'who, with little education else, was... deeply read in her Bible and *Paradise Lost*':

> When less than four years old, as I was standing with her, watching the shadows on the wall from branches of elm behind which the moon had risen, she transferred and fixed the fleeting image in my memory by repeating the couplet,
> 'Vain man, the vision of a moment made,
> Dream of a dream and shadow of a shade.'
> I never forgot those shadows, and am often trying to paint them.[2]

The nurse's rhyme was taken from the poet Edward Young's paraphrase of the Book of Job.

The poet's subject is evanescence – a vision here and gone. As the nurse's voice reaches the child's ear, it is night – bedtime, the verge of sleep and dreams. Her words 'fix' in his memory the transfiguring light of the moon. That light brings outdoor tree-shapes into the room where he is about to cast off once more upon the dark pool. Bringing the tree-shapes in, the moon's light reduces them to monochrome thinness – almost to lines.

Sam's father kept a bookshop in the City of London, north of the Thames. His mother (in the intervals between pregnancies which brought mostly disappointment and loss[3]) repaired south and eastwards through Kentish country to visit her brother's family at Margate. Sometimes Sam went with her: at the other end of life he would still attribute to Margate 'about the most restorative air in England'. In later years he returned there several times for inspiration.[4]

The boy accompanied one parent to the country, the other to the city. The house in Surrey Square made a meeting point between. It also made a setting for his education. More than sixty years later Palmer recalled his life beginning with 'good parents who, thinking me too fragile for school, gave me at home the groundwork of education'. To Latin and 'the rudiments of Greek', his father added English. Sam was set to learn by heart 'much of the Holy Scriptures'. *Pilgrim's Progress* became a lifelong favourite.[5]

Yet it was his mother's presence that defined the boy's sense of home. 'Home influence is maternal influence,' he was to write in maturity. And to maternal influence he coupled a religion of the country:

> When religion is made the basis of education – the sights, sounds and sentiment of the country shed a strong moral influence on the flexible and impressible minds of children – and in town they lose those fine wild exulting animal spirits – which seem to me essential to the healthy growth of mind and body.[6]

1. Sept 1828, in *Letters of Samuel Palmer*, ed Raymond Lister (Oxford University Press, 1974, 2 vols paginated continuously; hereinafter cited as *Letters*), 39.
2. 1 Nov 1871 (*Letters*, 823). The lines haunted his memory: in May 1870 he signed a letter to Frances Redgrave, 'ever affcy yrs. The shadow of a shade.' A decade earlier Palmer had characterised the whole memory as 'the first movement of poetic impulse... while the long shadows of moonlight were stealing over an ancient room' (*Letters*, 581). His own age of 'less than four', taken with the bare branches, would indicate Nov or Dec 1808.
3. In a genealogical letter written late in life, Palmer recalled only his brother William, 'besides many who died'. (*Letters*, 1024.)
4. *Letters*, 843; see below page 71.
5. Ibid, 646, 771, 822-823.
6. Ibid, 415 (1841); 619 (1861).

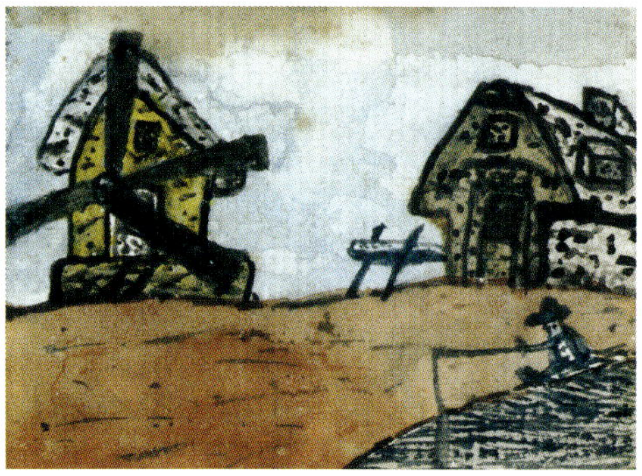

Plate 8. Windmill, cottage and fisherman, 19 December 1812. Wash

Courtesy of the Huntington Library, Art Collections, and Botanical Gardens, San Marino, California

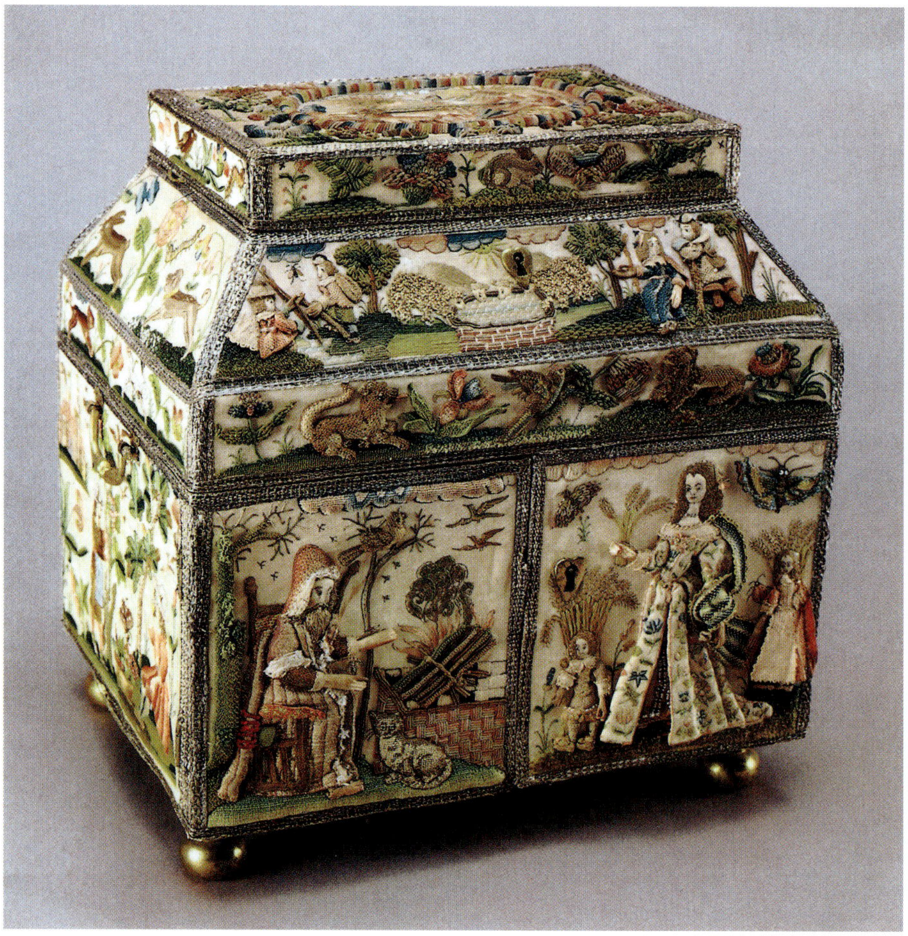

Below:
Plate 9. Pollard willow, Tottenham Marshes, *c.*1819. Pencil

Right:
Plate 10. Stump-work scenes from the story of David and Bathsheba, c.1700

Private Collection/Mallett

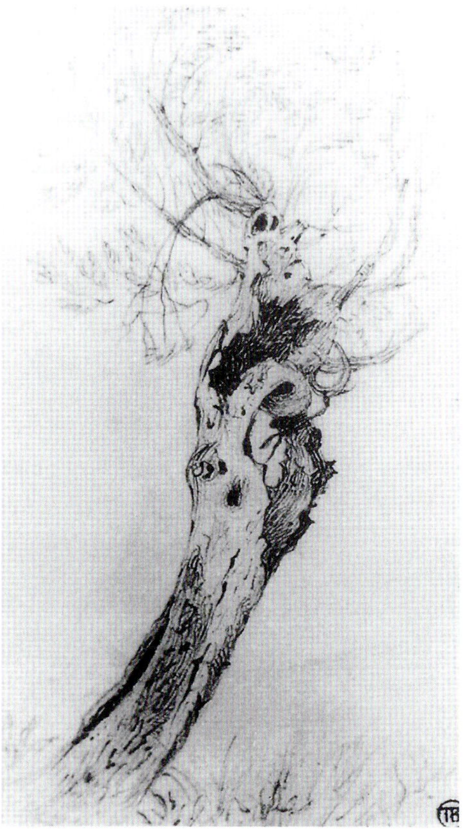

Some of this was clear to him even 'from my very early years'. 'I distinctly remember that I felt the finest scenery and the country in general with a very strong and pure feeling.'[7]

When mother and son visited Margate in June 1814, Mrs Palmer wrote back to her husband of nine-year-old Sam 'taking a sketch of Margate church'.[8] It may have been similar to his first surviving drawing, dated eighteen months earlier: a little wash landscape with windmill, cottage and fisherman (Plate 8). Only the human figure is wholly crude. Heavy outlines are fixed with decision, as if to compel the contrasting textures of nature and man's work into his own design. The whole design reveals already something of the rhythmic balances that were to inform Palmer's best work.

A pencil study of a pollard willow drawn four or five years later at Tottenham Marsh, in north London, shows similar heavy lines enclosing contrasted textures (Plate 9). Now they are managed with more control.

The contrast of plain with outlined textures could have been found in several sources of Palmer's early visual experience. One was the old English embroidery pictures known as 'stump-work' (Plate 10). They and their humble descendants, needlework pictures in thick and finer wools, were familiar to any gently reared child then and earlier. Human figures, houses, trees and plants were embroidered in contrasting areas of thick and thin threads to form bold islands of textured colours on a plain linen background. The worked areas were outlined with gold and silver wire. The materials themselves enforced simplicity – looking at every subject, whatever its elaboration, with the eyes of innocence. So it might touch a Church of England heritage enclosed within Baptist upbringing.

Further sources for Sam's outlined, textured drawings could be found in illustrated books of topography almost sure to come into his father's shop. The plates in Gilpin's 'Picturesque' *Tours* set off aquatint with etched line, to imitate ink and wash drawings. The last of the Gilpin *Tours* had appeared as recently as 1809, when Sam was four. New editions of the earlier *Tours* were still appearing.

Aquatint or mezzotint was similarly printed over etched line in Richard Earlom's renderings

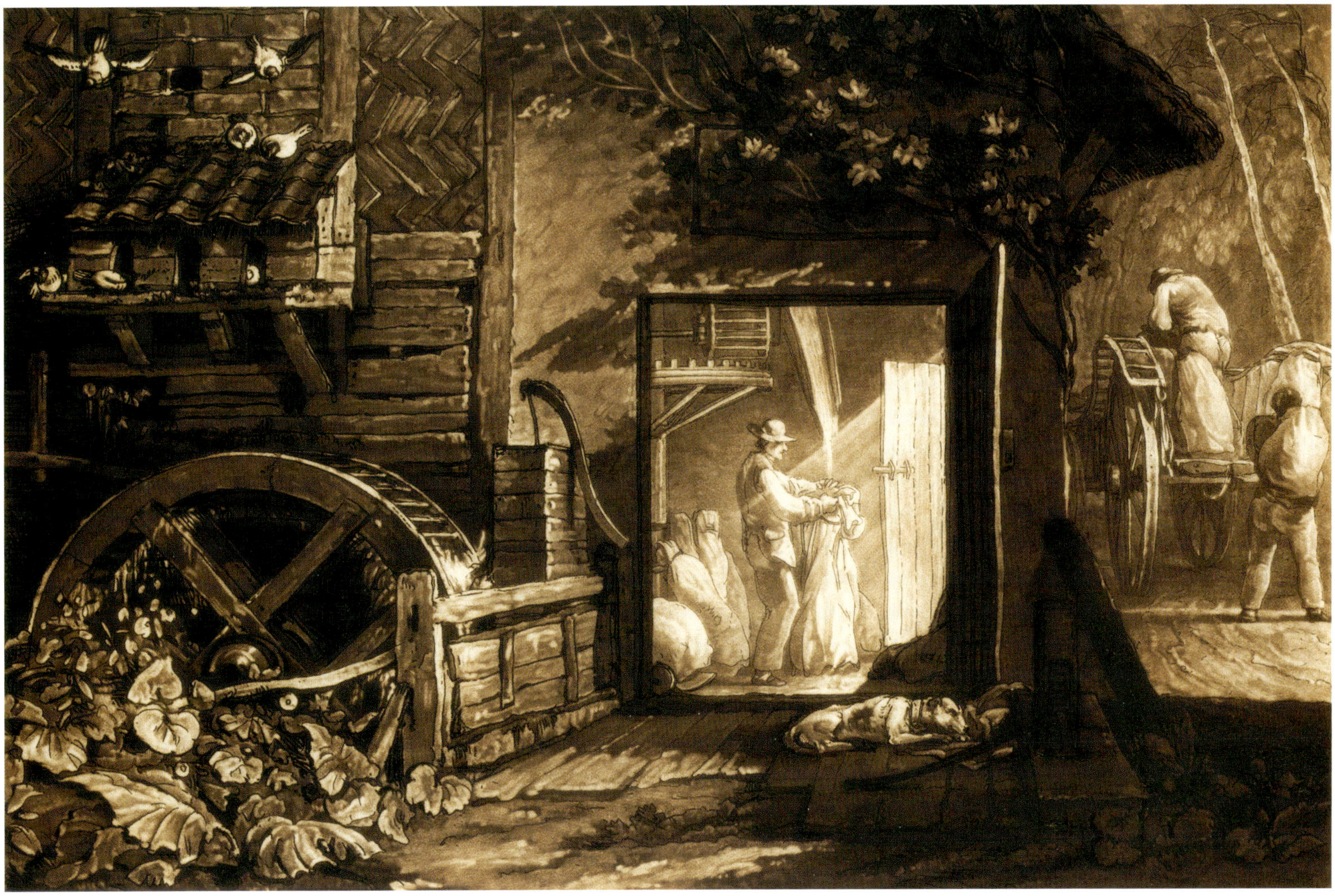

Plate 11. After J.M.W. Turner, *Pembury Mill* from *Liber Studiorum*. Etching and aquatint by Charles Turner, 1808

of Claude Lorrain drawings. A third volume of these was issuing in parts during Sam's childhood. The most masterly combinings of line with tint were seen in J.M.W. Turner's *Liber Studorium* plates, appearing in parts since 1807 (Plate 11).

Sam's agreeable world of home lessons and country visits came to an end in 1817, when he was twelve. His mother had succeeded in bringing to birth a second son, William; now she was pregnant again. So Sam was sent to the Merchant Taylors' School (then close to his father's London shop). His sight of older boys, he remembered, made him think of baboons. The nightmare lasted two terms before his parents yielded to his pleas and withdrew him.[9] He returned (in his son's words) 'to nestle in a corner with his cat "Watch" and a glass of home made wine, there to pore over a favourite author…'.[10]

Yet the horror of his wrench away from the family hearth had come home with him. It could have started his search for images of places that would be immune from change. Such places might once have been Catholic: no matter. Sam felt as 'instinct'

> a passionate love – the expression is not too strong, – for the traditions and monuments of the Church; its cloistered abbeys, cathedrals, and minsters, which I was always imagining and trying to draw; spoiling much paper with pencils, crayons, and water-colours.

This passion his parents were soon 'misinterpreting' (he felt) as 'an instinct' for drawing. The boy himself did not see it that way, as his next words make clear: 'Soon afterwards it was thought right that I should attempt painting as a profession.'[11] A teacher was found. William Wate of Southwark (a mile north-west of Surrey Square) had shown work at the British Institution and the Royal Academy. 'Honest upright and thoroughly respectable,' was Sam's assessment, 'industrious and frugal'.[12] Not, it seemed, a teacher to inspire him. Yet no hint emerged of any profession likely to suit him better.

7. Quoted in *The Life and Letters of Samuel Palmer* (Seeley, 1892; hereinafter cited as *Life and Letters*), 16. The compiler was Palmer's son, Alfred Herbert Palmer, who afterwards destroyed many of his MS sources. That fact makes it necessary to use the *Life and Letters* as a primary source. The original source of the quotation above seems to have been an early notebook later destroyed by the son.
8. *Letters*, 3.
9. *Letters*, 921; Merchant Taylors' School records.
10. *Life and Letters*, 5.
11. *Letters*, 823.
12. Ibid, 60. For the British Institution, see *Letters*, 48 n 4.

Birthdays, for such a boy, measured an ambiguous progress. In sight of his thirteenth, due on 27 January 1818, his mother was ill again.[13] Sam was sent to stay with his uncle at Margate. There was no sense of impending disaster before 18 January, when his uncle told him that his mother had died. 'It was like a sharp sword sent through the length of me,' he would write on the forty-fifth anniversary of the wound: 'and, like Cowper, "wretch even then life's journey scarce begun", I had in those years a secret foreboding that my end *in this world* would be calamitous.'[14]

His father redoubled efforts to provide companionship. Sam recalled:

> He carried in his waistcoat pocket little manuscript books with vellum covers, transcribing in them the essence of whatever he had lately read, so that, in our many walks together, there was always some topic of interest when the route was weary or unattractive.[15]

On Sundays and holidays their walks might extend to Greenwich or Dulwich – green country then, redolent of his mother. The weary unattractiveness came in their return through suburbs.

Soon the familiar comforts of Surrey Square itself were taken away. Palmer senior moved his widower's household (including the nurse Mary Ward, who became a second mother to the children) north of the river to a house close to his shop. Sam's childhood lay irrecoverable beyond the river.

He was driven to lonely searches after his mother's death:

> I was a freethinker at 14 and spent much time in controversial reading which ought to have been given to painting...
>
> I am acquainted with the whole scope of popular sceptical reasoning, and can therefore... find anchorage where Pascal Bacon Newton and Milton lowered their cables.[16]

To answer them, there was the King James Bible and *Pilgrim's Progress*.

A hint of pilgrimage emerges in the travels he recorded in a sketchbook begun in February 1819, just after his fourteenth birthday. He sketches country scenes up and down the Thames, with an excursion to Margate and a longer trip north-west to the country round Dunstable – in pencil, ink, and watercolours. There are cloud-studies with notes on surrounding lights.[17]

Another move brought the Palmers to a new shop with family rooms above, at 10 Broad Street. It was just east of Charing Cross Road in the 'rookeries' – already sliding towards the foetid slum pictured thirty years later in Dickens's *Bleak House*. Here they stayed.

The bookshop offered a varied stock. Gilpin's books had been so frequently and recently reprinted that there was no way the boy could fail to find them. He recalled specifically two commentaries on Gilpin's 'Picturesque'. Uvedale Price's *Essay on the Picturesque* (1794) he described as 'well worth reading'. Richard Knight Payne's *Analytical Inquiry into the Principles of Taste* (1805) he glossed extensively – sometimes mockingly.[18]

In January 1819 Sam had shown two oil paintings of country subjects at the British Institution. That spring three of his pictures were hung in the Royal Academy. There and then he came face to face with Turner's painting. It was a big oil entitled *Entrance to the Meuse: Orange-Merchantman on the Bar, going to pieces* with a sky of piled clouds and a green sea roiling under the survivors' boats. Turner's power fixed itself in Sam's memory: 'Being by nature a lover of smudginess,' he wrote more than fifty years later, 'I have revelled in him from that day to this.'[19]

Smudge, however, would not advance his own skills. He caught a glimpse of what might advance them in the copper engravings which converted Turner's brush strokes to lines and hatchings. The purpose of the engravings was to publish the great man's pictures. The copper plates were made by a little group of engravers chosen by him. Among them were the Cooke brothers in Soho Square, not far from the Palmer bookshop. The younger brother George Cooke 'would sometimes drop in of an evening for a talk about art,' Sam recalled. And thus 'the engravings of the brothers from Turner formed part of the pabulum of my admiration – lunacy I may almost say.'[20] The Cookes' chief work for Turner in those years was *Picturesque Views of the Southern Coast of England* (Plate 12). Sam varied his own landscape painting by trying his hand at seascapes.[21]

13. Possibly from the birth of his sister Martha in 1817. Aside from William, she seems to have been the only other surviving child: mentioned in letters of 1838, but not thereafter.

14. *Letters*, 676. On the back of an early drawing of a cottage with elms, Palmer wrote the quoted words again, with their identification: 'Cowper's poem, "On the Receipt of My Mother's Picture"'. See Raymond Lister, *Catalogue raisonné of the Works of Samuel Palmer* (Cambridge University Press, 1988: hereinafter cited as *Catalogue raisonné*), no. 32.

15. *Letters*, 823.

16. Ibid, 842; see also 817.

17. *Catalogue raisonné* no. 12. Geoffrey Grigson's *Samuel Palmer: The Visionary Years* (Kegan Paul, 1947: hereinafter cited as Grigson), 6, noticed affinities of Palmer's 1819 sketchbook with David Cox's *Treatise on Landscape Painting* (1813), and suggested that it might have been Mr Wate's teaching tool.

18. A.H. Palmer, *Samuel Palmer: A Memoir* (Fine Art Society, 1882: hereinafter cited as *Memoir*), 49; *Life and Letters*, 35-37.

19. *Letters*, 872.

20. *Life and Letters*, 7 (taken from Palmer's letter of 24 Jan 1880 to Frances Redgrave).

21. *Catalogue raisonné* nos. 31 and 33.

22. Ibid, nos. 17-19, 24-28, 31-32.

23. *Life and Letters*, 12, 14.

24. Much in the following paragraphs is based on information in David Linnell, *Blake, Palmer, Linnell and Co.* (Lewes, Sussex: Book Guild, 1994).

Within a year or two he was reverting to his boyhood monochromes of ink and wash.[22] He had attended no school of art, where he might have seen other students working at many levels and found dialogues with them. The result came soon enough:

> By the time I had practised for about five years I entirely lost all feeling for art… But it pleased God to send Mr Linnell as a good angel from Heaven to pluck me from the pit of modern art.

He would quickly come to associate the acquaintance of Linnell with 'my first trial': learning to draw.[23]

John Linnell (1792-1882), twelve and a half years older than Palmer, had grown up in a hard school.[24] He had practically taught himself to read and write. When he was nine he was seen to be a natural draughtsman: so his father, a carver and gilder of picture frames, had sent him out to copy drawings by popular artists for sale. The boy was seen at this work by a brother of the landscape painter John Varley – who made Linnell senior agree to his son's living in Varley's house.

There the boy's real mentor was Varley's young brother-in-law William Mulready, who introduced him to the Royal Academy Schools and oversaw his drawing there. After a year Linnell senior reached his son back to indenture him. But the boy gained enough success as a portrait artist to leave his father's house at seventeen and set up for himself. He never looked back, treating art as a profit-making business.

Plate 12. After J.M.W. Turner, *Lulworth Castle* from *Picturesque Views on the Southern Coast of England*. Etching and engraving by George Cooke, 1821 Hilary Gerrish

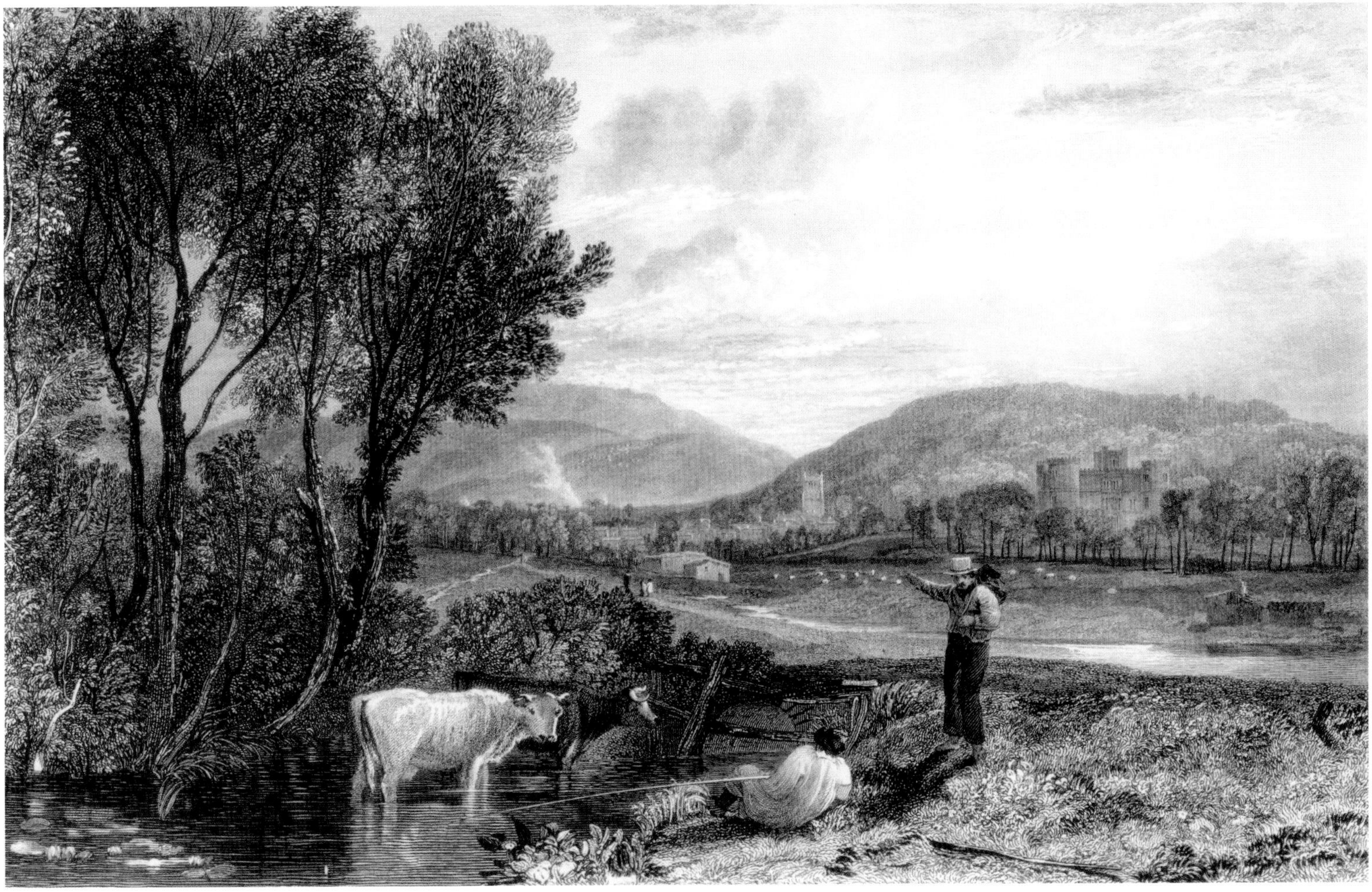

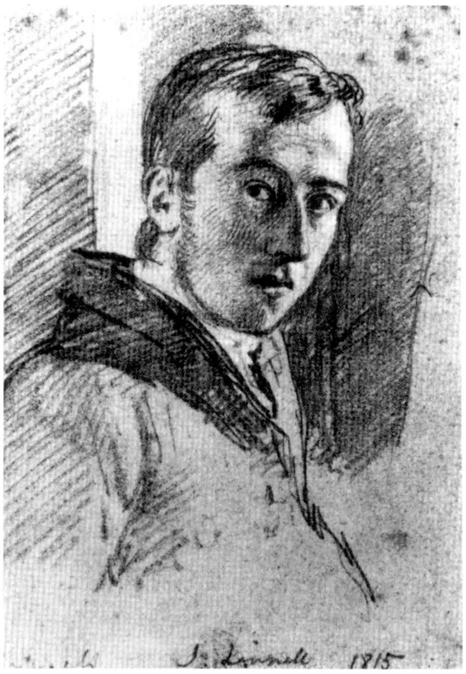

Plate 13. John Linnell: self-portrait, aged twenty-three, 1815. Pencil

Linnell's production of portraits (Plate 13) was alternated with landscapes lit with warmth and sometimes with drama. Their atmospheres draw interest away from incidental figures – to enter places revealed as enhancing experience in themselves (Plate 14). So Linnell's landscape art echoed the poetry of Coleridge and Wordsworth, as well as newer paintings by Turner and (in a lower key) Constable.

Linnell had found his spiritual allegiance when another Varley brother introduced him to the Baptist faith. Linnell had himself baptised. He became a martinet of Bible scholarship and distrusted every translation so deeply that he put himself through self-taught courses of Greek and Hebrew, so as to read the word of God untrammelled.

In the autumn of 1822 Linnell saw some of Palmer's small sepia landscapes. He asked to meet the seventeen-year-old youth, and began to give his struggles some direction. Linnell introduced him to Mulready – who showed him (in Sam's words) how 'to devote ourselves to each new undertaking as if it were our test – our first work and our last'.[25]

Mulready advised him to study anatomy, and in November 1822 Linnell sent him to draw from sculpture casts in the British Museum. Palmer started to work as hard as he knew how, charging himself to 'draw most severely, and to cry out for more and more form'. His 'first attempt at figure-drawing, 1823' was *St Christopher bearing the Sacred Child* – the world on his shoulders.[26]

The one clear benefit from Palmer's hours at the Museum came in a friendship with a boy of fourteen, George Richmond, who drew brilliantly from the sculptures. In comparison to Richmond's draughtsmanship, Palmer's own 'sedulous efforts to render the marbles exactly, even to their granulation' felt like a blind alley.[27] He lashed himself with the failure, even as he felt his short sight magnetised by country landscape. None of it seemed any good, as he wrote: 'I cannot execute at all. The least bit of natural scenery reflected from one of my spectacle-glasses laughs me to scorn, and hisses at me.'[28]

Linnell tried his own remedy. He took Palmer to look at pictures by old masters. In those days before the opening of the National Gallery, such pictures were mostly in private collections. Linnell had access to several. There was also the Gallery at Dulwich – south of Sam's childhood home, familiar from walks with his father and redolent of that time. The Dulwich Gallery was filled even then with pictures by artists Linnell called 'the grand old men'.

In a series of 'Memoranda, day after going to Dulwich', the young Palmer recorded a feeling that the old masters are superior somehow to more recent artists. His notes pursue the question of why. He finds pictures by David Cox (1783-1859) 'pretty… sweet, but not grand'. George Barret (1767-1842) 'has a beautiful sentiment and it is derived from Nature. But Nature has properties which lie still deeper…'.

This thought, rooted in the teachings of Linnell, suddenly takes young Palmer into a paradox. Here – a quarter century before the Pre-Raphaelites – he discovers the sheer multiplicity of nature's swarming presences. The very process of counting over and faithfully rendering their riches promises almost of itself to find again something of the open-eyed simplicity he thought he saw in the old masters:

> But Nature has properties which lie still deeper, and when they are brought out, the picture must be most elaborate and full of matter even if only one object be represented, yet it will be most simple of style.

That simplicity could show the record of an innocent eye. Accepting everything, rejecting nothing of a nature that is seen as basically good might lead to a new understanding – and so to a vision of God's goodness on and from the earth.

Palmer thought 'the grand old men' had realised this. For him they seemed to fill an almost prehistoric time – 'the early ages, when poetry was at its acme, and yet men lived in a simple pastoral way'. The memory of his own innocence was always keen in him.

He charged himself to 'remember always' Linnell's advice to *'Look at Albert Dürer'*. He meant the landscape backgrounds in Dürer's engravings. That emerged in Palmer's next sentence, as

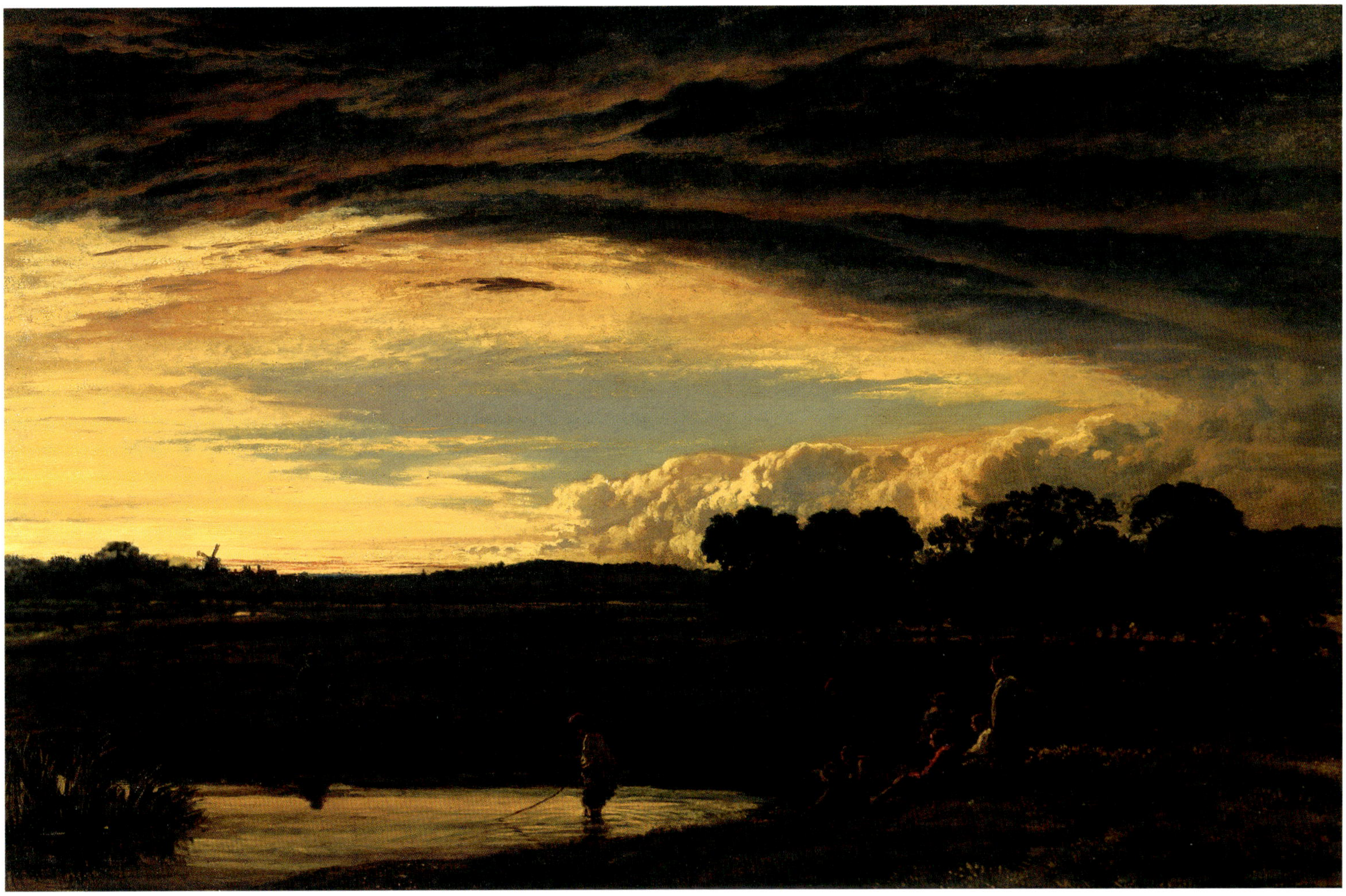

Plate 14. John Linnell: *Evening, Storm clearing off* (later identified by the artist as a view over what is now Regent's Park, London), 1818-19. Oil

Peter Nahum at the Leicester Galleries: www.leicestergalleries.com

his mind slipped southwards to Italy: 'In what a simple way landscape impressed the mind of Raphael; yet his little bits make me despair.'

Mulready had already told him that 'the old painters used the brightest colours they could get'. Brightness could suggest innocence in different ways. One Italian Renaissance panel at Dulwich portrayed a young man of about his own age. Palmer found it 'amazingly superior' to any other portrait there – because of an utterly simple background: 'The tone of the flat bluish sky… is the colour of the soul.'[29]

Could any such 'colour of the soul' be found in modern painting? Palmer's Dulwich Memoranda include this note:

> How superior is Mr Linnell's style of colouring to that of any other modern landscape painter, and yet not half so captivating to an ignorant eye as others.

Ignorant of what? Palmer's note turns immediately to an older artist Linnell knew – whose works Linnell had clearly shown to the young man:

> Look at Mr Blake's way of relieving objects, and at his colour.

William Blake (1757-1827) lived outside the mainstream of his country's art. As a child he had seen 'visions': one was of a tree filled with angels, their wings 'bespangling every bough like stars'.[30] Yet humble circumstances had dictated his artistic training as an engraver of other men's images. Throughout his life Blake had plied the engraver's trade to keep bread on the table he shared with his childless wife. They lived in two rooms of an obscure building off the Strand.

Those surroundings had done nothing to curb vaunting imagination. Through engravings, Blake had discovered Michelangelo. His heroic figures seemed to offer ideal embodiment for

25. *Life and Letters*, 8.
26. Ibid, 14n; Grigson, 43.
27. *Letters*, 824.
28. Early entry in a notebook of Nov 1823 to July 1824, later destroyed by Palmer's son (*Life and Letters*, 13).
29. *Letters*, 890: *Life and Letters*, 15. The Dulwich portrait, thought in Palmer's day to have been copied from Leonardo, is now attributed to Piero di Cosimo.
30. Gilchrist, *Life of William Blake*, 6.

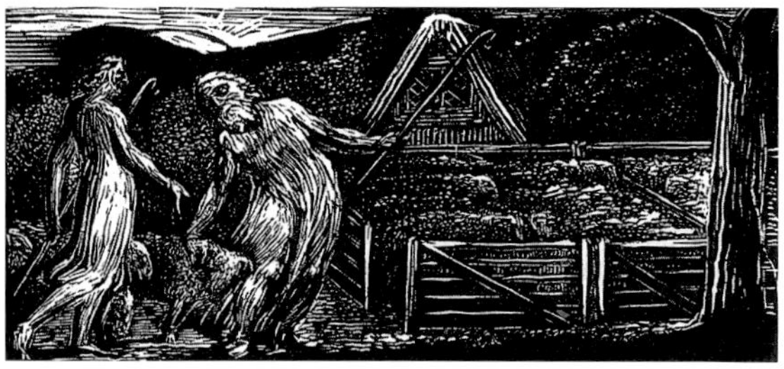

Plate 15. William Blake: *Colin and Thenot* from Virgil's *Pastorals,* 1821. Wood engraving

Blake's own visions. Blake's personifications of heroic allegory were begot on radical aspirations stirred by the Industrial Revolution at home, the American Revolution abroad.

In due course he had evolved his own form of Christianity. This side of him sought expression in poetic effusions long and dense. He printed them single-handed in books of texts with pictures interwoven, from plates elaborately engraved and afterwards hand-coloured by himself. 'Illuminated books', he called them, for they held 'prophecies'. But they found few purchasers.

Blake's little *Poems of Innocence and Experience* enshrined his equation of earthly life with innocence. These poems attracted the attention of Wordsworth, but their short lines and simple diction appeared to many people merely naïve. Blake 'illuminated' them too, with occasional borders of lawn or tree to record his landscape of innocence.

Yet the mature Blake was not deeply interested in the day-to-day world. To him, Wordsworth's worship of nature amounted to atheism. 'Nature', wrote Blake, 'is the work of the Devil'. He thought it distracted men's attention from the power to envision. Against Wordsworth's claim (in his Preface to *Lyrical Ballads*) that the first requirements of poetry are 'observation and description', Blake wrote: 'One Power alone makes a Poet: Imagination, the Divine Vision'. Against Wordsworth's section on the 'Influence of Natural Objects', Blake wrote: 'Natural Objects always did & now do weaken, deaden, & obliterate Imagination in Me'. 'Imagination', he added, came not from 'Natural Man' but only from 'Spiritual Man'.[31]

In Blake's drawings and paintings, the allegorised figure is everything and the landscape behind (if it exists at all) usually minimised or idealised to a vanishing point. Only in his engravings after other men's work, or when a specific commission dictated it, did Blake occasionally go beyond his linkage of childhood perceptions to any notice of earthly nature.

For all that, Blake remained an essentially gentle spirit. He was always ready to discuss his insights with any younger person who showed interest. So it had been when the twenty-six year-old Linnell knocked on Blake's door in June 1818. Linnell's errand was to hire the sixty year-old Blake to 'lay in' the etched base for an engraving from Linnell's portrait of a Baptist preacher.[32]

It soon emerged that they shared many interests. Blake had made his own studies of Greek and Hebrew. That gave wings to their discussions of religion. In time Linnell bought several of Blake's 'illuminated' books. He acquired them slowly because of their expense, but the expenditure itself was a measure of the value the younger man (always careful with money) found in Blake's work. It was also an expression of his friendship for the old man.[33]

Then Linnell had another idea to help Blake financially. One of Linnell's friends, Dr Robert Thornton, had published a cheap edition of Virgil's Pastorals for schools – in Latin, but illustrated by humble woodcuts. A new printing, due in 1821, was to include an English version of the first Eclogue. For it Linnell secured a commission for Blake to engrave some additional pictures on wood. They were to be of the same size as the little wood-block pictures retained from earlier editions.

Wood engraving is opposite to the metal engraving Blake had always practised. Metal engraving is an 'intaglio' technique, where anything cut into the surface prints black. Wood engraving is a 'relief' technique: the surface itself prints black, with excavations left white. Each cut Blake made in these blocks would light a little lamp against the ink's blackness.

Perhaps it had something to do with the fact that the book was for young people – a schoolbook; and also that the commission had come through Linnell, who so interested himself in landscapes. However it happened, this small commission more than revived Blake's old equation of earthly nature with childhood innocence. Landscape in Blake's little wood engravings for Virgil gained a presence that had no forerunner anywhere in the sixty-two year-old artist's original work (Plate 15).

Blake had no prior experience of engraving on wood. The results, cut by his own hand, are almost wilfully rough-textured. It is as if the textures of the wood-grain itself are shaping the lines of engraving. Long lines curve through the figures' gowns to animate their prophet-like gestures. The lines straighten to delineate cottage, tree-stem, gate and fence, as Virgil's pastoral scenes are brought home from their classical world and domesticated to rural England.

To counterpoint the lines, Blake's wood-engraved foliage everywhere exudes tiny points of light to twinkle through the printer's ink. And at the back of the little scenes a large rim of sun or large moon often haunts the horizon to give a sensation of transfiguring lights – perception on the change. So surrounded, the figures appear almost as spirits of the twilit rural places in which they find themselves: as if they would become part of these places and borrow their lights.

Blake's wood engravings for Virgil made a profound impression on the young Palmer when he saw them. They could touch back to his childhood memory of his nurse's night-time words about life itself: 'the vision of a moment made, Dream of a dream and shadow of a shade'. What came uppermost now for him were Blake's transfiguring lights in rustic places – showing as so many metaphors of innocence. The young Palmer wrote of these pictures:

> They are visions of little dells, and nooks, and corners of Paradise; models of the exquisitest pitch of intense poetry. I thought of their light and shade, and looking upon them I found no word to describe it...
>
> There is in all such a mystic and dreamy glimmer as penetrates and kindles the inmost soul, and gives complete and unreserved delight, unlike the gaudy daylight of this world.

Only then did he turn his attention to the figures:

> The figures of Mr Blake have that intense, soul-evidencing attitude and action, and that elastic, nervous spring which belongs to uncaged animal spirits.[34]

Those spirits were uncaged first by the long curving lines Blake had given their garments and gestures, but then by the country in which they found themselves – and its lights of perception on the change.

Palmer from his beginnings was a landscapist. A landscapist he would remain. He was never to record such unbridled enthusiasm for any other works of Blake (generously as he praised several). The value of the little Virgil engravings for the emerging artist is characterised by one of his creative heirs, David Inshaw:

> Palmer would have seen in those Blake Pastorals a reflection of what he himself was thinking: and it gave him a little fragment in order to go forward – a kind of companionship.[35]

The companionship was of vision itself – new to the teen-aged Palmer, despite his association with Linnell. Pastoral landscape opened the narrowest of doors in Blake's vision. It happened to be the only door in all of Blake's art that Palmer could walk through.

In Linnell's copy of Blake's *Marriage of Heaven and Hell*, among the 'Proverbs of Hell' Palmer could read: 'The road of excess leads to the Palace of Wisdom.' At the end of his response to the Virgil engravings, the young man writes:

> Excess is the essential vivifying spirit, vital spark, embalming spice... of the finest art. ...
>
> We must not begin with medium, but think always on excess, and only use medium to make excess more abundantly excessive.

The excess in Blake's art was in its line. The power of line to express the artist's individuality dominated Palmer's thinking when he wrote (in 1825):

> Though I hope we shall all be severe outlinists, I hope our styles of outline may all be different as the design of Michael Angelo from his equal, Blake, and the outline of Albert Dürer from that of Andrea Mantegna.

31. Quoted in Gilchrist, 239-240.
32. Linnell himself would then finish off the plate with an engraver's burin. For a brief description of the process, see below, page 62, note 111.
33. Linnell purchased from Blake *Songs of Innocence and Experience* (in Aug 1819), *Jerusalem* uncoloured (in Dec 1819), *The Marriage of Heaven and Hell* (in April 1821), *Europe* and *America* (probably in March 1822), and some smaller works. See Joseph Viscomi, *Blake and the Idea of the Book* (Princeton NJ: Princeton University Press, 1993) for details.
34. *Life and Letters*, 15-16.
35. Tape-recorded interview, July 2002.

Yet when he looked back to actual landscape, Palmer found: 'There is no line in nature, though excessive sharpness.' So the application of line to nature had to involve translation.

No mere translation, however, could account for Palmer's next assertion – which turns the gentle 'improvements' of Gilpin and all his tribe inside out:

> Nature is not at all the standard of art, but art is the standard of nature. The visions of the soul, being perfect, are the only true standard by which nature must be tried. ... As we enjoy and improve in imaginative art, we shall love the material works of God more and more.[36]

The beginning words frame just the sort of paradox that Blake set out in his 'visionary' writings. But then Palmer goes down a path that leads right away from Blake.

Palmer's goal is not an otherworldly vision. On the contrary: he wants to improve 'vision' in order to love 'the material works of God' – earthly nature – more and more. At the time he wrote these words, Palmer had only the beginnings of his creative individuality: but this was to be his path. These words of his show how wrong it is to treat Palmer as a footnote to Blake. Too much writing about Palmer has defeated itself at the outset by making that mistake.[37]

The young Palmer continues:

> Sometimes landscape is seen as a vision, and then it seems as fine as art. But this is seldom, and bits of nature are generally improved by being received into the soul.[38]

Here is no tweaking of details, such as Gilpin recommended to improve the whole landscape. Palmer wants to save the details – for taking into some synthesis yet to be found.

Palmer was to be one in a group of artists, all two or three generations younger, magnetised by Blake's notion of vision itself. They were not fired by the old seer's heroic allegories and myth-making. For they were to be men of the nineteenth century – the century of scientific impulse and observation. Any visions these young men might achieve were based on closer scrutiny of this world and its nature. Thus they would reaffirm English pragmatism. They would make pragmatism itself the basis of their vision.

For Palmer, the new vision he sought might open the door to some hoped-for synthesis of earthly nature with the continuing worship of God. The model of it had informed Haydn's late oratorio *The Creation* (1798) and his setting of Thomson's *The Seasons* (1801).

Where should the eighteen-year-old Palmer look for other examples to realise God in the sheer wealth of created details in earthly nature? Linnell owned a 'supernatural' panel picture by one of his 'grand old men', the Dutch painter Lucas van Leyden (1494–1533). It showed God with Adam and Eve in Eden. Eden regained, or something like a child's perception of nature, made an important part of Palmer's goal. So he now charged himself: 'Look for Van Leydenish qualities in real landscapes, and look hard, long, and continually.'[39]

Then it came over him where in his own world of experience he might look. He might look about Dulwich. Dulwich was rural. It had been one goal of his childhood walks with his father (and also, he would discover, close to where Blake had seen his early vision in childhood). And Dulwich held the Gallery filled with works by 'the grand old men'. Coming out of the Dulwich Gallery, Palmer looked at the actual nature surrounding him:

> Often, and I think generally, at Dulwich, the distant hills seem the most powerful objects in colour, and clear force of line: we are not troubled with aerial perspective in the valley of vision.[40]

'Aerial perspective' (in which things recede towards indistinctness) would now reverse itself for Palmer's quest: clarity should *increase* with distance. It could recall Bunyan's Pilgrim looking through the Shepherds' 'perspective glass' from the Delectable Mountains. The goal of Palmer's art was that identified by Haydn's successor Beethoven: a vision of 'God in Nature'.

On 9 June 1824 the nineteen-year-old Palmer set down a resolution to seek his vision directly through his inheritance of religious faith. It showed itself, after twenty months' trial of

36. *Life and Letters*, 16.
37. One of the first to recognise the presence of a crucial difference was the Neo-Romantic artist Keith Vaughan (see Chapter 8). Vaughan wrote in 1943: 'It is the greatest mistake to regard Palmer merely as the disciple of Blake. His work is absolutely original and his vision is totally different from Blake's.' (From 'A View of English Painting', in *New World Writing and Daylight*, Winter 1943–44; reprinted in *Penguin New Writing* 31, 1947).
38. *Life and Letters*, 16–17.
39. Ibid, 14 (probably written in 1823).
40. Ibid, 17.
41. Colin Harrison, *Samuel Palmer* (Oxford: Ashmolean Museum, 1997), 12.
42. *Life and Letters*, 12–13.
43. *Samuel Palmer's Sketch-book 1824*: facsimile, with introduction and commentary by Martin Butlin (Trianon Press, 1962).
44. *Life and Letters*, 14.
45. Nearly contemporaneous detailed views of all these places can be seen in John Thomas Smith, *Antiquities of Westminster, with Sixty-two Additional Plates* (London: for the author, 1807).

drawing under Linnell, as 'my second trial'. 'Draw near to Christ, and see what is to be done with Him to back you. … Ask Christ to manifest to you these things.' He listed three subjects from Christ's life. All were to be approached inductively: 'Lay up, silently and patiently, materials for them in your sketch-book.'

Meanwhile 'smaller subjects of separate glories of Heaven might be tried – hymns sung among the hills of Paradise at eventide.' One subject on the young man's list had already been drawn by Blake (for Blair's poem 'The Grave'): 'A family met in Heaven'. That for Palmer touched back to the loss of his mother.

He turned it into a picture of the Holy Family in Egypt – offering scope for landscapes of this world. Palmer assembled figures and 'palm' trees from northern Renaissance painting. His own medium was mixed: ink drawing on the panel, painted over in thin oils, which he then 'heightened with brilliant, jewel-like strokes of tempera mixed with gum'.[41] But he could not resolve the landscape background that should focus his vision. He stopped his painting 'in much distress, anxiety, and fear'.[42]

* * *

He opened a new sketchbook. Inside the cover he wrote his name, address (the rooms over his father's bookshop), and the date 'July 15th 1824'.[43] The new book's pages were to trace a pilgrimage. Its goal would gradually reveal itself as a 'valley of vision' which seemed to glimmer over and beyond the Dulwich hills. In his new sketchbook Palmer resolved to 'try to work with a child's simple feeling'.[44]

The opening page contains three drawings. They show immediately the range of weights he wants to give his line. Feathery outlines define a refulgence of summer trees at the front. In both the left-hand drawing and that lower right, the outlines of distant hill and waxing moon are heavy, as a promise of reversing perspective. Such outsized moons and suns had denoted time in European art reaching back to Carolingian drawing a thousand years earlier. They had been revived in several of Blake's Virgil engravings. Palmer's sketchbook drawings now elaborate the summer light (Plate 16).

In the right-hand upper drawing, hill and moon with a large star are set beside a city. A closer look shows Westminster Hall, before the Embankment, with the Abbey towers behind. So Palmer's moon-capped hill has been raised from the fields (as they were then) of Millbank. The whole prospect is seen from across a river. It is the Thames, and the artist's viewpoint is Lambeth, on the Surrey shore.[45] Thus to begin his journey, the nineteen-year-old sketcher has placed himself on the opposite side from the city of his present life – back once more on the shore of childhood, and of Dulwich.

Plate 16. Sketchbook, begun July 1824: from page 1. Ink

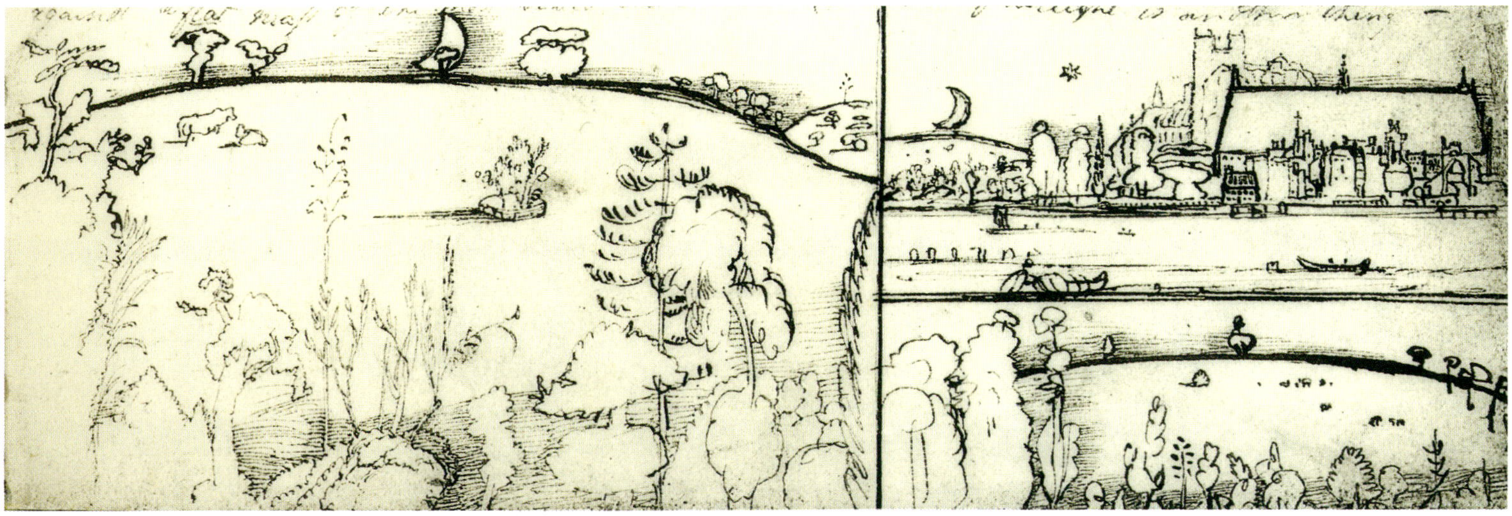

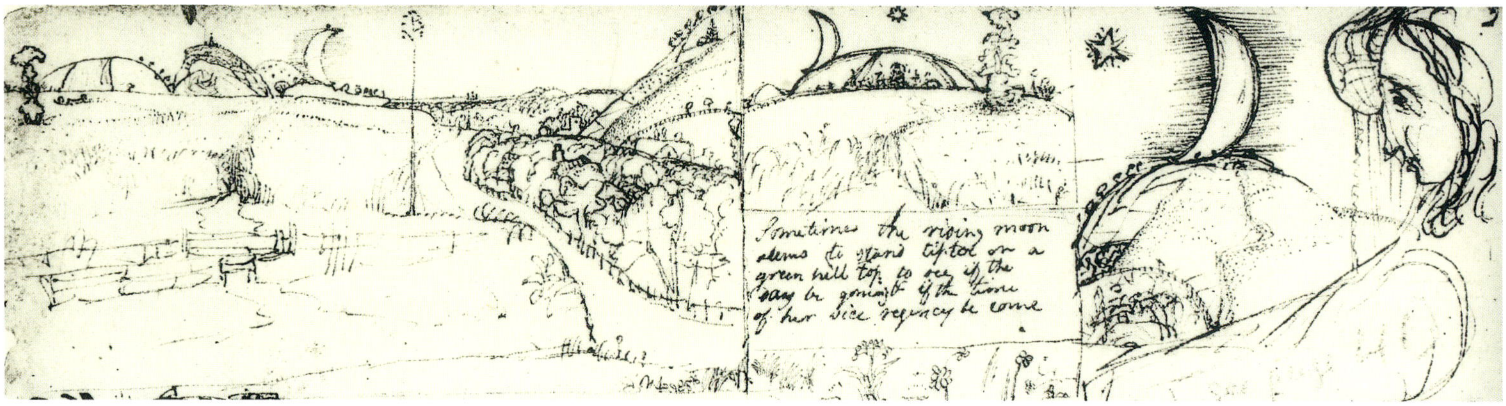

Plate 17. Sketchbook, begun July 1824: from page 2. Ink

Over these drawings on his first sketchbook page, Palmer writes a note about how the long evening light of summer appears to infuse a 'chastened glow' into a tower rising through it: 'the tower… seemed luminous in itself, & rather sending out light from itself than reflecting it.' Such 'inherent light' (he would write in the sketchbook a few pages on) sends 'a lustre into the heart of him who looks'.

Palmer's opening sketchbook drawings seek to capture their light within lines. So the art of drawing (which Blake manifested and Linnell insisted upon) might enkindle Palmer's inner light. Nearly fifty years later Palmer wrote of the kinship of line and texture:

> I should like an outline as deeply bitten as those in [Turner's] *Liber Studorium*; and believe that if we were to make an etched copy of a bit of near landscape out of one of Albert Dürer's wood-cuts, of the same width of line – and then on a new transparent ground, to add what we wished of shade – the lines would scarcely be too powerful to support them.[46]

The next pages of the sketchbook show him seeking that ground through the country beyond Lambeth and Surrey Square. The *verso* of the opening leaf has three drawings across the top (Plate 17). The first sets the smooth texture of ripening grain-tops through a field – before another moon-capped hill – side by side with a busy-ness of trees and cottages. Palmer's note below recalls the contrasts in stump-work embroidery and the pure needle-work pictures which followed them:

> A large field of corn would be very pretty with as it were islands peeping out of it – as a clump of cottages completely inclosed and shaded by trees[:] the corn being high[,] no part of the little isles in this wavy sea of plenty would be seen till they were perhaps 5 or six feet from the ground.

A clump of cottages – man's habitation – 'inclosed', almost lost in God's bounty approaching harvest time: Palmer could have seen this yearly climax in fields about Dulwich around the time of beginning this sketchbook on 15 July (as harvests tended to be later then). The note continues:

> A group of different sex and age, reapers, might be shewn in the foreground going down a walk in the field toward the above cottage island[;] & over the distant line that bounds this golden sea might peep up elysian hills, the little hills of David; or the hills of Dulwich [–] or rather the visions of a better country which the Dulwich fields will shew to all true poets.

Here is the idealism of Blake. But for Palmer, far more than in Blake's little Virgil engravings, the land overwhelms any people in it.

Palmer's second drawing along this page-top shows another full harvest field and path through it towards another hill, moon and star. He inscribes it:

> Sometimes the rising moon seems to stand tiptoe on a green hill top: to see if the day be going & if the time of her vice regency be come.

Had he read Keats's lines beginning 'I stood tiptoe upon a little hill', opening the *Poems* of 1817? It was not a common book: yet living over a bookshop can afford surprising chances.

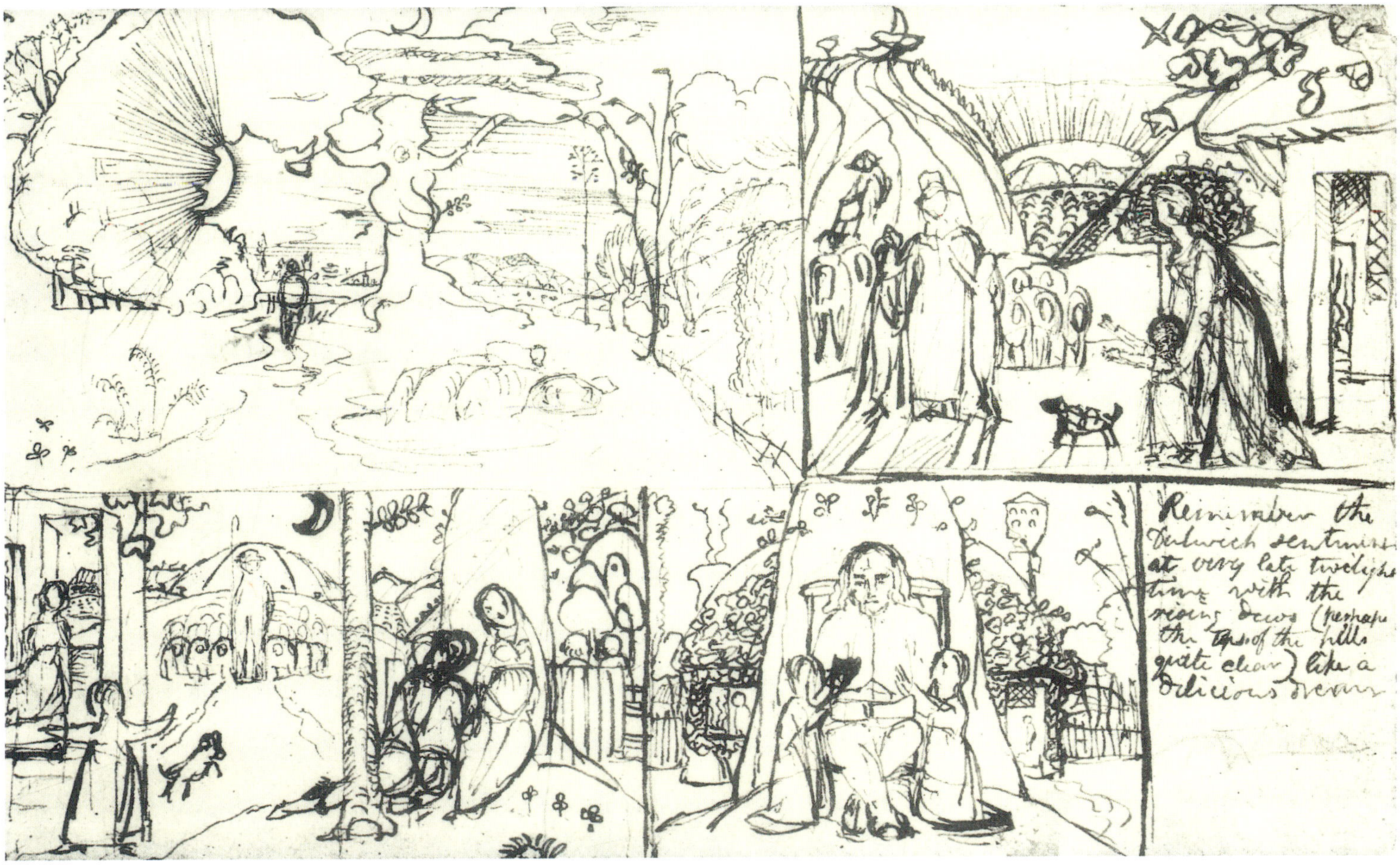

Plate 18. Sketchbook, begun July 1824: page 7. Ink

The right-hand drawing shows its hill touched by a still larger waxing moon, set beside a sensitive human profile of contemplation under a shepherd's hat. Who is this witness? The question is taken up several times in the following pages of sketchbook drawings. Pages 5 and 6 show the profile of a prophet-like old man under a tower intersecting a waxing moon. In a second drawing the old man reads from a large book.

On page 7 a group of drawings seems to record a journey (Plate 18). At the upper left, a solitary figure (not old) walks away past the sheep of pastoral tradition, towards light woods. Above him, an edge of sun is answered by a waxing moon directly over the central tree. In the left distance a tiny spire rises before hills.

The next drawings (upper right and lower left) show arrival and welcome at a country cottage – before a sun-edge at the horizon, and then under a waxing moon. A shepherd brings in his flock from fields – the grain now harvested and spread on the ground in piles to dry before stooking.

The drawing at bottom right suggests a further stage in the pilgrimage. Before a central tree-bole or tumulus with a thatched cottage behind it, an old man sits with an open book on his lap. On either side a child kneels with arms raised. The subject here is not so much knowledge as the heritage of wisdom. At the end of this far-journeying page, Palmer writes:

> Remember the Dulwich sentiment at very late twilight time with the rising dews (perhaps the tops of the hills quite clear) like a delicious dream.

There follows the faintest sketch.

Behind his work in the sketchbook, Palmer began two new pictures. He named their subjects in a rapid summary of work done in the later months of 1824:

> I resumed and finished my *Twilight*, and quickly took up my *Joseph's Dream*, and sketched in my new sketch-book.[47]

46. Oct 1871 to P.G. Hamerton (*Life and Letters*, 316).
47. Memorandum dated January 2nd [1825], quoted by A.H. Palmer (*Life and Letters*, 13) from a notebook which he afterwards apparently destroyed.

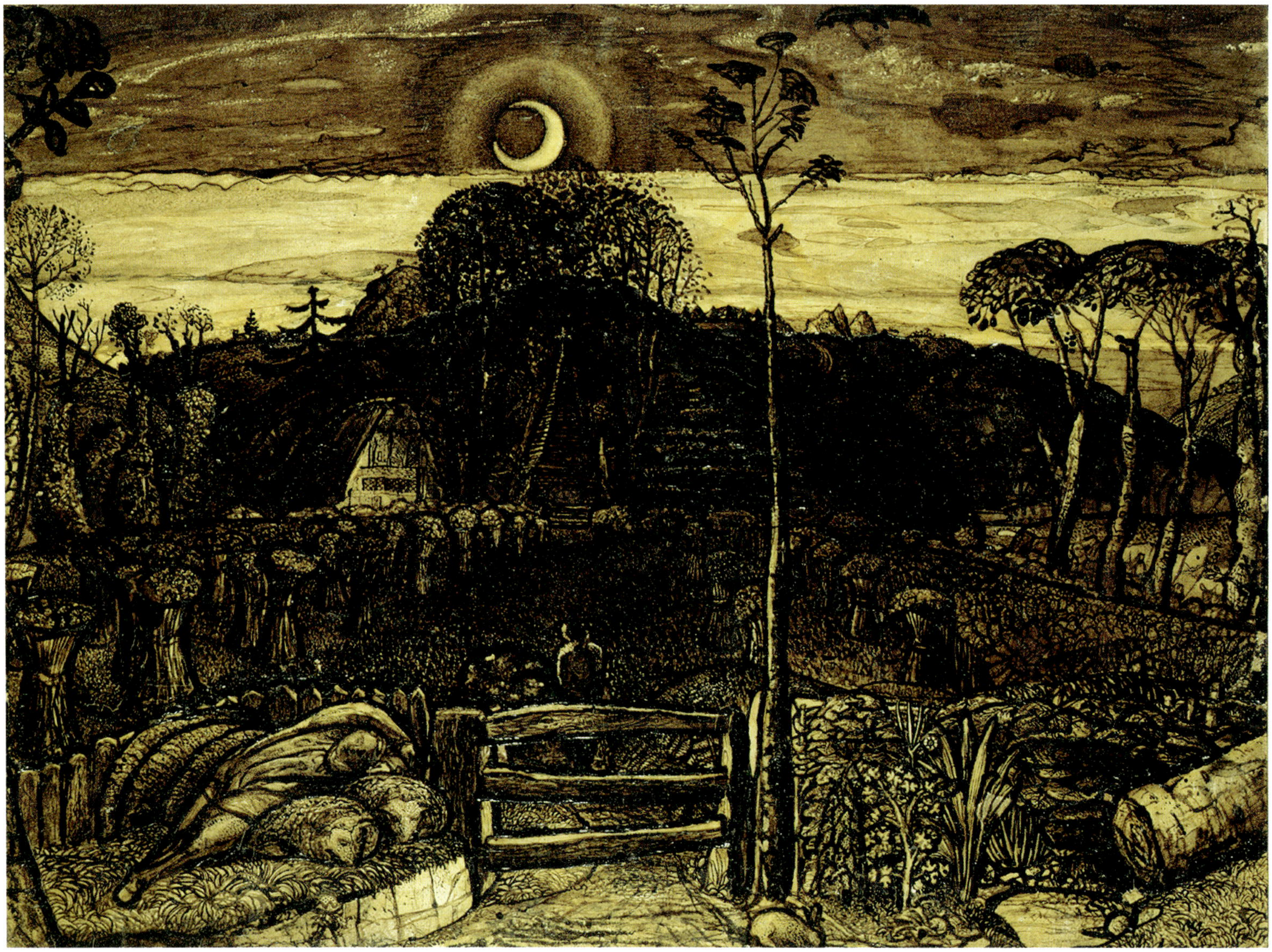

Plate 19. *Late Twilight,* 1824. Ink with gum arabic, varnished Ashmolean Museum, Oxford

These two pictures started his progress towards a set of six large drawings in very dark sepia which show his first surviving achievement of real individuality. They are patterned in contrasting textures closely worked and heavily outlined (as in stump-work embroidery). The effect is to imply some supernatural force driving the shapes and textures of its nature. Here is the beginning of an utterly new style of drawing (Plate 19).

There are some pictorial elements from Blake's Virgil engravings. One is the narrow, steep-roofed vernacular cottage at the back. The waxing moon is almost cribbed from the only Virgil engraving without figures (a huge-boled tree in a ridge-and-furrow field raked by rain and wind.[48] Blake's lone figure-less Virgil image is a significant choice for Palmer.

Palmer's ideal subject – sharply differing from Blake's ideals – is the immanence of nature. Man's presence is for Palmer only a detail within nature's visionary eye. When Palmer includes figures, they do not prophesy. In rest or activity, they fit themselves into the patterns and shapes which it is the business of his new linear art to articulate.

In this picture of twilight, Palmer's seeking eyes begin to find their own metaphor. The series of his dark brown sepia drawings will celebrate man's cultivation of his place in earthly nature as the key to his happiness. That cultivation will be expressed in the age-old time cycle of farming: ploughing, sowing, harvesting. The cycle of the farming year is thus the natural enlargement of the daily cycle of light and darkness already implied in this *Late Twilight*.

The next sentences of Palmer's Memorandum of work done in 1824 describe two encouragements. First:

48. Reproduced below, Chapter 6, page 171

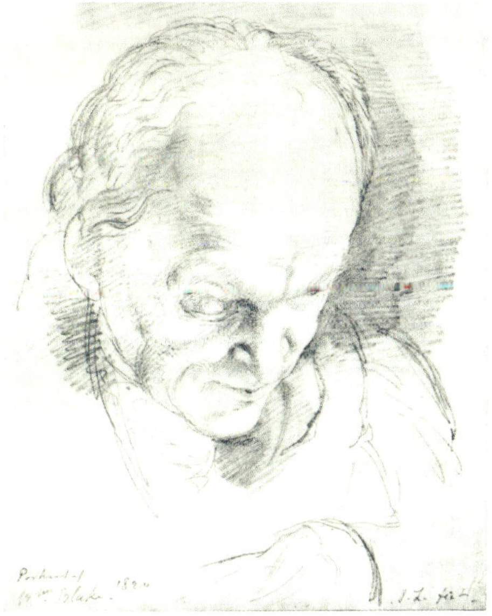

Plate 20. Linnell: Blake at work by candle light, 1820. Pencil

> Mr L[innell] called, and looking at my *Joseph*, sepias, and sketch-books, did give me indeed sweet encouragement.

Here are three levels of work: sketchbooks at the beginning of Palmer's process, at the end a formal picture; and between them, this half-way house of drawings in dark sepia.

Then came Linnell's second encouragement:

> Soon, by his desire, I went with him to Mr B[lake], who also, on seeing my things, gave me above my hope, over-much praise.

They found Blake and his wife that Saturday evening, 9 October 1824, in their two upstairs rooms of a building in Fountain Court, off the Strand (Plate 20).

Palmer took note of the old man's claim for innocence as the visionary's only honesty: 'He thought that no one could become truly great who had not humbled himself "even as a little child".' Yet Blake was no innocent in his understanding of art. Close to his engraving table hung an impression of Dürer's *Melancholy the Mother of Invention*. Palmer wrote: 'In him you saw at once the Maker, the Inventor… He was energy itself, and shed around him a kindling influence – an atmosphere of life, full of the ideal.'

On Blake's table lay the first copper plate for a new Linnell commission. Blake was engraving his own watercolour designs for the Book of *Job*. *Job* was the story which had started Palmer's childhood vision of tree-shadows silhouetted by moonlight on the wall of his nursery:

> At my never-to-be-forgotten first Interview, the copper of the first plate – 'Thus did Job continually' [Plate 21] – was lying on the table where he had been at work on it. How lovely it looked through the tissue-paper!

Plate 21. Blake: *Job:* 'Thus did Job continually', 1824. Engraving

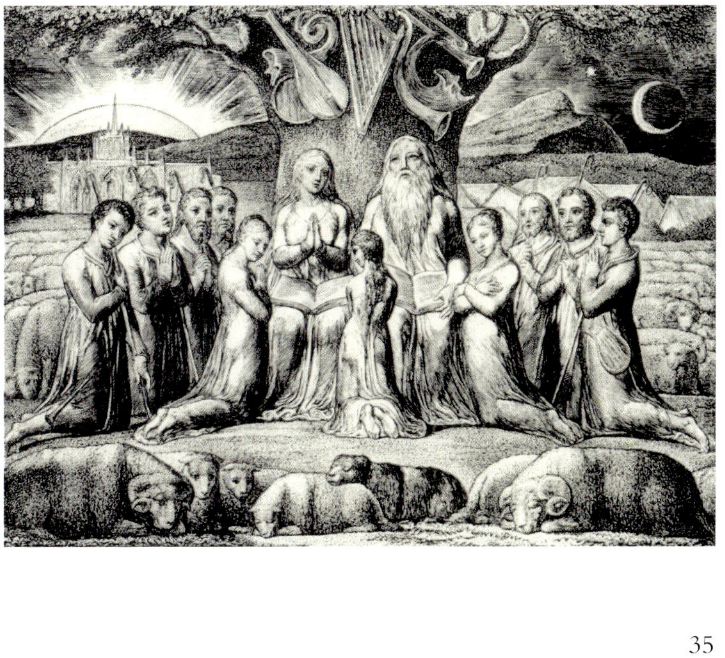

Here was engraving of a different order from the Virgil Pastorals on wood. In the copper of Blake's accustomed practice, outlines differ sharply from shadows. Enclosed areas are finely worked to varied textures. And here again landscape plays a striking role in the visual drama. The human figures front their landscape quietly, gathering almost as closely as the sheep before them and behind.

Blake follows the ancient practice of showing Biblical places as landscapes of home. A patriarchal tree spreads over all. In the left background stands a Gothic church (such as Palmer had tried to draw in childhood); on the right spread the roofs of an English village. The village nestles before enclosing hills under star and moon – while the church spire opposite pierces an edge of sun at the horizon. Sun and moon in balance suggest the equinox.

Blake told his young guest that he began his designs 'with fear and trembling'. Palmer responded: 'O! I have enough of fear and trembling.' 'Then', said Blake, 'you'll do!'[49] Palmer concluded:

> He ennobled poverty, and, by his conversation and the influence of his genius, made two small rooms in Fountain Court more attractive than the threshold of princes.

Blake's rooms became known to several young artists of Palmer's generation as 'the House of the Interpreter'. That reference to *Pilgrim's Progress* exactly described the relations between disciples and seer. The House of the Interpreter is a way-station: from there the Interpreter bids the Pilgrim go forward on his own journey of discovery. 'From his study window,' Palmer remembered, 'a glimpse was caught of the Thames and the Surrey shore.'[50] It was the shore of Palmer's innocence, and now of his pilgrimage to Dulwich and beyond.

Page 8 of Palmer's sketchbook shows its largest drawing thus far (Plate 22). It reworks Blake's 'Thus did Job continually'. Palmer scatters his figures to the four corners, leaving the centre open to landscape. A slim central tree roots hugely in the foreground. Behind it a cottage divides figures inside (right) from outside (left). At the upper left, the full orb of the sun above one hill is pierced by a tall shepherd-figure bringing home his flock. Opposite right, from another hill touched by a waxing moon at least as big as the sun, a family bring in sheaves from the corn now stooked on the hillside.[51]

Page 9 has the first full-page sketchbook drawing. The bottom foreground and right side are filled by a large reclining figure of contemplation, with hand resting on a book inscribed 'The earth is full of Thy richness'. The horizon is half filled by the grandest of Palmer's sun-edges. The central field (behind a church steeple virtually buried in its landscape) is now cleared – with the long stubble of Palmer's time left for gleaning.

The earlier drawings of the bald-headed old man seem to fructify on page 10 in a more vigorous man, reclining with a female companion in woods (Plate 23). He bears more than a passing resemblance to Blake. His prospect, in Palmer's sketch, includes a variant of the round-headed laurel which Blake had drawn and engraved for his *Songs of Innocence*. Here the laurel shelters yet another shepherd with his sheep: the embodiment of pastoral in the eye of the Interpreter.

The sketchbook leaves begin to fill more rapidly as the season turns toward winter. Ongoing pages show fields winter-ploughed in the curving furrows made by oxen. Under one drawing of a hill-field ploughed to its hedgerow (page 14) Palmer sets down in words the memory of a reflective walk in high summer – perhaps up this field and hill, towards his own Delectable Mountains. As his description extends, its prospects resolve into such close-textured areas as filled his *Late Twilight* sepia:

> Opposite the cottage was (across a little valley where they were cutting corn) a range of hills you walk up – the sheep bells going all the time – through several fields (of different sorts[:] rye, hops, fallow, meadow) of colour, form & texture various – then you come to the line of thick wood which runs all along the summit[,] very close wild & intricate yet such as you would wish to explore guided by one that knows its mazes...

The facing page returns the sketchbook to winter: a tall fir tree, its branches outlined in cloud-like shapes of wet snow, tells against a blue wash of chilly sky.

Linnell had moved his family to a farm on the far slopes of Hampstead, four miles north-west of London. When the weather grew warm enough he persuaded Blake, now sixty-seven, to walk up and visit. Sometimes Blake was accompanied by Palmer, and one of their conversations along the way glowed with special light in the younger man's memory. The topic was Claude Lorrain.

---

49. Quoted in Gilchrist's *Life of William Blake*, 299. A different recollection of Palmer's first visit to Blake (in a notebook quoted from and later destroyed by A.H. Palmer) had Blake working 'in a great book' at a hundred illustrations to Dante (*Life and Letters*, 9-10). Both this and Palmer's recollection of seeing the *Job* plate were genuine memories. But only the *Job* was being worked in 1824 (see David Linnell, *Blake, Palmer, Linnell and Co.*, 85-87, 97-99, 103).

The 'great book' of paper for the Dante drawings was given by Linnell to Blake only in Oct 1825 (Mona Wilson, *The Life of William Blake*, new ed: Oxford University Press, 1971, 358). Linnell's first payment for the Dante drawings was made on 21 Dec 1825 (David Linnell, 89); and few of the Dante drawings were finished when Blake died in Aug 1827.

Moreover the words 'fear and trembling' (associated in the destroyed notebook with the Dante drawings) are quoted from *Job*: a fact unlikely to have been overlooked by either Blake or the young Palmer.

50. 23 Aug 1855 to Alexander Gilchrist, quoted in his *Life of William Blake*, 301-304.

51. Just such a stooked hillside was to make a subject ninety years later for the young Paul Nash (see below, Chapter 5, page 147).

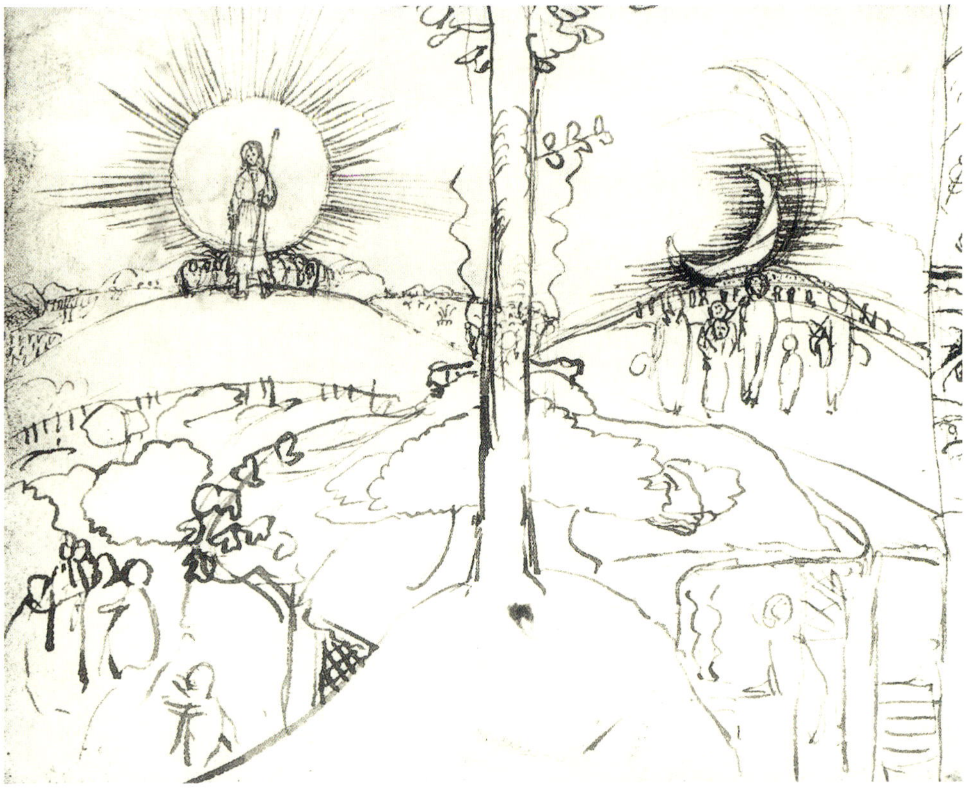

Plate 22. Sketchbook begun 1824, from page 8. Ink

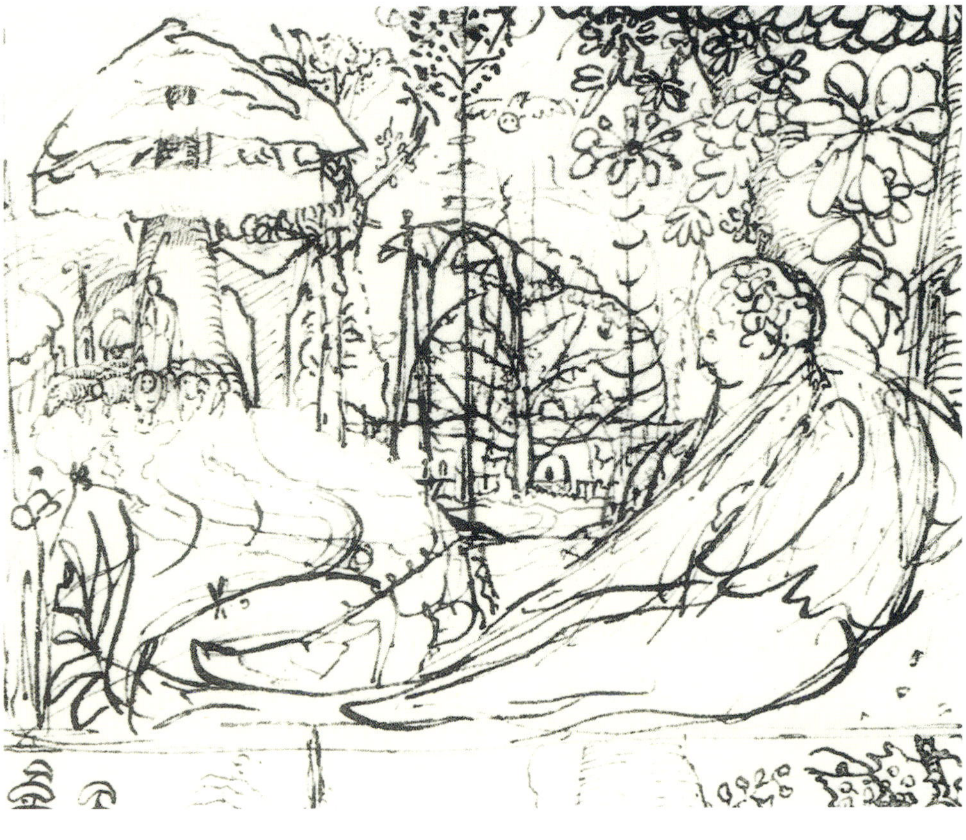

Plate 23. Sketchbook begun 1824, from page 10. Ink

Many of Claude's paintings, Blake said, had been ruined by overcleaning –

> but spoke of a few which he had seen, really untouched and unscrubbed, with the greatest delight; and mentioned, as a peculiar charm, that in these, when minutely examined, there were, upon the focal lights of the foliage, small specks of pure white which made them appear to be glittering with dew which the morning sun had not yet dried up.

Claude's white specks were like the swarming little white cuts in Blake's Virgil engravings – so many tiny lights in dark places. Palmer's recollection concluded:

> He warmed with his subject, and it continued through an evening walk. The sun was set; but Blake's Claudes made sunshine in that shady place.[52]

Slivers of lingering day defining the edge of night: opposite ends of life touching hands for a moment through fugitive lights of change.

Page 27 in Palmer's sketchbook holds its most finely elaborated drawing thus far, in a contrast of young and old. Below a smooth arc of horizon, a central 'island' is worked of new-growing grass and bushes with sheep, farm, milkmaid and swain. Near its centre an exotic 'palm' rises to pierce the horizon hill and touch the picture top. From beneath it a long-haired young man with pastoral pipe rushes forward, as if wishing to match his steps to the purposeful stride of an older man with hat and stick. But the old man's onward energy seems to signal his purpose to bypass the delights of the pastoral island.

Plate 24. Sketchbook begun 1824, from page 84. Ink

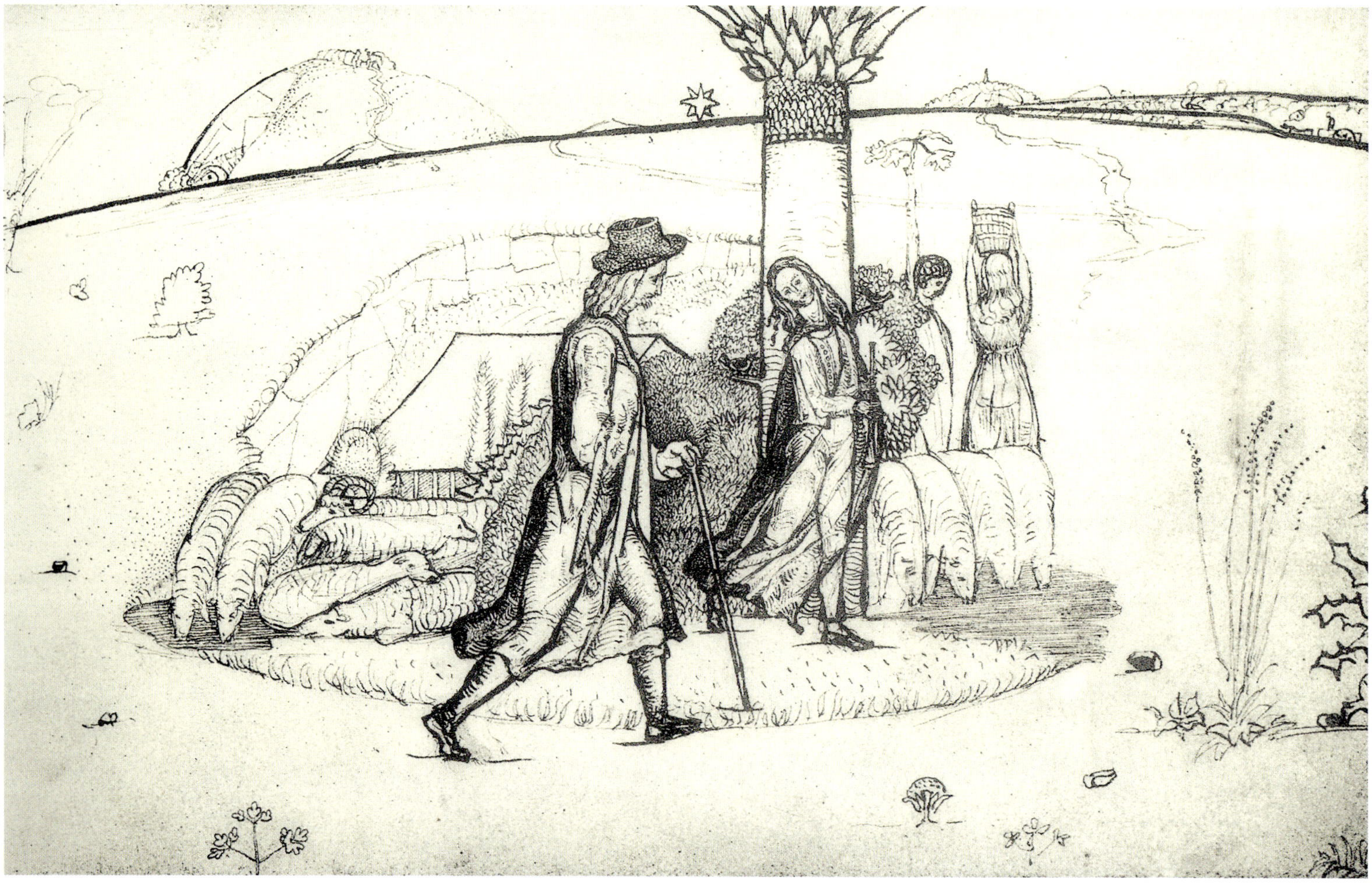

Overleaf Palmer writes:

Remember that most excellent remark of Mr B's – how that a tint equivalent to a shadow is made by the outlines of many little forms in one mass, and then how the light shines on an unbroken mass near it, such for instance as flesh &c.

Later in the sketchbook (pages 90–91) he applies Blake's formula to three attempts at an ideal female portrait: 'the firm enamel of a young face', he writes, surrounded by 'hair, wondrous sleek and silkily melting' into a further surround 'of the crisp mosaic of various leaved young trees thinnishly inlaid on a smooth sky'. Spring. Is he dreaming of such a girl in such a place?

So many interests competing for his notice drove the twenty year old Palmer to the alternative expression of verse. The poem he wrote bore so heavily on his own art that he wrote a fair copy of it into his sketchbook, filling nearly eight pages (74–81).

The poem's title, 'Twilight Time', signals another review of the subject of his elaborate sepia picture. Twilight brings change – mutability, perhaps development. Accordingly he begins in the midst of things:

And now the trembling light
Glimmers behind the little hills, and corn...

They might be the little hills and cornfields about Dulwich.

This landscape (as in many of his sketchbook drawings) acquires an observer – clad perhaps in a shepherd's smock:

The Faithful Witness, pure, & white,
Shall look o'er yonder grassy hill
At this village, safe, and still...

The village seen 'o'er yonder hill' may thus appear beyond the hills of Dulwich. It is a place of silence and folded sheep. How to see it better?

Methinks the ling'ring, dying ray
Of twilight time, doth seem more fair,
And lights the soul up more than day...

Is that impulse irreligious? God matures the harvest, after all, with the fullest sunlight. The young poet tries to resolve the conflict with a metaphor of tree-shadows:

Here I, (full oft forgetting Thee,)
Repose, beneath my cottage roof:
Outside, there spreads that ancient tree,
Thy emblem of the Book of Truth.

God's Book of Truth none the less opens widest for him at twilight:

The reason I must needs suppose
Is that we love a parting friend
And parting day draws near his close.

The notion of parting moves his thought to companionship – to women and marriage:

For sure, howe'er a poet young
Upon a fair young loving bride
Might doat and reckon ev'ry moment long
Absent from her faithful side...

What if the parting were made permanent by death? Even that notion does not extinguish his lingering light of inspiration: 'Still lovelier doth begin to Seam[*sic*] The vanishing light...'.

52. *c.* May 1860 to Alexander Gilchrist, quoted in his *Life of William Blake*, 311.

The end of this longish poem does at last move twilight into night. Here Palmer's visionary eye makes its most astonishing leap – to pagan spirits of wood and stream appearing as if from Shakespeare's *Midsummer Night's Dream*:

> The little crisped waves doth tip
> Where are the fairies wont to dip
> Then wrap them in a daisy's cup
> And by then the moon is up
> They all ready are and dry
> To trip and turn with lightsome thigh
> In magic circlets on the grass.
> Blythe their mystic hours do pass.

Thus moonrise turns the young poet's worship back to earth. He tries for a final synthesis with other-worldly faith:

> O would that man high in creation's class
> So innocently used the passing time!
> Then should heav'ns gates now dimm'd by fleshly veil
> Admit the blissful soul to joys sublime...

Yet all this poet's sublimities rise from a twilit marriage of faith with the rustic world.

Finishing the poem's fair copy midway down a sketchbook page, Palmer fills the remaining space with a prose exhortation to go beyond his now familiar ground:

> Note. that when you go to Dulwich it is not enough[,] on coming home[,] to make recollections in which shall be united the scattered parts about those sweet fields into a sentimental and Dulwich looking whole
>
> No[.] But considering Dulwich as the gate into the world of vision[,] one must try behind the hills to bring up a mystic glimmer like that which lights our dreams.
>
> And those same hills, (hard task) should give us promise that the country beyond them is Paradise –

Plate 25. Sketchbook begun 1824, from page 27. Ink

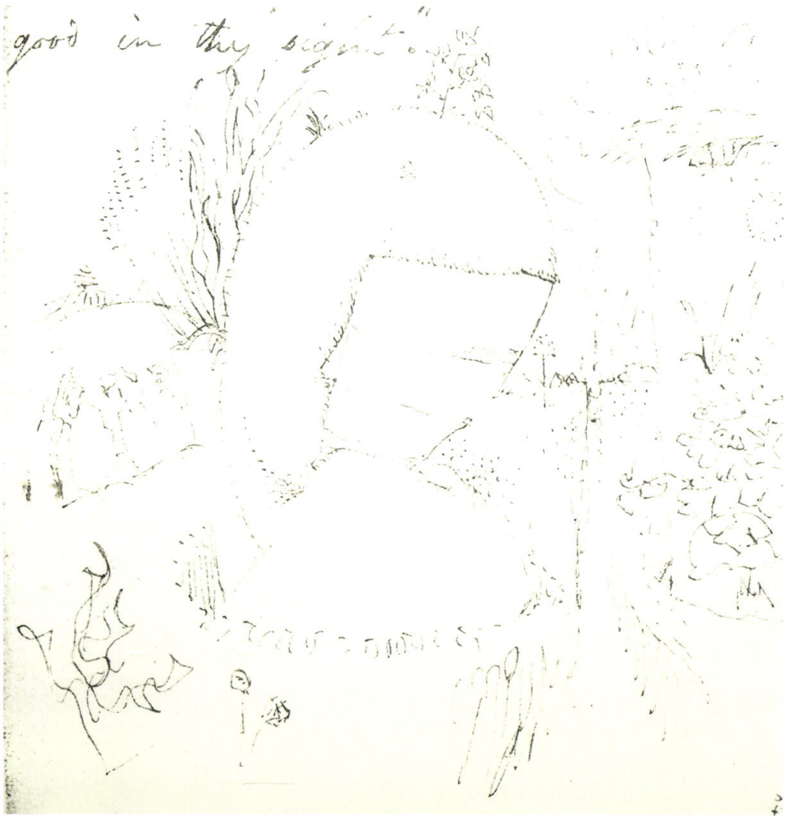

The country beyond Dulwich hills did indeed hold a 'village safe and still' where Palmer had access to a familiar 'cottage roof'. It was called Shoreham – not the seaside town in Sussex, but twenty miles down the Sevenoaks road in deepest, steepest Kent. At Shoreham, Kent his well-to-do Grandfather Giles had a cottage described by a later family friend as 'quite an Arcadian retreat'.[53] Grandfather Giles's main residence was close to Palmer's childhood home in south-east London. So the boy and his family might have visited the Shoreham cottage at almost any time.

In the spring of 1825 Grandfather Giles died. It made the cottage more available than ever. The country round Shoreham was hillier than Dulwich – less adapted to growing crops, more to keeping sheep. There a pastoral vision might be brought to focus.

Going to Shoreham for any length of time would mean putting distance between himself and Linnell and Blake and 'the grand old men' whose pictures filled the Dulwich Gallery. Palmer was not minded to hesitate. Right after his sketchbook words about the hills beyond Dulwich giving 'promise that the country beyond them is Paradise', he fills two entire pages with prose abuse of sophistication and incuriosity. Innocence is his touchstone:

> God reveals not the beauties of ancient art to the wise and prudent but to babes; to the self abased, to the mourners in Zion.

Immediately below those words comes an extraordinary drawing: a hill of spring, transmuting to an outline of head and shoulders bent in close looking or meditation: but the face is invisible (Plate 25).

Palmer's notes on intervening sketchbook pages had continued to insist on the importance of outlines. On page 48 there is a note about Michelangelo first scratching outlines into the wet Sistine fresco plaster, then filling the grooves with pitch to guide his painting. Ninety pages later Palmer condemns Raphael for using 'printer's black' in his shadows, as it 'spoils the other colours with which it is mingled'. Still it might be 'a good hint for outlines [–] which cannot be got too black'.

Many of his sketchbook drawings continue meditations on harvest and its long preparation from early spring. Spring and harvest are the times of radical change: fields full of crops growing almost visibly; and then – after standing up like a high smooth sea – suddenly cut and heaped, stooked and removed to leave the long stubble, before gleaning and then winter ploughing. These two seasons of rapid change most acutely amplify the moments of change in the daily cycle – dawn and lingering twilight.

Page 110 in Palmer's sketchbook begins a renewal of the annual cycle, with early spring returning to cottage fields. 'Try for the primitive cottage feeling', he writes opposite this drawing. Its foreground shows a huge log, symbolising past life readied for use again. That log would soon reappear in new large sepia drawings.

In his brief summary of work done in the later months of 1824, Palmer had differentiated his 'sepias' from pictures with titles (presumably paintings). The same differentiation appeared again around September 1825, when Palmer wrote out a bill addressed to a Mr Bennett. Bennett (probably his mother's cousin[54]) had commissioned the six drawings and five titled pictures (whose high prices suggest that they were paintings). Palmer wrote his bill thus:

Windsor	£5. 5. 0
Twilight	3. 3. 0
Scene from Kent	7. 7. 0
Rustic Scene	7. 7. 0
Harvest Moon	7. 7. 0
6 Drawings	1.10. 0[55]

None of the five titles appears to survive as a painting (with one possible exception: see below, page 44). But the '6 Drawings' are probably the set of six large drawings in very dark sepia, all but one dated 1825, now in the Ashmolean Museum, Oxford. A comparison of these drawings, and the titles later attached to them, with Palmer's painting titles on the Bennett bill suggests some fairly close relationships among them.[56]

The later history of *Joseph's Dream* (in progress in October 1824) may be contained in a sketchbook note on page 114:[57]

> Now begin to finish the corn-field picture bit by bit [:] finish it now as you go – and *execute* each bit with what refinement you can.

Palmer's next words are: 'In the coast drawings [two appear in his sketchbook, pages 30-31] try this way.' The formula he then writes out fits as a glove the six Ashmolean drawings:

> Begin[,] sparing no pains[,] to copy from the sketches carefully in pencil very faint and with the utmost correctness:
>
> then perfect those lines with a very fine pen so that the objects shall all be palpable and the outline very clean tho' faint

53. Samuel Calvert, *A Memoir of Edward Calvert* (Samson Low, Marston, 1893: hereinafter cited as Calvert *Memoir*), 17, 34

54. *Letters*, 454, 481 & n, 1022 & n, 1028 & n

55. Quoted in *Life and Letters*, 17 n 1. A.H. Palmer noted that he copied the bill from a sketchbook page that followed some poems. The copy-bill is no longer in the surviving sketchbook, but poems appear there on pages 74-81 and 127-129. The leaves containing pages 125-126, 137-138, 179-182 are now missing, and the leaf of 131-132 has had a portion cut away.

56. Of the six dark sepia drawings now in the Ashmolean, two may fit the two titles cited in Palmer's 1824 summary of work. *Twilight* (described as finished before his visit to Blake in Oct 1824) may correspond to the Ashmolean's *Late Twilight* (the only one of the six sepias not dated 1825, and the only one whose present title goes back with some certainty to Palmer himself: see David Blaney Brown, *Samuel Palmer* [Hazlitt, Gooden & Fox, 1982], 35.) The title *Twilight* recurs in the Bennett bill.

Joseph's Dream (in progress in Oct 1824) probably corresponds to the Ashmolean drawing now called *The Valley Thick with Corn* (a title derived from Palmer's quotation of Psalm 65 on an old mount for this drawing, preserved in the Museum). It is the only one of the Ashmolean sepias to fit Palmer's title 'Harvest Moon' in the Bennett bill.

Another title in that bill, *Rustic Scene*, is itself now attached to a third Ashmolean drawing.

Further correspondences may exist. The bill's title 'Windsor' could link to the Ashmolean *Valley with a Bright Cloud* through its distant castle turret. The bill's 'Scene from Kent' could touch the Ashmolean *Early Morning* or *The Skirts of a Wood*: both show the round-headed Portuguese laurel which still grows in Kent, but not much farther north.

57. Drawings on sketchbook leaves surrounding page 114 suggest early spring – i.e., 1825.

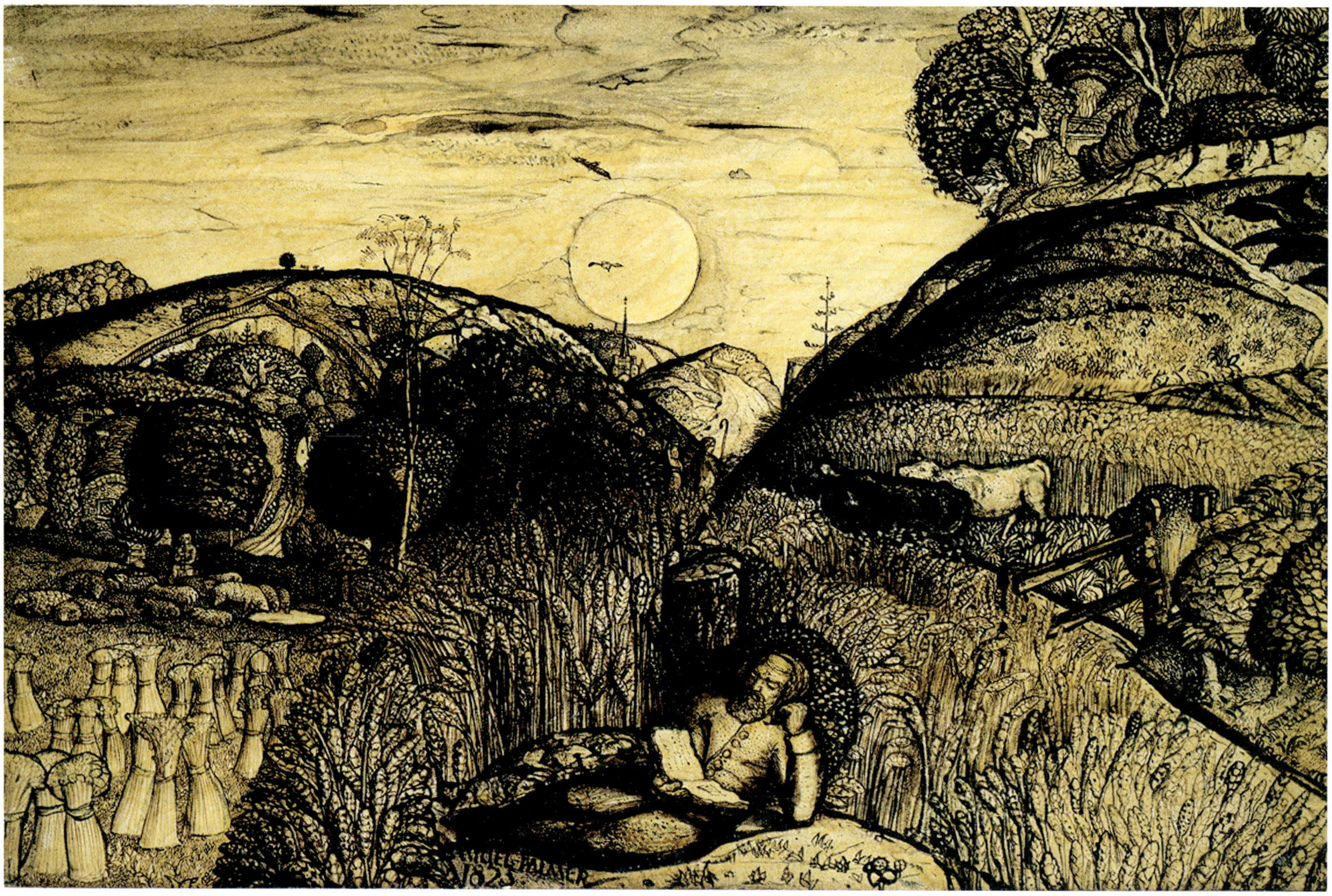

Plate 26. *The Valley Thick with Corn,* probably first called *Joseph's Dream,* 1825. Ink with gum arabic, varnished
Ashmolean Museum, Oxford

> Then presently begin to insert those masses of little forms like the leaves of a near tree which *serve instead of shadows & themselves make a tint*
> all this while fattening up the outline, till as near as you can get it[,] you make it like the prints of the Georgics [probably Blake's Virgil engravings] getting in the minutenesses too ere the colour [in the paintings] be begun.

Compare that with the expert description of the six Ashmolean drawings by Colin Harrison:

> The technique of these works is unique: Palmer has used a fine pen to draw in minute detail every element of the composition, and has mixed the dark brown ink with gum to give the thick outlines the relief found in etchings and some woodcuts.

The effect is also close to stump-work embroidery. Palmer's 'embroidered' areas in the six sepias are then re-illuminated with white ink applied to the interstices – as if to recall Blake's praise of Claude Lorrain's 'specks of pure white… upon the focal lights of the foliage'.

Finally Palmer applies his own form of dark 'sepia' tone:

> The addition of varnish unifies the composition, and gives the drawings the appearance of carved ivories, which has increased with age.[58]

Palmer's varnish recalls the mezzotint and aquatint washes printed over etching in Earlom's reconstitutions of Claude drawings, and in Turner's *Liber Studorium*, as well as the single tints Gilpin's printer imposed to unify his illustrations.

The six Ashmolean sepias trace two sequences of time. One covers the fertile months of the year in southern England. *The Valley with a Bright Cloud* shows trees with new leaves and a huge cut log beside a pair of courting birds. In *The Skirts of a Wood* the leaves are larger, the bird in

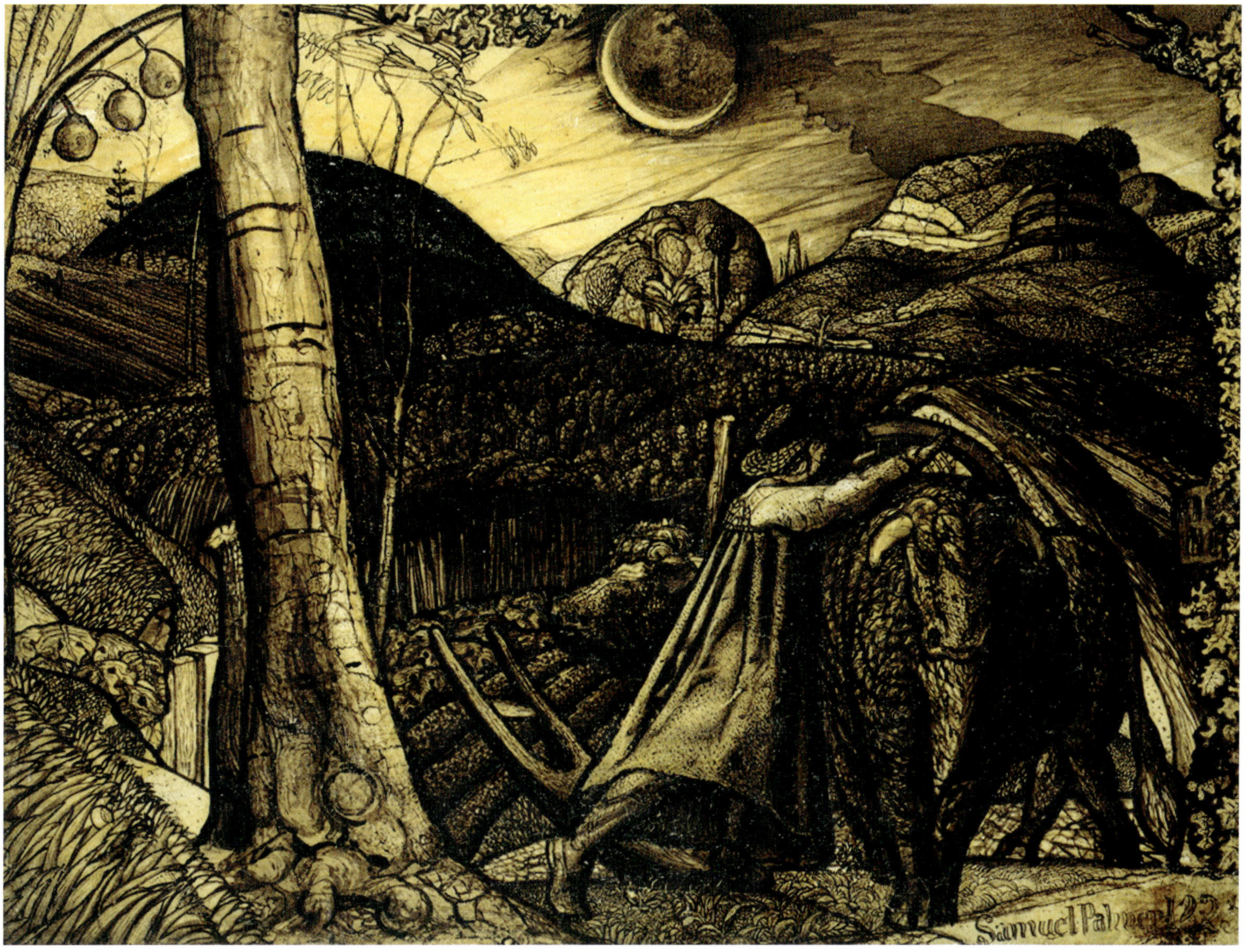

its nest with eggs and young. *Early Morning*, with another cut log and a hare symbolising fecundity, 'islands' a group of figures before ripening grain. In *The Valley Thick with Corn* the harvest is begun (Plate 26). It is nearly finished in *Late Twilight* (Plate 19, page 34, with yet another cut log and hare). *A Rustic Scene* shows its young farmer yoking bullocks under sun rays and a waning moon – at the autumn equinox, according to lines from Virgil's *Georgics* inscribed on its old mount – for ploughing until the winter solstice (Plate 27).

The six drawings move in a different sequence through the hours of the day, from *Early Morning* to *Late Twilight*. *The Valley Thick with Corn* shows an apex of double light. The huge harvest moon there reconciles earthly nature (the owl flying through it) with spirituality (the spire piercing its circumference). Yet the entire foreground is bathed in a frontal light which can come only from a low sun behind us. Here are no visible rays, but a pervading warmth to imbue each separate presence with its own particular glow as from within.

The lines and textures of Palmer's six drawings control even their largest figures. The young farmer yokes oxen with a movement fitting the patterned nature of which he is a part. The dreamer in *The Valley Thick with Corn* has no nervous spring such as Palmer found in Blake's Virgil figures. His spirit is 'uncaged' by the burgeoning textures of nature which immobilise his recumbent form. His book is the oblong shape of Palmer's sketchbook: the left-hand page appears to show a drawing, the facing page writing. Under the curve of the dreamer's leg, the young artist shapes the letters of his own name by way of signature.

Plate 27. *A Rustic Scene*, 1825. Ink with gum arabic, varnished Ashmolean Museum, Oxford

58. Harrison, *Samuel Palmer*, 14.

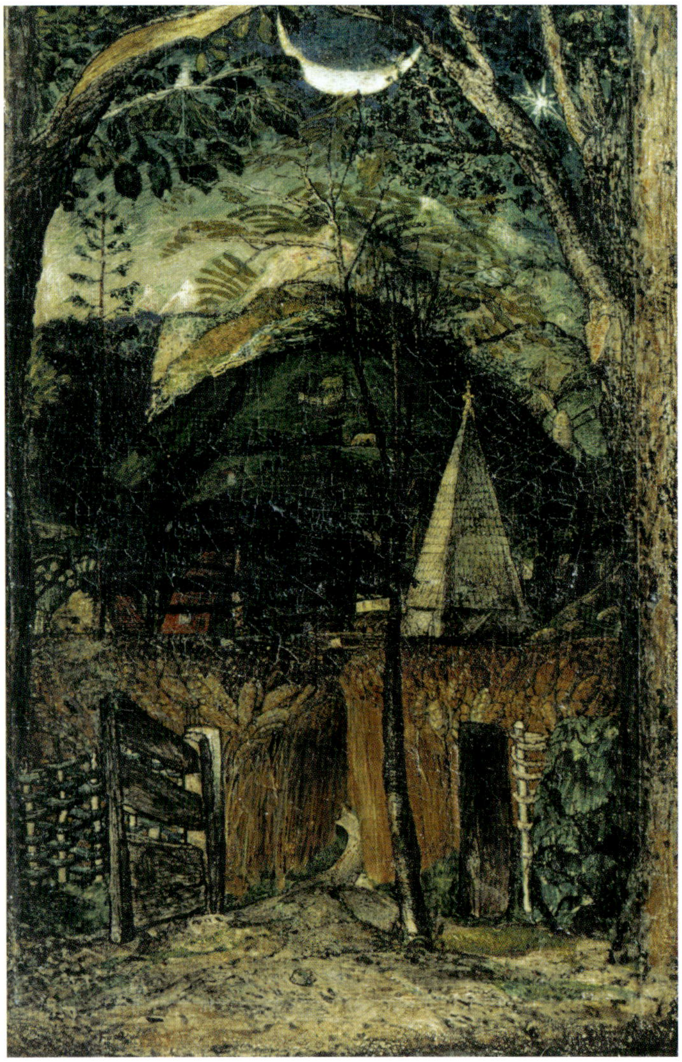

Plate 28. *A Hilly Scene, c.*1825. Ink, watercolour and tempera, varnished

Palmer's only surviving painting to share the full 'stump-work' vision of the six sepias is a small *Hilly Scene.*[59] Originally on paper (now mounted) it is drawn in ink, painted over in watercolours and tempera mixed with gum, and once again varnished (Plate 28). From under branches rising either side to meet in a rough gothic arch, a huge crescent moon and star almost touch the steepest hills. A rustic church steeple and cottage roofs lie half buried behind a field of bursting grain. The gate stands open, but no figure is here. The colours soften Palmer's ink textures only a little.

Every natural presence throughout the six sepias and *A Hilly Scene* ideally fits its 'island', enclosed in the rustic dance of Palmer's strong outlines. Aerial perspective dries away, in the enhancing warmth of interior lines and lights, to a harvest of innocence. It is a synthesis of utter individuality. In these pictures Palmer's Ruralist successor Graham Ovenden sees the one truly original style of drawing ever created in England.[60]

No such significance was seen by Palmer's contemporaries. Two of the pictures listed afterwards on his bill to Mr Bennett were hung in the Royal Academy Summer Exhibition of 1825. One critic wrote:

> We feel the most intense curiosity to see what manner of man it was who produced such performances. We think if he would show himself with a label round his neck, 'The Painter of *A View in Kent*', he would make something of it at a shilling a-head [61]

Such derision might have pushed Palmer into sending Mr Bennett an apologetic third-person note to cover the bill for the five titled pictures and six drawings. The young artist confesses that they have all emerged 'somewhat different in style from those he used to paint when Mr Bennett gave the commission'. He offers to take back 'any of the set that Mr Bennett may disapprove', or 'listen to any suggestion… towards the improvement of this set of pictures and drawings'.

Then suddenly Palmer feels impatient of all this cheese-mongering accommodation. A note to himself, written a year and a week after his first visit to Blake, draws a line on his own ground:

> It was given to me this morning (16th October, 1825) to see that I had done wrong in seeking for Mr Bennett's pictures, visions more consonant with common nature than those I received, at my first regeneration, from the Lord.
>
> I will no more, by God's grace, seek to moderate for the sake of pleasing men.[62]

There is no record of Mr Bennett ever buying or owning any of Palmer's work. Palmer kept his vow. He would concede various half-accommodations to Linnell. Blake had never asked for any accommodations. But now Palmer was making up his mind to move right away from all his mentors.

* * *

None of Palmer's six sepia drawings really reflects the Dulwich landscape. The two drawings with round-headed laurels hint at southern Kent. But *The Valley Thick with Corn* and *A Rustic Scene* in particular – and the coloured *Hilly Scene* – show sharp precipitous hills of the country round Shoreham.

Palmer's change of landscape finds its parallel in comparing the two poems he copied into his sketchbook. 'Twilight Time' (sketchbook pages 74-81) was set among Dulwich-like 'little hills and corn' – with the glimpse of another village beyond those hills. The later poem (pages 127-129) is set in this farther village among steeper hills. Here they keep sheep (studies of sheep's head appear on sketchbook page 132). The new poem's title is 'The Shepherd's home – old Churchyard'. Its geography is unmistakably Shoreham.

---

59. Could this *Hilly Scene* (now in the Tate Gallery) have been one of the five paintings listed on Palmer's bill to Mr Bennett – or a portion of one? The later histories of all these pictures strengthen that possibility. Bennett probably did not buy, for Palmer seems to have kept them all for much of his life. In 1873 he gave or sold *A Hilly Scene* to George Richmond. At around the same time he sold the six sepias to Joseph Watson Overbury (1839-1909), the junior partner of Palmer's cousin, the solicitor John Giles. (See T. Sturge Moore, 'Samuel Palmer's Happiest Designs', in *Apollo*, Dec 1936, 329). Overbury kept an annotated list of his picture acquisitions (MS in private hands). Against the six sepias he noted: 'Bought of the artist', without giving a date. From Overbury's son, Sturge Moore gathered that the transaction had taken place in Palmer's 'last years'. So it is interesting to find another early Palmer picture in Overbury's collection – 'Sunset' (later called *Going to* or *Coming from Evening Church* (see below, page 55) listed as bought from Palmer in 1873. That was the year in which *A Hilly Scene* went to Richmond. If Palmer had a clear-out of early works around 1873, it could suggest that he himself destroyed the remainder of the five Bennett-bill paintings about the time he let the others pass to friends.

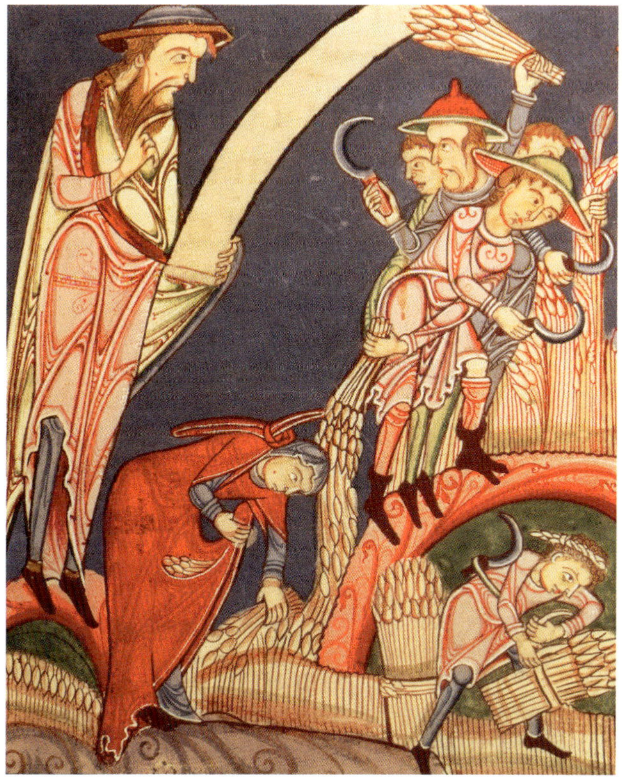

Plate 29. Ruth gleaning after the reapers of Boaz in *The Lambeth Bible*, mid-12th century. Illumination © Lambeth Palace Library, London, UK/The Bridgeman Art Library

> Low lies their home 'mongst many a hill,
> In fruitful and deep delved womb;
> A little village, safe and still...
>
> There, almost buried from the sight
> Of travellers on the higher ground
> Be rushing brooks, and sparkling bright
> Clear, shallow, pebbled streams...
>
> And intricate with fruit-bent boughs,
> And flowers, trim cottage gardens are...
> And there's a church-yard something raised
> Above the more unholier ground.

The little Darent River runs shallow under the bridge through the middle of Shoreham. Church and churchyard stand at the far edge of the village on rising ground. Here the poet asks to lie without any marker to distinguish his bones from surrounding nature.

Soon after finishing the six sepias and *A Hilly Scene*, Palmer took the decision to go and live at Shoreham. Set in a fold of the North Downs, it seemed a hundred miles and a thousand years from London. Even half a century later Palmer's son could write:

> Here were stately parks replete with antique oaks of giant growth; huge chestnuts with outstretched limbs sweeping the ground... The deeply hollowed lanes were fringed with luxuriant vegetation and gnarled roots, and at night were black with intense darkness.
>
> In sloping orchards, grey-stemmed patriarchs still fruitful, were covered in the spring-time with clotted blossom, to be afterwards bowed beneath an autumnal load of crimson apples, in rich contrast with the white fleeces of the sheep in the chequered shade beneath.
>
> The soil was tilled and the golden corn was reaped by sturdy villagers whose dress was picturesquely beautiful, their implements archaic. Their strenuous flails resounded in spacious, lichen-covered barns, where the thick masses of dark green moss half hid the deep overhanging thatch.
>
> They lived in oak-beamed cottages with ample chimney-corners, in which, on tempestuous winter nights, many a strange legend and weird superstition lingered still.[63]

Here the cycle of seasons was humanised in the immemorial round of ploughing, sowing, reaping, turning. It was far older than Christianity: yet the perspective glass of English vision remained the New Testament, and the Old. And thus Shoreham, for the young visionary, could touch the inspiration of the Bible itself. Here Palmer's vision might also meet a classical Golden Age – where the fruits of innocence remain forever ripening in an English orchard.

Palmer went down to stay at Shoreham in the spring of 1826, probably in May.[64] He took with him another young artist who shared Blake's friendship, Frederick Tatham. They nicknamed Grandfather Giles's gothick cottage 'Rat Abbey', spread the grandfatherly legacy paper-thin, and lived on enthusiasm.[65] Palmer's father made frequent visits, and was so charmed that he closed his bookshop and brought down much of its stock to a larger house by the river called 'Water House'.[66]

The atmosphere of Shoreham for the transplanted Londoners remained young. Tatham and other friends who visited all read the younger Palmer's favourite passages from Virgil and Milton to induce pastoral vision – each to himself, aloud to one another, or chanting the lines as they walked the hills by day and night. At home in the cottage and Water House, young Palmer would scrape away at old country tunes on a violin.

In later years he was to write of Shoreham as a refuge from illness (probably asthma). But Palmer had an immediate project there. In one of his 'pocket-books' he wrote a prayer 'On going to Shoreham, Kent to design from *Ruth*'.[67] *Ruth* is the Biblical Book of the harvest, a subject for illustration time out of mind (Plate 29). Moreover it had a connection with Blake – and Blake had promised to visit Shoreham.

60. Conversation with the writer, 2000.
61. *The European Magazine*, quoted in Grigson, 29.
62. Quoted in *Life and Letters*, 17. A.H. Palmer located the note of Oct 1825 in the sketchbook 'after another interval of poetry' (ie presumably the poem on pp 127-129). It is no longer there. After the second poem, three sketchbook leaves are missing: pp 137-138, 179-182; and one (pp 131-132) has had a portion cut away.
63. A.H. Palmer, *Samuel Palmer: a Memoir* (Fine Art Society, 1882: hereinafter cited as *Memoir*), 5.
64. All of Palmer's known letters from Shoreham are dated 1827 or later, except one. That one, addressed to Linnell, is superscribed 'Wednesday Septembr. 1824[*sic*] (*Letters*, 7-9). All its internal evidence – a considerable amount – fits with other Shoreham letters to Linnell of Sept 1828. The last Wednesday in Sept 1828 fell on the 24th: and that may probably account for Palmer's slip of the pen.
65. *Life and Letters*, 33; *Letters*, 956.
66. Calvert *Memoir*, 34-35; see also the superscription in Palmer's long letter of Sept 1828 to George Richmond (*Letters*, 32).
67. Written 'about April or May, 1826', according to Palmer's son, who quoted only these words before destroying the MS (*Life and Letters*, 33).

Blake himself had once drawn *Ruth and Naomi* before a typically summarised landscape. Palmer had never seen the picture or its purchaser, but Blake had offered to take him to see that collection.[68] Now Palmer listed in his sketchbook (page 136) five possible subjects from *Ruth*.

As the first summer at Shoreham drew to its end, he had not finished a single one of them. It was not for want of trying. 'A short, fragmentary journal' (partly quoted, before destruction, by his son) raises despair to puritanic appeal:

> At Shoreham, Kent, August 30, 1826. God worked in great love with my spirit last night, giving me a founded hope that I might finish my *Naomi before Bethlehem*, and (to me) in a short time... That night, when I hoped and sighed to complete the above subject well (it will be my maiden finished figure drawing), I hoped only in God, and determined next morning to attempt working on it in God's strength. ...

But the real spring of the young man's inspiration appears in his next quoted words:

> Now I go out to draw some hops[,] that their fruitful sentiment may be infused into my figures...
>
> August 31... I worked with but little faith on my *Naomi before Bethlehem* this morning, and succeeded just in proportion.
>
> After dinner I was helped against the enemy so that I thought one good thought. I immediately drew on my cartoon much quicker and better...
>
> Satan tries violently to make me leave reading the Bible and praying... O artful enemy, to keep me, who devote myself entirely to poetic things, from the best of books...

Here is the opposite to Blake's self-assurance, and to Linnell's commercial drive. Each of those elders based his work on firm training in figure-drawing. To try to compensate, Palmer charges himself to begin each day's work with a morning meditation on 'some short piece of scripture'. Yet the morning hour itself runs against his own promptings: 'Now, in the twilight, let Him come that at evening-time it may be light.'

Then as if suddenly waking to the naked enthusiasm in these sentiments, he adds:

> God bless my father and brother and poor old nurse: who, though a misled Baptist, shall sing among the redeemed for ever.

The chapel attracted Palmer less, the Church of England more and more as he looked for inspiration in the traditional life around him at Shoreham.[69]

Palmer's entire effort to make drawings from *Ruth* at Shoreham may have looked towards Blake's expected visit. In the single *Ruth* drawing to survive,[70] *Ruth Returned from Gleaning*, the big striding heroine makes Palmer's closest approach to a Blakean figure (Plate 30): it is not matched in any of Palmer's surviving work. A second figure reading by candlelight outside a cottage window (lower left) remains only a sketch. The landscape they share is faintly reminiscent of a Blakean whirlwind – with new sexual overtones.

Palmer's wish to please Blake might also be seen in this drawing's loosening pencil technique under its ink and wash (heightened with touches of white). Some outlines are as heavy as those in the six sepias of 1824-25; but the finer 'stump-work' textures are now partly washed over.

At last the inveterate old Londoner paid his visit to Shoreham.[71] Blake was accompanied by Edward Calvert (1799-1883), the eldest of his young disciples, whom Palmer had met that spring in London), by Calvert's wife, and by Samuel Palmer (probably senior). They travelled down in a heavy stage-wagon from Charing Cross.

All the signs point to the visit proving a sharp disappointment to the young Palmer still trying, against his inclinations, to make Blake his master. After welcoming the guests, young Palmer discovered two days later a need to take himself to London. He left Blake and the Calverts to his father and departed. He returned only because his coach had broken down outside Lullingstone

---

68. Listed by Blake as 'Ruth & her mother in Law & Sister': sold to Thomas Butts (Gilchrist, 163). Palmer recalled: 'Dear Mr Blake had promised to take me himself to see Mr Butts's collection, – but alas! – it never came off.' (5 Feb 1881 to William Abercrombie, in *Letters*, 1061.)
69. *Life and Letters*, 33-38. All the manuscripts of these notes and many more were afterwards destroyed by Palmer's son, embarrassed by their emotionality. For that, A.H. Palmer thought he knew where to set the blame: 'It must create no little wonder that even Blake could have infected any healthy mind to such a great degree with his own nebulous way of regarding simple things.' Yet in another mood Herbert Palmer saw a gulf between Blake's sublime assurance and Samuel Palmer's 'morbid and effeminate tendency of thought'.
70. A.H. Palmer almost certainly destroyed other drawings from *Ruth*. He confessed to finding them 'remarkable for exaggerated attitude, unwieldy muscular form, and a nightmare composition for which even the teaching of Blake could not be held responsible. The spectator is repelled before he has time to discover little nooks of landscape...'. The son then minutely describes as 'before me' two *Ruth* pictures which seem to have disappeared. *Ruth Returned from Gleaning* was spared perhaps because it showed its muscular female from behind. It may have been finished after the others, as it was shown at the Royal Academy in 1829.
71. Looking at the ups and downs of Blake's now fragile health, and at the seasons, the autumn of 1826 appears the only possible time after Palmer's arrival to stay at Shoreham in the previous spring. Laurence Binyon, in *The Followers of William Blake* (Halton & Truscott Smith, 1925) p 14, comes to the same conclusion.
72. The only source for Blake's visit to Shoreham is the recollection of Calvert's son Samuel, who related what he had been told (in his *Memoir* of his father, pp 34-36, written after all the eyewitnesses were dead).
73. Quoted in A.M.W. Stirling, *The Richmond Papers* (Heinemann, 1926), 18.
74. *Life and Letters*, 42.

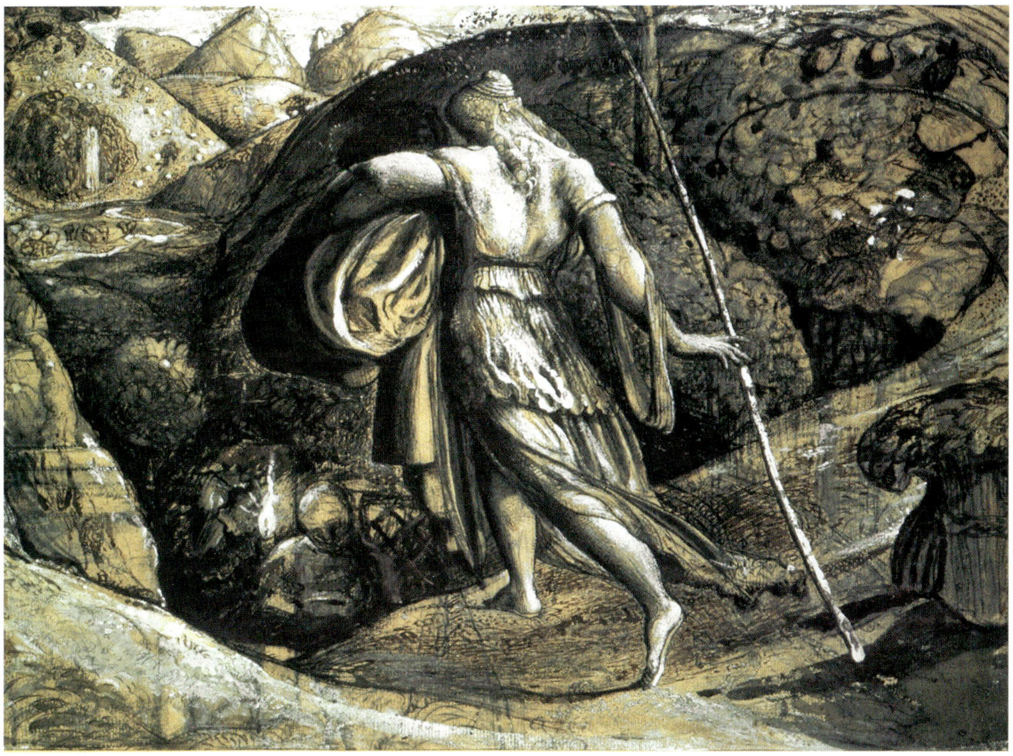

Plate 30. *Ruth returned from gleaning*, *c.*1826–28. Pencil, ink and wash
V&A Images/Victoria and Albert Museum

Park. In all the luminous recollections he set down in later years for Blake's biographer, Palmer never wrote a word about the old man's visit to Shoreham.[72]

The Shoreham visit was the last time Palmer is known to have seen Blake. When Blake died in August 1827, Palmer declined George Richmond's offer of a place in the coach to attend the funeral – leaving Richmond, Calvert, and young Tatham to follow the coffin to the cemetery. Grigson has suggested that Palmer could not bear to see a dear friend laid away. That is possible.

Yet all the history of Palmer's art thus far shows him making use of outside guidance when it happened to fit the emerging pattern of his own goals. Blake's influence was chiefly in awakening the notion of vision itself. Blake's late engravings for the Virgil *Eclogue* and for *Job* had fetched ancient Mediterranean landscapes home to English rurality; but they defined no special place. Now that Palmer had found his place and gone to live there, Blake's physical presence on Palmer's ground might show the younger man how little his clarifying vision here was to be helped by any teacher.

Young men take what they can from a helping hand, and then move on. There could be no doubt of Palmer's devotion to the memory of Blake. But Shoreham was opening its gates. Palmer was bound to enter in.

Each of the other young friends of Blake came to stay at Shoreham in 1826 and 1827. Calvert came again in April 1827, Richmond in June and once more in September. Joining Palmer's search after vision, they had dubbed themselves 'The Ancients'. Richmond recalled: 'The people of the village could not make out what we were after, for we walked much in the deep twilight and into the night, so "Astrologers" seemed much the most likely.'[73] The country speech turned it to 'Extollagers', and that seemed quite as good.

They were, Palmer's son wrote:

> … especially fond of those effects that gather in the sky with great summer tempests, and at the first mutter of approaching thunder, whether by day or night, they hurried out and revelled in the thickest of the storm.[74]

Storms alter the light as dramatically as any dawn or sunset – with rapid, concentrating violence. As Palmer's time at Shoreham extended, the lights of its darkness would hold him more and more.

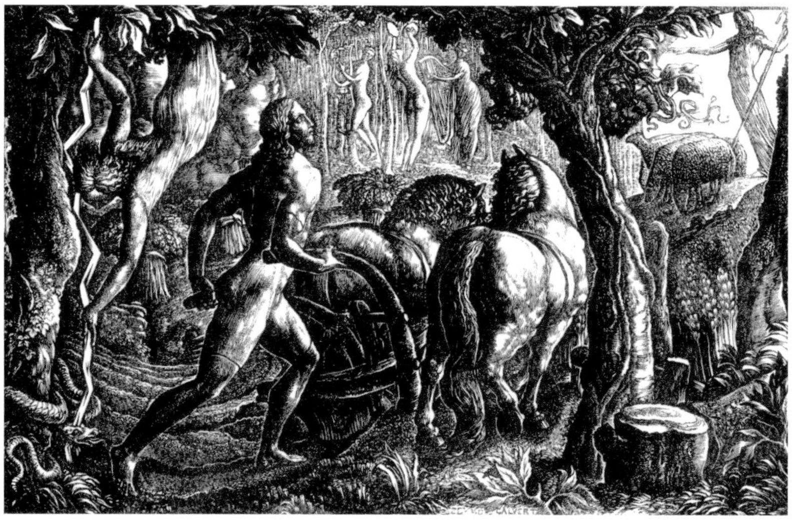

Plate 31. Edward Calvert: *Christian ploughing the last furrow of life,* 1827. Wood engraving The Fine Art Society

Calvert and Richmond tried to share Palmer's vision of the land and its keeping. Each was more skilled than Palmer at setting Blakean figures into their landscapes. In 1827 both Calvert and Richmond engraved inspired images on wood and copper. Yet those images proved to be few. Calvert's *The Christian Ploughing the Last Furrow of Life* (published in September 1827, a month after Blake's death) was one of hardly a dozen little pictures of comparable inspiration from his hand (Plate 31). Of Richmond's two copper plates, *The Shepherd* was actually engraved at Shoreham in 1827 (Plate 32).

Neither friend sustained his vision far beyond Blake's death. Richmond in 1828 began an extended study-visit to France and Italy. From it he returned to take up a career as one of the most successful portrait artists of his time. Married at twenty-one and soon the father of a growing family, Richmond lived his long life in and about London.

Calvert's equally long life with his large family was also lived in London. After making his visionary images (mostly on wood blocks the size of Blake's Virgil engravings, but going beyond them in complex counterpoints and finish) Calvert's art fell into a sub-Claudean stupor of weakening pastoral nudes. It proved lifelong. Another part of his brain pursued psychologic geometries as impenetrable as Blake's most gnomic writings.

Plate 32. George Richmond: *The Shepherd,* 1827. Engraving The Fine Art Society

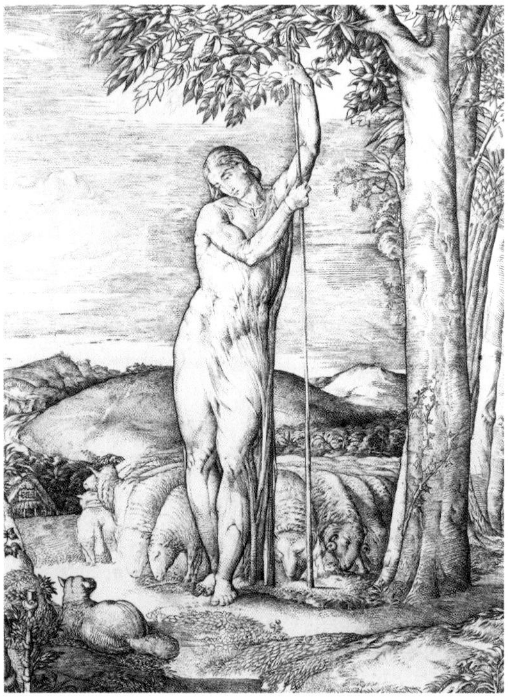

Palmer's art differed from his friends' in two ways. Ultimately Palmer was to find means to recover from a *stupor mundi* into which he too fell in the later 1830s. But before that, Palmer's art at Shoreham was to burgeon with a suddenness never experienced by any English artist before him. His Shoreham pictures would bring pastoral vision to a new definition in English art.

Most of Palmer's Shoreham pastorals are independent of any story. Their purpose is to concentrate the visions of rustic tradition and farming cycle which had brought him here. He was still only twenty-one when he had taken himself to live at Shoreham. At twenty-two and twenty-three his art began to overtake the arts of his friends.

Calvert and Richmond had pursued their Shoreham visions in highly wrought graphics. Palmer, who had already driven line to one kind of ultimate expression in his six sepias, now moved slowly away from pure line. He enkindled newer lights in a series of monochrome wash drawings highlighted with white. Several are nocturnes. Moonlit as well as twilit atmospheres amplify his delineations of mass and shadow (Plate 33). The widening range of his wash drawings at Shoreham would gradually lead Palmer towards the most astounding colours.

Once again, as when he was making up his mind to live at Shoreham, Palmer resorted also to the alternative expression of words. The young artist's exaltation mixed with uncertainty is set down in a long letter to Linnell. This letter is to be understood (Palmer writes) not as assertion, but 'putting forth a thesis by way of query'.[75]

His text is still his 'excessive' claim for art as 'the standard of nature'. First he separates them:

> I have begun to take off a pretty view of part of the village… though, at the same time I can't help seeing that the general characteristics of Nature's beauty not only differ from, but are in some respects opposed to Imaginative Art; and *that*, even in those scenes and appearances where she is loveliest…

To survey the opposing territories, his pilgrim prose sets up a House of the Interpreter. Struggling to clarify long long thoughts, Palmer's prose subdivides in rough strophes. So he anticipates the 'free verse' of Walt Whitman half a century later. Some such Whitmanesque repointing, to my mind, frees Palmer's lyric figures from the solid blocks of his letter-writing prose. Thus (in his words and virtually his punctuation) he writes to Linnell:

Nature, with mild, reposing breadths of lawn and hill,
shadowy glades and meadows,
is sprinkled and showered with a thousand pretty eyes
and buds and spires and blossoms, gemm'd with dew
and is clad in living green.
Nor must be forgot the mottley clouding, the fine meshes,
the aerial tissues that dapple the skies of spring;
nor the rolling volumes and piled mountains of light;
nor the purple sunset blazon'd with gold;
nor the translucent amber.

Most of this is light and colour, not line. And almost his next words question the formula which had achieved his linear 'stump-work' style of 1824-25:

But the leafy lightness,
the thousand repetitions of little forms
which are a part of its own generic perfection…

75. Dec 1828 (*Letters*, 47-51).

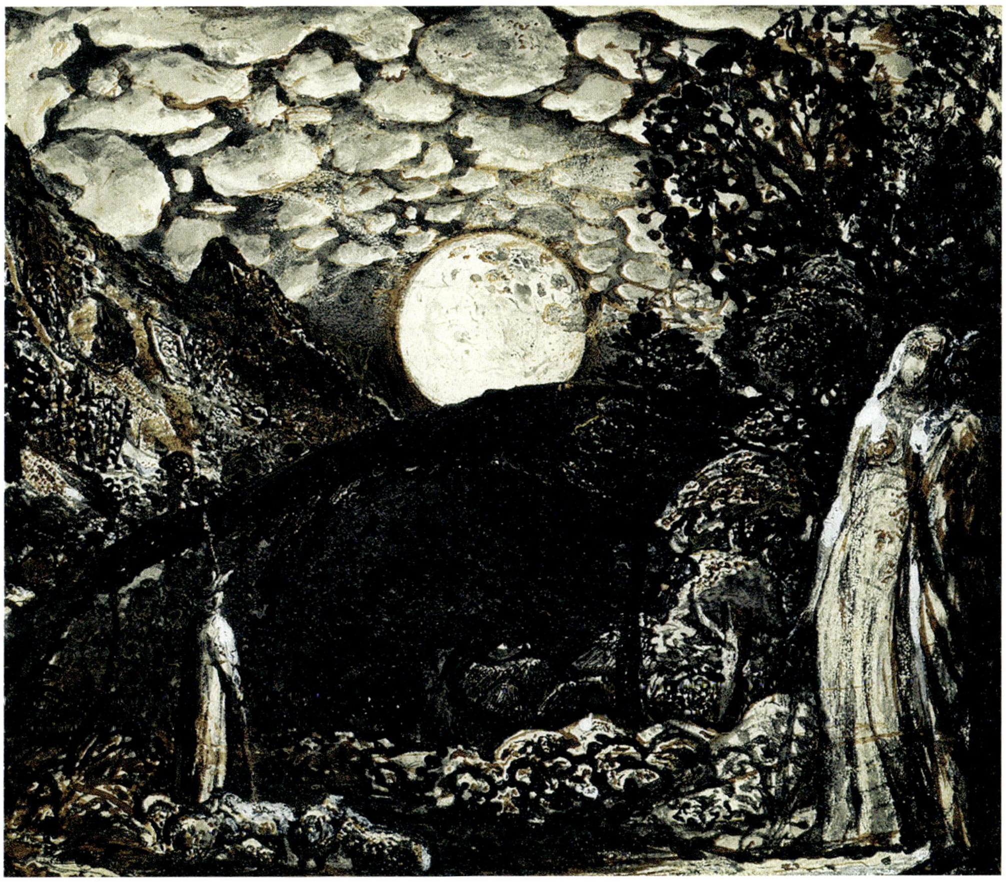

Plate 33. *Shepherds under a full moon*, *c*.1830. Ink and body colour
Ashmolean Museum, Oxford

seem hard to be reconciled with
the unwinning severity,
the awfulness,
the ponderous globosity
of Art.

This first try at setting his newest aspirations into words has brought his diction down with a bump.

He invokes exemplars from history. First literature, setting the single verse line within deliberate prose:

Milton, by one epithet, draws an oak of the largest girth I ever saw; –
'Pine and *Monumental* Oak' [in Il Penseroso];
I have just been trying to draw a large one in Lullingstone; but the Poet's tree is huger than any in the park:

(it is a matter of structure, not surface:)

there, the moss,
the rifts and barky furrows,
and the mouldering grey
(tho' that adds majesty to the lord of forests)
mostly catch the eye –
before the grasp and grapple of the roots;
the muscular belly and shoulders;
the twisted sinews.

The metaphor of a human body, introduced at the turn from appearance to form, broadens implications. Are details now the enemies of art? He thinks of Flemish painting, with its 'faces… exquisitely drawn' while 'the naked form, thwarted with fringes, and belts, and trappings' is 'neglected, or ill expressed'. Its *reductio* arrived for him in the over-domesticated Dutch painting that followed – where faces ('the least finished of any part') yield 'to the perfected finish of stew-pans and chamber pots'. Corruption lies in emphasising the man-made things.

'But nature is not like this.' The details of nature possess innocence.

I saw a lovely little rustic child this evening,
which took my fancy so much, that I long,
with tomorrow's light, God sparing me,
to make a humble attempt to capture some of its graces…[76]

Is innocence itself the key to this lock?

Sometimes, when the spirits are in Heav'n,
earth itself, as an emulation, blooms again into Eden;
rivalling those golden fruits
which the poet of Eden sheds upon his landscape…

God then as artist? or in the artist? Yet traditional religion seems powerless to help Palmer's aspiring philosophy:

Still the perfection of nature
is not the perfection of severest art:
they are two things: …
That, is graceful humanity;
This is Plato's vision.

The distinction seems to epitomise the difference between Palmer's two styles. First, the 'stump-work' drawings:

> General nature is simple and lovely…
> every where curious, articulate, perfect,
> and inimitable of structure, like her own etymology –

But now Shoreham opens a new breath to his vision:

> Nature does yet leave a space
> for the soul to climb above her steepest summits: …
> Creation sometimes pours into the spiritual eye the radiance of Heaven:
> the green mountains that glimmer in a summer gloaming
> from the dusky yet bloomy East;
> the moon, opening her golden eye,
> or walking in brightness among innumerable islands of light –

These things 'not only thrill the optic nerve,'

> but shed a mild, a grateful an unearthly lustre into the inmost spirits,
> and seem the interchanging twilight of that peaceful country,
> where there is no sorrow and no night.

Every light eternally on the change: yet no light finally extinguished.

So the end of all this catechism seems to show his goal as the paradox of representing change itself in an art of stillness – of capturing an essence of becoming more than being. Admitting the usefulness of Linnell's insistence that he study nature, the end of Palmer's letter deftly turns the elder's rule against him (as the letter reverts to prose):

> Those glorious clouds which you paint I do think inimitably, are alone an example of how the elements of nature may be transmuted into the pure gold of art:
> I would give something to get their style of form into the torso of a figure.

'Their style of form': it is a phrase worth pondering. Several pages in Palmer's surviving sketchbook, including three close to the end, show male anatomies in Blakean shapes: but they never translated into any known finished drawing or painting by Palmer.

For the first two years of Palmer's residency, Shoreham never saw Linnell. At first he had prophesied Palmer's ruin from rustication: 'Voluntary secession from artists will end in the withering of art in your mind.'[77] It needed time for Linnell to change his mind – or half change it. When at last he came in August 1828 and again in September, he was turned by Shoreham's beauty – and wanted to return once more to sketch hop-picking. But he remained sharply critical of Palmer's 'excesses'. He advised his former pupil to confine himself to close studies in Lullingstone Park. That could lead to income.

Palmer half acceded: for he himself was searching. But inviting Linnell to Shoreham again, he used a gently mocking tone to tell of close studies in Lullingstone Park:

> I have begun two studies for you on grey paper at Lullingstone – if you make haste you may prevent my spoiling them. …
>
> Have I not been a good boy? I may safely boast that I have not entertain'd a single imaginative thought these six weeks. While I am drawing from Nature[,] vision seems foolishness to me – the arms of an old rotten tree trunk more curious than the arms of [Michelangelo's] Moses… and Jacob Ruysdael a sweeter finisher than William Blake.

Yet Linnell must not conclude that Palmer was yielding an inch of the ground he had gained here:

> I dare say it is good to draw from the visible creation because it is a sort of practice and refreshes the mind tired with better things…[78]

76. For one possible result of this particular inspiration, see below Chapter 6, page 163.
77. As Linnell's message was conveyed by Palmer's father (*Life and Letters*, 39).
78. 'Wednesday [24] Septembr. 182[8]': see above page 45, note 64.

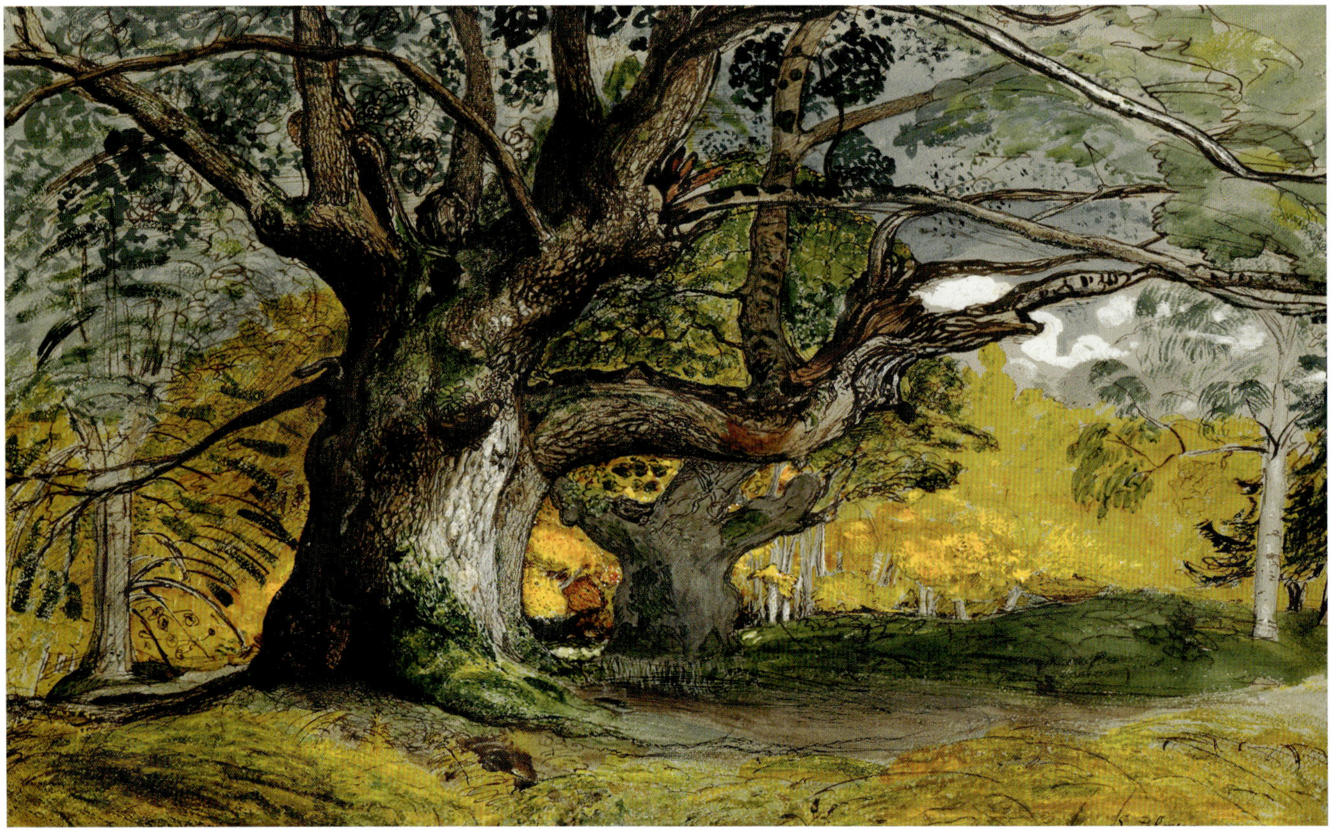

Plate 34. Oak trees, Lullingstone Park, 1828. Pencil, ink, watercolour and bodycolour with gum National Gallery of Canada, Ottawa

A few days later Palmer conveyed his fuller thoughts to George Richmond in France.[79] He recounts debates with Linnell over politics and religion: Linnell for low church and the 'peasantry', Palmer for 'high church' and 'the old high tories' who might keep country traditions. There was also the continuing debate over art itself. Palmer would have none of Linnell's monetary motives:

> By God's help I will not sell away His gift of art for money; no, not for fame neither, which is far better.
>
> Mr Linnell tells me that by making studies of the Shoreham scenery I could get a thousand a year directly. Tho' I am making studies for Mr Linnell, I will, God help me, never be a naturalist by profession.

Palmer's letter to Richmond looks back to older sources for inspiration. He longs for adequate engravings of Italian Renaissance pictures, and urges Richmond on to Italy: 'A visit, indeed, to Rome should reimpress upon us with the force of local retrospection the spirit and genius of Christianity.' As for Palmer's present art, 'the force of local retrospection' was exactly what he was pursuing at Shoreham.

Within weeks of writing that letter to Richmond, Palmer used part of his remaining legacy to buy the freeholds of several tenanted cottages as his own stake in Shoreham. He wrote to Richmond now of its 'inoppressive links of lenient penury' as purifying his soul. He drew analogy from the oaks at Lullingstone towering over the park walls to receive every wind:

> If my aspirations are very high, my depressions are very deep, yet my pinions never loved the middle air; yea I will surrender to be shut up among the dead, or in the prison of the deep, so I may *sometimes* bound upwards; pierce the clouds; and look over the doors of bliss.

In later years George Richmond was to say that he thought Linnell had got as much from Palmer as the other way. If so, it was slow learning, painful to giver and receiver. For too much of their lives there was only the older domineering character trying to impose itself upon the younger visionary imagination. An aggressor is often tempted to mistake vision for weakness.

Palmer's letters to Linnell through the autumn of 1828 show him trying to fulfil Linnell's

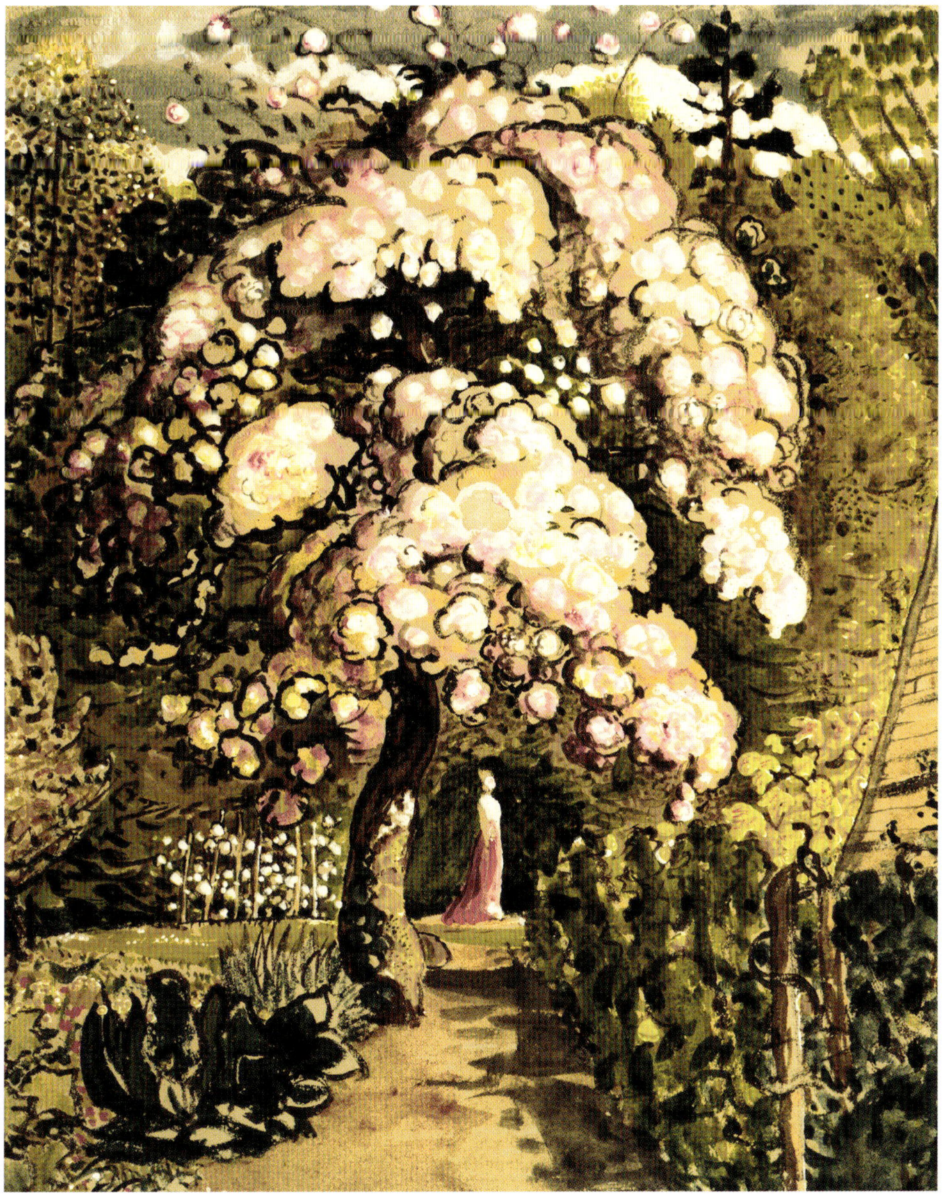

Plate 35. *In a Shoreham Garden, c.*1829. Water-colour and bodycolour
V&A Images/Victoria and Albert Museum

prescription for 'drawing the Natural Fact till I am cold in my extremities'. Line re-emerges, without regaining the patterning exuberance of his 'stump-work' drawings. The best of Palmer's Lullingstone drawings, however, begin to open his path to a new exuberance – colour.

Two of Palmer's Lullingstone drawings show additions of body colour and watercolours: greys and grey-blues, cool greens and browns. But the autumn distances are measured in rich bright yellows. The brightest colour defines the greatest distance (Plate 34). A year or two earlier the horizons of Dulwich had led his eye toward 'the most powerful objects in colour'. Now the environs of Shoreham begin to reveal the colours with which to reverse atmospheric perspective.

The first buildings about Shoreham to attract Palmer's new colours are rustic sheds and barns. Here, without much depth of horizon, his brightest colours go into showing things least worked by the hand of man: foreground grass, moss on the roofing thatch, and between them a rich brown cow.

Palmer begins to heighten his colours by preparing his boards with a white grounding formula given him by Mrs Blake. Stronger whites appear in a small drawing of a pear tree against a garden wall. Then white is joined with bright pink in a watercolour of blossom surrounded by golden yellows and greens *In a Shoreham Garden* (Plate 35). Here at the end of the prospect walks a female figure: not one of Palmer's rustics, but distinctly a lady. Who is she? and what is she doing at Shoreham?

79. 'Sept. 1828' (Letters, 32-43): written largely at the end of Sept, as Palmer writes of Linnell: 'He has been twice to the valley, and is coming again in a day or two.' (p 36). Illness apparently prevented Linnell's third visit. A later portion of Palmer's long letter to Richmond is dated 'OCTOBER' (*Letters*, 43-45).

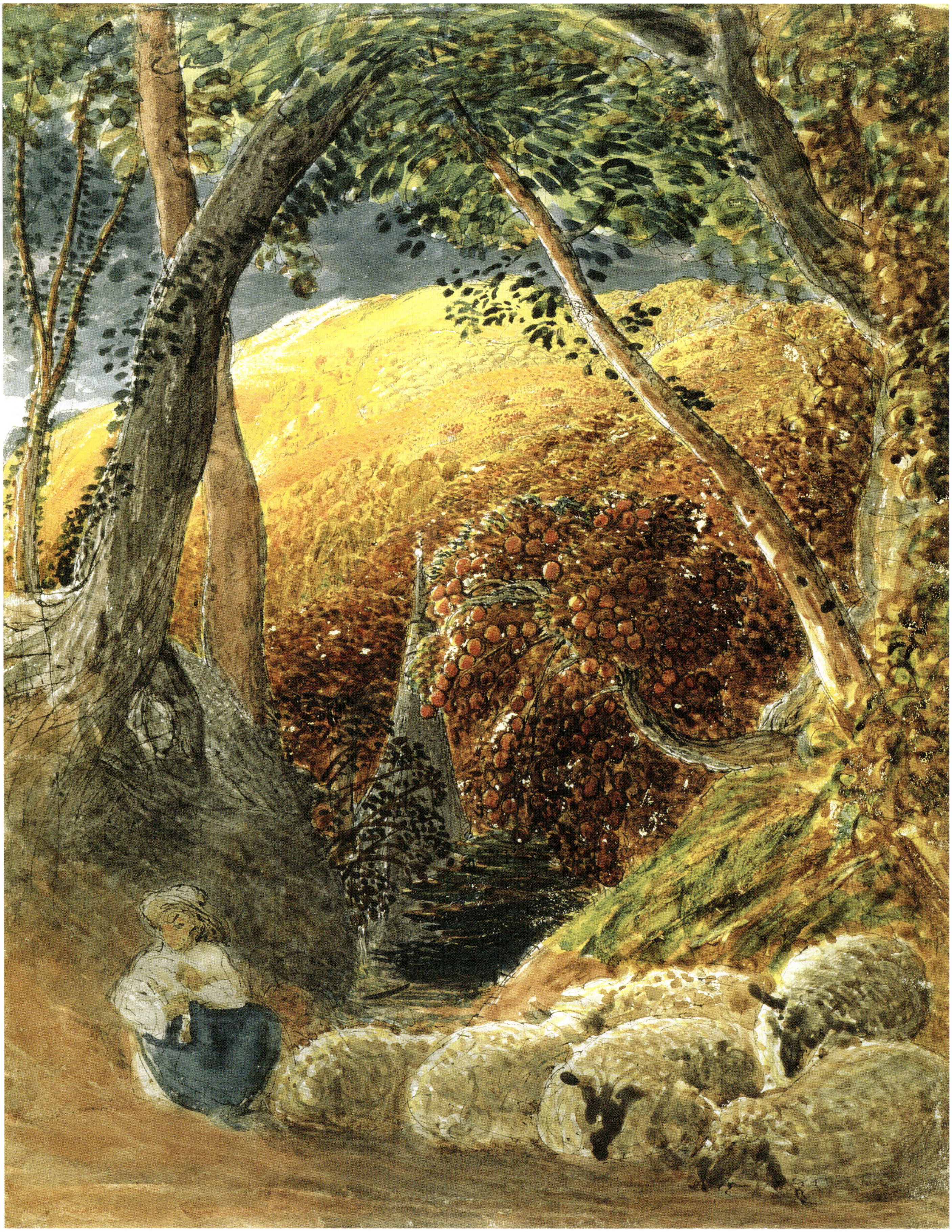

Plate 36. *The Magic Apple Tree,* 1830. Ink, watercolour and bodycolour with gum
Fitzwilliam Museum, Cambridge

Quite suddenly Palmer found himself able to complete his oil and tempera painting of *The Holy Family* (laid aside in 1824) with an ideal background which he found about a Shoreham paddock.[80] He lays on the oil colours in minute strokes side by side – a chrysalis of Impressionist techniques fifty years in advance.

As his colours spread and intensify, Palmer's brushwork takes on more dotting, dashing, and dappling: new translations of his earlier pen and ink 'stump-work' textures – to watercolour. In 1830 Palmer's dappled colouring touched unprecedented intensities in *The Magic Apple Tree* (Plate 36). Radiating round a steeple of puritan grey half buried in the surrounding colour, eye-opening brightnesses animate the surface in close-worked textures of pen and brush. Boundaries are softened and somewhat modelled at the edges. Again there is negative aerial perspective as the eye ranges through heating distances where textures gain intensity as they diminish in size.

Each of the foreground areas evokes a different texture of fruit hugely magnified – drupelets of berry, colour-flecks of apple, down of peach, sheen of rounded plum – all tumbled into a harvest basket. Here Palmer's art touches an ultimate 'excess'. He is twenty-five.

A luminous oil-and-tempera (also painted in 1830), of twilight beneath steep hills almost touched by an immense full moon, unwinds a long procession. Generations from babies to old men 'Coming from Evening Church' (as a later title has it) extend backwards. Palmer's letters for two years past had complained of loneliness and longing for a wife.

The biggest of his Shoreham oil and tempera paintings, *The Shearers*, opens vast distances. Against them, rustics move in a vigorous dance of shared work. Their ellipse separates the cool foreground barn interior from distances empty of all but light pastel colours. Through them Palmer's art begins to lose the enclosed intensity of *The Magic Apple Tree*. Other pictures at Shoreham reach for their lights over distancing horizons. So they seem to renew the quests and problems of Dulwich. Were his Shoreham achievements now also to be left behind?

Behind the flowering of Palmer's colours at Shoreham, a steady procession of monochrome drawings told a similar tale. His most finished ink and wash drawings now were often studies for coloured pictures. Their elaborated details seemed to look back to the linear 'excess' of his 'stump-work' drawings. But many of Palmer's new monochrome lights flatten towards the light of common day (Plate 37).

A vision based wholly on a narrow geography, however rich, can expand beyond a certain point only through memory and reflection. But the reflecting pool of a young man's experience is still too shallow to plumb the depths Palmer's art needed now if it was to drink deeper from the wellspring of Shoreham.

Through these years, moreover, Shoreham itself might appear to be withdrawing pastoral vision. As recently as 1826 the place had shown itself to Edward Calvert's astonished eyes 'as if the Devil had not yet found it out'.[81] By 1830 the discovery had clearly been made. Rising travel and its communications – the forces which had brought Palmer's grandfather, and then Palmer himself – were starting to make inroads into the traditions of rural peace.

The new forces were later characterised by the historian G.M. Young thus:

> A boy born… in time to have seen the rejoicings after Waterloo [in 1814] entered manhood with the ground rocking under his feet… From Kent to Dorset the skies were alight with burning ricks.

The cause lay in the outlook fomented by the Industrial Revolution in cities. In that thinking, 'the virtues of a Christian after the Evangelical model were easily exchangeable with the virtues of a successful merchant or a rising manufacturer.' Yet any progress that relied on competition reduced both profits and wages:

80. On the *verso* of an undated sepia wash landscape (*Catalogue raisonné* no 116) there is an early inscription referring to Palmer's cousin John Giles' subsequent ownership of this picture: 'The Background of Mr Giles's Holy Family/Shoreham paddock.'
81. Calvert *Memoir*, 33.

Plate 37. Drawing for *The White Cloud*, *c.*1831-32. Pencil, india ink
Ashmolean Museum, Oxford

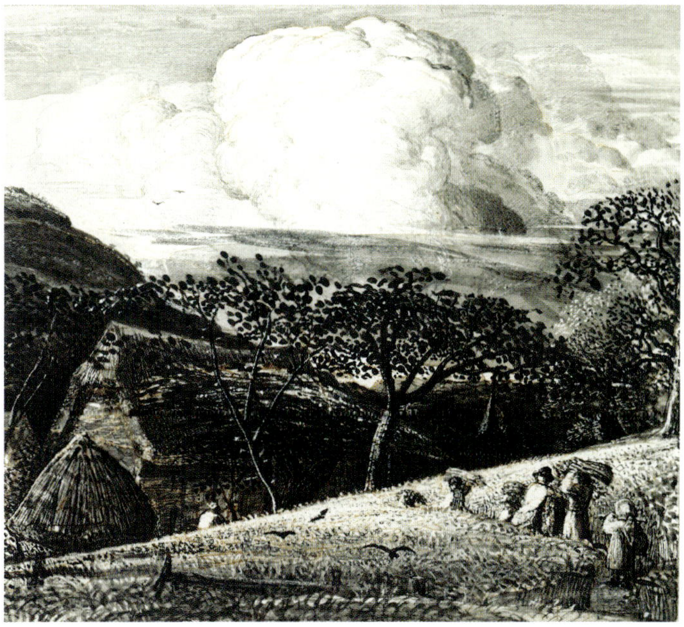

> Machinery had so reduced the value of labour that at any moment the workman might find himself starving in the midst of a plenty which his own hands had helped to create.

Repeated riots produced a voting Reform Bill in 1832. Its proposed broadening of the electorate was regarded by the poor as only an instalment on the margin.[82]

For Palmer the Reform Bill threatened to bedevil the traditional dialogue of rural man and nature which had focused his vision at Shoreham. One of his harvesting watercolours showed a red sky – thought by his son to be 'the reflection of one of the incendiary fires': it lent more than a sunset glow to 'harvesters hurrying away the last of the harvest'.[83]

In advance of a general election fomented by the 1832 Reform Bill, Palmer published an 'Address to the Electors of West Kent' urgently advocating their support for the Conservative candidate.[84] Behind his writing stands the fear of full-scale revolution on the French model of 1789. In the event, Palmer's candidate came bottom of the poll.

A growing apprehension that the vision of Shoreham might be receding could have made one motive for an entirely different kind of house-purchase in 1832. With the last of his grandfather's legacy, Palmer bought a ten-room house in west London. From there he might remedy the loneliness of Shoreham at the firesides of metropolitan friends. The clearest advantage of his house in the shabby suburb of Lisson Grove was its proximity to Linnell in Bayswater.

Linnell constantly chipped away at Palmer's 'excesses'. Blake would have dismissed any adviser. So probably would Linnell himself. But Blake's art and Linnell's were underpinned by secure training. Thus Linnell's continuing advice could lead Palmer into nervousness about his own vision.

The relationship was proving awkward for them both. Linnell found his best advice half mocked or ignored by the young semi-amateur who none the less seemed always to return for more. Palmer for his part began to suspect Linnell as the potential enemy of his vision. Yet should that vision fail, then Linnell might remain his only visible resource.

At Bayswater Palmer found what seemed to him a special welcome from Linnell's eldest daughter, fourteen-year-old Hannah. Despite a difference of nearly fourteen years in their ages, Palmer began to see in Hannah an embodiment of his wish for a wife. When he dropped hints, Hannah's mother showed disapproval. Linnell watched developments.

Palmer's returns to Shoreham grew onerous. One of his late paintings from there shows his trouble. *The Sleeping Shepherd*, with tasks to do in the day dawning behind him, sleeps on as if exhausted by yesterday. His lantern remains lit, but his sheep are gone. Luminous colour kindles over the distant hills, but Palmer's dappling and dotting about his foreground figure is beset by more conventional brushwork.

In Bunyan's *Pilgrim's Progress*, the way to extend vision is to extend its geography. The summer of 1834 saw Palmer leave Shoreham to make a sketching tour in Devon. There, in sight of the sea, he found a Shoreham-like harvest field beneath a sharp outcrop of rock. (It appears partly anticipated in a 'stump-work' study in the sketchbook begun in 1824, page 30.) This place, seen from varied angles in varied lights, fills several pictures he made in 1834. The best of them keep luminous their far and middle distances.

That autumn, back at Shoreham, Palmer wrote to George Richmond:

> I would not have been without the Devonshire reminiscences on any account – I hardly ever try to invent landscape without thinking of them…
>
> I long to see some firstrate distances… I believe in my very heart (but the heart's a great liar tho' it's the truest part about us) that all the very finest original pictures and the topping things in nature have a certain quaintness…[85]

Quaintness can be found in new experiences of the old-fashioned – of scenes whose grasp of modern life appears to be loosening.

In 1835 and 1836 he made summer tours through Somerset to Wales. The results are less and less distinguishable from topographic records. Trying to relight his lamps of vision, Palmer applied white highlighting until it began to vitiate such colours as survived within an increasingly commonplace draughtsmanship. From both tours he returned not to Shoreham, but to Lisson Grove and the Linnells.

* * *

Palmer was more eager to please Linnell because he wanted to marry Hannah. And it seemed that Hannah, now rising eighteen, wanted to marry him. Yet the disappearance of the last of Palmer's capital into the house in Lisson Grove meant that his only means of support henceforth lay in painting and teaching. Success in either or both (as Linnell would not fail to remind him) meant producing works to appeal to those with means to buy.

The most likely customers for artists outside the Royal Academy (where Linnell had fallen foul of Constable, who blocked his election) were self-made men of the Industrial Revolution. They now held much of the power which, up to a generation or two since, had gone with the inheritance of land. The money-maker of humble origin had no family tradition of taste to consult.

The new rich wanted pictures to reflect their own enhancement – pictures of impressive size and finish, clear in subject and moral. The last thing to tempt them would be small panels showing old-fashioned yokeldom painted with curious crudity. They had no time for 'visions'. Palmer was later to write of them:

> To a sharp man of the world, both verse and philosophy are superfluous: routine and the market have shaped and set him to a mediocrity for which epic is too high and the bucolic too lowly… with its… poetic sheep which never come to mutton.[86]

The results of that patronage were summed up by a later pastoral visionary, John Piper. He saw the Victorian era as producing a 'blight' that withered all of England's prior 'great conquests in romantic painting':

> Why did it settle everywhere, this blight? Smugness and the birth of the business instinct caused it.
>
> An artist of sensibility born round about 1800 had little chance of keeping his gifts whole in the face of the new materialism: a materialism that had young, vital, revolutionary zeal and power. … This patronage crystallised into the super-romance of the Great Exhibition.[87]

Palmer was later to recommend painting classical subjects 'as a protest against the degraded materialism which is destroying art'.[88]

In 1837, at thirty-two, he married Hannah Linnell. At first it seemed a match. Palmer took his bride for an extended honeymoon in Italy, centred on Rome. The attractions of the south went deep: here were ancestral landscapes of pastoral vision, which had once culminated in the art of Claude Lorrain.

Linnell accepted the long absence of his daughter. Such an exposure to Renaissance art should knock out of Palmer any remaining 'visionary' localisms. To aid that process, Linnell sent engravings after famous paintings in Italy, with orders for the couple to colour them from the originals. The results would be useful back in England – either for Linnell's collection or for sale. Hannah had become her father's apt pupil.

For Palmer's painting, the immediate effects of Italian light proved disastrous. The light of the south flashed off every surface with blinding resilience – except where shadows plunged dazzled eyes into undifferentiated black. To a northern visionary who had found lights twinkling and glowing with atmospheres and through shadows, every sight here shouted opposition.

The pictures Palmer painted in Italy have been vaguely praised. In fact they show him descending through dullness towards incompetence. Almost all of the pictures actually finished in Italy are panoramas in daylight – without a hint of Shoreham intimacy in dawn or twilight. The once firm line loosens sometimes out of recognition. Occasionally a pencil drawing recalls an old spontaneity. Anything at all worked turns stale.

82. G.M. Young, *Victorian England: Portrait of an Age* (NY: Doubleday Anchor, 1953), 11-48 *passim*.
83. A.H. Palmer, letter of 18 July 1930 to F. L. Griggs (Ashmolean Museum).
84. Reprinted in Raymond Lister, *Samuel Palmer: his life and art* (Cambridge University Press, 1987), 241-254.
85. 16 Oct 1834 (*Letters*, 66-67).
86. 'Observations on Rural Poetry', published as a prefatory essay to Palmer's translation of Virgil's *Eclogues*. See below, pages 72-73.
87. John Piper, *British Romantic Artists*, later included in *Aspects of British Art* (Collins, 1947), 191.
88. n.d. (*c*.1860) to Laura Richmond, who had been sent to study with Palmer by her father George Richmond (*Life and Letters*, 249)

After eleven months Palmer writes to tell Linnell that Italy has taught him 'how to make foregrounds… more of a piece with the whole'; and that he has 'found out the point of danger in yellow'.[89] The most brilliant yellows had lit his finest visions at Shoreham – which had been enhanced by the contrast of dark and secret foregrounds.

From Pompeii Palmer confessed to Hannah's younger sister that he was finding difficulty in doing anything well – 'this one begins to find at thirty':

> Where is the golden autumn of life? We are first green, and then gray; and then nothing in this world, and as far removed from the next generation as the busy people of Pompeii [before the eruption].
>
> I… am really glad I had a dose and glut of reading at Shoreham; some savour of which is yet within me like the relish of wine in an empty cask.[90]

'I can never paint in my old style again,' he wrote to Linnell after a second winter in Rome, 'even though I may paint worse.' At the same time he was feeling again his old impulse to go beyond mere transcribing:

> I have now had my fill of sketching from Nature for the present and wish when I come to London to do any drudgery to get money to go on with so that I can but get… a little leisure to try – sink or swim – Poetic Landscape…[91]

The scent of renewed danger twitched Linnell's nostrils. He sent a very mixed answer through Hannah:

> Pray tell Palmer that I will talk to him about the drudgery he mentions which he says he will be glad to do, when he returns.
>
> It is a mistake, I believe, to suppose that any great progress can be made in poetic landscape unless the whole mind and time is devoted to it.
>
> He ought to take warning by my pettifogging practice [Linnell was painting mostly portraits then], lest he fail of accomplishing the best he is capable of, as I have fail'd.[92]

Then the anxious father learned that Hannah had been ill through much of the second winter in Rome. He issued summary orders for the Palmers' return – Hannah to be nursed by her parents while Palmer sorted himself out at Lisson Grove. Palmer refused: 'I had better have staid at home… rather than begin my English labours in such a den of desolation.'[93] As to the time of their return, he would not be hurried.

Linnell was outraged. He took his aim:

> You know I have prophesied that our differences of opinion upon some subjects will one day cause a separation and I fear now that the latent qualities are about to be developed which will prove me a true prophet.[94]

When the Palmers returned at the end of November 1839 to a harsh winter in Lisson Grove, Linnell supplied money to Hannah and derision to the husband who could not make enough for himself. It began a pattern that lasted the rest of their lives. Years after both men were dead, Palmer's son (and Linnell's grandson) Herbert wrote: 'I, who knew them both so intimately, find it difficult to imagine two men more unlike and even antagonistic.'[95]

On Palmer's thirty-seventh birthday, 27 January 1842, Hannah presented their first child. Palmer named his son Thomas More, after Henry VIII's Catholic chancellor: Linnell would loathe that. The baby was subject to 'fits', and was afterwards a sickly child.[96] Yet almost from before he could understand anything, Palmer poured into him an unending stream of instruction, correction, advice and moral warning, making no allowance for a child's spirit. His purpose was to arm his son (as he himself had never been armed) with strengths to deal with such a character as Linnell.

89. *Letters*, 182.
90. Ibid, 156.
91. Ibid, 385-6.
92. *Life and Letters*, 69.
93. *Letters*, 349, 354.
94. Ibid, 368n.
95. *Life and Letters*, 21.
96. *Letters*, 223, 444-445.
97. *Life and Letters*, 85.
98. Ibid, 103.
99. So it impressed the memory of their younger son (*Life and Letters*, 87).
100. *Letters*, 462.
101. *Life and Letters*, 76.

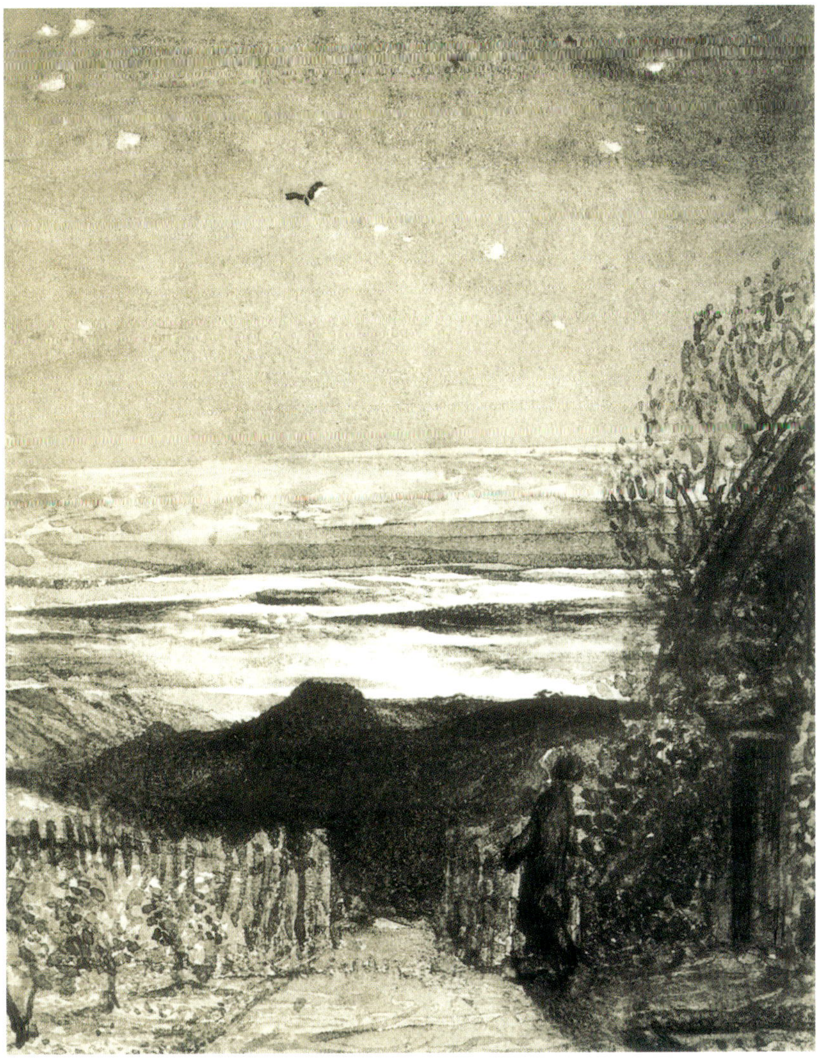

Plate 38. *The Skylark, c.*1832. Wash

Palmer's feelings of inadequacy, constantly reinforced by Linnell, drove endless notes lashing himself to change his art:

> I must, D[eo] V[olente], strike out at once into a NEW STYLE. SIMPLE SUBJECT; BOLD EFFECT; BROAD RAPID EXECUTION; ... blotting out little lights, when the leaving them precise and sharp would involve premature niggle...[97]

Those were just the 'little lights' which Blake had praised as making Claude Lorrain's paintings glitter 'with dew which the morning sun has not yet dried'. Another note asks: 'Why do I wish for a NEW STYLE?' Back comes the answer: '1st. To save time.'[98]

Yet in the year after his son was born, Palmer looked back to an old Shoreham sepia, *The Skylark* (Plate 38): the cottager turning upwards to listen, before a gateway opening on a glowing and starlit prospect of distant hills. He began to paint this emblem of interior escape in oils.

But in that year, 1843, his attention was taken back to watercolour painting, as he was elected Associate of the Royal Society of Painters in Water Colours. Thereafter he bent slow energies on producing a few highly finished watercolours for the Society's annual exhibitions.

In March 1843 Hannah bore a girl whom they named Mary Elizabeth. But the child fell ill in her fourth year and died in December 1847. After that Palmer found Lisson Grove intolerable, and forced their removal. He found an old thatched cottage barely surviving in a yard in Kensington – and took it from March 1848.

It was a little farther from Linnell's house in Bayswater, closer to Kensington Gardens – where great trees might recall the Lullingstone oaks near Shoreham. Not far from the cottage were a few fields with a lane or two remaining – 'an apology for the country'.[99] The cottage itself was decayed: that made it picturesque for Palmer. Hannah hated it. Its roughness defied the disorganised, extravagant housekeeping habits she had picked up from her mother. Palmer found her becoming a scold.[100]

Too many of Palmer's hours now went on teaching any pupil who would pay for lessons. He sought escape in sketching trips to the real country. There he sometimes found himself 'walking all night to watch the mystic phenomena of the silent hours'.[101] At first nothing of what he might recover in country sketching seemed to survive the return to work up finished pictures in London.

Then he began to find watercolour subjects that spoke (under the most sophisticated finishes) to his condition. He returned to nocturne painting in *A Gypsy Encampment* – fugitive figures round a fire in moonlit woods. It renewed some of the shadows of Shoreham. Another watercolour, from *Pilgrim's Progress*, showed *Christian Descending into the Valley of Humiliation*. The lonely pilgrim, armed only with sword and shield, turns to look at a single tower rising to reinforce his loneliness in this wild landscape.

A watercolour *Evening* shows a labourer trudging homewards in the dusk. The glowing horizon finds answer in a single light from the cottage window. His children run to greet him; but his wife remains within, absorbed in her household. *Farewell to Calypso* shows Ulysses' ship sailing away towards a luminous Claudean sunset.

The title of an 1849 watercolour from Spenser's *Faerie Queene* invoked his own name: *Sir Guyon and the Palmer Tempted by Phaedria upon the Enchanted Islands*, in the golden light of another low sun. A further brilliant sunset lights *Robinson Crusoe Guiding his Raft into the Creek* (Plate 39). The castaway's landfall is lit with overwhelming splendour.

So it came about, ten years after his time in Italy, that Palmer's memory of Italian light – now softened and enriched in renewing English atmospheres – went gradually through the secret places of his loneliness into the fabric of his art. In the high finish of the Victorian 'exhibition watercolour', Palmer burnished the Claudean sunset to a brilliance never before seen in watercolours. In 1850 the *Athenaeum* critic asked: 'What shall we say to Mr Palmer, who, with certain evidences of talent and a dream of truth, offers us such eccentricities of prismatic colour run mad?'

Yet these later visions were all most carefully calculated. Palmer had recalled Mulready describing the colours in early northern painting 'as resembling stained glass'. Palmer reasoned:

> The lustre of stained glass is produced by the light of the sky shining through from behind the colours. ... The nearest approach we can make to the light from the sky behind [is] *a pure white priming.*[102]

Priming upon what? After years of using ordinary papers, Palmer discovered a 'London-board' (six sheets of Whatman drawing paper hot-pressed together): 'it reflects light through the pigments', he wrote.[103] He grounded this board with white – adding more brilliance by mixing in a little cadmium orange. Palmer remembered all his life an early moment when Calvert had suddenly observed: 'Light is orange.'[104]

On this board and ground, Palmer drew his picture's guidelines in pencil or red chalk. Then he applied his colours pure – hardly ever mixed with each other, but with his preferred vehicle, gum arabic – in thin glazes, one on top of another:

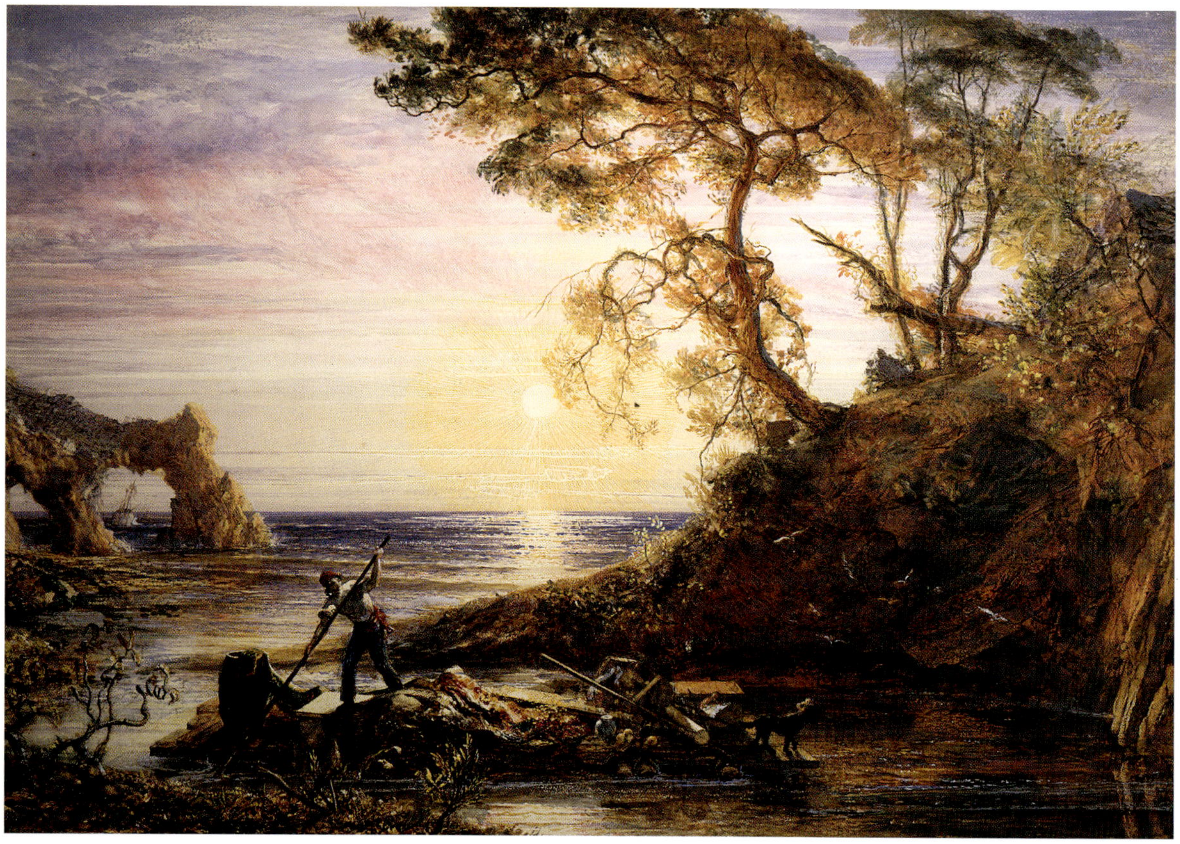

Plate 39. *Robinson Crusoe guiding his raft into the Creek,* 1850. Watercolour, wash and bodycolour with scratching out
City Museum and Art Gallery, Stoke-on-Trent

> I never mix two pigments if I can get the hue I want by laying one over another – for superimposition being necessarily unequal, there is endless variety and pulsation.

Proto-'Impressionism' again: yet concealing, not advertising the technique. The secrecy emerges in private notes Palmer made on superimposing colours in special sequences to capture different lights:

> Golden green, such as that caused by the sun's rays transmitted through leaves[:] either model with cool green, leaving here and there little sparkles and scratches of the white ground, and glaze with a gorgeous yellow (such as yellow cadmium); or reverse the process. It may be necessary to repeat two or three times, until the desired tint is obtained. …
>
> *Sun shining through leaves towards sunset.* Perhaps the most splendid yellow, which is the ground of the subsequent tints, is produced by raw sienna over yellow cadmium; over these, again (for autumn tints), come first the scarlets, then the reds, then the pinks – generally in that order, somewhat darker and darker.
>
> The things which by contrast enforce the splendour, are the *semi*-contrast of the transmitting greens, the *contrast* of the holes of dark, dark tree stems and branches, and particularly the opposite position of foliage in shadow, receiving a faint, coldish light on the shadowed side *behind* the spectator… from the blue sky.
>
> *Note* – When there are portions of pure sunlight, mirrored by polished leaves, leave the paper white, if possible; if not, cut them out afterwards (not deeply [from the board surface]) with a very sharp knife.[105]

Here is no opposition of art to nature, such as Palmer had cracked his prentice head against before Shoreham. All his harvested experience now is focused on getting the most out of what nature presents – at special times, to be sure – and using those intensities to create his art's vision.

Thus Palmer renewed his determination to capture again his old 'excess' of colour – to work out and preserve its formulas as permanent possessions to lay up against old age. And thus the colour half of Palmer's vision (however hedged by maturing experience) was enthroned once more in his art.

Palmer's recovery of brilliant colour came virtually with the appearance, in 1848, of a younger generation of painters also pursuing brilliance in nature, the Pre-Raphaelites. Yet theirs was a different quest. The Pre-Raphaelites sought to render every natural object with equal precision – 'rejecting nothing, selecting nothing', as Ruskin wrote. All would be seen by what one of the young painters called 'the enfranchised eye': what they aimed at was the levelling, demotic scrutiny of science.

Palmer sought no levelling. His early 'stump-work' pictures had differentiated little objects for working up into a texture: the whole texture enclosed within heavy outline, to contrast it with other such fields – and so hint at divine ordering. Now Palmer's recapture of richest colours gathered them for a kindred purpose. They were to evoke those moments when the sun's light finds unique enrichment against the gathering darkness of night – with all its implications for human life.

Palmer's deliberate, determined recovery of this side of his youthful 'excess' has no precedent in English art. The Victorian market began to reward him, slowly and grudgingly at first, with better prices. Linnell himself turned back to landscapes in the early 1850s. He introduced more and more of Palmer's high colouring, especially into oil-painted sunsets.[106] Still he lent Palmer money, so as to keep Hannah in the comforts she ought to expect.

At home Palmer had to fight for every inch of ground recovered. In 1851 they left the Kensington cottage. Its nearby fields were being built over. And Hannah loathed the little place more than ever since her prosperous father built a spanking mansion for himself and wife on the hills of Surrey. There they regularly required Hannah's presence. The Palmers, as an unhappy compromise, took a small semi-detached house with bad floors in a Kensington cul-de-sac.

102. *Memoir*, 54.
103. *Life and Letters*, 273-274. He noted a similar effect in tempera painted on vellum 'in the old missals' (Ibid, 316).
104. Ibid, 327.
105. *Memoir*, 54-56.
106. See e.g. David Linnell, op cit, plate opp. p213.

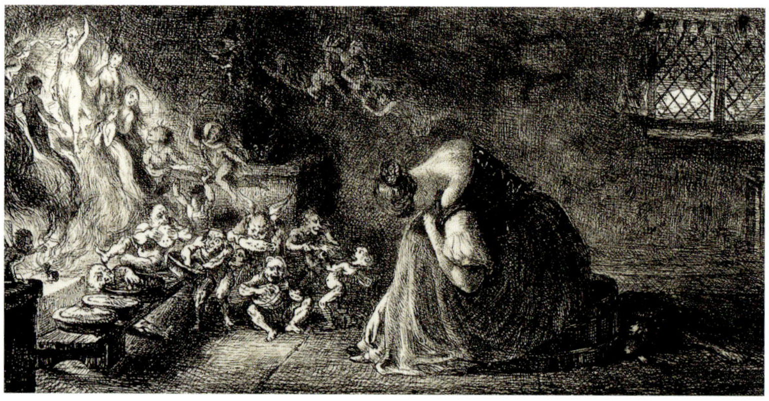

Plate 40. Charles West Cope: *L'Allegro:* 'How Faery Mab the junkets eat', 1848-49. Etching

There in September 1853 Hannah brought a last pregnancy to term, producing a second son. He was named Alfred (for the Saxon King) Herbert (for the seventeenth-century poet who had brought vision to English Church orthodoxy). The baby looked as frail as his eleven-year-old brother, who was being drilled by their father to achieve much – more – most.

The room Palmer had now for his studio looked out on house-fronts opposite. The thin party-wall resounded their neighbour's music. Yet Palmer set his stamp on the place, as his son recalled:

> Much to the astonishment of his neighbours my father often allowed the weeds and grass of the little back garden to reach maturity, in order that his pupils might draw them from the window; and the laurel-bushes did duty in the same manner.
>
> Underneath a chalk sketch of his own of some dandelions and grass-tufts on the back lawn are these words: -
>
> 'Farewell, soft clusters – the only pretty things about the premises – ye are to be mowed this evening, and to leave a scraped scalp of "RESPECTABILITY"!'[107]

Every year added weight to the yoke of his life in London. In the summer of 1856 he wrote to Hannah, away again at her parents' Surrey mansion: 'My summers are literally *wasted*, while almost all other landscape-painters are reaping some harvest from the country.'[108] Economy held him prisoner in the 'exhausted' city air. To another such protest two years later, Hannah replied (patently at her father's instruction) that he ought to be able to paint saleable things in London. Palmer answered:

> I can *begin* my subjects better in London, but when *Italian* weather sets in I should like to go out of town directly, if it were only for a week, and take my drawings with me.
>
> The weather from which I get my subjects and my suggestions for the remainder of the year is that dazzling weather when all the air seems trembling with little motes. A week of that is, to me, worth three months of ordinary fine weather. It is then I see real sunsets and twilights.[109]

A year after that: 'I seem doomed never to see again that first flush of summer splendour which entranced me at Shoreham.'[110]

Palmer did not stop with recovery of his art's 'excess' in colour. As he revived that climax of his old vision at Shoreham, now he reached still farther back to revive the other 'excess' – the excess of line which had shaped his earlier 'stump-work' pictures.

This newer, older revival began in his friendships with several artists about Kensington. They had formed an 'Etching Club'. To every meeting each member brought a new etching. At intervals of two or three years the Club produced a book of their work – sometimes a miscellany of subjects, sometimes all illustrating a single poem. In 1849 they published etchings for Milton's *L'Allegro*, a poem Palmer had loved from boyhood.

Some of the Etching Club images were vignetted with soft edges. Others were densely worked to the plate edge. Thus they recalled the 'engravings' after Turner. In fact both the Turner 'engravings' and the Club 'etchings' were worked in similar combinings of both processes.[111]

The dense textures in many Etching Club plates (as in Turner engravings) needed clean printing to prevent smudge. The Club's professional printers were so expert that paper-whiteness glimmered through all but the heaviest workings. Palmer always treasured a Blake-like remark made by one Etching Club member: 'Lose your line and you lose your light.'[112]

---

107. *Life and Letters*, 106. *Catalogue raisonné* no 537 (May 1856).
108. *Life and Letters*, 116.
109. 'Kensington, 1858' (*Life and Letters*, 117).
110. 'Hastings, 1859' (Ibid, 118).
111. Etching – lines drawn through a wax ground on to the metal plate and then bitten with acid – produced a base of bold work. Engraving – lines dug directly into the uncovered metal with a burin or 'graver' – then gave a fine finish. The difference between Turner 'engravings' and the Club 'etchings' was largely one of nomenclature.
The combination of etching and engraving went back to Rembrandt, whose prints were always called etchings. See Cynthia P. Schneider *et al*, *Rembrandt's Landscapes: Drawings and Prints* (Washington DC: National Gallery of Art, 1990) pp24, 83*f*, 154. In seventeenth and eighteenth century England virtually the same process was called 'engraving'. One of its practitioners, J.T. Smith (1766-1833), summarised: 'When the plate is sufficiently bitten in [with etching acid], the whole is finished up with a graver.' (*Antiquities of Westminster*, 1807, p 48). The extent of etching underlay in turn-of-the-nineteenth century 'engraving' can be seen in a special copy of Thomas Hearne's *Antiquities of Great Britain* (2 vols, 1786 and 1807) at the John Rylands Library, Manchester. Here the plates are printed in two states: first as etched work alone, comprising 75 to 90 per cent of the image; and then again with the engraving added to complete the images.
112. James Clarke Hook, quoted in *Life and Letters*, 100.
113. *Memoir*, 47; *Life and Letters*, 379.
114. Raymond Lister, *Samuel Palmer and his Etchings* (Faber, 1969), p 76 n 3.
115. *Letters*, 483.

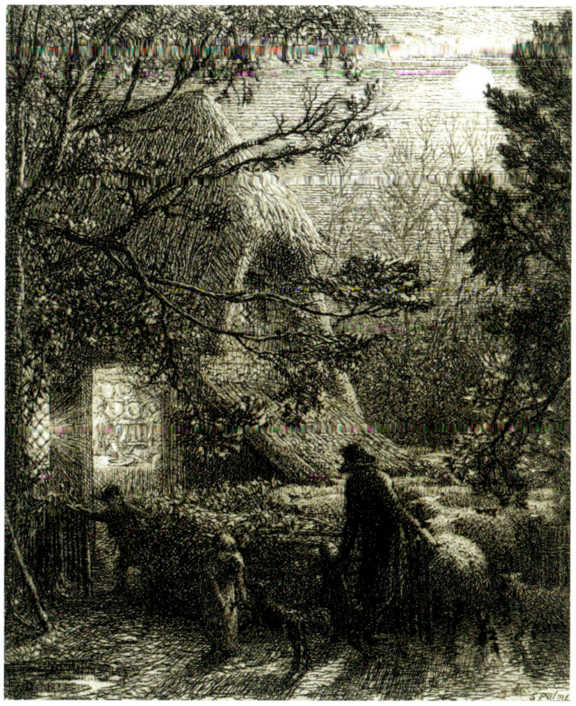

Plate 41. *Christmas,* 1850. Etching
The Fine Art Society

Light-in-darkness haunts several Etching Club plates for *L'Allegro*. A sunrise study by Thomas Creswick is built on Milton's reference to 'the Eastern Gate' of dawn. H. J. Townsend's goblin plying his 'ghostly flail' by moonlight was to remain vivid in Palmer's memory.[113] Night interiors by Townsend, Richard Redgrave, and Charles West Cope light fires and the moon with areas of paper left nearly blank amid the heaviest workings (Plate 40).

When Cope offered to act as Palmer's 'master in etching', a new prospect opened out. Soon after the *L'Allegro* volume appeared, Palmer tried his hand at etching a recent study he had made of a willow tree with cows by a stream. The conventional subject and technique could be given a range of lights through different inkings and pressures of printing. The little plate secured his election to the Etching Club in February 1850.

Yet Palmer's long horizontal sky-lines (an old-fashioned technique) drew criticism from Creswick, the Club's acknowledged master of landscape. Palmer began to break up his etched lines. It opened fresh horizons of close-swarming pattern making.

Through the remaining months of 1850 he etched three more small plates. In each, nearly the whole surface is worked to produce textured darknesses, with areas left white for lights. One of the new etchings revives again his Shoreham monochrome *The Skylark*. On one impression he inscribed a line from *L'Allegro*, 'to hear the lark begin his flight'[114] – as if to make his private addition to the Etching Club volume.

Another 1850 plate, entitled *Christmas* (from a sonnet by J.C. Bamfylde) holds Palmer's first etching of night (Plate 41). Extending the theme of his watercolour *Evening* with the father coming home, this father folds sheep as his children come out. Still the wife and mother occupies herself within. Her window of lamplight rivals the frosty moon: the two lights seem to immobilise the man between vision and domesticity. 'Wouldst thou know thyself?' Palmer asked George Richmond in a letter of March 1851: 'MARRY A WIFE!'[115]

Did Palmer's sense of isolation in his own house drive the sharp contrasts within his reviving 'excesses' in line and in colour? Each, as he used it now in maturity, strikes light against the dark. Yet each rises independent of actual topography. The vision of innocence once pursued through Dulwich to Shoreham is now annealed in the fabric of Palmer's creative maturity.

Palmer managed his one contribution to an Etching Club thematic project, *Songs of Shakespeare*, in 1853. The book holds several remarkable images. Townsend shows half-hidden sexual ferocity (*Midsummer Night's Dream* Fairies' Song) – counterpointed with an androgynous Ariel (*Tempest* 'Where the bee sucks') stretching his slim nudity along a morning-glory vine before the full moon. Creswick's 'Under the Greenwood Tree' from *As You Like It* almost touches back to Palmer's Lullingstone oaks.

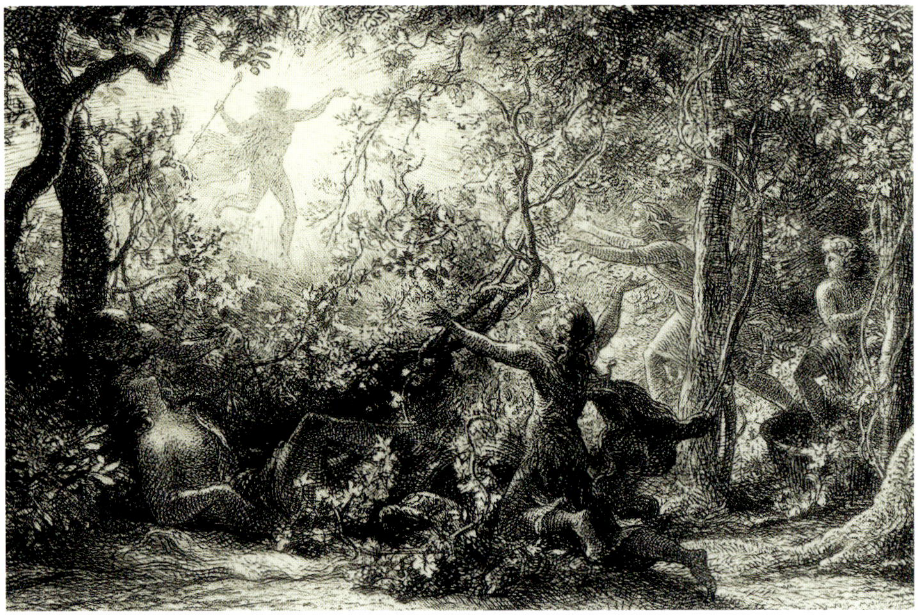

Plate 42. *"Come, Thou Monarch of the Vine'*, 1852. Etching Hilary Gerrish

Palmer's 'Come, Thou Monarch of the Vine' (*Anthony and Cleopatra*) pays covert tribute to the fellowship he found in the Etching Club by evoking golden memories of the youthful 'Ancients' at Shoreham.[116] Silhouetted in sunlight at the horizon, Bacchus lifts a spear to lead away his forest worshippers – his star-shaped form echoed in the foreground votary on his knees (Plate 42). Here uniquely in Palmer's etchings, nature invites pagan revelry.

As etching extended his vision again, so he seemed wilfully to extend its process. His son would recall him 'content to dwell day by day, and perhaps week by week, upon a work: till, to the uninitiated, the plate was a glittering chaos'. 'Stopping out' minutenesses already perfected (against re-biting for greater densities elsewhere on the plate) Palmer made an art as idiosyncratic as painting itself – 'sitting, sable in hand, hour after hour… pencilling in varnish silver cloudlets round a moon' [117]

He could never keep up with the Etching Club demand of a fresh plate for each meeting. 'I can do a sketch from nature in tolerably quick time,' he told Richmond in 1856: 'but when it comes to invention,' his 'finest thought' required 'laying the thing by and returning often to it with a fresh eye'.[118] It showed an invention slowly inductive – small particularities gradually joining one another, gathering perceptions to light lengthening paths.

In the mid-1850s Palmer etched his late Shoreham image of *The Sleeping Shepherd*. The morning horizon is now mounted by a ploughman and oxen, with the hint of fresh fields to open. And indeed Palmer's next etchings, begun in the late 1850s, will practically double the size of his early plates – to expand their pastorals of night and morning, to attract greater attention.

The Rising Moon (Plate 43) 'grew out of' his memory of 'houses at Margate with bars of moonlight'.[119] Margate touched the memory of his mother. His etching transfigures sheep and shepherd in the rise of a full moon. From dark hills a lonely tower (a hint from Milton's *Il Penseroso*, once planned as an Etching Club volume) half emerges as a focus for the shepherd's gaze. Between them opens a womb-like valley cradling a village asleep. Tower and valley will haunt Palmer's later etchings. In one of the last, he would identify the village of his vision with Shoreham.[120]

The dark village sunk among hills reappears in *The Weary Ploughman*. He follows his oxen to their rest beneath a moon beset by clouds blown to passionate textures. The right foreground holds Palmer's darkest etching and deepest biting.[121] Then he asked the Etching Club printers Gad & Keningale (whom he thought 'first rate', 'attentive and obliging') to wipe the plate of excess ink before printing, with different cloths. He wanted separate proofs to test the effects of removing more ink – 'acting on the etching as a glazing' to 'add mystery' by burnishing interior lights.[122]

Palmer's third large plate, begun around 1860, roused ploughman and oxen again to morning light. *The Early Ploughman* (Plate 44) adds a woman bearing a jar on her head. Taken together with the cypresses behind her, she touches back to Italy and the south. Yet oxen and plough drive towards a river valley below a new lonely tower. All are defined in an eruption of light.

116. This perception I owe to Michael Campbell.
117. *Life and Letters*, 93, 100.
118. *Letters*, 511. After the Shakespeare *Songs*, all the Etching Club books were miscellanies. To them Palmer lent odd plates conceived in separate circumstances.
119. *Life and Letters*, 112.
120. Ibid, 377-378.
121. Palmer made detailed notes of his work on this plate in 1858. Needling the design through the covering wax took him a month. Then followed various bitings over five days (in consultation with another Etching Club member, Thomas Barlow). At the end he finished details with the engraving burin. (*Catalogue raisonné*, pp 268-269.)
122. *Letters*, 500; V & A Catalogue, 77-78.

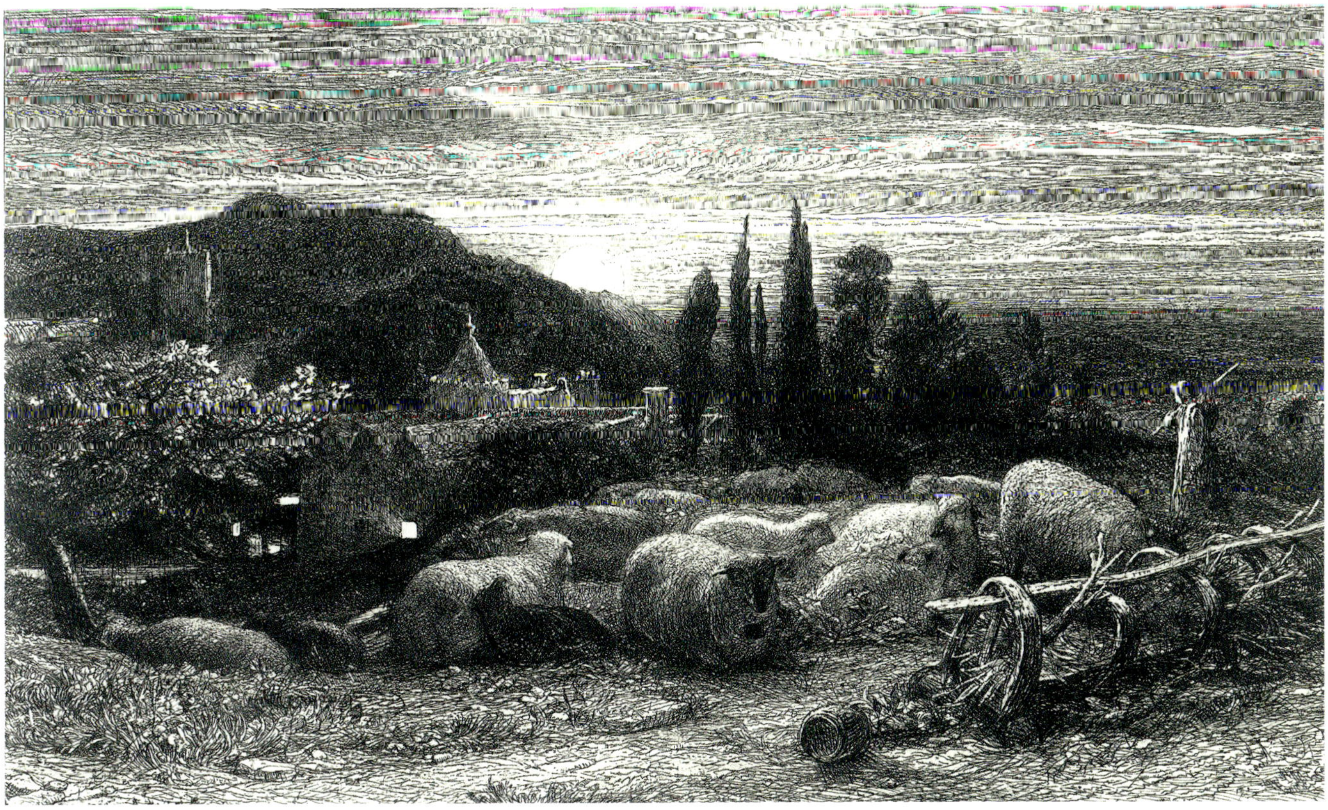

Plate 43. *The Rising Moon (An English Pastoral), c.*1860. Etching The Fine Art Society

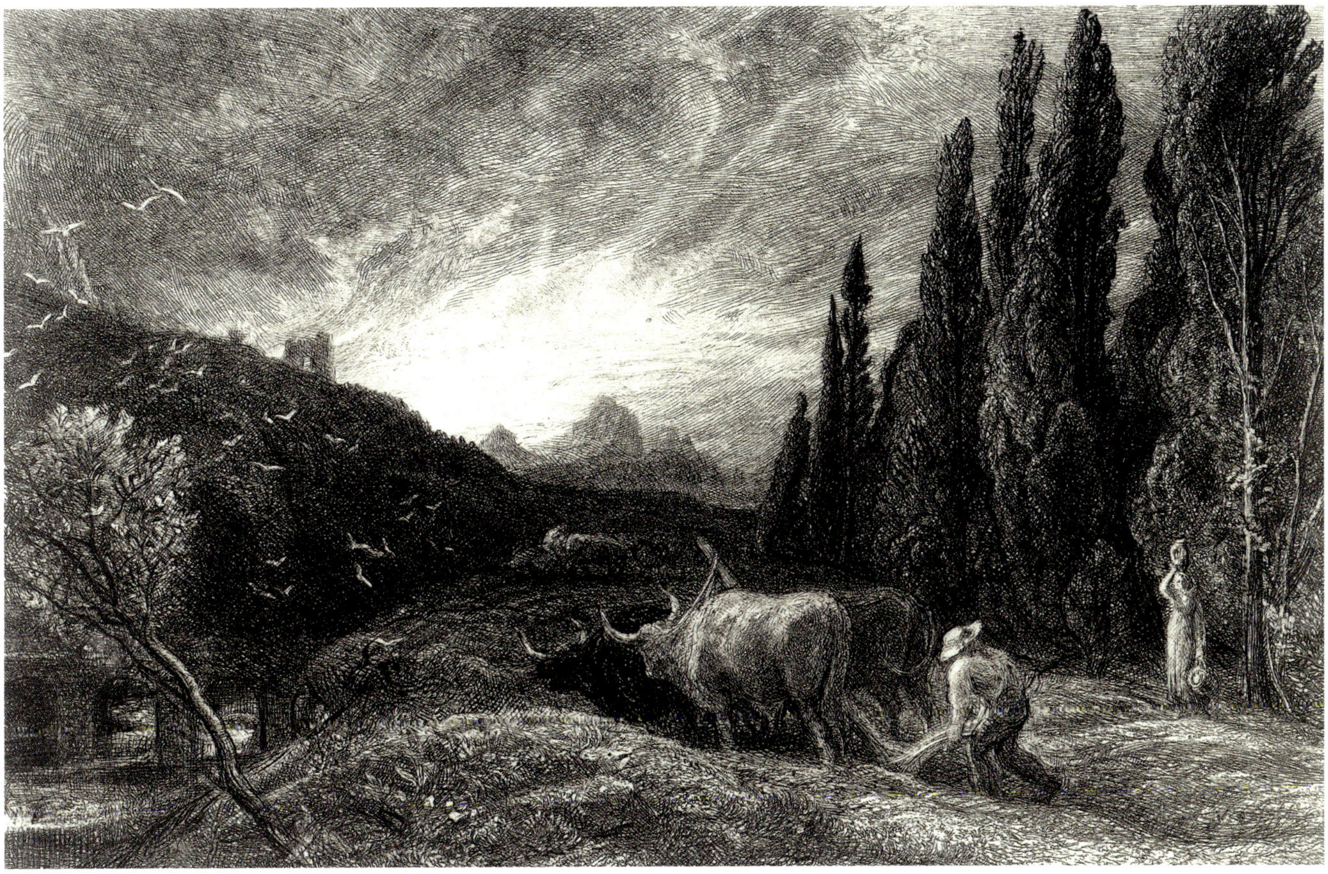

Plate 44. *The Early Ploughman, c.*1860–80. Etching The Fine Art Society

It is the sacramental torch, the lamp of creation's promise endlessly renewed. So it might yoke Baptist revelation to a tradition of Anglican heritage – the vision of Shoreham, and perhaps of Blake, to Palmer's lengthening, enriching memory of Italian light. His etching on this plate comes close to painting, in the perception of his friend, the critic and etcher P.G. Hamerton:

> In the bridge on the left, where a pure etcher would have given frank lines of structure, the utmost care is taken to avoid them; and even when, as in the black marking of the arches or of the tree trunk which comes across these, there are what appear to be something like lines, these are not true and simple lines, but elaborate imitations of brush-work with the etching-needle.
>
> All through the foreground we have the same steady resolve, carried out with infinite mastery of resource, to obtain as nearly as possible the results of painting; and you cannot find a pure etched line a quarter of an inch long that dares to stand on its own merit.[123]

So the textures of his early 'stump-work' drawing reappeared – contrasted but not outlined.

A fourth large etching began as a subject from heroic mythology. Midway Palmer changed it to make a pastoral *Morning of Life*.[124] Any synthesis was interrupted by what happened next.

* * *

Palmer's elder son Thomas More turned nineteen in January 1861: time to prepare him to win the scholarship needed to send him to Oxford. Yet More was far from well. Rheumatic fever in 1858 had weakened his heart. Scarlet fever a year later had kept him an invalid for months. Early in 1861 he began to suffer 'seizures', and by March he had to quit his school. His alarmed parents rented a little Surrey farmhouse on Leith Hill in hopes the high air would help him. By then he could hardly walk unaided. On 10 July he had a prolonged seizure, and early the next morning he died.

Palmer's grief and guilt were hardly to be borne. Again, as after the death of his daughter in 1847, he found his London house uninhabitable. This time the surviving family did move to the country – but on Hannah's terms: a suburban villa, close to her parents. They found Furze Hill House, a mile and a half from Linnell's mansion, in the hills between Reigate and Redhill.

It was a newish place in Gothic Revival brick, and they rented it. When the landlord wanted to sell, Palmer felt he could not afford the purchase. So Linnell bought it – and vested it in his own eldest son, to collect £75 annual rent for the rest of Palmer's life. Here Palmer cultivated quietness. His surviving child Herbert (then aged eight) was to remember it as 'the house of the mourning'.[125]

Hannah trained her servants to clip and prune every corner of the villa's geometric flower beds and serpentine gravel paths but one. Under the window of Palmer's combined painting and bed room, a small patch was told off to him to grow his weeds. Herbert recalled them: 'some gave us infinite trouble, and pined away, in spite of artificial irrigation suggested by a passage in the *Georgics*.'[126]

Inside the house Palmer's room, fifteen feet square, served his dreams and his memories. Herbert wrote:

> Here lay one of the beautiful smock frocks once worn by so many of the peasantry [at Shoreham], there a relic of [his nurse] Mary Ward – her battered tin ear-trumpet; and there again, unstrung and silent, the old violin, once eloquent with many an ancient air on the banks of the Darent. ...
>
> What with the old books, plaster casts, piles of portfolios [of old and new sketches], the rickety painting-table, and the bed, there was barely room for him to back away from the easel.
>
> The west light was so full of green reflections that the bottom of the window had to be obscured with white paint. The Venetian blinds worked *from the top*; and after 12 at noon, had to be lowered.
>
> Partly for these reasons all the most important part of his work – the creative part – was

done at night by the light of a small 'moderator' [lamp]. Few there were even among his friends who ever saw the inside of the 'painting room'.[127]

Palmer's sense of isolation was wilfully extended. Herbert added: 'The simplicity I have described was no longer a matter of necessity, for my father's circumstances were easier now, his prices higher…'.[128] His object was to surround himself with quiet to hear inner promptings. Those, after More's death, sent him away from etching and back to watercolours – to depths and brightnesses that might relight yet again, if still possible, his visionary lamps.

He remained open to hints from outsiders. In 1863 he had a letter from a Lincoln's Inn solicitor, Leonard Rowe Valpy, proposing to buy a watercolour *Twilight: the Chapel by the Bridge* if Palmer would consider lowering the light from the chapel windows. Palmer agreed that they 'glare a little and should rather glimmer'.[129] He made the alterations very slowly.

As he applied 'the last touch' in June 1864, there came another letter from Valpy. Was there any project especially close to Palmer's 'inner sympathies' which Valpy might sponsor? There was, Palmer answered: for twenty years it had touched him with 'sevenfold inwardness', and he had just begun to think of it again. It was a set of watercolours founded on Milton's 'L'Allegro' and 'Il Penseroso'. These early poems had shone as a tower light over Palmer's valleys, from the time Mary Ward had given him her old copy of *Milton* at Shoreham. In the 1850s Palmer had painted several watercolours founded on Milton's 'Comus', but had gone no farther.

A suite of pictures from 'L'Allegro' and 'Il Penseroso' might lead his art now towards some circle-closing synthesis. In the medium term, work on such a sequence could offer its own propulsion to ageing energies: for Palmer was in sight of his sixtieth year. Valpy agreed to support the project.

Palmer began his search for subjects by noting an image in 'Il Penseroso':

… the bellman's drowsy charm
To bless the doors from nightly harm.

Valpy responded with his own memory of once seeing just such an evening watchman in Herefordshire.

The patron began to send suggestions for Palmer's project. He asked whether one passage invited an amber sky. Palmer answered: 'Your thought of an amber sky rather haunts me. For Milton, space is essential… a *spread* of light.' That brought Palmer to lines in 'L'Allegro' evoking sunset and the approach of dreams:

Towered Cities please us then…
Such sights as youthful poets dream
On summer nights by haunted stream.

The ghosts of Shoreham could rise through those lines. Others touched Palmer's young time on Dartmoor, recalling 'morn… when the gust hath blown his fill'. His goal was still light: the finished watercolour would show 'the lull in a rain-and-wind storm *after* sunrise [with] *plates* of golden light wherever the sun can get through.'

An image from 'Il Penseroso' set Milton's 'lamp, at midnight hour, … in some high lonely tower'. It could not fail to kindle Palmer's thoughts of his own solitary nights. Those nights were connected especially with the Milton watercolours in the memory of Herbert Palmer:

> Many and many a time have I seen one or the other of these works on the easel late at night, and its author standing before it with a candle in his hand to catch, in that dim light, suggestions that a brighter light would not have given, for the next day's work.

The hints Palmer caught in his late lights were of things half seen, on the change. 'In breathless silence I am absorbed by it,' he wrote to Valpy of *The Lonely Tower* watercolour: 'We must reach poetic loneliness.'

123. P.G. Hamerton, *Etching and Etchers* (1st ed, 1868), 144.
124. *Life and Letters*, 323.
125. *Letters*, 675 n 2.
126. *Life and Letters*, 134.
127. Ibid, 144; *Letters*, 649 n 1.
128. *Life and Letters*, 145. 'There is not a better painter of sunsets in England', the *Athenaeum* critic had written in 1860, 'than Mr. Samuel Palmer.'
129. This and the following material about the Milton watercolours is taken from the *Memoir, Life and Letters*, and *Letters* (especially pp 694 *ff*), together with Herbert Palmer's Preface to *The Minor Poems of John Milton with Twelve Illustrations by Samuel Palmer* (Seeley, 1889). In most cases the sources provide no dates for their quotations.

Each of the Milton watercolours was started in two stages. First came the gradual formation of what his son called a design 'embryo'. Then came a search through old portfolios, for sketches from nature which might nudge the design forward. But nothing was taken over entire, Herbert wrote:

> Nature's material was absorbed by, rather than engrafted upon [the design. I] cannot call to mind a single instance in which a portion of the many hundred sketches from nature which filled Samuel Palmer's portfolios was drafted direct into a drawing.

Valpy, to assuage his impatience, asked for any sketches that Palmer might be finished with. But there were no such sketches. In Palmer's inductive thinking and feeling, anything might prove useful anywhere at any time. Thus every sketch from nature remained part of his working capital, as he explained to his patron: 'It is curious how, without my seeking, sketches of very picked scenery have pressed themselves into service' – and might do so again.

One subject from 'Il Penseroso' was particularly slow to find its form:

> I hear the far-off curfew sound
> Over some wide-water'd shore...

When Valpy asked about this picture's progress after several years, Palmer assured him:

> It is getting more and more, at every touch, of the solemn fusion belonging to the theme, and directly it reaches that point at which it is on even balance, and another touch may do harm instead of good, I will send it.

Another, the only 'Penseroso' subject in daylight, rose from the lines:

> ... The waters murmuring
> With such concert as they keep
> Entice the dewy-feathered sheep.

'I have for a long time been cultivating coolness in shadows, and that makes the lights more gorgeous. ... The moment supposed is that immediately before the poet (in the covert) wakes...'.

Sometimes an idea first thought of for one picture then seemed better in another. In June 1865 Palmer wrote to answer Valpy's pressure for results in *The Waters Murmuring*:

> I have no longer a difficulty about the brook; what I had, arose from attempting to combine it with the avenue of pine and monumental oak, which is distinctly another theme.
>
> Yet it is surprising how many indications, how much by play may suggest itself, if strict unity of main subject be secured. Thus, the cottage behind the aged oaks may find a place in the 'Prospect' or elsewhere.

The Prospect, seventh in the series, was the only full daylight subject from 'L'Allegro'. Here he took so long to find his median 'between a mappy Buckinghamshire treatment and a gentle poetic swoon' that he was still apologising for it in the last year of his life: 'I always, from a child, expected to see a great deal when I was taken to see a "prospect".'

His final Milton subject was *The Eastern Gate*. It owed nothing to Creswick's plate in the old Etching Club *L'Allegro*, everything to Palmer's own *Early Ploughman* images (together with an 1873 watercolour of *Lycidas*, which Valpy eagerly bought). For this ultimate *Eastern Gate*, Palmer went to the trouble of making a small wax model of ploughman and oxen to view from many angles in many lights.

Synthesis emerges finally in these late watercolours from the extraordinary depths of their colours – rich darknesses (never blacks) reaching up through every glowing light. Palmer's light concentrates in his passionate skies. Grand trees mediate to figures of the land below. His humans and animals find harmonising gestures and patterns within the pervasive shapes of hill and dell. Only man's buildings show edges and angles: and even they may be sculpted by light and shadow – or by the wind implied in several of the Milton watercolours.

130. *Letters*, 769.
131. 27 May [1868] (*Letters*, 755-756 n 6).
132. *Life and Letters*, 261.

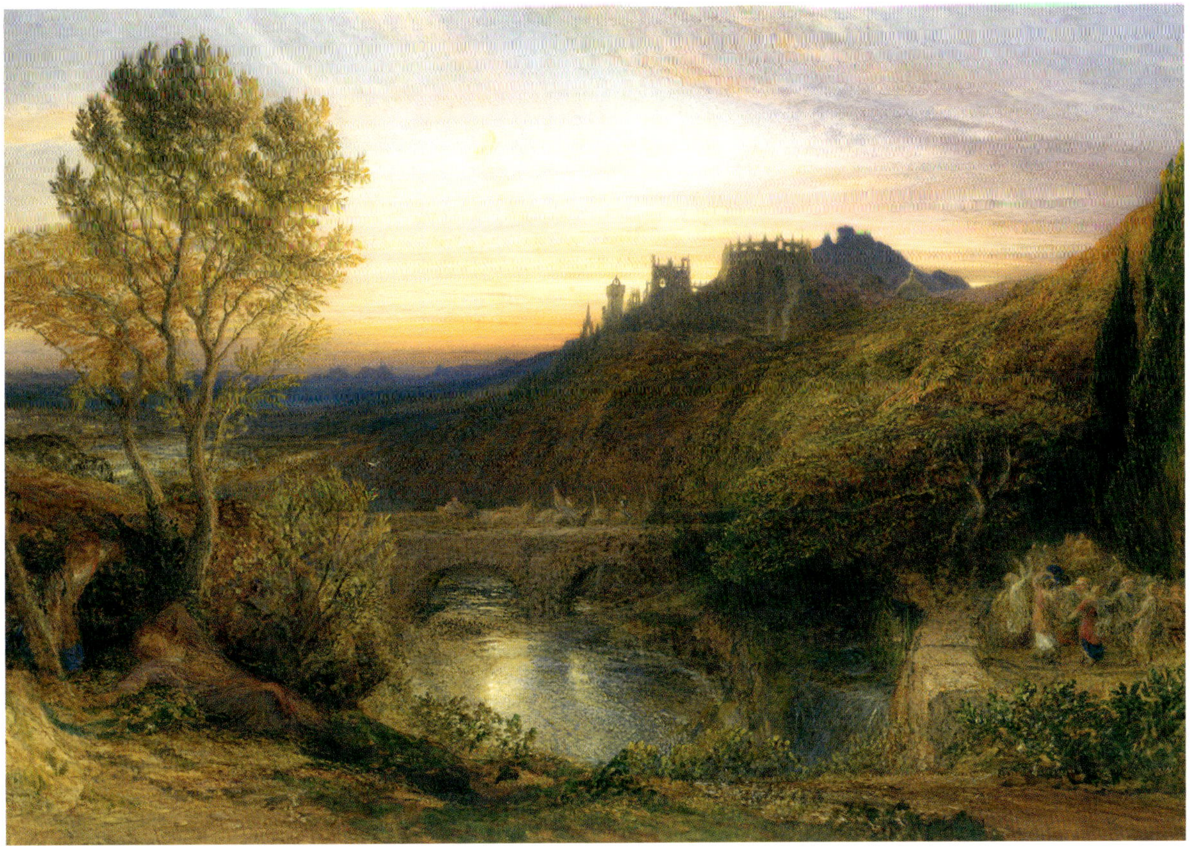

Plate 45. *A Towered City (The Haunted Stream)*, *c.*1865–68. Watercolour, wash and bodycolour with gum
Rijksmuseum, Amsterdam

In November 1867 the artist wrote to his patron about one of the first in the Milton series to approach completion, *A Towered City* (Plate 45). He was 'most tenderly breaking those delicate crimson tones' which had dominated the sketch, and were now 'merging the extreme distance… to a more mysterious purple gloom: and the result is that the city, which never pleased me, has sprung up and asserted itself (I fancy) as the poetic eye of the drawing.' He would release *A Towered City* and *The Lonely Tower* for exhibition in the spring of 1868, before they entered Valpy's collection.

The brilliance and burnish of his watercolours only strengthened, it could seem, against the dreariness that permeated every corner of his life at Furze Hill. In January 1868 Palmer wrote to a friend:

> For the last 3 years there has been scarce any sun or any colour. A cousin of mine was here in the summer from Rome where he has lived 14 years: I said how does our colour strike you? said he 'There is no colour.'[130]

Palmer in his sixties suffered renewing bouts of asthma. In the spring of 1868 he was brought low by his wife's insistence on sending in her household servants to spring clean his sanctum. He asked the Richmonds and other friends to take him in during the siege, and he stayed away a month. For her part, Hannah wrote to her father of getting a builder's man 'to colour and varnish the floor of Mr P's painting room whilst he is away, to save having carpet.'[131] Her husband's asthma seemed to weigh nothing in her calculations.

Two further Milton watercolours were 'surrendered' (as Valpy characterised it) and exhibited: *The Dripping Eaves* in 1869, *The Curfew* in 1870. Then seven years elapsed before Palmer finished *The Waters Murmuring*. Asthma now confined him to the house often for weeks at a time, and he never ventured out at night.

Perhaps to increase remuneration from this slowest of projects, he thought of making etchings after the Milton watercolours. He envisioned 'a set of highly-finished etchings the size of Turner's *Liber Studorium*', as he wrote to Valpy: 'a compact block of work which I would fain hope might live when I am with the fallen leaves'.[132]

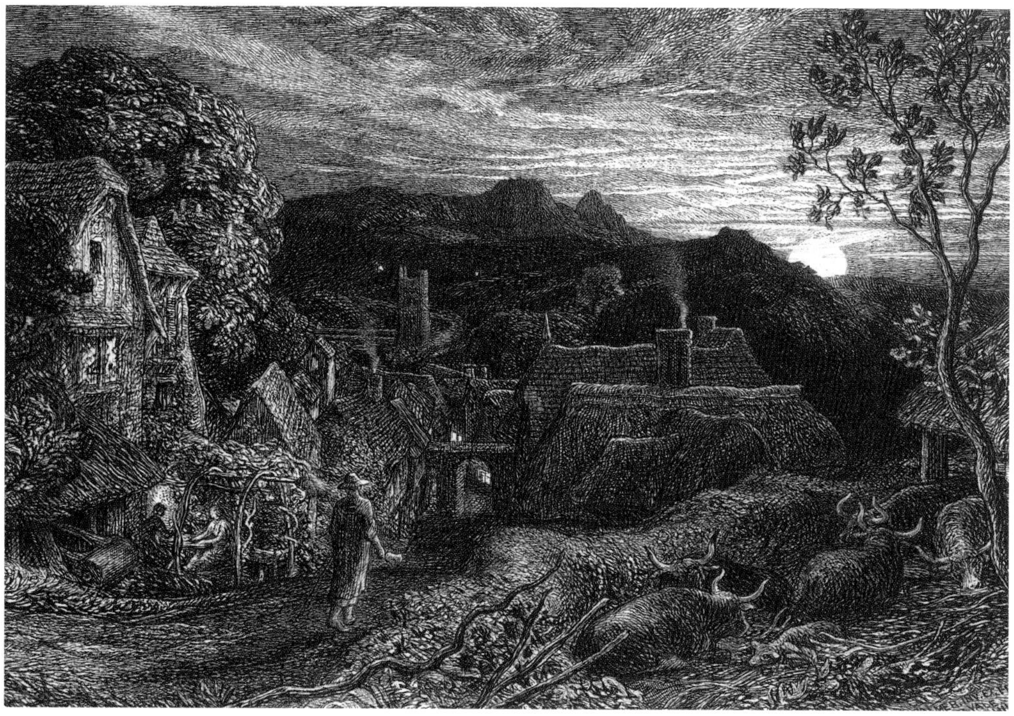

Plate 46. *The Bellman,* 1878-79. Etching
The Fine Art Society

The spark of his interest in etching had been kept alive, in the years since his son More's death, partly through a growing friendship with the etcher and critic Philip Gilbert Hamerton (1834-1894). When Hamerton had wanted a new etching in 1870 (to illustrate an article on Palmer in his *Portfolio* magazine), Palmer answered that his kind of etching needed time:

> I can get 100 guineas for quite a small drawing which does not occupy nearly the time of some of my etchings.
>
> But I am purchasable, perhaps, not only for one, but for a small series of larger etchings, which are in contemplation.[133]

The Etching Club in recent years had seen quarrels, following on the election of Seymour Haden in 1860. Haden had learnt to etch in France, where quite opposite fashions prevailed. He and his brother-in-law James McNeill Whistler etched in an open, linear style.[134] Palmer and his friends by contrast made careful preliminary studies, and then filled the plate to its edges with close-worked needling to secure 'the right construction of light and shadows'.

Haden's lighter etching invited a different kind of printing. The elaborate Etching Club plates needed very clean printing to preserve dense textures from blotting. Haden's more open textures favoured a new practice called *retroussage*, where the printer wiped the inked plate with a soft cloth in order to draw excess ink up over the furrows for impressionistic effects. Palmer felt that 'etching in the old sense' was threatened 'by the new art of retroussage added by the printer upon a comparatively slight fabric'.[135]

For an Etching Club miscellany to appear in 1872, Palmer lent *The Morning of Life*. The printer was a new man recommended by Haden, Frederick Goulding. He was another enthusiast for *retroussage*. Despite Palmer's careful instructions, the proofs appeared to Herbert Palmer as 'gobs of black and white, flopped here and there'.[136]

Palmer decided to try direct control of printing from his plates. He acquired a press of his own, and had Herbert trained to work it. The best teacher, it seemed, was still Goulding. So one day in 1873 Goulding came down to Furze Hill House. Within a few hours he and Herbert were producing, under Palmer's guidance, the best Palmer proofs ever seen.

Five years later, in the autumn of 1878, Palmer made up his mind to etch two of the Milton watercolour subjects. Both were from 'Il Penseroso'.[137] He worked their larger plates in a bolder way, suiting elderly eyes. It invited relatively 'pure' etching without much addition from the engraving burin, as he wrote to Hamerton. But he discovered all over again how etching 'makes havoc of my time':

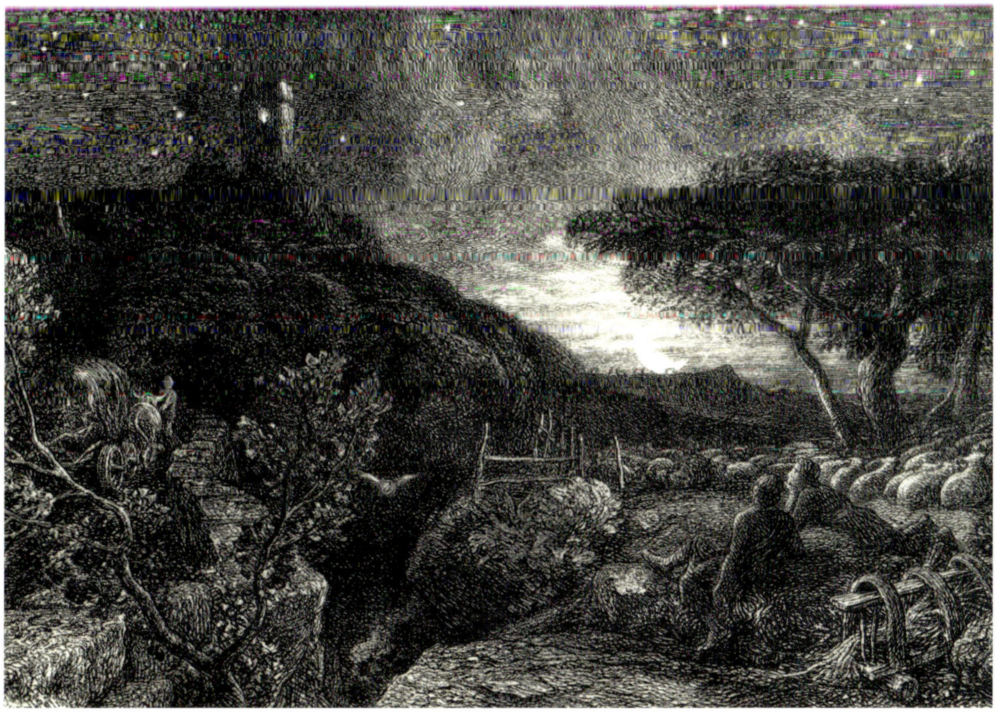

Plate 47. *The Lonely Tower,* 1878-79. Etching

> Outline, with its *local* shadows, can be etched rapidly; not so that mystic mass of enticement[,] ideal *chiaroscuro*, of which I think you will agree with me that etching is the best exponent.[138]

Each of the Milton etchings darkens its watercolour original. A study for *The Bellman* watercolour showed a warmth of richly coloured light that defined the orb at the horizon as the setting sun. In the etching it becomes the moon (Plate 46).

The Lonely Tower watercolour had shown a waning moon above the horizon, but the foreground flooded in low sunlight (reviving the paradox in *The Valley Thick with Corn* of 1825). The etched *Lonely Tower* enthrones its moon amid stars (Plate 47).

The Bellman plate received thirteen separate bitings, *The Lonely Tower* fourteen.[139] Each biting shows added work. 'Matter aggregates within matter', Palmer wrote then, 'till the copper looks as large as a half-length canvas.'[140] A half-length canvas connotes a portrait. Here indeed is self-portraiture.

The question of further Milton etchings was overtaken by a new etching project. From boyhood Palmer had worshipped at the shrine of the founder of pastoral vision, Virgil. That worship had been confirmed by his young sight of Blake's little wood engravings. Later in life Palmer told his younger son that Virgil's pastorals 'teach the wisdom of all life and the mysteries of intellectual discipline under the veil of agriculture, vintages, cattle, bees, so that the veil itself is glorious'.[141]

Virgil's *Eclogues* so attracted Palmer that he had begun, during the lifetime of his elder son, to write and translate an English 'version' of them. After More's death Palmer continued the writing 'as a resource in the deepest distress of mind'. The book was kept secret from his wife and everyone but the surviving son Herbert. Herbert thought that finding the right English words for the *Eclogues* at times overtook his father's interest in painting the Milton watercolours.

By the beginning of 1872, Palmer's version of the Virgil *Eclogues* was near enough finished to think of publishing it. He consulted Hamerton, in a letter containing this pregnant sentence: 'If Blake were alive and I could afford it, I would ask him to make a headpiece to each bucolic.'[142] So Hamerton answered that a Virgil translation by a man not known for his writing would become publishable only with Palmer's illustrations. Palmer returned to his charge over the cost of such etchings from his own needle.

Still he took pencils, pen, and Bristol board to Margate (to escape Hannah's latest spring cleaning) in May 1872. When he returned, Palmer brought with him 'the ten [Virgil *Eclogues*] subjects upon their cardboards', Herbert recalled, 'and one or two of them well advanced'.[143] They were drawn in ink lines carefully separated, with a view to photo-mechanical reproduction then in its infancy. Printing experiments proved hopeless. Valpy was pressing for his Milton watercolours, so the Virgil images were set on one side.

133. Ibid, 315.
134. Ibid, 336, 338-339. Of the Haden-Whistler style, Palmer's Etching Club friend J.C. Hook quipped: 'Some etchers nowadays dip a daddy long-legs into the ink, and start him on an adventure across a continent of papier vergé.' (Ibid, 97 n).
135. Ibid, 365. Ultimately Haden resigned from the Etching Club to found a rival 'Society of Painter-Etchers' – which secured a Royal Patent, knighthood for Haden, and wide praise for his *soi-disant* 'etching revival'.
136. *The Parting Light: Selected Writings of Samuel Palmer, ed* Mark Abley (Manchester: Carcanet, 1985), 234; *V&A Catalogue*, 81.
137. Perhaps Palmer's choices were made in deference to the old Etching Club *L'Allegro*. Although a companion *Il Penseroso* was mooted, no trace of any such book can be found. Several sources list such a volume in connection with the publication of Palmer's etched *Lonely Tower*. *The Lonely Tower* etching in fact appeared in Dec 1879 as a plate in the final Etching Club miscellany, a portfolio: copies survive with the contents sheet.
138. 17 Feb 1879 to Hamerton (*Life and Letters*, 376).
139. A.H. Palmer in *V&A Catalogue*, p 83.
140. 13 Jan 1879 to Hamerton (*Life and Letters*, 158).
141. 14 Oct 1866 (Ibid, 282).
142. 26 Jan 1872 (Ibid, 323).
143. Ibid, 156.

At length Palmer made up his mind to convert his Virgil drawings to etchings. By the time he finished his two Milton etchings in 1879, he had done enough etching on four Virgil plates to take preliminary proofs. His seventy-fifth birthday in January 1880 found him working slowly on a fifth plate, *Opening the Fold*, for Eclogue 8.

Opening the Fold draws elements from both the Milton etchings, with longer memories from *The Rising Moon* and *The Early Ploughman*. An English thatched roof in the right-hand middle distance is counterpointed by a distant town below Italian hills. From behind their geologic mass spread beams of a brilliant sunrise, to exude inspiration. The shepherd unfolds his sheep, while at the right a youthful Damon pipes paradoxically 'his last numbers'.

In the late summer of 1880 *Opening the Fold* had its first biting – of eleven, many interspersed by work added (once again) with the engraving burin. But no proofs were taken at Furze Hill. For his wife, Palmer wrote, had entered

> … a perfect crusade against all 'litter and lumber'; – now, next to myself, the most obvious piece of 'lumber' was of course the printing press.[144]

She packed it off to Herbert (now living in London), and it was damaged in the shipping.

Ultimately Herbert had to replace the damaged press with a larger machine which he kept in London. Palmer, separated again from proving his plates and controlling their printing, sent sheaves of instructions to guide his son. There were even detailed directions for Herbert to make some little additions to the image itself.[145]

That December Palmer sent holiday wishes to a young friend, with another wish less conventional: 'hoping? for the sake of my fellow creatures, that this may be the last Christmas of the present dispensation'.[146] He prepared the sixth and seventh Milton watercolours for exhibition in the spring of 1881, and wrote a memorandum 'in case of my death' that the eighth and final watercolour, *The Bellman*, could be shown in the following year.[147]

With the coming of spring he began to fail. Herbert saw his father on 18 May 1881, and promised to finish any Virgil etchings far enough advanced. Six days later Samuel Palmer drew his last breath. He had made his own summation a year earlier, when he described death as

> … the catastrophe of a being by all his instincts[,] all his enterprise, otherwise formed for immortality. Else why does he shun delights and live laborious days for the sake even of posthumous fame? Perpetuity is our ideal…
>
> *What* explores, what can possibly explore[,] but the ego [–] the immaterial self? Why the man is looking to the ends of the earth for the candle which he carries about with him.[148]

* * *

Palmer's great predecessors in English landscape painting, Turner and Constable, had also transfigured special places with qualities of vision. But they had not often sought deliberately to transcend time in their places. Palmer sought that transcendence in his art. Thus he regarded the art of Claude Lorrain:

> I do not think that it is either the truth of his colour or the charm of his trees, (unrivalled though they be,) or the gold of his sunshine, that makes CLAUDE the greatest of landscape painters, but that Golden *Age* into which poetic minds are thrown back – on first sight of one of his… pictures.[149]

The removal of time-barriers in Claude's pictures opened Palmer's prospect to farther fields of poetry:

> Ordinary landscapes remind us of what we see in the country; Claude's of what we read in the greatest poets and of *their* perception of the country, thus raising our own towards the same level.[150]

In the final months of his life, Palmer had set down his last thoughts on these things in an essay to preface his *'English Version'* of *Virgil's Eclogues*. The essay was called 'Some Observations on the Country and on Rural Poetry'.

144. 26 Oct 1880 to C.W. Cope (*Letters*, 1043).
145. *Letters*, 1038*f.*
146. 21 Dec 1880 to Thomas Howard Wright (*Letters*, 1052).
147. 9 March 1881 to Valpy (Ibid, 1068).
148. *c.*June 1880 (following the death of John Giles) to William Blake Richmond (Ibid, 1009-1010).
149. 3 Sept 1875 to F. G. Stephens (Ibid, 923-924).
150. *c.*1870 to Valpy (Ibid, 913).

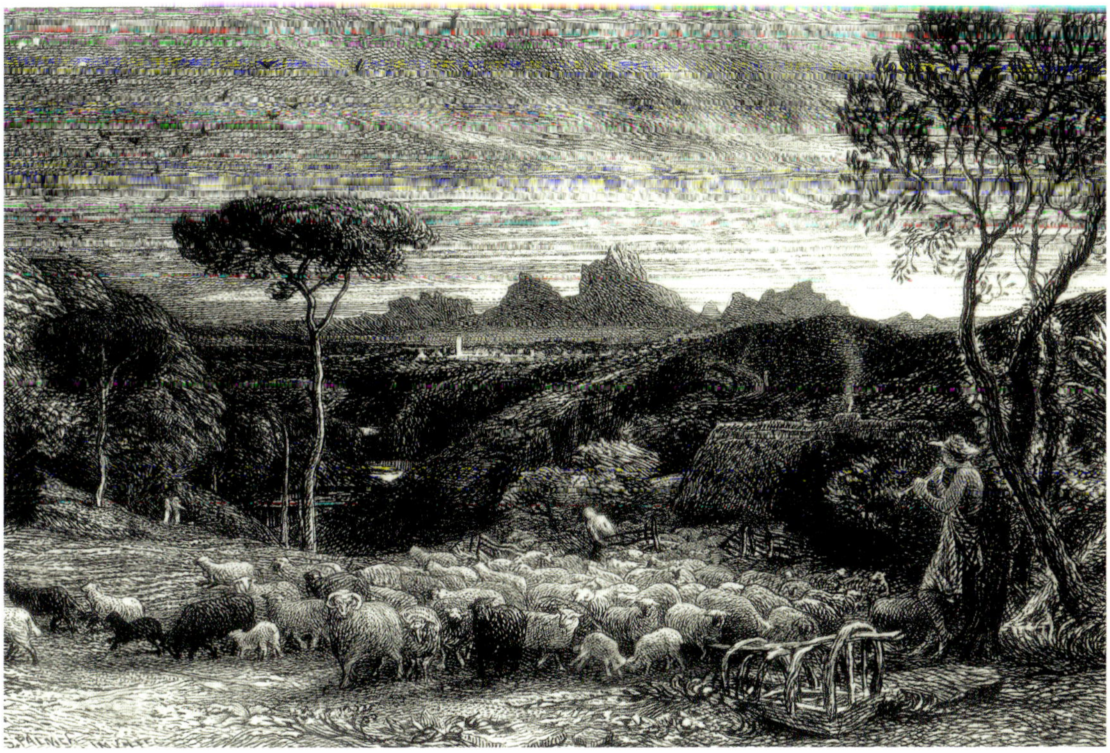

Plate 48. *Opening the Fold,* 1879-80. Etching

Poetry, Palmer writes, 'sets wit and philosophy to music'. He locates poetry among 'the useful arts', because 'it develops imagination':

> Disciplined imagination in equipoise with learning and judgement is very active, practical and materially productive; what it sees within, always desiring to make and embody without.
> Foreknowing the end, it can best devise the means, going to work the shortest way.

The alternative to inherited 'wit and philosophy' is fatuous novelty (where 'a more prosaic and tentative industry, rather feeling its way than seeing it, is officiously busy before it is quite known what is to be done').

Poetry, as the vehicle of imagination, thus equates for Palmer to civilisation itself:

> For no small portion of their renown, the greatest nations have been beholden to their poets… because their living words from age to age, continued to educate the leaders of the people, keeping before them the ideas of justice, magnanimity and fortitude, exemplified in persuasive story.
> Robust nations which were merely warlike, without arts or literature, though useful to weaker races by the infusion of new blood, after they had shed what they could of the old, muster in history without adorning it; they were formidable as locusts are formidable.

A poet's real concern, then, is his country in its widest prospects:

> We might be grateful to the poets, if the benign influence of their art did nothing more than make us love the country; and while we are yet uncorrupted, open to us a world of innocent pleasures; enriching us… with a new sense, which invests familiar objects with meaning and beauty.

New in old, old in new: the vitality of country experience to renewing seasons of innocence.

Finally Palmer's memory casts back fifty years to the picture of his young self at his grandfather's cottage in Shoreham. 'A young man of competent estate and education' will live best 'if he determines to begin life where the best and wisest men have desired to await its close':

> … if, with Cowley, he would choose 'a small house and large garden', rather than a large [city] mansion with none: if he prefer sunshine to smoke; bean-fields, violets and new-mown hay…

Palmer himself, if he had not lived the whole of his life in the country, had managed that its inspiration had filled all his pilgrimages to the country of vision. So he set perspectives for his successors.

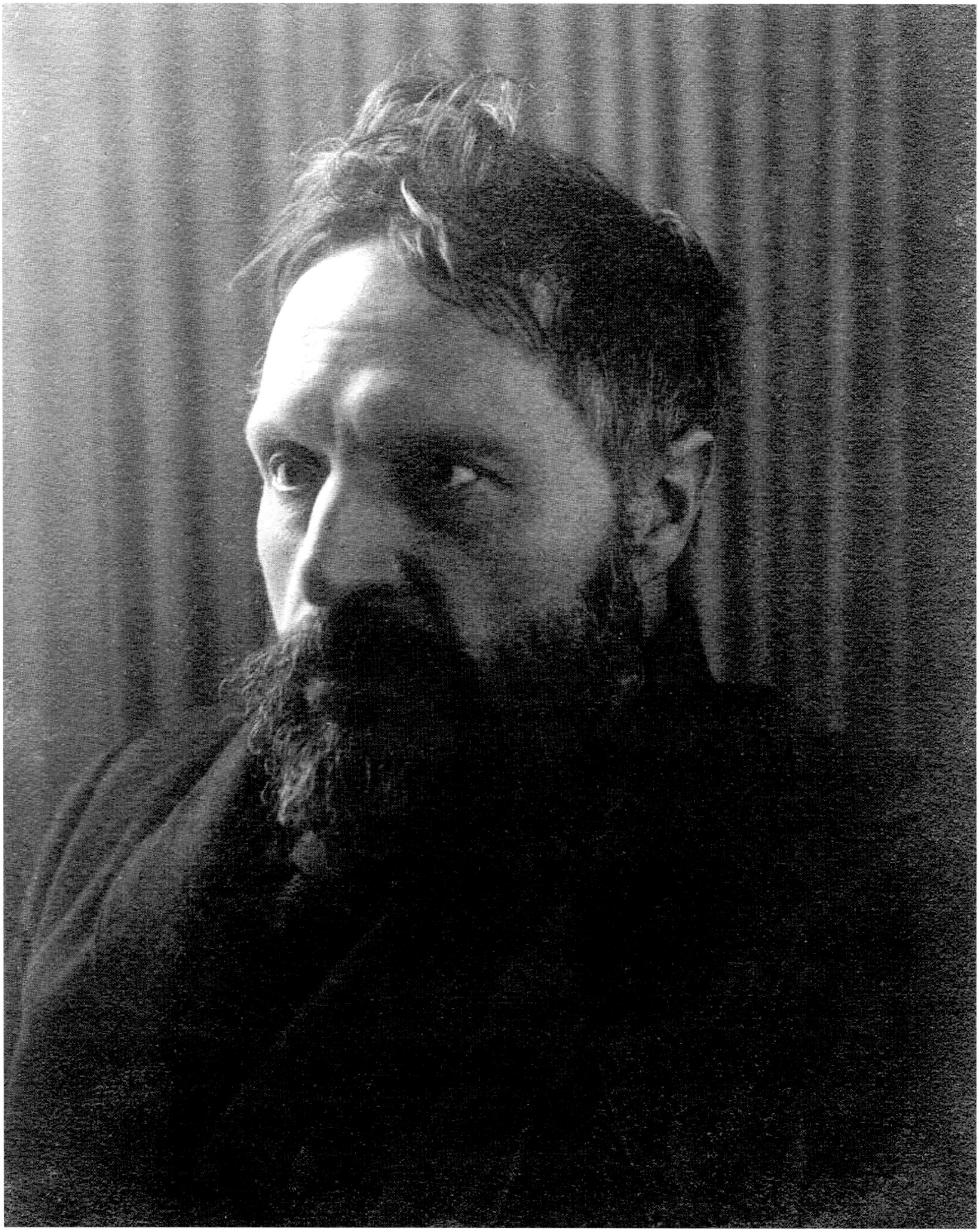

CHAPTER 2

William Hyde (1857-1925)†

Country Lights in City Darkness

Palmer's art had shown its rustic figures in their Edens, harvesting the fruits of faith in a benevolent Creator. It was only a step from the world hymned in Haydn's *Creation* and *The Seasons*, with romantic enrichments. In the art of William Hyde, born two generations after Palmer, that faith has blown away on a wind risen with gathering darkness.

Where Palmer had used darkness to define light, Hyde uses his lights to measure the spread of darkness. Hyde's London lamps flare against towering gloom to outline a rainswept figure or strike on a face in the crowd. Country figures appear as hapless intruders caught in the eye of nature. That eye may look through autumn winds, winter silences or the calms of summer, but its dominance is always implied. Ploughmen appear, but never a harvest – only weeds and nettles, overhung by trees grown huge in relentless rains. The moon reveals its phases in clear night or mist, but the sun shines for Hyde through angry dawns and dusks.

Of all the visionaries here assembled, Hyde lived farthest outside the art establishment. Two photographs of him at forty-six show a man far from the town. Eyes burn, hair and beard are windblown, and he is thickly wrapped against a cold he seems to look for without and within.

Opposite:
Plate 49. William Hyde, *c.*1904. Photograph by A.C. Curtis, Guildford, Surrey

* * *

Hyde's parents, William and Lydia, were from tradesmen's families in Southampton, where they married in 1856. They went to live in another place of shipping and docks, Thames-side Greenwich, where the young husband found employment as an 'eating house keeper'. In a small house at 7 Ashburnham Road, on the western side of Greenwich, their eldest child William was born on 2 October 1857.[1]

It was three miles east of where Samuel Palmer had seen the light half a century earlier. Here too the country was still close by, beginning at Greenwich Park and Blackheath. But the dominating presence was the tidal Thames: the Greenwich Reach lay half a mile to the north, with the Isle of Dogs and Essex marshes beyond.

Water was to fill the art of the man born there – interpenetrating land with river and marsh, thickening the air above with mists and smoke. Here was Hyde's pastoral, evoked by the mature artist in words from early memories and half-memories:

> A wide stretch of misty marsh-lands, bounded by soft grey hills, fading away into the distance… while the wind brings up from the river a dreary melancholy moaning from the syrens on the vessels passing… One sees a few sheep penned in by hurdles, here and there indistinctly catching on their fleeces grey lights from the sky.

At other times:

> Over the horizons of the Essex Marshes, like a great golden lamp, the full moon rose and tinted the soft grey air with amber tones, which were reflected in the broad limpid stream beneath.[2]

Before the boy's second birthday his family had moved over the River and into the City of London. They found rooms in a huddle of yards politely called Devonshire Square, behind the intersection of Houndsditch with Bishopsgate. There Hyde senior was serving as a 'tavern

†N.B. Not to be confused with the American portrait and genre painter William Henry Hyde (*b.* New York 1858, *d.* Albany 1943), who graduated Columbia College in 1877, studied in Paris, and lived virtually the rest of his life in New York (*NY Times* obit 8 Feb 1943; *Who Was Who in American Art*). Several books of reference conflate the two William Hydes; they are correctly differentiated in the Thieme-Becker and Bénézit dictionaries.

1. This and much other background material has been traced through official records by Barry C. Johnson, who is at work on a full-length biography of Hyde.

2. William Hyde, 'Autumn near London', in *Pall Mall Magazine* XXXI, no 127 (Nov 1903), 302; and 'The Thames at Night', Ibid XXXIV, no 136 (Oct 1904), 150.

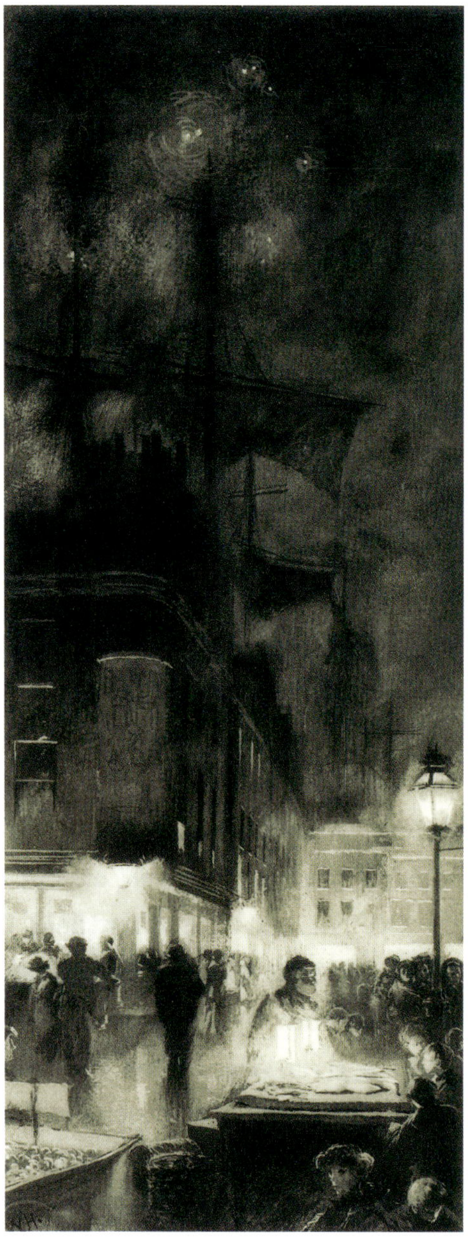

Plate 50. *Back Street* from *London Impressions*, 1898. Photogravure

waiter' at the time a second son George was born in 1859. At the birth of a third son Henry two years later, the father gave his employment as 'commercial clerk'.

As the eldest boy William grew, his impressions of Bishopsgate were permeated by swirling lights and ghostly shapes half-emerging from the fogs that gathered among the old buildings. Later knowledge traced their origins back to the marshes downriver. Hyde wrote:

> These emanations from the marsh, made visible by a drop in the temperature, are the unsmirched ingredients of the celebrated London fog... which happens when these pearly fleeces are allied with smoke and soot. ... One gropes one's way, a phantom among phantoms.[3]

Hyde's mature writings show education or self-education sound enough to publish his written impressions in a good magazine. His business letters defend his corners without suffering fools gladly. Family letters express deeply held affection. He may have owed something of his abilities to his mother's encouragement. He would honour her by naming his elder daughter Lydia after her. But he perpetuated neither his own name and his father's, nor those of his brothers, in the naming of his son.

Bishopsgate in the 1860s was a cockpit of past and present. The northern railway terminus at nearby Shoreditch contributed to the pall of smoke. And during William's boyhood they began to clear a wide swath of old houses west of Bishopsgate to extend the railway down to a new terminus at Liverpool Street, nearly opposite the entrance to where the Hydes lived.[4]

Yet the whole area was honeycombed with survivals from the past. Some of the City churches reached back to mediaeval times. The fifteenth century came alive in the magnificent Crosby Hall. The seventeenth century stood up in the elaborate carving and glazing of Sir Paul Pindar's mansion in Bishopsgate. From St Paul's Cathedral, a few streets west, ran part of the Roman Watling Street; and north by Moorgate stood a section of the old London Wall. As boy and man, Hyde haunted the Guildhall library and museum of antiquities (and sent his daughter there in later years).

He saw his ghosts most vividly after dark. At the Tower of London he observed:

> The mediaeval world peeps out as one sees the gleam of a bayonet, as a sentry paces steadily up and down, when the old walls and battlements are touched by the cold silvery light of a high moon... and the old Norman stronghold seems to have gathered back something of its past under the spell of night.[5]

Another magnet was over the river at Southwark – the end of the Roman road from Dover, and a starting point for mediaeval pilgrims to Canterbury (as in Chaucer's *Canterbury Tales*). Hyde's own sight of Chaucer's Tabard Inn lingered in his memory long after the last surviving fragment fell to the wrecker's hammer in 1875. Near the end of his life Hyde wrote to his daughter Lydia, then studying in London:

> Of course modern progress (???) has effaced many things I knew as a boy – nearly all the old Inns in the Borough [of Southwark] – but when I come up one day I will take you there; one or two are left.
>
> I also want to take you along the bank of the Thames eastward of Southwark Cathedral – one of the queer places amongst the Wharves and Docks. I don't think young ladies could go there *alone* quite safely.

Then he shared something more general that London had taught him:

> Always dear try to get a love of *places*. Very often we find them of more substantial interest than a love of people.
>
> Never forget to *see* things [–] that is the atmosphere – fog, sunlight, rain and colour and light and shade. Millions of people live in London who never *see* or have *seen* their immediate surroundings. They take them as a matter of course like the multiplication table. ...
>
> It is a great Pageant of Life in London. ... Don't let it make you unhappy or feel small. Vain people resort [to] being 'lost in a crowd' but this is quite through want of imagination – read the past by the present...[6] [Plate 50].

Hyde was still young when his parents moved again – a few miles north of London this time, to Edmonton. There the father seems to have tried some final employment as a gardening farmer, before he died in the 1870s.[7] Edmonton in those years was recalled by another artist as a 'sweet country village where quiet people lived and farmed and gardened amidst the orchards, fields and hawthorn lanes'.[8] After London fog and history, this experience of country brought fresh perceptions. Hyde was to write:

> Early flowers have associations and influences that touch all the springs of life: who cannot remember as a child watching with a child's unsophisticated vision the coming of some of the amaryllids, as they pushed aside the earth with their golden-pointed buds, and the wonder and instinctive imagination that an opening bud roused as it uncurled leaf by leaf?[9]

Those perceptions belonged to an artist in the making. William's difficulty lay in the fact that art was not a business for reliable remuneration. His answer was wood-engraving – the medium of Blake's Virgil illustrations, the medium by which artists' drawings were reproduced then throughout the journal press and humbler ranges of books. The journeyman-engraver's task was to cut away the wood surrounding the artist's lines drawn upon the block surface, until only those lines stood proud for inking and printing.

The engraver's training also showed young Hyde something else. Fifteen years later he shared it with a journalist friend:

> When very young I was placed under a man who was not only a splendid engraver but a man of taste, knowledge and professional pride. He had passed many years on the continent, in Paris and elsewhere, and had all the best traditions of the French Art world.
>
> From him I received both encouragement and instruction, and became acquainted with French engravers whose views on art enlightened though depressing me – so great was their contempt for English art.[10]

This incursion of French taste was coeval with Haden's 'etching revival'. Contempt for the art of his own country disturbed the young Hyde. It would drive him to scrutinise his country when opportunity offered.

Almost as soon as Hyde entered the trade, wood-engraving fell under threat from the newly perfected process of photo-mechanical engraving. In the 'new process', any original picture – drawing or even photograph if clear enough – could be photographed and engraved in a single operation on to metal. The photo-engraved plate could then be inked and printed in the same frame with text type.[11] Cheapness came before fine accuracy, but that was coming too.

So at twenty-four Hyde took a brave decision. He would equip himself as an artist of original work – for reproduction by whatever means might be or become available. He had wanted the change, as he recalled 'days spent in engraving work which too often was agonizingly uncongenial'. He set himself to study perspective and its geometries, but felt weakness in drawing the human figure.

A good place to seek instruction was the Lambeth School of Art in Kennington Park Road, a mile south-west of Southwark. Set up by the City and Guilds of London as a technical school to benefit young artisans, its classes were mostly in evenings and at weekends. On 10 January 1882 Hyde applied for admission to the class in 'Life drawing' at a cost of five shillings the term.[12]

The resident head, John C.L. Sparkes, ran the school on a shoestring, and personally oversaw every aspect of his students' work. 'He really knew his business,' wrote Laurence Housman (one of a brilliant group of students who followed on Hyde's heels at Lambeth), 'and his quiet biting remarks were enjoyed by all except the recipients.'[13] Hyde attended the School 'desultorily', he told his journalist friend, and kept steadily at his wood-engraving trade until the inroads of photo-engraving forced him out. But all the while he was developing his own expression.

---

3. 'Autumn near London', 304.
4. Information from my friend the late B.J.D. Walsh. The later widening of Liverpool Street station beginning in 1890 was to clear the west side of Bishopsgate Street itself.
5. 'The Thames at Night', 146.
6. 10 Oct 1921, with its 'PS Tuesday morning' [11 Oct] (private coll).
7. On Hyde's marriage certificate in 1895 he cited his late father's occupation as 'farmer'. The elder Hyde was dead by the time of the national census of 1881, which lists Mrs Hyde as a widow living in Hertford Road, Edmonton with the three sons: William (*ae* 23), wood-engraver; George (21), banker's clerk; Henry (19), in the wine trade.
8. Christopher Whall, *Stained Glass Work* (1905: rpr Bristol: Venables, 1999), 215.
9. 'A Sussex Valley in Spring', in *Pall Mall Magazine* XXIX, no 120 (April 1903), 470.
10. Quoted in Ford Madox Hueffer, 'William Hyde: an Illustrator of London', in *The Artist* XXI, no 217 (Jan 1898), 2.
11. Joseph Pennell, *Modern Illustration* (2nd ed, Bell, 1898), 40.
12. Lambeth School of Art archives. For access and help I am grateful to the present Registrar, Mrs Judith Maroon. Hyde's application shows him lodging at 1 Melbourne Square, Brixton Road, a mile south of the School.
13. Laurence Housman, *The Unexpected Years* (Cape, 1937), 35. Housman (1865-1959) entered the School with his sister Clemence (1861-1955) in Nov 1883. Charles Shannon (1863-1937) had entered in 1881 (a few months before Hyde): at the School in Oct 1882 he met his lifelong companion Charles Ricketts (1866-1931). Shannon's former pupil Thomas Sturge Moore (1870-1944) entered in 1887. The five later played a leading part in a revival of wood-engraving as an original art: they became known as the 'Vale' group.

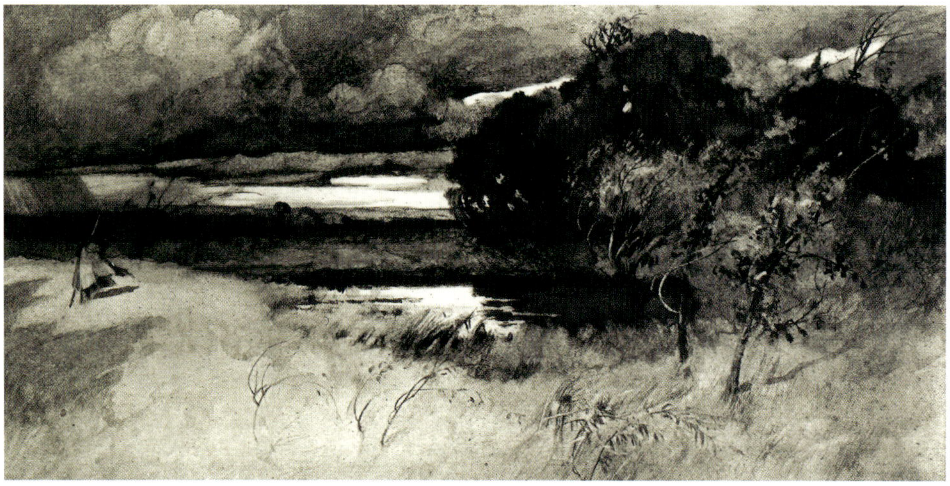

Plate 51. *The Falling of the Night* from *An Imaged World,* 1894. Photogravure

Hyde's power as an artist revolved round the black and white of his engraver's training, backed up by his experience of London nights and fogs. Out of these memories he honed two monochrome techniques that echoed the young Palmer, with Turner and Claude behind him.

One is a finely elaborated skill with pen and ink, with radical contrasts of light and heavy lines learned in the engraving trade. The other lies in broad washes and grisaille watercolour – which Hyde adapts brilliantly to capture the strongest weathers, the subtlest lights. His bright lights flare against darknesses in London. But in the country skies are broader.

In 1889 Hyde showed his first picture at a Royal Academy exhibition, *An Autumn Evening*. The next year he showed and sold *Light and Shade*, evoking a special place on the southern coast which caught and held his imagination – the eerie emptiness of Romney Marsh (Plate 51). Here the interpenetrations of land and water at dawn or dusk cast hints (as Thames-side and the Essex marshes had cast hints). Lights glimmering obscurely might hold special potency for a visionary of Hyde's humble background.

West of Romney Marsh rose the old 'Cinque Port' of Winchelsea. One of Hyde's pictures in the Academy exhibition of 1891 was of *Winchelsea Rocks*. Then in a secluded valley behind Winchelsea he came upon a large mediaeval and Tudor manor house, Brede Place. It was empty but for a caretaker – and the ghost of a murderer said to walk there. Such rumours had been encouraged by smugglers who had used the cellars and subterranean passages within living memory. Hyde drew the ancient pile with its overgrown park in moonlit washes (Plate 52).

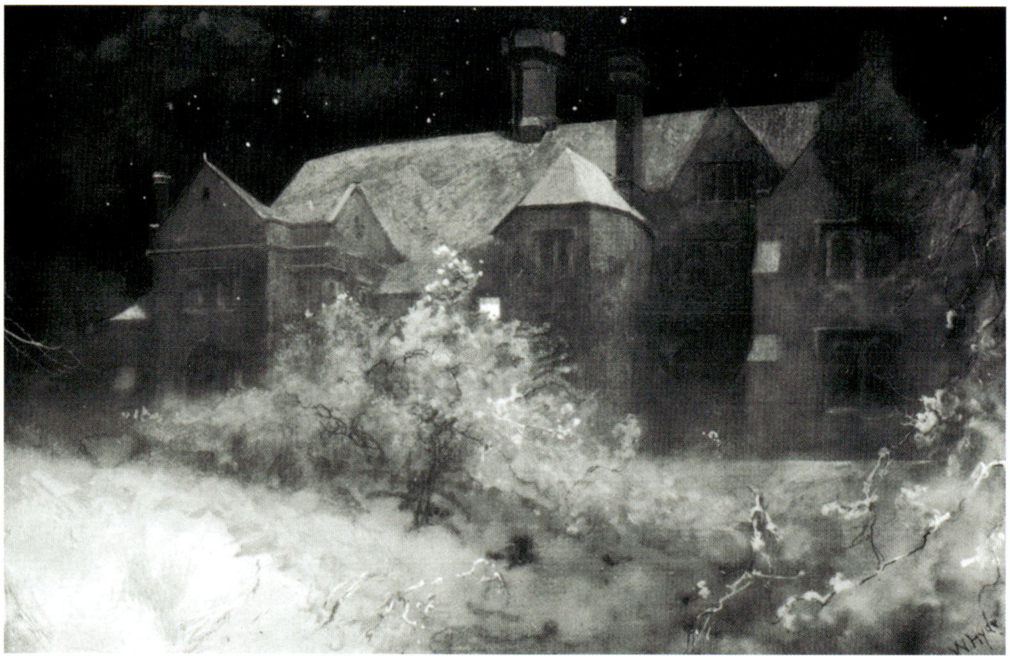

Plate 52. *Brede Place, c.*1894 (from *The Cinque Ports,* 1900). Grisaille watercolour

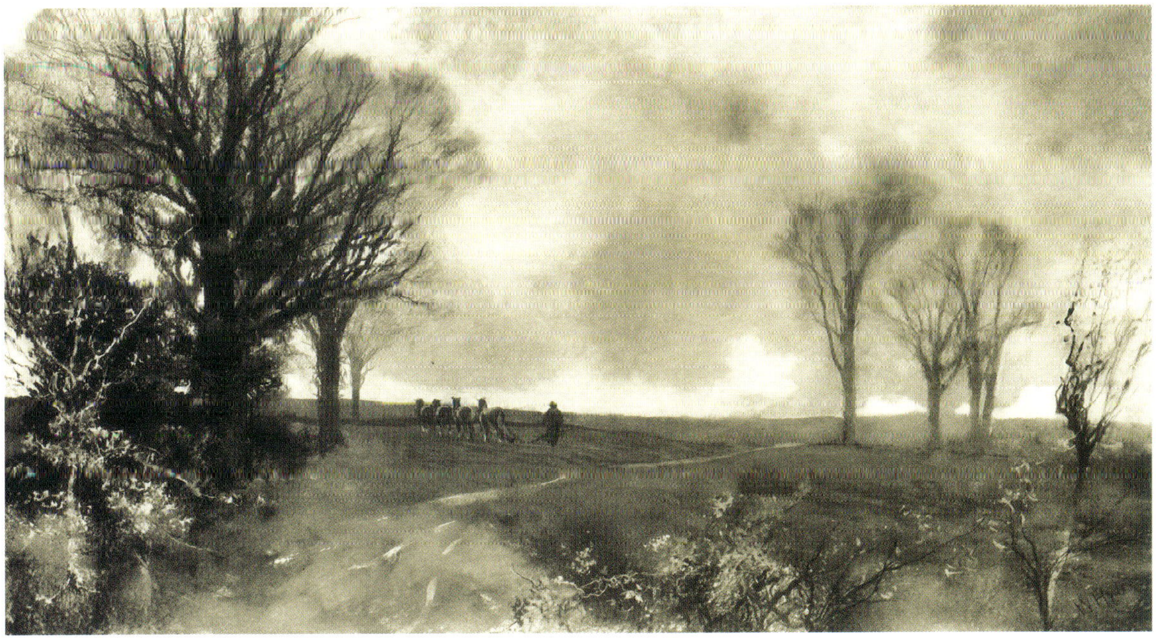

Plate 53. *The Ploughman* from *L'Allegro & Il Penseroso* [1895]. Photogravure

Brede Place so magnetised Hyde that he arranged to stay alone there 'for the better conception of these designs' (as he confided to his journalist friend Hueffer). He lived in a room over the porch, wandering out at any hour of dusk or night or sunrise. He stayed from the end of February to late April, and the memory of those weeks filled an article written years later.[14] Hyde's article translates to words the visions and techniques of his pictures there:

> The days of the valley begin in long rifts of silver light, inlaid in the dark grey shadows of the night – shadows that fade into the upper sky in infinite graduations of pencilled cloud, while the Marsh pastures are visionary in mists and frosty rime.

His article uses the manor house and its country to evoke a sequence of ideas gradually laying bare the springs of surrounding nature:

> The old house stood up with its high-pitched roof and clustered chimneys with the air of being there by right. ... Brick and grey stone, tiled roof and porch, were shaped in the spacious times before men had lost the instinct of building with craft. ...
>
> It was one with the row of tall poplars, with the oaks in the park, with the valley and the marsh; the bleating of sheep, the scent of burning wood, the cawing of the rooks belong to it as an inheritance

In the house he enjoys winter fires of oak from the park, before retiring to his lonely room to sleep – and awaken to morning vision reminiscent of the young Palmer: 'There, after a wild night, when February was all but March... a blurred image of a star glistened through the wet panes [as] the dawning light revealed the shape of the old mullioned window... gleaming sapphire with a promise of warmer tints as I opened the casement... Men and horses moved over the brown earth with plough and harrow.' (Plate 53)

He leaves the house to follow an old track winding towards the hilltop – 'now pasture for sheep, where the shepherd had made his fold of wattles and hurdles under a sheltering bank':

> I had often seen the shepherd outlined against the rising morning on the ridge of the hill... He was one of those significant figures that were often seen about the valley and the marsh... a figure which has walked through many ages.

Another such figure rises to his view – 'the sower coming up the furrows of a field with steady, measured tread, sowing the seed broadcast with his swinging arm... an everlasting symbol of man's hopes and efforts personified. He seemed a vision, this Sussex farmer in his cords and leggings, in an age of patent drills and fizzing engines.'

Yet his own humble origin turns Hyde away from easy sentiment. 'Machinery may yet rob us of this symbol... One cannot say *No* to Science, or old Adam, or those of his children who

14. 'A Sussex Valley in Spring' (1903). The year of Hyde's two-month stay at Brede Place is uncertain, but before 1895 (possibly before 1893: see note 24 below). In 1895 he was in London in early March (see below pages 85-86), married in Richmond on 30 April, and immediately took his wife to Shere, Surrey, where they lived the rest of their lives. A two-month absence from his wife in 1896 or 1897 seems unlikely; and in Dec 1897 Hueffer wrote in his article of Hyde's stay at Brede.

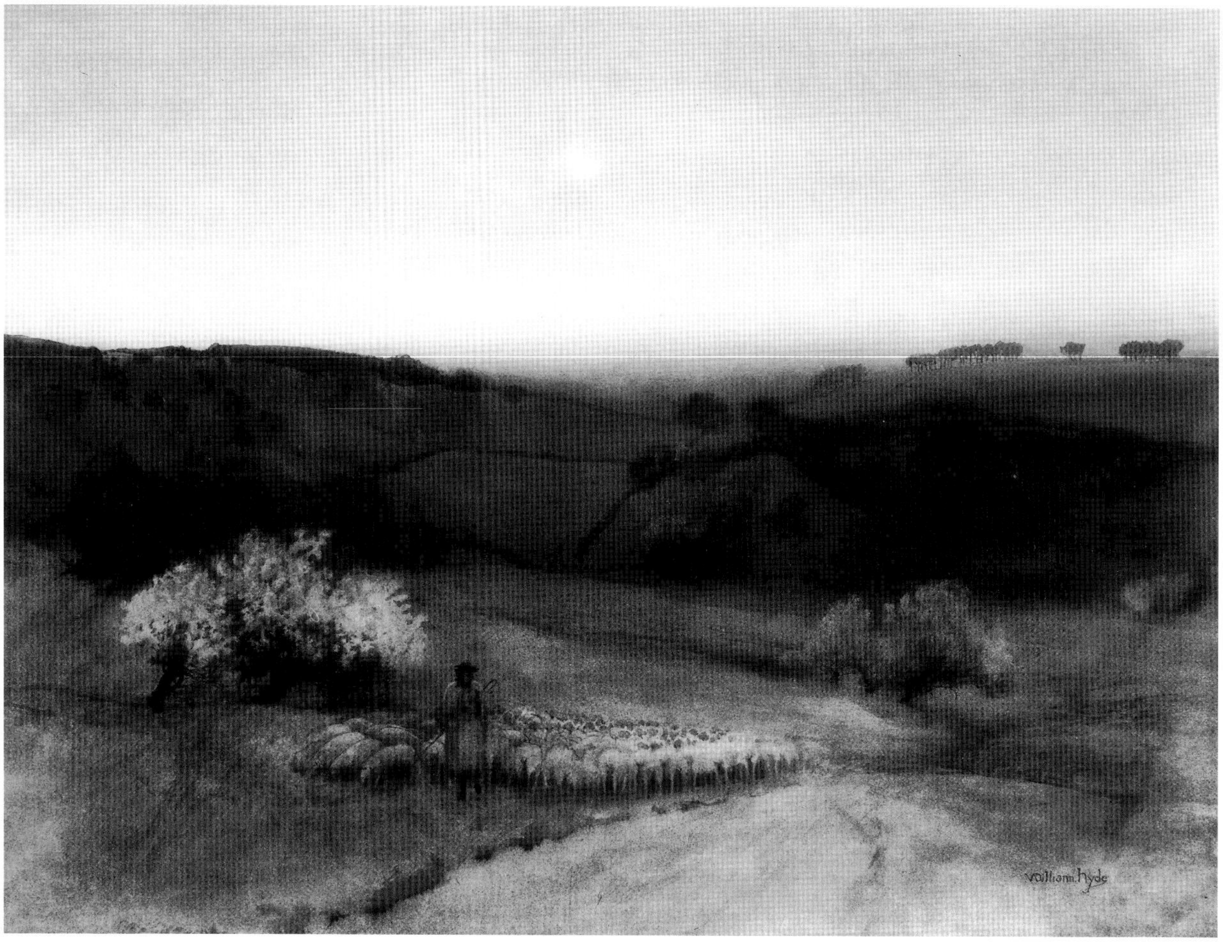

Plate 54. *Summer*, *c.*1896. Grisaille watercolour with pencil and wash

hunt for the red gold through all the crannies of life; for even in remote pastoral valleys man's needs must be satisfied, and the everlasting want of pence is one [:] the short story of labour come to the cottage, though the wedded beauty of earth and sky is at the door.'

Still the traditions surrounding humble country lives (seen with Hyde's city-bred eyes) shape an inheritance of national history:

> Here man's old struggle to get and to keep is tempered by a philosophy that is bred in the open air, and its influence on brave and kindly hearts [in] yeomen of a nation whose birth-pangs were there, beyond the silent wave of downland at the head of the valley.

(He looks westward to Hastings.)

The same country has shaped English pastoral literature:

> Seen from the higher pastures is a landscape that brings reminiscences of early Miltonic verse naturally into the mind; the sweetness and gravity of the breadth and tone which dwell in the repose of the sunlit hills as the cloud shadows pass over them…

By those lights and shadows Hyde reads the country above Brede for his own pastoral vision:

> From one of these higher pastures, above the slopes of the old park, where the shepherd had made his fold, the greater hills surrounding the valley were seen in all their relations with the sky, from the earliest dawn to the last fading glimmer of evening, and with the shadowy scented night and its great expanse above.

Palmer had seen such things at Shoreham.

The prospects in Hyde's art from its outset were large. From above Brede, thirty miles south-east of Shoreham, he sees the history of the land in its days and seasons:

> Lower yet, and the twilight came, a long April twilight: and the merged tones and colours gathered closer together, where the sheep-bell came from the now glimmering flock… The

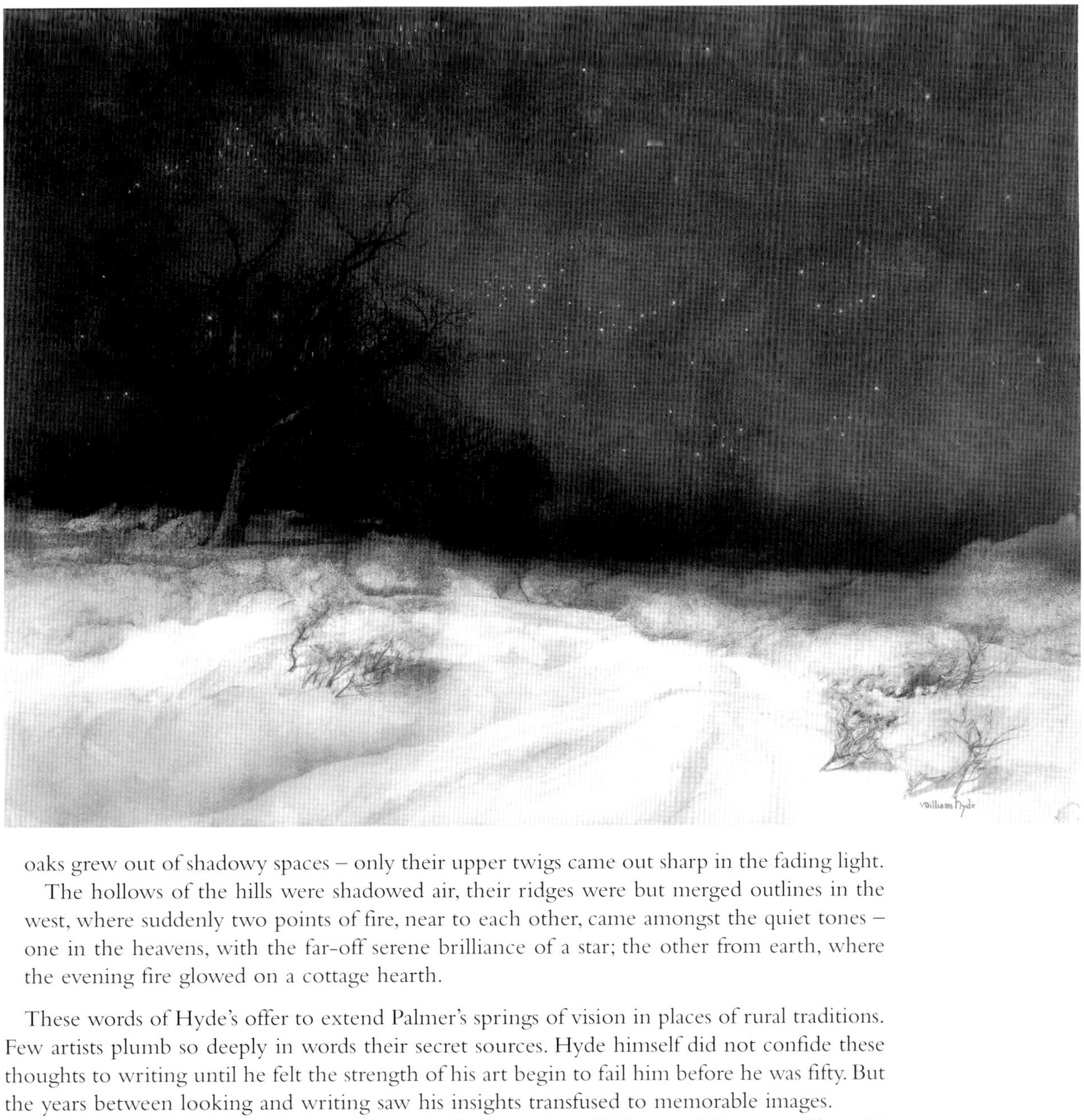

Plate 55. *Winter*, *c*.1896. Grisaille watercolour with pencil and wash

oaks grew out of shadowy spaces – only their upper twigs came out sharp in the fading light.

The hollows of the hills were shadowed air, their ridges were but merged outlines in the west, where suddenly two points of fire, near to each other, came amongst the quiet tones – one in the heavens, with the far-off serene brilliance of a star; the other from earth, where the evening fire glowed on a cottage hearth.

These words of Hyde's offer to extend Palmer's springs of vision in places of rural traditions. Few artists plumb so deeply in words their secret sources. Hyde himself did not confide these thoughts to writing until he felt the strength of his art begin to fail him before he was fifty. But the years between looking and writing saw his insights transfused to memorable images.

Hyde's early vision emerges in two large grisaille nocturnes of Winter and Summer (Plates 54 and 55.[15] They are worked in wizard-like grey washes and line to capture secrets of moonlight over the land. *Summer* is lit by a soft half-moon above a glowing horizon. It exudes the 'long rifts of silver light, inlaid in the dark grey shadows' seen about Brede and remembered. With his sheep gathered close about him (as they gathered in pictures by Blake and Palmer), Hyde's shepherd stands smocked and hatted and faceless. He holds the crook neutrally across him – a figure of ageless guardianship rising out of this ancient topography. The guardianship reaches both downwards and upwards through this pure light-in-darkness – the light without colour.

A sharper loneliness touches Hyde's *Winter* nocturne. Here the light is on the foreground snow below heaven's darkness – where stars clarify in a thin freezing haze descending to the black horizon. Out of the middle ground rise tree-shapes in recessive rhythms. The foreground is almost empty. No human path marks the snow – only faint tracks opened by strong wind. No earlier artist but Turner (unless Constable in a few cloud studies) had set the wind to dominate a picture.

* * *

The question facing Hyde in his thirties, as it had faced Palmer earlier, was how to expand a vision drawn from one place to fill a career. Hyde could not do it either. He turned his own

15. Private coll. Sight size of each, 425 x 550 mm; undated; each signed in full with elaborate lettering (contrasting with the simple capitals 'W HYDE' he used in work intended for reproduction).

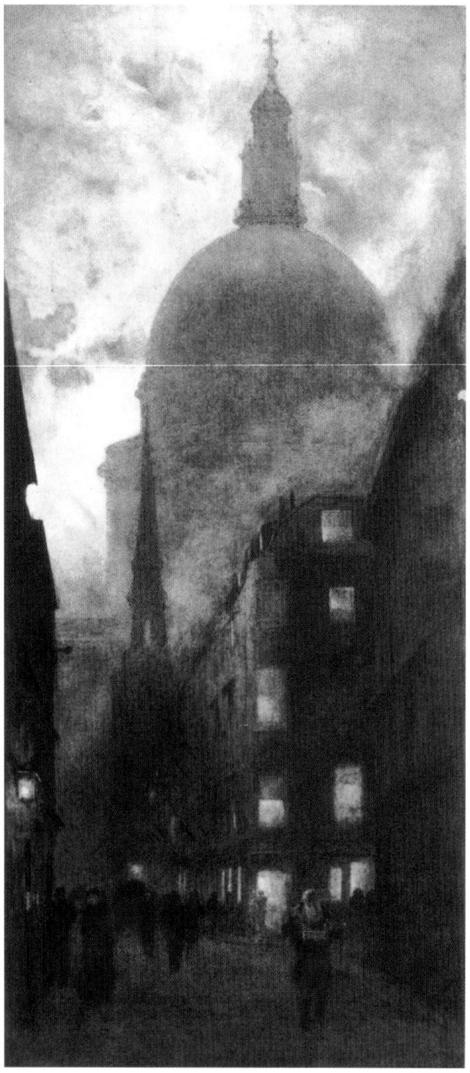

Plate 56. *St Paul's from Watling Street* from *London Impressions,* 1898. Photogravure

way – back to the city. He took a London studio in New Court, Carey Street (behind the Law Courts), and garret lodgings.[16] 'The City of Dreadful Night' showed itself instantly. He told the story to E.V. Lucas, who retold it thus:

> On the first night of his tenancy, on arriving home very late [Hyde] found on the doorstep, in an unconscious condition, the body of a man. Thinking it might be some one who lived there and had been overtaken, he rang for the landlady.
>
> Not in the least surprised, she merely asked her new lodger to help her get the 'poor gentleman' in. 'You see,' she said, 'It's Dr Jekyll.'
>
> 'Dr Jekyll?' said Mr Hyde.
>
> 'Yes, the organist.'[17]

Such experiences focused Hyde's darkness-in-light to pictures of London which exuded the rich greys and blacks that had filled his childhood. His London pictures found purchasers. One of the keenest was Frederick H. Evans (1853-1943). He was a well-known City bookseller, so ready to share his enthusiasm for Meredith, Stevenson, and other modern authors with young browsers that his shop became known as 'the university of the City clerk'.

One City clerk who had found his way to Evans's shop was the very young Aubrey Beardsley (1872-1898). Evans had traded books for the boy's drawings – and shown the drawings to the publisher J.M. Dent. Evans put it into Dent's head to publish a new edition of Malory's *Le Morte d'Arthur*, and to commission Beardsley illustrations for it: the young man's first book.

In 1893 Evans introduced Beardsley to another publisher, John Lane, and *The Yellow Book* was born. There two of Hyde's monochromes were included, before Beardsley was removed as art editor at the time of the Oscar Wilde trials in 1895.

Outside shop hours Evans pursued an interest which drew him towards Hyde's monochromes: photography. Evans was secretary of 'The Linked Ring'. Many of its members employed soft-focus camera-techniques that paralleled impressionism in painting and *retroussage* in the printing of etchings. Evans himself specialised in photographing church interiors, where he sought to capture 'rich deep shadows, full of soft detail'. Yet to Evans 'No photography can ever give us the same sense of absolute authority, as progenitor, as creator, that a drawing, or an etching, or a lithograph, or other monochrome method of graphic art can.'[18] Hyde's monochromes most of all (Plate 56).

Evans showed his Hyde drawings to Dent, with the idea of a grand folio of London images. Evans himself proposed to commission twenty,[19] but Dent fought shy of expensive photogravure reproduction on such a scale from another 'new' artist.

Then Dent was offered a small book that asked for Hyde illustrations. The book's author was Edward Garnett (1868-1937), a son of the British Museum's Keeper of Printed Books, Dr Richard Garnett. Both father and son were friends of Evans.

Edward Garnett and his wife Constance were Fabian socialists. He worked as a publisher's reader. She was learning Russian with the idea of translating Russian novels – and had fallen in love with her teacher, an anarchist who called himself 'Stepniak'. When Stepniak demanded that Constance visit Russia, she had left the Garnetts' baby son with relatives.

Edward Garnett repaired to a lonely cottage in the Surrey hills below Dorking. Wandering alone through an autumn and winter, between country and city, he set down his reflections under the title *An Imaged World*:

> To a man when the sun has set in fire, watching from some quiet hillside the black rim of the flying world bearing fast into the darkness the burden of another day, there comes a moment of solemn hush running up from the faint horizon of quivering light.[20]

Many of Garnett's verbal landscapes seemed to recompose in Hyde monochromes of darkness and light. Dent wanted to publish the book, he told the young author on 30 October 1893, 'because I am very desirous to have in Mr Hyde's drawings the interpretations of your beautiful word pictures'.[21]

Dent produced an elegant little book with a cover design of foliated leaves by Hyde.[22] The artist revived his old skill as wood-engraver for several vignettes (Plate 57). But his illustrations for *An*

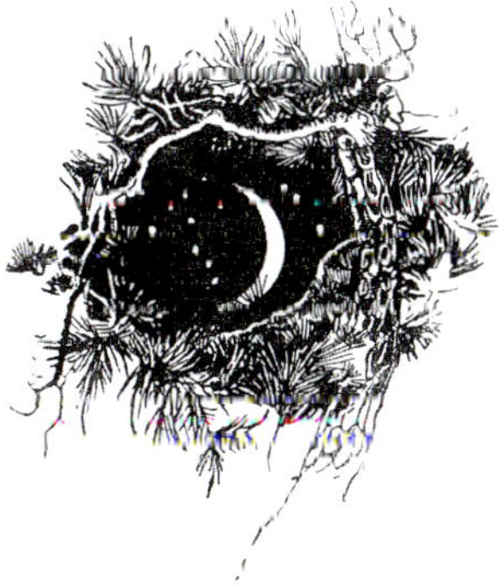

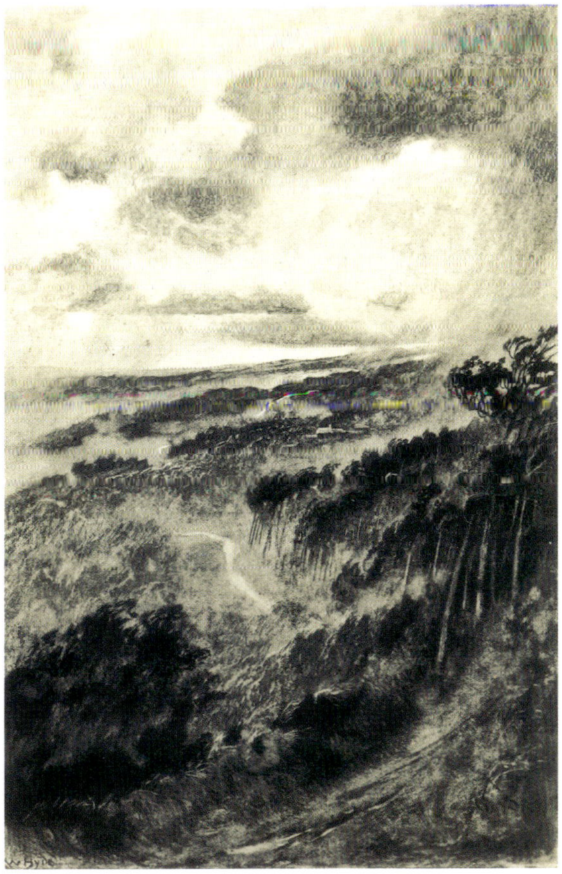

Above:
Plate 57. Headpiece from *An Imaged World,* 1894. Wood engraving

Right:
Plate 58. *The South-West Wind* from *An Imaged World,* 1894. Photogravure

Imaged World centre in five monochromes printed in fine gravure. Two of them draw on Romney Marsh and its coast. Of those, *The Falling of the Night* (reproduced above, page 78) inverts the paradox of lights in Palmer's *Valley Thick with Corn*: here foreground moonlight seems to shine over the back of Hyde's windblown traveller as he looks away to an angry sunset.

Two other monochromes show Hyde's vision finding a new and rougher country in the Surrey hills about Garnett's cottage. The book's frontispiece opens a prospect from pine-covered escarpment under rainy skies, to evoke *The South-West Wind* (Plate 58).

Dent next commissioned Hyde to make a new suite of illustrations for Milton's 'L'Allegro' and 'Il Penseroso'. They would be the first illustrations to these poems since Palmer's watercolours had been printed as gravures in 1889 (a book Hyde would surely have looked at). His own Milton gravures draw again on the hills of Surrey, Sussex Downs and Romney Marsh.

September 1894 found Hyde back on the Marsh. One day he walked thirty-two miles with Edward Garnett and his brother Robert, their friend Eustace Hartley, and the young Ford Madox Hueffer with his wife of four months.[23] The Hueffers had taken a house on the northern edge of the Marsh at Bonnington, and the others were visiting them. Hueffer's later recollection suggests that Hyde was back at Brede Place (which was about thirty miles from Bonnington).

Hueffer remembered Hyde imagining the old house as still harbouring its smugglers, who tried to thwart his work:

> There were mysterious noises in the cellars, remote explosions, rumblings, sounds resembling gunfire. But Hyde stuck it out until he had finished the illustrations and I daresay longer.[24]

Hyde kept a lifelong fascination for smugglers. Years later he would chant Kipling's lines:

> Five and twenty ponies
> Trotting through the dark –
> Brandy for the Parson,
> 'Baccy for the Clerk.
> Them that asks no questions isn't told a lie –
> Watch the wall, my darling, while the Gentlemen go by![25]

16. Of a picture of Westminster at night, Hyde wrote in 1902: 'I have seen this effect from my own garret window often.' (To F.M. Hueffer: MS at Cornell University Library, Ithaca NY.)
17. E.V. Lucas, *Reading, Writing and Remembering* (Methuen, 1932), 155. Charles Sherwood Jekyll (1842-1914) was organist of the Chapels Royal at St James's Palace and Whitehall until his early retirement in Oct 1891. Robert Louis Stevenson's sensational story had appeared in 1886.
18. Quoted in *Frederick H. Evans: Selected Texts and Bibliography, ed* Anne Hammond (Oxford: Clio Press, 1992), 51, 100.
19. *The House of Dent 1888-1938* (Dent, 1938: expanded from earlier editions of *The Memoirs of J.M. Dent*), 68; *The Studio*, June 1894, 85.
20. Edward Garnett, *An Imaged World* (Dent, 1894), 93-94.
21. Quoted in George W. Jefferson, *Edward Garnett: A Life in Literature* (Cape, 1982), 29.
22. *The Studio*, May 1894, 21. Portions of the cover design reappear as half-borders to the book's pages.
23. This is the first reference to Hyde in *Olive and Stepniak: The Bloomsbury Diary of Olive Garnett 1893-1895, ed* Barry C. Johnson (Bartletts Press, 1993), 121. Olive, a sister of Edward and Robert, had not been of the party at Bonnington, but wrote from a report by the Hueffers soon after. Hueffer was a Garnett family friend from childhood. Hartley was a Fabian living opposite the Garnett house in the British Museum.
24. Ford Madox Ford (as Hueffer was later known), *Mightier than the Sword* (Allen & Unwin, 1938), 45. The noises, for which Brede Place was notorious, could have been caused by coastal winds driving up the narrow valley, roaring down chimneys and through crannies to loosen casements, doors, and panelling. Hueffer thought in 1938 that Hyde's work at Brede Place had been for *The Cinque Ports*, but most pictures for that book are dated 1899. By then the house had passed to new owners, who made extensive repairs and then let it from Jan 1899 to May 1900 to the American writer Stephen Crane and his mistress. Nor would Hueffer's memory have reached back to Hyde's earlier residence at Brede Place. Until he married in May 1894, Hueffer had lived with his family in north London: and his frequent letters to his fiancée from 1892 onwards make no mention of any visit to Brede. (Information from Hueffer's biographer Max Saunders)
25. Recalled by Hyde's daughter Lydia (1901-1980) for Mr and Mrs Eric Earle, who shared it with me in 1999. 'Gentlemen' in the poem refers to the fact that much coastal smuggling was carried on with active help from the local gentry.

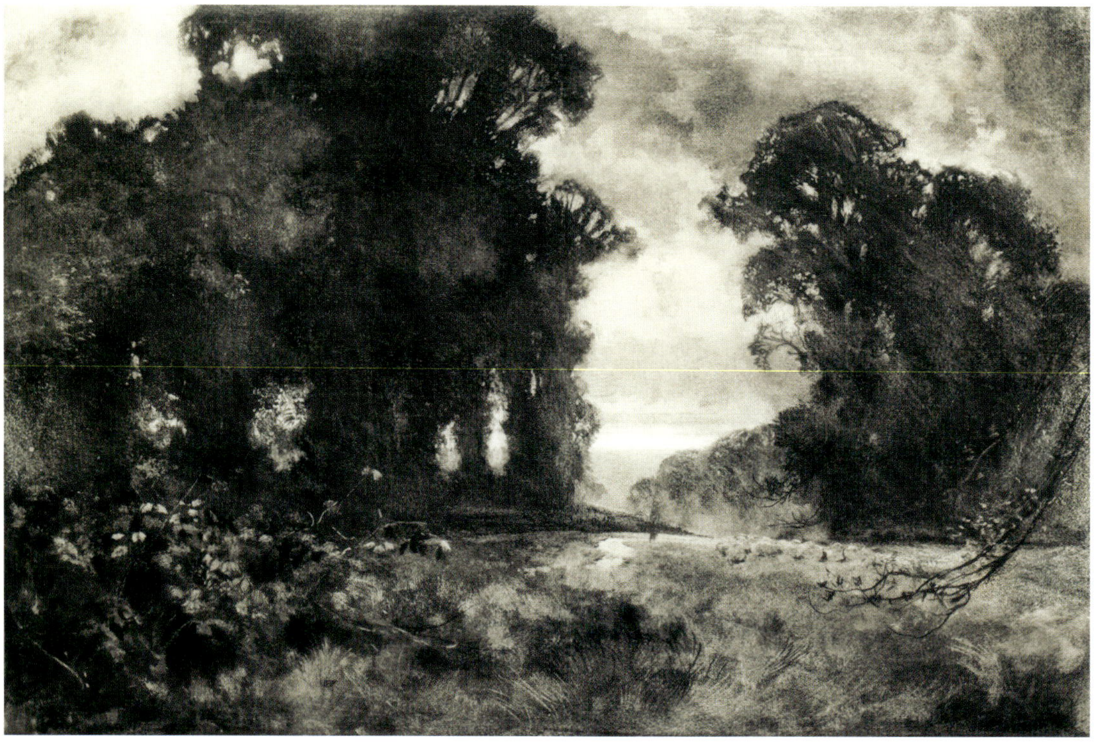

Plate 59. *The Eastern Gate* from *L'Allegro & Il Penseroso* [1895]. Photogravure

Hyde's Milton pictures show little of Palmer's kindly community of man in nature. Here are no gardens, and even the summer woods in transfiguring lights of Hyde's *Eastern Gate* hint at forces waiting to overtake the solitary wanderer (Plate 59).

Hyde's Milton monochromes are younger work than Palmer's, and less even. Palmer's *Eastern Gate* comprehends ten lines of the poem in masterly synthesis. The same ten lines generate three separate Hyde images. Palmer's *Early Ploughman* drives his oxen through Italian hills before a spectacular sunrise. Hyde's ploughman with horses (reproduced above, page 79) breaks an empty horizon against an English expanse of rain clouds: they unify his composition in evocative washes, driving damp wind into the bones even as spring light invites the spirit.

The rainy morning in 'Il Penseroso' inspires one of Hyde's strongest images (Plate 60). The lines had drawn from Palmer a complex ensemble of English farm, distant water-carrier, tumbled hills and angry sky. Hyde's rain-soaked lane through windswept Surrey hills speaks directly to Milton's

Kerchieft in a comely cloud
While rocking winds are piping loud.

Hyde made this image his book's frontispiece.[26] He tried for extra emphasis with an elaborate border incorporating female figures of Wind, Night, and Dawn, shapes of briar, owl's mask and claw, flying bat and steaming bowl. A smuggler's journey through gypsy eyes? But such decorations sort uneasily with the raw strength of the central image.

The bigger scale of west Surrey landscapes offered scope for projecting grander emotions. The Surrey hills so possessed Hyde that he made up his mind to go and live there as soon as he was married. His fiancée was Kate Rogers (1861-1942). Descended from a Huguenot family once settled at Rye by Romney Marsh, her grandfather had been a woodcarver of national repute.[27] Yet Kate and her younger sister Isabel were orphans, brought up by an aunt at Lewisham. The Lambeth School head John Sparkes had taken a hand in Kate's education – with the result that she became a leading flower painter for Doulton's Pottery in Lambeth. Somewhere between school and factory Kate and William Hyde had met.

On Sunday evening 14 October 1894 Kate and her sister went to supper with Mr and Mrs Eustace Hartley, opposite the British Museum. Edward Garnett's sister Olive came in, and wrote in her diary afterwards: 'One of the Miss Rogers is betrothed to Mr Hyde; both girls are commonplace, slightly vulgar & plain. It was a pleasant evening.' Olive, who was not engaged to anybody, might feel some jealousy over this artist of romantically humble origin whom she

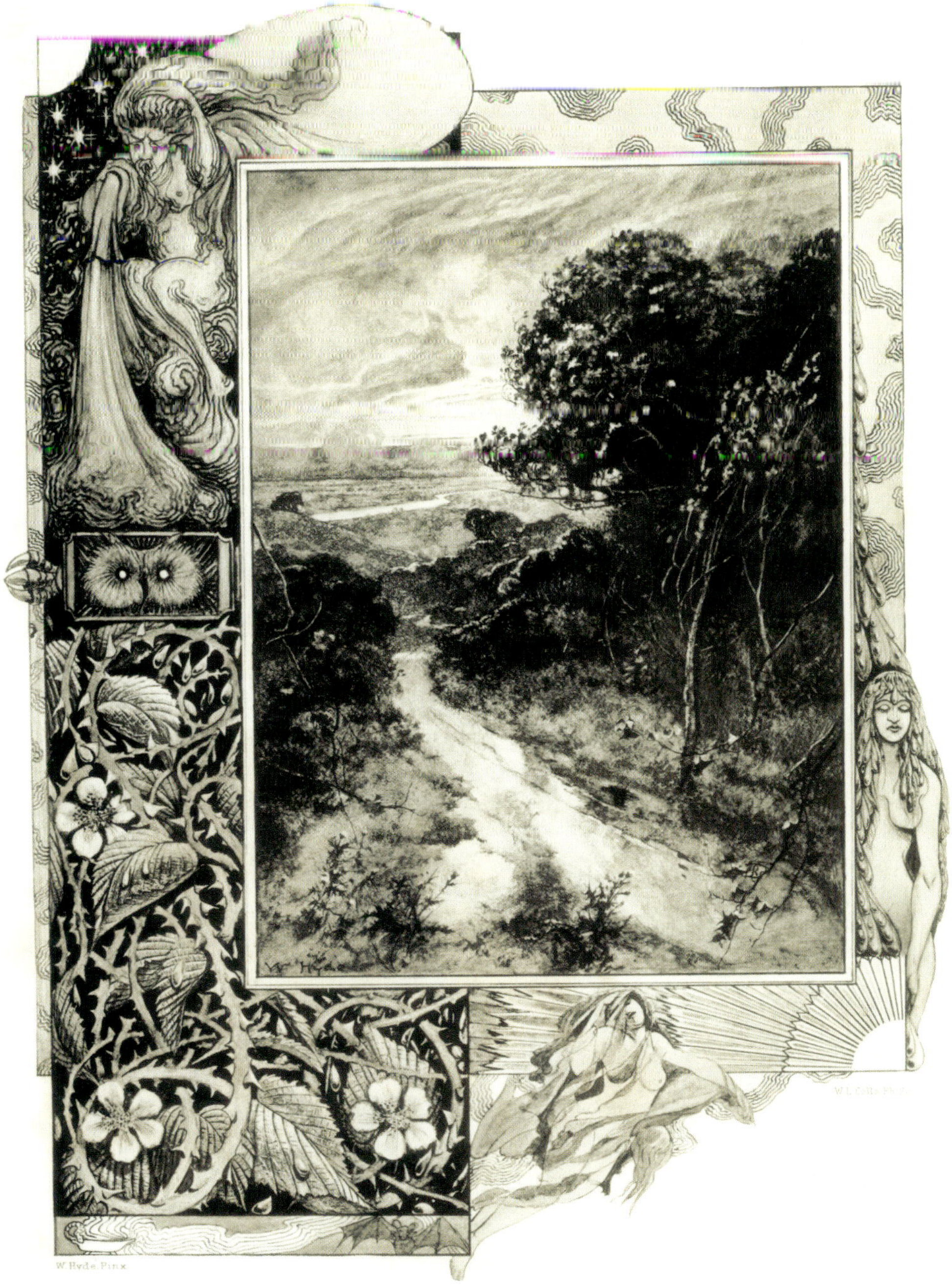

Plate 60. 'Kerchieft in a comely cloud, While rocking winds are piping loud', frontispiece to *L'Allegro & Il Penseroso* [1895]. Photogravure

had yet to meet. She saw his work every day, since her father owned a fine Hyde monochrome of Romney Marsh.[28]

Five weeks later Olive Garnett visited the young Hueffers at Bonnington with her brother Edward. Her diary describes a walk across the Marsh as 'Hyde land':

> Mud, dykes, sunset, mist effect, berries, black ruin silhouette, willows, peewits. As we neared the coast we heard the waves breaking & saw dotted lights. … We were silent & then talked of Hyde's work.

On 3 March 1895 the man himself came to dinner at the Museum. Olive wrote: 'Mr Hyde… is going to marry & settle down at Shere [Surrey] in the red brick house near the church & wanted Papa's name as a reference. He talked very well & we spent an interesting evening.' When she next saw her brother Edward, 'I told him how much I liked Mr Hyde.'[29]

Hyde's fiancée Kate had her own souvenir of his eloquence in a little letter written the morning of their wedding, 30 April 1895. She would keep it all her life.

26. *L'Allegro & Il Penseroso of John Milton* (Dent, *nd*: the Introduction by T. Gregory Foster is dated June 1895).
27. William Gibbs Rogers (1792–1875), in *Dictionary of National Biography*.
28. *A Passing Storm* (*The Artist*, Jan 1898, 8).
29. *Olive and Stepniak*, 126, 134, 155–6.

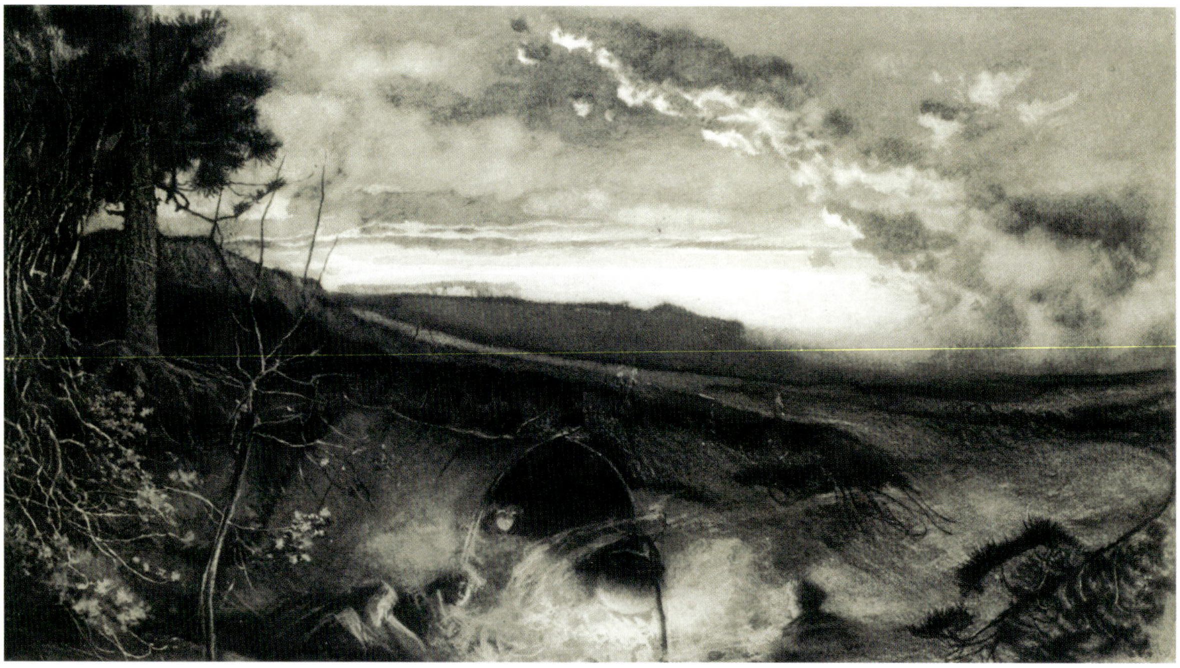

Plate 61. 'The moor-faced sunset' from *Nature Poems,* 1898. Photogravure

My True Hearted Darling

These last few lines to you as Kate Rogers. God bless you dear. You have my whole heart and I am deeply aware of how much you are going to give me today at the altar. I am so glad that the sun shines today and our dear little home looked lovely yesterday.

Be *Brave* today dear – don't be nervous and when we are at last alone we shall be happier than most mortals today.

I have no more time to write longer – but within a few hours make those promises that it will be as much my delight as my duty to keep – God bless you my brave sweet bride

Your own

Will[30]

The choice of rural life carried a risk. The young Palmer had found Shoreham ultimately too narrow a base for his vision. Afterwards in Kensington he had made friends among the Etching Club artists; yet his late return to this country made him almost a hermit again.

Now Hyde, at thirty-seven, was taking himself into the country without any such base of professional friendships as Kensington gave Palmer. London in fact had opened Hyde's way to some fine visions: Frederick Evans constantly urged him to make a book of them. And Kate's own career had depended on London. In the face of all this, Hyde's choice of Surrey as their permanent home showed his need for those higher hills.

The village of Shere (a few miles from Garnett's cottage) was a place of craftsmen serving estates round about. It had become a haunt of artists who paid their bar bills in kind – as the local inn's walls of pictures testified.[31] The house Hyde rented was called 'Burnside' for its position beside the little Tillingbourne River. But the modest eighteenth century building is strangely placed: it is half in the village and half in the churchyard, whose wall divides the house-front in two. So the inmates of the house pass constantly back and forth between the communities of living and dead.

Hyde's daughter recalled in later years that no outsider was allowed into the house. Even so the artist's studio was upstairs at the back, in the smallest of three bedrooms, with north light reflected up from the river flowing past the cellar door below.[32]

Exploring the country around Shere opened Hyde's way to the finest of all his suites – for a book of *Nature Poems* by the seventy year-old George Meredith, living on the nearby slopes of Box Hill. Hyde's introduction to the old poet could have come from the Garnetts (who were Meredith's old friends) or from Frederick Evans, a Meredith enthusiast who had taken atmospheric photographs in Redland Woods. Evans knew Meredith's publishers, Archibald Constable, who commissioned the book. The firm gave it out that the choice of Hyde as illustrator was the poet's own.[33]

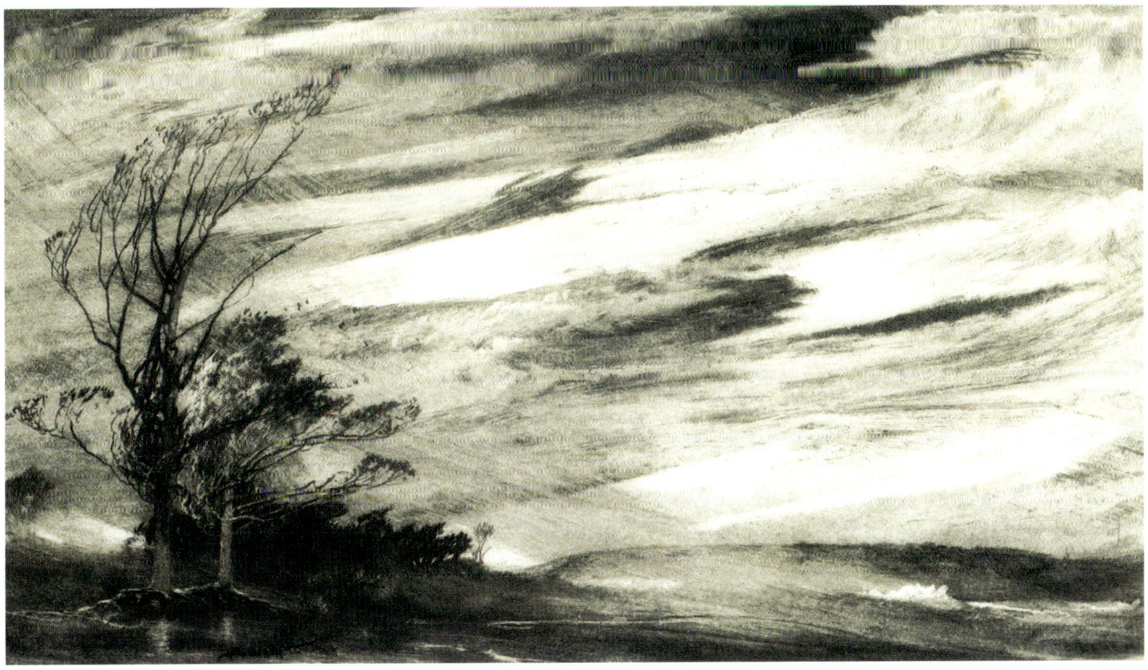

Plate 62. 'Clouds… as if swift the Furies flew' from *Nature Poems,* 1898. Photogravure

Hyde later set down his own reflections on the country he now shared with Meredith. He noted 'the pine woods silhouette upon the moving brilliance above them, and the beech-copses patching the long, sweeping down lands'. Below such a scene in one of his Meredith images he set a gypsy group round an evening fire (Plate 61).

The wide Surrey prospects drew Hyde's thoughts of pastoral tradition from Italy into northern art:

> At times it appears as a brown land, a land of classic poetic moods, where pines, yews, and hollies simulate the cypress and the olive, where mysterious shades become the haunts of nymph and faun.
>
> Then melancholy Ruysdael landscapes compose before one, larch-woods, beyond a heath, browns, greys and green standing up against a sky of cumulus cloud.
>
> Then, in the turn of a lane, suddenly a vast stretch of valley scenery will open out below a ridge – the Thames valley… with dim blue hills beyond a grey castle tower.

Yet Hyde's interior landscapes reinforced the strife revealed to his generation by Darwin:

> Even the golden gorse on the bank-side is armed. Ages have gradually evolved spines for its protection, just as in the human world skill, brains, wealth, laws, fight an endless round. …
>
> There a bee or a mouse will… reproduce, in the visible loneliness around, on a smaller scale the aspirations and struggles of men. …
>
> There are woods of mystical silence, oaks buried in ravines, in gaps of the downs, where last year's leaves cling, brown and rustling to the branches, until the spring sap sends them falling upon the banks of primroses beneath.

Thus he is drawn to darknesses and dusks in Meredith's poems:

> Darker grows the valley, more and more forgetting:
> So it were with me if forgetting could be willed.
> ('Love in the Valley')

Yet darkness turns them both to seek the lights to define it. One of Meredith's 'most insistent notes is *light*', Hyde writes: therein he sees the poet's bond with Turner.[34]

The twenty monochromes Hyde made for Meredith's *Nature Poems* send endless brilliant cloud-forms over their lands. Some are driven by the wind towards abstraction. In such images Hyde opens a path for pastoral vision to engage perspectives of destruction and ruin in the Great War barely fifteen years in the future (Plate 62).

30. Private coll.
31. *The British Isles Depicted by Pen and Camera*, with an introduction by Harold Spender (Cassell, 3 vols, *nd* [*c.*1900], III, 92.
32. All this was shown me in 1999 by Kenneth Chard, who has lived in the house (now called 'Sayers') for many years, and had the information from Hyde's daughter Lydia.
33. Scrapbook of news cuttings (many of the sources unnamed) begun by Hyde when the Meredith pictures were exhibited in 1898 (private coll).
34. 'An April Day on the Surrey Hills', in *Pall Mall Magazine* XXXIX, no 168 (April 1907), 387, 388, 390.

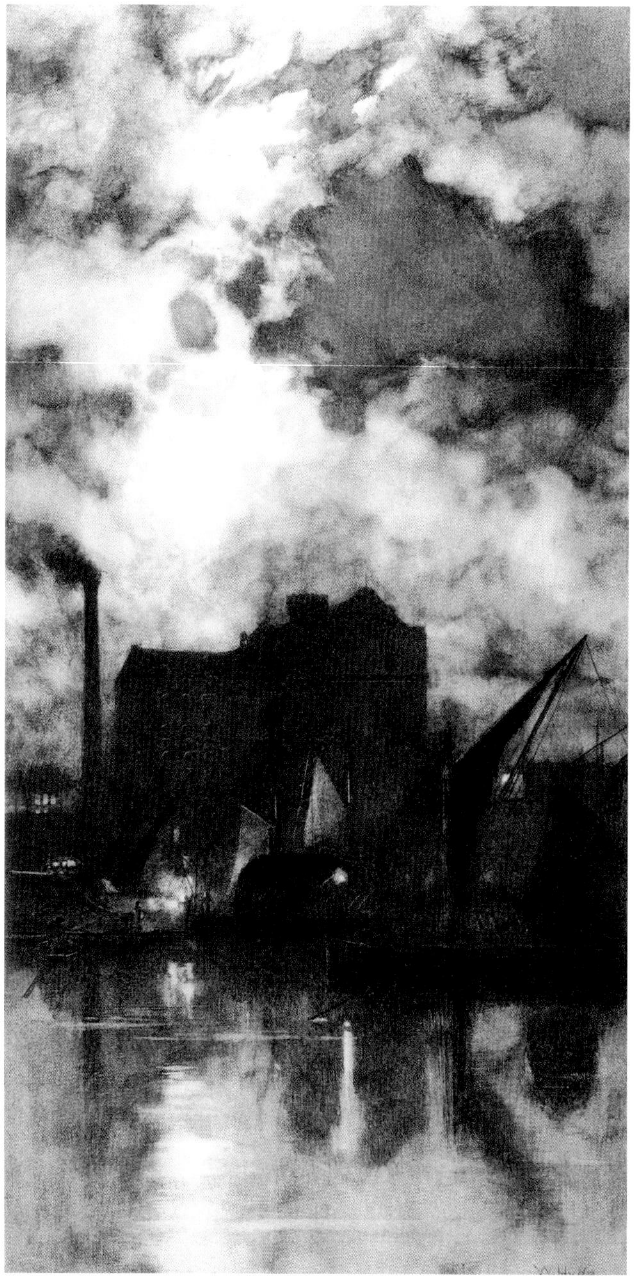

Left:
Plate 63. *Below Bridge* from *London Impressions,* 1898. Photogravure

Opposite:
Plate 64. *Kensington Gardens* from *London Impressions,* 1898. Photogravure

The publisher Constable also agreed to produce Hyde's London pictures in an expensive folio.[35] In due course Constable's monthly magazine *The Artist* carried an article about Hyde by Ford Madox Hueffer. Hueffer drew attention to London atmospheres which Hyde 'has made his own' (Plate 63).[36]

When Hyde's *London Impressions* were published and the original monochromes shown in December 1898, the artist told the press he had attempted neither 'elaborate topography' nor 'architectural detail' – both, he said, better left to 'photographic artists' such as Evans. In his own pictures, the 'impression which the eye receives is that, more or less, of a vision, resultant from the atmosphere… London is unique in this respect.'[37]

Hyde's most celebrated recent predecessor in depicting the Great Wen had been Gustave Doré, thirty years earlier. Doré had concentrated on the seamy side; and that was by no means neglected in the new book. Yet many of Hyde's best images recall Miltonic grandeurs in the work of John Martin and Francis Danby – but wrapped in a softness of his own. In *Kensington Gardens* two tiny points of lamplight in the gathering dusk define the solitary figure's loneliness between the last daylight and its pale reflection in the shadowy snow (Plate 64).

35. Signed contract, dated April 1896, calling for twenty London pictures, 'one being at this date in the possession of Mr F. H. Evans, who has undertaken to hand over the same'. (Archibald Constable archives.)
36. Ford Madox Hueffer, 'William Hyde: an Illustrator of London', in *The Artist* XXI, no 217 (Jan 1898), 1-9.
37. Quoted by a reviewer of the exhibition (from Hyde's cutting book, started at this time, but not identifying many sources: in private coll).

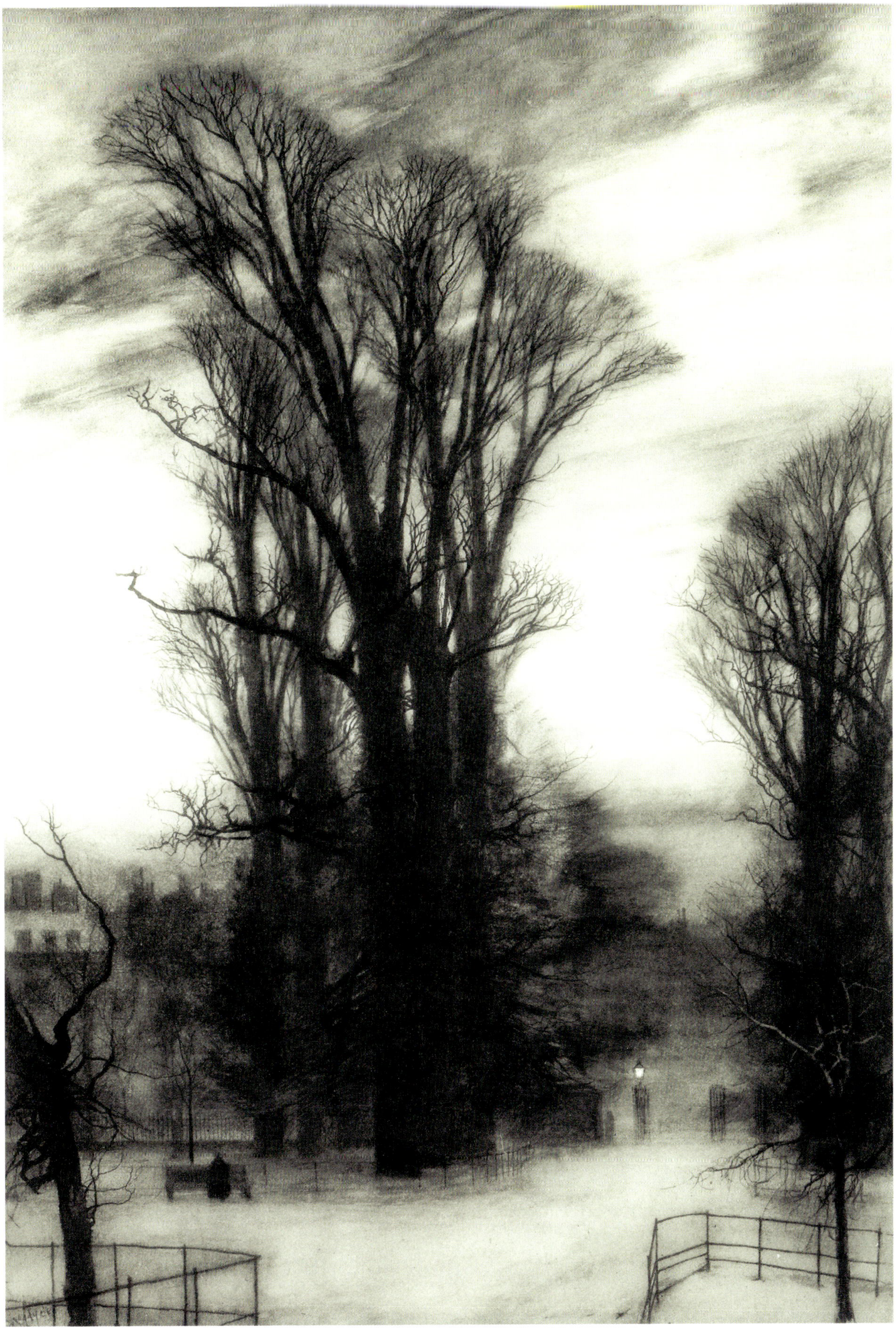

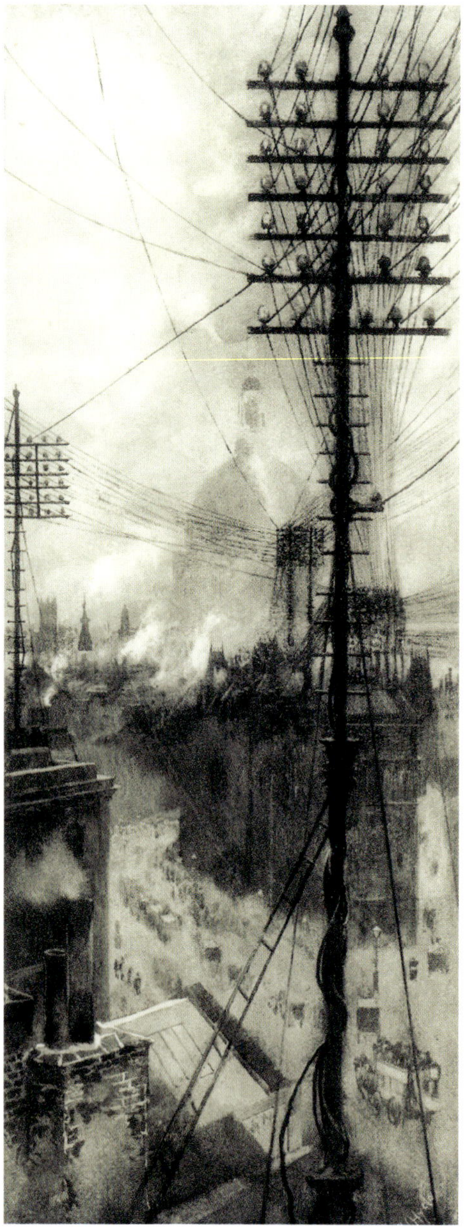

Plate 65. *The Nerves of London* from *London Impressions,* 1898. Photogravure

Three of Hyde's *London Impressions* are experiments in etching. But the best are still his monochrome drawings, described by one critic at their exhibition as 'charcoal, chalk and wash'. Full folio page and smaller plates finely printed in the text show lights qualified by fog, rain or snow, clouds and darknesses. Several push towards abstraction (Plate 65).

The book's text took form in a series of essays by Alice Meynell with such titles as 'The Climate of Smoke' and 'Below Bridge'. But the cover and title page of *London Impressions* print Hyde's name first. The price was eight guineas – equal to a house servant's wages for a year.

At the same time, Constable brought out *The Nature Poems of George Meredith* at two and a half guineas – a tall octavo with twenty full-page Hyde gravures and a title-page device by Laurence Housman. Both sets of original drawings were shown in Bond Street, together with twenty other Hyde monochromes reaching back to Romney Marsh days. The venue was the Dowdeswell Gallery, whose walls had shown Whistler and the French Impressionists. The Dowdeswell brothers framed Hyde's pictures in green oak.

The private view on Saturday afternoon 3 December 1898 attracted a select company headed by the aged Meredith's son. The guests included Arthur Balfour – Leader of the House of Commons, heir apparent in the Conservative government of his uncle Lord Salisbury, and well-known patron of the arts. Balfour bought two of Hyde's pictures on the spot. The event was widely reported:

> Mr William Hyde and Mrs Alice Meynell were chatting with their many friends, and comparing the illustrations in the handsome volume of 'Impressions of London' [*sic*] with the originals on the walls.

Another paper noted:

> A good many people have been asking, who is Mr William Hyde?... The conflict of light and gloom is eloquent in Mr Hyde's work. Every shadow seems to hold a secret.

The *Telegraph* noted Hyde's ability to differentiate electric from gas lighting in the same picture. The *Echo* critic wrote:

> The smoke beaten down about the chimney-pots... brings the sting of the raw gust with it, and one feels the soaking drizzle of the streets about the docks, with the bright steamy patches from the flaring naptha lamps of the costers' barrows breaking the murkiness...
>
> The London in which the Londoner gets his living, and which is most familiar to him, has never been handled before with such consummate technical skill or such grasp and mastery.

The artist himself might have been still better pleased by a book review which saw his pictures as bringing 'London into fair competition with the cities of dream'.

The two books kindled Hyde's lights in city and country. The artist himself had drawn attention to the point by penetrating one with the other. *London Impressions* finds a quiet centre in the ghostly rurality of *Kensington Gardens*. Meredith's *Nature Poems* holds two London images. One shows Westminster from Lambeth – just upriver from where Palmer had opened his 1824 sketchbook – against a gash of sunset. The other evokes St Paul's as Meredith has it 'clothed in snow and soot, With lamps for day in ghostly rows'.

* * *

Here, in man's will to reshape nature through the city, was a plenary subject for Hyde's art. His friend Evans had tried to convince him of it. Yet Hyde himself had moved away to the country. So the question rose, as it had risen for Palmer at Shoreham, of how to take his vision farther. Hyde was now forty-one, with a wife and baby son. The loyal Evans (recently retired from bookselling to pursue his photography) was no Linnell. Apart from him and a friendly author or two, there were only publishers – and Hyde's own poverty – to trim his lights.

He devoted much of 1899 to a new suite, the largest of his career. *The Cinque Ports* was planned by another publisher, William Blackwood, as a large quarto limited edition to sell at three guineas. Its text was being written by Ford Madox Hueffer, self-indulgently

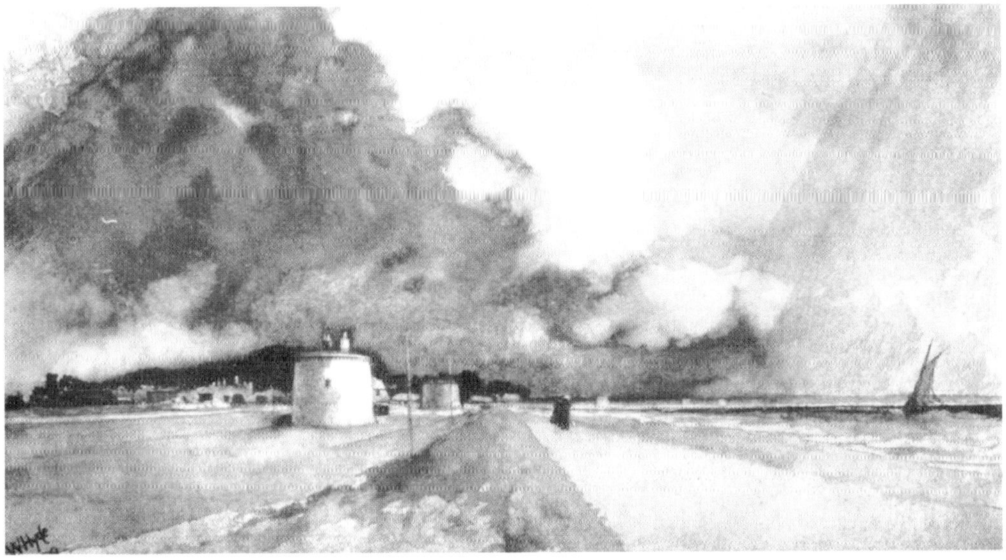

Left:
Plate 66. *Dymchurch and Seawall,* 1899; from *The Cinque Ports,* 1900. Pencil and wash

Below:
Plate 67. *Near Sibertswold* from *The Cinque Ports,* 1900. Ink (imitating black-line and white-line wood engraving)

filling four hundred pages. Scattered through them, Hyde's drawings would make less impact.

There were other diluting factors. The whole subject of the Cinque Ports was retrograde, taking him back yet again to coastal Sussex and Romney Marsh when his impulse had moved on. One of the book's finest gravures (a pastoral of Winchelsea under the rising moon) is undated – and probably earlier than the majority of Hyde's *Cinque Port* images dated 1899.

Not all of these monochromes were printed in gravure. Several were reproduced by the cheaper half-tone process, losing depth and definition. Some of the wash reproductions hint at a falling off of draughtsmanship (Plate 66). Draughtsmanship is stiffly kept, but not extended, in a number of ink drawings which revive techniques of wood-engraving, including white-line drawing (Plate 67).

In June 1900, before *The Cinque Ports* was published, Hyde signed a new contract with Constable. It was for a suite to follow the southern pilgrim track to Canterbury: from Southampton by Winchester, under the North Downs and along the Tillingbourne valley through Shere Churchyard past his own front door. He wanted to call it 'The Pilgrim's Way' and issue it as an expensive portfolio.[38]

Constable was not convinced. The expensive *London Impressions* sold very slowly. So the new contract limited Hyde to thirteen gravures, with a further twenty line drawings for printing 'by the zinc process' (in effect photographic etching). The contract specifies 'a work', but its clear intention is another book. The publisher offered £200 for the drawings and another £100 if Hyde would write the text. He felt unequipped to do that. From further negotiations he emerged with only 130 guineas spread over eight months for his drawings, plus another 50 guineas in royalties if and when sales passed 350 copies.

It proved a bad contract for both sides. Constable specified that the original drawings should become publisher's property. Hyde interlined a contract note to retain half the drawings: his motive, he told Constable, 'was to control or prevent any kind of exhibition… as they were made for engraving & not as exhibition drawings'.[39]

Everything about the new suite shows Hyde trying to isolate his problem and surmount it. He wrote to Hueffer:

> It is late of course – but one has to get a footing – mine has been a very difficult task – starting with many disadvantages – getting a piece of luck here and there while steering my bark amidst the shoals and quicksands of trade & greed, fashions, cranks, egotists, my own ignorance and disponibilité, and diffidence.

He feels it 'time to take another step':

> Black and white landscape is not the end of my tether – circumstances alone have left me to this – and heaven knows how much longer it will do so unless I make some efforts.[40]

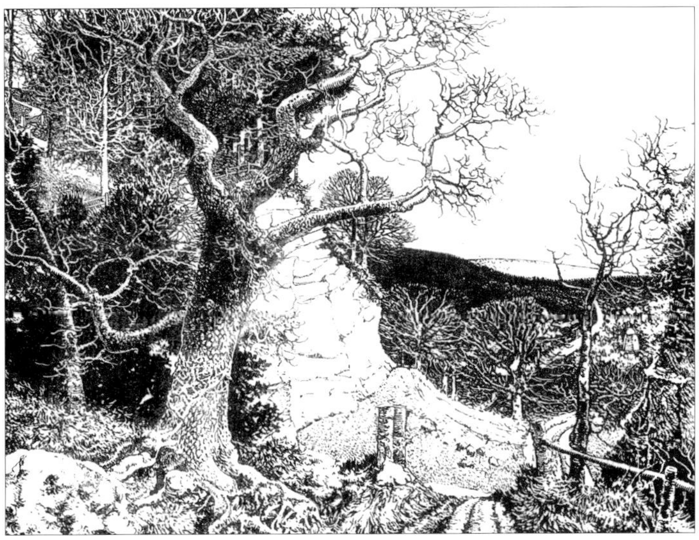

38. Hyde anticipated that several hundred subscribers 'would take in a half-yearly portfolio at about ten guineas a year' (17 Feb 1903 to Hueffer). Hyde's letters to Hueffer (in Cornell University Library) have guided my following discussion.
39. 27 June 1903 (Constable archive). Several critics of *London Impressions* had noted that drawings made for reproduction were not necessarily so effective in original form.
40. 29 Dec 1902.

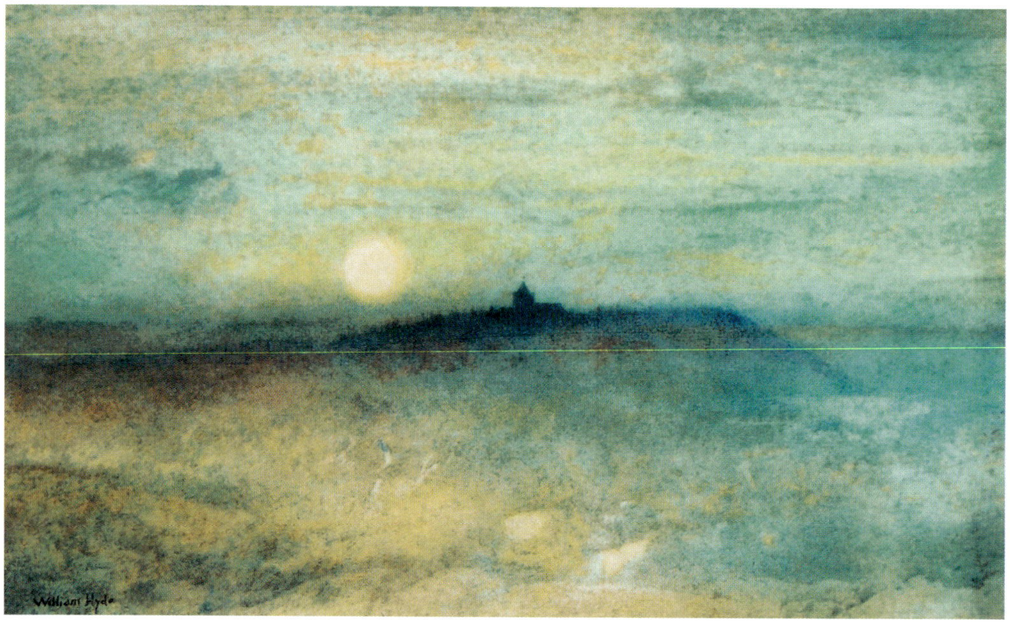

Plate 68. *St Martha's Chapel* (in Surrey Hills between Shere and Guildford) *by moonlight, c.*1900. Watercolour

He went right outside the world of printing to paint a small watercolour of an ancient chapel-of-ease in the hills close to Shere.[41] Its moonlit vision is luminous in soft colours (Plate 68). Yet there was no exhibition of Hyde's watercolours.

His monochromes for 'The Pilgrim's Way' show no advance, and some ink drawings show weaker draughtsmanship. His best drawings for the project avoid human figures and buildings (as Hyde himself avoided them through lonely nights and days about the Surrey hills and valleys). In evocations of distance and light, his pen reaches through clouds towards new line patterns (Plate 69).

When Hyde realised that the contract effectively stopped much payment for his 'Pilgrim's Way' line drawings until after many copies had been sold, he became angry. Constable sought to mollify him by meeting his wish for a printing press of his own. A press at home, such as Blake and Palmer had enjoyed, might open all kinds of graphic experimentation to his art. The firm sent a press and printing materials to Hyde as a loan.

He set it up in his cellar, where land falling away to the riverbank at the back gave the house an extra storey with north-facing windows and door. To reach it you went down an outside staircase on the churchyard side. To keep the press, Hyde bartered away his contingent royalty on 'The Pilgrim's Way' and his claim to half the drawings. He asked Constable not to exhibit them. They promised only to make clear that the drawings had been conceived for reproduction.[42]

More than a year after finishing those drawings, there was still no text. Constable had approached Maurice Hewlett, who seized the theme of Canterbury pilgrims for his own work but refused to write a text for Hyde's pictures. Hyde wanted Hueffer, but Constable was chary of that young author's self-indulgence. At the end of 1903 the publisher commissioned the well-known Liberal journalist, Catholic, and amateur artist Hilaire Belloc (1870–1953).

Belloc spent several weeks in the winter of 1903–4 actually walking the Pilgrim's Way with two friends. He produced a text of close topographic description fortified by a series of Ordnance Survey maps, and retitled it *The Old Road*. Hyde's complaints of 'totally opposite desires to mine' were overridden, and four years after the contract had been signed the book at last appeared. Relations with Constable were frigid.

This long interruption in what had been a steady production of books since Hyde's marriage sharpened the bite of poverty. One Christmas a local farmer sent a chicken to give the family a good meal. Hyde proudly returned it.[43] In the autumn of 1902 he had written to Hueffer (now living at Winchelsea) from Shere:

> I sometimes wish I could get a cottage near Rye – so that the boy could go to school. I am, we all are, very tired of this place – it will never inspire me to do anything, beautiful as it is [;] and our neighbours are either rich and dull or tiresome.

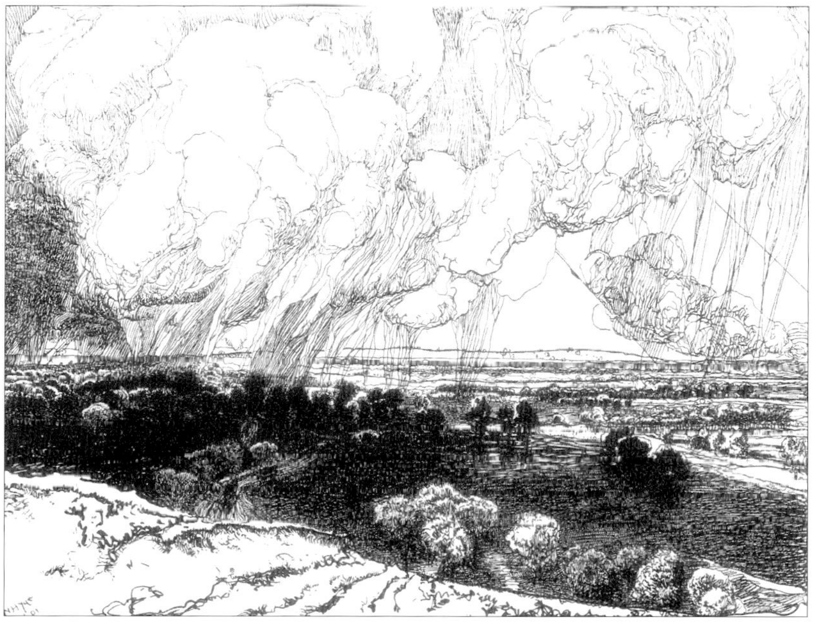

Plate 69. 'I might be lying on the crest of my own Downs', 1901; from *The Old Road,* 1904. Ink

He involved Hueffer in plans for a new and cheaper book about London, and wrote in October 1902:

> I have been up in town two or three days – getting material. I wish you had been with me. The wonder of it never ceases – there is so *much* of it – 'the Bedlam of Creation'.
>
> I have bribed servants to let me look out of back windows in Westminster and have had my pocket picked in Wapping – two days would suffice to show enough material for a dozen pictures.

Constable was not interested, but gave an introduction to John Murray. Murray hesitated, dodged, and finally admitted to feeling that there were too many London books in the market. The newest was Macmillan's *Highways and Byways in London*, illustrated in part by the young F. L. Griggs. Hyde judged it 'good (of the Guide book kind but well illustrated)'.[44] Then he discovered that Constable still had such stocks of *London Impressions* after four years that they had drastically reduced the price.

To support his family, now including a baby daughter Lydia, Hyde took to journalism. He wrote to Hueffer: 'I am not equipped for writing anything like literature it is true, but I hope to be able in time to put some of the things I see into plain English.' He approached the *Pall Mall Magazine*, one of the best illustrated monthlies,[45] with a piece about 'The Surrey Woods in Winter'. Its opening words explore the country about Shere in near-monochromes of intense privacy:

> Brown leaves whispering, a murmur overhead, grey oak stems toned by their lichens into the subdued richness and colour of a moth's wing… Spaces of solitude, and in winter scarcely crossed by a human being for days.

When figures do appear in Hyde's writing, they are of the country's immemorial textures, like Palmer's workers or travellers. Hyde had drawn them for Meredith's *Nature Poems*. Now he wrote:

> See a tramp's fire at night in a grove of yews, a rough head bent down catching a glint of the fire: visions rise of men who lived with trees in the past, glimpses of him with the matted hair and flint hatchet.

The oldest presences are trees. One above the rest spoke to his loneliness:

> A tangled oak in winter, with the ivy tendrils clinging round it, always impresses one with the feeling that trees are not only things of vegetable growth, with botanical names in due order arranged, but companions and friends.

Hyde's article, with six illustrations, was accepted. The *Pall Mall* editor sent proofs, followed by a cheque, and then the January 1903 issue containing the article handsomely printed. He

41. Private coll.
42. Letters of 22 June to 6 Aug 1903 (Constable archive).
43. Recalled by Mr and Mrs Eric Earle from Lydia Hyde's conversations with them.
44. 4 Dec 1902 to Hueffer.
45. See James Thorpe, *English Illustration: The Nineties* (Faber, 1935), 163-70; and A.S. Hartrick, *A Painter's Pilgrimage through Fifty Years* (Cambridge University Press, 1938), 119-30, 165.

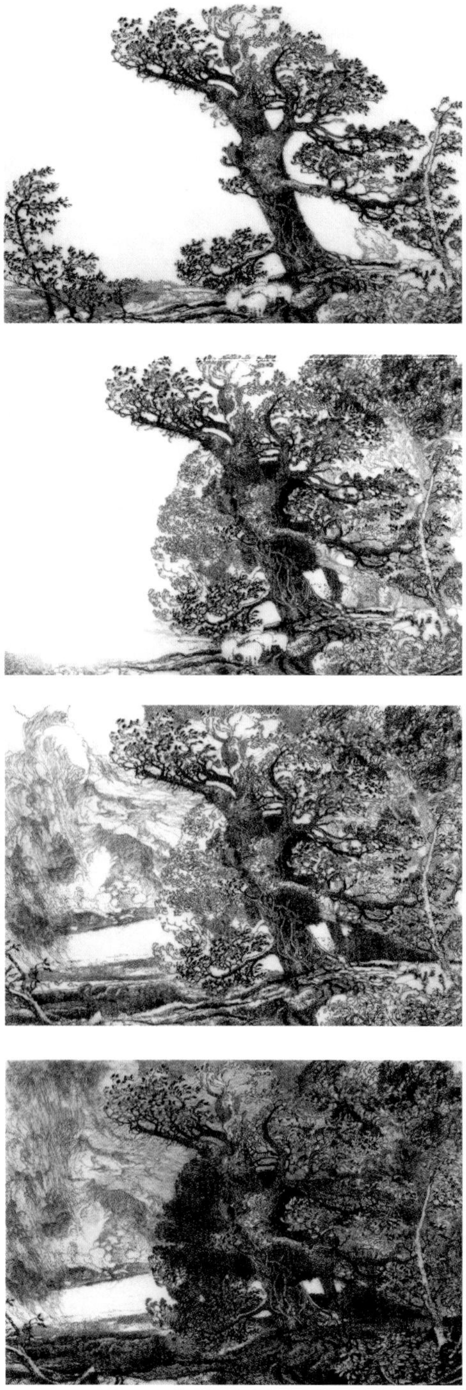

Plates 70–73. 'Kerchieft in a comely cloud, While rocking winds are piping loud' for *The Poetical Works of John Milton,* 1904. Etching: four successive states

wanted another piece for April. For that, Hyde assembled his impressions of the late winter and spring weeks at Brede Place a decade since. Another piece in November on 'Autumn near London' rakes together memories of Essex marshes and London streets before returning to Surrey woods in early morning to study drops of dew at eye level. To make the sketch he must have got right down into the soaking grass.

He kept fighting for vision in his art. In 1903 a private press owner nearby in Guildford proposed a folio edition of Milton's Poems with twelve plates by Hyde in any graphic processes he chose. With the new press Hyde produced etchings, engravings, and mezzotints for the book.

One mezzotint for 'Lycidas' shows a wide watery sunset behind mermaids and spectacular rocks: it looks forward to later experiments. Other mezzotints for 'Paradise Lost' reach towards Blake: success comes closest in an image of Satan among the worlds. Several suffer from weak drawing, and one or two seem hardly finished. An engraving for 'Samson Agonistes' limply recalls woodcuts of the 1860s.

Hyde's new etchings, however, reveal a technique mastered. Some of his Milton etchings use Palmerish elements, and the best are for 'L'Allegro' and 'Il Penseroso'. The first, as frontispiece, shows the young poet beneath tall trees looking towards a brilliant sunrise. That for 'Il Penseroso' evokes again the morning 'kerchieft in a comely cloud'. In 1895 those words had shaped Hyde's rain-swept Surrey lane.

The etching now to replace it evolved through a series of working proofs, kept by Hyde for the rest of his life (Plates 70–73).[46] The first shows a quiet landscape with sheep under twisted trees. The second state removes the comfortable prospect from the left, at the right adding finely needled background trees to thicken the forest. The third state removes the sheep. It adds a darker landscape left, below new wind-wracked clouds of an approaching storm. In the fourth state, the storm darkens the entire scene but for a gash of light at the horizon. The finished etching intensifies the blackened storm (Plate 74) – dwarfing a wraith of shreds at the lower left whose humanity is hinted only by its pilgrim staff. New highlights open a rutted track dividing the waif from the raging forest.

It seems to enact a darkness gathering in the artist himself. Pastoral calm withers before the approaching catastrophe of a man strong in feelings and gifts, who has touched real success in the battle to raise his vision above poverty and obscurity – only to be overtaken by his own limited training, in a pastoral isolation largely self-imposed.

Anger and fear boil over in a letter to the friendly printer of the new Milton, A.C. Curtis. Hyde pours wrath upon the commercial printers of his proofs, who seem now to prefer newer, easier, cheaper processes. His anger is such, he says, that he cannot trust himself with the pen but dictates to his wife about proofs 'disgracefully printed':

> A boy apprentice has probably done it & not a clever boy either... The cheapest Christmas cards are printed better... Photogravure people don't want a revival of Mezzo.[47]

It was at this time that Curtis made the photograph of Hyde at the head of this chapter. Here is the man who would haunt the memory of Ford Madox Hueffer: 'Hyde was a mysterious and, with his black beard and his secret process, a ferocious, gipsy-like figure.'[48]

Neither anger nor fear could get over the fact that the world of illustration was moving on. It was turning towards younger artists (led by a later Lambeth school graduate, Arthur Rackham) who mastered a 'three-colour process' by which illustrations could be printed in colours with the shapes neatly outlined.

An article for the *Pall Mall Magazine* in October 1904 assembles Hyde's inveterately monochrome perceptions of 'The Thames at Night'. Standing on a City bridge above the darkest flow at dead of winter, an hallucinatory pastoral ends in secret violence. Through 'frozen nights'

> miniature icebergs, like glittering flocks and herds, emerged from a silver mist to vanish in a silver mist. There were fogs too – Cimmerian darknesses that stifled the cry of unwary benighted river folk as they found a watery end.

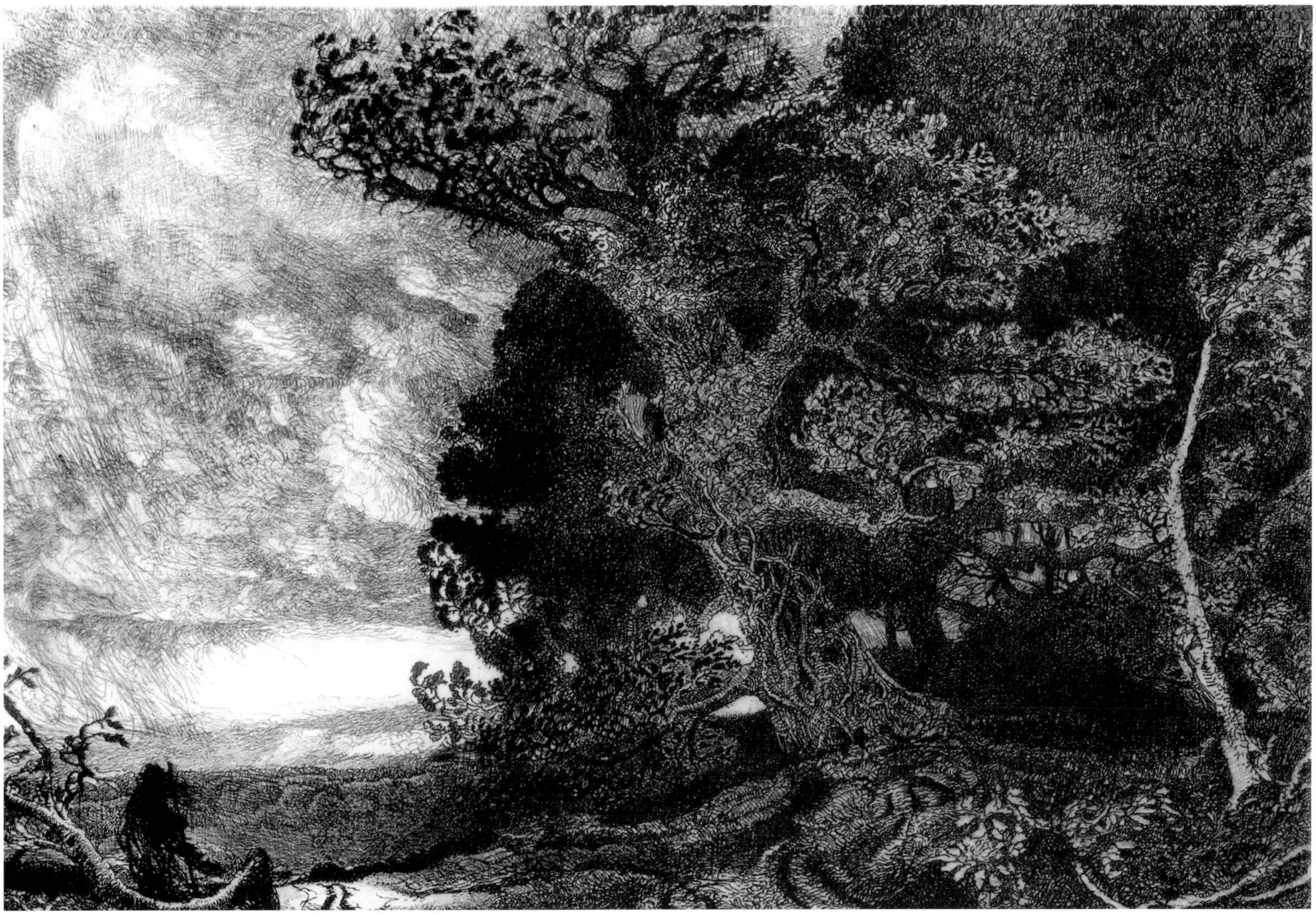

Plate 74. 'Kerchieft in a comely cloud, While rocking winds are piping loud' for *The Poetical Works of John Milton*, 1904. Final state

He just wrenches it back to polite inheritance:

> There were fogs that created Rembrandtesque masterpieces of tone amongst the huddled wharves and warehouses.

Did anyone care for monochrome visions any longer? On the cliffs at Dover early in 1905 to write another illustrated article, Hyde saw a winter sun shine on the water 'a silver streak of light that pointed straight across to Calais'. A sentry challenged him and he recalled working here on a *Cinque Ports* picture only five years ago 'without hindrance'.[49]

In book illustration the three-colour process was suddenly everywhere. It could only have raised in Hyde a secret sympathy with the waif of Kensington Gardens, looking into the Darling nursery at lock-out time in J.M. Barrie's sensational West-End success *Peter Pan* produced at Christmas 1904 (and soon to be immortalised again in Rackham's three-colour illustrations). But Hyde was in sight of his fiftieth year – a waif on the verge of old age.

In 1907 he took a commission to illustrate a small book in colour. It was a first illustrated edition of A.E. Housman's *A Shropshire Lad*. Hyde made a fine cover design to print gold on white buckram: a rim of sun edging past cloud and castle, the rays radiating upwards to branches of blossom. Monochrome endpapers of city and country showed obvious weakness only in the figure of a ploughman. Most of the eight colour plates were indistinguishable in the flood of coloured topography pouring from the presses. A smaller colour commission, for Maurice Hewlett's *The Spanish Jade*, could not avoid pasteboard figures.

A final colour suite for Shelley's *Nature Poems* appeared in 1911 from the publisher Hutchinson. Several of the pure landscapes show a sharpened understanding of how to drive sunrise and sunset colours through the printing process. Yet Hyde's *Shelley* was also lost in the welter of such things.

46. Private coll.
47. 'Thursday morning', *c.*winter 1903–4 (private coll).
48. *Mightier than the Sword*, 45. The words preface Hueffer's account of Hyde at Brede Place in the autumn of 1894. But Hyde's 'secret process' probably followed his acquisition of the printing press in 1903.
49. 'Dover and Calais', in *Pall Mall Magazine* XXXVI, no 148 (Aug 1905), 151–2.

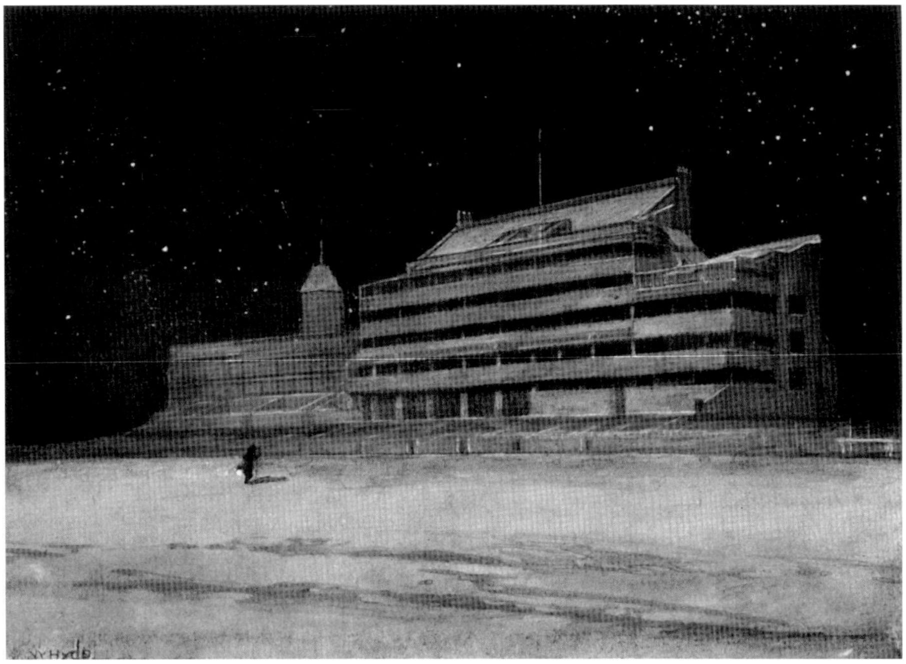

Plate 75. *The Grand Stand, Epsom Race Course* from *The Stane Street,* 1913. Grisaille watercolour

Constable reissued *The Open Road* in smaller format, for inclusion in a series of books on the ancient tracks of Britain. So Hyde asked Hilaire Belloc to renew their monochrome collaboration. Belloc produced a text on the Roman *Stane Street*, running from Chichester through Surrey east of Shere and up to London Bridge. Hyde's frontispiece shows a favourite subject of Evans's photography in *The Redlands, Moonrise* – a gravure whose quality suggests its origin in earlier years. The other *Stane Street* monochromes were all printed in half-tone (which now defined an illustrated book of the second rank). Hyde's vision flares once. *The Grand Stand, Epsom* (Plate 75) keeps the starlit sky and moonlit foreground of his old pastorals. The lonely lamp-carrier here might almost be a shepherd searching for his flock. But his way is barred: his whole horizon is blocked by the monstrous erection dedicated to amuse the modern crowd – and deserted. It is blind despoliation of ageless tradition.

The outbreak of the Great War in 1914 found Hyde isolated and forgotten, out of employment yet with his wife and three children to support. The youngest, Isabel, was only eight, her brain slightly weakened by infant meningitis – yet able to go with her elder sister Lydia to the Guildford Girls' High School when a generous lady in Shere provided funds. But their poverty was spitefully noticed by the other girls pointing out that the Hyde daughters lacked knickers: the family could not afford them.[50]

Their house had no conveniences. The old pump which drew water from the little river at the back remains in the cellar to this day. The house furnishings consisted of scraps of carpet, sticks of furniture, the roughest crocks.[51] Hyde barred entry to any outsider. 'Temperamental?', his daughter Lydia responded half a century later to a journalist's query: 'he exploded at a touch. And if he thought he was being patronised…'.[52]

To make ends meet he went back to Bankside Thames and took factory war-work. While there he painted a picture in oils of the Woolwich Arsenal, and persuaded the Imperial War Museum to buy it. When he offered a second oil of the Cloth Hall at Ypres in ruins (from a photograph), it was declined.

There was another side to Hyde's late work that no outsider saw after his final entries in Royal Academy exhibitions (one item each in 1906, 1911, and 1915). The 1906 entry, *The Storm Cloud,* was a mezzotint,[53] and the others were probably graphics as well. On his printing press in the cellar he drove restless experiments of light through darkening textures of tree and water and wind – memories laid up over seasons and years of wandering by day and night.

With his daughter Isabel helping at the press, Hyde worked and reworked these ultimate images. Self-criticism pushed him on: there was no one to praise or damn him as he altered a tree-shape, light from the moon, the stance of a figure (Plate 76). The only resonances among the work of Hyde's contemporaries might be seen in lithographs of Fantin-Latour or paintings by the American Albert Ryder. A few sheep by dark waters touch back to Claude Lorrain – or to Hyde's half-memories of Greenwich. These final graphics kept the private places of his vision, with darkness gathering ever more closely before illness and death took him on 28 August 1925.

The oldest residents of Shere repeat a story that near the end Hyde set fire to his remaining works – and that his fiercely loyal daughter Lydia snatched from the flames anything that survives from his studio. It is known that on his deathbed Hyde gave his engraving tools to a young artist who had been his daughters' schoolmate.[54] So he tried to hand on the grip of his torch, and perhaps the wick of its flame.

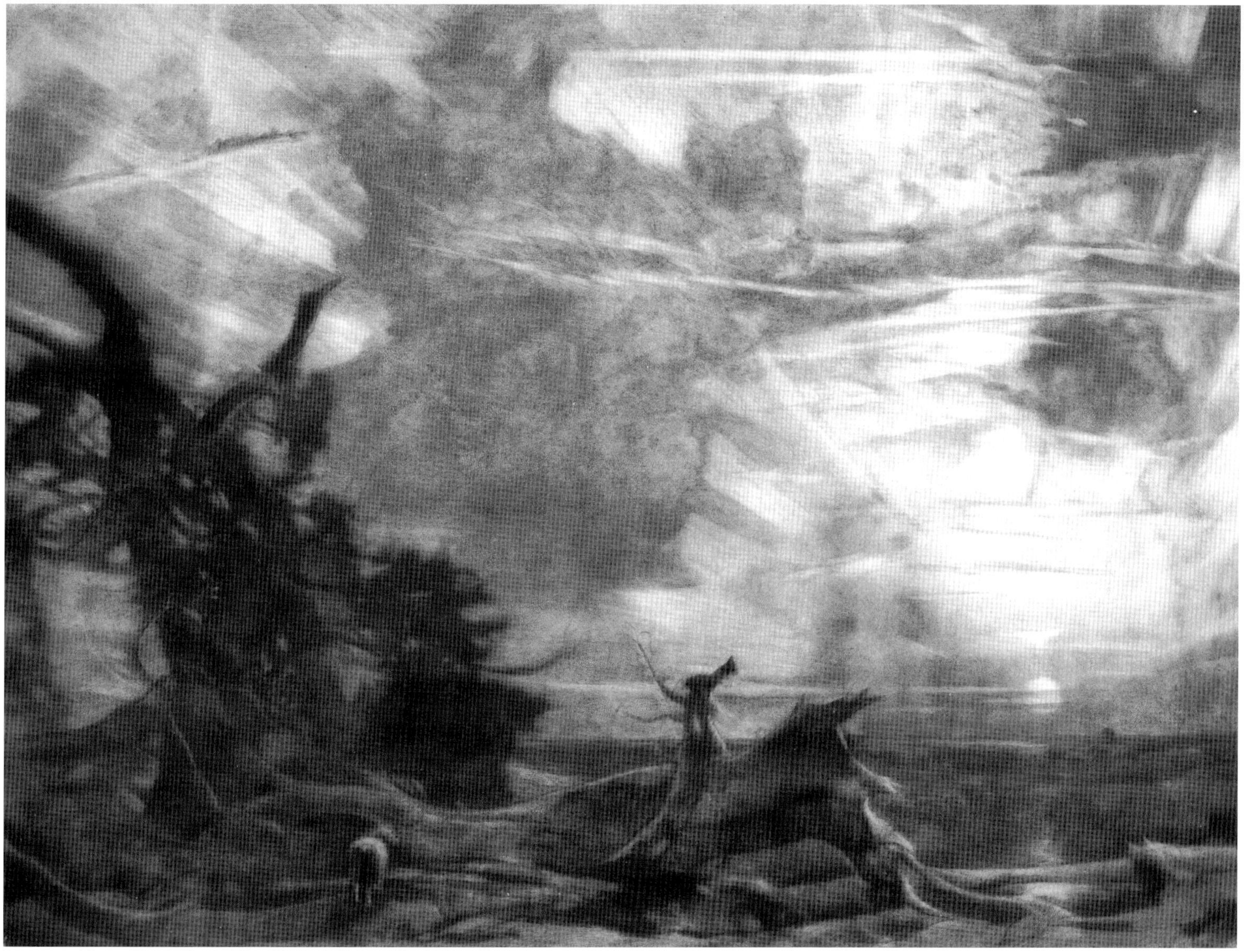

Plate 76. Fantasy, *c.*1905-18. Mezzotint

Hyde's art expanded the pastoral vision planted by Palmer – through dark and savage weathers, and even into the city. His achievement was to show these as the paradoxes of pastoral vision, not its destroyers. Thus Hyde's images expanded and deepened the prospects of English pastoral – as if preparing its vision to face half a century of wars. It was Hyde, among pastoral visionaries, who caught the wind of that future.

Postscript note

This is the first attempt at a connected account of Hyde's career. It was begun more than seventy years after his death, and could not have been done at all without generous help from the legatees of Hyde's daughters, Mrs Auriol Earle and Mrs Joan Hamilton; from Kenneth Chard at Hyde's old house; from my old friend the late Joseph Cooper, and from Elizabeth Rich at the Shere Museum. I owe a particular debt to the research skills of Barry Johnson, who has kindly shared his discoveries with me.

Yet I am conscious that this chapter's judgments are heavily based on reproductions, fine though many of the gravures in Hyde's books appear to be. Very few originals from his best years are presently known, and he is unrepresented (to my knowledge) in any major museum. For these reasons the judgments made and conclusions presented here must remain tentative – in the nature of advertisements to encourage further discoveries in the work of a man who was clearly an important artist.

50. Recalled by Lydia Hyde for Mr and Mrs Eric Earle, who shared it with me in 1999.
51. Recalled by Mrs Joan Hamilton, whose memories of 'Burnside' go back to 1942, immediately after Mrs Hyde's death.
52. Quoted from an untitled TS article by Russell Chamberlin (Shere Museum).
53. Reproduced in *The Studio*, June 1906.
54. Mrs Mary Webb to Nicholas McDowall, 22 May 1980 (private coll.).

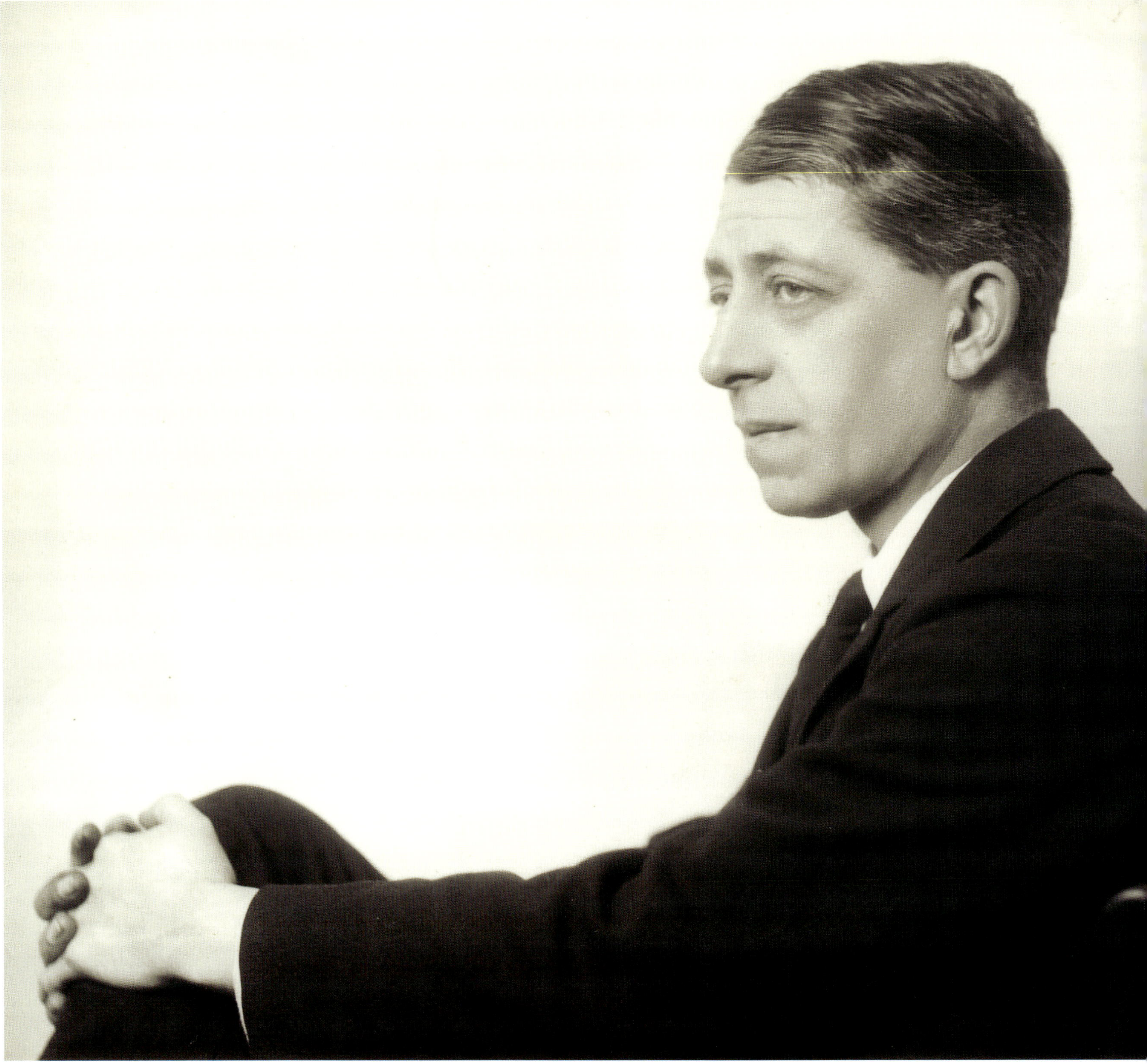

Chapter 3

F. L. Griggs (1876-1938)

Towers of Eden

Frederick Landseer Griggs was Palmer's first disciple. In the midst of his own career, Griggs wrote:

> My love for the things Samuel Palmer loved is my first & last love, & I know no other artist who loved them so well, & whose love so showed forth in his work.[1]

The bond was acknowledged equally by Palmer's son Herbert, who wrote in his old age to Griggs: 'Possibly even you do not know how immeasurably different is your utter sympathy with S.P., from anything which he ever met with in any other man *including* "The Ancients".'[2]

Before Griggs there was no Palmer-tradition. No one then saw William Hyde's art in such a light. Before much of Hyde's work appeared, the schoolboy Griggs had found the Virgil *Eclogues* with the impressions of Palmer's etchings printed in the book. Etching soon became the goal and soul of Griggs's own art.

Griggs was born and grew up in the Hertfordshire town of Hitchin, thirty miles north of London. Hitchin was even then an urban place of narrow streets. Here the boy saw little enough of the ageless agriculture which had fused Palmer's vision sixty years earlier. Palmer's landscapes, however, had also shown vernacular buildings made of local materials – cottages, inns, farmhouses and barns, the occasional church spire. Where such buildings survived about Hitchin, they were often disused or ruinous. The surrounding country churches were beginning to look like sole survivors.

English churches touched back to the mediaeval Catholic inspiration which had built them. The old religion, after a ban of three centuries, had been relicensed in England in 1829 – when it was judged no longer a threat to the Church of England. Roman Catholicism was then lumped with the 'dissenting' chapel religions. Griggs's parents were Baptist (more exclusively than Palmer's parents had been). So young Fred could feel doubly an outsider when he watched the bell-ringers' evening practice in Hitchin's grand old Parish Church, close to the family's rooms over his father's High Street bakery.

Griggs's pastoral vision gathered first about the churches and traditional vernacular buildings in the country round Hitchin. He saw them more and more in late nights and approaching darkness. Where Palmer's late lights had celebrated survival, Griggs's hinted at impending loss. In his middle years, he compounded his vision by becoming a convert to Roman Catholicism.

His art made no conscious anticipation of twentieth-century wars. Yet when the Great War came, it invested Griggs's art as with a prescience. Here was an artist who had recognised a fall of darkness before Sir Edward Grey saw the lights going out all over Europe.

After the War, survivals of the old faith and rustic life in England seemed to be receding towards extinction. From then on, one side of Griggs's art was dedicated to repairing and rebuilding the derelictions of this world in the eyes of vision. Yet the gothic places of Griggs's vision showed themselves almost always too large for any people making use of them. His great churches and castellated towns are peopled, if at all, by two or three ecclesiastics or a lonely pilgrim. They contemplate large places of the spirit overtaken, not by nature's violence as in Hyde's vision, but by human abandonment.

⋆ ⋆ ⋆

A narrow passage at the side of the Griggs bakery still leads to the big tree-shaded churchyard at the centre of Hitchin. There the boy found implications beyond the ancient church: 'That

Opposite:
Plate 77. F. L. Griggs, 28 December 1921. Photograph by Hay Wrightson. The fingers of Griggs's right hand are deeply stained with etching inks

1. Quoted in the writer's *F. L. Griggs: The Architecture of Dreams* (Oxford University Press, 1999), 15. Quotations in this chapter not otherwise attributed are from this book.
2. 22 March 1927 (Ashmolean Museum, Oxford: Griggs archive).

farther end of the great churchyard, under the trees by the river, was almost frightening to me as a youngster – it was so quiet and mysterious, especially at dusk.'

His mother was a gentle, perceptive woman who devoted some of her energies to teaching the illiterate poor of Hitchin. She understood her son well, and sent him to one good school after another. It culminated in his day-attendance at The Woodlands School, with acres of gardens dotted by little folly buildings in varied styles hidden behind the School's sober Georgian street-front. Fred was to remember all his life his good fortune in finding teachers who extended his mother's encouragement to think and feel, and to draw.

His drawings of old buildings about the town soon led him into surrounding country. At the other end of his life, after many years away, his memory still traced a secret path from a ruined chapel at Minsden to the little church of St Ippolyts, three miles from Hitchin: 'As a boy I used to regard it almost as my own, it was so unfrequented.' That church, those ruins, and the path between them were all to come into his mature art.

Yet as Griggs's words hinted, arrival was less for him than the pilgrimage itself. At fifty, when his etched vision of the mystic city of Sarras in *Le Morte d'Arthur* fell short of his dream, he turned back to St Ippolyts Church as a signpost:

> St Ippolyts is one of the places that pilgrims to Sarras see, & I don't think it's very far away. For me it's in the heart of that lost country – oh God, how lovely it was!
>
> There was a wonderful road, difficult to find, – it seemed to have no beginning, & I, for one, never knew the end; one never saw anyone there, it was small-stony & smooth & mossy; it ran by woods & meadows with untrimmed hedges rich in flowers & birds, & seemed to avoid even farmhouses... It was called St. Alban's Highway.

Such places even then seemed fragile and threatened. So he had begun to draw them. It offered two advantages. A drawing was itself partial preservation, whatever might happen later to the place itself. And if there were already unhappy aspects, they could simply be left out.

A light to guide his drawing shone from a house just beyond the Woodland School gates. There Mr Lawson Thompson had a famous collection of etchings and engravings. He welcomed high and low to enthuse with him. In that house Fred could see original impressions from plates and blocks by graphic masters from Dürer and Rembrandt to Charles Meryon, Whistler, and the latest practitioners.

Mr Thompson had placed the copy of the Virgil *Eclogues* with Palmer's etchings in the local library. There Fred Griggs found it. His schoolboy discovery was to prove the first straw in a wind which thirty-five years later would open a national exhibition to rediscover Palmer's vision for everyone.

Fred's best drawing teacher was a well-known architect, Walter Millard. (Millard had been trained by two masters of the Gothic Revival, William Burges and G.E. Street – who had also been master to William Morris.) He was a brilliant draughtsman, adept at 'forced perspectives' – sharpening angles and declinations to create drama. It was a skill he passed on to Fred Griggs.

Griggs shaped the skills he learned to his own purposes. One early series of drawings depicts the Boot Inn at Hitchin 'before alteration'. He took it first from an old photograph. But as he drew and redrew it, the old Inn emerged in better and better repair – not as patched in reality, but following principles of William Morris's Society for the Protection of Ancient Buildings. Griggs's drawings carried out secret repairs of the mind's eye, until the whole place fairly glowed with love and care and enjoyable use. Yet the memory of its dereliction and shoddy actual repair haunted him. Vast and ruinous old inns were to make another recurrent theme in Griggs's art.

Some of his young drawings of Hitchin were reproduced in the local press, or circulated in photo-engravings. Whatever the printing process, the results dissatisfied him:

> Again and again I had to deplore the loss of quality through ordinary methods of reproduction. It was that more than anything which determined me to try my hand at etching – because by that method of duplication there's gain rather than loss.

Nothing about Hitchin in the 1890s promised a secure living from art. Young Griggs refused to follow his father into the bakery. The best solution might have been an architect's training, but his family could not afford the fees attached to an articled pupilage. As a compromise Fred was sent to an architect's office for 'perspective drawing'. In that pre-computer age, it was a vital part of architectural practice: to create views of proposed works for securing contracts to build. The best perspective-drawings from all over the country were shown each year at the Royal Academy Summer Exhibition in London.

Griggs entered the office of Walter Millard's friend, the well-known Arts and Crafts architect C.E. Mallows in Bedford. Mallows saw that his new junior was more than a perspective-artist. He encouraged the young man to write magazine articles for his own illustration (as Mallows himself had done).

Griggs made one venture into the genre. It took him in the summer of 1897 to a lonely stretch of the Suffolk coast. His article is entitled 'Churches by the Sea: Notes at Some Dead Seaports of Sole Bay'.[3] It opens with a modern pilgrim's journey: 'Almost noiselessly the trains pursue their course across the still country… to the moribund places beyond it.'

Once arrived, his drawings show no figures. His attention is all for the churches and the 'strange interest' of their slow decay. The intact church at Southwold interests him so little that he does not draw it, but merely provides a photograph for the editor to reproduce. The ruined churches he draws assiduously. One, at Dunwich, is gradually falling into the sea as the coast beneath it washes away (Plate 78).

In every case the tower survives. Griggs's article asks why – and answers the question thus: 'The reason we would like best, and believe the true one, is that [the towers] have always been appreciated as beautiful objects – something to be proud of, and worth preserving for beauty's own sake.' So the young man renews Keats's equation of beauty with truth. Applied to buildings, that equation might prove costly.

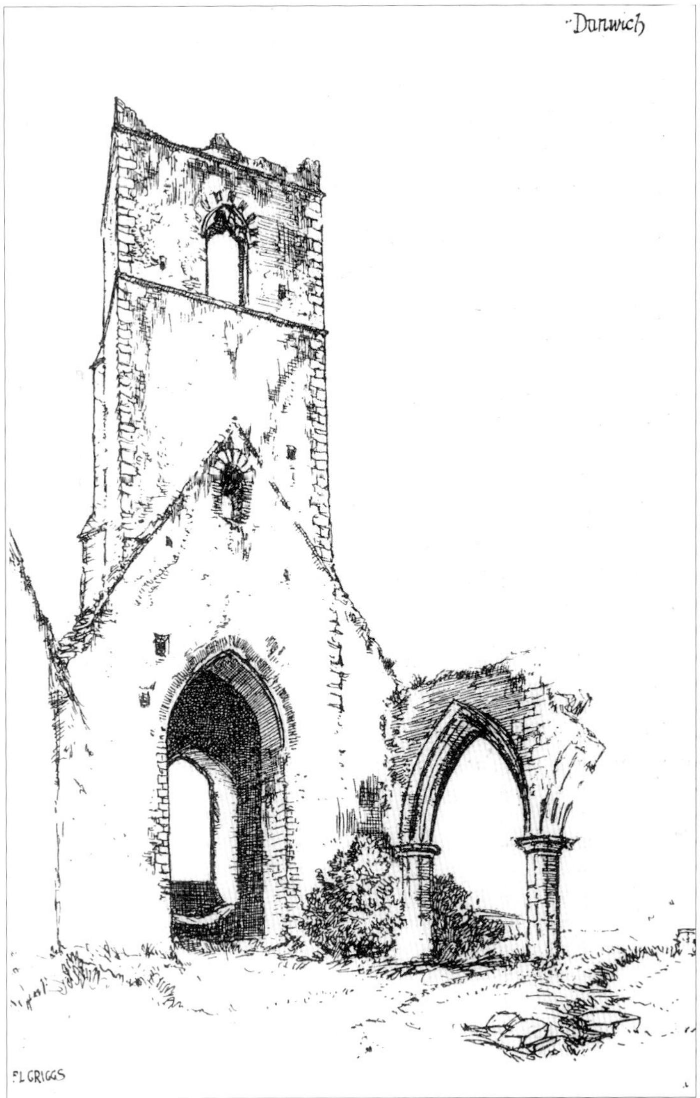

Plate 78. *Dunwich Church,* 1897 (for Griggs's article, 'Churches by the Sea: Notes at some dead seaports of Sole Bay', in *Architectural Review* XLV, 8 August 1900). Ink

Who had there been, in these 'moribund' places, to save the church towers or appreciate them? The answer was: no one, until young Mr Griggs arrived to make his equation. So Griggs's art began to show a loneliness that was different from the fierce loneliness of Hyde. Here was the historian's secret warmth of coming upon – of 'inventing' in its root meaning – something once achieved and afterwards partly lost. Such a way of looking can invest an older world with new fineness, burnished by retrospection.

He finds one hint in the church at Blythburgh, outwardly intact but inwardly stripped bare:

> Where once was a rich and solemn interior that glowed with colour and gilt; lighted by glass which sparkled like precious stones and by lamps which flickered and shone like stars before the altars… for our inheritance we have now only large white windows, and damp white stones – white everywhere, relieved by such fortuitous colour as red floor-tiles and old oak can afford.

Puritan whitewash and its shadows focused the black and white of his own art. Catholic colour had preceded that.

Griggs began to sample Catholic services at the unfinished Cathedral of Westminster in London. He could have pursued its colour in his art had he wanted it. He showed that in a small, intensely romantic *Study for 'Boston'* (Lincolnshire) painted in oils around this time. Amid glowing colours ranged before a setting sun, the great 'stump' tower of Boston Church stands

3. Published in *Architectural Review*, XLV, 8 (Aug 1900), 69-79.

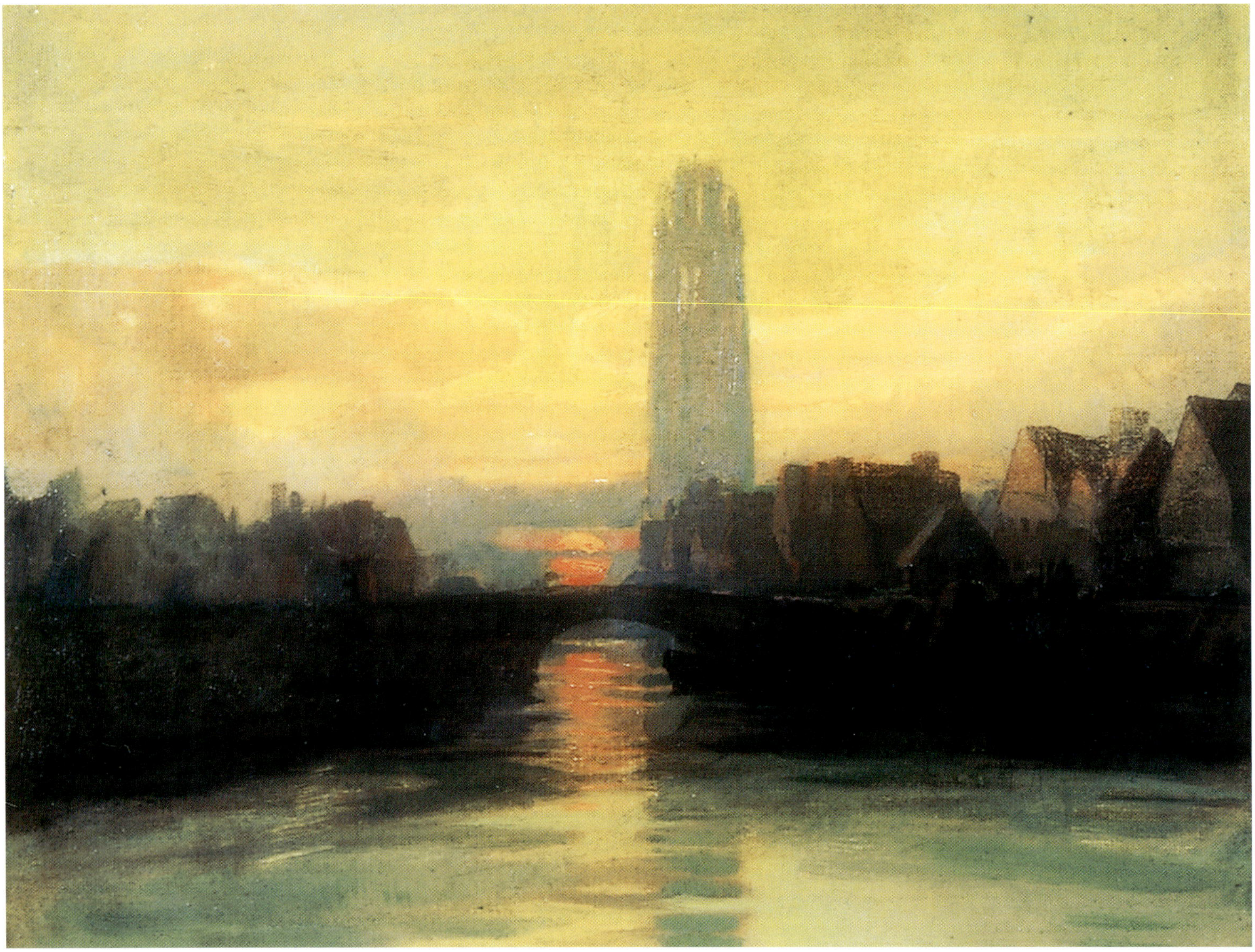

Plate 79. *Study for 'Boston',* 'about 1895'. Oil

up in grey atmospheric distance. It recalls the grey spire at the centre of Palmer's *Magic Apple Tree*. But the height of Griggs's grand tower is nearly doubled by its reflection in his painting's foreground water (Plate 79). Tower and reflection are then crossed by a horizontal of old houses ranged either side of their connecting bridge. The cruciform might have been barely deliberate.

Fifteen years were to elapse before Griggs embraced Catholicism for himself. During those years, the bridge emerged as another theme in his art. That art kept largely its black and white. So it continued to witness a puritan heritage. Near the end of his life Griggs acknowledged it thus:

> I have always thought that a certain Puritanism was a part of our national make up, & that the Puritans were not the first people to give it expression. The remains of the various Cistercian Houses up & down the country are as English as they can be.

Griggs left the architect's office after two years, with his chief's recommendation to a famous illustrator. Joseph Pennell had illustrated several of Macmillan's 'Highways and Byways' County guides. Now Pennell passed the torch to Griggs. The career of a topographic artist opened out. Macmillan commissioned a book of Griggs's native Hertfordshire. The text was to be written by someone else, but from the beginning Griggs wanted to choose his own subjects.

His portfolio of Hitchin material yielded several usable drawings. Farther afield the young artist took sketches – to work up at home in the ink textures needed for strong reproduction. His perspective-drawing outstripped every other *Highways and Byways* artist in the illustration of buildings. In gardens and woods, he paid his tribute to Aubrey Beardsley (recently dead of tuberculosis at an age hardly beyond Griggs's own), shaping varied dark textures against daring expanses of white.

In head-pieces and tail-pieces for *Highways and Byways in Hertfordshire*, Griggs reached beyond what could be seen. A century earlier Gilpin had encouraged his artists to make little improvements to nature for the sake of the design. Griggs's perfectings had an added intent. For the end of his *Hertfordshire*, he drew a fantasy of old Hitchin at dusk under snow, and noted: 'Hitchin might possibly have looked like this in the XVII cent[ury] from where the New Post Office stands.' (Plate 80) It was the formula of Palmer, of Coleridge and Wordsworth – 'to let imagination and memory work together'.

Other *Highways and Byways* commissions followed. On a motor tricycle bought with the publisher's advance, Griggs reached remote places to draw for *South Wales* (1902 1903). All his choices of subject were rural, no cities or mines. He worked harder and took longer than any other artist drawing for the series. But he grew restive in the shackles of topography.

Through early experiments, Griggs had already explored the slow processes of etching – grounding the plate, drawing with the burin, biting in acid, cleaning and proving, revising and perfecting the image in Palmer's way, through minute accretions. It was as if deliberation itself might open a magic casement on 'the realms of the imagination', as he confided to a friend: 'Oh the richness, the warmth, the seductive shadow, the laziness, the colour[*sic*], the atmosphere – the heaped-up glory of it!' He etched one plate from a visionary *South Wales* tailpiece of castle ruins on distant escarpment, and attached to it a phrase from Coleridge's 'Kubla Khan': *'A miracle of rare device'*.

Yet as he finished it, he found himself 'forced to the conclusion that my art is far from ripe enough to tackle the sort of landscape I dream of'. Like the young Palmer at Shoreham, Griggs at twenty-seven lacked the breadth and depth of experience to sustain and expand his vision.

Two surviving friends of William Morris befriended him. Emery Walker and Sydney Cockerell, now sharing a photo-engraving business, recognised dedication and the beginnings of distinction in Griggs's art. Cockerell emphasised the weight Morris had attached to natural materials, and the crafts for working them. Such an understanding was as vital as perspective skill, Cockerell pointed out, to any faithful recording of old buildings. In Griggs's new *Highways and Byways* project for *Sussex* (1903), some plain cross-hatching for the roof of Sompting Church tower caught Cockerell's disapproval:

> I am not sure about the material of the roof of Sompting Tower – that of the main building is so very well rendered & explained. … The mind tires of anything that has a mechanical look – anything that is taken in at a glance & contains no mystery… In a perfect drawing every touch is alive.

Griggs redrew that tower roof to show the varied shapes of hand-hewn stone tiling.

Cockerell sent Griggs to see Morris's oldest surviving friend, and co-founder of the Society for the Protection of Ancient Buildings. Philip Webb (1831-1915) was father of the Arts and Crafts building revival. Webb praised Griggs's drawings of old buildings, and enlarged the younger man's observation: to 'black & white work' Webb would add 'the intermediate term of "grey" – which I feel is of *great* importance, when striving to make pen and ink drawings… more like nature'.

Through these friendships Griggs became the youngest and last of all the 'Morris men'. Though he could not follow Morris's socialism as the others did, Griggs held high Morris's ideals of workmanship and vision through country traditions. His next *Highways and Byways* project, *Oxford and the Cotswolds*, would take him into their midst.

Plate 80. Old Hitchin under snow, 1901 (tailpiece for *Highways and Byways in Hertfordshire).* Ink

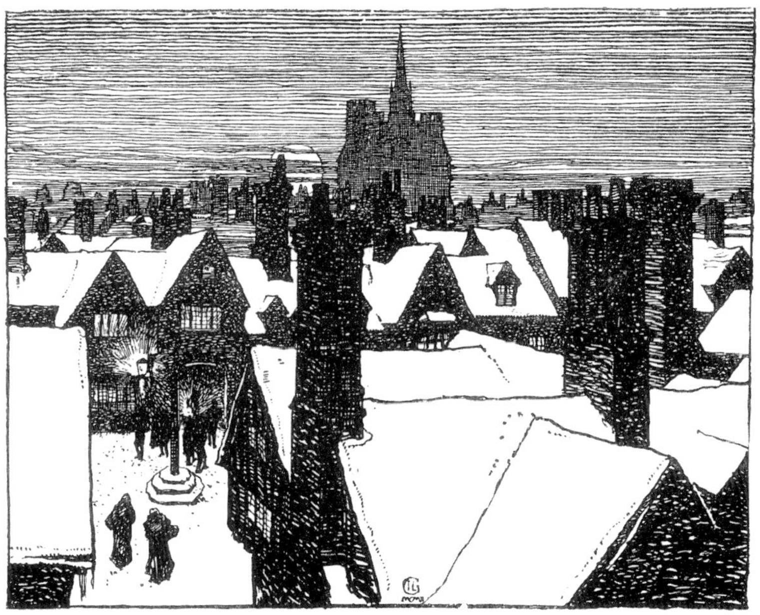

Riding westward from Oxford one afternoon in November 1903, Griggs came to the north Cotswold town of Chipping Campden. There, amid the mellow stone buildings of what has been called the finest High Street in England, he found C.R. Ashbee's Guild of Handicraft. Here was the most successful craft community actually operating on Morris lines. Its members included two friends from Hitchin. In the young craft-fellowship Griggs found what seemed a heaven on earth. He decided to move to Campden. He would live there the rest of his life.

Griggs worked at his *Cotswolds* drawings as if his life depended on them. A drawing of Gloucester Street, Winchcombe (an ancient town south-west of Campden) shows how hard he worked. With fewest, lightest strokes of the pen to shadow architectural members on an otherwise blank surface, he spreads shimmering sunlight across the church tower (Plate 81). Below the tower, darker shadows are made from textures of short ink lines (echoing Palmer's etchings) – and then the interstices are re-opened with tiny dots of Chinese white. So the shadows seem to vibrate, revivifying Palmer's 'thousand little luminous eyes' of paper twinkling through heavy etching, and the morning dew Blake had seen in the flecks of white across the painted landscapes of Claude Lorrain.

After two years' work, Griggs had finished only seventy-two of the eighty drawings commissioned for *Highways and Byways in Oxford and the Cotswolds*. In October 1905 Macmillan closed the book to go to press for the Christmas market, and reduced Griggs's payment by a proportionate ten per cent. The young artist was outraged. But he spent twelve guineas of his reduced fee on a trial proof of Palmer's *Lonely Tower* etching, as he wrote: 'This picture gives me more pleasure than any black & white I've ever seen.'

Having stayed a year in the bachelor quarters of the Guild in Campden, Griggs took a lease on Dover's House three doors away. There he would live for nearly twenty-five years. He fell in love several times. In 1908 he proposed to a clever, pretty daughter of the land agent for the Stanway estate a few miles south-west of Campden. But Griggs at thirty-two wanted a wife unformed enough to receive the impress of his own tastes. The girl saw that and rejected him.

Three years later he transfused the pain of rejection into a vision. Visiting the girl's father in his retirement home close to the ruined Abbey of Hailes near Winchcombe, Griggs met a time-dissolving experience. The season was early summer. Late one evening he had not gone to bed, but sat up reading and nodding off. Looking up then and seeing the sky pale blue, he wandered out along a field path as a revenant:

> The light of early dawn is so ghostly & curious that things don't get definitely fixed in one's mind somehow – or perhaps I wasn't quite awake. I walked to Hailes Abbey, & almost conjured out of those rank weeds & heaps of shapeless stone the *'House'* that once was there!

It showed again the character of his vision: to rebuild in his mind's eye the grandeur of old achievements from the ruins made of them by a lesser age.

By 1909 he had made *Highways and Byways* drawings through a dozen counties of southern England and South Wales. His buildings attained their grandest scale when juxtaposed with small human figures. To perfect his figure-drawing, early in 1910 Griggs went to the Slade School of Art in London for a mature term. His teacher was a gifted martinet of life-drawing, Henry Tonks. Younger Slade students all around him were being distracted by new mannerisms from France. Griggs stuck it out.

He had already sought to lighten the burden of *Highways and Byways* recording by changing from laborious pen and ink to pencil. The pencil's quickness could touch springs below conscious thought. At length Macmillan found a block-maker in Vienna with the skill to reproduce pencil lines well enough. Griggs's topographic drawing took on new subtleties of expressive line and atmospheric shadow in drawings completed on the spot, for *Highways and Byways in Cambridge and Ely*.

His pencil-drawing campaign for *Lincolnshire*, through the summer of 1912, was beset by huge thunderstorms. Such storms, as with Palmer's 'Ancients' at Shoreham, extended Griggs's

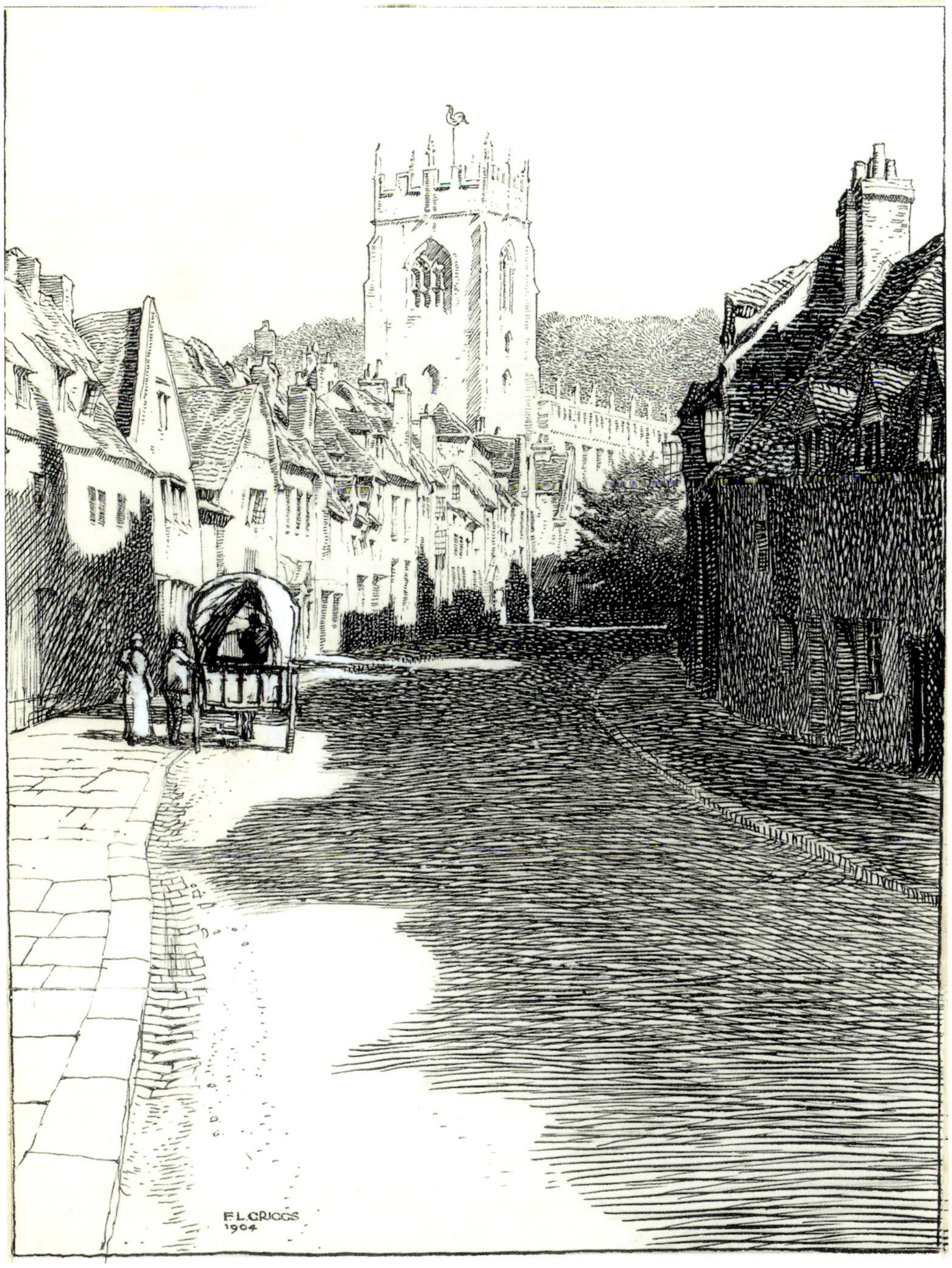

Plate 81. *Gloucester Street, Winchcombe,* 1904 (for *Highways and Byways in Oxford and the Cotswolds).* Ink, with white highlighting

perceptions of light. The pencil's immediacy divided his topographic drawing more decisively from dreams of careful etching.

Between those first two *Highways and Byways* excursions in pencil came an event to draw a heavier line under Griggs's past. In February 1912, after years of doubt and atheism, he embraced the Roman Catholic faith. It was no quick decision. Catholicism had built all the finest churches he had drawn through the past decade and more. The faith that built those living testaments of local stone and wood spoke to Griggs as no other evangelism ever spoke.

Catholicism, still classed in England with Non-conformity, ministered to the visionary's loneliness. On his reception as a Catholic in February 1912, Griggs took to himself the name of Maur. On St Maur's Day in 1361 a mighty wind had blown away the plague, according to an inscription in the once-Catholic church at Ashwell, between Hitchin and Cambridge. Griggs had drawn (and even painted) Ashwell again and again. Now at thirty-five he sought to make the wind of Maur his own. And within a month he set about his mature etching.

* * *

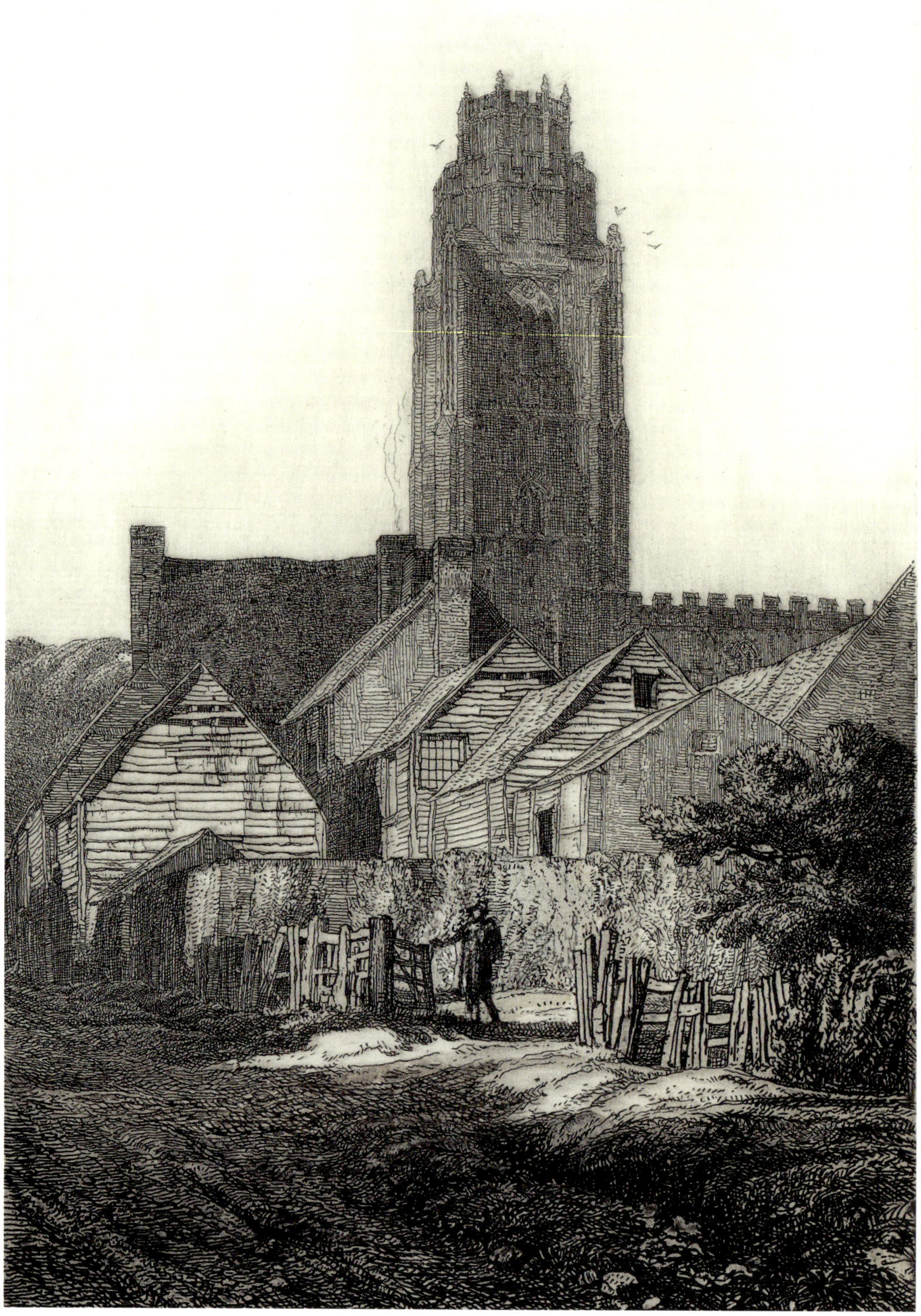

Plate 82. *Sutton,* 1912. Etching, state 2, touched with wash with a view to later state

Griggs's first mature etchings trace a conversation from topographer to visionary. The earliest, etched in March and April 1912, translates a *Cambridge and Ely* pencil drawing of Sutton Church. The drawing's flat spring light ripens in the etching to a richly shadowed late summer afternoon (Plate 82). This later light intensifies the image of the church – raising its tower through nave and choir as the top of a great cruciform over the hovels below.

A secret strength emerges in Griggs's etched stone building. The etching shows its masonry mortar lines hand-drawn (rather than ruled): so they express the stones hewn by hand in the old builders' craft. It is Palmer's texturing etched to new purpose. Griggs's etching adds a figure with pilgrim's staff and (in its second state) a burden on his aged back. The pilgrim will haunt Griggs etchings to come.

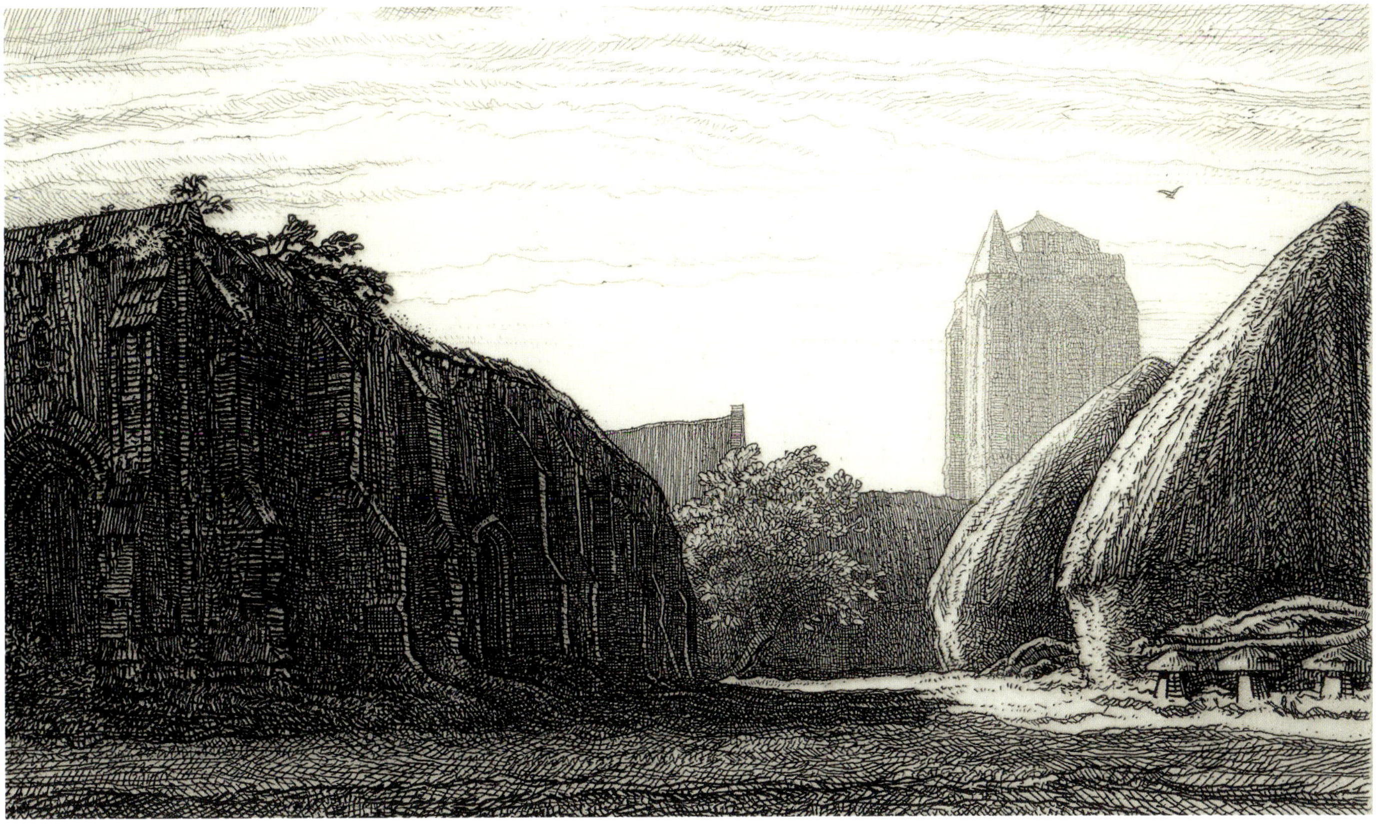

Plate 83. *Maur's Farm,* 1913*f.* Etching, state 2 (printed by Griggs)

Afternoon light advances farther in his next etching, started the year after *Sutton.* This smaller plate is founded on another *Highways and Byways* drawing, of Helpringham in *Lincolnshire.* The new etching supplants the drawing's steeple with a tower massively distant. Where the drawing showed men repairing a wagon wheel under haystacks, the etching's later light leaves the stacks lonely – in the words of Gray's 'Elegy in a Country Churchyard' (Griggs's favourite poem) 'to darkness and to me'. The etching is given a suggestive new title, *Maur's Farm* (Plate 83).

Soon after it, Griggs fetched from farther an early tailpiece in *Hertfordshire* to make a miraculous late-afternoon pastoral in drypoint, of a shepherd moving his sheep through *The Coppice*. It is his closest approach to the world of Samuel Palmer.

From the Minsden Chapel ruins of his boyhood walks (drawn with seeming accuracy for *Hertfordshire* in 1901) Griggs conjured a derelict bishop's palace in etching: *Minsden Episcopi.* 'It started out to be a grange', he confessed, ' – but became too important-looking (the Grange must come later).' So it would. Many such private thoughts were shared now with the man who was becoming Griggs's closest friend. Russell Alexander (1877-1951) kept his young family by journalism in London, while his dreams and his poems sought Griggs's world.

In the first year of the Great War, Griggs returned to larger plates for a new series of etchings. The new plates invent town-scapes, touching lightly back to the half-English Meryon – and behind him to Piranesi. Griggs envisioned his town from a poem by a young fellow-convert to Catholicism and the Cotswolds, Wilfred Rowland Childe (1890-1952). Childe's 'Song of the Little City' found its vision

> … under lonely towers
> Where silences of noons
> Cover their sacred flowers
> In places no one knows.

Griggs's 'Little City' plates show a new presence in his etchings. Water across the foreground divides us from these scenes (as it had divided the little boy gazing across the stream at the far end of Hitchin Churchyard from what lay beyond).

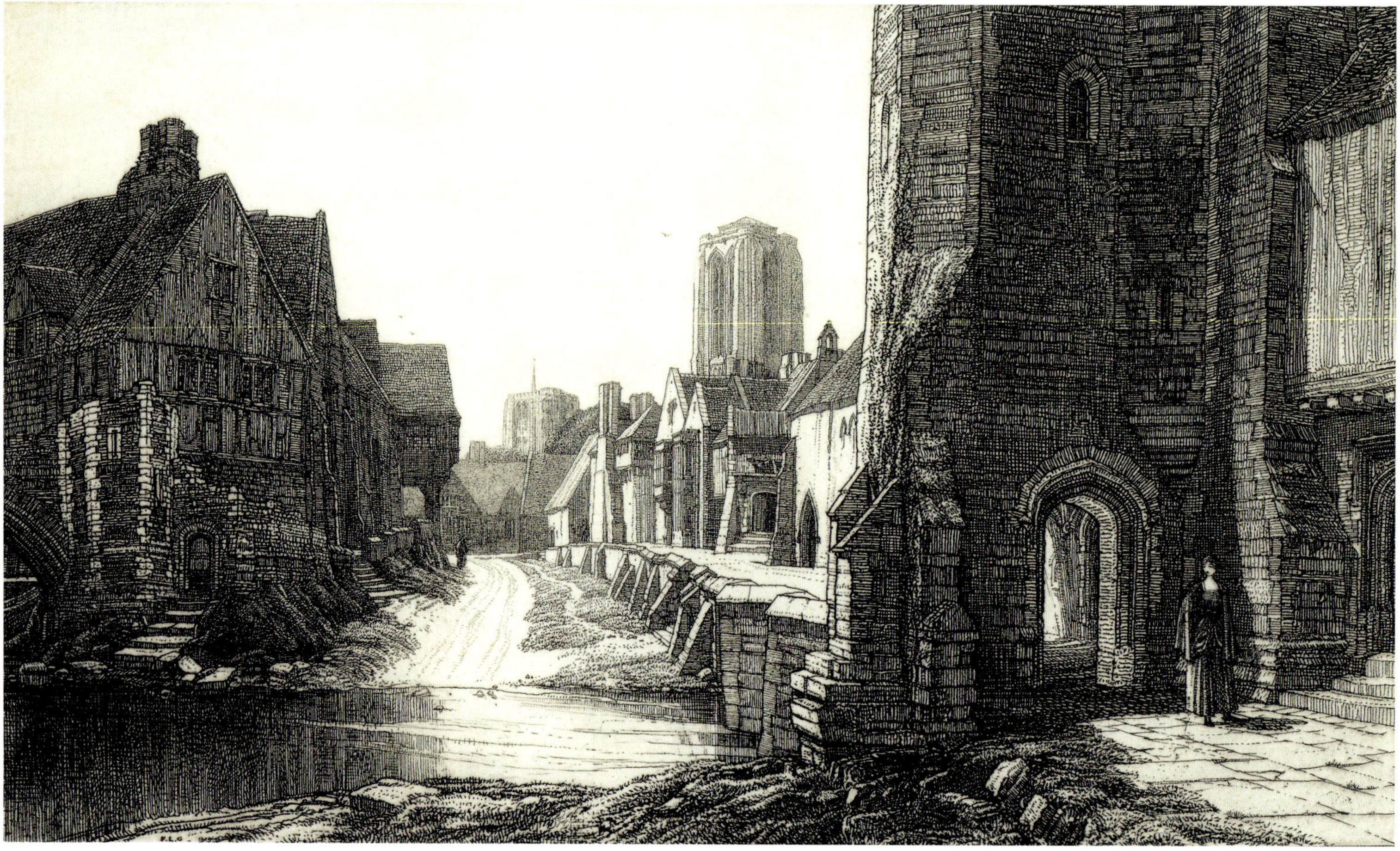

Plate 84. *The Ford,* 1915-24. Etching, state 6

Beyond the stream in his first 'Little City' etching, *The Ford* (1915), stands 'an imaginary English town before the Reformation & the Renaissance had had visible effect' (Plate 84). Griggs acknowledged the role of *Highways and Byways* experience in the making of his town: 'Very likely the character of the scene owes something to what survives at Winchcombe & Campden, as well as to East Anglian preferences.'

The water in his next etching, *The Pool*, flows under a gothic bridge stretching almost across the long plate. Behind it rises a hill town of triangular shape, to recall Dürer's towns. Here several small presences watch and wait.

A third 'Little City' etching, *The Cresset* (1915), shows its bridge overwhelming the plate – to end in a gatehouse so huge as to block much view of any town behind it. Defence itself is now the etcher's obsession. Three figures in a boat try to hail a solitary on the bridge: but he only draws his cloak about him. Here is apprehension of a kind Palmer's art never had to face. Still Palmer's spirit haunts him, as Griggs quotes: 'Matter aggregates within matter till the copper looks as large as a half-length canvas.'

When the first 'Little City' etchings were shown in London, the artist Walter Bayes wrote in *The Athenaeum*: 'There is something very impressive in Mr Griggs's slow, pertinacious, accumulative manner, producing the result of so much thought in so little space.' The achievement is astonishing in 'an etcher of only some two years' standing. … He will probably rank among the great little masters.' That in the face of English etching now gone largely over to the sketch-style imported from France.

With the sketch-style went *retroussage* in the printing of etchings. Every commercial printer now did it automatically. Griggs liked it as little as Palmer had done: all their close workings depended on clean printing. So Griggs began to print for himself on Goulding's presses. For a new state of *Maur's Farm*, his own printing produced a golden glow never seen through the sooty blacks of the old commercial proofs. Griggs resolved to do all his own printing – as Blake had done, and as Palmer had sought to do with his son. Griggs would print every impression of every new plate. He made himself the most accomplished etching printer in the Palmer style.

In *The Quay* (1916) the hill town grew larger. But any reaffirming civility is undercut in two ways. A shower of rain casts a storm-shadow across half the foreground. And the people here are at odds. A lone woman on a high balcony watches a man standing below at the water's brink. Behind him, another man points across to a couple on our side of the water – still in sunlight but approaching the shadow line. Nothing is clear in these human webs, except that the Little City no longer offers the ideal refuge Griggs had tried for early in the War. One way and another, the War is in them all.

He had fallen in love again. In the summer of 1915 he met Theresa Browne, visiting from Ireland. She was thirty-two: yet she radiated an innocence possible perhaps only in remote Ireland where Catholicism reigned in mediaeval authority. Again Griggs dreamt of a wife compliant to his dreams. Theresa invited him to visit her family home at Ballynabola, Co. Wexford, where she lived with her widowed mother.

Griggs went over several times – against a background of threatened military conscription at home, despite his thirty-nine years and indifferent health. At Easter 1916 rebellion swept Ireland. Griggs was so worried about Theresa that he went out once more in May. But Ballynabola remained inviolate.

He stayed two months. And there, galvanised by the displacements of love and distant war, he achieved a unique concentration of visionary drawing. Churches, fortresses and towns, bridges and rivers, manor houses and farmsteads lie often derelict, sometimes transfigured in shafts of rich low sunlight amid engulfing shadow (Plate 85).

The Irish drawings also showed their artist a paradox, which he described to Alexander in the midst of making them:

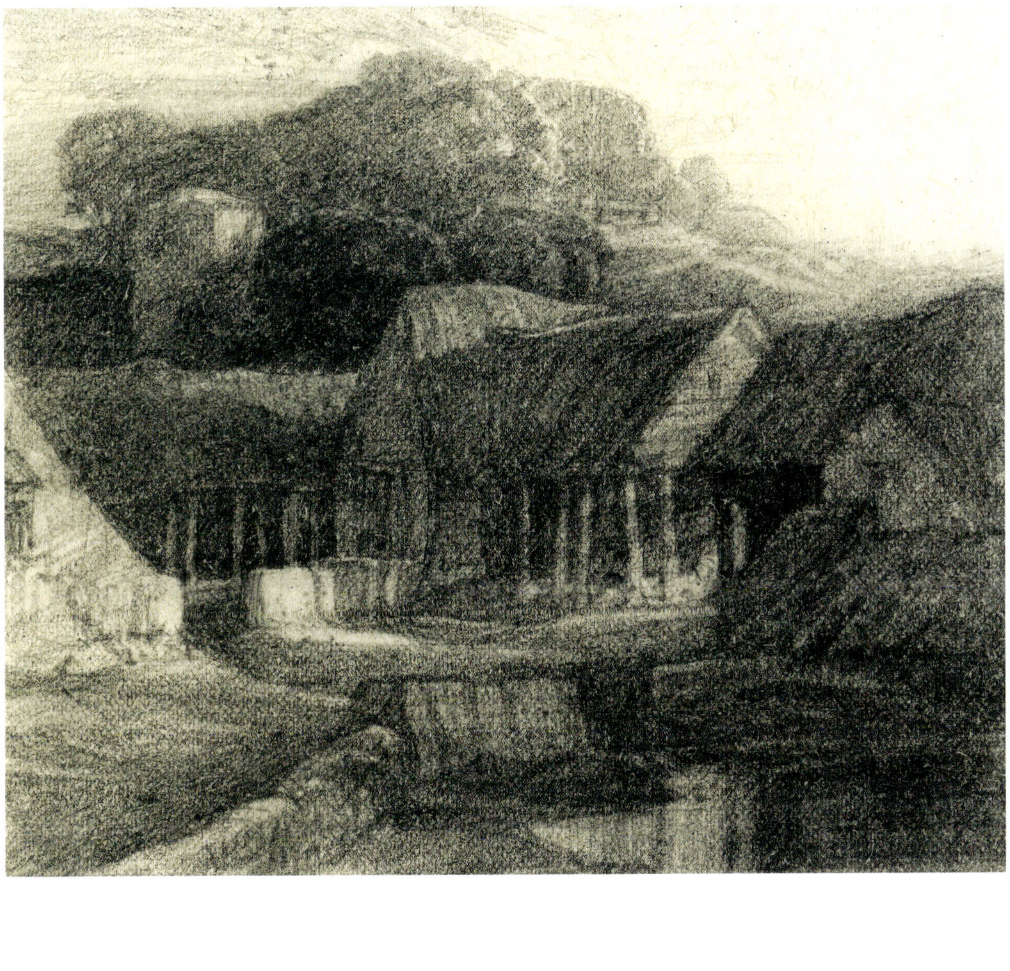

Plate 85. Farmstead, 1916. Pencil on sugar paper

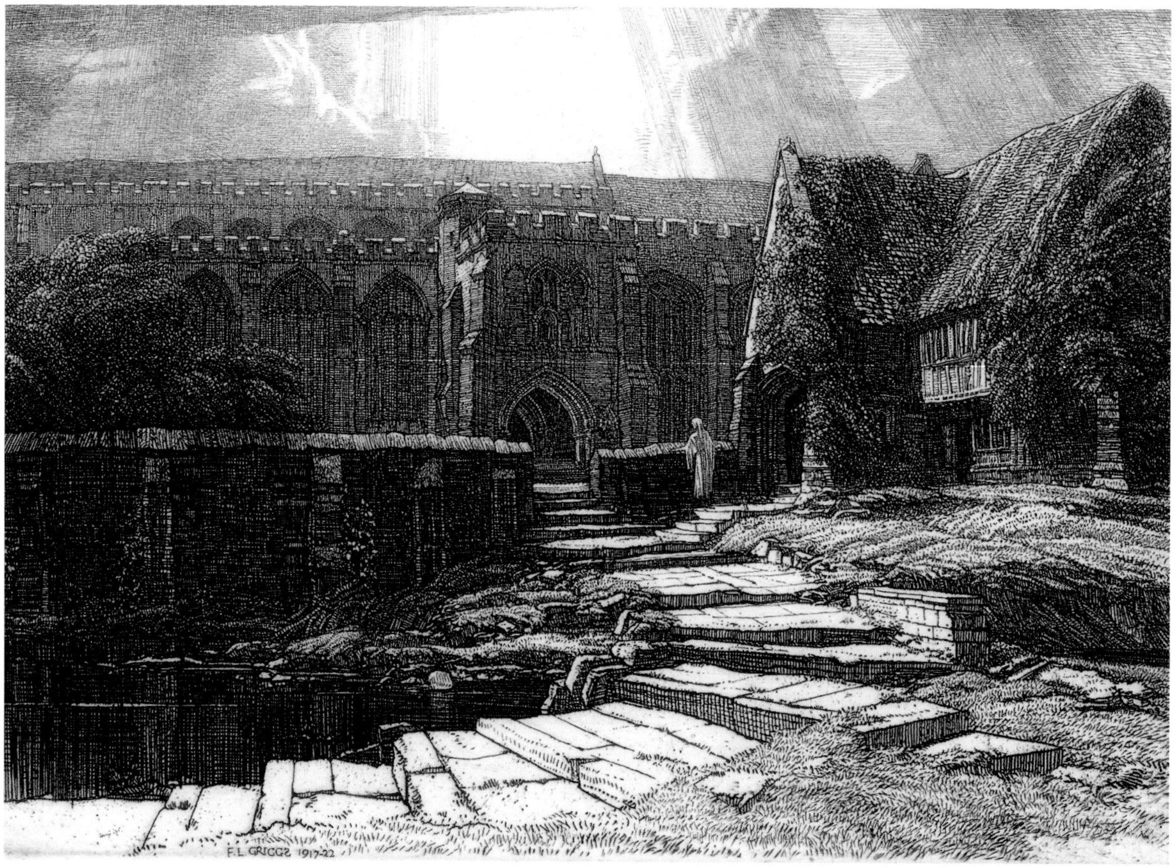

Plate 86. *Sellenger,* 1917-22.
Etching, state 6

> All my studies here are intensely English.
> There's one, a perfect riot of old English gothic houses in all the picturesqueness at my command. ... There are many studies for a scene that so far eludes my grasp... 'The Lanterns of Sarras', with the evening sunlight coming through the lanterns and belfries.

A third was to show a 'broad upland landscape, with a hint of the Cotswolds, The Cross Hands'. That was a type of old sign at crossroads, pointing the four ways. He had drawn one in a lonely *Lincolnshire* landscape. Such an actual sign still stood along the London road above Campden.

Yet it had taken his visits to another country to focus these visions of home. 'I've learnt a lot about my work here,' he confided to Alexander near the end of the long Irish visit. The seeds sown there and then were to germinate visionary etchings throughout the rest of his career.

After the War cut ties with Vienna, his ongoing pencil drawings for *Highways and Byways* books suffered from reproduction by English firms – often so bad as to force their printing as half-tones. Griggs offered himself for war work, and in 1917 the manager of the Lacre motor-chassis works at Letchworth, near Hitchin, took him. It meant a partial closing up of his house in Campden.

Through it all the affair with Theresa unwound. She had attached herself so deeply to the man she saw that she grew jealous of every change – change that is vital to an artist's development. In December 1916 Griggs's apprehension set into a new etching a pair of disjunct figures. Before another bishop's palace, a man unfolds what may be architectural plans; but the kerchiefed woman beside him half turns away. Behind them stretches the nave of a great Perpendicular church.

That church's other side seems to fill the background of his next visionary etching, *Sellenger* (Plate 86). In place of the kerchiefed woman, a lonely diaphanous figure turns her back to contemplate the grand edifice. She was identified by Griggs as a ghost – the only such figure in all his etchings. Foreground steps curve round a dark pool of unfathomable depth. On the etching's first state he set two lines from Childe's 'Song of the Little City': 'silences of noons – In places no one knows.'

In the spring of 1918 Griggs came upon a terrace of half-timbered houses in the Essex village of Clavering that touched back to one of his Irish visions. As he sketched it, from across the

English Channel came a distant sound of the guns. He did not etch 'Clavering' then. The house he etched that autumn was a moated manor with dereliction in its sinister title – *Mortmain.*

For a new etching at the end of the War in late 1918 Griggs set at the apex of a triangular bridge (drawn in 1912 at Croyland, Lincolnshire) a standing cross. This etched cross rose through a night sky brilliant with stars over snow and roofless houses. Below this image he set a Latin inscription of high irony, which he translated:

'In the Feast of Our Lord's Epiphany:
The year of salvation 1919.'

He had made an informal architectural partnership with the Morris disciple Ernest Gimson. Most of their commissions were for war-memorial crosses in villages. But Gimson died in the summer of 1919, leaving Griggs to carry on the work alone. The one commission that produced trouble was in Griggs's own Campden. He offered a cross-design as his gift to the town. A local doctor organised opposition, with the object of taking the money for a nursing station. Energetic canvassing divided the town. Griggs was appalled: it was as if the actual 'Little City' where he had chosen to make his home was bedevilled. 'It would be horrible', he wrote, 'if now they erected a cross out of so much squabbling.' It was precisely what they did.

In the midst of it he etched a new plate, long and narrow like a coffin lid. *Totterne Inn* (Plate 87) shows an old hostelry at the end of its empty town, falling into shadow as the last light strikes a headless cross-shaft. On its plinth – the very image of his Campden cross-design – sits a disconsolate pilgrim leaning on his shaft.

In 1921 he started a large etching of a visionary church dedicated to the vanished bells of Croyland Abbey, Lincolnshire. Its study drawing showed vandals' ladders rising over the great nave roof, with smoke pouring from a tower. The attack disappeared from the copper plate, which he called *Ex Anglia Perdita.* He etched invocatory inscriptions top and bottom: but the centre foreground remained an obstinate blank.

That summer *The Studio* magazine published the first serious attempt to place Griggs in the context of his nation's art. Its author was the Turner scholar A.J. Finberg. 'Nature and man's work are to [Griggs]', Finberg wrote, 'what the human figure has been to most artists.'

> To us to-day man is no longer the centre of the universe, the hero of existence, as he was in the glow and pride of the Renaissance. Man we know now is complete only… as a moment in that Nature which surrounds him.

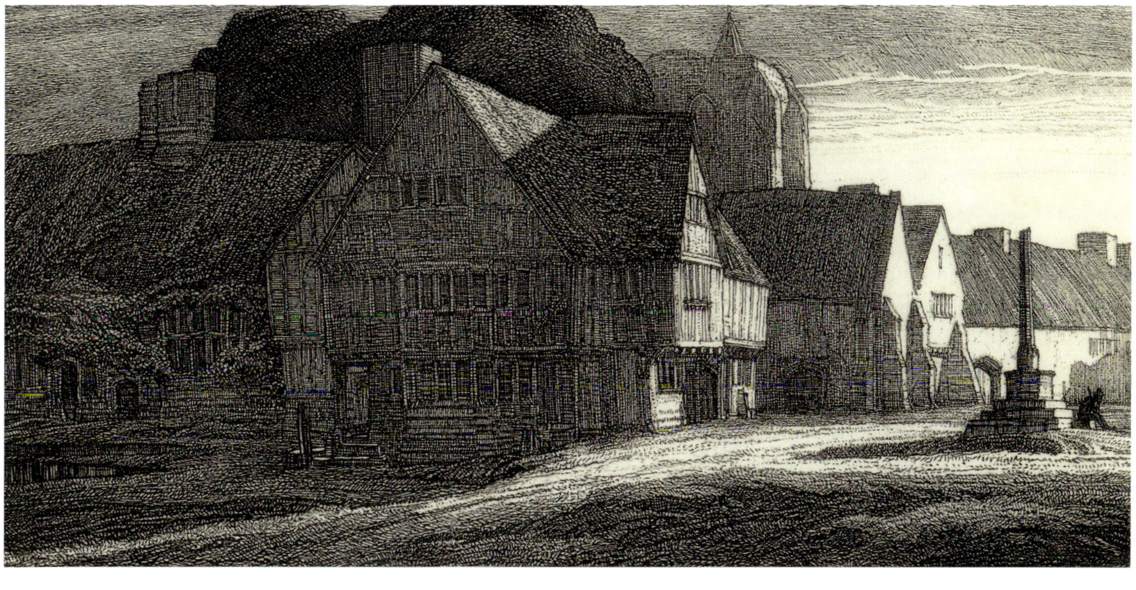

Plate 87. *Totterne Inn,* 1919. Etching, state 4
The Fine Art Society

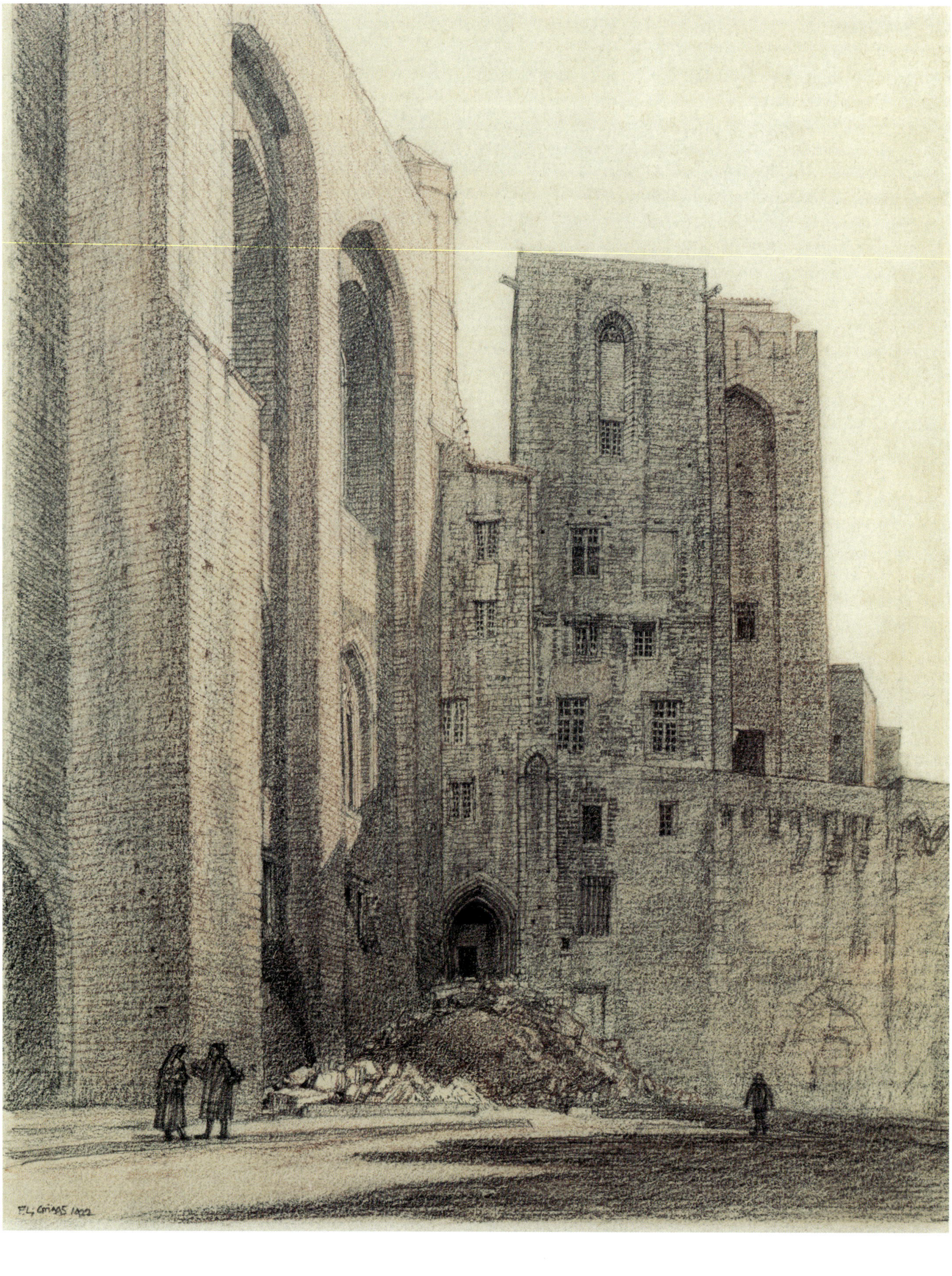
F.L. Griggs 1922

Opposite:
Plate 88. *Place de l'Amirande,* Palace of the Popes at Avignon, 1922. Red and black conté crayon on light green paper

Finberg described Griggs as 'a born etcher', citing 'that marvellously supple, delicate and thoughtful line of his':

> He seems to think and feel in line… In the whole range of present-day etching I know of no more thoroughly individual works than these… or more perfect in their workmanship.

In June 1921 Griggs met the woman he was to marry. Pretty, grey-eyed Nina Muir was the sister of a local artist at whose house Griggs was a familiar guest. She was twenty-one, he was rising forty-five. Yet both experienced something like instant recognition. Nina wrote later: 'I felt then that I had met someone utterly different from the ordinary run, someone vital and real, and whatever he said or did I'd approve of.' Griggs for his part wrote to Russell Alexander of walking home after their first meeting to a sleepless bed, and rising at 3 a.m. to walk up Dover's Hill above Campden to greet 'the silver-gilt of a new day'.

Both were Catholic. Nina, scant of education though she came of a good family, brought him a light heart: he called her his 'laughing wisdom'. Less than five weeks after they met, he proposed during a walk on Dover's Hill, and she accepted. They would be married early in January 1922.

Their honeymoon took them to Avignon, with its vast fourteenth century Palace built for the Papacy during its exile from Rome. Griggs spent the days, with Nina at his side, making a series of large drawings that marry black and red crayon across their visionary surfaces (Plate 88). After the Avignon drawings were shown in London, Griggs was made Associate of the Royal Academy.

A quest for some new definition began in an obsessive revising of his older visionary etchings. Between 1920 and 1924 he made changes to twelve of the fifteen etched thus far. The plate revised most persistently was *Maur's Farm* (1913). Changes in 1921 and 1922 darkened skies and shadows. Then in the autumn of 1924 he transfused that darkness into morning rays of a summer sun.

The old evening states had reflected the slow decay of tradition – tradition which now seemed decimated by the War. Younger artists and writers were denouncing 'Edwardian' values in which they looked for causes of the War. If Griggs in his mid-forties was to find a new day for his more traditional art, its dawn must break over some accumulated experience. 'To my thinking,' he wrote now, 'reconstruction, like Charity, must begin at home.' It was the new dawn over *Maur's Farm.*

Barely a month after achieving it, he found his foreground for *Anglia Perdita*. Below the great monastic church, in a little courtyard two monks feed their pigeons. The moment shown (Griggs decided as he etched) is just before 'the last conventual High Mass there. Yes, & the monk is saying goodbye to his house doves.' That vision crystallised a new understanding. The real destruction had not been wrought during the War: it was coming now.

By the time he finished *Anglia Perdita* in late 1924, Griggs had three masterpieces in view to crown his etching career. The oldest was to be founded on the most desolate of all his visions in Ireland: a monastic church in ruins, back-lit by the setting sun. Its etching would be called *Fen Monastery*. The church's crumbling east end appeared detached, and whitened as a skull.

A second masterpiece would show the great 'stump' tower of St Botolph's Church, Boston – based on his 1912 drawing for *Highways and Byways in Lincolnshire*. Recalling the huge thunderstorms that beset him then, Griggs's etching-study blackened the sky with 'a very devil-made storm': he scratched forks of lightning right through the heavily pencilled paper surface. 'Three hundred feet of noblest English Architecture upreared above the fens', he wrote to Alexander: ' – white & unhurt by lightning, wind or sea-flood' from what had once been called 'the German Ocean'.

Yet as he etched the tower, the sheer achievement began to speak for itself. 'Perhaps this will not have the sky after all,' he thought in January 1924. Such uncertainties are difficult to live with. Two months later he wrote to another friend of the merciless grip:

> For myself I seldom know what Content is, and it is as if I had been made to adopt my adopted motto from St Augustine,
> 'Quum dixeris sufficit periisti.'
> ('When you say it is good enough, you will have died.')

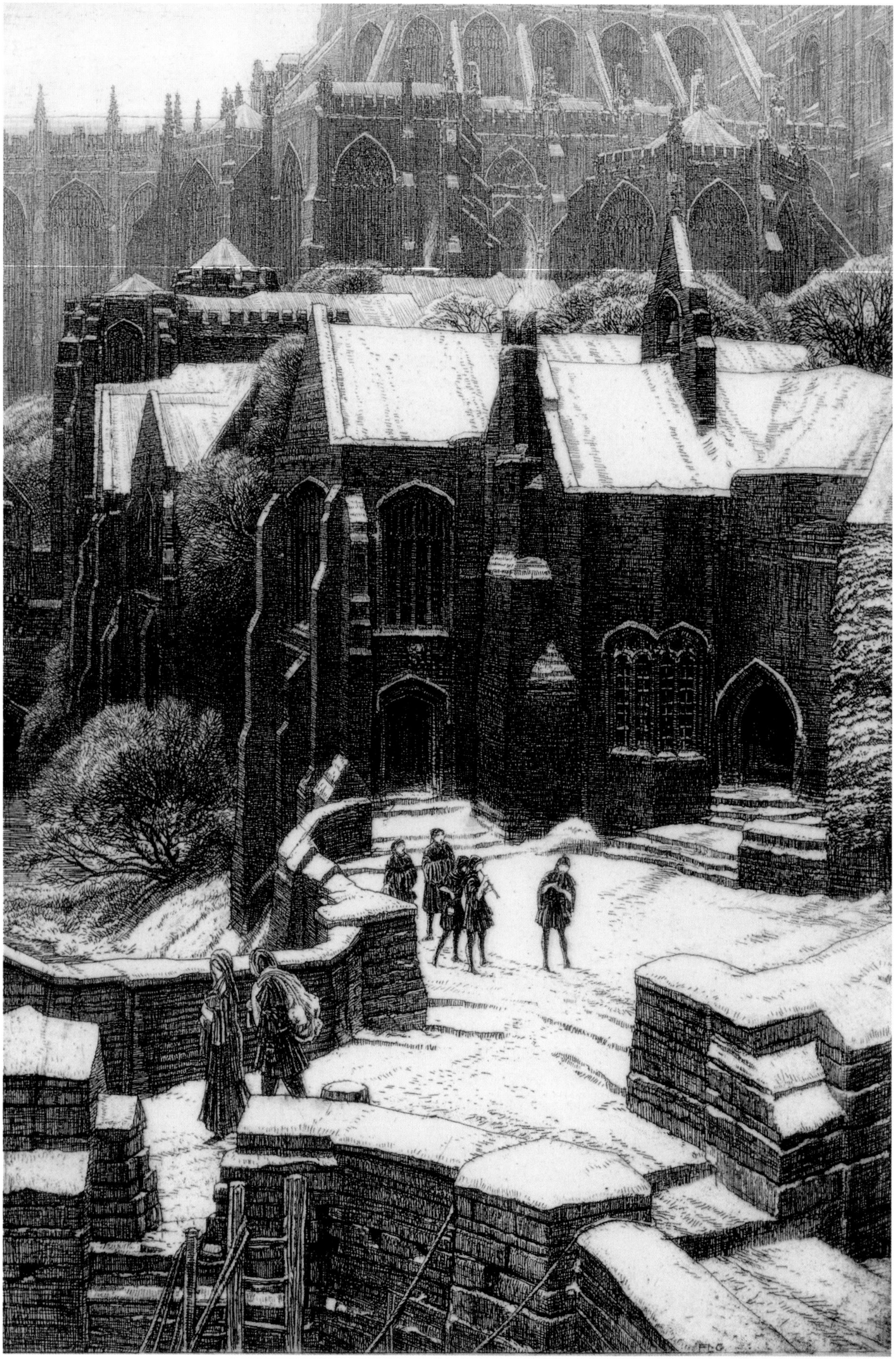

Plate 89. *The Almonry,* 1925. Etching, state 5

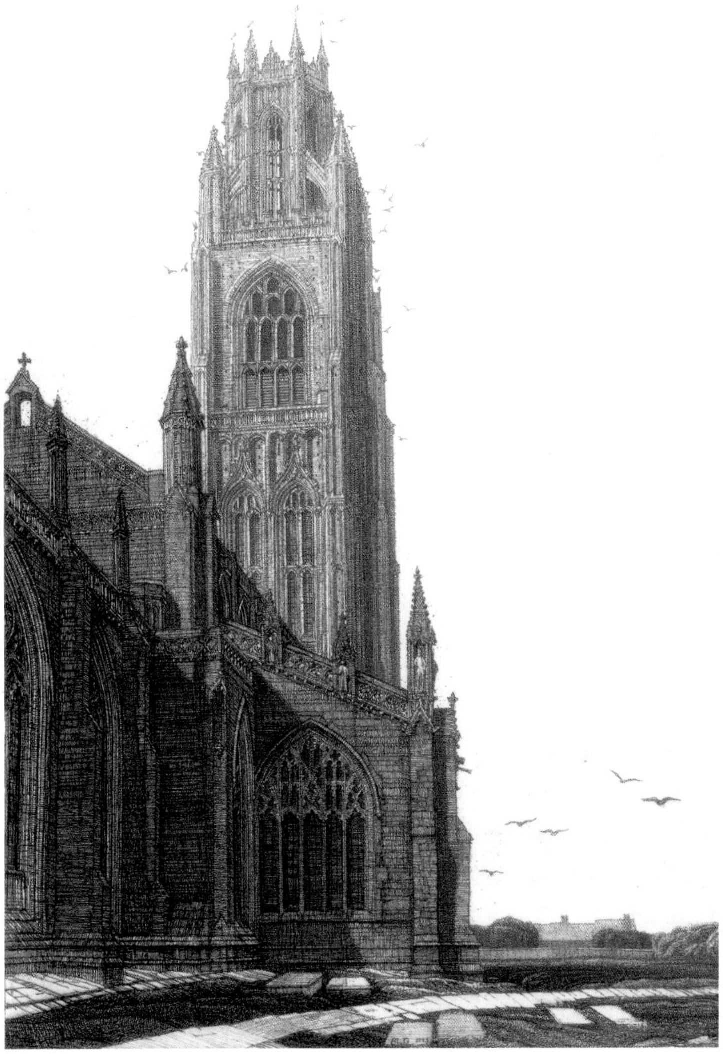

Plate 90. *St Botolph's, Boston,* 1924–25. Etching, state 5

Already he had compared himself to Blake's 'Man & the Moon, crying "More, more"'.

The counterpoint was his private happiness at home with Nina, their little son born in 1922, and a daughter a year later. (Yet even Nina, young as she was, had begun to characterise anything good or agreeable as 'very pre-war'.) The opening of 1925 found Griggs making a study for a third masterpiece – sprung this time from the intimate textures of home.

Across the lane behind Dover's House in Campden stands a tiny late gothic structure facing a noble row of almshouses. So the little building had come to be called 'the Almonry'. That hint, fertilised by the spirit of Christmas just past – and perhaps a memory of the 1901 *Highways and Byways* tailpiece evoking old Hitchin under snow – now shaped his crowning vision of an old English Perpendicular gothic high-point before the Dissolution (Plate 89).

The spectacular church fills its prospect to the top of its image and beyond. Choir, transepts, chapter house and buttressed nave rise in receding planes as a vision of Heaven itself – enlarging as they move away in refinements of snowy purity, diminishing as they return towards clarity in our earthly sight. Before a broad gothic doorway, a handful of little almoners and waits in the courtyard of this visionary *Almonry* points the theme of transcendent generosity.

Immortality had made a leading subject for Blake. It had come to the fore again a century later with Elgar's setting of *The Dream of Gerontius* in 1900. Ten years after that the elderly Henry James had written an essay asking 'Is there life after death?'. James had come down on the side of possibility, purely through analogy: the experience of having been led by his art repeatedly into dimensions not previously apparent. Since the Great War and its losses, many grieving survivors pursued the painful fascinations of spiritualism. Now Griggs's *The Almonry* was emerging through all this palimpsest of speculation and wish.

Even unfinished, an impression of *The Almonry* shown at the Royal Academy in the spring of 1925 made a sensation. More subscribers put down their names for it than the biggest Griggs edition could compass. Almost as soon as he printed the edition of eighty-two that autumn, impressions began to change hands at rising prices – from which only purchasers and dealers profited.

Before completing *The Almonry*, Griggs finished *St Botolph's, Boston* without the storm (Plate 90). He added simply a flat landscape beneath a vast open sky, and wrote to Alexander in July 1925:

> It's meant to be one of those days in the Fens near the sea when all the objects are clear & full-coloured as they are when there's much rain about. I wanted to suggest the sea air too, & the *neighbourhood* of the sea, &, dammy, I believe I've done it, & reconciled it all to *line*.

Ten days later he wrote again: 'I've got nearer to the soil of England in it, I think, than ever before.' The nightmare thunderstorm, it seemed, had all gone into the world of light. The edition of seventy-six sold out immediately. Within two years impressions would be changing hands at £120.

The new year 1926 brought the seeming promise of another visionary masterpiece. It was a city of churches rising behind outer walls to evoke the Arthurian dream-citadel of Sarras: 'hidden & mystical', Griggs wrote to Alexander in February, '& all that our highest ideals would paint it'. But this ideal proved delusive. 'It's as if I could *see* Sarras,' he wrote a month later, 'but could not hear the sound of its heavenly bells.' He laid it aside, and that autumn finished off the remaining plate of the great trio, the desolate *Fen Monastery*. Printing its edition in November and December 1926 seemed to close a circle.

* * *

As late as the War years, Campden had remained so quiet that dogs slept in its High Street at noon. No longer. Now motor traffic here as everywhere wound up the springs of noise and speed. Older residents wanted only to jog along. Their children aped the antics of various Smart Sets whose self-advertising vulgarity seemed to guarantee their success.

Again and again Griggs tried to galvanise the citizenry of Campden to defend what appeared more vital to him than to them. Some of his objects were achieved, or half-achieved. Not many of them improved Griggs's popularity with old residents whose families had tilled Campden earth time out of mind.

Gradually Griggs began wishing himself away from the High Street – into some place from which he might see the beauties of Campden and hear its church bells, without having to deal with the residents except on his terms. Such feelings fomented a dream of building his own house – of working out the perspectives of his visionary etchings in actual stone and mortar.

In the aftermath of the European War that shredded his generation's dreams, Griggs also wished to build an earthly refuge for his family. He wanted a house of local stone and fine wood to rise by the richest vernacular lights. Never mind that by then such building had become 'odd' and therefore expensive.

Then came an unprecedented threat to Campden. The entire town is overlooked from the west by Dover's Hill. The Hill held Griggs's favourite walks and the site of his engagement to Nina. In the spring of 1926 the owner of the Hill put it up for sale, with the hint that such a site invited the building of a profitable hotel.

Griggs opened a campaign to buy the Hill for the town as permanent open space. He and Nina started it with £50 they could ill afford. When the appeal was posted in the town, the postmistress observed: 'They don't rush much.' Griggs's desperate canvassing of local magnates yielded a little.

He applied to the National Trust. The secretary came down, walked the Hill and adjoining fields with Griggs, and agreed what should be purchased. But the Trust could only come in *after* a purchase was made. So Griggs himself would have to meet most of the purchase price with his own overdraft.

He hesitated not an instant. 'I will *not* give it up,' he wrote to Alexander: 'even if I become bankrupt over it, for I could retrieve, D[eo] V[olente] my own fortunes, but could never recover the Hill.' On the day of the auction, he bought Dover's Hill with every field and wood needed to protect it. The bill amounted to £4,400 (perhaps half a million pounds in today's money).

Then the National Trust announced a purchase in Suffolk that took all its current funds. Griggs was left to carry the huge burden for two years. Relief came then only through the conscience of one of the great men of the Trust, the historian G.M. Trevelyan, who at last used his private fortune to bail Griggs out.

Three months after buying Dover's Hill in the spring of 1926, the ideal site for building his house presented itself. It was a farm, with a big farmhouse and a cottage fronting on Campden's upper High Street (known as Leysbourne). Griggs would sell on the farmhouse, but keep the cottage as his secret gateway to the town.

The acreage behind was his real quarry. There, on steeply elevated land, stood an old stone barn with orchards and fields reaching west to the base of Dover's Hill. Looking east from the orchard, he could see the Perpendicular tower of Campden Parish Church and hear its bells – away from town stews.

He would build his house up there, beginning from the stone barn. He would build it on strict Arts and Crafts principles, using traditional materials and local labour, sketching his own plans as the building went on. It must be big enough to accommodate his growing family, with Nina's house servants. A separate wing rebuilding the old barn itself would become his studio, with rooms for etching materials and the large press on which he now printed the editions of his etchings with the help of an assistant.

How could the man who had just bought Dover's Hill with his overdraft – an artist in his fifties with a young family and perhaps further children to come – contemplate such building? He would manage it in the ways visionaries find, utterly mysterious to those not so driven. Griggs had sailed close to the financial wind all his life, and had survived to live decently with his family and his vision intact. The market for his etchings in 1926 was buoyant. And building so large a house by traditional methods would proceed slowly enough to spread the cost.

He would himself control the evolving design, would hire and pay the hand-picked local craftsmen individually, and would act as his own clerk of the works. The plan contained a hidden trap. There was nothing to protect Griggs the client from Griggs the visionary.

He took the precaution of consulting Norman Jewson, a pupil of Gimson. Since Gimson's death, Griggs and Jewson had shared several projects to buy and repair Campden buildings in a worthy manner – using their overdrafts to achieve spectacular results (which they then sold on). Most spectacular of all had been Jewson's purchase and repair of a remote Gloucestershire manor house called Owlpen, which but for his intervention would have been lost. He had dreamt of living there, but knew he must sell it once repaired. He was a more practical man than Griggs.

Through their repair work about Campden, Jewson and Griggs had built up a team of Cotswold craftsmen builders, all hired individually. This team were currently restoring an old Campden house for a wealthy friend. As soon as the master mason George Grove finished his work there in the summer of 1927, Griggs sent him up to build a high garden wall of select stone to protect his site's privacy. Beginning with the garden wall, Griggs said, would avoid the worry that he might not be able to afford it after the house-building began. That was Griggs the visionary of finance.

Even with such craftsmen as Grove, Griggs went up every day to inspect the work. If anything fell below his standard, he ordered it pulled out and redone. He treated his building works as he treated his etching: each was an expression of creative induction. Building this way proved slow and very expensive.

The rest of the team came up over the winter of 1927-28 to begin at the old barn. For months it looked less like a building site, one friend observed, than a barn in ruins. 'The Ruins' it then became in Griggs's thinking. He kept that name for it all, practically to the day he moved his family into the house two and a half years later. Ruins invite repair – revision – new vision for the artist.

As his studio rose out of the old barn, in the late spring of 1928 Griggs finished his etching of *Sarras* in frustration. 'The conception was a rose,' he wrote, 'but the achievement was a rose grown grey.'

He began a new etching of ruins amid trees with sheep and grass. He called it *Launds*, after an old word for 'lawns'. The tall masonry fragments were based first on a memory of Bramber Castle by the River Arun. He had drawn Bramber village for *Highways and Byways in Sussex* in 1903. The Castle fragments had seemed to guide an experiment in drypoint around 1910. Six years later he had seen similarly tall ruins at Rosegarland in Ireland. The etching of *Launds* in 1928 began in summer light. But it changed under his hand (he told a friend) to autumn: 'I was going to say "& my own Autumn".' He turned fifty-two that October.

He worried constantly at the outflow of money on the house, but could not stop himself buying quantities of choice materials. To raise more money, he sold portions of his own collection of etchings and engravings assembled over half a lifetime.

Jewson insisted on installing an experienced foreman. Edward Poole was a master mason of 'placid' temperament. Griggs summarised their contests:

Poole: 'A beam must go there; 9in. by 7in. deal would do.'
Griggs: 'Would it? Then let it be 12in. by 12in. oak, and will defy time.'
Poole: 'You'll never use that floor.'
Griggs: 'Perhaps not, but we'll have it in elm, all the same.'

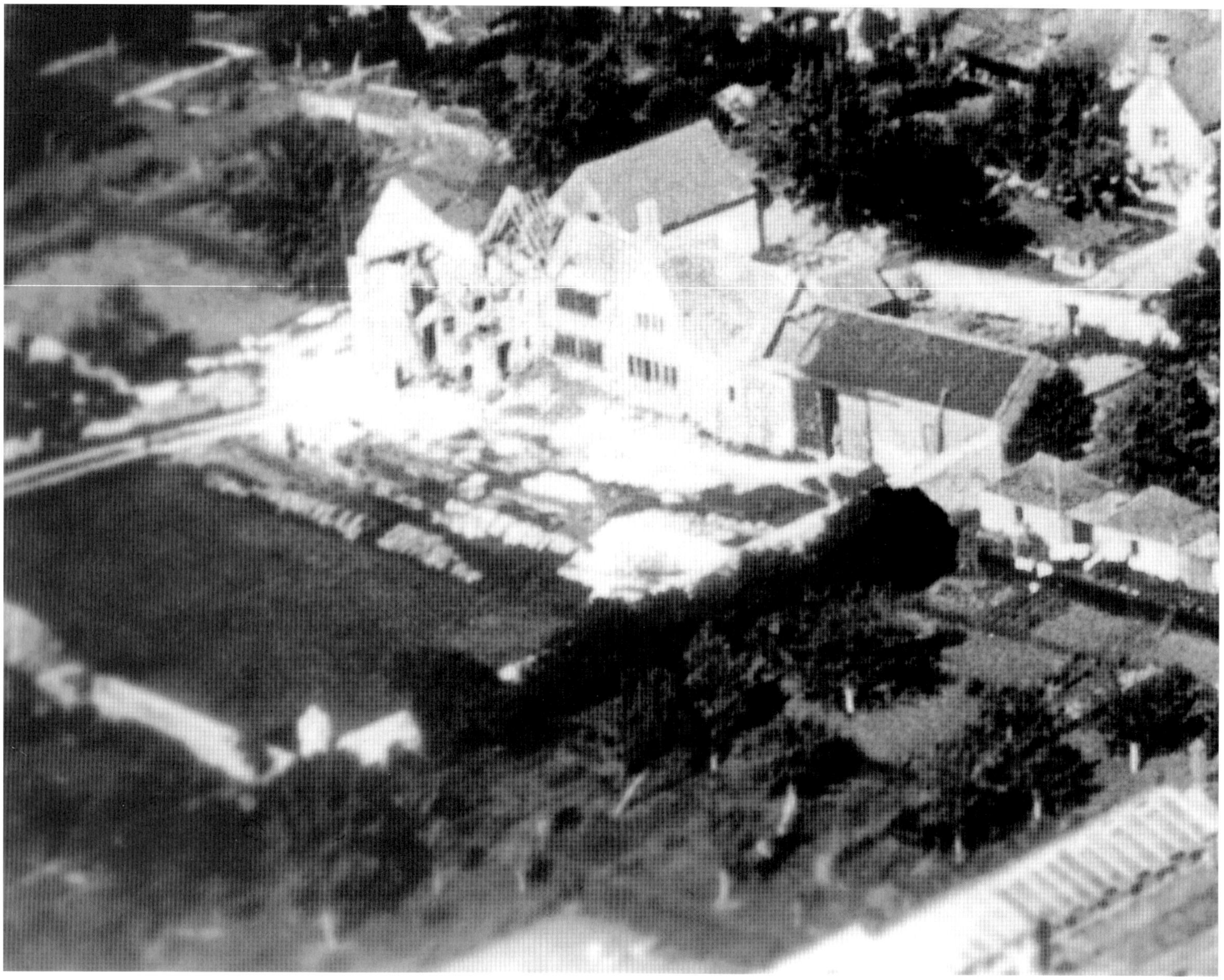

Plate 91. New Dover's House under construction, summer 1929. Photograph by Aero Films. South and west garden walls complete; length of old barn (later demolished) remains right. East range of House almost complete, ready to start the higher north range. In the courtyard lie stone and stone roofing tiles ready for use.
Mrs P. Haines

At last Poole persuaded Griggs to relinquish the ordering of materials to a professional (Plate 91). Griggs hated to lose this control, fearing the results would show in the house.

They chose a young Campden builder, Joe Warmington, willing to work with so extraordinary a client. The old-fashioned materials and methods Griggs insisted on had almost disappeared since the War. Motor lorries now brought cheaper supplies from elsewhere, and builders had grown accustomed to their use. Griggs's was to be the last great Arts and Crafts house ever built.

The private cost in anxiety and weariness shaped a new etching in the autumn of 1929. *The Maypole Inn* is Griggs's ultimate evocation of a big old hostelry going to ruin (Plate 92). The identifying maypole has lost its top (like the standing cross of *Totterne Inn* a decade earlier). The three-sided plan of this Maypole Inn round its courtyard shows alarming resemblance to the house Griggs was building. In the etched vision, rotting thatch reveals bare joists, windows are blocked up, and only a track leads to the gaping gothic doorway. Here the alms are not given but taken. In this etched courtyard through gathering dusk, a pilgrim-turned-tramp cooks his own supper over a tiny fire of wood probably torn from the decaying grandeur behind him.

As Griggs worked at his *Maypole Inn*, news came of a catastrophic crash in the American stock market. Its impact in the art world was instant. The long rise of values following the end of the War stopped dead. The entire market speculation in etchings collapsed. *The Maypole Inn* attracted only twenty-eight subscribers, most of them friends. No one had anything but praise for the image or its execution. It was a matter of 'cash-flow'.

Recoveries were predicted, and one or two appeared to begin. So Griggs allowed his men to round the house's second corner and go on to build its final wing – a drawing room of hostelry proportions with a noble library above. When Warmington presented his next interim bill of more than £1,600 in April 1930, Griggs had no money. He was forced to agree to pay interest, and had to mortgage the unfinished house. Yet its achievement seemed so close.

As the walls of the completing wing rose, across the courtyard in his new studio Griggs sat alone. He began another etching. A roofless Cistercian monastery church stands next to its grand tithe barn. In a rutted track leading to the barn, a horse and empty wagon have stopped: from the wagon a solitary figure gazes over a low range of deserted buildings. Griggs called it *Lone End*. From an edition of sixty, printed over several months by his own hard labour (now he had let his printing assistant go), his London dealer Colnaghi sold hardly more than half by the end of 1930 – and then returned several impressions from an over-ample stock.

Pressure came from a new direction. The long lease of the old house in Campden High Street was expiring. The owner wanted it back, and virtually forced Griggs to move his family into the unfinished 'New Dover's House' at the beginning of October 1930.

Plate 92. *The Maypole Inn*, 1929. Etching, state 4

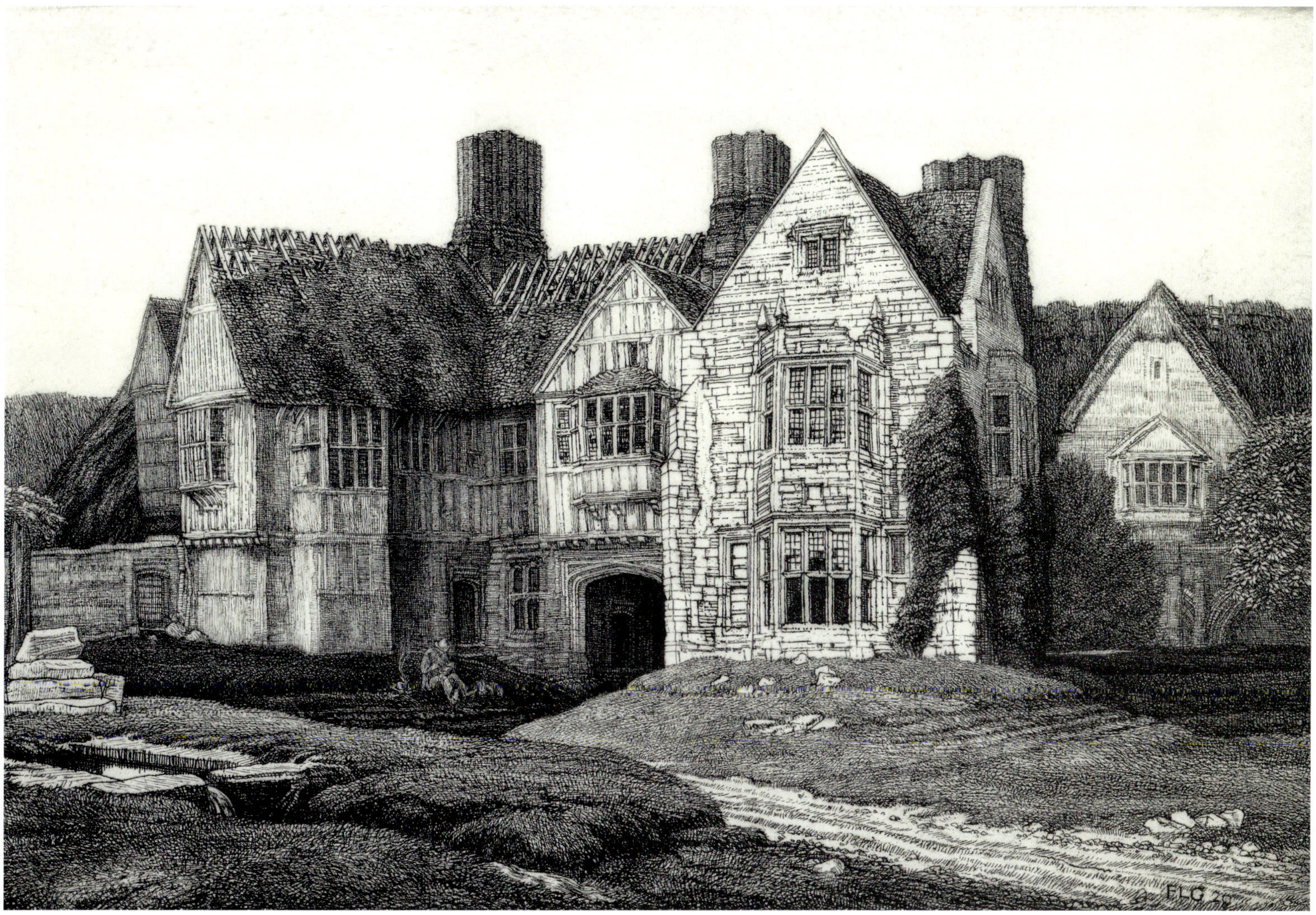

Amid much discomfort, Griggs etched a large plate of *Tattershall* (from a *Lincolnshire* drawing of a fine Perpendicular collegiate church across a summer meadow beyond a stream). He dedicated it to Samuel Palmer's son Herbert, now living his last years in western Canada – 'kind unseen friend of many years'. Herbert Palmer was moved by the dedication of Griggs's new etching as by nothing else in his old age. He wrote to Griggs:

> The etching appeals to all I love most strongly – what an accomplishment it is in the tawdry old world, given over to 'speeding' & record breaking. ... You have abundant measure of S[amuel] P[almer]'s detachment.

Griggs needed every ounce of detachment to print the edition of *Tattershall* in the new press room he could not afford to heat through the frigid January of 1931. The impressions sold hardly at all.

Three months later Nina presented a fourth child, their third daughter. Griggs loved his children deeply and tried to rejoice. He was at work on another masterly etching – of Jewson's *Owlpen*. Here distant sunlit gables seem to float between huge dark yews cut in shapes of towering menace. Below them on a terrace two modern young ladies show off their bobbed hair and short skirts in the exiguous sunlight: they are incongruous here as happiness itself.

In November 1931 Griggs was made a full Royal Academician. A 'diploma work' was expected. For a culminating etching, he turned again to the Irish drawings now fifteen years old. There lay his sketched 'dream of a startling collection of towers "the lanterns of Sarras", with the evening light coming through the lanterns & belfries'. The etching he now made of the *Lanterns* (in contrast to his etching of *Sarras* itself) emerged as the finest of all his late images (Plate 93). It showed again how much more the journey meant to Griggs than any arrival.

The sun at the horizon gains focus shining through the three towers. Across the foreground extends a bridge joining three ways. At their junction, three cowled figures show contrasting attitudes, as if disputing the way forward. As he finished it, Griggs reckoned *Lanterns of Sarras* 'my best plate'. Posterity ranks it beside *The Almonry*.

Throughout the 1930s depression years the burden of debt about his house gradually broke his health. Attempts to sell the house came to nothing. Two further children arrived, the last affected by spina bifida.

In 1934 he etched *Memory of Clavering* from the half-timbered houses seen there during the War. The etching shows sunshine after rain: but even that simple pleasure came now under the rubric of *Memory*. A final drypoint of the vanished mediaeval bridge at Evesham remained unfinished. In the distance a single tower just emerges over the shadowy gothic arches spanning undefined depths. Griggs died in June 1938.

The question dominating Griggs's art is how and where earthly vision may be found. Its vehicle for him remained the gothic and vernacular buildings of England in their traditional settings. Averse from the dreams and nightmares of the 1930s and almost alone, he carried indigenous tradition towards a Sarras receding as a mirage.

Griggs felt the richness of the past and the threat of every future with a sharpness no younger visionary was to find. Griggs's *discordia* was that which sounds through Elgar's music and Housman's poetry. By the very richness of his vision, Griggs lighted the past for visionaries yet to appear.

Opposite:
Plate 93. *Lanterns of Sarras,* 1932, Etching, state 3

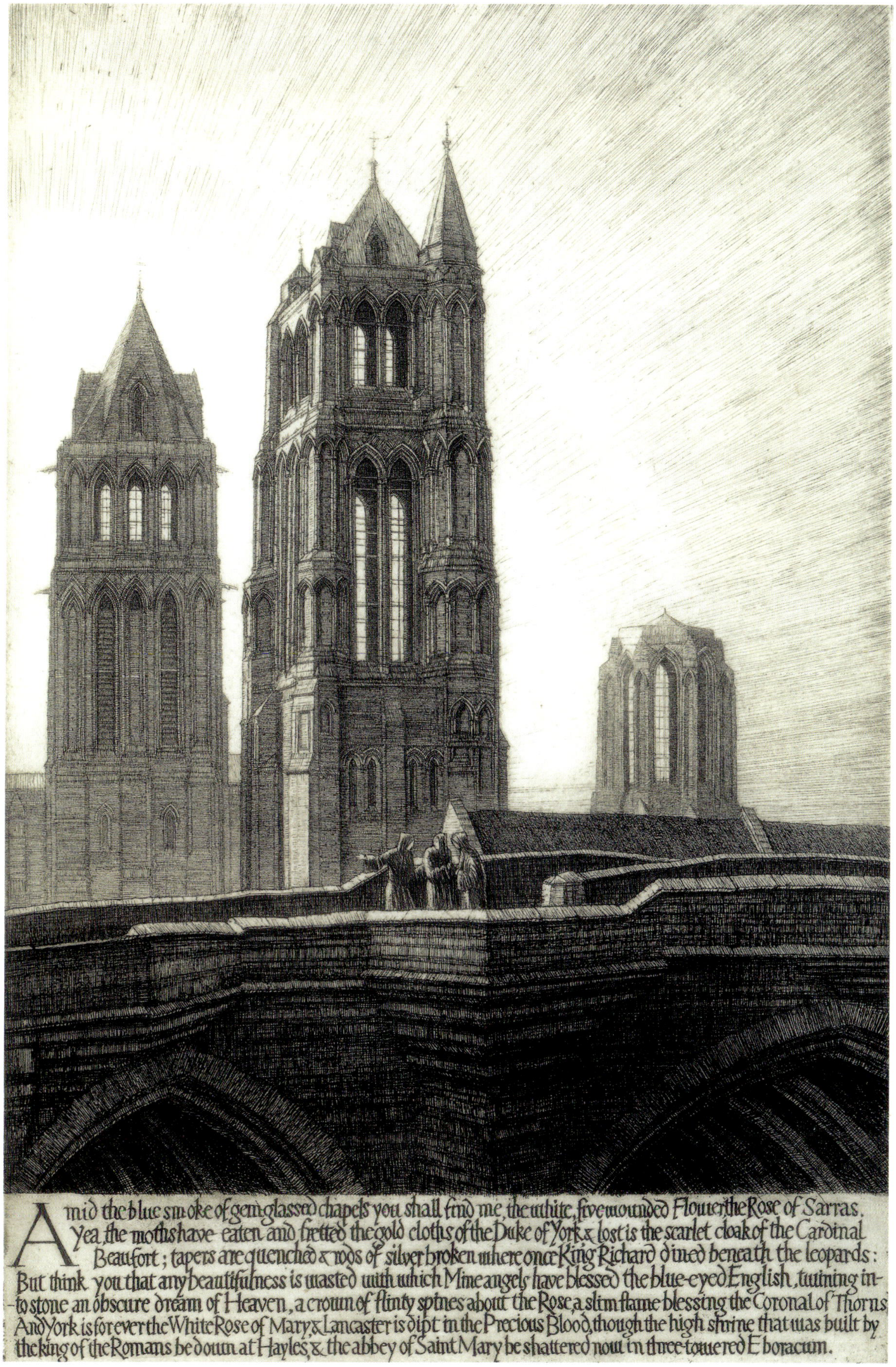
Amid the blue smoke of gem-glassed chapels you shall find me, the white, five-wounded Flower, the Rose of Sarras.
Yea, the moths have eaten and fretted the gold cloths of the Duke of York & lost is the scarlet cloak of the Cardinal
Beaufort; tapers are quenched & rods of silver broken where once King Richard dined beneath the leopards:
But think you that any beautifulness is wasted with which Mine angels have blessed the blue-eyed English, twining in-
-to stone an obscure dream of Heaven, a crown of flinty spines about the Rose, a slim flame blessing the Coronal of Thorns;
And York is for ever the White Rose of Mary & Lancaster is dipt in the Precious Blood, though the high shrine that was built by
the king of the Romans be down at Hayles, & the abbey of Saint Mary be shattered now in three-towered Eboracum.

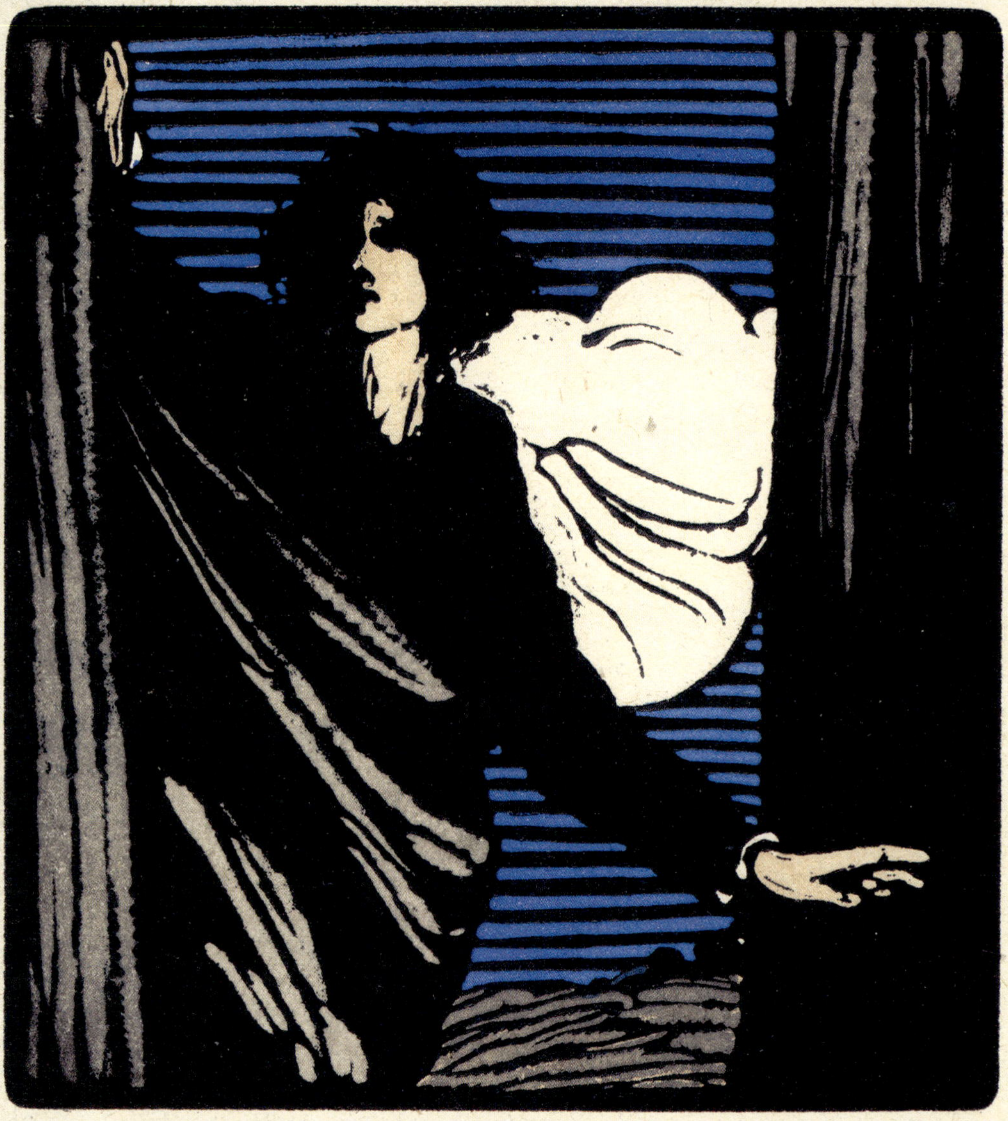

CHAPTER 4

Edward Gordon Craig (1872-1966)

Theatres of Vision

Griggs had imbued Palmer's vision with elegy. To kindle another dawn, English pastoral needed new lights. The first of them were lit by Griggs's least understood contemporary, Gordon Craig. Craig's birth at the centre of the late Victorian theatre turned his energies to the stage. Yet the mature man came to condemn that dramaturgy for the very success of its imitation. He wrote in 1913:

> The modern Realistic Theatre... drags back a curtain and exposes to our view an agitated caricature of Man and his Life, a figure gross in its attitude and hideous to look upon. ...
>
> There is no poison more swift than that which eats into the mind – this falsewitnessing Realism – this traitor of the Imagination...
>
> It has never been the purpose of art to reflect and make uglier the ugliness of things, but to transform and make the already beautiful more beautiful. And in following this purpose, art shields us with sweet influences from the dark sorrows of our weakness.[1]

Weakness is realism. Strength lies in a vision of the ideal.

Craig never much interested himself in human plots. To reduce the impact of plot on the stage, he studied every abstracting means – dance, pantomime, the old *commedia dell'arte*. He wanted to turn human figures into super-puppets to animate successions of moving patterns on the stage. What he saw behind the patterned stage-movements was light. 'The true and sole *material* of the art of the Theatre', he wrote in 1914, is '*Light* – and through Light, Movement.'[2]

Light and movement, for a child of Craig's generation, came first from the great luminaries, the sun and moon. Craig took his inspiration especially from the feminine cycles of the moon. This emerged with particular clarity in an art he made his own, wood engraving. Therein he honed his vision – both before he could take that vision into the theatre (see the young self-portrait, Plate 94, opposite), and again after the theatre as he felt rejected him (Plate 95).

The catalyst for Craig's vision in the theatre came when light could be controlled by electricity. He filled his theatres with illumination from coloured lights each separately changing – waxing, waning, combining – as he projected them through or on to gauzes stretched over the scene. These lights became his palette. Human figures were his brush-strokes. On his stages they approached closer and closer to the anonymous labourers in Palmer's valley of vision.

As Craig moved farther from conventional drama, his chances to realise his art in the theatre grew less. One of his few mature stage productions was his *Hamlet* in Moscow (1912), achieved

1. Craig, *A Living Theatre. The Gordon Craig School...* (Florence: Tipographia Giuntina, 1913). Foreword.
2. Craig, MS Daybook 3: 13 Feb 1914. Quoted in Denis Bablet, *Edward Gordon Craig*, trans Daphne Woodward (Heinemann, 1966), 176.

Opposite:
Plate 94. Self portrait from *The Page*, I, iv, April 1898. Wood engraving with hand colouring The Provost and Fellows of Eton College

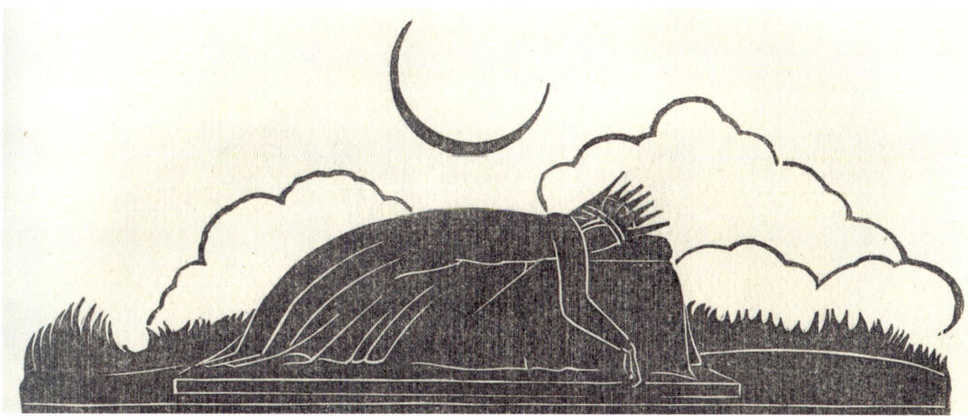

Right:
Plate 95. The murder of Gonzago, Act III scene 2 of *Hamlet:* Cranach Press, 1929. Wood engraving The Provost and Fellows of Eton College

with the vital help of Stanislavski. The *Times* correspondent observed:

> Mr Craig has the singular power of carrying the spiritual significance of words and dramatic situations beyond the actor to the scene in which he moves.

That sentence met my reading eyes in a country cottage bedroom one night. Then my attention was taken from the book by an odd light coming in at the uncurtained window. Switching off the reading lamp, I looked out on a night still and clear but for a slight haze. It seemed at once to enhance and diffuse the light of a moon that was full (as it happened) on the night of the autumn equinox.

The moon hung in the south over an old orchard field freshly mown. It was bounded at the right by a line of tall conifers receding down its western edge. Looking out over the scene at different times through the night, as the moon went westward, the tree-shadows reached gradually eastward across their moonlit stage – to touch at last its opposite side. No other movement met my eyes, yet the drama was utterly complete.

It seemed to offer an essence of Craig's vision – to mount pageants of the grandest phenomena. These are the lights and shadows which measure our lives in their patterns of change and return. Such lights, and the movements within them, made Craig's drama – his theatre's 'revelation'. 'In silence', he wrote, 'we will reveal the Movement of Things.'[3]

Whatever Gordon Craig added to the history of the theatre, to the history of pastoral vision he added the movement of time before our eyes. Thus Craig's art carried implications forward to Surrealism and beyond: disparate, often remote objects and figures brought together in unifying lights of new times and places.

* * *

Craig's parents were the most famously gifted of any parents in this book. The father, Edward Godwin (1833-1886), was a well-known architect, designer of furniture and theatrical productions. The mother was Ellen Terry (1847-1928), the greatest English actress of her time. But mother and father were not married, and they parted when their son was three.

His mother gathered round her a household of women to look after her children by Godwin – five year-old Edith, and Teddy. He wrote later about having

> ... a guilty sense of something being wrong with me... It was brought about by the so many dear women all around me. Never a word from them about my father.
>
> Every other boy I knew had his mother *and* father. Not having mine – not hearing of mine – this grave sensation of *something being wrong* grew and grew into a fixed sort of small terror.[4]

In the Victorian world of the 1870s and 1880s such a boy had a defective identity – no name to call his own. And this boy had wide public exposure from early childhood. His illegitimacy was to trouble him always.[5]

His namelessness seemed later to make a kind of inevitability about his entry into acting. From the outset he would work under pseudonyms. 'Edward Gordon Craig' was the first of them – chosen by himself in boyhood, afterwards registered by Deed Poll. It did nothing to stop his continuing self-inventions, until his pseudonyms reached a number of more than seventy. In later life he carried a pilgrim's staff in the streets of Paris.[6]

He grew up almost entirely in London. The first house he remembered was in Kensington – tall, with high ceilings and long staircases. His bedroom was at the top rear. He would be taken up there each night, after his mother had departed for the theatre, and put to bed by a servant: 'Then she would take the light away, and I would hear her descending the stairs... descending and finally, afar off, a distant door closed.'

'Afraid of the dark', he lay still. From behind the curtains came what might be a secret sound. He would call and call. If the servant returned, it was only to tuck him up, and take away the light again. Sometimes he screamed himself to exhaustion: 'My dreams were often nightmares – and often I would walk in my sleep.'[7]

When Ellen Terry was at home, she tried to be both mother and father. Her son recalled a scene several times repeated when he was about four: 'Whenever E.T. took a fancy to torture me' he was made to recite, like a miniature actor. One poem in the enforced repertory was the Nurse's Song in Blake's *Songs of Innocence*. Both mother and son remembered Teddy's refusal to complete the line 'And the hills were all covered with…' by the word 'sheep'. That was, he said, because his mother 'grew Poetic about it'.

Yet *Songs of Innocence* became so familiar to him that Blake came to seem 'one of our family'. The presence confused him, as he wrote more than sixty years later:

> But that was all a dream – and I soft and silly as a sheep, heard that piping down the valley, as a sheep hears and heeds it not. NO – but to have heard it so early was ever to hear it – toiling and in tumult and desperate and unkind, still I would hear it.
>
> Happy in the sunlight, later in my life, the sound was farther off – but it was there. Come this, come that, and pass – it *was* and never went.[8]

His early recollections contain little enough about what he called 'London's stony streets'. His memory was all for holidays in country places. For summers when he was between six and eight, his mother took Rose Cottage at Hampton Court. The recollection of it evoked in his memoirs the first in a series of lyrical set-pieces.

The rear windows of the cottage opened directly on to Bushey Park. Ted would sit on the sill, 'one leg inside, one out of the window'. From there he watched deer 'against the background of many big trees', and went out after stag fights to pick up pieces of antler. The green grass and tended spaces gave near total emancipation from the adult supervision in London streets and houses.

Then sister and brother made friends with the keeper of the Hampton Court maze. They climbed with him to the tower from which he called directions to visitors lost in the maze. The children saw how an audience can be manipulated, and began to call the directions themselves.

At the boy's school, however, the light itself seemed to search out his 'guilty sense of something being wrong with me'. 'I was made to feel very guilty about everything.' The Ten Commandments read out in morning chapel by the clergyman headmaster focused the menace:

> 'He is looking at me …'. The white light of day glared on to my guilty face, and I could hardly bear to think of what everyone was thinking of me…
>
> At evensong, with the lights less searching, I felt more at ease; but I was always unhappy in church.[9]

Too much light exposed guilt; too little could breed terror. The ideal would be to control the light, as they did in theatres where his mother acted.

In 1878, when Ted was six, his mother married an actor. She asked Ted and Edy to think of the man as their father. His stage name was Kelly, but his real name was apparently Wardell: the children themselves should use that name. It reawakened yet again the 'guilty sense of something being wrong'. Then Wardell disappeared, after Ellen Terry accepted an invitation from Henry Irving to be his acting partner at the Lyceum Theatre.

Irving (1838-1905) was coming to be recognised as the greatest actor-manager on the British stage. When Ellen Terry joined him at the end of 1878, Irving was playing Hamlet; she became his Ophelia. Ted did not see the play then, but everyone talked about it so much that the figure of Hamlet stamped its image on him.

When his former nurse married a blacksmith at Brancaster, on the north coast of Norfolk, the country opened again. Impressions of visits to Norfolk from the age of seven kept fresh all his life: the blacksmith's forge and shoeing of horses; honey bees 'under hood-like hives made of straw'; 'the cutting of corn by an old-fashioned machine' followed by a steam roller to thresh it. He was taken on day trips to Walsingham – 'as I have since learnt, the haunt of pilgrims that have come, that have gone. … So very pretty then that I don't think I want to risk going there again. Probably not one pilgrim now.'

3. Craig, 'Geometry', in *The Mask* I, no 1 (March 1908).

4. *Index to the Story of My Days: Some Memoirs of Edward Gordon Craig 1872-1907* (Hulton Press, 1957; hereinafter cited as *Index*), 48

5. Edward Anthony Craig, *Gordon Craig: the Story of his Life* (Gollancz, 1968, hereinafter cited as EAC), 333.

6. *Index*, 94.

7. Ibid, 5-7, 32-33.

8. *Index*, 25, 106. There he describes the Blake as 'a book of verses and of drawings, flowing the one through the other'. An illustrated *Songs of Innocence* would have been difficult to find in the 1870s (except in scattered pages of Gilchrist's biography of Blake). Pickering's edition of 1866 was unillustrated.

9. *Index*, 34, 37, 39-40.

One visit to Brancaster in September 1879 showed him something strange:

> I was very much alone there, because everybody had work to do... So I used to wander along to the marsh...
>
> The marsh used to fill up regularly each night or morning when the tide... overflowed the entire place, so that looking out of the window in the morning, you would wonder what had happened, because the whole place was transformed. ...
>
> And then, when the tide began to recede, I would walk down this winding path, crossing several stiles, I remember, until I reached the sea. The great beach of Brancaster was huge, and the sea was very, very far off.[10]

Such a total change in the whole setting was unmatched by anything in the city, except when scenes were shifted in the theatre. Ted was first taken by his mother to the Lyceum backstage in the following year. There he saw the heavy scenery moved, and low-lit rehearsals. It forced one to think about change – and about what might only appear to be real.

Always he learned less from words than from pictures. He remembered Irving bringing to their Kensington house a big book of pictures of the Wagner productions at Bayreuth:

> I recollect few things of those days more clearly. He sat at the large dining-room table, turning over the pages and speaking. What he said I can't recall, but I got peeps at the pictures.[11]

In the winter of 1884-85 Irving took the Lyceum company across the Atlantic for a tour of America. At Christmas he brought the twelve-year-old Ted out to join his mother. Irving gave him a book of *Robin Hood*, told in words and pictures by the American artist Howard Pyle. The printed ink drawings were heavy with north European engraving traditions from Dürer onwards.

Craig remembered Pyle's *Robin Hood* as 'one of the first books I ever read. I didn't care for reading, but this book's pictures helped, so I read it all; and for Howard Pyle I developed a thorough admiration.'[12] A few months later, when Irving took them all to Nuremberg as background for a new production of *Faust*, the city of Dürer and the mediaeval towns in Pyle's *Robin Hood* came alive for the boy.

At fifteen he was sent to Heidelberg College to learn German – and found a new romantic countryside:

> The valley of the River Neckar, which passes through Heidelberg, was a very romantic spot. It was bordered by little hills... at a certain time of year covered by a mass of lilies of the valley. ...
>
> I could not study, I could not settle down – the romance and the sentiment were too much for me.

He spent hours looking across the river at the old town and castle – because he was under arrest. 'First I was arrested for a day, being late for breakfast.' Playing with matches got him a week. Blunders in class increased the penalties. He made a moonlit escape by bicycle: and for that little escapade in October 1888 he was expelled and sent back to England. Looking back in later years, he wrote that he had 'learnt nothing, but received from the German soil and the river and the hills something which I retain till now.'[13]

Two and a half years later Irving gave him another book. It was the volume in a new 'Henry Irving Shakespeare' which contained *Hamlet*; and it was inscribed 'To the young Lord Hamlet from Henry'. The illustrations were by Gordon Browne (a son of the famous Dickens illustrator 'Phiz'). As part of a final attempt at formal education, young Craig was set to copy Gordon Browne's drawings, by way of art lessons. From his real father Godwin (who had died in 1886, still away from the family), he had clearly inherited 'an eye for proportion'. He found copying Browne's drawings 'child's play'.[14]

His mother was so worried about her son's future that it began to affect her work at the Lyceum. So in 1889 Irving did the only sensible thing: he acceded to Ellen Terry's plea to let her seventeen-year-old Ted join the Lyceum company on trial. Mother and son appeared

10. Ibid, 41-46.
11. Ibid, 51.
12. Ibid, 66.
13. Ibid, 80-81, 103.
14. Ibid, 85; EAC, 63.
15. *Index*, 152 (with the ellipsis printed thus). See also *Index*, 72.
16. *Index*, 100, 122. Herkomer's play was produced, and all of its nine performances given, in June 1889. But Craig later associated his memory of it with a visit to Bushey in Sept 1890.
17. Sir Hubert von Herkomer, *My School and My Gospel* (Archibald Constable, 1908), 198-200, 207-208. Herkomer's London lecture was given on 28 Jan 1892, a few days after Craig's twentieth birthday.

together in *The Dead Heart*, a melodrama of the French Revolution, playing a mother and her son. Audiences loved it. It ran and ran.

Irving still tried to be a father to Ted. But the young man gradually saw that Irving was all sagacity and policy, where his real father Godwin had been an artist of the imagination. When Craig began to find 'an impediment' in himself to an acting career, he identified it with the absence of his father:

> For my father might – would – have taught me what I had to discover for myself. The 'impediment' was in my bones, in my blood, which cried out vaguely that an artist is... well, not what an actor is.[15]

The longer he remained in the theatre, the stronger became the pull of his imagination – and its prompting to look beyond conventional stage drama. In 1891 young Craig saw a mimed production of *The Prodigal Son*, imported from France and suddenly popular in London: father and son were both dressed as Pierrot, the moon-struck clown of the old *commedia dell'arte*. Craig was deeply impressed. (So was Aubrey Beardsley, just Craig's age, when he saw it.)

Before that, Craig had gone with his mother and Irving to an experimental theatre actually in a country landscape. A few miles north-west of London at Bushey there was a school of art founded and run by the painter Hubert von Herkomer. He had built the school theatre to his own design. In it, with his students, he produced a 'pictorial music-play' called *An Idyl*, set in a mediaeval village. The words, music, choreography, and setting were entirely by Herkomer himself. But its real originality lay in his stage lighting.

Herkomer eliminated footlights, 'as light does not come from the ground in nature'. Instead he set electric lights behind either side of his proscenium. From there, trained stagehands varied electric currents and colours to produce endlessly changing atmospheric effects on gauze stretched across the stage at distances in front of the backcloth.

Afterwards Herkomer lectured in London on his scenic effects. Irving and Craig both attended.[16] The event was noticed by *Punch* with a sketch by Linley Sambourne (Plate 96). But Herkomer was in deadly earnest:

> Light is the most potent factor in scenic art. By its magic the most trumpery materials are transformed into priceless fabrics... and a few feet of canvas into vast distances.

He cited the Bushey production of his own *Idyl*:

> The painted sky became atmospheric by being seen through the gauze. This gauze gave me an additional surface upon which to play with colour by means of limelight. ...
>
> Clouds were reflected upon it... clouds that moved. The last rays of the sun (which had cast real shadows from the corn shocks, hedges, and trees) had ceased to illuminate the distant hillock, and the whole background was bathed in that mystic tone of grey which causes form to become indefinite, and melt together into mere tone.
>
> Then rose the great red, solemn harvest moon in the pink sky. Imperceptibly it moved upwards and gained in brilliancy as it ascended – not perpendicularly, but on a line true to nature.[17]

It was as if Herkomer had made up his mind to fill his theatre with Samuel Palmer's valley of vision – but with nature on the change. To concentrate this vision, stage action and plot were reduced to mime and lyric.

Irving thought it impractical for a commercial theatre on the scale of the

Plate 96. *'A Moonlighter at Bushey':* Hubert von Herkomer lecturing on the scenography in his student theatre, with Augustus Harris and Henry Irving in the audience. Woodcut after a drawing by Linley Sambourne for *Punch*, January 1890

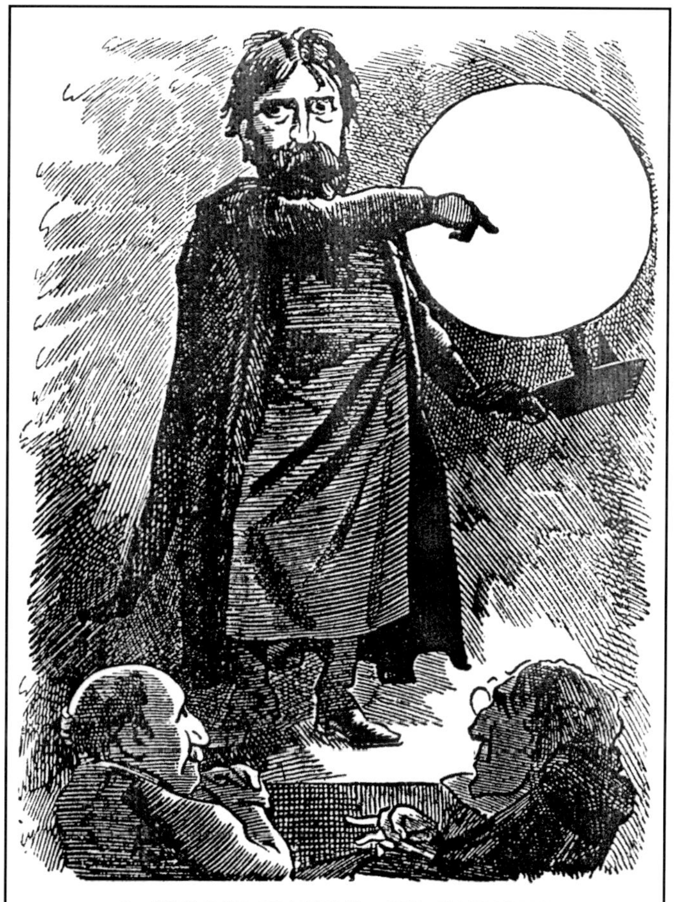

A MOONLIGHTER AT BUSHEY.
PROFESSOR H-RK-M-R, A.R.A., INSTRUCTING MASTER HENRY IRVING AND MASTER GUSSIE HARRIS HOW TO ILLUMINATE "THE INCONSTANT MOON." (*"The Moon was not like the Moon ordinarily seen on the stage."—Vide general journalistic opinion on the "Herkomer Opera."*)

Lyceum (though he did make some use of gauze). But young Craig had seen something he could not forget. More than fifty years later he wrote of seeing Herkomer's *Idyl* at Bushey: 'The day – the dark theatre – I thanked my stars. Most moving it was – perfect realism.'[18] It was the realism of nature in the eye of pastoral vision.

Herkomer had enhanced the art of stage lighting until its naturalism rivalled plot and action. Craig would take his own lighting farther, to where it could have no rival. He would control everything in his theatre – as Irving controlled everything at the Lyceum – but for this revolutionary purpose. In 1890 Craig was poor, and commanded few of the world's goods. But he was young with energy.

Craig's sense of the power of youth kept his vision intact for the whole of his maturity – if his later life could ever be so described. Was the commercial theatre built in wrong ways to accommodate him? Then he would demand its wholesale rebuilding. Craig was to pay the heaviest price for his vision. But throughout the rest of his life, extending another three-quarters of a century, it would never cross his mind to sacrifice vision to any 'practicality'.

* * *

In summers, when the Lyceum was closed, the young Craig went with provincial touring companies who billed him as 'Mr Gordon Craig (of the Lyceum Theatre)', and gave him larger roles. Private recitals beckoned in fashionable London houses. His handsome good looks brought flattering letters. One from Oscar Wilde was confiscated by his mother, but women and girls plied the waters unimpeded.

He used Irving's announcement of another American tour to ease himself out of the Lyceum. He had no plan. One of his following girls was May Gibson, whose parents were friends of his mother. May was several years his senior, and she talked him into marriage. In March 1893, two months after his twenty-first birthday, it made a fine gesture of independence. The knot was tied in a Registry Office and his mother informed by telegram. They took over a cottage his mother owned at Uxbridge (another leafy suburb west of London) and lived on savings from his Lyceum wages she had made him put by. By the autumn May was pregnant.

Loosed from regular work in the theatre, Craig's attention was taken by black-and-white illustration of radical stripe: masterful line showed how few details were indispensable. In June 1893 he bought the first instalment of Dent's new edition of *Le Morte d'Arthur* with Aubrey Beardsley's drawings. Nine months later came a sly quarterly with Beardsley as art editor, *The Yellow Book*: Craig recalled its appearance on the newspaper stand at Uxbridge as 'a blaze of yellow'. Both publications showed many of their subjects liberated by bold design.

A similar style was invading posters, taking advertising into 'art'. An exhibition of such posters from several countries was to be mounted in London the following autumn. Two new friends of Craig would contribute to it. He had met them almost by chance.

Returning from London one evening in the train, Craig had encountered James Pryde (1866-1941), a young Scottish artist whose parents knew Irving. Pryde was staying just beyond Uxbridge at Denham with his newly married sister Mabel and her husband, the young painter William Nicholson (1872-1949). Nicholson was exactly Craig's age, married to his Mabel four weeks after Ted and May. The young Nicholsons had met as students at Herkomer's school. The brothers-in-law were to form a partnership over the signature 'Beggarstaff' (a name seen one day on an old sack in a stable yard). Craig was fascinated.

In the year since his own marriage, Craig had run through most of his savings. The money disappeared faster after the birth of his daughter in April 1894. His wife took to reminding him of his duties as breadwinner. Seeing an advertisement for experienced actors to join a provincial Shakespeare tour, he found that they had not yet cast the leading male roles – including the title part in the opening vehicle, *Hamlet*. When Craig told them he had been with Irving at the Lyceum, he was given all the leading roles sight unseen.

His first thought was to ask Nicholson and Pryde to design a splendid poster. Nicholson cut

18. *Index*, 100, 107.
19. Ibid, 155. There is evidence of inspiration shared by Pryde and Craig. Both as children had been struck by the tall shapes of antique royal beds. Both later used tall architectural shapes as foils to lonely figures. But the fragmentary state of known chronology in Pryde's career makes it impossible to establish precedence – and therefore, patterns of influence one way or the other.
20. *Index*, 171.
21. Ibid, 176.
22. Ibid, 179.
23. Ibid, 164.

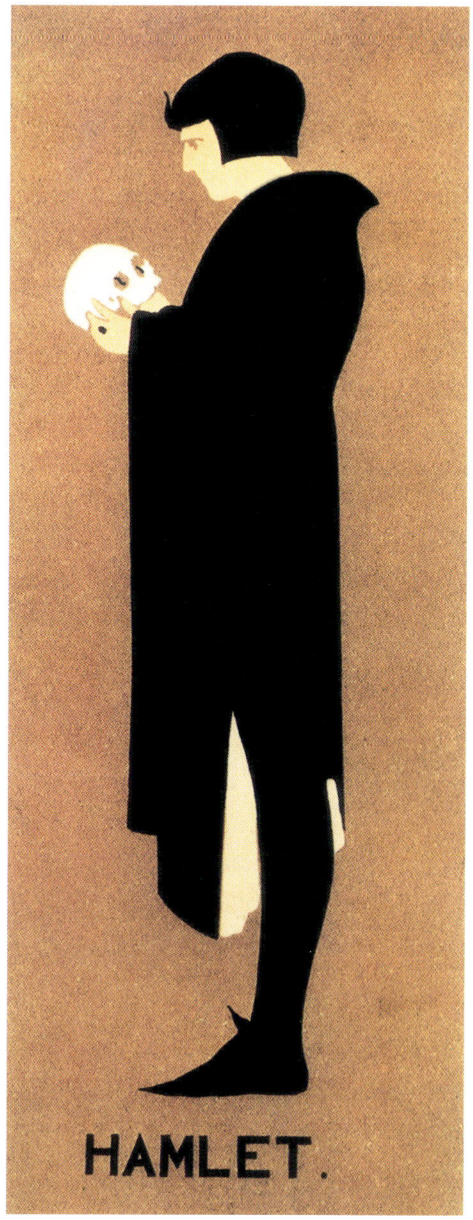

Plate 97. William Nicholson and James Pryde: *Hamlet:* poster for Gordon Craig's tour, 1894. Stencilled and cut papers

out a marvellous silhouette of Craig's tall figure holding a skull. Then he 'stencilled the life-size figure of Hamlet over and over again' on a roll of brown paper suggested by Pryde (Plate 97). (Pryde lay asleep upstairs.)[19]

The posters went up and the tour began in the autumn of 1894. Craig snatched a day to go with Nicholson to the London poster exhibition before it opened. The *Hamlet* poster was there, already attracting attention. They caught sight of Toulouse-Lautrec, in charge of the show's French section.

In late November 1894 Craig's tour reached Rugby. One night after playing Hamlet, he walked through fields to his lodging. In his room over a solitary supper, he picked up a copy of Defoe's *Robinson Crusoe*. 'Within a couple of pages I realised I had never come across anything that I loved so much in a book.' It told of a boy full of wanderlust, his father urging caution; but the boy would pursue his dream and be wrecked amid the loneliest splendours of nature (Plate 98).

When his wife bore a second child, Craig was on another tour. One of the company was an old girlfriend, Lucy Wilson. Now she would not respond to the advances of a married man. At Yarmouth on the Norfolk coast in May 1895, 'the stage door led straight out on to the sands… I would go out between the scenes [of Sardou's *La Tosca*] in my red silk dress, and sit on the sands and listen to the sea… in the moonlight.'[20] As at Brancaster in childhood, as in *Robinson Crusoe* six months ago, the sea of imagination spread before him.

A few days later, when the tour came to Ryde in the Isle of Wight, he wandered into a second-hand bookshop. There he found copies of two picture books he had owned in childhood: *The Three Bears* and *Cinderella*, both illustrated by Walter Crane in strong outlines and gentle colours. Craig bought the books again.

Yet instead of returning to his own children when the tour finished, he signed on for a third acting tour at a lower wage – because Lucy Wilson was in it. August 1895 found him 'always drawing. L.W.' He made himself ill with longing. Between tours he tried writing music (as Herkomer had done). Craig set ballads by Heine; and then 'My Father is dead, I do not know how'.[21]

During a season of badly paid acting at Chatham in the spring of 1896, he took a separate room in which to try 'to make posters *à la Beggarstaff* (utter imitation!)'.[22] When his wife heard of it, she made clear her view that he was wasting his time. In the stage company at Chatham was another old girlfriend, Jess Dorynne. She did not discourage him on account of being married.

Craig's attraction to women, and theirs to him, showed him something about himself and his acting:

> The women and girls I met took me right out of myself – I then ceased to be Hamlet – I became any character I wished to be – and hoped one or another would please one or another. For to please women became my deepest real delight – and one or two I did please. Yet often I felt it was all acting – not real.[23]

He tried a week of his own theatre-management in January 1897 at Croydon. His lavish production ideas ate up any profits in advance. At his mother's urging, Irving invited him back into the Lyceum company for a season. But Irving was running into financial trouble. In a reorganisation soon forced by his backers, Craig was one of several actors who had to be let go.

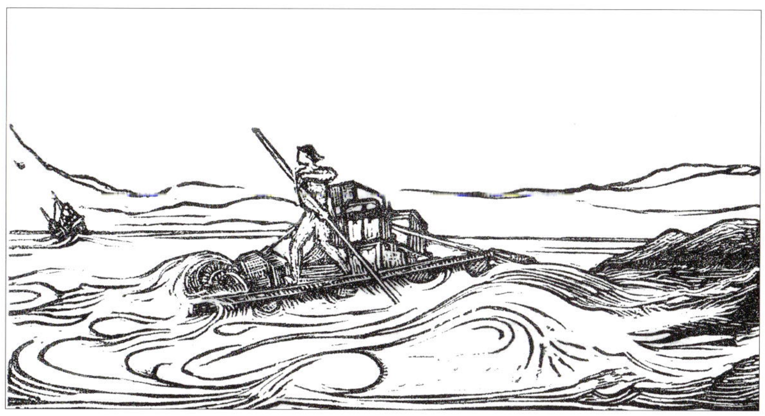

Plate 98. *Robinson Crusoe approaching the island.* Wood engraving, *c.*1938

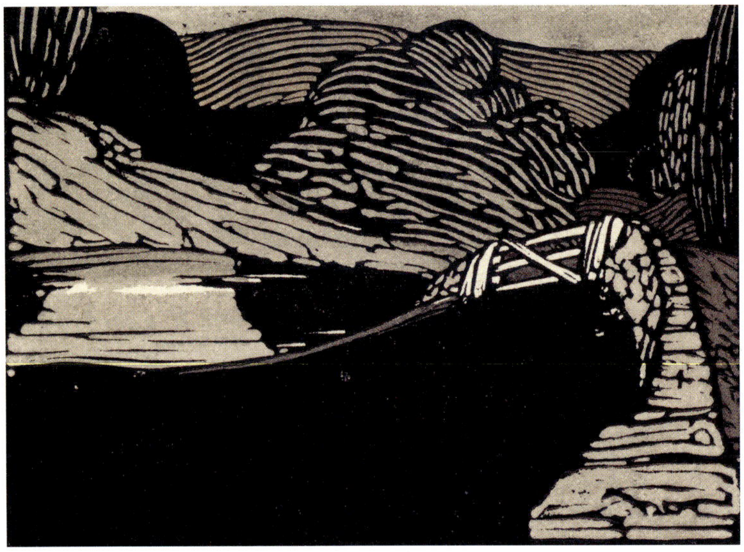

Plate 99. *The White Gate, Ednal, Cumberland,* from *The Page,* I, iv, April 1898. Wood engraving with hand colouring
The Provost and Fellows of Eton College

With his marriage nowhere, he took a rural cottage for himself at Thames Ditton, by Hampton Court. He re-named it 'Rose Cottage' after the beloved cottage of his childhood. There he welcomed Jess Dorynne and Jimmy Pryde. One day Jimmy's conversation turned on starting a magazine.

Nicholson had begun to make woodcuts.[24] He had stumbled on some crude old woodblocks (probably for chapbooks), and from them had picked up the art for himself. 'He was skilful beyond words,' Craig recalled.[25] Publishers clamoured for Nicholson's woodcuts. Could Craig teach himself to make them for his new magazine?

Craig's skill at drawing had led him to sketch actors for other magazines. His draughtsmanship might not be equal to anything on the scale of a poster, but a woodcut was something of manageable size. And engraving on wood held a secret appeal for a man of the theatre.

Nicholson made use of the white-line technique that Blake had employed in his Virgil engravings. When the block was inked across its surface for printing, what was cut away made light in darkness. Nicholson said: 'You just cut out the highlights. It's like coming into a dark room with a candle and noting what parts of things pick up the light first: then slowly you add more and more light.'[26]

It was just how you began to light a darkened stage. Engraving on wood in this way was like entering a dark theatre of the mind, where everything depended on the making of light. When Craig later recalled his first sight of a Nicholson wood engraving, he instantly associated it with his own frustration in the Victorian theatre where the 'comfortable ones' forbade change. So, 'groping – puzzled – in the midst of will-o'-the-wisps calling from all sides', wood engraving beckoned to him:

> What a blessing to be able to turn to this rather difficult craft; teach myself through its slow ways how to design scenes and how to delineate characters better… and how to keep from heart-break. And this it did teach me.[27]

Craig bought wood blocks and tools. His struggles had no success until Nicholson suggested he find a photograph where contrasts of light and dark were sharp, trace the outlines on to a block, and cut out their pattern. Craig found a profile photograph of one of his favourite revolutionary spirits, Walt Whitman. The result of this tracing and cutting was vivid: suppressed detail dramatised the character of face and beard.

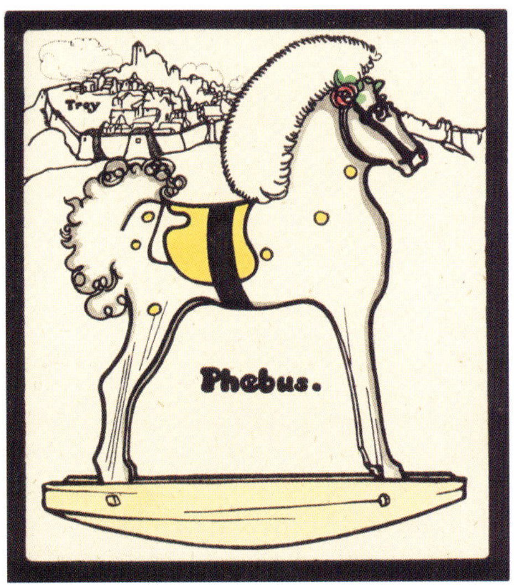

Plate 100. *Phebus,* for *The Book of Penny Toys,* from *The Page,* I, x, October 1898. Wood engraving with hand colouring
The Provost and Fellows of Eton College

By the time Irving let him go, Craig had cut about ten blocks. They suggested a character for his magazine. It would be a limited-edition monthly, with illustrations and texts all made and assembled by Craig under a panoply of fresh pseudonyms. Thus the whole thing would hold up so many mirrors to the self Craig was trying to see. He would call it *The Page.*

The fourth number, in April 1898, carried two woodcuts of astonishing mastery from a hand of no more than eighteen months' practice. One is the ideal self-portrait at the beginning of this chapter: a long-haired young romantic parting stage curtains to reveal himself side-lit against the richest fleecy cloud of nature.

The other is a landscape (Plate 99). White lines in quasi-parallel (an old technique broadened) curve to fill and shape areas of contrasting textures. The lines and shapes may limp here and there, but there is real resource in suggesting perspectives. The foreground hillock of solid black under the curving Lakeland stone wall and gate takes Beardsley's boldness into pastoral landscape. Many of Craig's images in *The Page* were enhanced by restrained hand-colouring applied to every copy by himself and Jess Dorynne.

For a holiday in June he went to the Suffolk coast. Jess joined him at Dunwich, eaten away by the sea: 'A street of not more than some ten or twelve cottages', Craig remembered, 'led up to the edge of the cliff, and there, far below, the sea making a queer noise. Into one of these cottages we

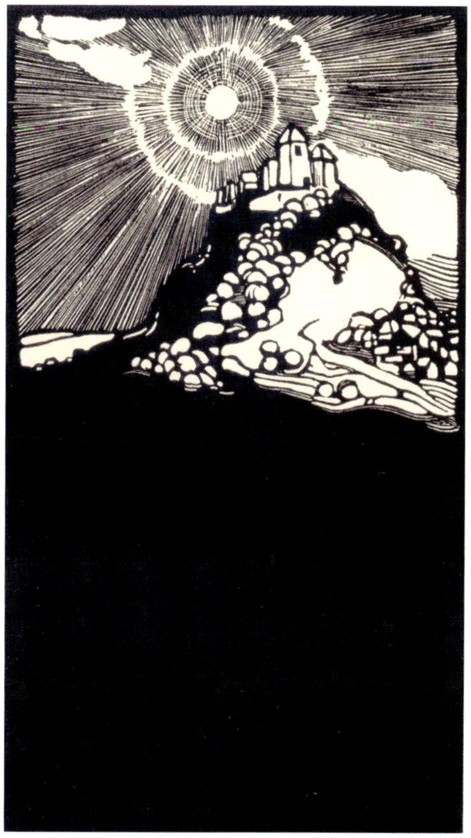

Plate 101. Book-plate from *The Page,* I, xii, December 1898. Wood engraving
The Provost and Fellows of Eton College

stepped.' They were pursued by detectives hired by his wife. He did not care: 'I let them do as they wished – the whole crowd. The moral wife, the moral mother-in-law, the moral lawyers…'.[28]

Jess vowed to stand by him. After they returned to London he found another Rose Cottage, this time at Hackbridge in Surrey. From there they could issue *The Page* 'At the Sign of the Rose'. The July number had published his wood engraving of a Dumas character in bold outline, facing water and a headland with the stance of Robinson Crusoe. The September magazine printed a thought attributed to Robert Louis Stevenson: 'Never allow your mind to dwell on your own misconduct: that is ruin. … You will always do wrong, you must get used to that.'

The October issue carried some childlike verses for '*The Book of Penny Toys*: an unpublished folio'. Craig conceived it as a present for his children. His wife would not allow them to visit when Jess was about, which she usually was. Remembering the wooden toys of his own childhood, he had bought old ones from gypsies for a penny each, and made woodcuts of them – mostly in outlines brilliantly expressive of the wood. If the child is in them, so is the man. Labelling the rocking horse 'Phebus' and the walled city 'Troy' raises a juxtaposition of ideas which can point forwards both to Surrealism and to Pop-art (Plate 100).

The December 1898 *Page* carried an engraving to extend Craig's romantic vision (Plate 101). From a solid black bottom half rises a rock-strewn hill crowned by a little towered town. White clouds yield to radiant beams from a central sun. A dozen years later Craig would write: 'If there is a symbol of heaven that I can bend my knee to it is the sky, if there is a symbol of God, the Sun.'

Yet *The Page*, at the end of its first year as a monthly, was threatening to become a sorcerer's apprentice. With the new year 1899 he converted it to a thicker quarterly. The first 'double issue' gave a page to Walt Whitman. At the top a woodcut (signed with Craig's legal name) shows another facet of his invention (Plate 102). 'Idly dreaming that grey would be an addition to black and white, I began to cut fine lines close together which would form a grey when printed.'[29] It recalled the advice given to Griggs by Philip Webb for drawing nature. The lines to print grey Craig cut closer and straighter than those to print black. Grey softens the poet's figure as he gazes towards black-printed trees and cloud-capped towers of romance. Below the image Craig prints a visionary passage attributed to Whitman:

> Out of the same silent beauteous miracles that envelope and fuse me – trees, water, grass, sunlight, and early frost – the one I am looking at most to-day is the sky.
>
> … As noon approaches the colour gets lighter, for a spell till sundown – which last I watch dazzling through the interstices of a knoll of big trees… the transparent shadows, shafts, sparkle, and vivid colours…

Here speaks a spirit kindred to Griggs and Hyde and Palmer.

Yet Craig remained restless. Through the summer of 1899, in a holiday cottage at Cleeve in

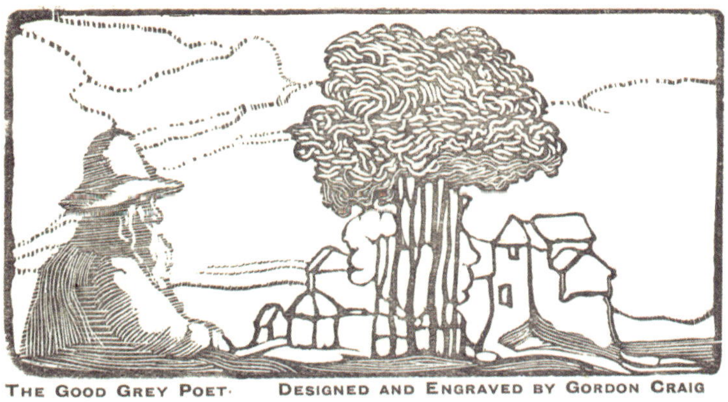

Plate 102. *The Good Grey Poet* from *The Page,* II, i, 1899. Wood engraving
The Provost and Fellows of Eton College

24. Most sources associate Nicholson's first woodcuts with his life at Denham, where Craig met him in 1893. But Nicholson's first real woodcut seems to have been made in the summer of 1896. See Andrew Nicholson, ed., *William Nicholson: painter* (Giles de la Mare, 1996), 17, 57*f.* Craig made clear that Nicholson was his only instructor in woodcutting. See Craig, *Woodcuts and Some Words* (Dent, 1924), 8.
25. *Woodcuts and Some Words*, 8
26. Quoted in Edward A. Craig, Introduction to Daniel Defoe, *The Life and Strange Surprising Adventures of Robinson Crusoe*, illustrated by Edward Gordon Craig (Basilisk Press, 1979), 15.
27. *Woodcuts and Some Words*, 21, 22, 25-26.
28. *Index*, 198-199.
29. *Woodcuts and Some Words*, 14.

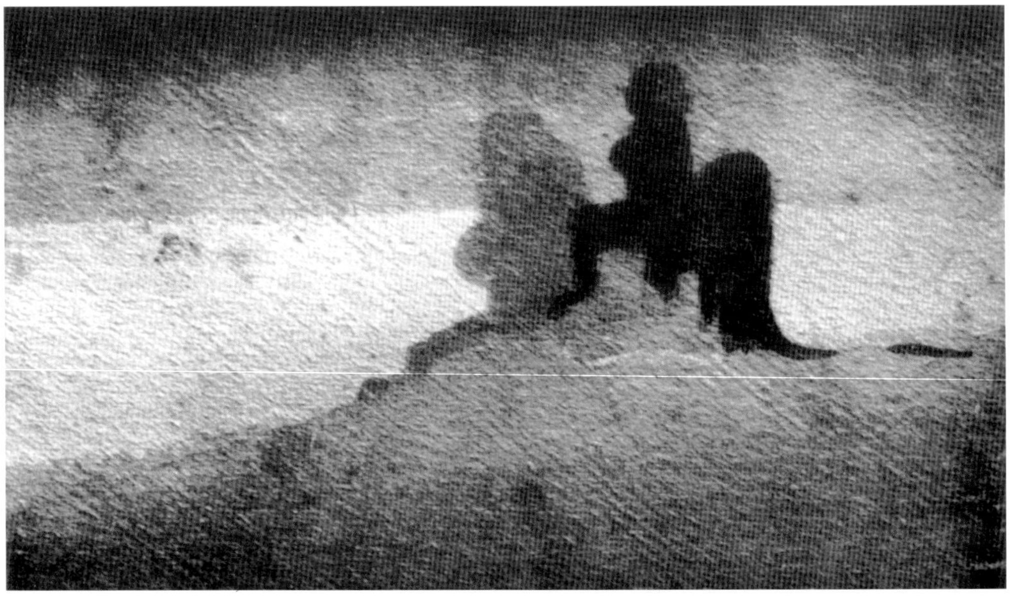

Plate 103. Sketch of a set design for Ibsen's *Peer Gynt*, 1899. Oil on paper

Somerset, he set himself to read Nietzsche, Wagner, Goethe, and Ibsen – 'and to think about that which I loved beyond all other things – theatre – *my theatre*.'[30] Suddenly he saw himself as Ibsen's Peer Gynt. On Broadfield Downs through long afternoons, looking at cloud formations away to the distant sea, he painted shapes which sought to abstract the stage back towards nature (Plate 103).

* * *

One of the advertisements printed at the end of *The Page* for February 1900 announces a 'Purcell Operatic Society'. The first production is to be *Dido and Æneas*, its 'stage director' Gordon Craig.

The roots of the enterprise lay in a walk over Hampstead Heath with another friend, the musician Martin Shaw. Shaw had enthused over Bach's *St Matthew Passion*, which Craig did not know. When they came to the heathside inn Jack Straw's Castle, Shaw found a piano and played and sang enough of Bach's masterpiece to fascinate his friend. Craig later described the vision that this music raised in him:

> Great flights of steps, crowds of moving figures, crowds that opened up as a single figure ascended to his destruction, figures wandering in darkness, shafts of light appearing as great chords brought them forth, pink skies turning blue, then to purple and indigo, against which a solitary figure stood out in gold.[31]

It was far from any conventional stage drama – closer to Herkomer's illuminations or the broad textures of wood engraving: choric contrasts of one against many, their movements defined in changing lights and colours.

Craig's staging of *Dido and Æneas* used no elaborate sets or gas footlights, but gauzes and electric lights as Herkomer had used them at Bushey. Again Craig went farther: 'I'll make a dance of arms', he wrote to Martin Shaw, 'white *white* arms – the rest of the scene dark – and out of it, the voices – with arm accompaniment...'.[32] He lay awake at night 'watching the shadows on the walls and ceiling', as the child Samuel Palmer had watched them in his nursery ninety years earlier.

Craig devised and controlled every detail of his production, even as Herkomer had done: stage proscenium, settings, costumes, figure movements, lighting. An elaborate printed programme was illustrated with his woodcuts. One of them shows the shore of Æneas' shipwreck, as seen from the Witch's cave. On the stage Craig used old grey clothes to suggest 'some long, low waste of dunes', such as might have confronted Robinson Crusoe.

The production of *Dido and Æneas* (supported by Ellen Terry and a few backers) made a *succès d'estime* at its little theatre in Hampstead. The next year a *Masque of Love* was added: it was devised by Craig for Purcell's *Diocletion* music.

30. *Index*, 200.
31. EAC, 115.
32. Ibid, 117-118.
33. 'The Masque of Love': summary of action by Christopher St John (a lifelong companion of Craig's sister Edith), printed in the *Souvenir* programme designed by Craig.
34. EAC, 85
35. Ibid, 152

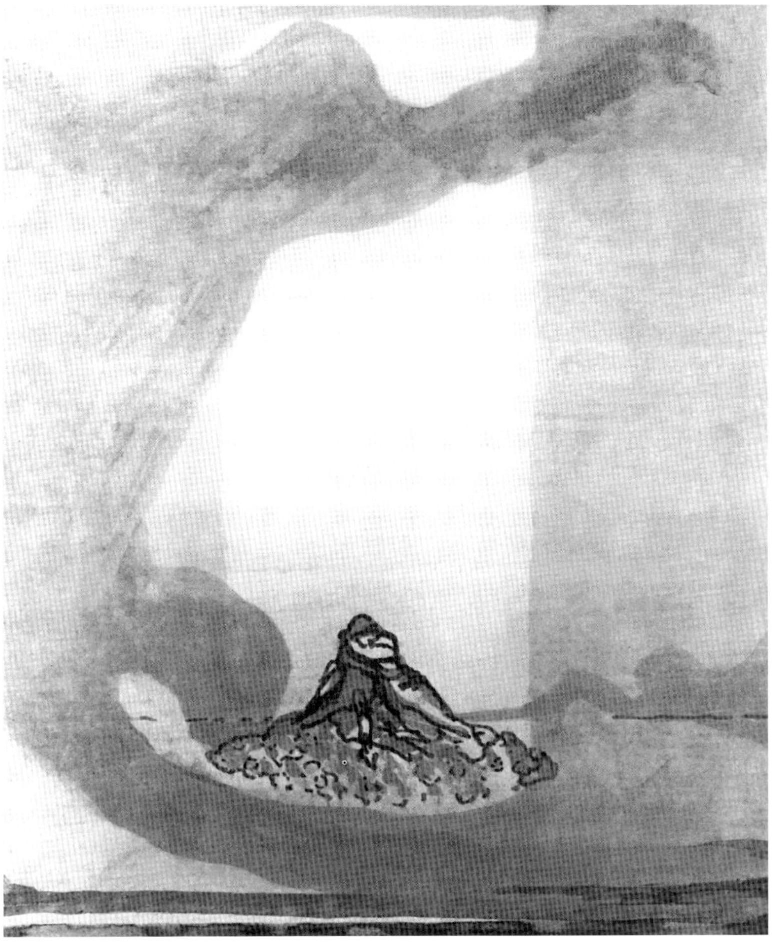

Plate 104. *Acis and Galatea: Wretched Lovers* menaced by the giant Polyphemus, from the Souvenir programme, 1902

Craig's *Masque of Love* is set in a 'palace of shadows'. Behind 'the bars of an immense window', Cupid and the children with him appear as jailers 'to do the god's bidding unvexed by whip or chain'. They call nymphs and fauns from the wood. Comus and Bacchus appear, with masks and disguises. At the fall of darkness, the procession of Love's captives enters 'between sleeping and waking... drugged by one only less powerful than Death'. To convince them that 'their slavery is perfect freedom', Love has their fetters struck off by the children. At the reappearance of Bacchus, 'the maskers resume their chains' – but with a final reversing illusion that Captivity itself has been enslaved.[33]

The new printed programme (March 1901) showed up the limitation of woodcuts, when linearity is called upon to suggest changing lights and shadows. Then Craig recalled another trick of Nicholson's:

> You scribbled and scribbled away at an idea, then put a piece of black (not blue) transfer paper under the scribble, and, selecting certain lines from amongst the scribbles, transferred them to a piece of sugar paper; then, with a paint brush dipped in water, you went over these few lines and gave them a soft edge; the result was delightful, and so simple.[34]

The simplicity lay in the way the process induced and shaped an idea which might not otherwise have emerged. Craig added areas of wash among his lines – again with deft success.

The quick power of Craig's wash drawing went far to focus the next production of the Purcell Operatic Society in 1902, Handel's *Acis and Galatea*. Handel's third character is the monster Polyphemus. He seemed to rise before Craig's eyes one night in the Lyceum after a rehearsal. As the stage-hands moved about the darkened stage, the single 'working light' cast their shapes in huge shadows. Out of those shadows Craig created his Polyphemus from 'the cunning adjustment of shadows over light' (as Max Beerbohm described it): 'the only real and impressive giant ever seen on any stage'.[35] The sheer scale of the shadow expanded character into setting (Plate 104).

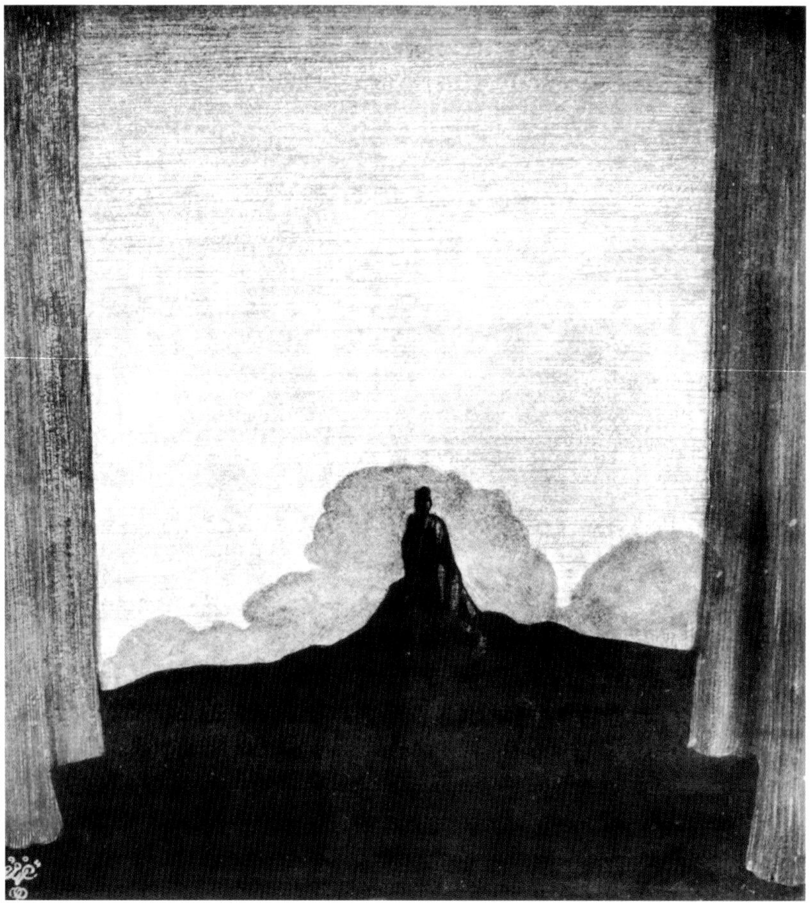

Plate 105. *Hamlet,* Act V, scene ii, 1904. Wash drawing

Ellen Terry was just terminating her long partnership with Irving (since his later productions had held less and less for her). So she took the Imperial Theatre in Westminster – rather remote from theatreland – to let her Ted loose on two plays. *Much Ado About Nothing* was repertory to fall back on. Before it would come Ellen Terry's first venture into 'modern drama', Ibsen's *The Vikings*: 'I was not thinking so much of the play for me', she wrote, 'as for my son.'[36]

He demanded sweeping changes to the theatre – practically reconstructing its proscenium and other parts of the building. Yet even then the commercial theatre would not yield Craig the control his vision demanded. Three weeks after *The Vikings* opened, it began to lose money. His mother closed the theatre for a fortnight to bring on *Much Ado*. To help his ideas for this, Craig bought a 1545 folio of architectural designs by Sebastiano Serlio. He would treasure it for the rest of his life.

Much Ado About Nothing had to be cobbled together with almost no money remaining from the *Vikings* expenditure. It fared no better, and before the end of June 1903 the little season closed with sharp losses. The only lesson Craig drew from it all was a perceived need for wholesale re-education: 'I announced that I would open a School for the Art of the Theatre. This did not interest anybody.'[37] He sketched a Masque of Hunger and a Masque of Lunatics in powerful wash drawings, without any prospect of staging either.

Craig's few briefly running productions had none the less attracted a few influential people. One was the young diplomat and aesthete, Count Harry Kessler (1868-1937). The son of a German banker (who had been recently ennobled) and an Anglo-Irish mother, Kessler lived at Weimar and cast a wide net. He had seen the Purcell Society productions. Now he wrote of *The Vikings*:

> The stage seems to be hung all round with cloths which are almost invisible behind the changing light effects and coloured veils of light. … The action… takes place in this (so to speak) sidereal infinity.[38]

He saw in Craig's *Much Ado* the same 'almost fanatical simplification and… turning away from realism'.

36. Ellen Terry, *The Story of My Life* (Hutchinson, 1908), 325.
37. *Index*, 248.
38. Quoted in Lindsay M. Newman, *The Correspondence of Edward Gordon Craig and Count Harry Kessler 1903-1937* (W.S. Maney, 1995), 6.
39. *Index*, 260, 263.
40. 15 Feb 1907 to Martin Shaw (EAC, 227).

Kessler thought Craig would be an ideal designer for the lyric plays of his friend Hugo von Hofmannsthal. Craig accepted an invitation to visit Berlin in the summer of 1904. (It offered a convenient escape from his wife, who had commenced an action for divorce to involve him in endless money payments.) Craig took with him deft drawings for a production of *Hamlet*: one showed the solitary visionary silhouetted against refulgent nature (Plate 105). But Berlin, like London, would not give him the total control his art craved.

The real result of Craig's Berlin visit was a meeting and instant affair with the American dancer Isadora Duncan. She was revolutionising the dance in exactly the ways Craig wanted to revolutionise the stage. He wrote:

> She threw away ballet skirts and ballet thoughts. … She put on some bits of stuff which when hung upon a peg looked more like torn rags than anything else; when she put them on they became transformed… One had but to see her dance for one's thoughts to wing their way, as it were, with the fresh air.

He connected her to Blake's 'Piping down the valleys wild', and added: 'The whole great singing follows.'[39] So it did for a season.

In March 1905 Kessler asked Craig to design a production for Hofmannsthal's version of *Elektra* to star the great Italian actress Eleanore Duse. Craig's wash drawing raised a grand hooded figure, defined in solitude by distant dim figure-groups suggesting a sort of choreographic scenery. But Duse put it all off, fearing perhaps that the monumentality of such a set as Craig had washed in behind the crowd would prove hard to move from one theatre to another for her tours.

Eighteen months later, in the summer of 1906, Craig designed a set for Duse's performance of Ibsen's *Rosmersholm* – 'graduated streaks of colour, indigo merging into ultramarine, into Russian green'. His set caged the light in another tall barred window at the back (as in *The Masque of Love*). Again it hinted at the prison of human relations.

Craig's set made a sensation when built for Duse's production in Florence. But when transferred to Nice, its proportions were brutally altered for the theatre there. Craig exploded with rage, cursing everyone including Duse for letting it happen. Duse is said to have retorted: 'What they have done to your scene they have always done to my art.' She refused to work with Craig any more. So a third nation's theatre rejected him.

A week after the angry parting, Craig wrote as he watched a star in the night sky beyond his window: 'Slowly but surely, just as that star outside, … I shall pass out of the Theatre to the new Land of Beauty. A place of my own creating.'[40] He was just thirty-five.

He turned back to graphic art. He took up dry-pointing on copper; and a year later, etching. The magnetism of Italy brought him back to Florence in February and March 1907. Italy was the home of all that Craig valued most in the heritage of stage performance – dance, mime, *commedia dell'arte*, Serlio. 'It was then that my hour struck.'

Walking at dusk among the tall old buildings of Florence, with every sense sharpened by solitude and loss, he suddenly saw 'the whole city – one marvel of architecture'. It reminded him of designs by Serlio for a stage floor in squares blackened to show where walls should stand (Plate 106). From this, Craig thought of a floor where the squares could be raised or lowered

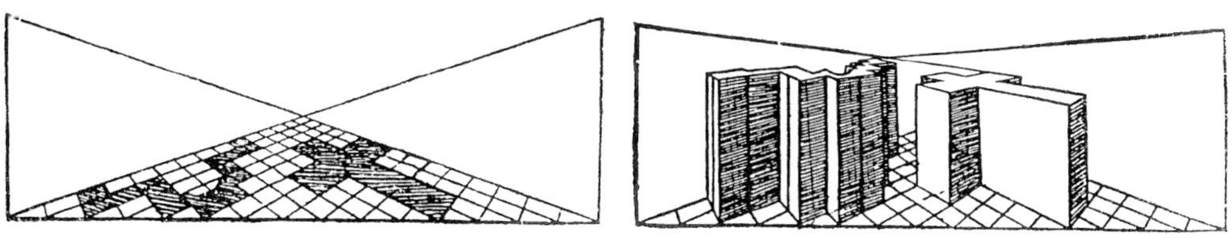

Plate 106. Sebastiano Serlio: Designs to show screens rising from a stage floor, from *Five Books of Architecture,* 1545. Wood engravings

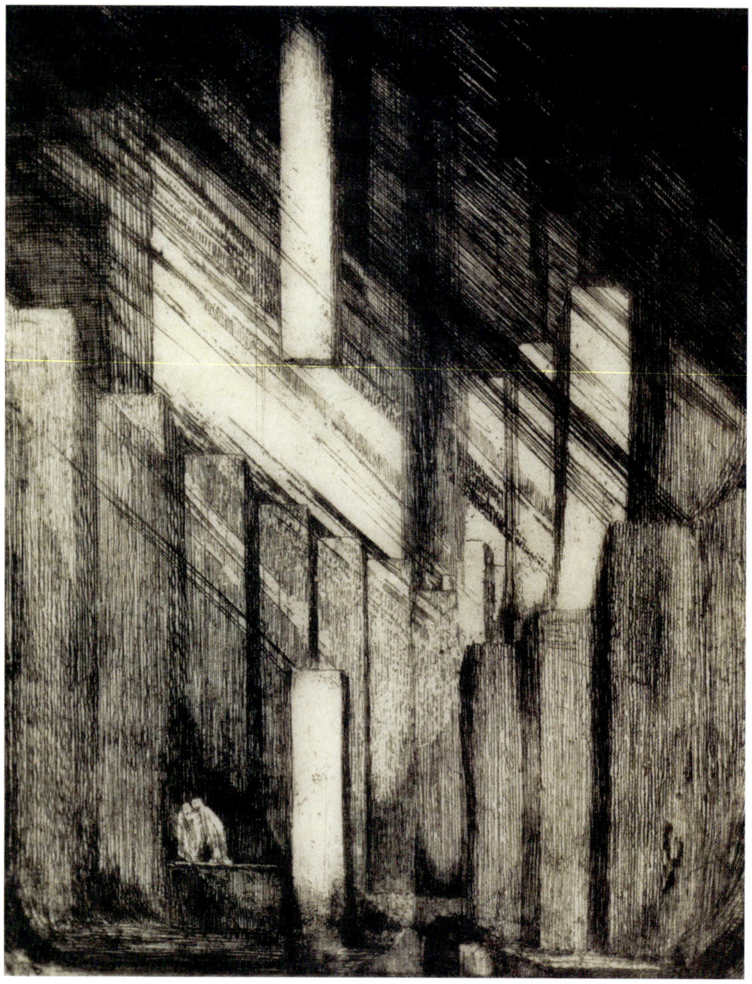

Plate 107. Study of stage lighting, 1907. Etching The Provost and Fellows of Eton College

at will: to make 'steps – platforms or seats… deep wells – open spaces – raised squares of all sizes – raised walls'. Answering squares might descend from above. Craig used his skill at etching to study effects in raking light and shadows (Plate 107).

In these years Picasso, a decade younger than Craig, was beginning to experiment with Cubism. There is no evidence that Craig knew of it, or of Picasso then. But Craig's idea is literal cubism. The thought of it inspired a description of his own creative process – nearly abstract, yet rooted in his sense of protean nature:

> The place is without form… Even as we watch, in the very centre of that void a single atom seems to stir – to rise – it ascends like the awakening of a thought in a dream… Near it, yet further back, a second and third atom seems to have come into a half existence…
>
> Some spirit seems to work there in the space, as in a gentle mind – A wind which blows open the void and calls it to life – And now, to right and to left, one chain of life moves like a sea before us, while slowly breaking from atoms into pairs, slowly shapes, all alike, none less nor more than another, continue to arise in endless numbers… mounting one higher than another, others falling, until there stand before us vast columns of shapes, all single yet all united – none resting. Until like a dew it settles – no more – enough.
>
> … As I write it is not easy to refrain from singing – the moment is the most lovely the most hallowed in my life – For in a few moments I shall have given birth to that which has for a long while been preparing – far back before I was born, and all during my life.[41]

Those words practically evoke the act of procreation. They can suggest the double helix in which the discovery of DNA was to be expressed after Craig's time. Yet his thinking is for the stage. And thus, before all his near-abstractions, move the human figures on which both mime and drama depend.

None of it found any permanent place in the commercial theatre of Craig's time. He was to pursue his later visions largely on a model stage. He translated the rising and falling squares into vertical blocks and screens. To suggest actions, he carved little profile-figures in low relief to be moved about at will. Yet the figures move less in dramatic action than as elements in changing scenic pictures.

In Craig's model stage and figures, the poet Yeats recognised an aid to the very conceiving of his own poetic dramas. With Craig's little stage, Yeats wrote:

> I can all but 'produce' my play as I write it, moving hither and thither little figures of cardboard through gay or solemn light and shade, allowing the scene to give the words and the words the scene.[42]

But Yeats' plays exerted no more direct influence in the commercial theatre than Craig's ideas and designs had done.

The best advertisement for Craig's work, and the fairest promise of income, lay in a new monthly magazine he now devised. To create the illusion of strength in numbers, he invented a fresh range of pseudonyms to represent fictitious 'correspondents' and 'stage managers' posted across Europe. Each must have an individuality: and there were so many that he cut them out in little cardboard figures to stand on a shelf and remind him of who they all were.[43] Everything recommended the title he chose for the new magazine: *The Mask*.

The first number, published in March 1908, opens with a Craig woodcut of a hill town illuminated in the rays of a low sun. It heads an article under his own name entitled 'The Artists of the Theatre of the Future'. The young idealist should aim not at acting, but at stage-

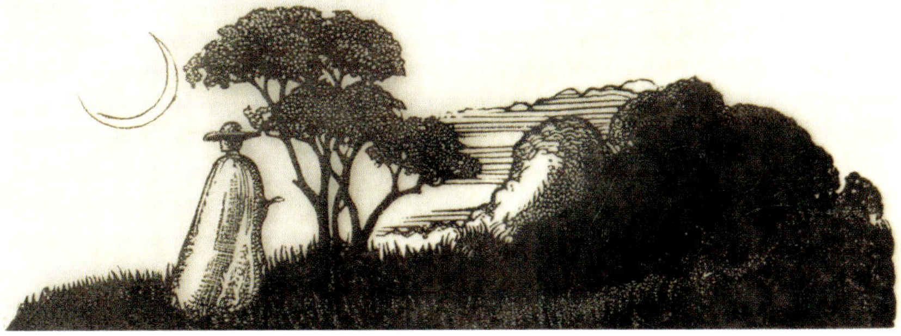

Plate 108. A pastoral poet, 1907. Wood engraving

managing and designing. Craig instances *Macbeth*, and draws out two opposing entities:

> I see a lofty and steep rock, and I see a moist cloud which envelops the head of this rock. That is to say, a place for fierce and warlike men to inhabit, a place for phantoms to nest in. Ultimately this moisture will destroy the men.

The entities dictate two colours – brown for the rock, grey for the mist. 'Touch not a single other colour through your whole progress of designing your scene and your costumes, yet forget not that each colour contains many variations.' The aim of vision, he asserts, is 'not to *reproduce* nature, but to *suggest* some of her most beautiful and living ways'.[44]

Pastoral vision emerges directly in a Craig headpiece for the second issue of *The Mask* (Plate 108). Here the cloaked visionary contemplates a new moon while his prospect seems still partly sunlit. So it touches back to Samuel Palmer's *Valley Thick with Corn*.

The Mask made an impact across theatrical Europe. From Berlin came an overture from Max Reinhardt for a Craig production of *King Lear*, to be followed by the *Oresteia*. In London Beerbohm Tree wanted to produce his *Macbeth*. From Moscow Stanislavski telegraphed an invitation to come and discuss a production of his choice. Only the last came to anything, and Craig chose *Hamlet*. It would become his testament in the theatre.

The Moscow *Hamlet* occupied nearly four years in its making. Through repeated visits Craig exhaustively discussed every scene with Stanislavski. Each costume and property and set had to be especially made to Craig's design. The total cost of the production ate up £14,000.

Craig's idea was to go beyond the words – to advance (as he characterised it) from 'impersonation' to 'representation'. The actors would approach his idealised concept of an 'Übermarionette'. (Marionettes, he wrote, might be stage 'men without egotism' – a power reserved in Craig's view to the producer.) He clothed his Moscow actors in heavy materials that fell in sculptured folds to catch the limited light.

Everything was done with light. Not naturalistic light, like Herkomer's, but shone from above, or raking sidewise – whatever would form or enhance successive dramatic pictures. Total removal of light would signify the end of a scene or act: so no curtains were wanted. Painted sets were replaced with proscenium-height screens. At the centre rear rose a platform two or three steps above the rest.

On this rear platform, in the Court scene of Act I, sat the King and Queen:

> From their shoulders a huge golden cloak fell down, its folds spreading over the entire width of the stage. Holes were cut in this gigantic cloak, and through them emerged the heads of courtiers... The lights were dimmed, and the rays of projectors glided over the surface of this degenerate world.

All the minor actors were thus drawn into Craig's setting – itself a psychologic projection of the hero's viewpoint:

> In the foreground sat the black-garbed figure of Hamlet, lost in thought.

So Craig achieved the paradox of practically converting drama to the novel's new 'stream of consciousness' centring on a single character.

In the Play scene of Act III, the King and Queen were enthroned again at the rear. The stage actors in front turned their backs on the audience to play their 'Murder of Gonzago' to the King. When the King began to tremble and rose, Hamlet sprang after him across the fore-stage in a blaze of light.

At the play's end, Craig's rear-stage platform filled with soldiers, the front with courtiers facing the biers. Mediating between the two stood the light-haloed figure of Fortinbras.

41. Ibid, 236-238.
42. Yeats, *Plays for an Irish Theatre* (Stratford-upon-Avon: A.H. Bullen at the Shakespeare Head Press, 1911), xiii. The book's plates reproduce Craig drawings.
43. EAC, 242.
44. *The Art of the Theatre* (1905).

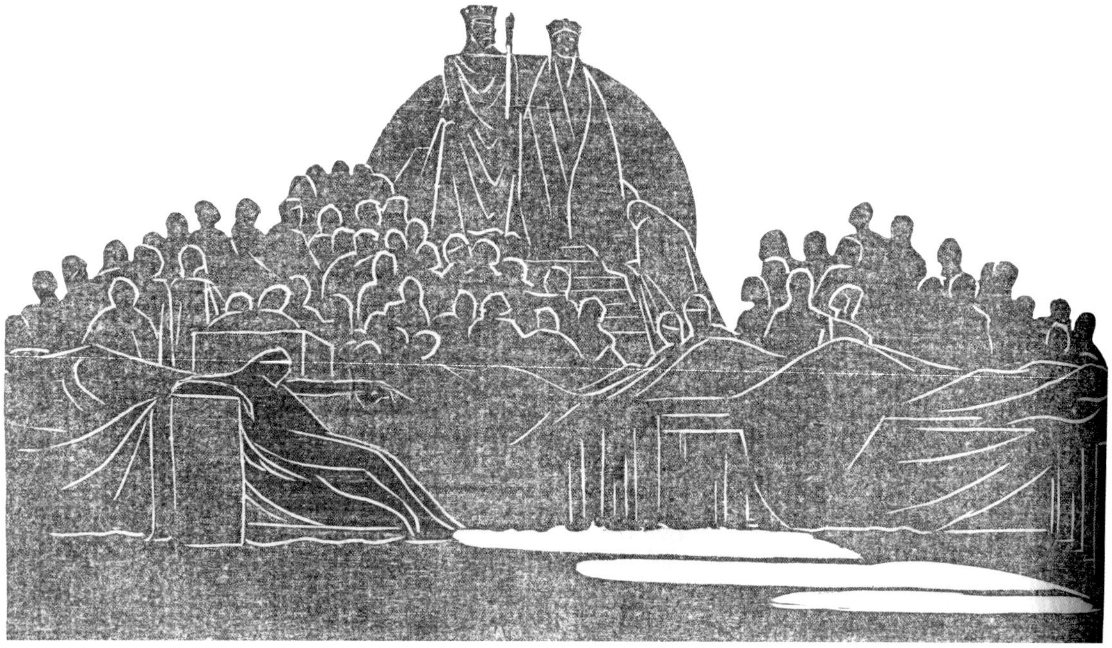

Plate 109. The first Court Scene, Act I scene ii of *Hamlet:* Cranach Press, 1929. Wood engraving
The Provost and Fellows of Eton College

Throughout the play, produced at last in January 1912, the *Times* correspondent noted: 'Only two colours are used – a neutral cream shade and gold.'[45]

Not all of Craig's vision proved translatable to the Moscow stage. Some disappointments went with him as he returned west. In Paris Craig began to plan with Count Kessler the further translation of his visionary *Hamlet* into a finely printed book.[46] His little figures carved in low relief could be inked for printing, with screens and steps and crowds and moons to be cut in wood for their settings on the page (Plate 109).

The book took longer than any other Craig project to finish. It did not appear until 1929 (in German) and 1930 (in English). By then it made a threnody for the private press movement, whose crafts had been doomed by the decay of apprentice-training with the rise of trade union influence in the wake of the Great War.

Craig had spent the War years in Italy – largely with Elena Meo, the woman whose love had lasted longest, and whose children by Craig included the devoted son who would write his father's biography. When Count Kessler visited them in Italy after the War, he saw Craig as a Robinson Crusoe, 'living like an island exile while festival playhouses, international drama exhibitions, and revolutions in theatrical production still draw on his capital'.[47] Kessler's observation echoed another by the actor-manager Granville-Barker, fifteen years earlier, that Craig was 'good to steal from'.[48] Yet every borrowing brought its adulteration.

Invited to join a new Society of Wood Engravers, Craig made in 1920 the most powerful of all his graphic images, *King Lear – The Storm*. Like some of William Hyde's best work, it shows the wind measuring the smallness of man (Plate 110).

After a time Elena Meo went to live in England. Craig did not return there, since his English wife was still alive. Instead he moved in 1935 to Paris. There his dreams slowly focused on the 'beloved book' *Robinson Crusoe*, whose hero more and more mirrored his own isolation. He began cutting illustrations for it in boxwood – perfect material for the subject. As Craig wrote now of this ultimate hero, his vision touched back to his boyhood memories of the north Norfolk coast:

> It was late at night, and it seemed to me that outside my window a high sea was tossing and rolling... and there, in this sound, came to me the cue to all the illustrations in the book. What is it but the sea – its many voices, its hundred faces, its whispering and crying... It does not intrude, or change anything – but it is there all the time – illustrating.
>
> And what else is there? Robinson's face.[49]

One day in a little Paris antique shop he found a mask of wood carved in the South Sea islands. It was an odd concave face, dominated by a long nose – not the nose of a native. Who then? It flashed on him: this must be the miraculously preserved portrait of none other than

45. This description is based on 'The Moscow *Hamlet*' chapter in Denis Bablet, *Edward Gordon Craig* (Heinemann, 1966), 133-160. Craig gave Bablet access to his archives. The English translation was made by Daphne Woodward, Craig's long-time secretary, mistress, and the mother of his last child.

46. Craig's wish to make a fine book of *Hamlet* went back many years. In July and August 1908 *The Mask* carried an advertisement for an edition of Hamlet to include

> '... Descriptions and Designs for each Scene, each Costume, each piece of Furniture used... ground plans of each scene and full directions as to how to light the play. Every movement of the Actors will be noted at the side of the Text, and at times a design will help the student to the full significance of the movements. The designs will be engraved upon wood... This Edition will be the work of Mr Gordon Craig...'.

Comparison of this plan with the Cranach Press *Hamlet* which emerged twenty years later may suggest the extent of Kessler's contribution to the final result.

47. Count Harry Kessler, *The Diaries of a Cosmopolitan* (Weidenfeld and Nicolson, 1971), 195.

48. *Index*, 289.

49. Quoted in E.A. Craig, Introduction to *Robinson Crusoe*, 47.

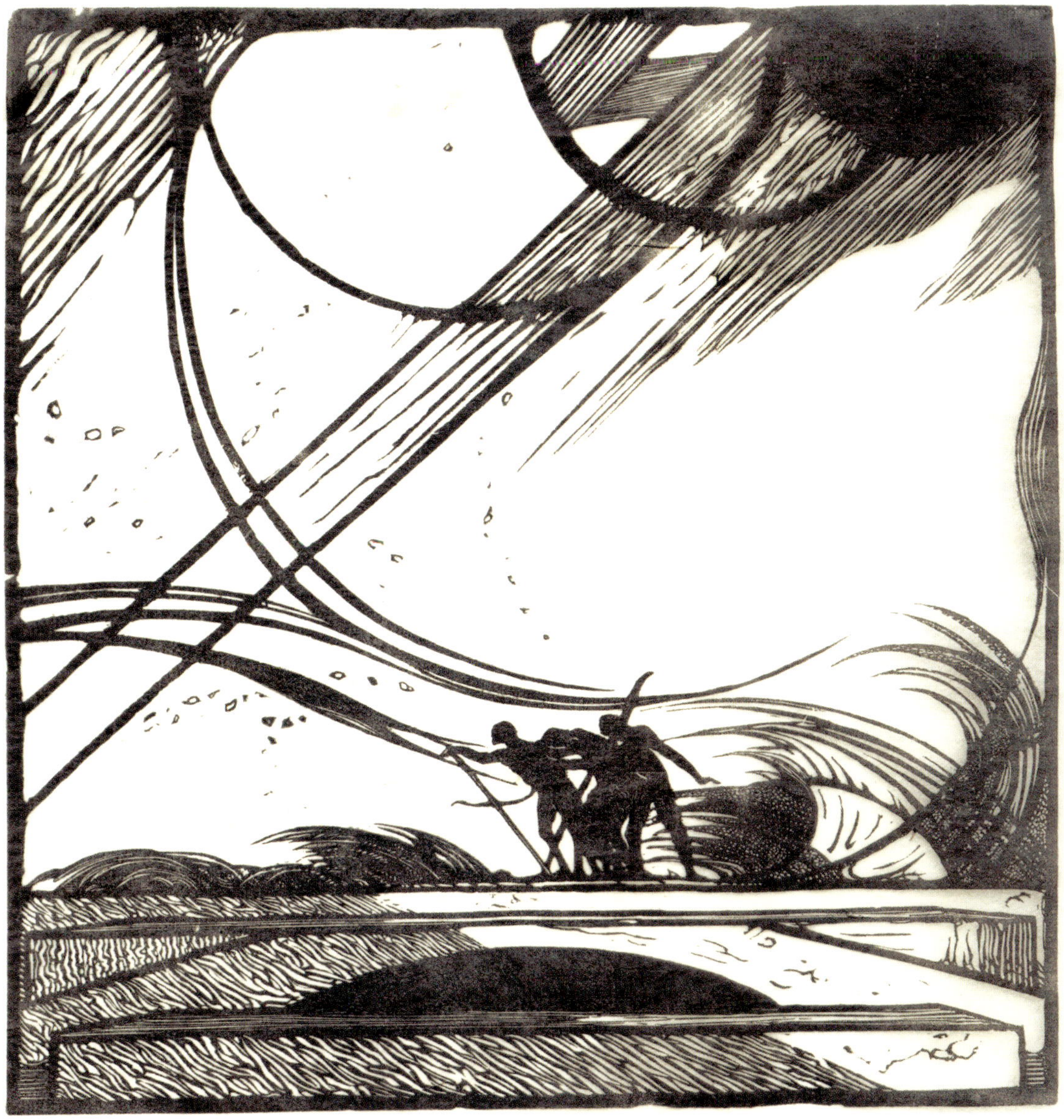

Plate 110. *King Lear: The Storm*, 1920. Wood engraving
The Provost and Fellows of Eton College

Robinson himself. Instantly he began to base his woodcut illustrations on the mask seen from all angles (Plate 111).

Through another European war he worked on in desultory ways. After the war he migrated to the south of France, where he passed his eightieth birthday – and his ninetieth. At ninety-one he no longer had the strength to cut blocks, and he gave the tools to his son. He lived on, receiving theatre historians and friends or not as the mood took him, until he died in his sleep at ninety-four in July 1966.

Plate 111. *Robinson Crusoe:* portrait from the mask, *c.*1938. Wood engraving

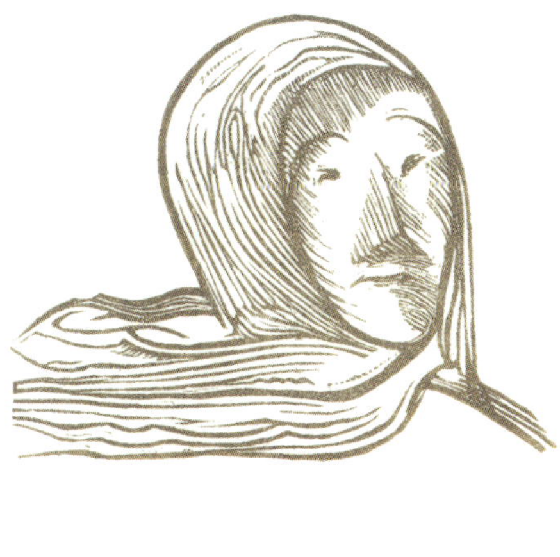

Craig's pastoral vision, when noticed at all by theatre historians, has always been treated as a side-issue. In fact it is the key to his genius and its influence. Throughout his long life, Craig's wood engraving drew its central theme in the relation of lonely man to the nature around him and within. In the theatre, his designs and visions systematically deduct attention from much dramatic interplay of characters to show loneliness drawing vision often from the world of nature.

To mount pastoral vision as a near-abstract drama of loneliness was to take its lyric to places far from grazing sheep. Setting this drama in a theatre, even of the mind, could extend the action through a new dimension of nature's time. That touched back to the Claudean hints of a golden age which had so galvanised Palmer. Yet Craig's extension also pointed forward. It was to drop a vital hint to a younger generation – a generation whose direct experience of war might otherwise have closed out any future for pastoral vision in England after the Griggsian farewell.

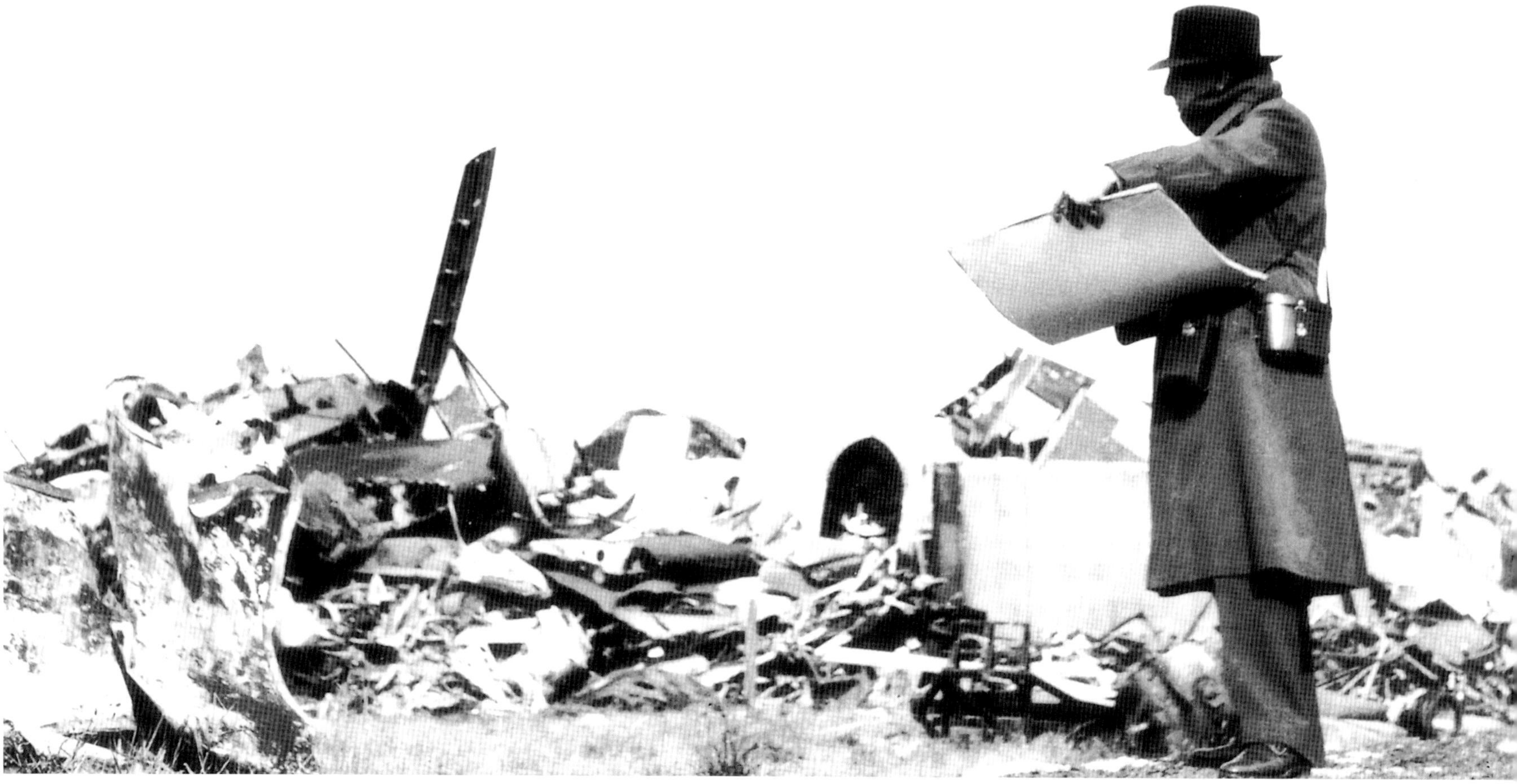

Plate 112. Paul Nash sketching at a wreckage dump of German aircraft, Cowley, *c.*1940. Photograph Tate, London

CHAPTER 5

Paul Nash (1889-1946)

Pastoral at War

'What appealed to me in the work of Gordon Craig', wrote Paul Nash, 'was the abundant evidence of poetic insight.' For his younger self and contemporaries, Nash recalled:

> We were conscious only of three rather more than life-size personalities... Augustus John, the painter; Jacob Epstein, the sculptor; and Gordon Craig, [who] possessed imagination in a degree far beyond John or Epstein.[1]

The most suggestive aspect of Craig's art for Nash was its paradox of time dissolved and surmounted. By contrast, Nash did not respond at all to the vision of F.L. Griggs.[2] Griggs was only a dozen years Nash's senior, but his was a vision of the gulf opened by the Great War.

Nash served in the War, and was just under thirty when it ended. Creative maturity lay still ahead of him – but only if he could find a way to incorporate his own experience of war into his art. The path Nash opened shows, none the less, a secret kinship to Griggs.

Griggs, building his house in the 1920s, looked on its phases of reconstruction and new building as 'ruins' challenging the creative spirit to vision. Nash had found his own ruins in his sight of war destruction. Murdered nature – shattered trees, polluted land and water, shards of buildings – so pervaded Nash's wartime drawing and painting that it could seem his postwar art's primordial ooze.

For Nash's generation, the worldwide growth of communications fomented dissatisfaction with localisms, and an insistence on radical change. Nationalism still pervaded it – with Futurism in Italy, Cubism in France and Spain, Vorticism in England. But behind them all loomed Abstraction. Nash found his best help in Surrealism – disparate objects assembled from remote contexts with the aim of inventing (in its root meaning of 'coming upon') new insight.

In the aftermath of the War, Nash sought borderlands where opposing elements of nature met. He followed William Hyde to coastal Romney Marsh. There a vast breakwater, of long straight sections ranging through distances in a shallow curve, separates land from sea – slow from rapid change. Nash's postwar art studied the breakwater from every angle, in every darkness and light.

In the 1930s Nash's art began to search for 'equivalents' which might link mineral, vegetable, animal substances through symbols. Such metaphysical, surreal 'equivalents' became building materials for Nash's house of the spirit. 'The landscapes I have in mind', he wrote in 1938, 'are neither moral nor sentimental nor literary, but rather something strange and... poetical.'[3]

Nash never commanded the draughtsmanship of Griggs or Craig. His battles to frame his vision ultimately wore him out. Only in his last phase, with health collapsing against a second European war, his scrutinies of earthworks and shadows, trees and flowers finally annealed the dimension of time into the fabric of his art. Craig's art had evoked time's passage through human presences. Nash's late landscape art made time its fourth dimension.

Therein Nash advanced a poetic solution to the quest for a unified field theory which so occupied the science of his time. The scientists and philosophers never solved their equation. But Nash's visionary solutions, worked out in the teeth of renewed violence darkening his world, lit another lamp for his successors in pastoral vision.

* * *

His paternal roots were in the farms of Buckinghamshire, where his grandfather still lived. But Paul's father was a London barrister who had settled his family in an overbuilt house in

1. Paul Nash, *Outline* (Faber, 1949), 166–167. This unfinished autobiography offers the richest account of any pastoral visionary childhood and youth. Quotations in the present chapter not otherwise noted are from this source.

2. Both Griggs and Nash separately visited the home of the collector Percy Withers. His daughter Audrey recalled Nash standing before a Griggs etching and saying 'Poo-oor Mr Griggs.' (Conversation with the writer, 1999.)

3. 'Unseen Landscapes', in *Country Life*, 21 May 1938; quoted in *Paul Nash: Modern Artist, Ancient Landscape*, ed Jemima Montagu (Tate Publishing, 2003), 66.

Kensington. 'Ghuznee Lodge' was too big for its closed-in site. As Craig's night nursery had been high up in his mother's house in Kensington, so was Paul's in his father's house there. Paul's fear of the dark took form as a black dog lying in wait about an upper landing. To escape its horror he had dreams of flying.

Yet another of his boyhood horrors seemed to parallel Craig's stagecraft. Nash recalled his own young sensation of 'being hemmed in by vast perpendiculars of changing dimensions about to envelop and overwhelm one'. That melancholy found its focus downstairs in Paul's late afternoon 'hour with my mother': 'I see her great agate eyes change and become overwhelmed with misery.' No one admitted that she might be ill.

A young nanny, a country girl from his grandfather's village, took Paul with his younger brother and sister to Kensington Gardens. There, following in the footsteps of Samuel Palmer and William Hyde, Paul found a primal landscape for himself:

> In all other environments you were conscious of circumvention, either imposed or implied. … With a shout and a sudden turn of speed you had broken through the invisible barrier. … It was an escape, not only from the others, but in some queer way from oneself. …
>
> Here I became aware of trees, felt the grass for the first time, saw an expanse of water, listened to a new kind of silence.

It was a still centre in the world of surrounding noise.

Later Nash would imagine himself lucky to have known it 'before Barrie took over Kensington Gardens with *Peter Pan*'. Barrie's inspiration was drawn from two small boys he met in the Gardens when Paul was eight and his brother John was four. One of the *Peter Pan* boys would be killed in the Great War, in which Paul and John would also fight. At the Round Pond, meanwhile, Paul sailed his boat – 'and wished I had a boat hook'.

Beyond the Round Pond at the skirts of a wood he found an ancient beech tree which seemed to capture changing lights:

> It was conspicuously ghastly on dark days in the beam of a low sun, or it shone steely blue in its metallic mood in early spring. Sometimes it was poetically pale and enchanted and could suggest a magical presence.

Its deepest magic lay in the fact that it guarded for Paul 'the threshold of a domain' – a domain of form:

> There was a peculiar spacing in the disposal of the trees, or it was their height in relation to these intervals, which suggested some inner design of very subtle purpose.

He remembered this place as 'charged with sweetness beyond physical experience'. When called away, the spell was broken: he found himself looking at 'nothing except a few sooty sheep cropping the thin grass'. Back at home, Paul and John made drawings with 'pencil and waxy coloured chalks'.

To shield him from his mother's illness, he was sent to relatives in the country. One visit renewed his nightmares. Paul and John went to their maternal grandmother's dark house and overgrown garden in Hampshire. The place was alive with snakes: 'In the orchard I went to pick up an apple when, almost from under my hand, a snake rose up hissing.' Both boys sickened there with whooping cough. It was, Paul remembered 'like being pursued by a demon'. Years later the demon returned as chronic asthma.

Yet the country brought happiness when Paul went to stay at his grandfather's big farm near Langley in Buckinghamshire, just beyond Uxbridge. Coming here, where his father had grown up, was 'like finding my own home, my true home'. In the 1890s the farm could show Old England alive and healthy in ways to have touched Palmer and Griggs – had their families rooted so deep as the Nashs. 'My Grandfather', Paul wrote later, 'was a true yeoman with the authority of a squire.'

The Old Rectory which served as farmhouse overflowed with treasures. Here was the family *Pilgrim's Progress*, 'thought by some to have been Bunyan's personal copy'. There were odd vegetable specimens – and eggs 'ranging in shape from almost round to long ovoid', showing an abstract beauty in their 'supreme glaze covering the lovely solid form'. When he drove to church in his grandfather's brougham:

> From the family pew in the choir... my eyes strayed to the clear glass east windows where the branches of trees showed through, or to the lovely painted vault above – pale, clear blue painted with golden stars and bunches of corn.

The city-contrast of Kensington sharpened when he was sent to school. One sensation predominated then: 'My liberty had been taken from me.' Never from that moment did any sense of freedom return until he left school at seventeen. In those years 'I suffered greater misery, humiliation and fear than in all the rest of my life.' That included two World Wars.

As many another dreamer, he found an escape in theatrical things. His special fascination, like Gordon Craig's, was in 'pantomime and scenes of phantasy and transportation'. A model theatre at school led him farther into Craig perspectives, as Nash remembered: 'I invented, coloured and illuminated all the scenes, and was especially good at caves and rocky coasts.'

When Paul was eleven, his grandfather died at Langley. The farm was sold, the family roots torn out. Some relief appeared when his mother inherited a legacy. With it, in hope of relieving her distress and transplanting his family, Paul's father built a house near Langley at Iver Heath – a six-bedroomed 'inoffensive villa' with acreage.

Paul led his brother and sister in exploring the country round about. 'The peak of our discoveries' was a sinister place three or four miles to the north:

> It was known to us as Hawks' Wood, from the fact that nearly always there would be a sparrow hawk or a kestrel hanging in the sky overhead, or, nailed to a tree in the Keeper's Larder, a dead hawk hanging among the dead jays in the dark aisles of the wood.

One day towards the end of his schoolboy captivity in west London, Paul wandered into the School's gallery filled with casts of antique statuary. Perched on a stool before an easel was a senior boy named Eric Kennington 'knocking off likenesses of the plaster casts... I watched Kennington's skilful pen running and pausing, cross-hatching and dotting as the spit-image of Caesar grew upon the page.' Sunlight fell on the young artist, showing an icon of independence and privacy with self-expression beckoning at the end of the prospect.

At seventeen Nash emerged from the 'long and complicated purgatory' of school, and an abortive cramming for the Navy, 'more or less ignorant and equipped for nothing'. He lived quietly at home, drawing bookplates for family friends and neighbours interested to encourage him with small payments. His designs followed Edwardian illustrators' elaborations of romantic and pastoral themes.

The country had not cured his mother's illness. At last she had to leave them and go to an asylum. Life can hold few experiences worse than the gradual dissolution of that fundamental bond through the years of youth. It hardened the elder son: Paul described his own emerging temperament as 'rather careless and sanguine'. When he proposed to earn 'my living as a black and white illustrator of some kind', his distracted father raised no objection.

In December 1906 he enrolled at the Chelsea Polytechnic. After a year and a half, a teacher there suggested the London County Council School at Bolt Court in Fleet Street. So he went. On school evenings he cycled three miles from Iver Heath to Uxbridge, caught a train to Paddington, and then on by Underground. The return journey took him back to his country, as he re-crossed the bridge over the little Alderbourne River 'talking in its limpid tones in the still night'.

He found himself writing poetry 'for the strange pain of being in love'. Her name was Sybil Fountain and she sometimes visited neighbours at Iver Heath:

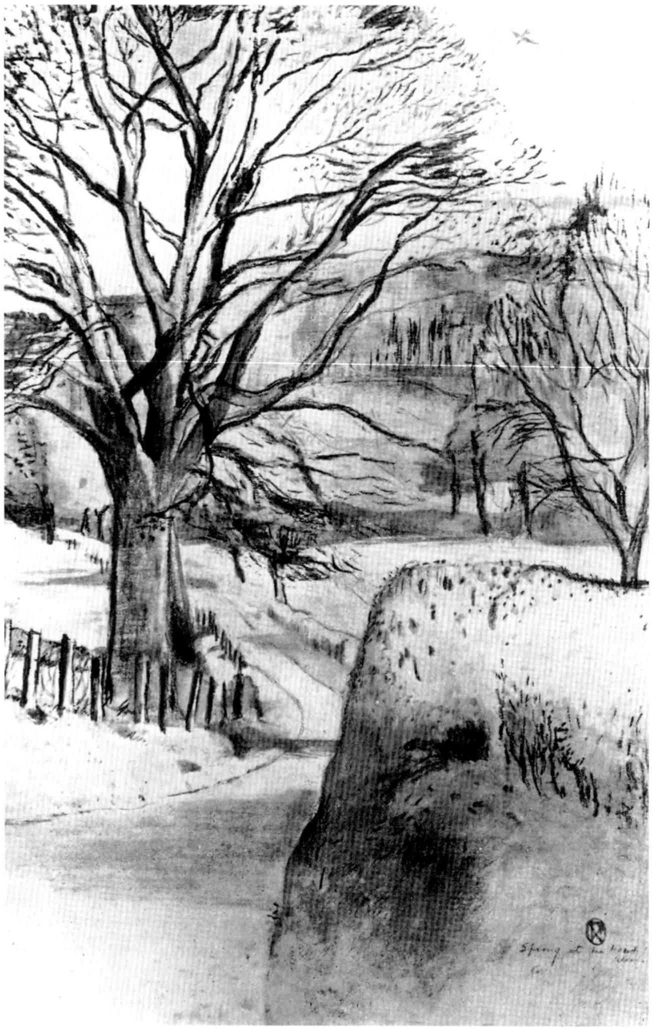

Plate 113. *Spring at the Hawks' Wood,* 1911-12. Pencil, ink and chalk

> My world became inhabited by images of a face encircled with blue-black hair… When I reached home I drew an immense figure of a woman whose head and body were partly articulated by stars, but whose feet were composed of the reflection of stars in a pool.

Many of his drawings now were of sunset and night. Some traced allegories of flying. Several showed obscure conflicts.

One drawing reflected his mother's hopeless state – leading towards her death in 1910. He called the drawing *Flumen mortis* – a river of human heads upturned in sleep. Later he destroyed it. Before that, he showed it at a Bolt Court exhibition in January 1910. Two visitors came in. One was the distinguished artist William Rothenstein. He was accompanied by the tall figure of Gordon Craig. Nash watched them approach his drawing:

> Craig pounced from the skies, peering myopically at my drawing with an increasing smile. Then Rothenstein passed sentence in a few memorable words…: 'I shall give it ten.'[4]

Not for draughtsmanship, as Nash himself knew too well. Seeing more of his work, Rothenstein said: 'You should go to the Slade and learn to draw.' The resident genius at the Slade School was Henry Tonks. For Tonks the essence of art was drawing; the essence of drawing was from the human figure. Yet Nash found that 'the human figure as represented by the models at the Slade did not interest me'.

At the Slade he met new European movements in art. Tonks and his colleagues were disturbed by a show of 'Post-Impressionist' pictures arranged at the Grafton Galleries by Roger Fry. The artists were mostly French: none of them was much concerned with draughtsmanship in the Tonks sense. Tonks appealed to his students not to 'risk contamination', but stay away. Being young, they gloried in the uproar.

One of Fry's younger friends, Clive Bell, soon wrote a little book called simply *Art*. It advertised Fry's premise that art was defined by the presence of 'significant form'. Manner – the way you looked at an object – was everything. Matter – the object you looked at – was practically irrelevant. The fact that literature, and therefore subjects, had always played a central role in the English imagination appeared to Fry and Bell as a sacred cow fatted for their new critical abattoir.

As Cambridge undergraduates both Fry and Bell had belonged to a self-perpetuating little elite known as 'the Apostles'. In Bell's time they were in thrall to the philosophy of G.E. Moore, exalting the ethics of private friendships over everything else. Another 'Apostle' of those years, the novelist E.M. Forster, once famously wrote: 'If I had to choose between betraying my country and betraying my friend, I hope I should have the guts to betray my country.' (An art-critic 'Apostle' of the next generation, Anthony Blunt, would do just that.)

Fry's friends and acolytes gathered themselves together in London's Bloomsbury district. Many of the 'Bloomsbury' artists showed draughtsmanship as weak as Nash's, but their relentless mutual promotion made a cell of influence. They pretended that nothing of importance in English art or literature could now happen outside the ellipse of Bloomsbury.

One Slade friend, Claughton Pellew, shared Nash's love for the country. In Pellew's company 'the individual beauty of certain things, trees particularly, began to dawn on me.' In the spring of 1911 Nash looked again at his boyhood haunts in Hawks Wood. His eye was taken by an oak tree standing in silver light (Plate 113):

> The spring sunlight struck across the wide shoulders of the oak, glancing down its great limbs which reflected the beams in a pale glow; the round trunk in sunlight was as white as paper.
>
> I did not find it difficult to draw this tree, as I had found the models at the Slade difficult to draw. … There stole through me a peculiar thrill as I realised the forms taking life under my hand.

4. The exhibition can be dated from the fact that Craig left England to return to his home in Italy in late Jan 1910. He did not revisit England during the rest of Nash's time at Bolt Court.

5. 2 Oct 1800, sent to his patron Thomas Butts; quoted in Nash's *Outline*, 79-80.

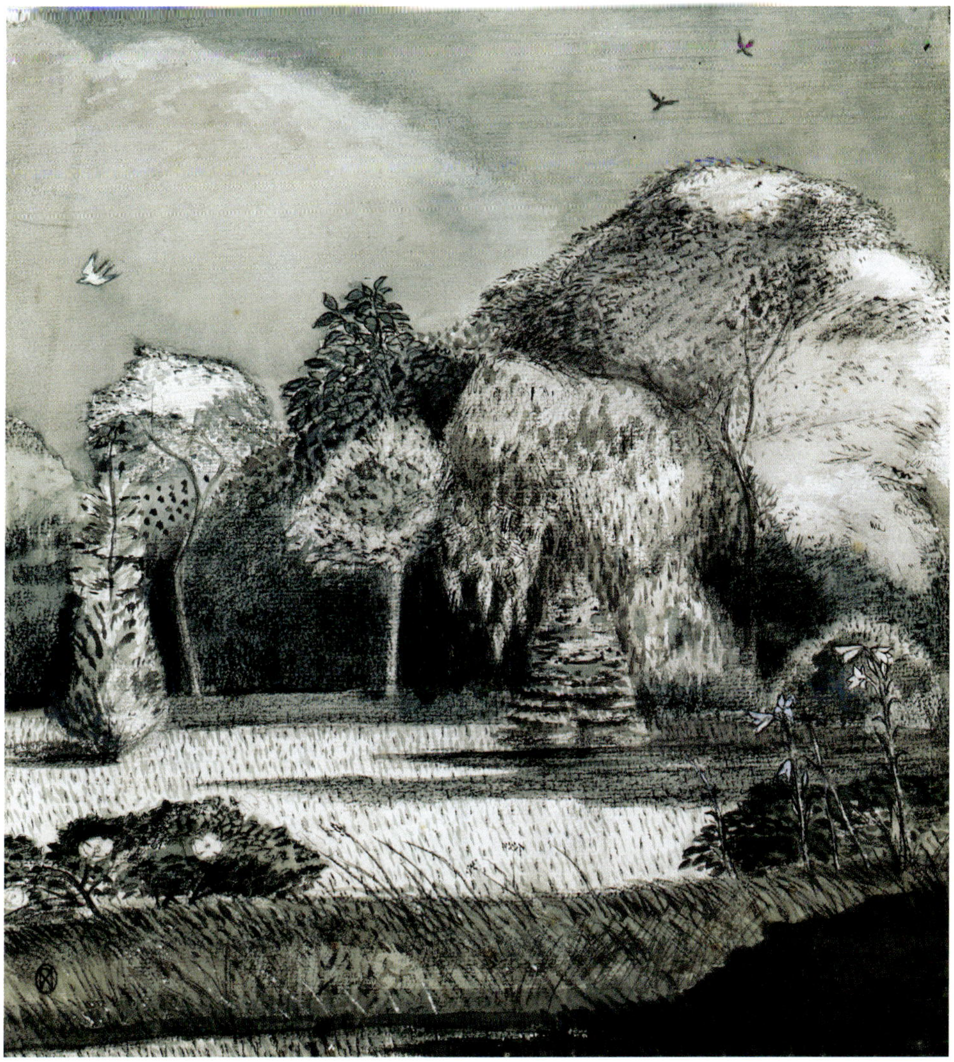

Plate 114. *Bird Garden*, 1911. Ink, watercolour and chalk National Museum of Wales

He ventured farther. 'With nervous strokes I painted in the washes of pale colour, trying to convey the sense I had of the landscape's bodily structure. … I deliberately sought to simplify.' He remembered some lines written by Blake in the country:

> Over sea, over land,
> Mine eyes did expand
> Into regions of air,
> Away from all care;
> Into regions of fire
> Remote from desire.[5]

Nash's draughtsmanship was primitive, yet his drawing captured and held its light.

During the summer of 1911, the view from the morning room at Iver Heath began to show itself as a stage platform for inspiration. The wide windows looked on to a rough garden bounded by different trees and shrubs at the back. The family called this 'the bird garden', as birds were always there. For Paul its keynote was cyclic time:

> Each year the grass grew up and flowered and was cut down and made into hay-cocks. Thereafter it was an open space of meadow invaded… by the shadows cast by the laburnum, the chestnut, the tall acacia and the little conical silver fir.
>
> These… made up a group that had a curious beauty of related forms [which] seemed to respond in a dramatic way to the influence of the light [Plate 114].

The changing lights did not portend loss (as they would have done for Griggs). For Nash they were more like the lights of change projected on Gordon Craig's model stages.

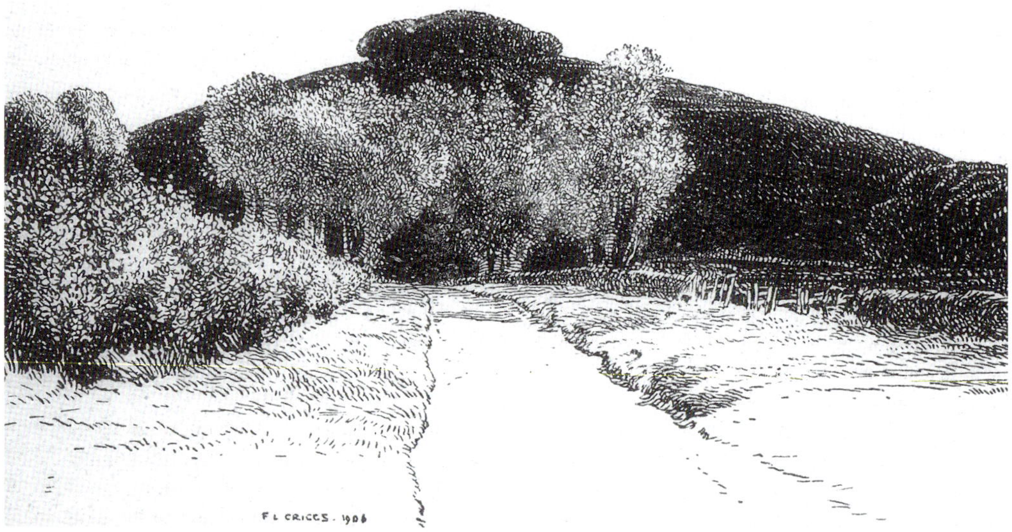

Plate 116. F. L. Griggs: *Wittenham Clump*, 1906, for *Highways and Byways in Berkshire*. Ink

Nash's platform stage of nature expanded in a watercolour of late summer afternoon fields and trees. He called it *The Wanderer* (Plate 115). His wake remains visible through the high foreground wheat as the distant figure, casting his shadow behind him, mounts a hillside through trees towards late light. Nash in these early years found paradoxic expression, like Griggs, in lateness.

Some early autumn shooting with cousins took him up the Thames Valley to a place dominated by two hills of ancient earthworks, known as the Wittenham Clumps. From them he returned to London – to see Gordon Craig's exhibition of designs for *Macbeth*. It was the project Craig had limited to two colours, brown and grey. He showed not only drawings, but stage-models. Nash wrote: 'Once I had seen his models, I could believe unhesitatingly in his drawings. Seen alone, the latter often seemed too stylised, too exquisite to support credible reality.'

Plate 115. *The Wanderer*, 1911. Pencil, ink, watercolour and chalk British Museum

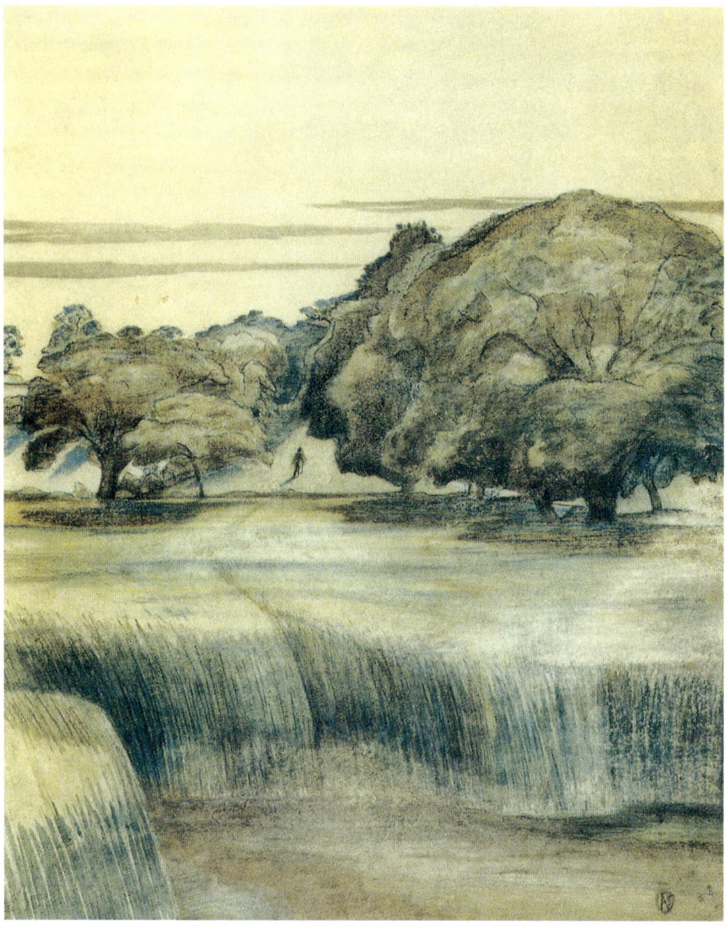

The younger man found himself distrusting drawing that might be too fluent. Deft draughtsmanship might civilise the loneliest scene. At the Slade that autumn, Tonks said that Nash's drawing was 'like a man trying to talk who has not learnt the language'. Nash left the Slade at Christmas 1911 – still with the wish to support himself as an artist.

He took up a friend's introduction to an elderly Royal Academician with an extraordinary heritage. Sir William Blake Richmond was George Richmond's son. Named for his father's first inspirer, Sir William at sixty-nine was a last link to 'The Ancients' of Samuel Palmer. Looking over Nash's drawings, Richmond confirmed the young man's attraction to 'Nature' before all else.

One of Nash's experiments was a nocturne of *Falling Stars* seen through canopies of awkwardly drawn cedars. It was a palimpsest of uncertainties, as the artist himself remembered it:

> Blue crayon first, then chalk, then Indian ink then conté [crayon]. The holes & scars are the places where a moon, some too-many stars, two embracing figures, & a fairy have been not quite successfully obliterated.[6]

Then something near despair produced a 'queer drawing of pyramids crashing about in uncanny eclipsed moonlight'. The two sharp shapes rise side by side over waves before and behind them.

September 1912 brought another shooting visit to the Wittenham Clumps. Now the Clumps appeared as 'the Pyramids of my small world'. Their slopes were harvested bare, but a clump of trees remained at the top of each. Griggs had drawn one of the Wittenham Clumps half a dozen years earlier for *Highways and Byways in Berkshire*, emphasising the mammary shape (Plate 116). Looking at the Clumps now in 'sweet September sunlight', Nash left the sportsmen to find his own vantage. He remembered thinking here:

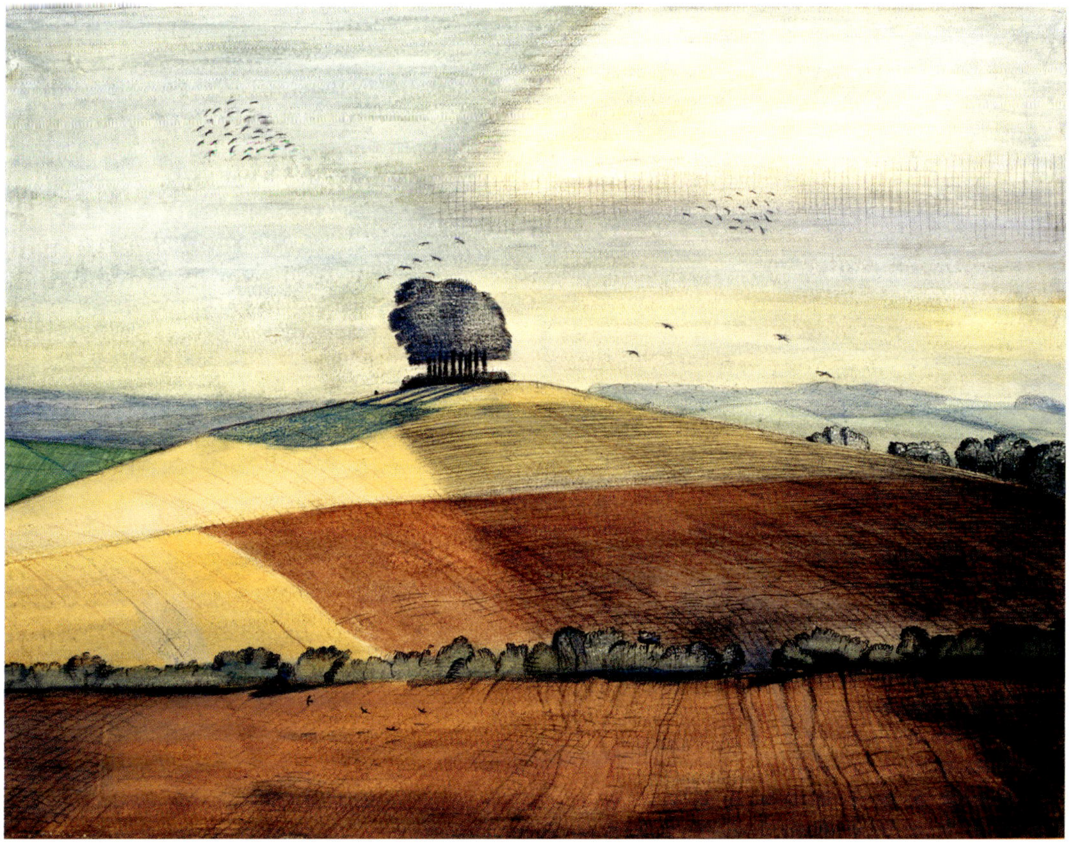

Left:
Plate 117. Wittenham Clump, 1913.
Pencil, ink, watercolour and chalk
Tullie House Museum & Art Gallery

Below:
Plate 118. *Cliff to the North,* 1912-13.
Ink, watercolour and chalk
Fitzwilliam Museum, Cambridge

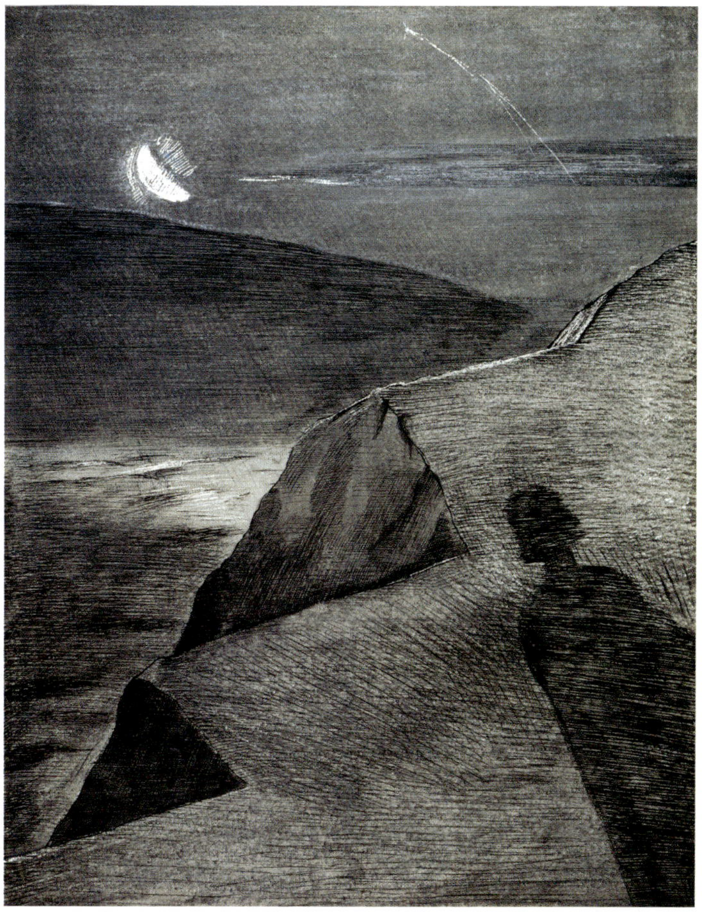

What better life could there be – to work in the open air, to go hunting far afield over the wild country, to get my living out of the land as much as my ancestors had done.

One of his drawings isolates a Clump summit between lines and shadows (Plate 117). Diagonals of cloud-shape and shadow across the hillside set the top-most trees within their counterpoints. These are not the square angles of Cubism. Instead, they anticipate by a year or two the more acute, gothic angles of Cubism's English cousin, Vorticism. Near the bottom, a line of foliage stretches across the base of the hill to cut it off from a more level foreground.

In November 1912 Nash showed twenty-one pictures in an exhibition he arranged with a small but influential West-End dealer. The Carfax Gallery had been founded and was still run by friends of Oscar Wilde, and the little show brought some distinguished visitors. William Rothenstein bought *Falling Stars* – and offered to teach Nash to paint in tempera.

As the show ended, Nash went to visit his Slade friend Claughton Pellew on the north-east coast of Norfolk. Here, forty miles east of Gordon Craig's boyhood vision at Brancaster, Nash drew the cliff edge in sharp angles 'above the cold, bitter sea'. Beyond a dark hill-shape rises a Palmerish waning moon (Plate 118). Across a jagged headland strikes 'the shadow of a figure approaching', cast in a lighthouse beam. Neither the lighthouse nor the figure itself is seen.

The shadowed figure came to life two months later when Nash met the woman he would marry. Margaret Odeh was an Oxford graduate, who held within her darkly attractive little person the determination of a suffragette. Within a month they were engaged. But they did not hasten the marriage.

6. *Poet and Painter: Letters between Gordon Bottomley and Paul Nash 1910-1946*, ed Andrew Causey (Bristol: Redcliffe Press, 1990), letter dated 21 Aug 1912, p 48.

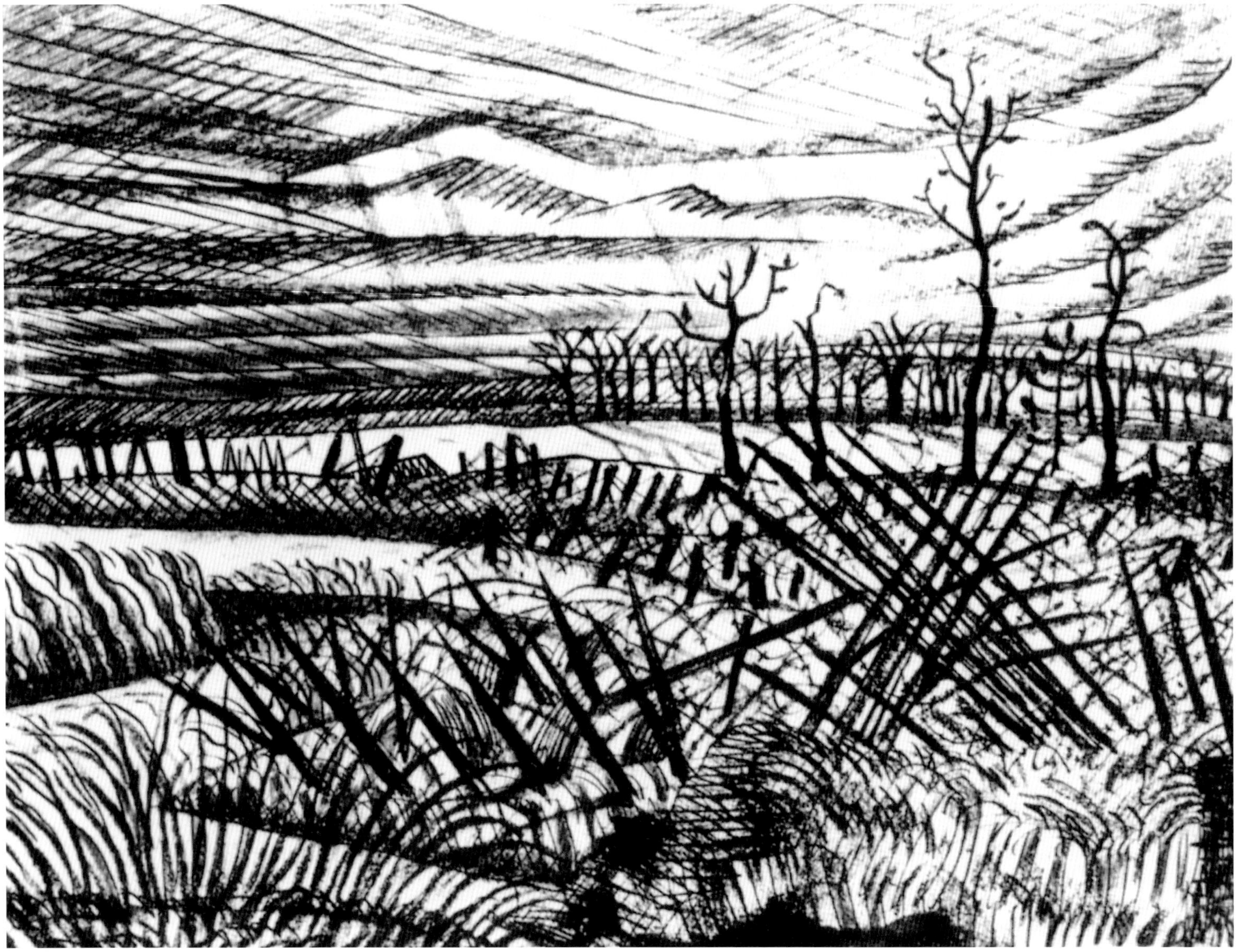

Plate 119. *Obstacle,* 1917-18. Ink, watercolour and chalk

In the autumn of 1913 Nash tried a joint exhibition with his brother. John Nash had found a talent of his own – by Paul's advice, without any formal training at all. The brothers hired the walls of a Kensington lamp shop for just over a week. They designed a poster to show them both cutting natty profiles with friends (in John's style) among wheatstooks before the Wittenham Clumps (in Paul's style). One patron, known as a formidable collector of young English art, was Winston Churchill's private secretary Edward Marsh. He differentiated the Nash brothers thus:

> When Jack sits down before a landscape, his only desire is to do his best for it; whereas Paul, who likes to order Nature about, uses it as a spring-board for some construction of his own.[7]

* * *

Less than a year later the Great War broke over them all. Paul and Margaret made up their minds to marry in December 1914. Before that he volunteered for the Artists' Rifles Territorials, guarding the country at home. He proved adept at keeping the thread of his drawing going through various postings during the first eighteen months of the War.

One artist from Nash's time at the Slade was making a big impression with his War pictures. Christopher Richard Nevinson (1889-1946, exactly Nash's years) had joined the Vorticists just before the War. Now he used the acute angles to show men shaped to their killing machines, and the War's impact on civilised country and town.

When Nash was sent to the Belgian Front early in 1917, he recognised essential truths in

7. Edward Marsh, *A Number of People* (Heinemann, 1939), 360.
8. 21 March 1917, quoted in James King, *Interior Landscapes: A Life of Paul Nash* (Weidenfeld and Nicolson, 1987), 80.
9. Nevinson acknowledged his debt to Hyde's *London Impressions* image 'The Nerves of London' (see Chapter 2, page 90) in *Among the Nerves of the World*, a similar view of St Paul's Cathedral behind wires crossing high above Fleet Street.
10. 18 or 25 Nov 1917 (*Outline*, 210-211).

Nevinson's pictures. He asked Margaret to buy a Nevinson etching of Ypres after its bombardment, as he wrote to her: 'How interesting in form these once stiff houses look, a rhythmic ruin of tumbling forms.'[8] A fall in the trenches invalided Nash home – to be sent back later as an official War artist.

Nash found his own War subject in displaced and destroyed nature. It tore up Griggs's evocations of ageless decay. One wiry Nash drawing entitled *Obstacle* (Plate 119) was acquired by Nevinson. Their careers made a counterpoint. Nash's drawing was spiky, while Nevinson deployed linear mastery. One strand of Nevinson's work extended the atmospheres of William Hyde. Before the end of the War Nevinson painted, and then mezzotinted, an evocation of *Wind* through writhing trees in sculpting forms (Plate 120). After the War Nevinson would paint London nocturnes which took Hyde's riverside warehouses into Vorticism.[9]

November 1917 found Nash back in Belgium, sketching devastations at Passchendaele. He was exposed to greater danger than in the trenches, in murdered landscapes through which the road from Ypres to Menin had once passed. What he saw there poisoned the pastoral roots planted at his grandfather's farm and Iver Heath. He wrote to Margaret:

> Evil and the incarnate fiend alone can be master of this war, and no glimmer of God's hand is seen anywhere. Sunrise and sunset are blasphemous... The rain drives on, the stinking mud becomes more evilly yellow, the shell holes fill up with green-white water, the roads and tracks are covered in inches of slime, the black dying trees ooze and sweat and the shells never cease.
>
> They alone plunge overhead, tearing away the rotting tree stumps, breaking the plank roads, striking down horses and mules, annihilating, maiming, maddening, they plunge into the grave which is this land; one huge grave, and cast up on it the poor dead. It is unspeakable, godless, hopeless.
>
> I am no longer an artist interested and curious, I am a messenger who will bring back word from the men who are fighting to those who want the war to go on for ever.[10]

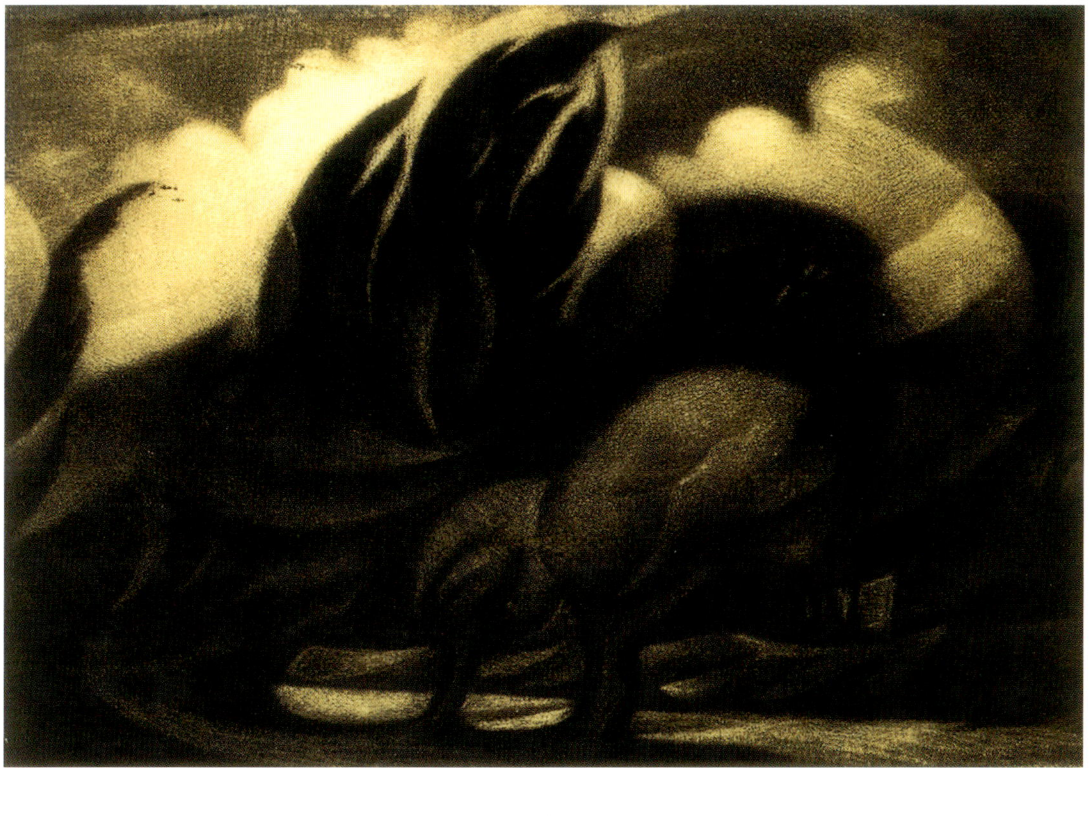

Plate 120. C.R.W. Nevinson: *Wind*, 1918. Mezzotint

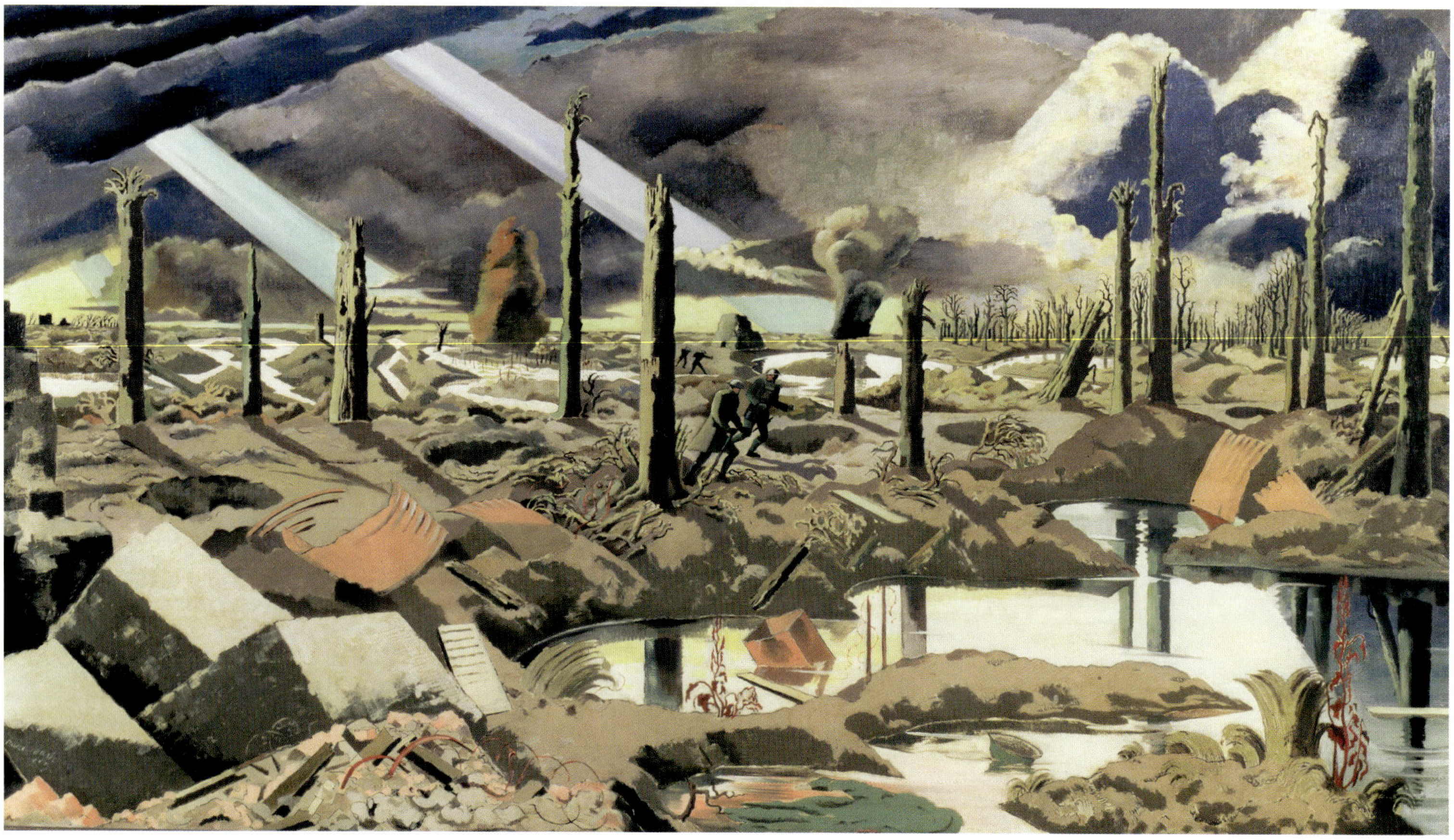

Plate 121. *The Menin Road,* 1919. Oil
© Imperial War Museum, London, UK/ The Bridgeman Art Library

Plate 122. *The Paths,* 1919. Ink and watercolour

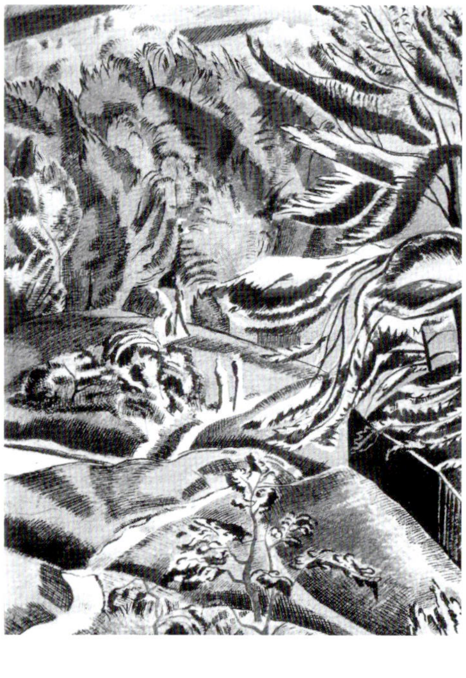

He had shown the finished results of his sketches in May 1916 in London, under the exhibition title 'Void of War'. In a catalogue note, the novelist Arnold Bennett wrote that Nash's pictures gave 'form and coherence… to the formless and the incoherent'. Herbert Read, who had been there and seen it for himself, said that Nash 'could convey, as no other artist, the phantasmagoric atmosphere of No Man's Land'. Nash's subject was still the earth itself. Thus his art brought its pastoral inheritance even into the devil's den.

The Imperial War Museum commissioned a huge image of *The Menin Road.* It was Nash's first very large work in oils, and he brought it off triumphantly (Plate 121). Through heavy clouds, garish beams light an endless waste in which two pairs of dwarfed and isolated soldiers advance with ironically purposeful strides. They are pilgrims progressing to nowhere – Robinson Crusoes in Hell.

The deformation entered Nash's private life. Up to his marriage at the War's beginning, his relations with women had been decorous. No longer. Staying with his wife at Chalfont St Giles in the summer of 1918, he started an affair with a married woman. It was terminated by a threat of murder from the woman's husband. But it marked the beginning of endless affairs and concomitant quarrels with his wife. His brother John, also married, and also a War veteran with farther-flung service, behaved in the same way.

After the Armistice, Paul put the War as a subject behind him. But its influence was inexorable. An ink and watercolour drawing of 1919 shows *The Paths* – twisting and disappearing beneath heavy branches extending their shapes – to re-emerge at angles leading nowhere (Plate 122). A distant pair of figures is nearly engulfed in nature's menace. At the top left, a tiny corner of rounded hill-harvest touches back to Palmer's *Magic Apple Tree*: but all the old Eden-like quietness is shredded through the roughest textures of Nash's most disturbed drawing.

His art found further broadening and suppression of detail at Dymchurch, beyond Romney Marsh. There coast and sea are separated by broad breakwaters – sets of steps in long segments curving across the distances. Nash insisted on moving there, to draw and paint the man-made division of elements from every angle in all lights. Several images called *Platform Facing the Sea* give his own view of Nevinson's wartime 'rhythmic ruins of tumbling forms'. One shows Craig-like uprights falling away to form horizontal steps, backlit from a mysterious source. The harsh stage-

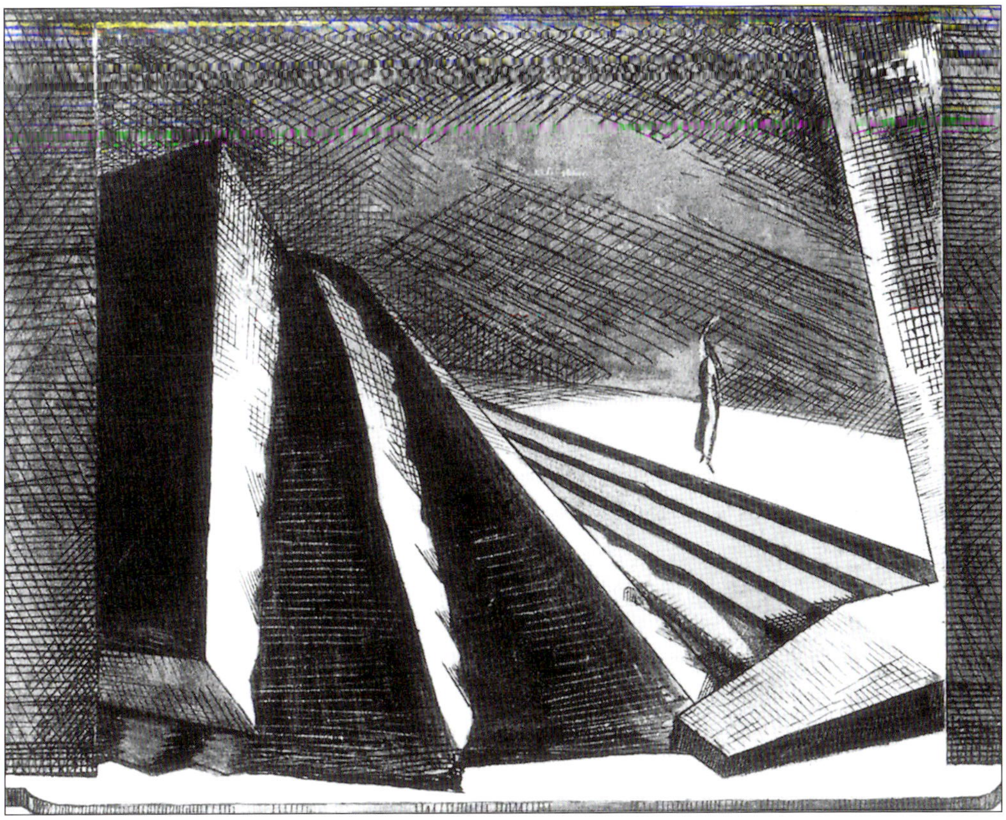

Plate 123. *A Platform facing the Sea,* 1920. Pencil and ink

lighting increases the sense of an overwhelming brutality threatening the lonely figure (Plate 123).

At Dymchurch Nash sickened to nervous collapse. Behind the War lay a fear of inheriting his mother's madness. No doctor would help him until Margaret put him into a London hospital for nervous diseases. Slowly he seemed to recover. But he was never to enjoy unclouded health again.

Partly as therapy, partly in tribute to Gordon Craig (with whom he was now in touch), Nash took up two of Craig's crafts – wood engraving and building stage models. One of Nash's models won Craig's special praise at an international exhibition. Later Nash broke up all his own stage models, when he recognised that the platforms for his art needed to find extension within himself.

Wood engraving promised better. Like Craig (whose *King Lear – the Storm* appeared in 1922), Nash found the technique lent itself to broadening. Nash's woodcut breadths lit hard-edged planes. He cut them through several suites. Trees and water with occasional attenuated figures shaped a little book of country *Places* in 1922. Then came a commission to illustrate the Book of *Genesis*. One image, 'The Dry Land Appearing', took his pre-War *Pyramids in the Sea* through Vorticism to the edge of Abstraction (Plate 124).

Nash was seeking his own way to take into his art developments on the Continent. French artists seemed to him 'able to create a beauty independent of subject-matter suggestion'.[11] One of Nash's written articles in 1919 had even used the Bloomsbury tag 'significant form'. But Nash's art showed little of Bloomsbury domesticity.

After Margaret had a miscarriage in the spring of 1925, they made up their minds to leave Dymchurch. Before leaving, Nash began a big oil *Winter Sea*. The waves, seen over a low diagonal of strand or sea wall, advance in abstracting lines and acute angles of light and darkness. It would take him a dozen years to finish it.

From 1925 to 1930 they lived at Iden, a wooded place near Rye on the western fringe of Romney Marsh. There Nash set schematised nature with ladders and scaffolds – means to process, models for work. In 1929 he made two Surrealist deployments. *Swan Song* shows dead leaves and mushrooms lying as if in wait for some composing resurrection. In *Dead Spring* a potted plant wilts between a window and a draughtsman's set-square.

His father's death in 1929 brought the task of breaking up the household at Iver Heath, and selling the home whose 'bird garden' had set an early stage for his vision. It seemed to break Paul's heart. In the year after Iver Heath was sold came the first attacks of bronchial asthma. Over sixteen years it would slowly kill him.

11. *Poet and Painter*, 136.

Plate 124. *Genesis: The Dry Land Appearing,* 1924. Wood engraving

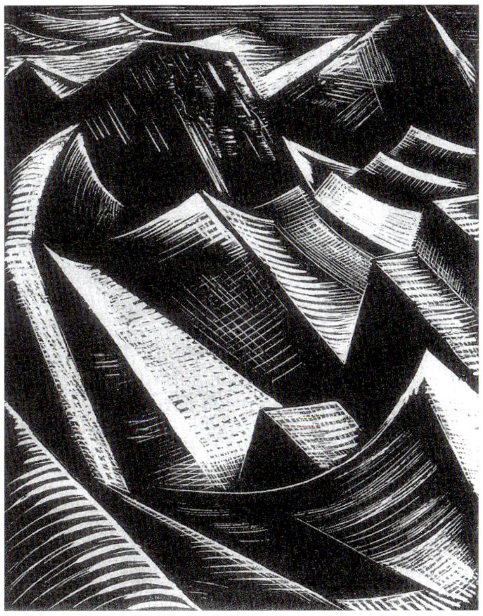

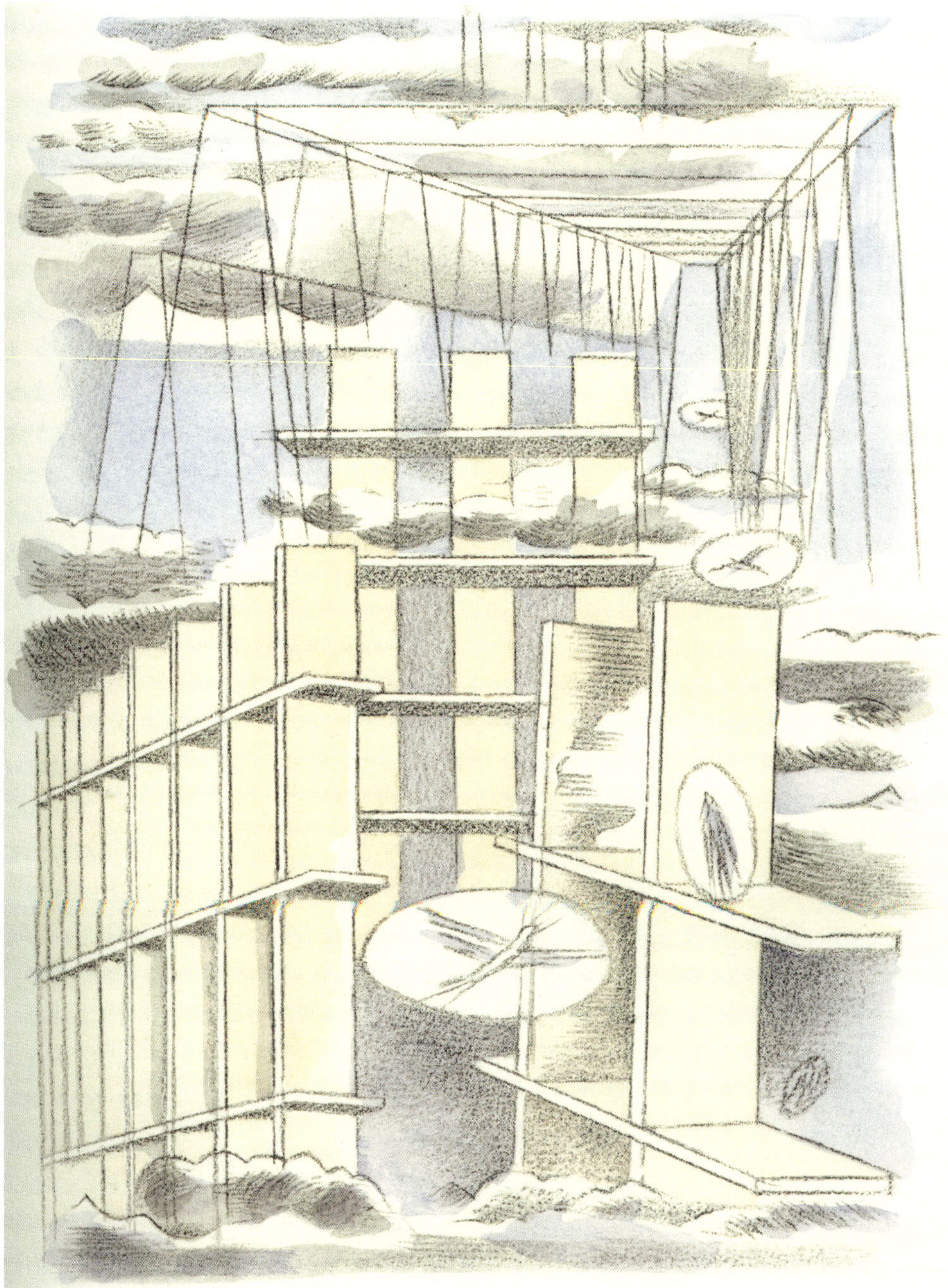

Plate 125. *Urne Buriall* and *The Garden of Cyrus: The Soul Visiting the Mansions of the Dead,* 1931-32. Collotype reproduction of watercolour

The Provost and Fellows of Eton College

It was also in 1930, when Nash was forty and forty-one, that the theme of death appeared under its own name in his art. A plan to illustrate Bunyan's *Pilgrim's Progress* was overtaken by the chance to make a set of images for Sir Thomas Browne's *Urne Buriall* and *The Garden of Cyrus* (Plate 125). 'The Soul Visiting the Mansions of the Dead' enters a series of constructs in dimensions more apparent than real. Colours are near monochrome. Emotion is ice cold. It was (Nash recalled at the end of his life) 'my first attempt to express the sensation of *being in space*'.[12]

A move in 1930 into the town of Rye signalled a change. From now on Nash was to be a dweller in towns. Puzzlement and dissatisfaction with his own art emerged in a compulsion to write. In 1931 he published no fewer than fourteen articles – on topics from Picasso to American cartoonists. In 1932 he wrote six further articles, and another six about design and home decoration to fill a small volume, *Room and Book.*

Confusion haunts the opening chapter, where he calls for 'greater mental independence', and in the same sentence for 'an intelligent, unprejudiced study of modern movements'. 'Almost everyone to-day is part of an impoverished state, a sort of incalculable bankrupt stock.' Hence, he feels, the continuing wish for 'the human note' sounded by recognisable subject matter. It kept a special resonance in England: 'There are still a great number of people who are unhappy with a non-representational picture.'[13] The tale of his own pictures continued to testify that he himself was one.

In 1933 he joined the sculptor Henry Moore to found a group of artists called 'Unit One'. The avowed aim was to find some accommodation between Surrealism and Abstraction. They recruited Barbara Hepworth and Ben Nicholson. But Nicholson was a committed Abstractionist, and demanded total unquestioning loyalty to his faith. It echoed too acutely the political fascisms, including communism, rising across Europe. Within two years 'Unit One' fractured hopelessly.

Nash and Margaret had already decided early in 1933 to leave Rye – without any plan of where to go, beyond perching in Margaret's tiny London flat (kept on since their marriage). Paul was so weak and dispirited from winter influenza and bronchitis that he could not face packing. Margaret took it on single-handed, and sent him for a holiday with their friend Ruth Clark.

He chose Marlborough on the Wiltshire Downs. He took the camera Margaret had given him: it was invaluable, when asthma limited his time out of doors, to record scenes and objects for further study. One day he and Ruth went in a local bus to Avebury. When he saw the prehistoric arrangement of huge stones, he was deeply struck. While Ruth climbed the nearby cone of Silbury Hill (an effort beyond Nash's strength now), he sat 'cross-legged in the stubble… drawing and painting all the time'.

As at Dymchurch, this landscape showed nature overlaid with human shaping – 'a fusion of cultural with artificial design'.[14] Here the artist's eye met the 'rough monoliths' of Avebury, juxtaposed with the 'green pyramid' of Silbury casting its 'gigantic shadow' just beyond; while close at hand 'the white trumpet of a convolvulus' turned on its spiralling stem to follow the sun. 'In my art', he wrote, 'I would solve such an equation.'

A trip to France early in 1934 only seemed to point him back to English nature. (Griggs's experience in Ireland, eighteen years earlier, had similarly clarified his English vision.) From Nice Nash wrote to his future biographer Anthony Bertram:

> I am beginning now to find my way between the claims of 'Abstractions' and pure interpretation. As you know, I am far too interested in the character of landscape and natural forms… ever to abandon painting *after* Nature of some kind or other.[15]

Back for a short stay on Romney Marsh, he wrote to another friend in August 1934 about picking up a fragment of wood during a walk over the Marsh:

> Yesterday I found a superb piece of wood sculpture (salvaged from a stream). Like a very fine Henry Moore, it is now dominating the sitting room waiting for a bright sun to be photographed.[16]

He added a further found fragment, drew the assemblage as *Wood Fetish*, and later showed the assemblage itself in a Surrealist exhibition under the title *Marsh Personage*. It was pushing the terminology to call it sculpture; nor was it any ordinary portrait. Scrutinising such fragments of nature was also beginning to open a way for a younger pastoral visionary, Graham Sutherland, on whom Nash had his eye. For Nash himself at forty-five, *Marsh Personage* yielded only fragments of the vision he still sought.

Another friend offered the loan of her house in Dorset for four months from October 1934. It stood on a coastal headland of the Isle of Purbeck, practically due south of Avebury and Silbury. Nash's presence there attracted the attention of John Betjeman, who was editing for the Shell Oil Company a new series of County guides for the motorist, to replace Macmillan's old *Highways and Byways*. Betjeman asked Nash to create pictures and text for a new Shell Guide to Dorset.

Nash's *Dorset* aims less at the tourist than at an artist in pursuit of natural and human geologies. He writes of the earthworks at Maiden Castle as having power 'to strike awe into even the most vulgar mind'. His own interest centres on Dorset hills and earthworks: 'Sudden pyramids are thrown up – actually conical in form and sometimes topped by clumps of trees.' (Shadows of Wittenham Clumps, rarely visited in these years.) The configuration appears again

12. 'Aerial flowers', in *Counterpoint* I (1945); reprinted in *Outline*, 262.
13. Paul Nash, *Room and Book* (Soncino Press, 1932), 8-9, 42.
14. *Outline*, 230.
15. 14 April 1934, quoted in Bertram, *Paul Nash: The Portrait of an Artist* (Faber, 1955), 216-217.
16. Quoted in Bertram, 220.

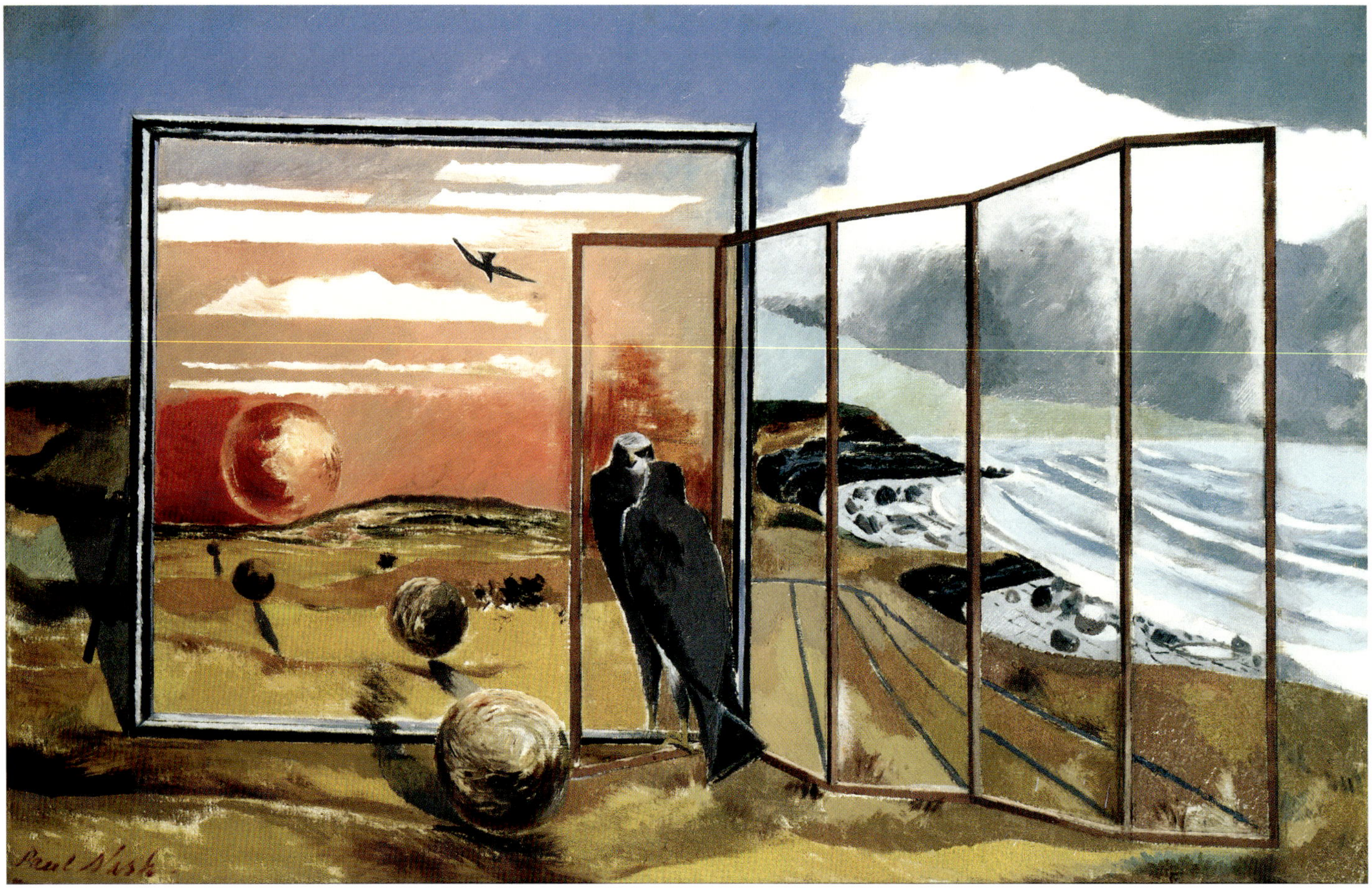

Plate 126. *Landscape from a Dream*, 1936–38. Oil Tate, London

in Nash's description of the stone-age fort within Bradbury Rings: 'round rather than oval, [with] the dread peculiarity of a crown of dense trees planted in concentric circles'.[17] Dread because suggestive – of what?

A violent attack of asthma brought the doctor's pronouncement that the Dorset coast was impossible for Nash. He made up his mind to live closer to artist friends about London. Ben Nicholson, Barbara Hepworth, and Henry Moore all lived in Hampstead. In 1936 the Nashs found a house there well up the hill. Many days in its airy studio he spent now with a brush in one hand and his nasal inhaler in the other.

He began to write his autobiography – concentrating on 'my encounters with places rather than with people'. He thought of calling it 'Genius loci', but settled on the more austere *Outline*. Yet after recounting his first twenty-four years, he seemed to run out of energy: his later struggles and evolutions still lacked any definite issue.

The state of Nash's art during the later 1930s emerges in a complex painting begun about the time he settled in Hampstead. This *Landscape from a Dream* shows a long background of recollected Dorset headland and coast (Plate 126). But coast and sky in the right half are seen caged through a folding screen of transparent panels. Overlapping the screen is a large mirror: it reflects a distant hill with the red ball of the sun at the horizon. The sun's roundness is repeated in several balls of grass also reflected, and another (at least as large as the reflected sun) actually standing in front. The contrast of blue sky above and behind, with red sky in the mirror, makes a surrealist play on Palmer's foreground sunlight and distant moon in *The Valley Thick with Corn*.

Nash's mirror does not reflect the viewer. But near the centre, where screen and mirror overlap, a shadow hovers of the hatted artist with his drawing pad (as seen in the frontispiece to this chapter). Below his shadow stands a hawk with its reflection. (Nash took it from an Egyptian carving which had touched his boyhood memory of Hawks' Wood.) The mirror also reflects a distant hawk flying through the reflected sunset. The colours show new brightness. Yet there is no integrated vision – still no integrated self to reflect.

* * *

Over all of Nash's experiments arched one vital concern: his interest in light and its courses through the English day and year. This perception made the beginning of an article on Nash's art by the future wife of John Piper, Myfanwy Evans, late in 1936. She wrote in a way to recall the 'free verse' of Palmer's letter to Linnell more than a century earlier; and so her lines are set out here:

> Paul Nash has absorbed the English climate…
> Abstraction in his hands becomes a weather-gauge,
> Surrealism the hailstones like pigeons' eggs
> that startle the midlands' summer sheep. …
> His violence is always the violence of an English storm,
> his clarity that of the Purbeck hills before rain,
> his brilliance the intermingled contrast of frost and sun
> and the whiteness of wet stones on ploughland.
> The English climate is his universaliser. …
> He has enclosed the morning mist in a birdcage.

Thus, she concluded, he had made time his own. That enabled him to keep his own way through 'these sectarian days' when 'the individual is subjected to the class'. So Nash met 'the problem of keeping some kind of thread going, some kind of continuity'.[18] That was continuity with the past. But was his present art a birdcage?

Nash seemed to measure the cage in a series of watercolours painted in 1937. They all try to envision one element of nature through another: *The Nest of Wild Stones, Stone Sea, Wood Sea*; and in 1938 a dreadful prescience: *Landscape of the Death Watch.* All are more or less terrestrial. One alone hints at the synthesis he will find through a Second World War: *Voyage of the Fungus* floats in the English Channel before the white chalk headlands of the south coast.

In May 1938 Nash entered a new landscape – his most frightening since the Great War. Staying with friends in Gloucestershire, he came into a field with two fallen elms – 'felled by lightning during a furious storm':

> The roots of one had been torn out of the ground. The other had broken off from a splintered shaft upon which it was leaning, its great limbs sprawled backwards over the grass. … Horizontally they had assumed, or acquired, the personality of monsters.

As he photographed them for drawing, one of the monsters took on a resemblance to the headlong horse in Blake's *Pity*. The other made a mate for the beast in Picasso's violent anti-war painting *Guernica*: 'it seemed as mystical and as dire.'[19]

By August 1939 the Second War was so close that Margaret insisted on their getting out of London. Paul wrote to his Gloucestershire friends: 'We… nearly killed ourselves packing… We watched our lovely home break up and vanish under our eyes. … We have enough to live on for a while and a year's supply of my drug. … I do not look very far ahead.'[20]

They went to Oxford just before War was declared. As a veteran of First War fighting and destruction, Nash measured the likely dimensions of what they faced: 'No new, better world will come of… this mighty effort of blood and pain and heroism.' Yet he knew it had to be fought and had to be won.

Ill as he was, he gave every ounce of ebbing strength to contribute his art. During most of 1940 he served as an official war artist for the Air Ministry and after that for the Ministry of Information. A medical board forbade him to fly, but they gave him every other access.

He painted aeroplanes flying and crashed, linking childhood dreams of flying to the Monster Field. The sight of a huge dump of wrecked German aircraft near Oxford (see chapter frontispiece) raised the memory of his *Winter Sea* (begun at Dymchurch, but only finished in 1937). The aircraft dump showed another sea, once threatening England but now dead. He painted it with the title *Totes Meer*, and wrote of its nocturne:

17. *Dorset*. Shell Guide compiled and written by Paul Nash (Architectural Press [1936]), 10*f*.
18. Myfanwy Evans, 'Paul Nash, 1937', in *Axis* 8, 12-13.
19. Nash, 'The Monster Field', in *Architectural Review* 88 (1940); reprinted in *Outline*, 244-247.
20. 2 Sept 1939 (quoted in Bertram, 227-228).

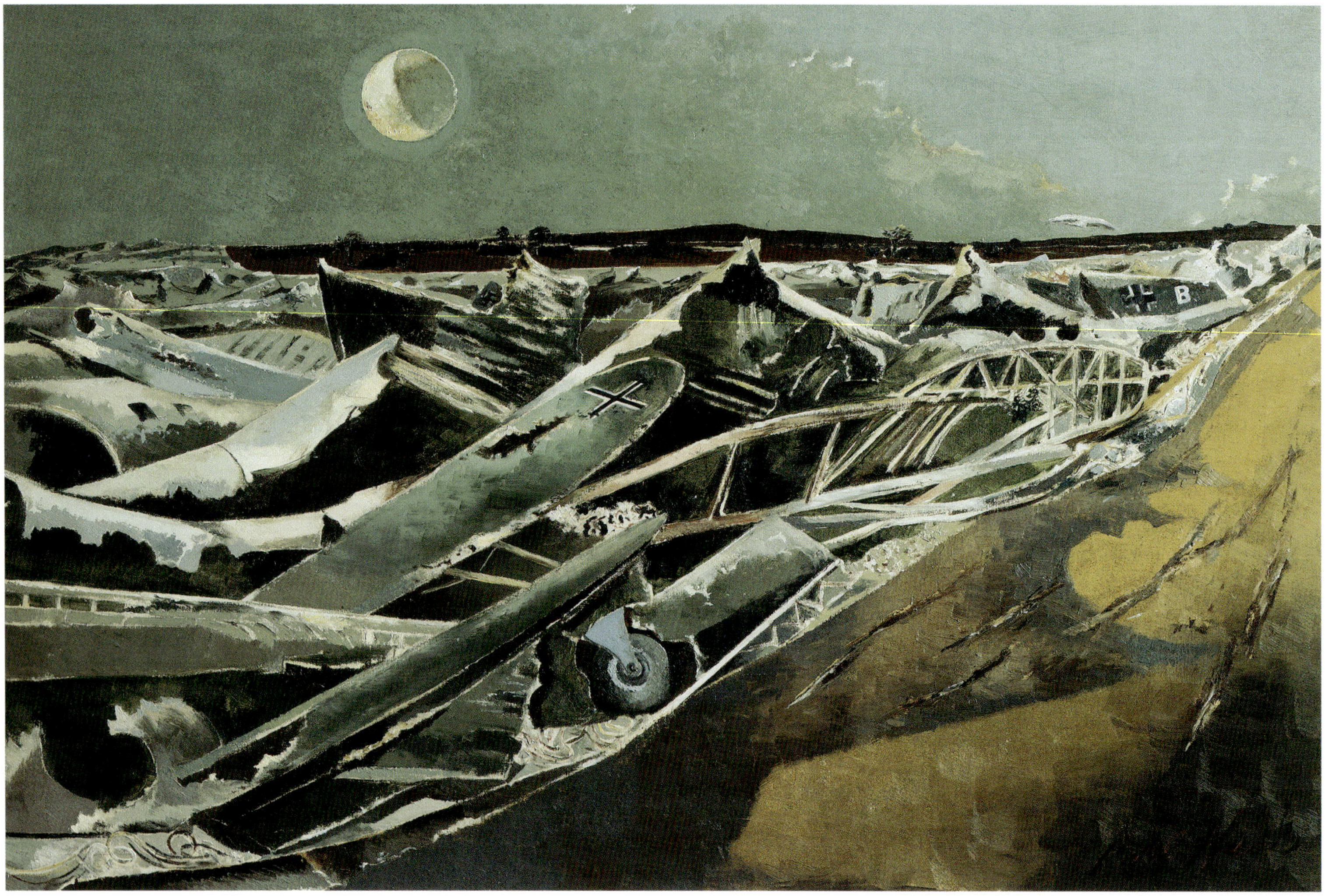

Plate 127. *Totes Meer,* 1940-41. Oil
Tate, London

> By moonlight, the waning moon… the only moving creature is the white owl flying low over the bodies of the other predatory creatures, raking the shadows for rats and voles.[21]

Man's wreckage – still under Palmer's moon, with his owl (Plate 127).

'He couldn't be idle for a single moment,' a friend recalled for me sixty years later: 'always working, always drawing.'[22] Whole aeroplanes challenged his draughtsmanship enough to recommend starting some with photo-collage. But to one heroically large oil of British aircraft flying he gave the Blakean title *Defence of Albion*.

Painting the lights of World War II from his own ground showed Nash that his pastoral vision must make some synthesis of earth and the air above it. Now he felt 'the sky was upon us all like a huge hawk, threatening.' He found himself 'hunting the sky for what I most dreaded… a white flower' signifying aeroplane fire or explosion, with the stem of its trail.[23] Explosion and vapour-trail showed Nash a monstrous *Sunset Flower* surmounting even the setting sun (Plate 128).

In 1941 he painted a large *Battle of Britain* in daylight colours enriched again. A map-like foreground of Kent, the intervening Channel and distant foreign coast spreads below a luminous sky – a field for the calligraphic vapour-trails of planes to map their courses as they do battle and plummet. An answering *Battle of Germany* three years later would show the English coast distant and serene under a full moon, while the foreground continent is bombed from its sky into abstraction.

Nash's creative life began to come full circle in November 1942, when he visited the house of a friend near Oxford on Boar's Hill. Through the wide windows overlooking garden and woods, his field glasses (his constant companion now he could no longer walk distances) took his vision right through one of its oldest mirrors. On the distant horizon rose another side of the Wittenham Clumps, which had first focused his vision of distances thirty years since – before both Wars.

21. 11 March 1941 (Bertram, 273).
22. The late Audrey Withers Kennett in conversation with the writer, 29 June 2001.
23. 'Aerial Flowers' (*Outline*, 260-262).

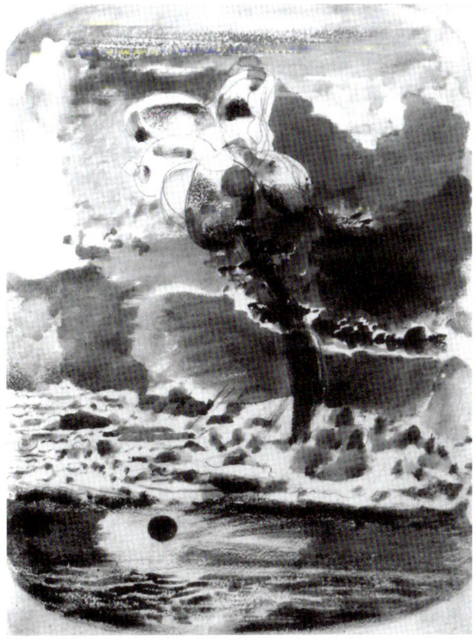

Plate 128. *Sunset Flower,* 1944. Pencil, watercolour and chalk

In further visits to Boar's Hill, Nash slowly retook the old visionary ground. As with his early 'Bird garden' drawings from his father's morning room, his vision through these late windows looked first at the near horizon. He painted it under a rich subdued *November Moon*, waxing egg-shaped over a pale blue and brown prospect of varied trees. Below them a sill or terrace holds two forms: a mushroom cap, and what appears as the trumpet of a convolvulus – death and life alongside (Plate 129).

Then the mushroom idea drew Nash's art to another opposite – the sunflower, with Wittenham Clumps now on the distant horizon. In *Sunflower and Sun* (1942), the foreground flower turns to meet the sun's rays, strong even from a cloud. He painted alternative versions: a watercolour of sun and distant rain in summer, an oil of pure sunlight in autumn.

So the dimension of landscape time opened fully in Nash's art. From 1943 he began to paint the distant Clumps under special conjunctions. *Landscape of the Summer Solstice* replaces the sunflower with convolvulus and three successive blooms of St John's wort ranged in the foreground: opening, in full flower, seeding.

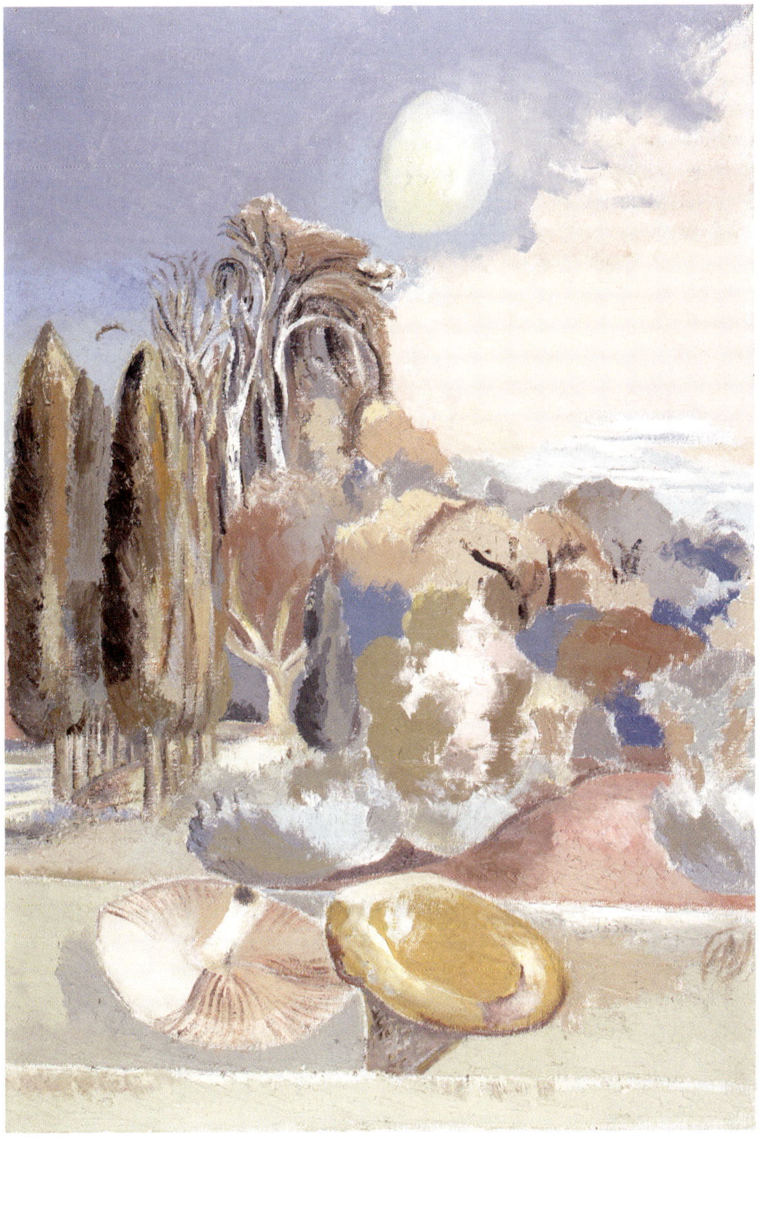

Plate 129. *November Moon,* 1942. Oil
Fitzwilliam Museum, Cambridge

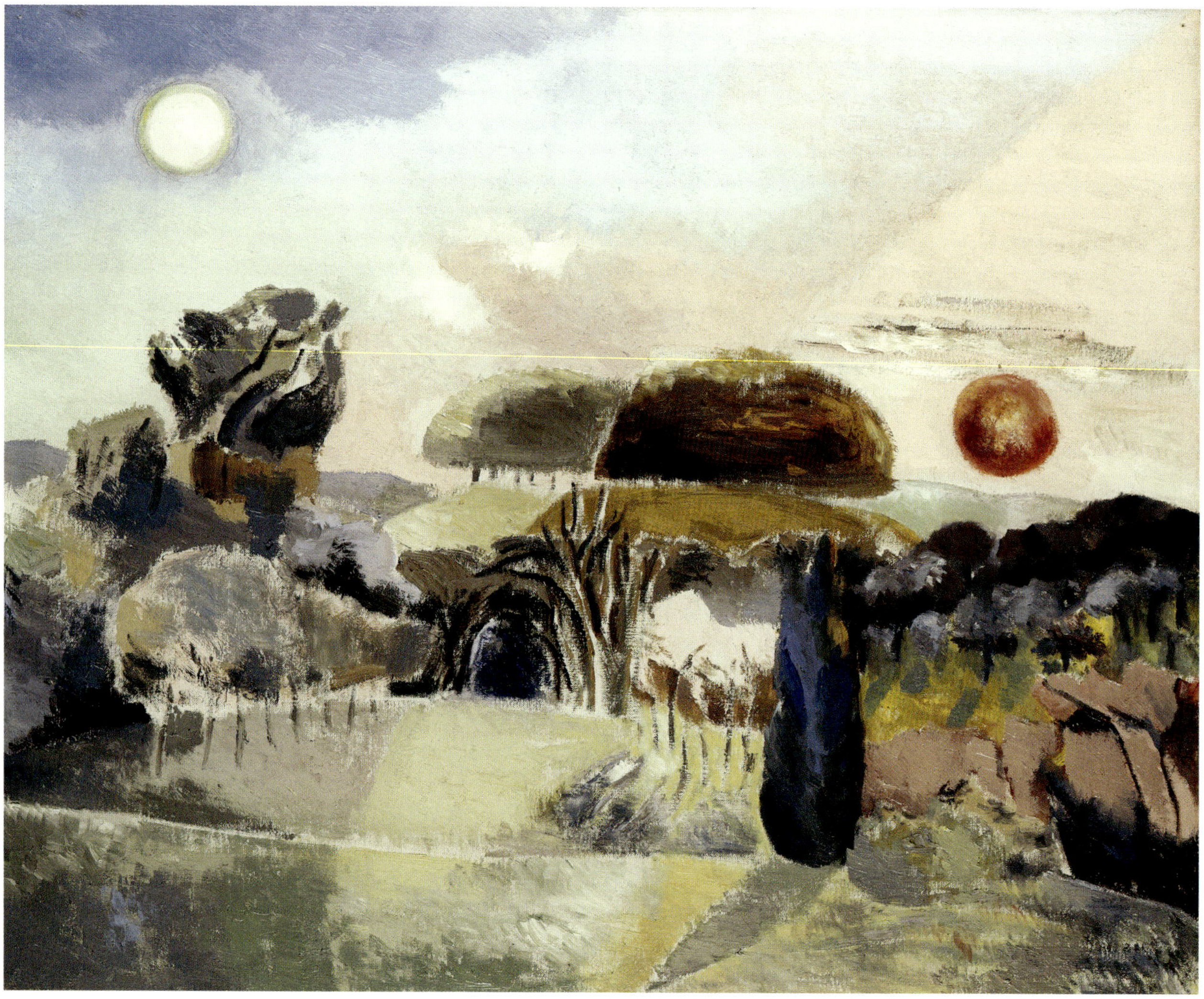

Plate 130. *Landscape of the Vernal Equinox*, 1944. Oil
Scottish National Gallery of Modern Art

Landscape of the Vernal Equinox (painted three times in refining lights) sets a white ascendant full moon opposite a red setting sun. The nearer Clump holds late sunlight: the farther is cold under the moon. The moonlit half of the picture takes its colours from *November Moon*; the sunlit half draws on the mirrored portion of his earlier *Landscape from a Dream*. Now they are fused in a single composition (Plate 130).

Then his conjoining of earth and sky revealed the goal of Nash's pastoral vision – at nearly the last hour, against all the weary worsening odds. Below the endlessly returning sun and moon, terrestrial nature – repeatedly violated by the wars of Nash's time – renewed itself through the seasons.

Time and its seasons had been glimpsed as Nash's key to his personal vision. Now he grasped it. In a late series of 'Picture History' notes, Nash paid tribute first to 'the spaces of the skies and the miraculous cloudscapes that constantly form, change, and disappear':

> But beyond any condition of the scene and its passing figures, I have become increasingly absorbed in the study of light and the drama of the great luminaries – particularly the moon and her influence upon all nocturnal objects whether on earth or in the heaven.[24]

It lighted him back over his own history. In the young nocturnes painted beyond the Bird garden, 'I shared with Samuel Palmer an appetite for monstrous moons.' This 'strange greed' had been forced to earth in 'the mud crater landscapes of Passchendaele and the nightmare of No Man's Land'. After that war he had used the sea wall of Dymchurch, ladders and windows at Iden, 'Mansions of the Dead' and *Landscape from a Dream* to mount experiments through Surrealism and near-Abstraction. 'I realise now', Nash wrote in 1944, 'that these were actually my first attempts to fly.'

24. Quoted in Bertram, 280.
25. Piper's review of *Paul Nash: The Portrait of an Artist*, by Anthony Bertram, in *The New Statesman and Nation*, 8 Oct 1955.

That year he painted the Wittenham Clumps under moonlight. *Landscape of the Moon's Last Phase* shows the orb egg shaped and cold at the horizon right. From the left, the dawn sky reddens the nearer Clump and yellows the night blues to fire: 'Very full-blown and frightening' he saw the newest dawn. His alternative *Landscape of the Moon's First Quarter* is weaker, as if hardly able to sustain so late a beginning.

Yet Nash's painting returned to full strength and to sunflowers in a final pair of oils painted late in 1945. They are his last and largest 'equivalents' – aerial flowers in *Solstice* and *Eclipse*. In *Solstice of the Sunflower*, the huge yellow head rises before two hills paired as the Wittenham Clumps, but with bare tops almost white in the sun's brilliance. Under *Eclipse*, the hills give way to clouds above water (Plate 131). Over it floats the flower, faded to a fungoid. Its glory appears memorialised in the flame-like petals radiating beyond the penumbra of moon and sun in final conjunction.

These paintings, achieved in the penumbra of Nash's own death from asthmatic heart failure in 1946, resonate with colour and symbolism hard won. His scrutiny and worship of earth's oldest survivals, and civilisation's – and his determination to set them in the lights of his own time – had raised a new Lonely Tower. Its prospects extended beyond Surrealism. In the eyes of John Piper, most of a generation younger, Nash's achievement lay in

> … deflecting the impact of the most powerful twentieth century art from abroad, filtering it through an English sea-mist of grey pebble and dead leaf colours… He was still basing his performance on the small natural truths that he had been discovering for years.[25]

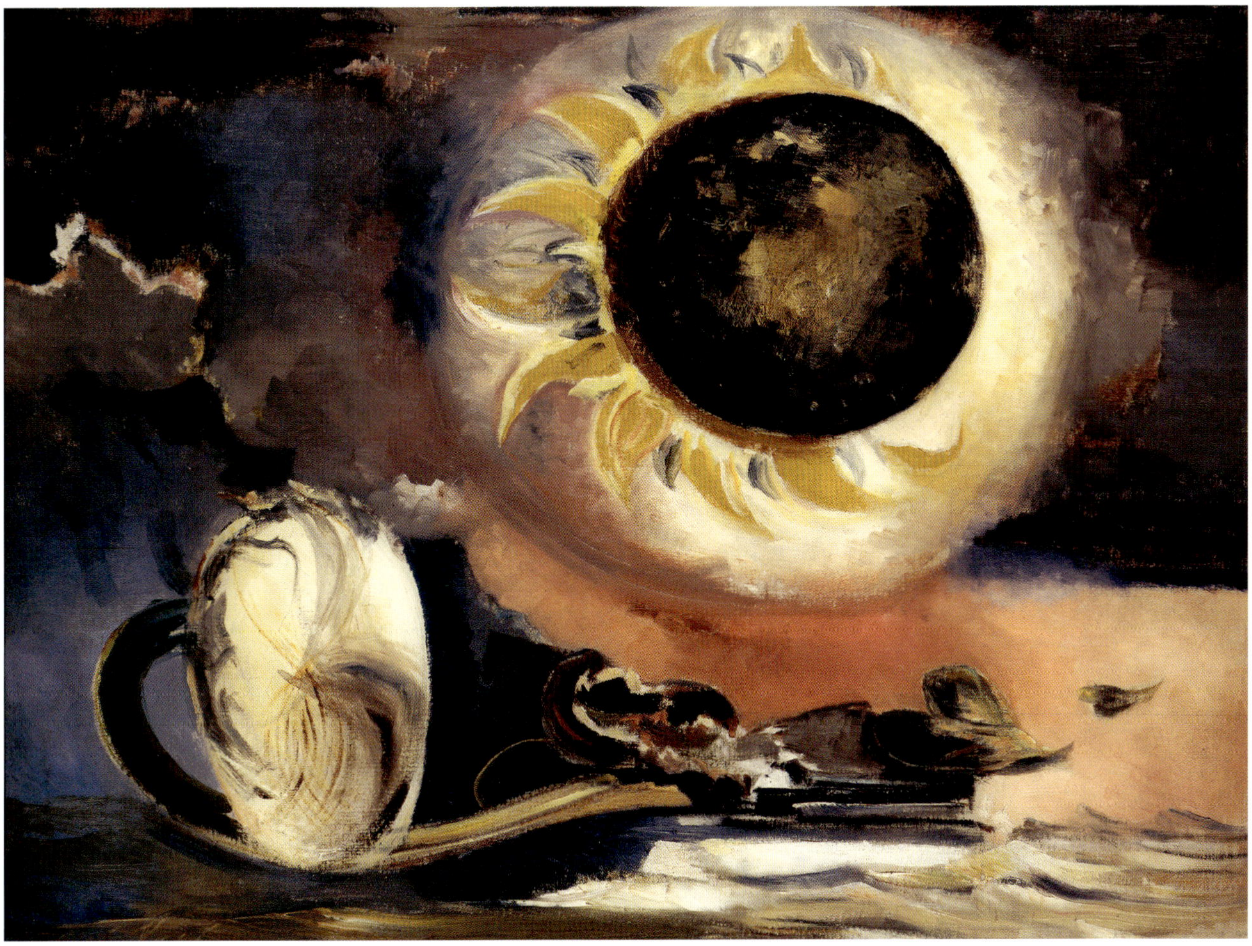

Plate 131. *Eclipse of the Sunflower,* 1945. Oil
British Council

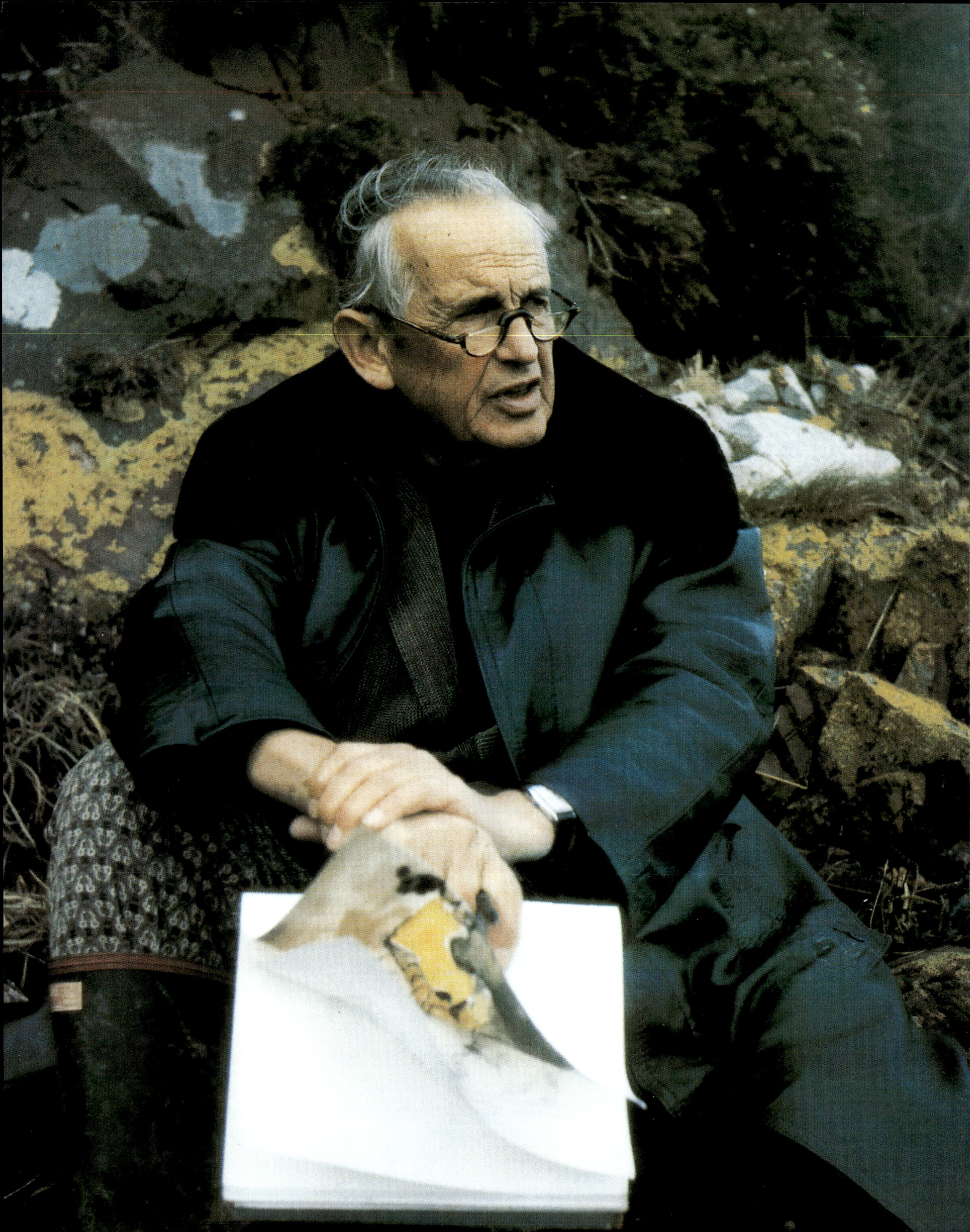

Chapter 6

Graham Sutherland (1903-1980)

Geologies of the Spirit

Opposite:
Plate 132. Graham Sutherland in Pembrokeshire, *c.*1975. Photograph Lutterworth Press

Graham Sutherland was half a generation younger than Nash. He was too young to fight in the First World War: but the reports, even censored for home consumption, reached into his formative years. Across the generations, young Sutherland was to know Griggs. And the pastoral vision of Palmer revived in Sutherland's early etchings.

Yet the experience of maturing through the 1930s pulled Sutherland inexorably past Griggsian elegy. It pulled him past Paul Nash's searches for an 'equation' among the twining convolvulus, the 'green pyramid' of Silbury Hill, and the monoliths of Avebury.

In 1934 the thirty-year-old Sutherland journeyed right across the British island from Kent to the Welsh coast of Pembrokeshire. There, instead of individual objects offering themselves for art's arrangement, lay a 'Surrealism' of shards and hills arranged by nature. Here was also the fourth dimension of time, in the fragments of bone and wood decayed to renew fertility.

The apparent chaos of fragments about the Pembrokeshire coast could reflect the fragmenting of human spirit that more and more dominated the decade running towards a Second War. Yet this fragmentation did not distance subject matter for Sutherland. On the contrary, it invited the artist's scrutiny. And so it opened a new chapter of English response to the abstracting pressures of continental art.

After the Second World War (in which Sutherland served as an official artist), the exhaustion widely felt in Britain tempted him to live in the south of France. There he would grumble at the English public's continuing interest in the works of an historical figure he called 'G. Pembrokeshire Sutherland'. Yet in the end he found his own way back to work again in Pembrokeshire, and accept the English judgment. 'I'd like to presume to call it innocence,' he wrote then, 'for that is what we all want to preserve.'

* * *

The Sutherlands were a Derbyshire family, risen from labouring into the middle class. Graham's father Vivian had been trained (like Nash's father) as a barrister, but then migrated to the Civil Service. Vivian Sutherland had a good but careful mind, loving music and literature as amenities. But he married a woman to whom they were central.

Graham's mother was the daughter of a man who had risen from office boy to company secretary of Macmillan publishers. She pursued music lessons even after she had married and borne Graham, her first child. Really she was stage-struck, and lived a life of restless fantasy. She and her husband quarrelled quietly, ceaselessly as Graham remembered: 'It was not a happy household at all.'[1]

His mother's restlessness fomented repeated movings of house. The houses were all on the southern edge of suburbanising London as it faced more or less country. From Streatham, where Graham was born in August 1903, they went to Merton Park and then to Sutton. There a younger brother was born five years after Graham. Five years after that a sister completed the family. Their father built them a new house in Sutton – and later a holiday house near the south coast.

Graham was schooled by a governess and then as a day boy at nearby preparatory schools. 'Not a dull boy by any manner of means,' a cousin recalled: 'He used to rather keep to himself, and didn't appear to have a lot of friends, but he had a good sense of humour and fun.'

The garden of one of their houses provided his 'first taste of landscape', when his attention was taken by a stand of elms with stems like columns. It was like Paul Nash's boyhood sight of trees in Kensington Gardens. Then Graham discovered 'my first conception of one space

1. Roger Berthoud, *Graham Sutherland: a Biography* (Faber 1982), 26. The authorised biography: quotations in this chapter are from Berthoud unless otherwise noted.

opening into another' when he crawled through a hedge into the neighbour's garden: 'The difference between one garden and another was enormous.' Sunlight there showed him 'a quality of enclosure' – of 'being inside (as it were) a jewel in a way which a sunlit landscape seems to have'. It was the luminosity which had led the mature Samuel Palmer to associate watercolours with stained glass, and which had lit Gordon Craig's visionary stages.

There was art in the Sutherland family. His father's sister admired Beardsley, Graham would recall, and 'did minute, very beautiful drawings of illustrations to poems'. But the illustrations which took his attention were those in the Macmillan books his grandfather gave them.

The most celebrated of Macmillan's illustrators, Arthur Rackham, appeared himself on the Sutherlands' doorstep when Graham was fourteen. Wartime air raids in London had caused Rackham's wife a heart attack, and he arranged to take the Sutherlands' holiday house near the Sussex coast at Rustington for her recuperation. 'A funny little gnome of a man,' Graham's younger brother would remember. Rackham's drawings were self-expression in line. Graham found himself 'mad' on them: 'I used to copy them, or try to.'

Then he found Macmillan's *Highways and Byways* books. 'They had some jolly good illustrators, and I think that was another influence.' He remembered especially the *Sussex* volume with its drawings by Griggs.[2]

There was no thought of Graham becoming a professional artist. In the summer of 1917 he entered Epsom College, where the emphasis was on science. 'It was disaster from my point of view.' So he came to feel like the young Nash – that anything of value had to be learnt for himself after he got clear of school. He left Epsom College in the summer of 1919 (and so missed meeting John Piper, who entered there that autumn).

Young Sutherland was not considered university material. He accepted his father's plan to send him as an engineering apprentice to the Midland Railway Works in Derby. There he saw 'the transformation of blocks and sheets of metal into the modern steam locomotive at its highest point'. It gave him 'a feeling for great machines which I have never lost'. Yet he knew instantly that he was 'on the wrong track'. After several months of it, he told his father he could stand no more, and wanted to become an artist.

The elder Sutherland was appalled at the implications for his son's ability to earn a living, but Graham's mother pressed her husband to find an art college for their son. No places were available at the Slade. (Graham, already a good draughtsman, was always to regret missing the guidance of Tonks.)

He was admitted to Goldsmiths' College, on the Surrey side of the Thames at New Cross. Entering in 1921, he found about two hundred students, mostly part-time. Goldsmiths' was more conservative than the Slade, less liable to upset at the latest French fashion. The best friend he made at Goldsmiths' was Paul Drury, son of the distinguished sculptor and Royal Academician, Alfred Drury. Drury senior knew Griggs – who was already a hero of Paul's. At Goldsmiths' they also met Kathleen Barry, at sixteen one of the youngest students, and as pretty as young Sutherland was handsome.

His Goldsmiths' teachers included E.J. Sullivan (a distinguished contemporary of Rackham) for book illustration. The School's head, Frederick Marriott, showed Sutherland basic techniques of etching, now approaching its greatest popularity: later etching teachers included Malcolm Osborne and Griggs's friend Stanley Anderson. Only one of the Goldsmiths' staff showed the students reproductions of Cézanne and Matisse. These puzzled Sutherland:

> One began to feel there was more to drawing than copying more or less what we thought we saw. [Yet] I for one thought the work he showed us superficial (a word then much in currency) and inept.

Sutherland began to make drypoints in the English tradition. He progressed so well that in 1923 his *Barn Interior* was accepted for the Royal Academy exhibition. It was hung close to a trial proof of Griggs's *Fen Monastery.* In the next year Sutherland started to etch. Some of his

2. Sutherland's praise of the *Highways and Byways* books (Berthoud, 30) carries his impression that all their texts were by E.V. Lucas. In fact Lucas wrote only *Sussex*, which Griggs illustrated.

subjects, assigned at the College, included well-drawn human figures. His own choices embraced rural scenes. Many were taken from the neighbourhoods of Sutton, towards Palmer's Shoreham.

When Sutherland had enough etchings and drypoints to make a little show, he persuaded Griggs's old dealer Mrs Bernhard Smith to hang them in her Twenty One Gallery in October 1924. Reviews were welcoming. Soon Sutherland was made an Associate of the Royal Society of Painter-Etchers.

One day that autumn a friend brought to College an etching by Samuel Palmer. It was the tiny *Herdsman's Cottage*, which he had found in a Charing Cross Road bookshop. None of the Goldsmiths' students knew anything about etching of this kind, as they had been taught the Haden-Whistler sketch-style. Sutherland recalled:

> It was unheard of at the school to cover the plate almost completely with work, and quite new to us that the complex variety of the multiplicity of lines could form a tone of such luminosity.

Few drawings by Palmer were in public collections then. One Shoreham drawing in ink and wash had recently come to the Tate Gallery – and was reproduced in Laurence Binyon's new *The Followers of William Blake* (1925). *Little Girl in a Ploughed Field* (Plate 133) 'astonished me', Sutherland wrote, 'with its total disregard for conventional composition. The drawing was almost… naïf.' But Sutherland could not then see enough of Palmer's early drawings to measure their impact: that bold pen-work still awaited a real inheritor.

Palmer's etchings were a different matter. Sutherland wrote:

> As we became familiar with Palmer's later etchings, we 'bit' our plates deeper. We had always been warned against 'over-biting'. But we did 'over-bite', and we burnished our way through innumerable states.

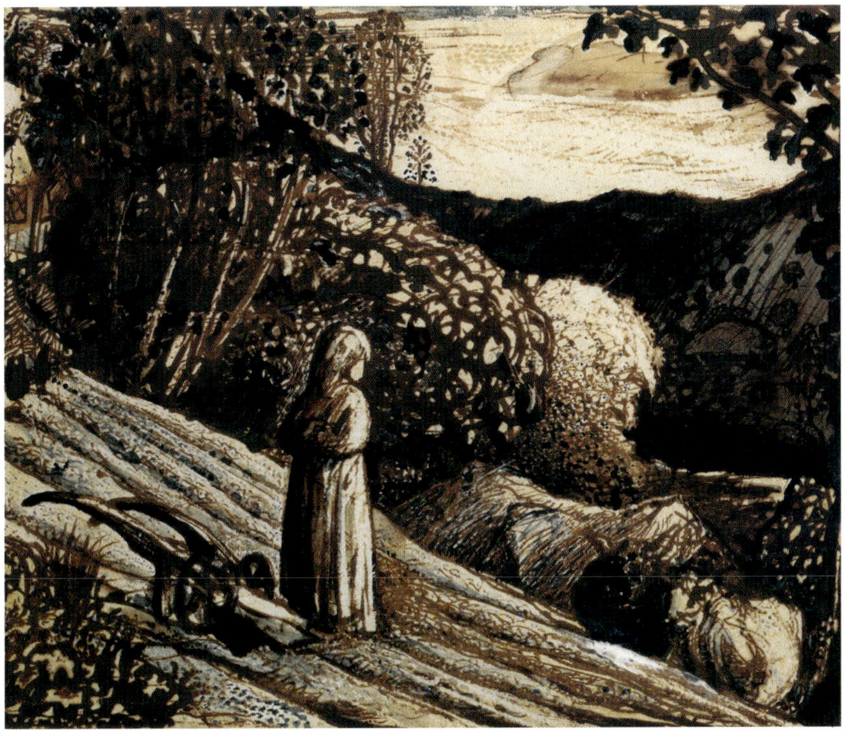

Plate 133. Samuel Palmer: *Little Girl in a Ploughed Field, c.*1826. Ink and wash

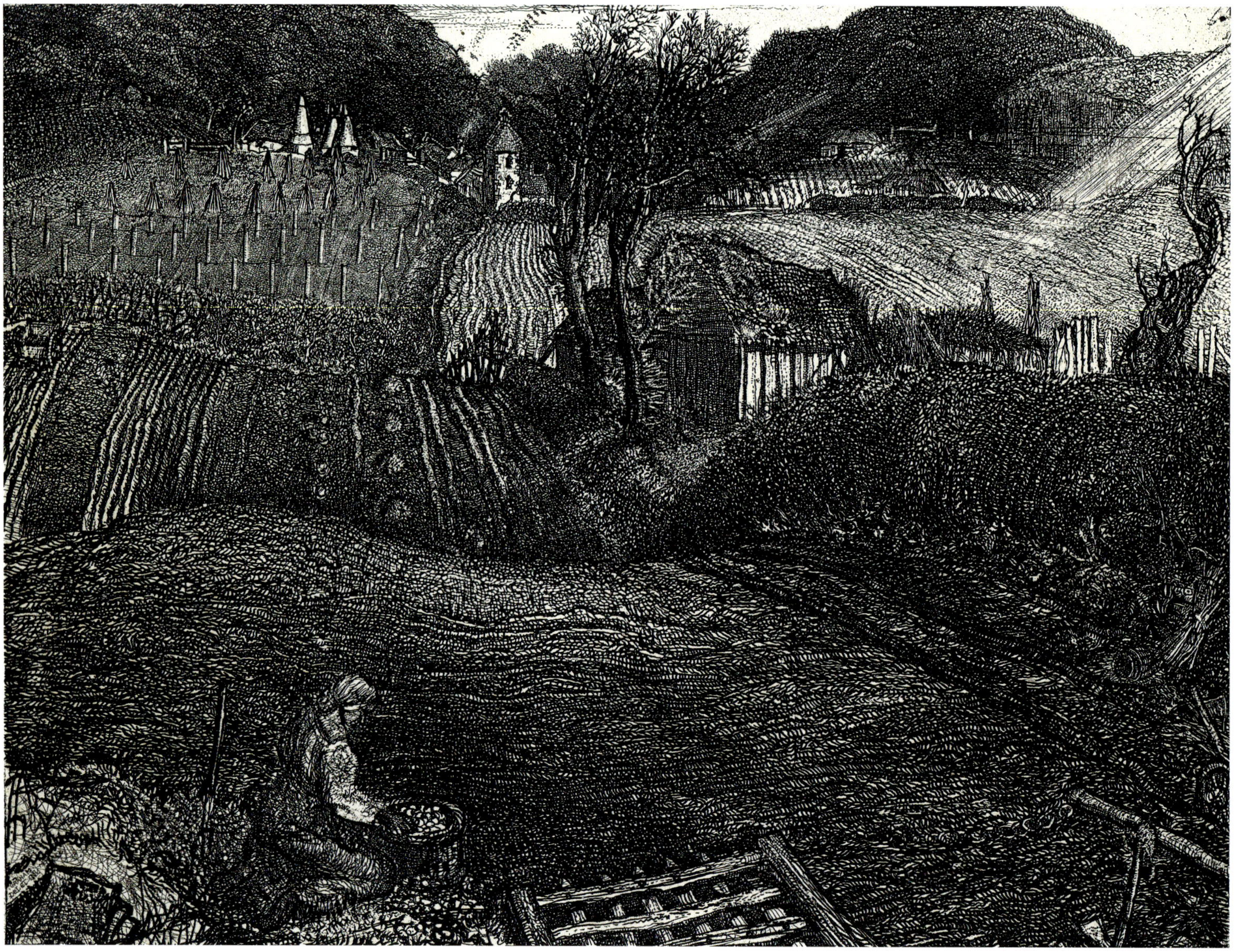

Plate 134. *The Village,* 1925. Etching
The Fine Art Society

He himself began a new series of etchings, each exploring the dense textures and enfolded intimacies of Palmer. He printed them on a small press installed in rooms shared with a fellow student. In *The Village*, sunrays lead the eye down to a lone contemplative harvester and antique harrow in the foreground (Plate 134). It was hung in the Royal Academy in 1925 near a proof of Griggs's still unfinished *The Almonry*. On Varnishing Day, Paul Drury's father introduced Sutherland to Griggs.

Over the next three years – during his last year at Goldsmiths' and after leaving in the summer of 1926 – Sutherland made pastoral etchings lit by sunsets and dawns. Paul Drury made a few of his own. The fifty year-old Griggs delighted in this emergence of new Palmer disciples. He bought impressions of both the young men's work, including *The Village*, for his own collection.

Griggs thought their printing might be improved. He invited Sutherland and Paul Drury to bring a plate each for printing on his own big press in Chipping Campden. They went at the end of November 1926. Sutherland would remember to the end of his life the sight of Griggs printing from his *Lammas* plate:

> Everything I know about printing I know I owe to him: how thick the ink should be, how to use the hand in wiping it off (Griggs had a palm as delicate as gossamer), how many rags one had to use, and at what kind of stages… We never came across a [professional] printer who had that particular acumen.

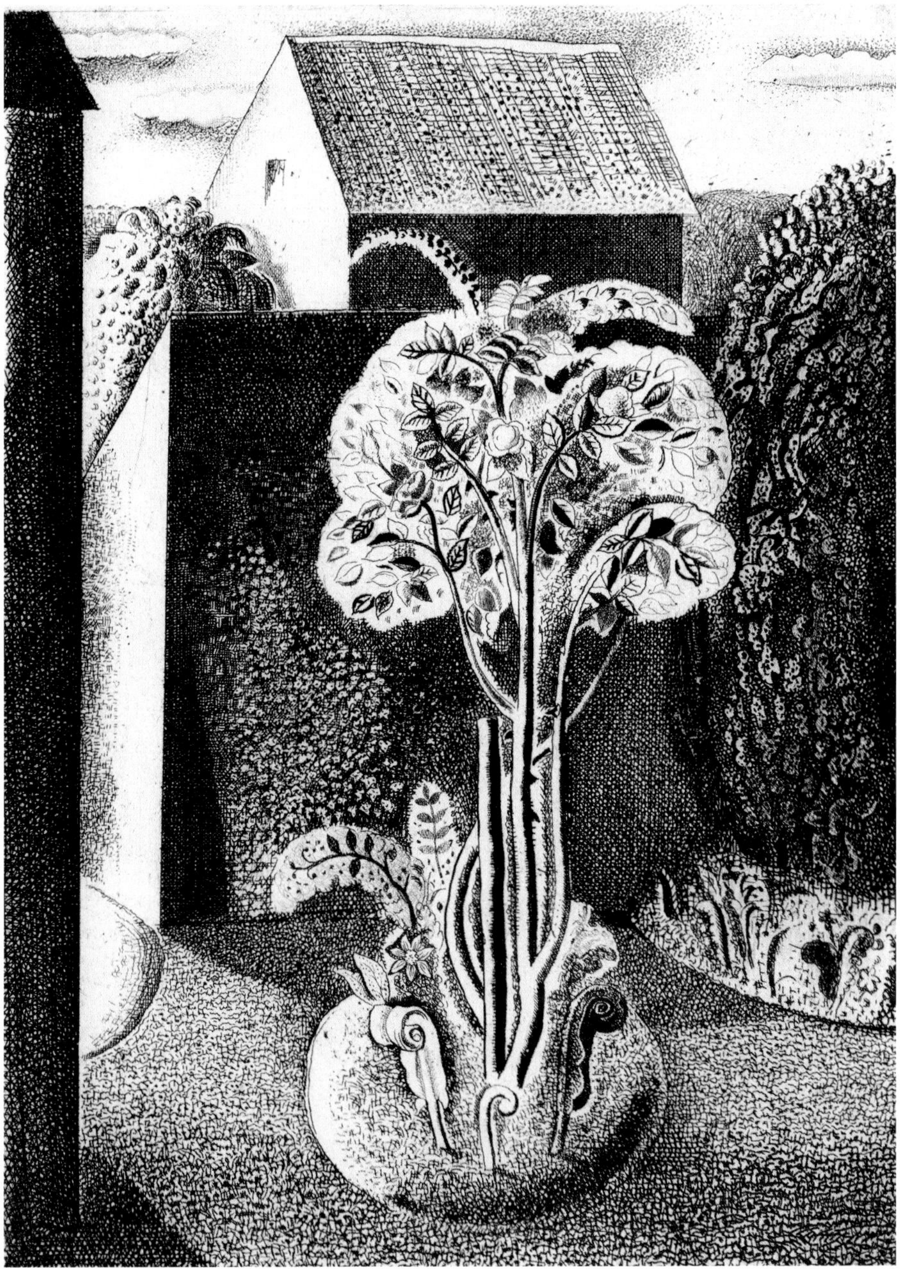

Plate 135. *The Garden*, 1931. Etching
The Fine Art Society

As for Griggs's own art, Sutherland was less certain. He was himself in the process of conversion to Catholicism (at the instance of Kathleen Barry, to whom he was now engaged). But the Catholic element in Griggs's art worried Sutherland. He thought that one etching-title showed Griggs 'thought real England had been damned': *Ex Anglia Perdita*. 'Lost' might equate to 'damned' in a young man's spirit.

Gradually Sutherland came to feel that the Palmer-Griggs tradition could entrap him in 'a total cul-de-sac'. He sharpened the edges of contrast in his own etched buildings and trees and shadows. Brighter lights whitened broader areas, and textures hardened, as Sutherland deliberately roughened his work. An etched *Pastoral* of 1930 sets rug-like hedge textures against white tree-skeletons and a massive shell of dead oak.

After the etching market collapsed, he sent to the Royal Etchers' show of 1931 a schematised rose bush (Plate 135). When it was rejected, Sutherland allowed his membership to lapse. Griggs wrote to Paul Drury: 'What is Sutherland up to? I wish he would leave Nash alone.' But a young English artist of pastoral then could not 'leave Nash alone'. When Nash's *Urne Buriall* illustrations appeared in 1932, Sutherland saw in them 'a poetic and imaginative achievement without equal to-day in this country'.[3]

3. Sutherland, 'A Trend in English Draughtsmanship', in *Signature* 3 (July 1936), 12.

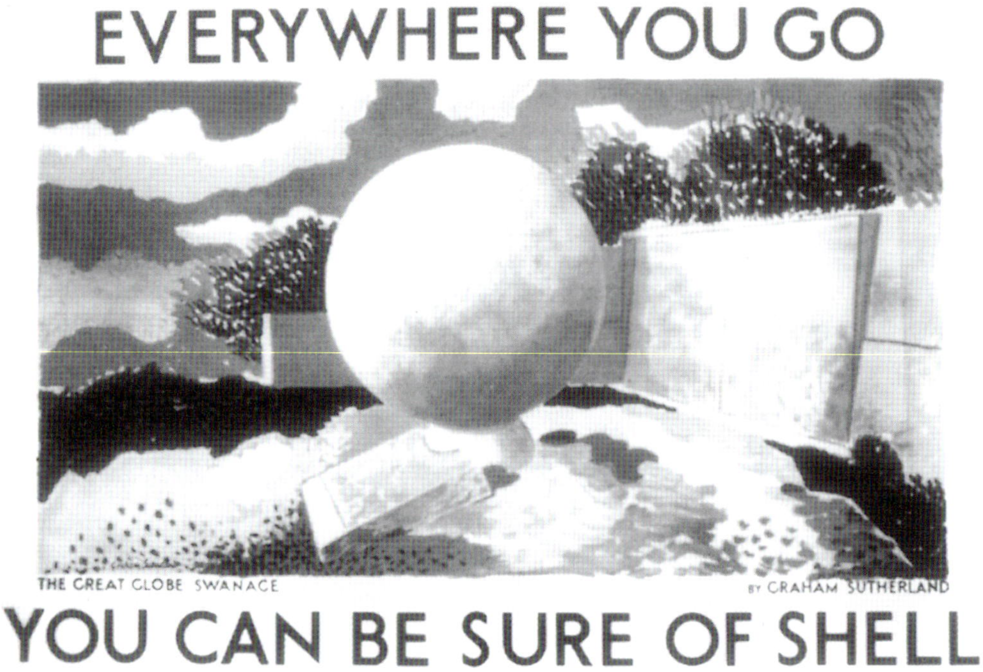

Plate 136. Shell poster: *The Great Globe, Swanage,* 1932. Lithograph

He was drawn not so much by Nash's surreal assemblages as by the elder artist's concentration on certain isolated forms of nature. Sutherland later recalled: 'Surrealism helped me to realise that forms which interested me existed already in nature and were waiting for me to find them.'[4] 'I did not feel that my imagination was in conflict with the real, but that reality was a dispersed and disintegrated form of imagination.' It echoed the young Samuel Palmer's 'Nature is not at all the standard of art, but art is the standard of nature.'

At the end of 1927 Sutherland had married Kathleen Barry. A son was born, but the baby had a defective heart and lived only three months. With him seemed to go any further wish for children. Graham and Kathleen drew closer together – a handsome couple determined to move well and hide any hurt. It grew (in the words of Sutherland's biographer) to a 'fierce mutual protectiveness'.

Sutherland turned away from etching, 'to broaden my horizon' with watercolours. His early watercolours were of places near their Kentish homes, using pale colours and streamlined textures in the Nash manner. He tried oils, but destroyed most of the results.

One means of support lay in teaching. Sutherland had taught at the Chelsea College of Art since 1926. A colleague there from 1931 was the sculptor Henry Moore. On country walks Moore, like Nash, picked up natural objects as suggestions for his art: mineral moving towards animal. Sutherland found in Moore's drawings a quality of 'discovering one thing with the help of another'.[5]

One modern application for pastoral art lay in designing posters. The Shell Oil Company (before any thought of the *Shell Guides*) was commissioning posters from young artists, to show where your car might bring you. In 1932 Sutherland did two posters for Shell. One was of Kentish oast houses. The other took him to Dorset (two years before Nash's stay there). At Swanage Sutherland centred on a huge municipal garden globe. He emphasised its surreal placement in the garden – recorded with Nash-like broadenings, but in his own crisp drawing (Plate 136).

The Swanage poster went into a London exhibition of such work in June 1934. It was opened by the young director of the National Gallery, Kenneth Clark. Clark was just Sutherland's age, and rising rapidly in the councils of British art. He thought Sutherland's poster 'stood out', and asked to meet the artist. Within a year Clark's interest was opening a patronage that would establish Sutherland as a leading English artist of his generation.

Others had already seen his potential. In 1932 a young gallery owner, Robert Wellington, had been eager to show Sutherland watercolours: there were not enough. But a Sutherland

4. Interview with Andrew Causey, in the *Illustrated London News* 19 Feb 1966 (quoted in Berthoud, 84).
5. 'A Trend in English Draughtsmanship', 12.
6. Robin Ironside, 'Painting since 1939' (Longmans, Green for The British Council, 1947), 28.

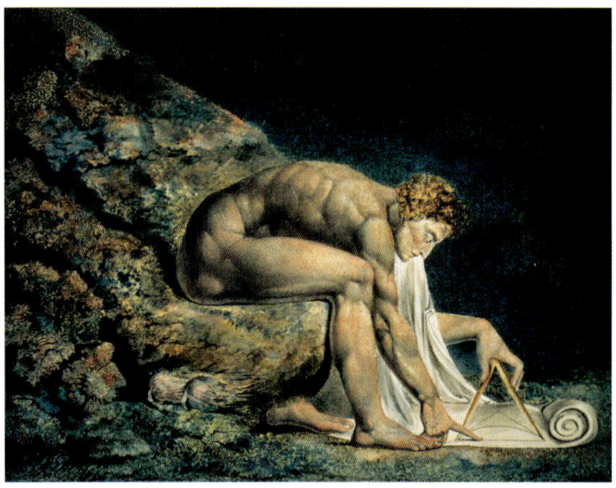

Plate 137. William Blake: *Newton, c.* 1804-05. Coloured print with pen and watercolour

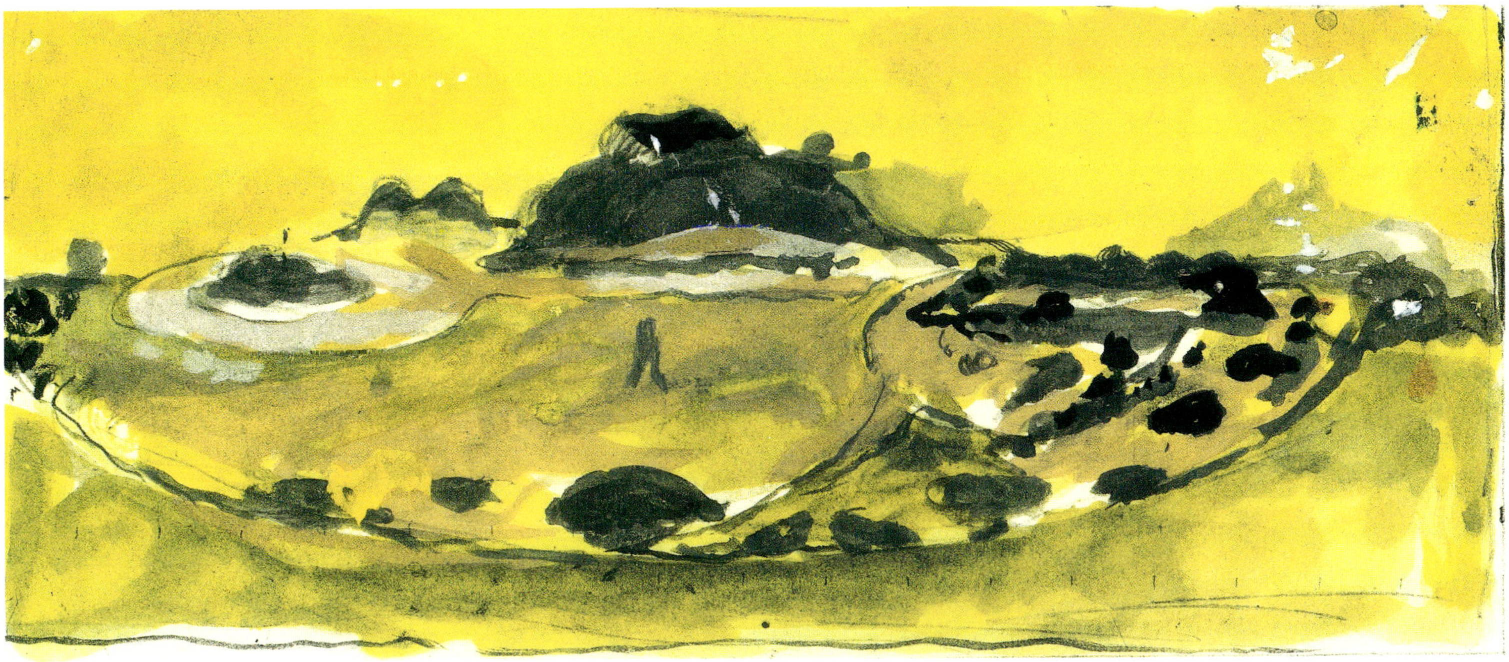

Plate 138. Sketch-book page: Rocks and fields near St David's, 1968. Watercolour and wash

drawing of chalk pits near Gravesend sprang to Wellington's mind during a summer holiday in 1933 on the western Welsh coast of Pembrokeshire: 'I thought it had the same sort of feeling', he wrote to Sutherland, 'which you had enjoyed so much in the chalk pits.' He recommended Sutherland to go to Pembrokeshire. The summer of 1934 found Graham and Kathleen motoring westward to spend several weeks amid 'the noble but ominous scenery of Pembrokeshire'.[6]

* * *

The distance of Pembrokeshire from Sutherland's home in Kent was suggestive, as the distances of Dulwich and Shoreham had been suggestive to Palmer in the slower travel a century earlier. Palmer's journey had seemed an expedition into older times. Sutherland's journey took him to where they spoke another language and lived almost prehistoric lives.

Coastal Pembrokeshire showed Sutherland two special 'passages of country'. Northwards the horizon was shaped by a pair of hills (Plate 138) – a pairing reminiscent of Nash's Wittenham Clumps. Sutherland found these hills 'so classically perfect' as to shape a climax. Below them 'the ground rises to a vast congregation of rocks, fallen cromlechs, and goats' caves…'. Through it all, 'the complexity of the roads… form strong and mysterious arabesques as they rise in terraces, in sight, hidden, turning and splitting as they finally disappear into the sky.' Then Sutherland's reflections touched back to Palmer:

> To see a solitary human figure descending such a road at the solemn moment of sunset is to realise the enveloping quality of the earth which can create… a womb-like enclosure.

Another 'womb-like enclosure' made Sutherland's way to his other special 'passage' of coastal Pembrokeshire, to the south. There the roads plunged down towards the water (Plate 139):

> We… found ourselves descending a green land buried in trees, which, quite unexpectedly, led to a little cove and beach by the banks of a narrow estuary.
>
> Here is a hamlet – three cottages and an inn crouch under the low cliffs. A man is burning brushwood cut from a tree, bleached and washed by the sea. The flame looks incandescent in the evening light.

The high left bank showed 'an impenetrable damp green gloom of woods which run down to the edge of low brackish moss-covered cliffs,' he wrote to a friend. 'Do you remember the rocks in Blake's "Newton" drawing? The form and scale of the rocks here, and the minutiae of them, is very similar [Plate 137].'

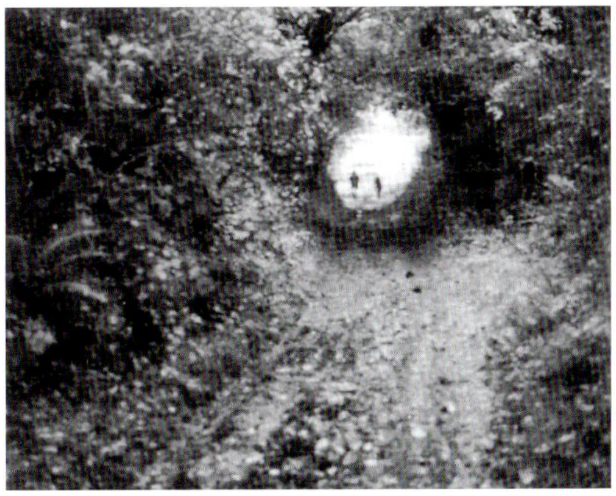

Plate 139. Sutherland with a friend in Pembrokeshire, *c.*1975. Photograph by Gilbert Adams Lutterworth Press

Blake's figure of Newton seems to generate its own light. The light in the Pembrokeshire estuary, Sutherland wrote, was from a low sun

> ... hinged, as it were, to the tops of the trees, from where its rays, precipitating new colours, turn the red cliffs of the right hand bank to tones of fire.[7]

Sutherland saw an 'exuberance of darkness and light – of decay and life'.

The special quality of light came from the fact that it was coastal light, filled with iridescence from the nearby water. Griggs had found it in coastal Lincolnshire – where it had reached up to give his etching of *St Botolph's, Boston* a sky 'near the sea when all the objects are clear and full-coloured as they are when there's much rain about'.[8] In Sutherland's Pembrokeshire vision:

> The quality of light here is magical and transforming. ... Watching from the gloom as the sun's rays strike the further bank, one had the sensation of the after-tranquillity of an *explosion* of light; or as if one had looked into the sun and had turned suddenly away.

The fields above these banks offered further echoes of Palmer: 'some covered with ripe corn, others with rough gorse-clad pasture'. But the 1930s, under gathering threats of a second war, forced themselves in: 'Cattle crouch among the dark gorse,' Sutherland wrote:

> The mind wanders from a contemplation of the living cattle to their ghosts. It is no uncommon sight to see a horse's skull or horns of cattle lying bleached on the sand.[9]

Here was anticipation of Nash's 'Monster field', and of Sutherland's sight of Picasso's *Guernica* four years later.

Sutherland recalled for a later friend the young struggle to make one's living as a painter in the 1930s. Failure at this time especially would mean starvation. Accordingly Sutherland had 'carefully observed the European art scene' of the moment: Cubism and Abstraction were both meeting with success in London.

In Pembrokeshire 'I learnt that landscape was not necessarily scenic.' Yet he kept his impulse to 'represent' even this landscape 'in other terms than those of abstract art'.[10] He shared that avoidance with Nash. Nash's First War images of bombed and 'murdered' nature could have set their artist towards Abstraction. But Nash had found that a total elimination of subject matter denied English closeness to the real world and its soil. Pure Abstraction suggested a double-mindedness – a hiving off of art from daily experience. That offended English pragmatism.

'It was in this country', Sutherland wrote of coastal Pembrokeshire, 'that I began to learn painting. ... I found that I could express what I felt only by paraphrasing what I saw.'[11] 'I believe that a new vision must grow out of reality': but to avoid the 'scenic', the vision had somehow to be synthesised.[12] A way forward began to appear when he looked at the trees hereabouts:

> I simplified the elements of tree forms. Trees have extraordinarily beautifully varied and rich shapes which detach them from their proper connotation as trees. ... They have the same urgencies as figures in action.[13]
>
> The forms are based on the principles of organic growth, with which I have always been pre-occupied. ... They give me a sense of the shock of surprise which direct evocation could not possibly do.[14]

Sutherland's 'shock' implied growth. But it was far from the 'regeneration' that had inspired the seventeenth century poet Henry Vaughan and other traditional pastoralists. For them regeneration conveyed the kindly workings of nature. Sutherland's vision recognised horror side by side.

Nash, in the work he had done after his First War painting, had hinted at that. But Sutherland saw a way to avoid surrealist assemblage in what he described as 'the extraordinary completeness of the scene' in Pembrokeshire. Here everything that met the eye, whatever its growth or ossification, was a product of the place. Here nature was creator, destroyer – perhaps above all, arranger.

---

7. Gilpin's Tour of the Lakes had recorded a chasm seen from above, where 'the sun-beams, unable to enter, rested only on the tufted foliage of the trees which grew from the sides.' (3rd ed, II, 49).
8. Chapter 3, page 115.
9. Sutherland, 'Welsh Sketch-Book', in *Horizon* V, no. 28 April 1942 (hereinafter cited as *Horizon*), 234.
10. Rosalind Thuillier, *Graham Sutherland Inspirations* (Guildford: Lutterworth Press, 1982), 103, 110.
11. *Horizon*.
12. 'Thoughts on Painting', in *The Listener* 46 (6 Sept 1951), 378.
13. Conversation with Bryan Robertson, *Kaleidoscope* (BBC Radio 4, 1978), quoted in Thuillier, *op cit*, 77.
14. 'Thoughts on Painting', 377.
15. 'Thoughts on Painting', 378.
16. *Horizon*.
17. See Chapter 1 (above), pages 60-61.
18. Sutherland, 'An English Stone Landmark', in *The Painter's Object*, anthology ed Myfanwy Evans (Gerald Howe, 1937), 91-92.

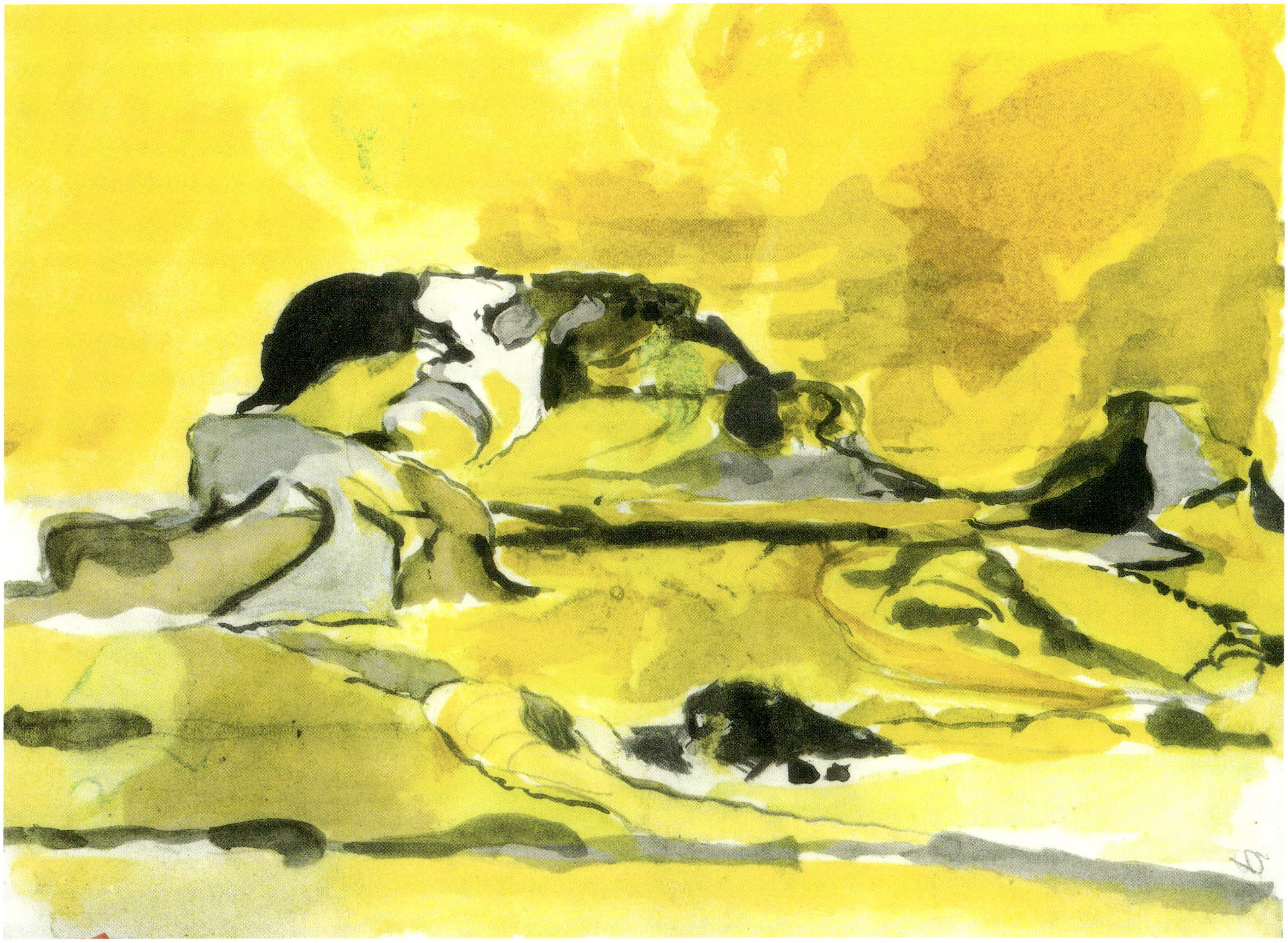

Plate 140. Sketch-book page: Outcrop of rocks near St. David's. Ink and wash, *c.*1970

To be on this ground was 'to notice how an infinitely small form at the foot of a tree is reproducing, in miniature, the whole structure of the surrounding landscape'.[15] He did not draw the coast itself, but used the coast as a low platform to look inland. He would lie 'on the warm shore'

> … until my eye, becoming riveted to some sea-eroded rocks, would notice that they were precisely reproducing, in miniature, the forms of the inland hills.[16] (Plate 140)

A different horizon of sequences arose when he went north to Brimham, Yorkshire in the summer of 1935 (in quest of material for a new Shell poster). The scene made a painterly vision to revive Palmer's formulas for obtaining brightness.[17] Sutherland wrote:

> The setting sun, as it were precipitating new colours, turns the stone, rising from its undulating bed of bright green moss and blackened heather, yellow, pink and vermilion.

Sutherland found more than coloured surfaces at Brimham. Here was another 'congregation of rock forms'. Among them he took a further step:

> Each intricate grouping unfolds the limit of another. Every space establishes the interest which gives to each form its significance.

It defined a third dimension, as Sutherland observed: 'Melancholy, impressive and integral such as this, is the basis of sculpture.' And in its wake followed the fourth dimension of time: 'Here it is as if, by a kind of prodigy of nature, the natural processes must add to the patterns inherent in matter.'[18] Sutherland's dimension of time, like Nash's, is geologic.

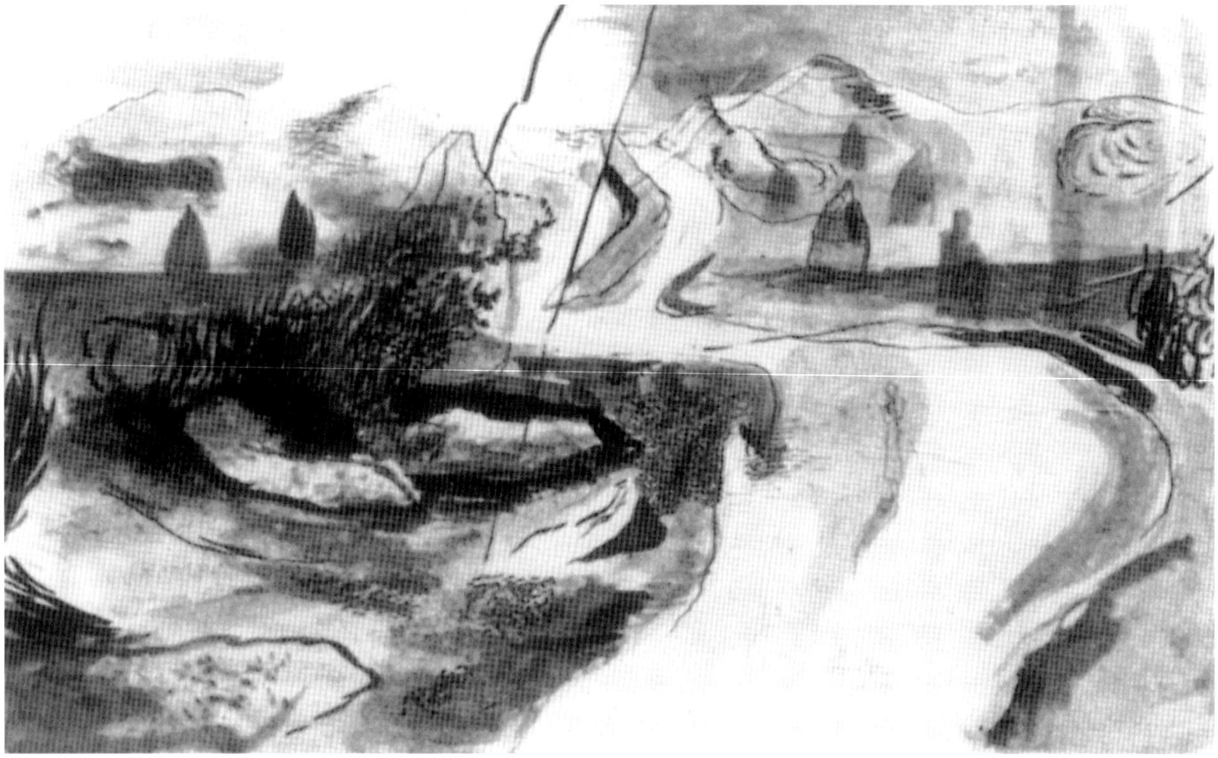

Plate 141. Road with Rocks, 1935-36. Ink and wash

He remembered trying to make finished pictures in Pembrokeshire especially – and giving it up. 'The spaces and concentrations of this clearly constructed land were stuff for storing in the mind.' So he began to make 'small sketches [of] forms that interested me'.[19] It 'helped to nourish my ideas and to keep me on good terms with nature'. (Blake's refusal to re-study nature, Sutherland felt, had held his art back – until the late Virgil wood engravings at last broke through.[20])

Sutherland used his sketchbooks to pursue 'the sequence of structures before my eyes [in] relationships between one form and another'.[21] As natural forms reduced to shapes and colours, Sutherland's process compelled his art back within the two dimensions of the sketchbook page.

A concentration on two dimensions could reach towards continental Cubism. One critic who interested himself in such connections was the Australian Douglas Cooper, who later befriended Sutherland. Yet even Cooper recognised Sutherland's 'romantic temperament' as linking him indissolubly to subject matter – indeed to the English 'picturesque' tradition. The critic counted over the English feelings which led Sutherland there:

> an attitude to nature which is ambivalent in its reverence, suggesting at once fascination, awe, and horror;
> a certain fear of vast open spaces and of the peculiarities of natural formation and growth;
> a pantheistic acceptance of the cycle of growth, fruition and decay.[22]

If a sketchbook image matured, it could be squared for transfer to watercolour paper – or later to canvas. At this point Sutherland would take his work from its scene of origin away to his studio:

> In the studio I react afresh. The original images dissolve, objects lose their normal environment and relationship. Then things seem to be drawn together and redefined in the mind's eye – in a new life and mould.[23]

Sutherland's finished pictures were made at home in Kent. But every summer he returned to sketch in Pembrokeshire.

One of the first Pembrokeshire drawings to be finished was an ink and wash *Road with Rocks* (1935-36) (Plate 141). Here the twisting rising road can hint at a further way forward. *Road with Rocks* shows a new kind of Sutherland line. Since the 'stump-work' drawings of Samuel Palmer, only Griggs and Gordon Craig had brought a personal line to English pastoral vision. Sutherland's new line in *Road with Rocks* caught the notice of Paul Nash, who wrote of it:

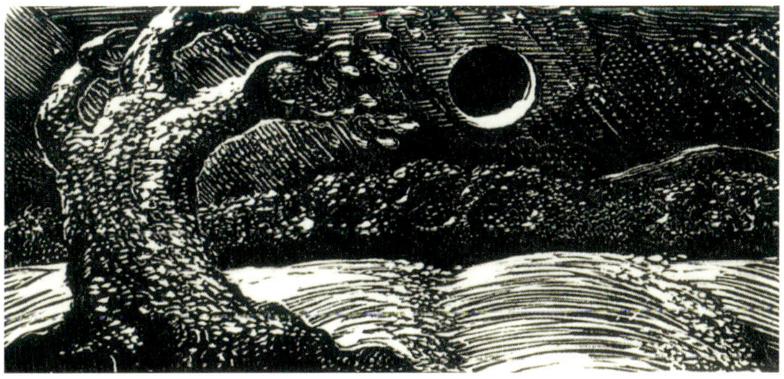

Plate 142. William Blake: Wood engraving for *Virgil's Pastorals,* 1821

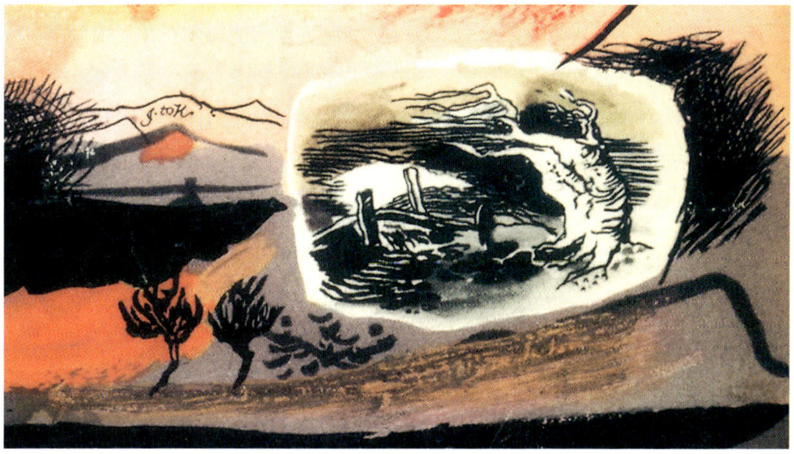

Plate 143. 'Winter' portion of book jacket for Kenneth Clark's *Landscape into Art,* 1949

> The whole conception is nebulous and abstract, the method fluid, almost precipitate. A feeling of nervous, scarcely controlled energy pervades the drawing, yet it achieves a subtle harmonious unity.[24]

It was the drawing's line that appealed also to Kenneth Clark, when he bought *Road with Rocks* for his own collection. 'Graham', he wrote, 'had considerable influence on me, by showing me a way out of the virtuous fog of Bloomsbury art.'[25] Clark saw both Palmer and Turner behind the vision now opening in Sutherland's art.

Sutherland himself acknowledged the heritage in an article of 1936 called 'A Trend in English Draughtsmanship'.[26] He dealt first with Blake's release from his own 'theological ideologies' in the late Virgil engravings: here 'nothing matters except the self-contained vitality which they manifest[:] mysterious grandeur and a flaring ecstasy.' Of Blake's ancient oak breasting the Virgilian storm (Plate 142), Sutherland wrote:

> This tree, so like yet so unlike the trees of our visual knowledge, so universal yet so intimate, obeys no laws except those of its creator. These stark forms... are strangely familiar yet disturbingly unprecedented.

A few years later, in drawing 'Four Seasons' for the dust jacket of Kenneth Clark's historical study *Landscape into Art*, Sutherland set his own mirror to Blake's tree. He inscribed the little drawing's distant mountain top: 'G. to K.' (Plate 143).

In 1936 Sutherland painted in oils, from flotsam washed up on the Pembrokeshire coast, several versions of an image he named *Red Tree*. Its form is closer to a cage of bones – on a blood-red ground, divorced from any natural context. One of the *Red Tree* paintings was also bought by Kenneth Clark. For men of their generation now, every second thought went to the encroaching threat of new war.

A sight of Picasso's *Guernica*, shown in London with all its preparatory sketches in October 1938, made a huge impression on Sutherland. He recalled later:

> By a kind of paraphrase of appearances... the forms I saw in this series pointed to a passionate involvement in the *character* of the subject whereby the feeling for it was trapped and made concrete.

Only Picasso, he thought, had realised 'the true idea of metamorphosis whereby things find a new form through feeling'.[27]

Gradually Sutherland's painting had concentrated, like the Cubists, on single objects and presences. They were usually mineral or vegetable, but endowed with hints of metamorphosis tending towards animal menace. Reviewing Sutherland's first one-man exhibition in London in September 1938, one critic wrote:

> Mr Sutherland's world is an unfinished thing, as though it had been abandoned half-way through the fifth day of creation.

A critic of our own time, Andrew Graham-Dixon, takes this farther, in the after-knowledge of how close the Second War was then. He writes of 'the anguished, totemic character that such forms assume' in Sutherland:

19. *Horizon*.
20. 'A Trend in English Draughtsmanship', 12.
21. Prefatory note for *Graham Sutherland's Sketchbook* (Marlborough Fine Art, 1973).
22. Douglas Cooper, *The Work of Graham Sutherland* (Lund Humphries, 1961) 2, 63. Cooper had been asked by Sutherland to write this introductory text to an imposing volume of Sutherland reproductions clearly aimed at the definitive (up to the time of publication). See Cooper's 'Author's Foreword' to the book.
23. 'On Painting: notes by the artist' in Arts Council Sutherland exhibition catalogue, 1953 (quoted by Cooper, *op cit.*, 21.)
24. Nash, 'New Draughtsmanship', in *Signature* 1 (Nov 1935), 28.
25. Clark, *Another Part of the Wood* (Murray, 1974), 254.
26. *Signature* 3 (July 1936), 7-13.
27. Quoted in Douglas Cooper, *The Work of Graham Sutherland*, 17 (without citation of source).

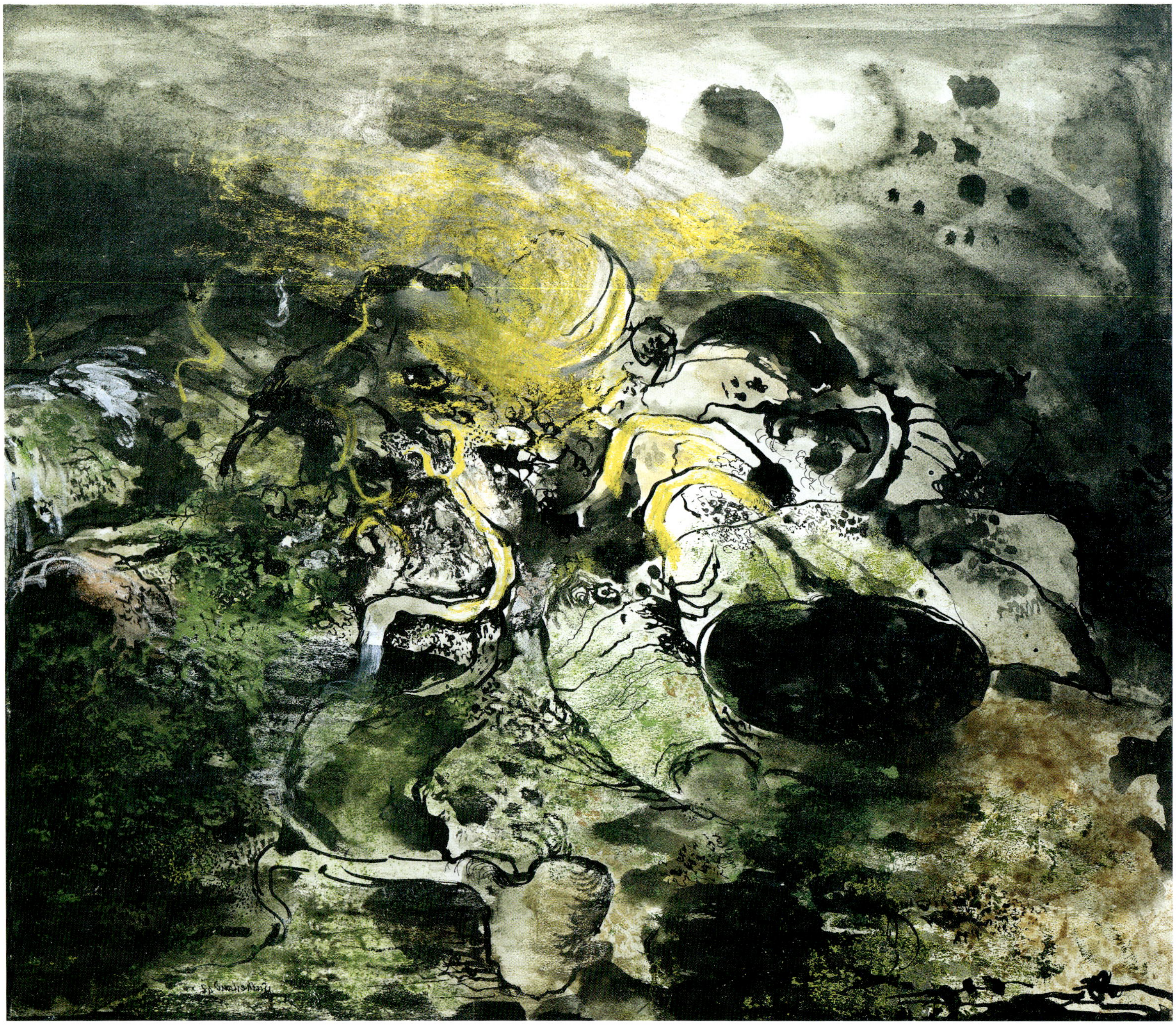

Plate 144. *Landscape with undulations and undergrowth,* 1939. Ink and wash

He pushes English pastoral towards the expressive intensity of *Guernica*, turns landscape painting into a medium for reflections on atrocity. …

Sutherland was an artist of great honesty and consistency of purpose. He never lost his feeling for the natural world.[28]

Horizon disappears – a loss of perspective eloquent of the Second War's close inevitability now. Sutherland's intensified colours went to greens exuding both decay and renewal (Plate 144). Exactly this paradox was informing the poetry of Sutherland's younger contemporary Dylan Thomas:

> The force that through the green fuse drives the flower
> Drives my green age: that blasts the roots of trees
> Is my destroyer.
> And I am dumb to tell the crooked rose
> My youth is bent by the same wintry fever.

* * *

28. *Sunday Telegraph* 19 June 2005.

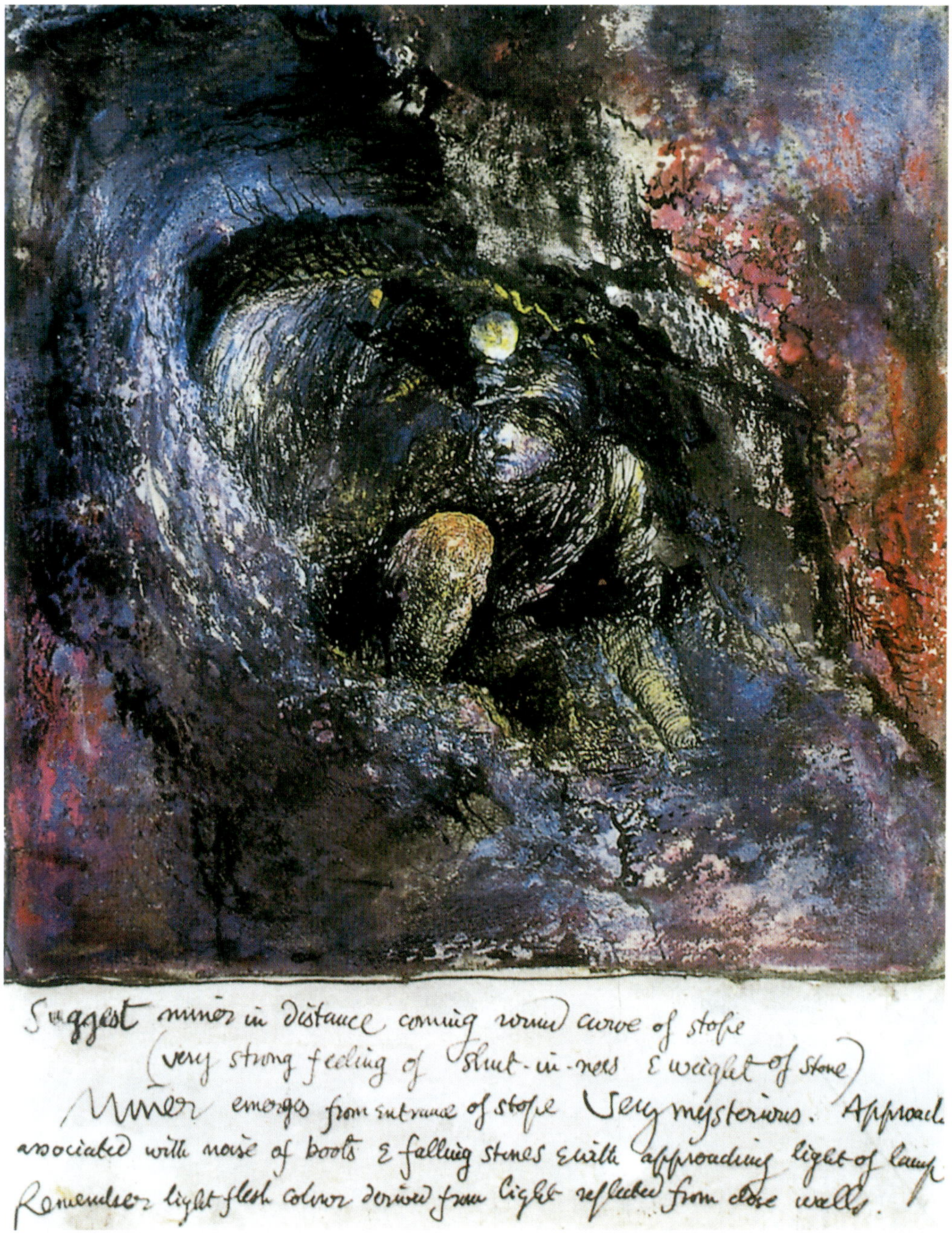

Plate 145. *Miner,* 1942. Ink, pastel and wash

Ten days after the declaration of World War II in September 1939, Sutherland wrote: 'I cannot believe that any war today can bring anything but further evil in its wake.' Nash felt the same. Sutherland, half a generation younger, agonised over the contribution he should make.

Kenneth Clark reassured him. Sutherland's contribution must be his art. Clark proposed a government scheme to employ the best British artists to make a unique record of the War for the nation's history (while increasing chances of those talents' survival: at least that lesson of the First War seemed to have been learnt). Clark's scheme was accepted, and he placed Sutherland's name on the list.

Assignments came in phases. From September 1940 to May 1941 Sutherland drew bomb-damaged South Wales and the East End of London. He was moved by the working class terraced house-fronts still standing shell-like, hiding the bombed chaos behind. Here were processes of Surrealism and Abstraction violently accelerated. Although this War work interrupted the course of Sutherland's development, he found in it a secret sharing with the natural histories of Pembrokeshire and Yorkshire:

> Gradually it was borne in on me amid all this destruction how singularly one thing would impinge on another. A lift shaft, for instance, the only thing left from what had obviously been a very tall building… a very strong lateral fall.

When a Government inspector applied the word 'abstract' to the finished pictures, Sutherland disagreed. The drawings were 'a very close and exact study of what these bombs do.'

His next assignment, to steel and munitions factories in South Wales, called out new colour intensities. At Port Talbot, Sutherland walked a parapet between blazing furnaces of molten metals. Nature's reds and oranges within blacks came here, he wrote, to 'Dantesque' meaning.

July 1942 took him into Cornish tin mines – down twelve hundred feet to tunnels a mile long. Black was pervasive, colours mutable in uncertain lights. But here he found new proportions:

> The diagonally descending shafts which followed the veins of metal… revealed precipitous perspectives of extraordinary beauty.

'Often one would come across a miner sitting in a niche in a wall,' he wrote (Plate 145), 'ennobled under ground.' It forced the human figure back to the centre of Sutherland's art for the first time since his pastoral etchings of the 1920s. Yet these ensembles of figures in their 'landscape' kept moving him forward. In limestone quarries near Buxton, in the spring of 1943, came the idea of a quarry and what it stands for '*transcending* nature, and formed by the mind and emotions.'

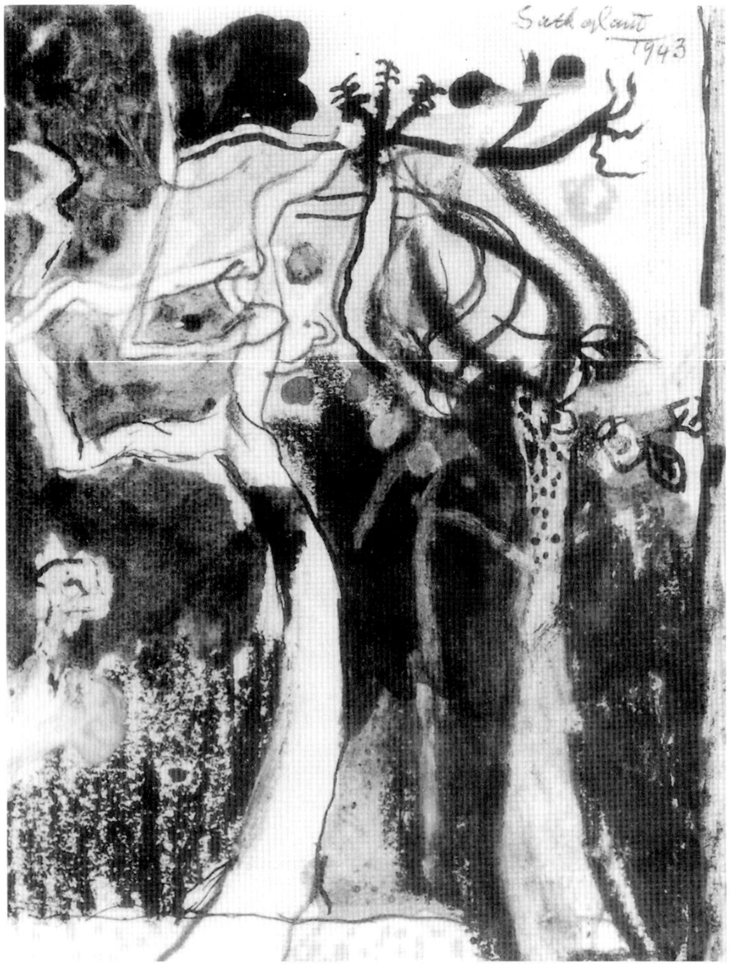

Plate 146. *Trees in an Apple Orchard,* 1943. Ink and wash

He returned when he could to Pembrokeshire, and also to his home in Kent. One study of *Trees in an Apple Orchard* (1943) touches back to Palmer's *In a Shoreham Garden* (by then in the South Kensington Museum); it also catches something of Rackham's trees mocking human shapes (Plate 146).

The sense of endangered pastoral vision now appearing in Sutherland's work (along with that of John Piper, Henry Moore, and several younger artists) had recently drawn from the critic Raymond Mortimer the epithet 'Neo-Romantic'. It was borrowed from a passing fancy in French art of the 1930s. In 1940s England the label stuck: everyone here recognised in Neo-Romanticism more than a flaking etiquette.

In the summer of 1943 Sutherland and Kathleen took the youngest 'Neo-Romantic', twenty-one-year-old John Craxton, to Pembrokeshire. Craxton was at Goldsmiths' College through Sutherland's influence. As Sutherland showed him how to extract landscape detail for private vision, Craxton asked whether such images were made of 'flesh and blood'. 'No,' said Sutherland, 'flesh and spirit.'

Henry Moore, to relieve his own war art in 1944, carved a Madonna and Child on commission from a Northampton vicar. The vicar wanted, for his church's other transept, a painting. Moore recommended Sutherland. With the end of the War coming in sight, there was a compulsion to commemorate its suffering in a large Crucifixion. Through the summer of 1944 in Pembrokeshire, Sutherland studied tree-stumps suggesting a twisted body.

The next summer there found him 'preoccupied with the idea of thorns and of wounds made by thorns'. He noted how thorns 'pierced the air in all directions, their points establishing limits of aerial space'.[29] Even after shaping his *Crucifixion* painting, the idea of thorns generated new tree-forms for Sutherland. But those designs of 1946 proved to be his last direct inspirations from Pembrokeshire for more than twenty years.

With help from Kenneth Clark at the end of the War, Sutherland and Kathleen had bought their own house in Kent. The White House at Trottiscliff was not far from Samuel Palmer's Shoreham. It was closer still to a prehistoric cromlech and suggestive Romano-British remains.

Yet as post-war shortages bit deeper in Britain, many who could manage it sought to escape. A fortnight in Paris in 1946 whetted Sutherland's appetite for more continuous living on the continent. A year later, encouraged by wealthy friends, he and Kathleen set off for the Riviera and Monte Carlo.

He loved the southern light, as Palmer had loved it before him (though it had upset Palmer's painting for much of a decade). But Sutherland was not thinking of Palmer now, as he wrote: 'To see Provence for the first time is to know Cézanne properly, and the painting of Van Gogh had suddenly for me a new excitement.' Kenneth Clark, who knew more of history, feared the effect on Sutherland's work. Others were reassuring.

A longer French visit in the autumn of 1947, in company with young Craxton's friend Lucian Freud, included calls on Matisse and Picasso. Against bright yellow backgrounds, Sutherland's newest thorns began to hybridise into grasshopper legs and cicadas. They looked to the young Neo-Romantic artist John Minton like products of 'hectic weekends at Antibes with Pablo'.[30]

So Sutherland's art moved away from landscape and towards the territory of still-life which brought it closer to Cubism. He began attracting attention from critics who showed renewing eagerness, since the War, to make a European Union of art with France holding permanent presidency. Robert Melville saw farther than many. He recognised in Sutherland's 'all-over pregnancy of the picture space' a link with Samuel Palmer's 'feverish vision of prodigality'. This aspect of Sutherland's art, Melville wrote, arose from 'the deliberate reduction of three-dimensional illusion'; he identified that with Cubism. Yet it is as visible in Palmer's six sepia drawings of 1824-25 as in seventeenth century English stump-work embroidery.

Sutherland's real link with Cubism may lie in his later treatment of objects (in Melville's words) 'as clichés', to the extent he does that. The critic writes of 'the vigilance with which [Sutherland] stares an object into instability'.[31] In a late letter Sutherland would quote Thomas Hardy's 'The exchange of international thought is the only salvation of the world.' The significant word for Sutherland was 'exchange'.

One day in 1949 the Sutherlands lunched at Cap Ferrat with the wealthy old novelist Somerset Maugham. Such was the light there after a festive meal that Sutherland found himself yielding to a proposal that he should paint Maugham's portrait for an experiment. Human images made another theme for Cubism, though Sutherland worked here in strictly traditional terms. He had trouble drawing trousers and shoes, but Maugham's face yielded a palimpsest of experience, with hooded eyes mocked by an ostentatious downturn of mouth. Sutherland asked £500. Maugham economised on £300.

The publicity proved endless. Other celebrities and new wealthy friends queued up to commission their own portraits. When he painted the press baron Lord Beaverbrook, Beaverbrook newspapers boomed and re-boomed Sutherland.

The 1951 Festival of Britain ordered a gigantic *Origins of the Land*. From thin flames below a basal crust, Sutherland painted greyish forms working upwards through plant-sections to a prehistoric bird skull and thorns reminiscent of Pembrokeshire. He went there no more, but surrounded his new vegetable-animal evolutions with Mediterranean yellows and oranges.

Evenings at the Monte Carlo gaming tables afforded distracting relief from another gigantic commission. It was to design an immense tapestry for the new Coventry Cathedral, rising as a symbol beside the bombed-out mediaeval shell. The woven *Christ in Glory* was to be surrounded by the four Evangelist symbols, with the Cathedral's patron St Michael also coming in. Design and weaving took ten years. But when the date arrived for the royal dedication, Sutherland found himself too busy preparing his newest exhibition of paintings for sale at unprecedented prices.

Having rented houses for longer and longer stays in France, in 1955 the Sutherlands bought a designer's concrete box perched above Menton on the French-Italian border. They re-named it 'Villa Blanche', to tie back to their 'White House' in Kent. Yet Sutherland's work responded more and more to the hot climate. In the thickening scrum of international collectors and dealers eager to invest in Sutherland's work, Italians led the pack.

Private insecurities still fed self-doubt. When he received the Order of Merit in 1960, Sutherland wrote to a friend:

> The old neuroses and paranoia still envelop me like a cloak, and however much one may groan at one's products, I hope there are a few signs of madness – I'd like to presume to call it innocence: for that is what we all want to preserve.

A new exhibition in June 1962 at the Marlborough Galleries in London showed his plant-animal hybrids combining with hints of machinery. The show sold out within hours. In the following year, inner doubt shaped his painting of a strange beast. It was inspired he thought by the Lion of Venice, yet its fore-feet were chained. He named it *The Captive*. Its cell is dark, the windows barred.

Worried that invention might dry up, Sutherland took the suggestion of an Italian gallery owner to draw and publish lithographs, which could be multiplied in sets. They comprised a bestiary and images of the life of bees in hot colours behind black lines. The issues were quickly taken up at prices averaging £100 a print.

* * *

29. Quoted in Rosalind Thuillier, *op cit*, 58.
30. Quoted in Frances Spalding, *Dance till the Stars Come Down* (Hodder & Stoughton, 1991), 131.
31. *Graham Sutherland*, with an Introduction by Robert Melville (H.P. Juda, 1950). Melville's essay, 'The Imagery of Graham Sutherland', is unpaginated. The quotations above are taken from its second, third, fifth, and sixth pages.

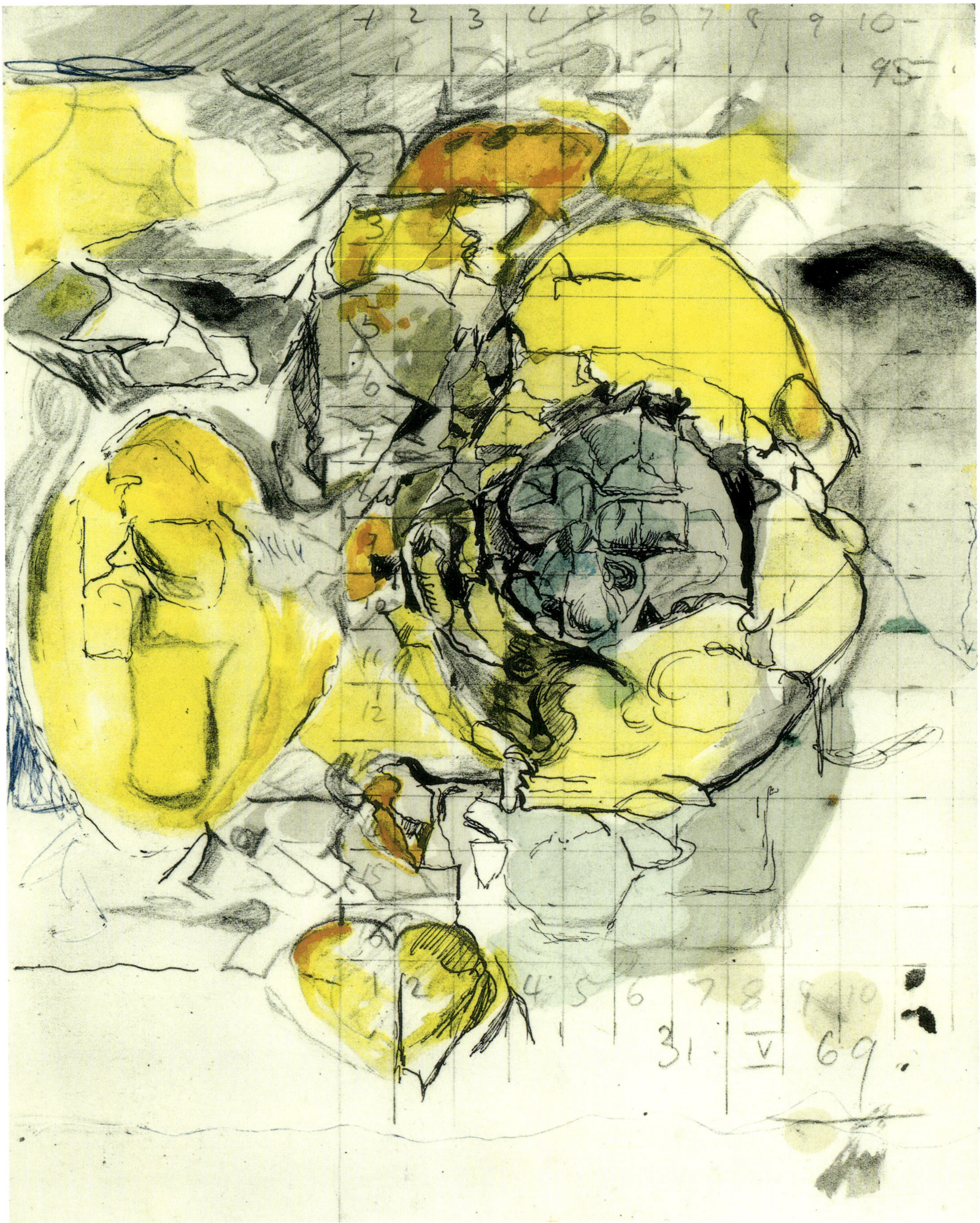

Plate 147. Sketch-book page: Forms in a cliff face, Pembrokeshire, 31 May 1969. Ink and watercolour

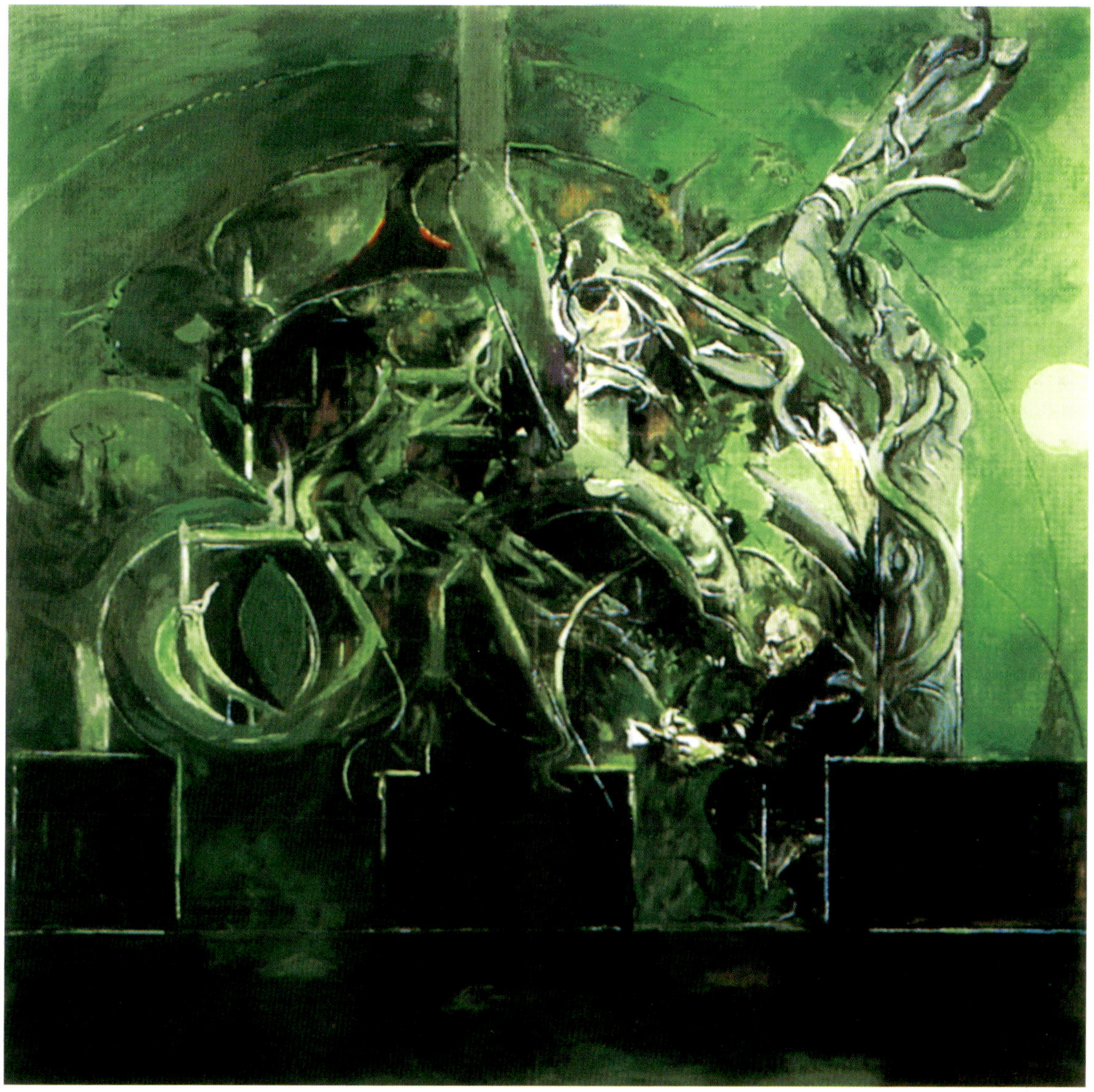

Plate 148. *The Thicket,* 1978. Oil

In 1967 one of his Italian friends planned a film about Sutherland's career, and asked for addresses in Pembrokeshire. Sutherland looked again at the 'found objects' from there still kept in his Villa Blanche studio – and decided to revisit Pembrokeshire with the producer. Late August 1967 found him once again among the rocks and lichen, tree roots, rotting shipwreck, bones and heather and grey buildings, in the clean air. 'It's extraordinary,' he observed to the Italian: 'the light here is as intense as it is in the south of France.' (Plate 147).

It opened a final phase. Regular visits to Pembrokeshire recommenced. Reds persist in these late paintings, and yellows. But there is a new dominance of strong greens, lightly caged now in black outlines hinting at other presences. Simple recapitulation could not satisfy him.

After a decade of renewed visits to Pembrokeshire, Sutherland set a small self-portrait into one painting. *The Thicket* (1978) weaves one of his greenest comminglings (Plate 148). Within it the old artist crouches over his sketchbook, drawing what looms in his mind. The ensemble raises orbiting geometries. Just outside them, above and behind the man, hang the great luminaries: the larger is dark, the smaller glowing at the picture's edge. Thus Sutherland echoed again the long-dead Nash – less than two years before his own death in February 1980. In that echo, he also touched back to the English vision encoded by the seventeenth century poet Andrew Marvell:

> Meanwhile the Mind, from pleasure less,
> Withdraws into its happiness…
> Annihilates all that's made
> To a green thought in a green shade.

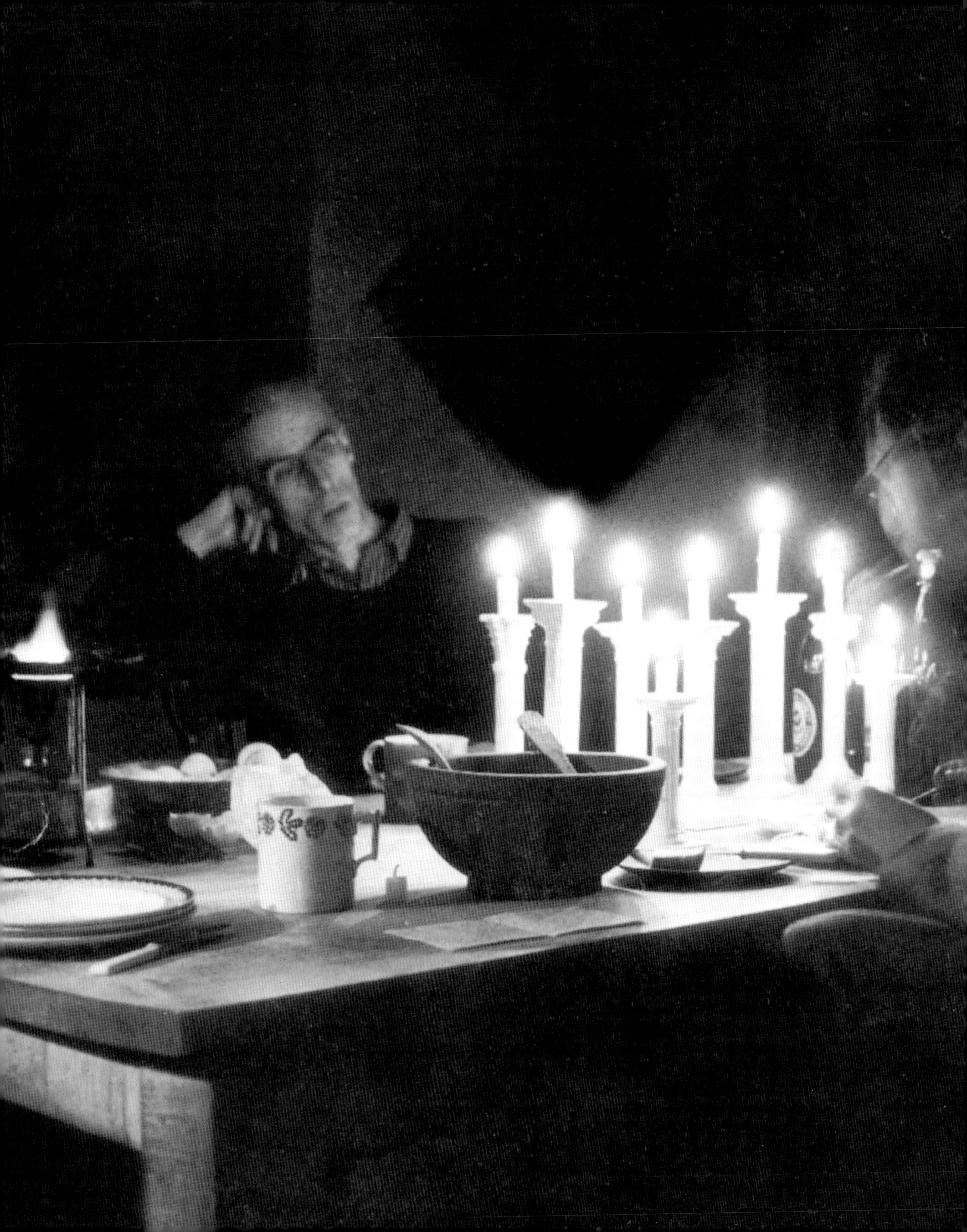

CHAPTER 7

John Piper (1903-1992)

Pastoral as Defence

John Piper was born three months after Sutherland, in December 1903. His young years were deeply influenced by Griggs's *Highways and Byways* drawings, and he collected the books from boyhood.[1] As a young artist Piper would feel the need to engage Abstraction. Yet ultimately his mature vision was less reductionist than Sutherland's.

Piper's art views shards and ruins as passing phases in the land's heritage. His vision, fused by the Second World War, equally embraces man's buildings especially in country places. This art has less of a specialist's intensity, more a half-holiday atmosphere of chance discovery amongst riches. So Piper became, more famously than any other artist in this book, the nation's visionary.

Opposite:
Plate 149. John Piper in the kitchen at Fawley Bottom, 1940. Photograph

* * *

His father was a London solicitor. The family lived much as the Sutherlands, in a comfortable new house with servants, on the southern fringe. The Pipers were at Epsom, three miles south-west of the Sutherlands' Sutton. Fifteen miles beyond them, William Hyde was living in poverty at Shere. Not much farther to the south-east of Epsom and Sutton, Samuel Palmer had found his pastoral vision at Shoreham.

The Pipers' house, like the Sutherlands', bordered open country. From Lord Rosebery's farm opposite came the Pipers' milk, butter and eggs. The lane between house and farm led on to Epsom Downs. John, the youngest of three brothers, explored the summer country on his bicycle.

He read Belloc's *Stane Street* with Hyde's illustrations.[2] Belloc traced the Roman road as far as Epsom Downs – 'very nearly' to the Race Course Grand Stand of Hyde's nocturne. That was an easy cycle ride from the Pipers' house. From there the old track was lost underground; but Belloc asserted that it 'cut through the heart of Epsom' on its straight way to London Bridge. John recalled 'trying to draw trees to go with it'.[3]

Piper's young exploring was guided, as Sutherland's had been, by the *Highways and Byways* books. The first was *Surrey*, inscribed in 1909 to 'Charles' (either his father or his eldest brother, killed at Ypres in 1915). *Kent* is inscribed by an aunt for John's eleventh birthday, 13 December 1914. Then (perhaps his own purchases) came *Dorset* and Griggs's *Sussex*, both dated with John's signature 1918. All are well used, some with his manuscript notes.[4]

In the summer of 1918 he explored Rye and Romney Marsh with a school friend. They camped at the western end of the Marsh near Snargate – whose church (according to *Highways and Byways in Kent*) had served as a smugglers' storehouse. Young Piper was fascinated, as Hyde was, by tales of smuggling. Many Marsh churches had figured in it.[5]

In the autumn of 1919 Piper followed Sutherland to Epsom College. His acquisition of *Highways and Byways* books went on. In November 1920 he dated his copy of *Wiltshire*. Next came Griggs's *Berkshire* which he dated 'Oxford 9/8/21'. He bought it on a trip with his parents and surviving brother Gordon up the Thames to the Cotswolds and Stratford-upon-Avon. At Hurley (below Nash's Wittenham Clumps) Griggs had drawn for the book a dovecote

1. *Books from the Library of John and Myfanwy Piper*, Part 2: Maggs Bros catalogue 1241 (1997), item 282 (18 books). Piper's copies of the *Highways and Byways* books, many bearing signs of heavy use, are now in a private collection.
2. The family copy of *Stane Street* is inscribed to Piper's father at 'Xmas 1917' from his brother-in-law William Harrison (private coll).
3. Quoted in *John Piper* [retrospective exhibition catalogue], (Tate Gallery, 1983: hereinafter cited as *Tate Catalogue*), 16.
4. Private coll.
5. John Piper, *Romney Marsh* (Penguin, 1950), 12.

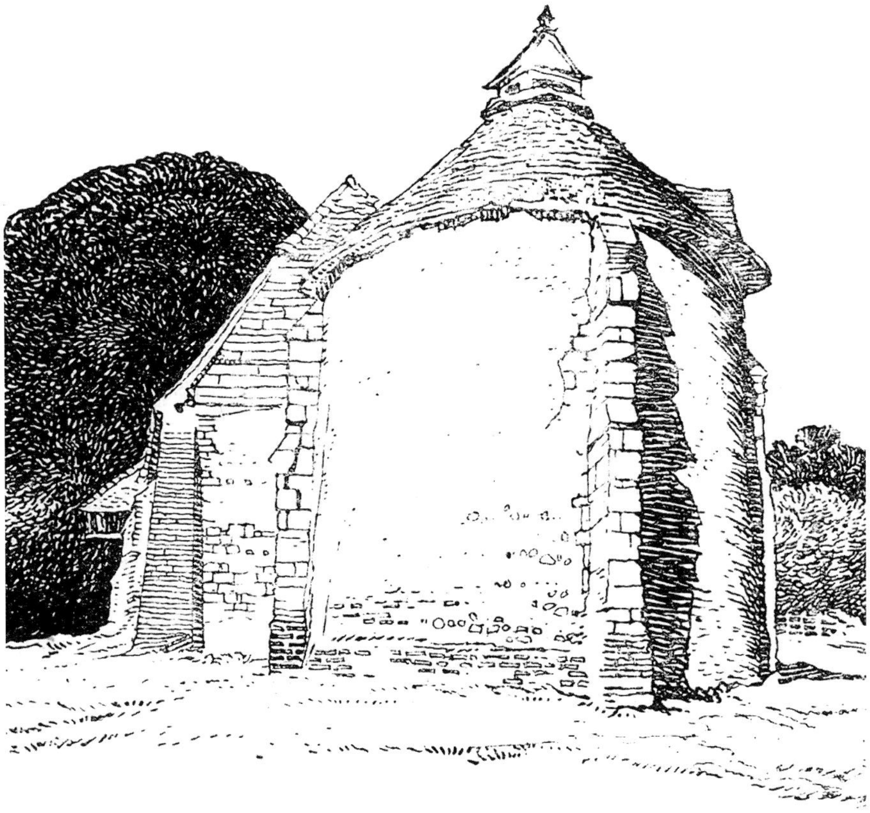

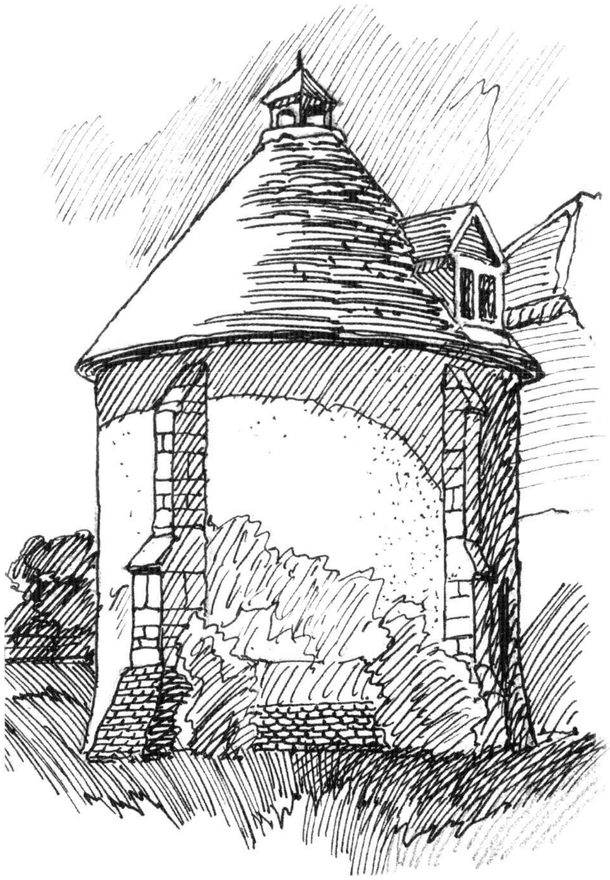

Above:
Plate 150. F.L. Griggs: Dovecote at Hurley, 1906, for *High ways and Byways in Berkshire.* Ink

Above right:
Plate 151. Dovecote at Hurley, 1921. Ink

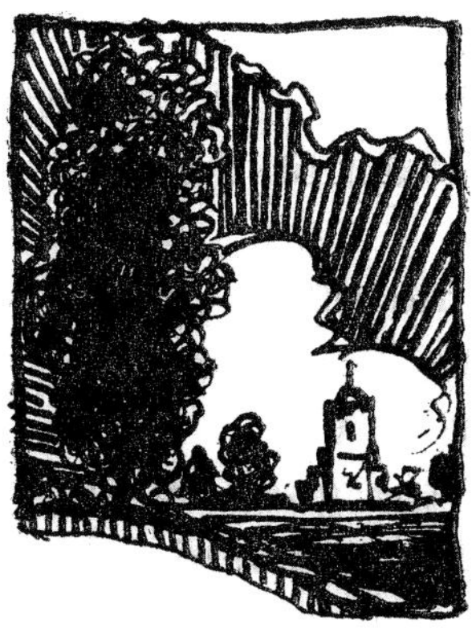

Plate 152. Autumn morning: vignette for *The Gaudy Saint and Other Poems,* 1924. Ink

remaining from a Benedictine monastery once there (Plate 150). John drew it again from his viewpoint (Plate 151).

He was 'collecting' churches – twelve to fifteen on a good day – in sketches with notes on the buildings outside and in. A special interest was old stained glass, which he began to copy in drawings. Altogether he compiled a detailed record of the family's fortnight tour, which returned through Cambridge and East Anglia. In an album he handwrote the finished notes, round his own illustrations or mounted photographic prints from negatives taken with his own camera.

His father noted John's 'very different tastes from both the other sons… He has of his own volition developed a taste for drawing, music, painting, poetry and architectural lore… showing us all sorts of interesting places which otherwise we should never have visited.'[6] Afterwards John himself recalled trying to write a novel 'full of people going to places in the upper Thames Valley and descriptions of sunsets and thunderstorms'.[7]

For his eighteenth birthday in December 1921 he acquired *Highways and Byways in Middlesex*, and three months later Griggs's *Buckinghamshire*. In the spring of 1922 he left Epsom College after three years as a day boy. His father had determined that John should follow Gordon into his law firm; and the office doors now closed behind him. Still John bought *Highways and Byways* books: *Normandy* (the only non-British volume) in December 1922, in 1923 *Yorkshire*.

Piper senior tried hard to convince his youngest son that art as an avocation could be combined with real work in the law office. Mr Piper himself attended art classes near the Tate Gallery to develop an enjoyable hobby.

As further consolation the parents took John to Italy in the spring of 1923. They followed Maurice Hewlett and Joseph Pennell's *The Road in Tuscany* (1904) through Venice, San Gimigniano, and Venice. In May John wrote a poem about a painted Saint's image glowing in the candlelit interior of Santa Maria della Salute while a gale of rain howled and stung without. Everywhere he drew and drew – and was to be grateful always for this first sight of Italy still much as Ruskin had known it. Returning through France the mediaeval glass at Chartres 'knocked him sideways'.[8]

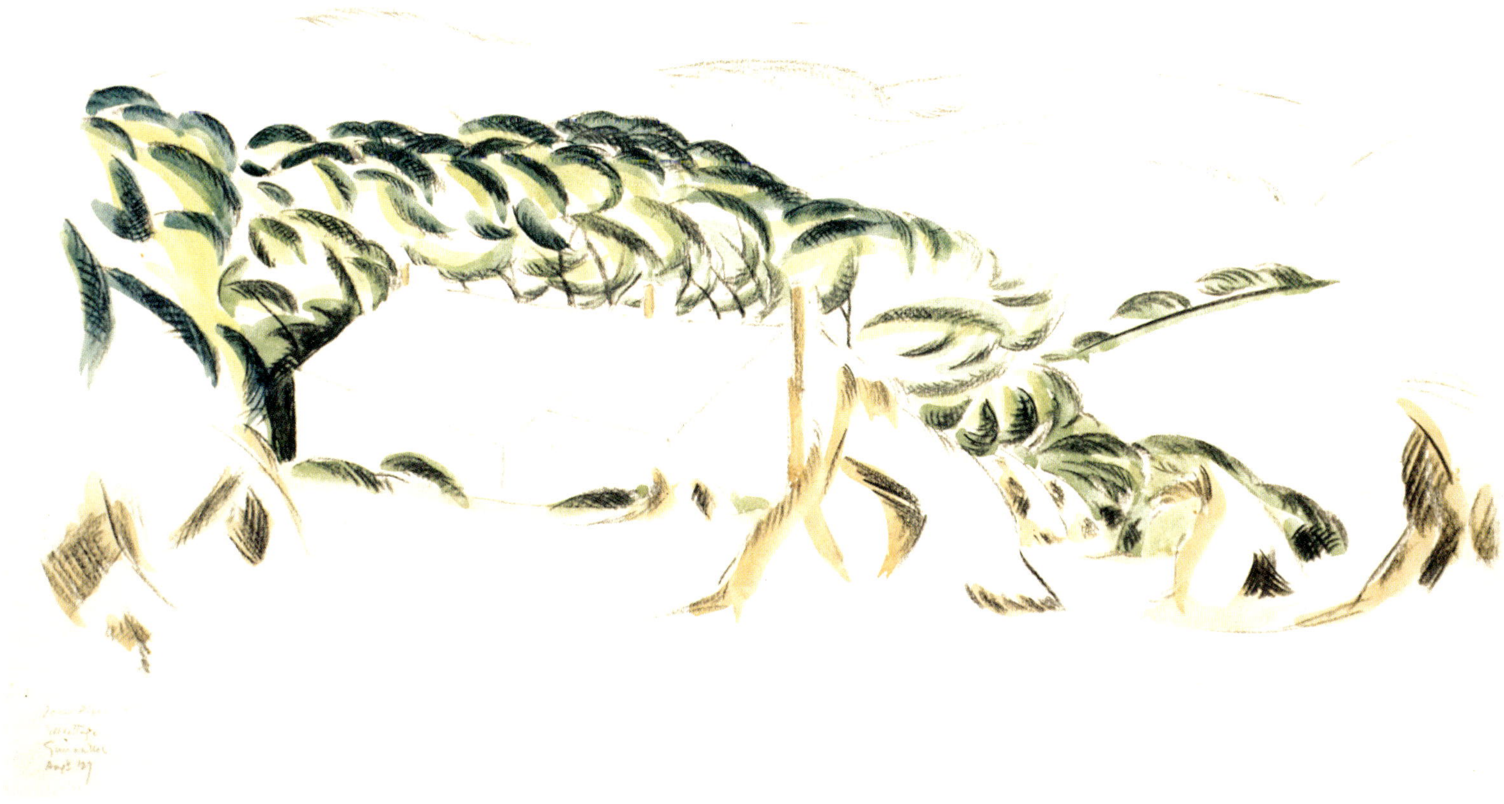

Plate 153. Cornish cottage, 1927. Ink and watercolour

In fact this holiday, undertaken as consolation for John, had the opposite effect. Drawing and writing through Italy and France convinced him (if he needed convincing) that art was his business. His father would not listen – just as Graham Sutherland's father had not listened at first.

The end of 1923 saw the private publication of John's first book of poems, with his own vignette drawings. Many were inspired by places visited abroad, but also at home. 'Cotswold Gables' anticipates Griggs's etching of *Owlpen* by several years:

> … The dark, sombre shade
> of close-clipped yews: …
> Up they rise
> with slight-advancing bays:
> latticed and straight;
> criss-crossed in light and shadow…

Some of the young man's lines touch back to Palmer:

> The moonlit waves across the standing corn
> Go dancing down the valley in the night.

A second collection of John's poems, published with further vignettes in 1924, reprinted several poems and added new ones. Near the end, opposite a new vignette (Plate 152), the voice of the aspiring visionary sounds in a poem he called 'Shy' – at the sheer wealth of an autumn morning:

> As though it all were done for me –
> The falling leaves, their rustling sound,
> And the grey-trunked hedgerow tree.[9]

In the spring of 1925 Piper sat the Law Society's examinations – and failed them. Less than two years later, in March 1927, his father died. Without hesitation John left the law firm to his brother. A drawing made that summer of a holiday cottage in Cornwall shows the influence of Paul Nash set in deft draughtsmanly rhythms with a nod towards Cubism (Plate 153).

6. Charles Alfred Piper, *Sixty-three Not Out* (Curwen Press, 1925): autobiography with illustrations by John Piper.
7. Quoted in *Tate Catalogue*, 16.
8. Quoted in Malcolm Yorke, *The Spirit of Place* (Constable, 1988), 70.
9. John Piper, *Wind in the Trees*, with Decorations by the Author (Privately printed, 1923); *The Gaudy Saint and Other Poems*, with decorations by the author (Bristol: Horseshoe Publishing Co., 1924).

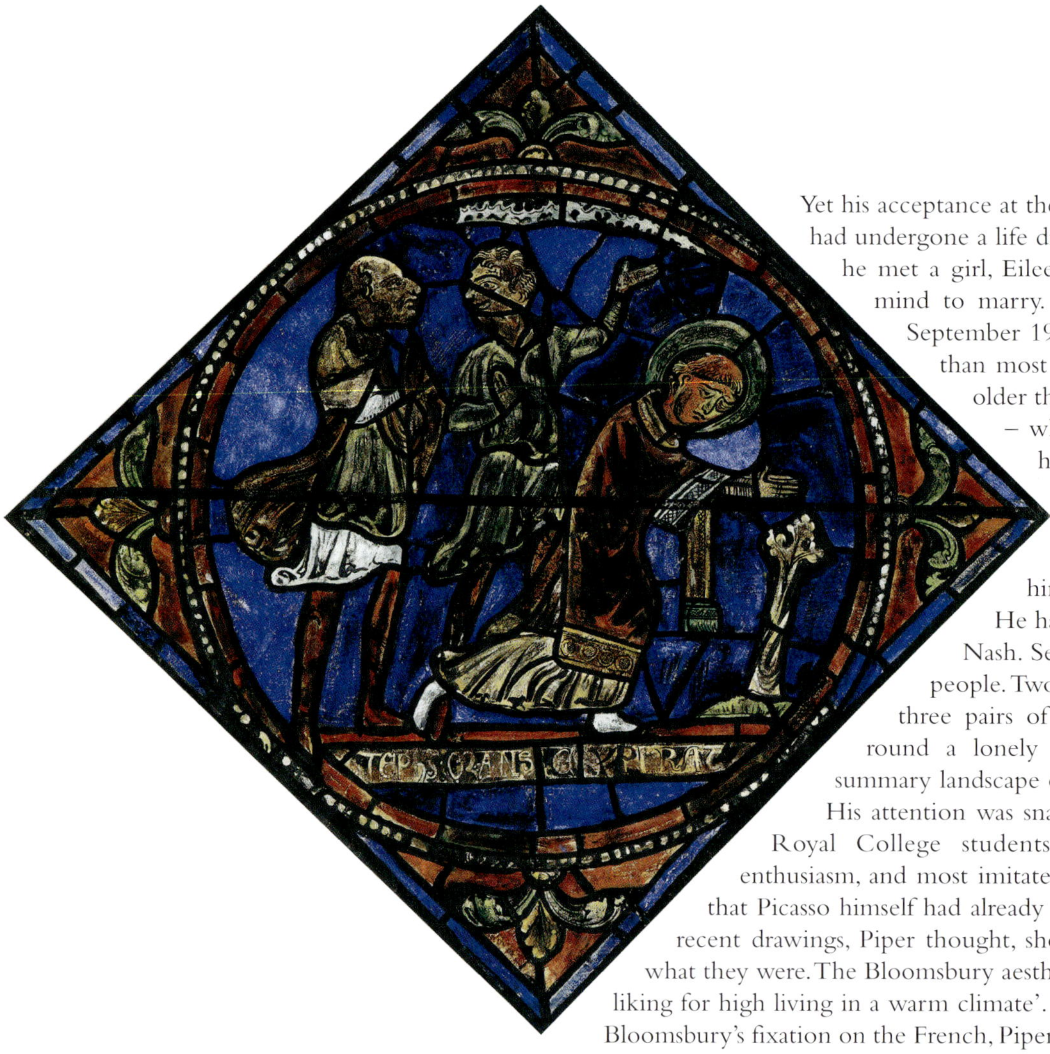

Plate 154. *The Stoning of St Stephen*, 1929. Watercolour after mediaeval stained glass in Wiltshire

Yet his acceptance at the Royal College of Art was delayed until he had undergone a life drawing course at Richmond College. There he met a girl, Eileen Holding, whom he would make up his mind to marry. Arriving at the Royal College of Art in September 1928, Piper found himself several years older than most of the students. In fact he was three years older than his painting teacher, Maurice Kestleman – who formed the idea that Piper knew what he wanted, and left him to seek it.

Piper was drawn to the School of Design, where subject matter counted for less than form and pattern. There he set himself to study stained glass and lithography. He had begun to make woodcuts, following Paul Nash. Several showed vernacular buildings without people. Two others held nude figures: the larger shows three pairs of women mutually absorbed – but ranged round a lonely male figure who looks away towards a summary landscape of hill, tree, and church.

His attention was snagged for a moment by French art. All the Royal College students discussed Cubism with Fry-and-Bell enthusiasm, and most imitated it. Yet a visit to Paris then showed Piper that Picasso himself had already moved on. The invention of Picasso's most recent drawings, Piper thought, showed up the *idées fixes* of Bloomsbury for what they were. The Bloomsbury aesthetic, he concluded, had been 'shaped by the liking for high living in a warm climate'.

Bloomsbury's fixation on the French, Piper reckoned, was 'quite deadly in its effect' on English students of his time:

> It bolstered the idea of France as… the only place civilised enough – cultured enough, in the German sense – to support a school of painting. Fry does actually say in one of his letters that it isn't possible to paint in England…
>
> The pressure we were under, to make ourselves mental expatriates, put my back up, and turned me against that whole line of Bloomsbury-hedonist country.[10]

By 1929 he felt ready to marry Eileen Holding. Finding that the Royal College of Art did not approve of married students, he left without a diploma. The couple lived first in a thatched cottage at Betchworth, five miles south of Epsom. John's mother built a studio for him there after his brother Gordon began to make difficulties about John's art and the dangers it might pose to family finances.

Eileen felt they should be in London, so they moved into a flat in Hammersmith. But John used the studio in the garden at Betchworth to keep some painting there. He continued to pursue 'Highways and Byways' travel. In the summer of 1929, at a little country church near Salisbury, he found a mediaeval stained glass panel of the stoning of St Stephen. He had been absorbing Herbert Read's recent big book on *English Stained Glass*, and this actual thirteenth century window so touched him that he copied it in vivid watercolours (Plate 154). The experience taught him (he wrote afterwards) 'more about using colours… than I ever have learned before or since'. It showed how colours could respond to changing lights with 'the glow of controlled fire' – the perception which Samuel Palmer had applied to his own watercolour painting.

The quantities of mediaeval English glass fragments scattered across the country began to show themselves to Piper as 'small symbols of man's unforced relationship with the past'. He found the same thought in Ruskin's observation of 'that agedness in the midst of active life which binds the old and the new into harmony'.[11]

* * *

10. Quoted in Anthony West, *John Piper* (Secker & Warburg, 1979), 55-6.
11. John Piper, *Stained Glass: art or anti-art* (Studio Vista, 1968), 19, 21-22.
12. John Piper, 'Aspects of Modern Drawing', in *Signature* 7 (1937), 33.
13. Written by John Betjeman for Kenneth Clark's *Penguin Modern Painters* (1944). The picture is now in a private collection.

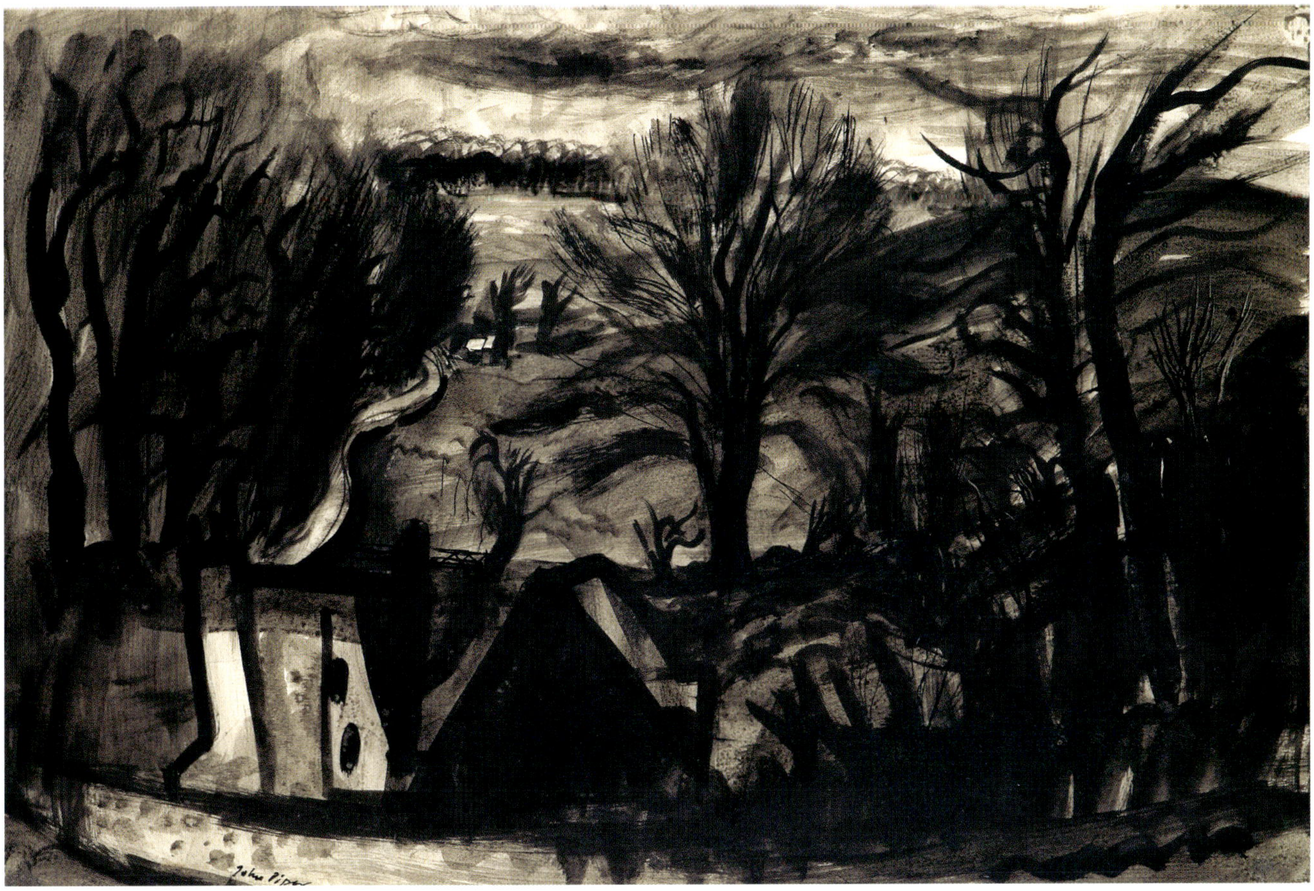

Plate 155. *Westwood Manor Farm,* 1933. Ink and wash

A young artist facing the 1930s needed more than bonds with the past to capture public attention. Piper had to confront, as Nash and Sutherland confronted, the range of current fashions and doctrines. Neither Surrealism nor Cubism (which Piper associated with the Great War and its 'destructive temper'[12]) seemed to offer him much. But his study of stained glass showed how materials themselves could impose pattern – and to that extent, Abstraction. Abstraction, he gradually saw, was the ground his art must fight.

His experiments kept a margin of topography. He began along the coasts of Romney Marsh (following in the footsteps of Hyde and Nash). Around 1932 Piper painted a watercolour of *Rose Cottage, Rye Harbour* standing beside a coastguard station with sand before it and water behind – using black and muted colours in broad techniques. To other beach paintings he added collage of paper doily amid pure colours applied with childlike crudity.

All these techniques were used by a '7 & 5 Society' of advanced English painters and sculptors verging on Abstraction. Their leader was Ben Nicholson. Piper wrote about their work in an article for the BBC *Listener* magazine. He himself experimented with 'painting using string glued to the canvas'. One such work outlined a nude girl on the beach schematised to the edge of Abstraction. The '7 & 5' accepted it for one of their exhibitions in the following spring.

Yet at nearly the same moment in 1933 Piper drew *Westwood Manor Farm* (beyond Henley in a remote corner of south-east Oxfordshire) in a Palmerish ensemble of dark sepia washes and indian ink (Plate 155). The near-monochrome captures light and weather to show (as Piper would later define Romantic art) a special place in a special hour. The mood is secret, set deep in a land far from any coast. It was Orpheus turning back, against the rules, to look again. Piper kept this drawing all his life, and included it in the first published study of his art a decade later.[13]

Still he plunged on. The winter of 1933–34 saw him turning sketchbook notes of figures and places towards abstract angles and planes. The results emerged in a series of 'constructions with straight and bent rods and discs' over varied surfaces. In January 1934 Piper joined the 7 & 5 Society at their invitation. Two months later Nicholson made him the group's secretary. When the Society adopted a 'revised rule' to show only non-representational work, Piper's future seemed defined.

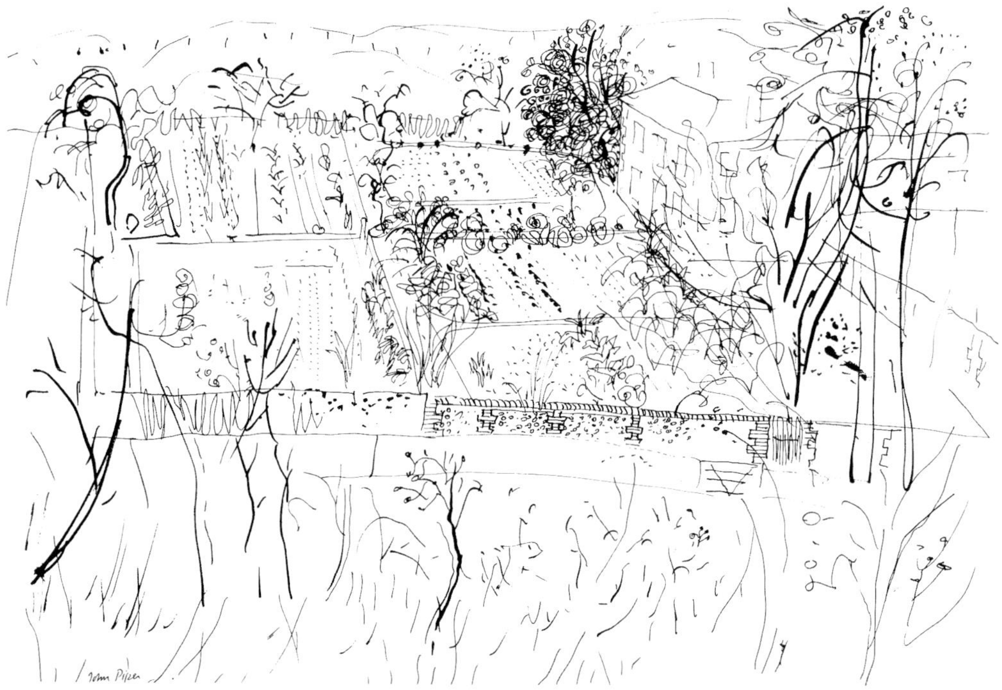

Plate 156. Fawley Bottom farmhouse and garden, 1971. Ink

In the spring of 1934 he paid another visit to Paris with his wife. But he and Eileen were finding less and less common ground. When an invitation came to spend a weekend with the 7 & 5 painter Ivon Hitchens at his cottage on the Suffolk coast at Sizewell (then undefiled), Piper left a note for Eileen to tell where he had gone. While there he had a postcard to say the arrangement suited her well enough.

That weekend on the Suffolk coast – close to where the young Griggs had drawn his Sole Bay churches and Gordon Craig had gone with Jess Dorynne – proved momentous. Hitchens sent Piper to meet another guest arriving at Saxmundham railway station. She was Myfanwy Evans, a twenty-three-year-old Oxford graduate, fascinated by modern art and lecturing part-time at Morley College. Myfanwy had gained her Oxford blue in swimming. As she and Piper walked back along the sands, they decided to strip and swim. The association of coasts with Piper's abstracting art seemed to gain Myfanwy as its mermaid. She remembered:

> The summer night was warm and the sea phosphorescent. We… dried ourselves by running along the strip of sand between the shingle and the shining water. We were late for supper and were received rather sternly by Ivon.

Hitchens wanted to make drawings of Myfanwy that weekend, but she and John 'never stopped talking'.

Later that summer Myfanwy made her own visit to Paris. Then she and Piper decided to start a new 'quarterly review of contemporary "abstract" painting and sculpture'. They planned the first issue for January 1935, and fixed on the name 'Axis'. (That in due course fetched an enquiry from the Italian fascist government.)

Both John and Myfanwy wrote for the new magazine. Other contributors included Paul Nash with a provocative article on Abstraction entitled 'For but not With'. They reproduced works by Nash, Nicholson, Hepworth, Henry Moore, continental artists from Mondrian to Picasso – and Samuel Palmer. To work on the magazine, Piper and Myfanwy rented a room near Weymouth on the Dorset coast, close to where Nash and his wife were staying. By Christmas 1934, Myfanwy wrote, she and Piper 'decided we must find somewhere to live' together permanently.

Their searches went inland, away from coasts. 'Not Essex nor Surrey nor Sussex nor Hertfordshire,' she remembered; not too far from London, for her lectures at Morley College – but not within London, because John 'couldn't bear to live in it'. So they drew a ring on a map round an area near Westwood Manor Farm, and stuck a pin close to Turville near Henley. Myfanwy recalled:

14. Dec 1993 to Leslie Waddington.

15. Quoted in *Piper's Places*, 22.

> We set out on the 31st December 1934 on a horrible raw day… Fawley Bottom Farmhouse [Plate 156] was under our pin.
>
> It was empty, no water, no electricity but, yes, we could rent it. There was delicious drinking water in a well a field away…
>
> The rest is the story of our life.

Fifty years later, still living there in her old age, Myfanwy wrote:

> It has a numinous quality, perhaps because it has remained untouched by development, perhaps because the road leads past us to… Cymbeline's grave or tumulus…
>
> It has, and always had a *genius loci* – that mysterious magic presence that collects the dreams of the past which, like wasp stings accumulating in the blood, accumulate in the mind and the imagination.[14]

Early in 1935 they moved in. Practically with the first issue of *Axis*, Piper began abstract oil painting. He showed with the 7 & 5. He would later join Paul Nash in showing 'found objects' in a Surrealist exhibition. Meanwhile a visit to Paris with Myfanwy in March 1935 to see collages by Picasso made another big impression.

In 1936 Piper restarted his own collages – not to exhibit for the time being, as they made recognisable landscapes again. He collected portfolios of scraps, for working anywhere. Many of Piper's collages (except for one he called *Avebury* in tribute to Nash) continued to evoke coastal places. He revisited old haunts on the west coast of Wales, north of Sutherland's Pembrokeshire. He began a series of collages centred on Welsh chapels.

Yet working in 'this whole painting/collage procedure', Piper decided, 'one was living in a protected world which very few people understood at the time, or had any desire to share. It was a means of isolating oneself for a time' when menacing politics dominated every other thought.[15]

Gradually a new direction began to emerge. In October 1936 the *Architectural Review* published an article by Piper. Its subject was 'England's Early Sculptors', illustrated with his own photographs. In Saxon and Norman church carvings from Yorkshire to Dorset by way of Wiltshire, Herefordshire, and Wales, Piper sees 'from the eighth century onwards for about five hundred years… forms very like those used by artists in our time'. 'Many a Picasso-like profile is to be found on twelfth-century fonts and capitals.' 'Non-figurative' decorations on early crosses look forward to Abstraction.

All this led Piper to reaffirm 'the well-known parallel of man in present-day world chaos [with] primitive man… oppressed by the seeming chaos of the unknown world around him, developing a "will to form"'. There the old sculptors had found guidance from their subject matter:

> For the primitive artist the Deity, ruler of the outside unknowable world, is above all awe-inspiring and majestic; powerful, and very unlike powerless man himself. So there is very little that is knowable, touchable or 'human' about these associates of the primitive English God on a village font.

The old sculptors' devotion to this view of things 'guarded' them against 'diffuseness and detail'. That drove their 'instinctive control' of 'a line tracked with feeling… through undiscovered country in every inch of its course'. Piper saw the old sculptors' 'interlaced ornament' of natural forms as 'symbols of the continuity of life in a dangerous world'. He reproduced his own photograph (Plate 157) of a ninth-century cross-shaft at Codford St Peter in Wiltshire. (It had been carefully described in the *Highways and Byways* volume on his shelf.) The shaft shows a sculptor with his mallet, reaching up to grasp the patterned vine or tree above him.

Piper also photographed (and later drew) a Romanesque tympanum over the church door at Rowlstone in Herefordshire. Its 'Christ in Majesty' shows 'sustained line' used to 'charge a design which is at once rhythmical and rigid – as if Christ enthroned is both a seated,

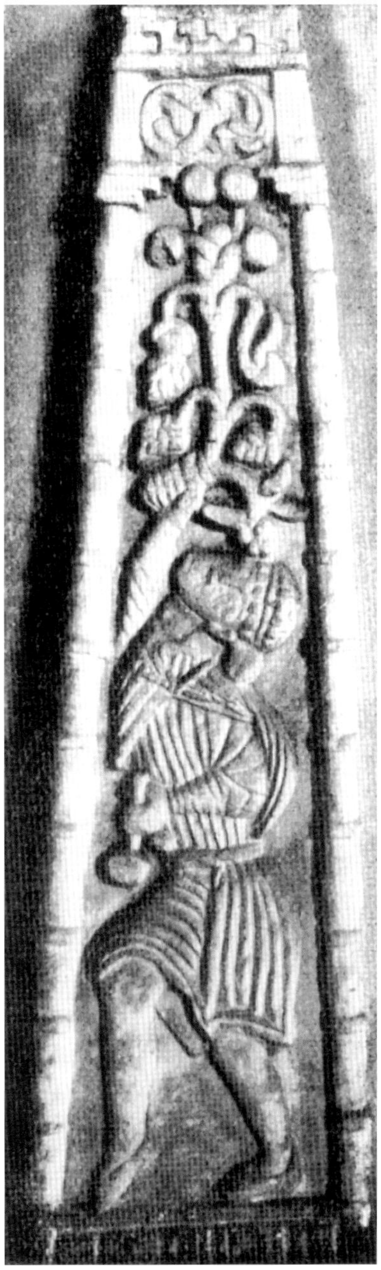

Plate 157. Mediaeval scripture at Codford St Peter, Wiltshire. Photograph by John Piper, *c.*1936

immovable Majesty and a flowing, abundant Life'. In later centuries this English strength of linear design had yielded to an 'age of sentiment' which 'humanised' its images of God. 'Not again until Blake', Piper wrote of the powerful line, 'did this specially English genius show itself so well.' And he quoted Blake's famous words:

> 'Leave out this line and you leave out life itself; all is chaos again, and the line of the Almighty must be drawn out upon it before man or beast can exist.'[16]

The goal of such a line for Piper returned to the 'man or beast' – or place – it could bring to representation. He was later to see both Surrealism and his own years of Abstraction as 'classical exercises' – 'disciplines' which might 'open a road to one's own heart, but they are not the heart itself. I doubt if under their complete domination one masterpiece will ever be created.'[17] To paint Abstractions always, he concluded, 'is to paint the same picture always' – because the artist has no subject but his own feeling of form.

Thus Abstraction became for Piper 'a luxury'. 'One felt that the things one was producing lacked the richness, the fulness, the ripeness of life.' To ignore subject matter, he wrote a decade later, 'was to look at painting for itself alone, for its manner and its past and present habits, for its language of form, discounting its message.'[18] What was painting's message for him?

The reality that showed itself to Piper, as menace gathered towards another European war, was that 'the whole pattern and structure of thousands of English sites [appeared] more precious as they became more likely to disappear.' So he found himself pulled back towards the Griggsian vision galvanised by the First War, with all those hopes and fears remagnified. Here, Piper wrote, lay 'our whole Romantic tradition'. In Britain 'it has always been possible for meaningful details to shine like beacons in the damp, misty evanescence of our beautiful island light and weather.'[19]

In the days of Griggs's youth, those words would have been greeted with understanding, even enthusiasm. Now they provoked bitterness in both Abstractionist and Bloomsbury camps. Piper was unrepentant. For a symposium devoted to *The Painter's Object*, edited by Myfanwy in 1937, he wrote a new article with the advertising title, 'Lost, A Valuable Object'. The 'object' was subject matter.

It was, Piper said at the outset, an excellent idea to link 'an artist with his place'. In this context he poured contempt on the 'isms' and their 'ists':

> The cubists had smashed the objects into fragments, ... collected the fragments carefully, made them up into a parcel, tied it with the sky-blue ribbon and posted it to oblivion.
>
> The abstractionists who followed held their noses in the air, and said they'd never been interested in the object anyway.
>
> The dada-ists and later the surrealists (all premeditatedly scatter-brained) looked for it and failed to find it.

All of them shared 'an absolute horror' of showing any object 'in its proper context'. 'But the object must grow again; must reappear as the "country" that inspires painting.'

Until the advent of Cubism, Piper wrote in another article of 1937, 'the *character* of the model was the point':

> The character of a face (Manet),
> the character of a tree (Constable),
> the character of a European town (Turner),
> the character of a religion (Blake),
> occupied painters and then produced masterpieces.[20]

The implication was: No longer.

The 7 & 5 were outraged. In a series of *putsch* actions to expel dissidents, they made Piper their exemplar of a word coined by 'George Orwell' to describe the anathema promulgated by both Fascism and Communism against anyone of less than perfect faith in the doctrine: a 'non-person'.

16. 'England's Early Sculptors', in *Architectural Review*, Oct 1936; reprinted in Myfanwy Evans, ed, *The Painter's Object* (Gerald Howe, 1937), 116-25. Piper could have recalled the phrase 'age of sentiment' from his copy of Herbert Read's *English Stained Glass* (Putnam, 1926), where those words head a chapter devoted to later Gothic styles.
17. 12 June 1943 to Paul Nash (quoted in *Tate Catalogue*, 38).
18. Piper, Introduction to the catalogue of a New York exhibition of his works (Ibid, 39); 'A Talk with John Piper', in *Encounter*, 116 (May 1963), 61.
19. Quoted in *Piper's Places*, 22.
20. Piper, 'Aspects of Modern Drawing', in *Signature* 7 (1937), 33.
21. The 7 & 5 also had a French apostate. One of their heroes, the painter Jean Hélion, announced after two years in a German prison camp: 'You don't dream about angles or surfaces' in prison. 'You dream about women, bread, smokes and trees.' When Hélion reverted to subject matter, the 7 & 5 ostracised him too. Hélion reflected: 'They all had a taste for the convent.' (Quoted in Malcolm Yorke, *The Spirit of Place*, 81.)
22. West, *John Piper*, 90.
23. Michael Northen, 'Designs for the Theatre', in *Tate Catalogue*, 32.

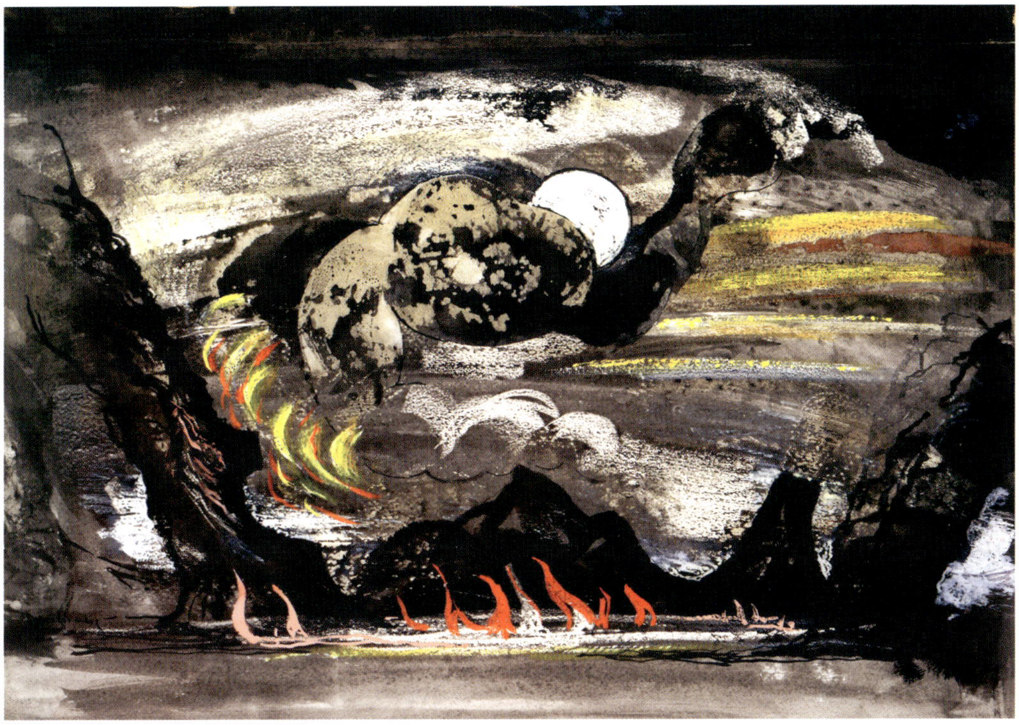

Plate 158. *Job:* Hell. Design for stage backcloth, 1948. Ink and Wash
V&A Images/Victoria and Albert Museum

Ben Nicholson actually called Piper 'traitor'. To the extent that Abstraction was allied to Roger Fry's Anglophobia, in fact the shoe was on the other foot.[21]

The Abstractionists' motive was fear. The relentless politicisation of everything in the 1930s had pitchforked them. Any patriotism for one's own land, they feared, could smack of Fatherland-worship and the Nazis. Erase every national past, then. Create an 'international' style to abrogate any reference to the past – and, therefore, to subject matter.

Yet this pitchforked choice, Piper had begun to feel, was the logician's 'false dilemma'. Between the extremities, he opened his own path through a formalised pastoral vision. That aspired to no leadership beyond spiritual reflection. It saw all nature as interdependent, and thus sacramental.

Piper was not alone. All the pastoral visionaries were with him. Nash was about to find the crown of his life's work in solstice and equinox, sunflower and moon over Wittenham Clumps, up the Thames from Fawley Bottom. Sutherland was finding his lights among the geologies of Pembrokeshire.

Piper's instinct now was to move right away from what his biographer Anthony West called 'the rôle of the bohemian intellectual that writers ever since Baudelaire have done their best to force upon the painter'.[22] Piper turned back to the workmanship of crafts. Abandoning abstract constructions, in the later 1930s he joined two new enterprises.

One was a *Group Theatre* bringing together younger men in several arts – Auden, Isherwood, Spender, and Benjamin Britten. Piper designed a production for them, and designed others elsewhere. From 1938 he produced a succession of back-cloths, drop-curtains, and costume drawings. Ultimately his work embraced a revival of Edith Sitwell's *Façade*, half a dozen Britten operas (three with librettos by Myfanwy), ballets by Frederick Ashton and John Cranko.

One of Piper's best achievements in the theatre would be his sets for a 1948 revival of Vaughan Williams's 'masque for dancing' *Job*, based on the Blake engravings. Piper's 'Earth' redeployed elements from Blake's 'Thus Did Job Continually' under the Tree of Life (the image young Samuel Palmer had seen on the copper during his visit to Blake in 1824). It was so successful that Piper used it years later in an equally fine stained glass window.

Piper showed Job's 'Hell' in a Palmerish design of moon and hills in sepia, with flames in controlled rhythms (Plate 158). Several times he moved the action through lighting on Craig-like painted gauzes. One director found it all so finely tuned that any addition 'destroyed the atmosphere that Piper intended'.[23]

He had also joined Robert Wellington in 1936 to organise *Contemporary Lithographs*, reviving

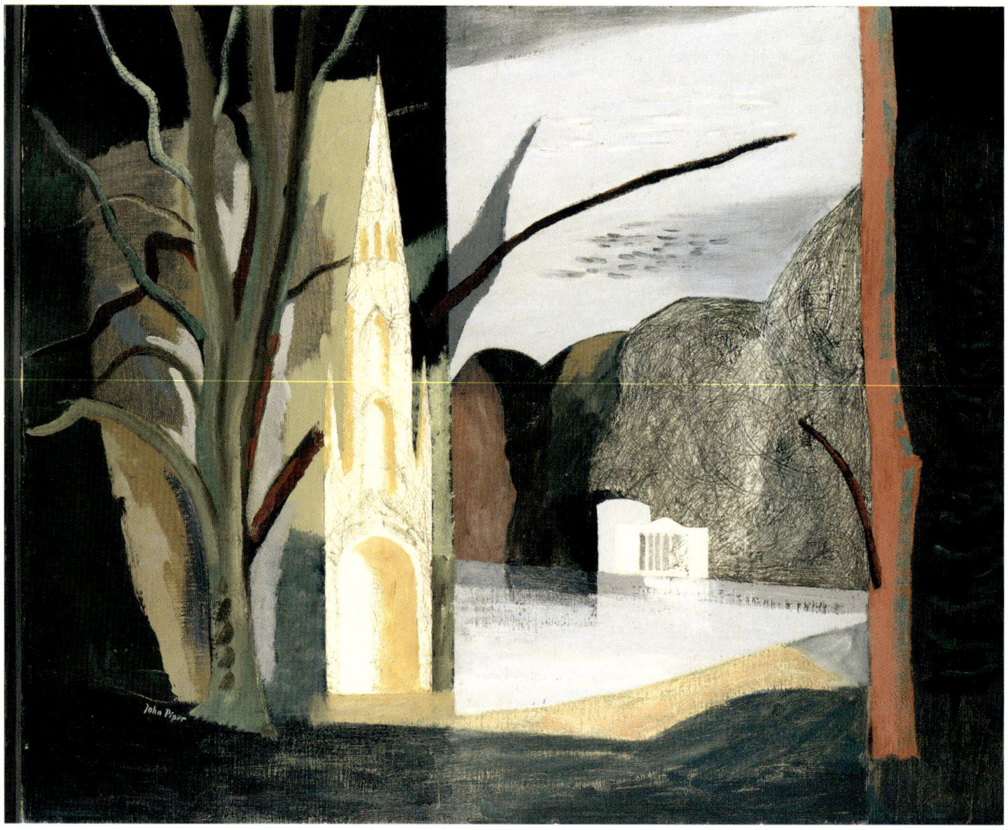

Plate 159. *Autumn at Stourhead*, 1939. Oil
Manchester City Art Galleries

an old technique to publish the work of young artists. Piper produced one brightly coloured abstract print and two gentle seaside designs for a nursery frieze. Then he reduced his colours virtually to the tan and black of classic lithography, for a series of evolutions based on real topography: they went on and on.

He studied etching and aquatinting – Gilpin's old medium – to produce what proved to be his farewell to coastal themes, in a series of *Brighton Aquatints* in 1938-39. The images were drawn over soberly blocked tints of brown and grey. Fifty copies were hand-coloured by Piper – with one plate coloured by John Betjeman, whom Piper had met at the *Architectural Review*.

Both aquatint and the theatre informed a 1939 oil painting of *Autumn at Stourhead* (Plate 159). Broad areas spread barely modulated colours and textures as on a stage backcloth. Yet the pale warm light is not so much of the stage, as of a nature enriched by history and dream. The upright Gothic presence of the Bristol Cross now at Stourhead counterpoints the garden's distant Pantheon.

At the same time a third craft came to the fore: Piper's writing. He delved into historical topography, with huge encouragement from Betjeman. Betjeman's nostalgia for places appealed to Piper's deepest promptings. Soon Betjeman commissioned Piper to write and illustrate a Shell Guide to *Oxfordshire* (whose south-east corner nearly touched Fawley Bottom). Then Piper and Betjeman together did *Shropshire* – finished in 1939, but not published until 1951.

It became one of the great friendships of Piper's life. Together he and Betjeman collected old guidebooks and theorists of the 'Picturesque' art which had lain behind Palmer's vision. Piper bought Gilpin's works. Kenneth Clark gave John and Myfanwy a book of impressions of Blake's engravings for *Job*. Ultimately the Pipers' library brought together books of graphic art and historic topography which rivalled Griggs's collections.[24]

* * *

The outbreak of the Second World War in 1939 found Piper making his own images of British lakes and hills, townscapes and cottages, ruined abbeys and parish churches under darkening skies or moonlight. He joined a group of artists drawing for a big project of *Recording Britain* against threatened destruction.

A year into the War Piper wrote an article under the Griggsian title 'Towers in the Fens'. Since it was for the *Architectural Review*, it is possible that he knew Griggs's 'Churches by the

24. The extent of Piper's collection appears in three catalogues of his library issued by Messrs Maggs in 1997-98. Even these three catalogues do not include some items such as the Blake *Job*, apparently sold privately.
25. Piper, 'Towers in the Fens', in *Architectural Review*, Nov 1940, 131*ff*.
26. In *The Architect and Building News*, 9 May 1941.

Sea' published there forty years earlier. Piper's churches continue up the coast from Griggs's Sole Bay into Norfolk and Lincolnshire.

Piper illustrated his article with his own photographs, and from early nineteenth century etchings by John Sell Cotman. These old images of still more ancient places raised in Piper's words a simile redolent of Palmer's *Magic Apple Tree*:

> Most country churches were then at an extreme of beauty. Ready to drop like over-ripe fruit, they were in an exquisite state of decay. ...
>
> Clear glass windows let in the sunlight that streamed over the faded umbers, ochres and greys of the walls, furniture and floor, and the whole scene was enriched by the splash of brilliant red of the tattered hangings on the high pulpit. There was, too, the jewelled colour of fragmentary glass in the tracery lights.

Re-emerging into 'the clear light of East Anglia', Piper sees that 'such a church was at least half the product of nature. Half-ruinous, it had indeed become almost one with nature.' The exteriors showed surfaces weathered by wind and rain – 'carved by nature with intense feeling and mastery' to a 'sculptural whole'. Such a church then became almost like one of his or Nash's 'found objects'.

Seen from a distance, these church towers celebrate a further aspect of English mastery. Each tower 'shows the mediaeval builders using majestically the Fens as a plinth – the best plinth for sculptural architecture in the whole country'. Here distance itself endows nature as a colourist of infinite resource:

> Grey and gold and brown, and sometimes none of these, the towers are always afloat on a sea of Fen-green. Changeable skies give them bodies of infinitely varying light, sometimes pale and almost white against heavy clouds and shadowed marsh, sometimes burnished, sometimes glimmering, sometimes vivid, sometimes dim.[25]

It is the Griggsian vision of towers seen through eyes seeking the subtlest colours. A few months later Piper wrote:

> I would rather paint a ruined abbey half-covered with ivy and standing among long grass than I would paint it after it has been taken over by the Office of Works, when they have taken all the ivy off and mown the grass with an Atco [machine].[26]

Those were the contrasts to War damage and destruction. For Kenneth Clark's War Artists, Piper went into Coventry on the day after the worst air raid in the nation's history, there to sketch the burning ruins of the mediaeval Cathedral – 'redder as one came nearer, and still hot and wet from fire and water' (Plate 160). Hurt and horror sharpened his accustomed colour-restraint to set off pervasive blacks with orange, red and violet in the painting he produced. In 1941 he was called to London to draw the bomb-ruined House of Commons.

Side by side with his War drawing and painting Piper was asked to write, for a reminding and recording series of 'Britain in Pictures', a little book on *British Romantic Artists*. In a text of less than thirty pages, heavily illustrated, he traced the history from the Picturesque to Sutherland.

Romantic art focused always, Piper wrote, on 'the particular'. So it found again the same 'sense of drama in atmosphere, in the weather and the seasons inherent in Shakespeare and Milton. The foothold of classical art in Britain has always been uneasy'. Thus England had become the home of landscape gardening on one hand, and of the quest for a natural sublime on the other.

Plate 160. *Coventry Cathedral, November 15th 1940*. Oil, 1940

Transferred to Manchester Art Gallery from the War Artists' Advisory Committee, Ministry of Information (1947)

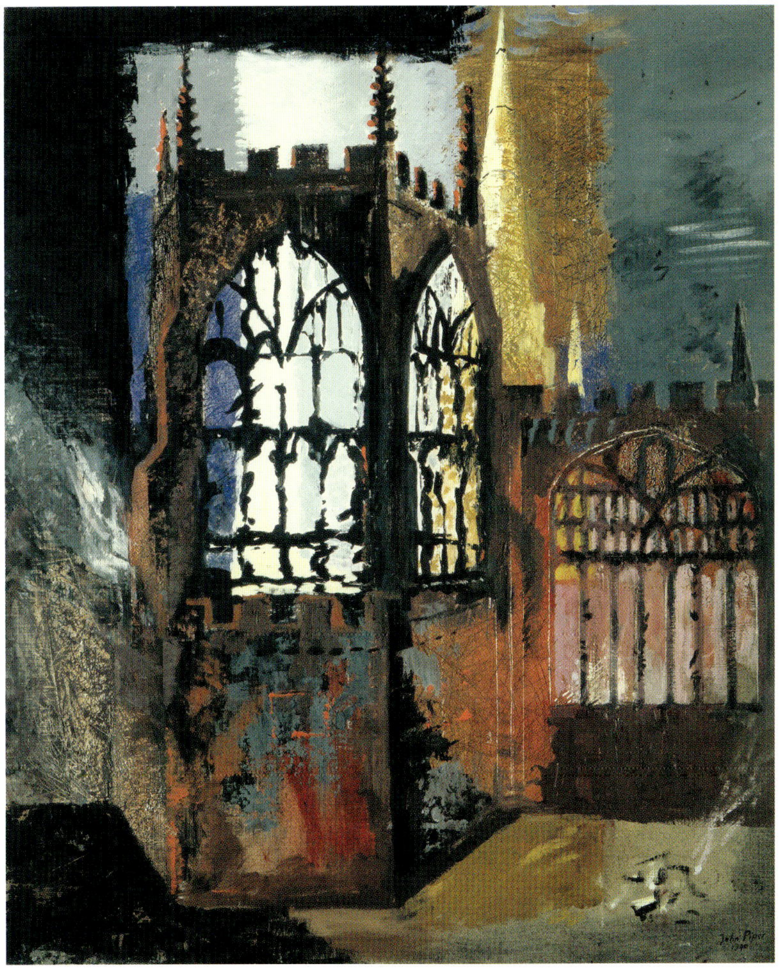

And thus, Piper wrote, Turner had been moved by what Santayana later called 'the weather in our souls' 'to substitute colour for perspective'. Girtin had drawn 'the picturesque part of an ancient town' by day – and returned at twilight to find the buildings 'had assumed so unexpected a mass of shadow… that the reflections in the water still increased the vastness of the mass'; which in turn had sharpened the contrasting 'bright gleam on the horizon'. All this had opened ways to visions for both Griggs and Gordon Craig a century later.

Constable had struggled all his life to resolve the conflict between what Piper called 'passion for nature' and 'passion for painting'. His art walked a tightrope over the 'abyss' where nature and art 'get confused'. But Constable 'explores every passage of light between the trees':

> Ground and sky become lively and full of meaning for one another in his paintings, trees plait their leaves into cages against space, their branches carve space into rich shapes.

All found its focus in Constable's lifelong attachment to his own corner of East Anglia. So he found an entirely personal enrichment of time past and passing. Yet Constable's enrichment had paradoxically enriched the inheritance of every English pastoral visionary.

Piper devoted the central section of *British Romantic Artists* to 'Vision and Imagination'. He began here with the master wood engraver Thomas Bewick (1753–1828), who 'noticed many things that absorbed later English visionaries' – and quoted Bewick's words evoking the seasons:

> … the grasses powdered or spangled with pearly drops of dew, the continued succession of plants and wild flowers… the yellow harvest of the fields, and the produce of the orchards, the varying foliage of the fading woods.

There Bewick had anticipated the 'particular eye' of Palmer. 'Against the machinations of the early nineteenth century,' Piper wrote, 'Palmer pitted his visions of England "where shepherds piped… and the clouds dropped fatness".' (Piper felt so strong an identification with Palmer that he took himself to Lullingstone Park near Shoreham, there to make his own drawings of the same 'groves and glades of very old trees with enormous boles' which Palmer had drawn more than a century earlier.) And he quoted Palmer's friend Edward Calvert:

> How sweet to see wagons, still destined for long journeys, in rest, and to watch slow preparations under sheltering thatch and woodwork. Wheels that have made many revolutions in wilderness and desert, now motionless and half-buried in dry shavings of the joiner's shed, or straw from the harvest threshing floor.

One of Griggs's earliest visionary etchings had shown just such a wagon in its thatched and open shed.

Later sections in Piper's *British Romantic Artists* begin to confront the problems of his own time. He quotes a warning from the minor Pre-Raphaelite James Smetham, which applied with treble force to the councils of Abstraction:

> Don't get into the focus of Criticism. Many men spoil their enjoyment of Art by looking on it as something to pull to pieces, rather than something to enjoy and lead them to enjoy nature, and through nature to enjoy God.

Here is the ideal of Haydn's *Creation* and *The Seasons* (both written midway between Gray's 'Elegy' and Palmer's years at Shoreham) persisting still. Smetham's words hold in their nutshell the whole 'existential' debate with inherited values newly envisioned.

Piper's concluding judgments on his own time began with 'Post-Impressionism' – which had been 'applied with too much austerity' in England:

> The accent on design, form, structure, … and the suppression of literary interest and atmosphere, tended to squash all that was most natural to English painters, and produced a new and artificial academism.

Against that academism, Piper wrote, Paul Nash and Sutherland had 'identified the romantic with the remote – of time or place'. And there, in the midst of the Second War for Britain's continued existence as an entity, Piper rested his history. The little book came out in the autumn of 1942.

Even before the publication of *British Romantic Artists*, Piper's art had begun to find its own place in the nation's identity. That was signalled in 1941 by a commission from the Queen to make two series of large watercolour images of Windsor Castle, in case of its destruction. Deliberate limitation of bright colour to yellows on black and white in these pictures led King George VI to make a celebrated remark about Piper having had 'bad luck with the weather' (Plate 161).

Plate 161. Windsor Castle: *The Quadrangle looking West,* 1942. Ink, watercolour and wash
The Royal Collection © 2006, Her Majesty Queen Elizabeth II

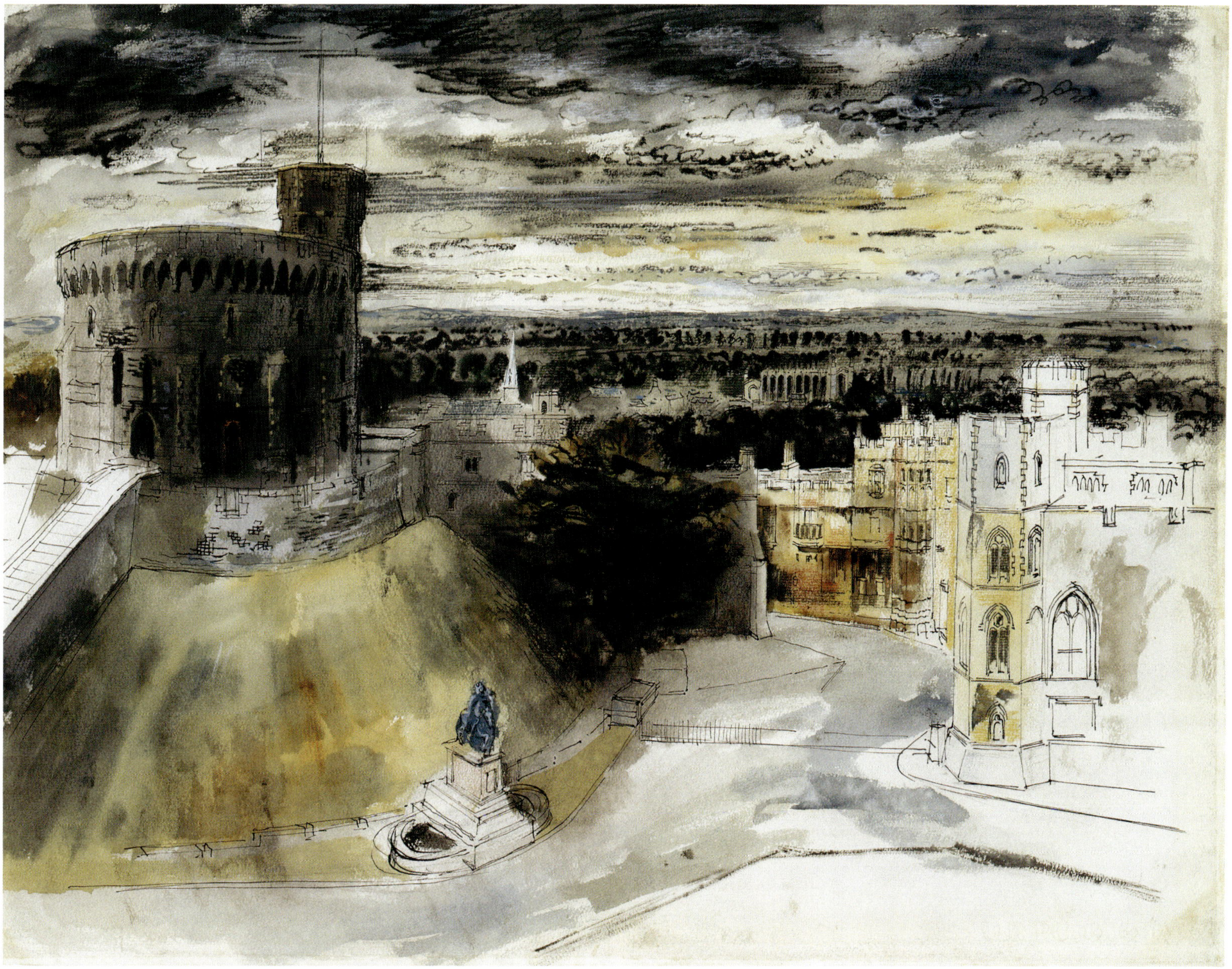

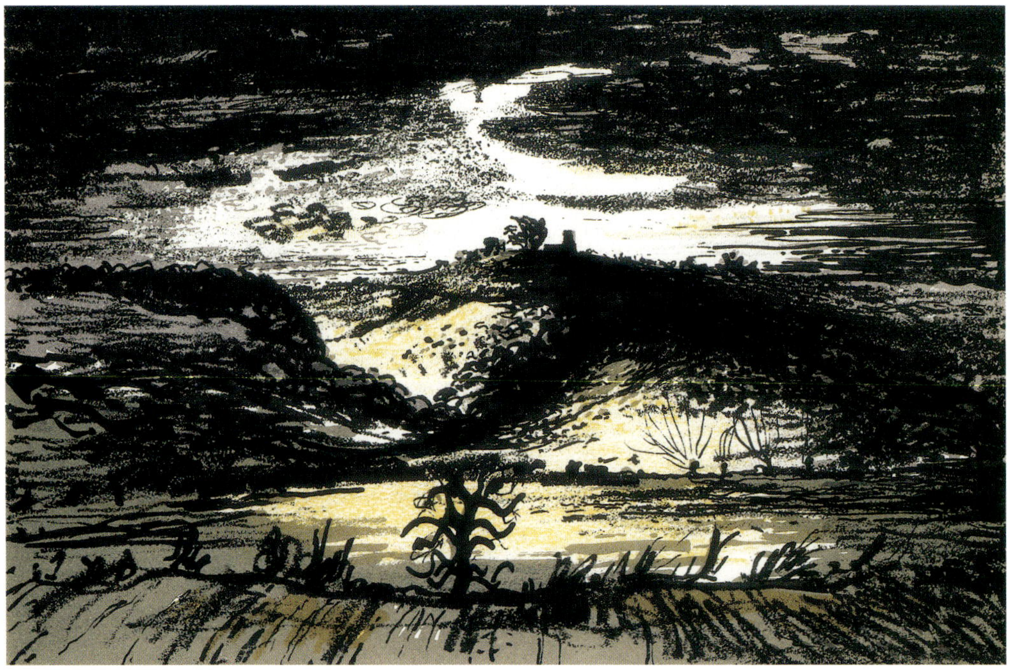

Plate 162. *Stonesfield, Oxfordshire,* 1942-43, for *English Scottish & Welsh Landscape Verse chosen by John Betjeman and Geoffrey Taylor.* Lithograph

Evelyn Waugh (whom Piper met while drawing the grim old Derbyshire seat of the Sitwells at Renishaw) had one of his characters write in 1943: 'We turned to buildings, and gave them the place which our fathers had accorded to nature.' Griggs's art had done that through the corroded peace between the Wars. Now Piper recaptured for an embattled nation the secret affinities between the buildings and climate of what Churchill proudly called 'our island'.

Piper returned to yellow and white, grey and black for a series of small powerful lithographs to illustrate a Betjeman anthology of *English Scottish and Welsh Landscape Poetry*. Like Hyde and Griggs and Nash, Piper's places continued to show few human figures. A Roman amphitheatre still reshapes its land before a more transitory Welsh cottage and barn. A hovel in Oxfordshire rests the wood and thatch of its decaying lean-to against a length of Georgian wall. At Stonesfield, light gleaming from behind a church-crowned hill sharpens a foreground range of tree shadows (Plate 162), answering both Griggs and the young Nash in the 'rapid handwriting' of Piper's drawing. The little book made an icon of Britain's will to survive, as Churchill quoted: 'Westward look, the land is bright.'

At the end of the War in 1945 Piper summarised his experience at life's mid-point:

> I believe it is necessary in these days to like, and even if possible to love, your subject: 'in these days' because there is a great deal of hate about, and there are many temptations to paint 'hate' pictures.[27]

The war on subject matter was bitterly renewed by his former friends the Abstractionists. Piper's growing fame in Britain and America, as his art continued to touch a widening public, was gall in Abstractionist mouths. They never forgave him for his success in the hearts of the people, who increasingly revered him.

* * *

Piper devoted the second half of his long life to ploughing his furrow. Where Sutherland went to live and prosper abroad, Piper visited and came home. In the place of Sutherland's aggressively modern concrete box in the south of France, Piper later bought a vernacular cottage for holidays near the north coast of Pembrokeshire. Even here his pictures now rarely showed coastal scenes, but repaired inland to fields and hills. There and from Fawley Bottom, his vision sought out country houses – decaying because their heirs had been killed in the Wars, or because of crippling Death Duties needed (it was contradictorily claimed) as a contribution to repairing the damaged national life. Here Piper's art took the 'Picturesque' into an alien age.

Piper's colours gained new brilliance in the 1950s when he began to design stained glass. He collaborated with a professional 'interpreter', Patrick Reyntiens. (Matisse, Rouault, and Chagall did the same for their glass.) The art became so important for Piper that he converted the old

27. 'The Practical Business of Painting', in *The Artist and the Public* (British Government Publication, 2 June 1945).

barn behind Fawley Bottom Farmhouse to a studio for it. There he annealed again the promise implicit in Samuel Palmer's comparison of watercolours to stained glass – as painting with colours through light.

Tapestries were woven to Piper's designs. With another collaborator, Geoffrey Eastop, he started a pottery studio in 1968. The brighter colours began flowing also into the lithographs he had never ceased to produce. The stream of lithographs became a flood. Sometimes the light of vision took second place behind Piper's apparent wish to record all of old England and Wales in his art. Some of his later landscapes reapproached Abstraction.

During these years Piper added two new subjects to his armoury. One was the 'foliate head', based on the traditional Green Man of the forest. The other transubstantiated his 'Towers in the Fens' to glowing colours in paint or lithography. Piper's later church towers stand singly, in visions of two, three, or even six to a single picture.

In November 1982, close to his seventy-ninth birthday, he finished an extraordinary picture. It juxtaposes a luminous church tower with a dark, bardic self-portrait (Plate 163). This may stand as a mirror of pastoral vision in twentieth century England. It is given to few artists so to sum up an era in his nation's experience and in his own life within a single image.

Plate 163. Self-portrait with church tower, 12 November 1982. Ink, pastel, watercolour and wash

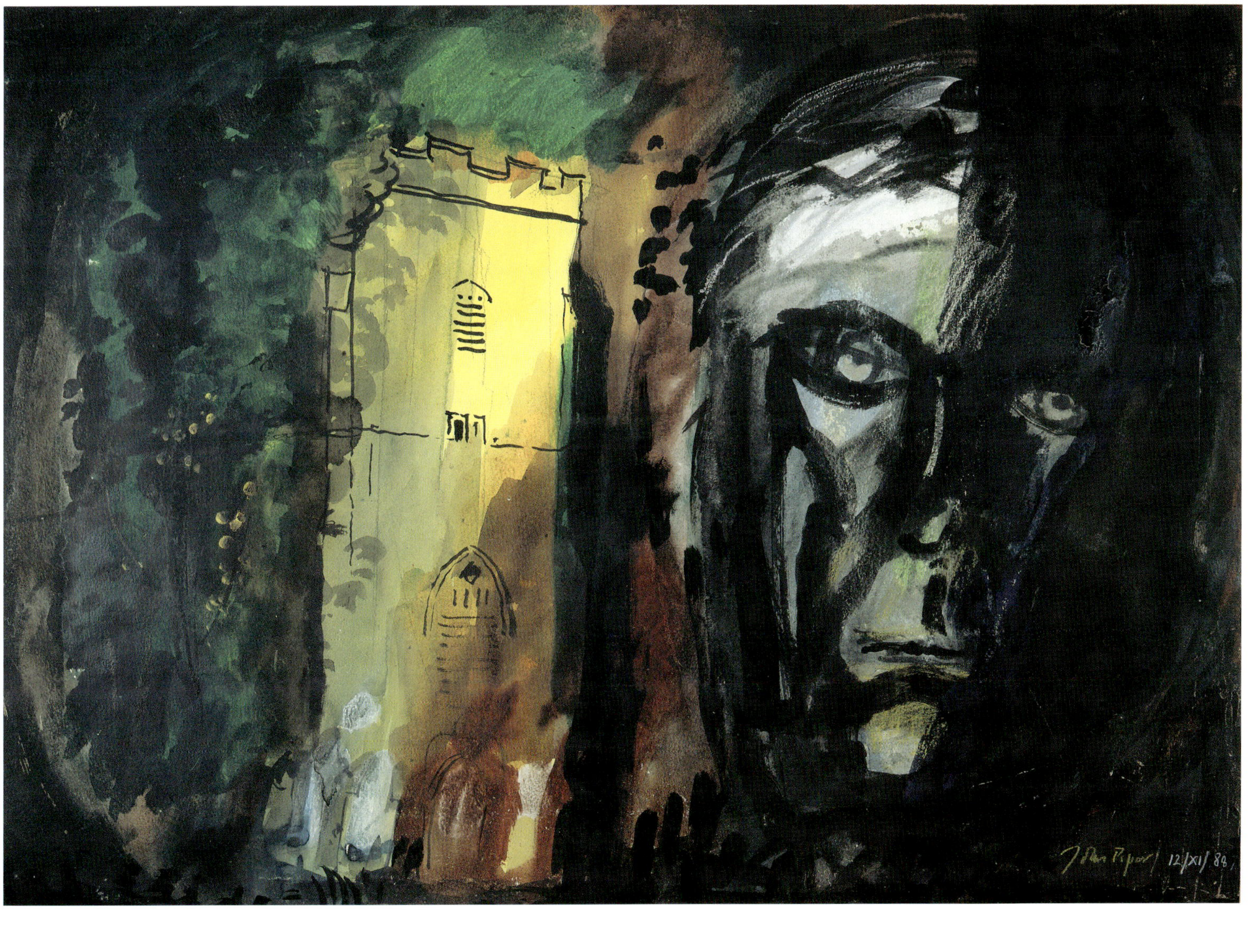

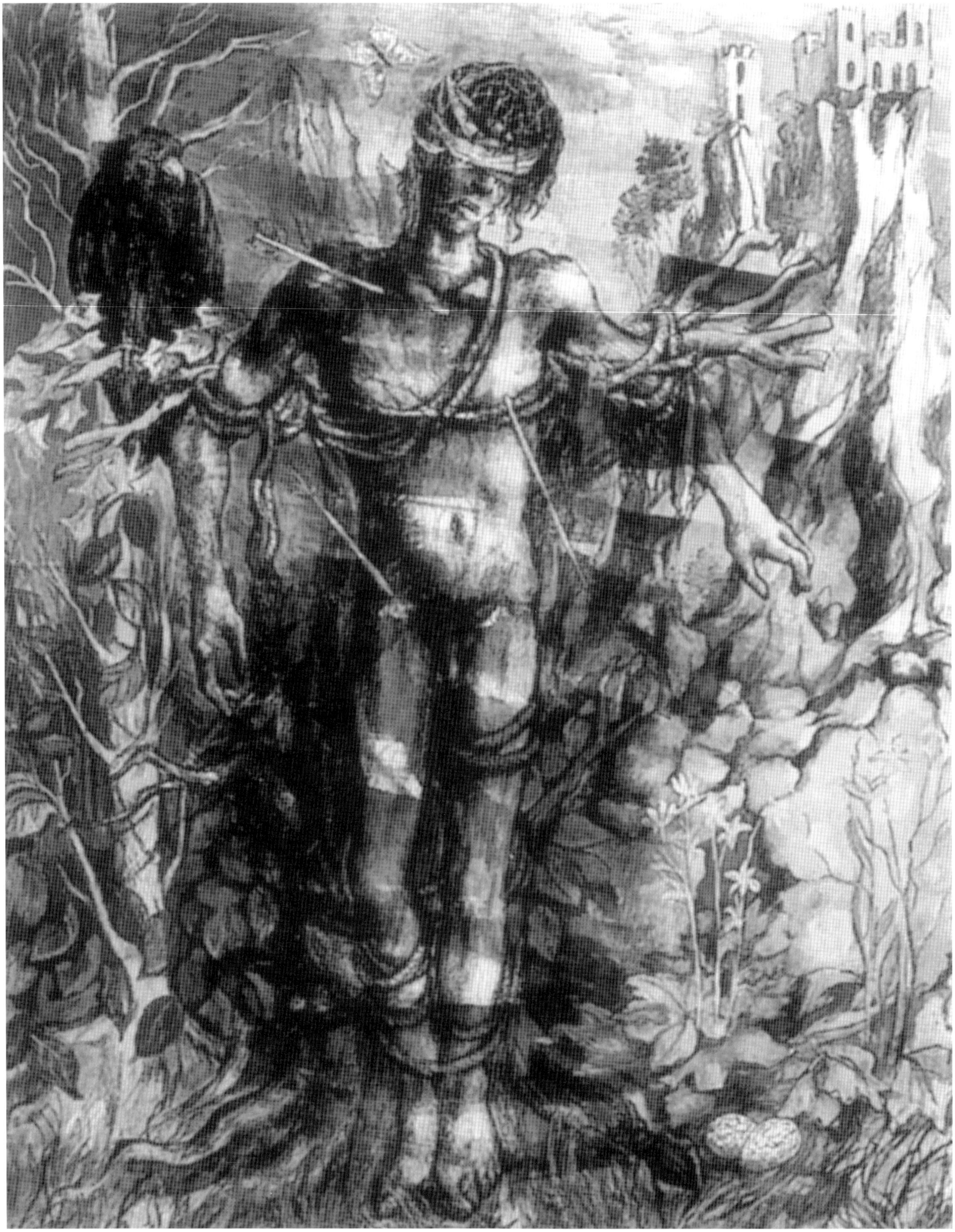

CHAPTER 8

John Minton (1917-1957) and the younger Neo-Romantics

Innocence on the Rack

The twentieth century had increased communications until nearly every person in nearly every place knew something of how the others lived: and every aspect of life was politicised. Before the Second World War, England and Germany were producing arts of seemingly opposite aims. Kenneth Clark looked across at Germany and concluded:

> Totalitarian art must be a form of Classicism. The State which is founded on order and subordination demands an art with a similar basis...

Despite Hitler's claim of a German artistic ancestry going back to Caspar David Friedrich, Nazi Romanticism went entirely into notions of the Fatherland.

Real Romantic art was just what the Nazis tried to suppress. For as Clark wrote: 'Romantic painting, however popular, expresses the revolt of the individual. [Its] inspiration is outside State control.'[1] Neo-Romantic art came to its fullest focus during the Second War in England. There it gained something paradoxically approaching official recognition. An historian of the style has written:

> We must give credit to the British Government and [Clark's] W[ar] A[rtists'] A[dvisory] C[ommittee] that the art produced during the nation's time of peril was, by and large, romantic in nature; and no artist felt coerced into abandoning his own style or viewpoint.[2]

That view was endorsed by the artists themselves. John Piper wrote, in his *British Romantic Artists* (1942), that virtually all recognisably British art is romantic. Piper was quickly backed up by an artist of the next generation, Michael Ayrton: 'One is hard put to it to think who, other than Reynolds, could be included in a hypothetical companion volume of "British Classical Artists".'[3]

Before and during the Second War, Sutherland scrutinised the smallest fragments of nature to reflect the atomising times. Piper reconnected the shards to the continuing development of human building throughout the history of the British island. Both artists lived long and productive lives.

Not so the next generation of 'Neo-Romantics'. Their young lives were shaped by what the poet Auden called the 'low dishonest decade' of the 1930s. Their pastoral visions were born of renewed war, and blown away by its aftermaths. The young Neo-Romantics brought human figures to the foreground in their pastorals. But their figures were shaped by the fact that most of these artists (unlike all their predecessors) were homosexual – at a time when acts of that love were against British law.

Sometimes the Neo-Romantics' figures multiplied to crowd out every hint of sheep and shepherd. Yet the loneliness they projected through the densest crowd still drew on the pastoral heritage. John Minton's pastoral, like Griggs's, rose out of memory and half-memory. But Minton's vision was utterly without Griggs's hints of some flashing mirror of history and faith only waiting to be recovered.

In the art of Minton and the other Neo-Romantics, innocence became like a Sutherland shard – ossified or petrified, reduced to a state which seems to exclude resurrection. Innocence, in the art of the Neo-Romantics, is there to be damned.

* * *

Opposite:
Plate 164. Self-portrait as St Sebastian, *c.* 1943. Ink and wash

1. Kenneth Clark, *The Romantic Rebellion: Romantic versus Classic Art* (Murray, 1973), 32.
2. Malcolm Yorke, *The Spirit of Place*, 80.
3. Michael Ayrton, Introduction to *Aspects of British Art*, which includes a reprint of Piper's *British Romantic Artists* (Collins, 1947), 7.

John Minton was born on Christmas Day 1917.[4] The First War had still nearly a year to run. Yet his family background offered many of the fairest promises of middle-class life. The father, Francis Minton, had a partnership in a firm of London solicitors. A year after John's birth, the solicitor moved his young family to a comfortable house on the North Downs at Caterham, a few mile west of Palmer's Shoreham.

John's mother was the daughter of a man who had raised himself from draper's assistant to Managing Director of the West End department store D.H. Evans. This grandfather, after the death of his first wife and mother of his children, had married another woman who loved his family. They lived in a mansion on the south coast surrounded by servants and acreage.

These promises for John were soon compromised and sullied. An elder brother suffered from birth defects so severe that the family had to send him to an asylum – where John was forced to make visits which horrified him. Then their father was overtaken by a gradual paralysis which would destroy his profession and ultimately kill him at fifty-four in 1930, when John was twelve. There was one more child, Richard, born in 1924. This brother, more than six years younger than John, could not offer close companionship to what was already a lonely childhood.

John's mother, to compensate her loss of conjugal pleasures, took up with a taxi driver. After her husband's death the man more or less joined her household – which she moved from the expensive comforts of Caterham to a ground-floor flat in a suburb south of London. She sent her two sons to spend much time at her father's and step-mother's estate. There they dressed formally each night for the servanted dinner.

The gardener's boy seduced John when he was about eleven. He was, he later admitted, a willing victim. In some moods he would refer to his homosexuality as 'nature's dirty trick'. Yet homosexuality may appear to offer some holding on to innocence, in a crucifying world which promises no resurrection.

For this boy, pencil-thin and already concealing nervousness with manic energy, homosexuality opened a gap between dream and nightmare which he could never finally close. But he might bridge it with art. 'I hate families', he said to one of his pupils in later years, 'and all the possessiveness and false loyalties and frustrations they cause.'

Preparatory school at Bognor and public school at Reading (both chosen and funded by his step-grandmother) encouraged John's reading and quick gift for drawing. A friend's parents took him to see the chapel at Burghclere painted by Stanley Spencer as a First War memorial. John revelled in the paintings of soldiers' domesticities. For himself, he collected reproductions of Samuel Palmer from the few magazine articles beginning to appear, and shared them with anyone who would look. He wanted an artist's career for himself.

In September 1935, when not yet eighteen, his grandmother took him to St John's Wood Art School in north London. It was an independent institution with some eminent Royal Academicians as patrons. But a young, energetic staff had recently taken over. The principal was Patrick Millard, at thirty-three as enthusiastic about Samuel Palmer as his new pupil. Millard had grown up with a background of Ruskin and Sickert. He had also studied in Paris side by side with his friend Anthony Gross (1905-1984), a virtuoso draughtsman (Plate 165). Together they exposed students at 'the Wood' to all the fashions and trends. Their friend John Piper made visits to the School. When Vanessa Bell visited, she gave a prize to young Minton and arranged for him to call at her Bloomsbury-decorated house in Sussex to collect it. Summer school outings took him to Yorkshire, Dorset, and Kent. There he painted 'oast-houses, barns, farmyards'. He turned his drawing pen to any subject with the readiness of Gross himself.

At 'The Wood' Minton made two particular friends. One was a breezy domineering matron twenty years his senior but still studying, Mrs Edith Lamont. She supplied a kind of maternal strength. When later she bought a house in the Kentish country south-east of Palmer's Shoreham, a more continuous experience of the Weald opened to Minton's eye and pen.

His other close friend at the School was four years younger. Michael Ayrton, even at sixteen, was ebulliently self-assured and shrewd in ways Minton would never be. The friendship was

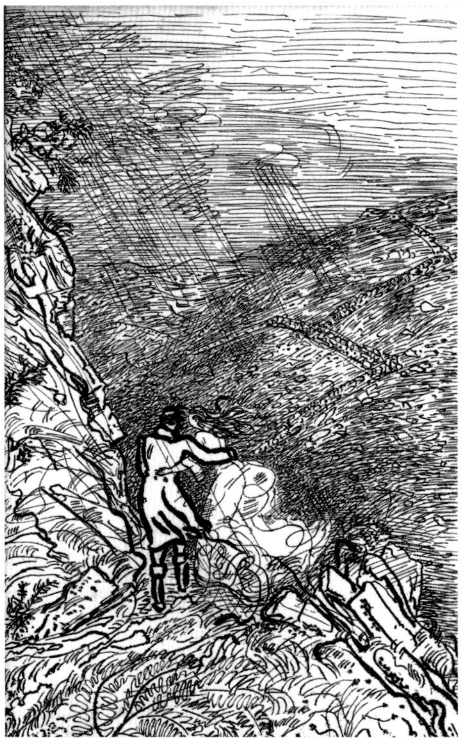

Plate 165. Anthony Gross: Heathcliff and Catherine, illustration for *Wuthering Heights*, *c.*1946. Ink

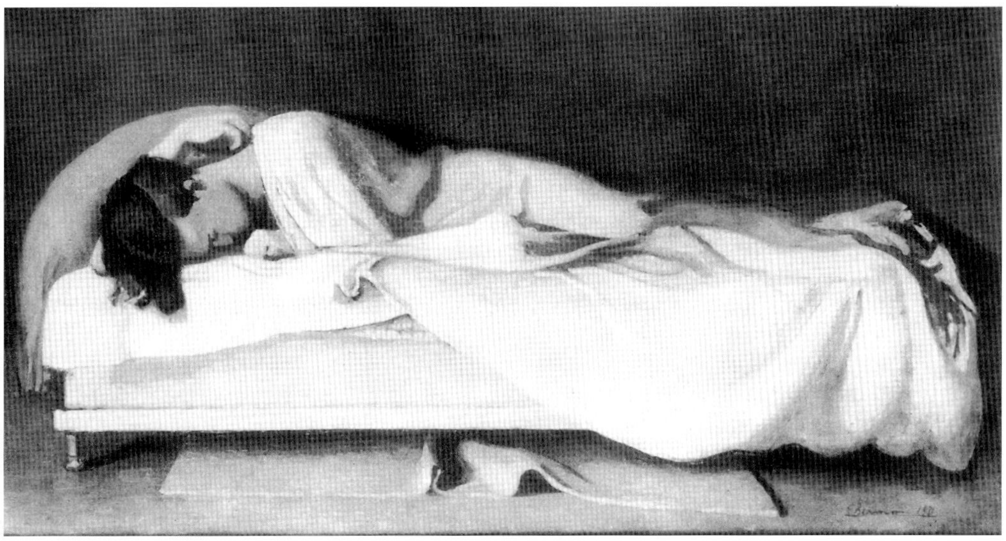

Plate 166. Eugène Berman: *Jeune homme couché,* 1931. Oil

confirmed over a School outing to Paris in April 1938. The two boys agreed that there was nothing for it but to get clear of school and return to Paris.

Behind that wish lay a shared distrust of English Abstraction and its influence. Together with another friend, Michael Middleton, they had read an American book with the provocative title *After Picasso*. 'It hit us in the midriff', Middleton would remember, 'and became our Bible'. The author, James Thrall Soby, distinguished two movements. One was Surrealism. The other belonged to a group of mostly Russian painters living in Paris.

They were called 'Neo-Romantics'. A generation younger than Picasso, they had revived the clowns and ballet dancers of Picasso's early 'blue' and 'rose' periods (now dismissed by the master of Cubism). These 'Neo-Romantics', the book's author wrote, were 'filling their canvases with unashamed poignancy'. In place of Abstraction's 'enforced intellectuality', they offered 'the futility and the sweetness of escape'.

Here were appeals to Minton's still secret homosexuality. He channelled his feelings into the theatre and ballet. *After Picasso* reproduced paintings by the Neo-Romantic Eugène Berman. There were slightly surreal stage-set prospects of 'Venice' and 'Ischia'. One dark painting showed *Statues in a Park* verging on animation. When Berman painted actual life, his *Jeune homme couché* (1931) seemed to show Minton another secret shared (Plate 166).[5]

Although the Neo-Romantic group had fragmented, several of the painters including Berman remained in Paris. To Paris Minton went at the end of December 1938 for 'independent study'. He had just turned twenty-one. He responded to the 'ordered design' of the city 'and of course the fantastic and florid statuary,' he wrote back to Ayrton. But he avoided newspapers through those months of extra 'peace' bought by Chamberlain's paper from Hitler. 'So if my ivory tower is going to be shattered any minute I shall be blissfully ignorant.'

When Ayrton joined him in April 1939, they saw Giraudoux's play *Ondine*, with sets and costumes by another Neo-Romantic, Pavel Tchelitchew. Like Gordon Craig, Tchelitchew projected images from behind screens: he turned hills to heaps of bones, and apparent mother-of-pearl to swirling water with mermaids. But the man himself was surrounded by parasites. Quitting Paris, the two young Englishmen spent some weeks drawing rock formations at Les Baux in Provence, where Berman had worked before them.

In August 1939, on advice from the British consul, Minton returned to England. News of his handicapped brother's death was overtaken by the beginning of the Second World War in September. Minton pleaded conscientious objection – which lost him his grandmother's financial support. He stayed in a flat owned by Ayrton in Belsize Park.

The two friends began to work at designs for a possible production of *Dido and Æneas* (following in Gordon Craig's footsteps). It did not come off. But Ayrton's thrusting self-advertising ultimately landed them a commission to design a *Macbeth* for John Gielgud. When it was staged in 1942, Gielgud found that the sets 'tended to dwarf the actors'.

Minton found a similar relation of setting to figures when he drew and painted London's bombed docklands with ragged waifs. Sketching War sites was forbidden, but he went back by

4. Much of this chapter relies on Frances Spalding, *Dance Till the Stars Come Down: a Biography of John Minton* (Hodder & Stoughton, 1991). The book snatched Minton's history from near oblivion at the last possible moment. Quotations not otherwise noted are from this source.

5. James Thrall Soby, *After Picasso* (New York: Dodd, Mead, 1935) 6-12, plates 18-21.

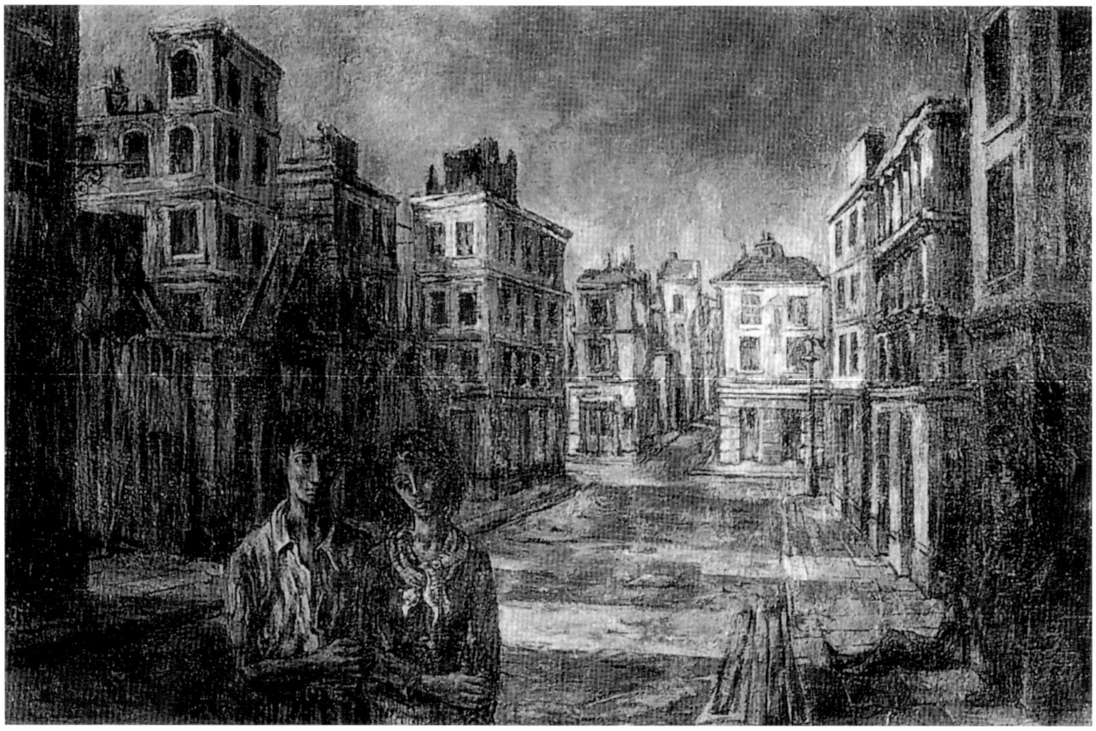

Plate 167. *London Street,* 1941. Oil

day and night for impressions to be worked up in the studio (Plate 167). Moving through blacked-out streets at night, he drifted into the promiscuity that came to play an obsessive role in his life: 'I would wander around the streets on summer nights feeling desperate and pick up any boy that would have me. It is all there in my paintings.'[6]

Fundamentally opposed to the War, he felt a refugee in his own country. He had written to Michael Middleton as early as October 1940:

> I cannot accept the existence of right or wrong, good and evil, only those things I feel... unhampered by the fallacy of moral valuation...
>
> The realisation of oneself in paint is... so different from the way in which Messrs. Bell, Read, Wilenski, Fry et alia talk about it... Nothing is more revealing about Berman and Tchelitchew than the pictures they paint, nothing more revealing about Picasso than *Guernica*.
>
> I often idly wonder if my preoccupation with adolescence in painting leads you to wonder what incentive, besides that of obvious influences, I have to paint pictures like that.
>
> The physical aspect of things has always been of great importance to me, and with it the touching and melancholy impermanence of all physical beauty – a sort of hopeless aching nostalgia – and the despairing transitory nature of all physical unions.

For a time he lodged with his mother and brother Richard in a barely furnished semi-detached house in south London. John felt cool towards his mother. His affection concentrated on seventeen-year-old Richard. With Richard now in sight of call-up age, John felt he could no longer sustain conscientious objection. In December 1941 he was drafted into the Pioneer Corps – largely non-combatant and therefore held in contempt by the Army, who trained them with rigour. Quartered in a Nissen hut, Minton drew his own *Jeune homme couché*, with an empty military overcoat hung from a peg to keep watch over this boy's bed (Plate 168). It is Samuel Palmer's *Sleeping Shepherd* a century on. The boy's self-contained quietude persists through rough textures and harsh angles in Minton's assured pen-work: there is no nature dripping fatness here.

From successive postings in Liverpool, Devon, and Kent ('Wrotham-in-the-mud'), Minton managed a slim presence in the London galleries. In March 1942 his work was included in a London Museum show of 'New Movements in Art'. Remarking the sheer diversity of styles in English art then, the critic Raymond Mortimer distinguished Post-Impressionists, 'Euston Road' realists, Abstractionists, Surrealists – and another group including Piper, Sutherland, and Henry Moore 'which I tentatively call the "Neo-Romantics"'.

The name stuck in England (as it had never done in *émigré* Paris) because it described the newest

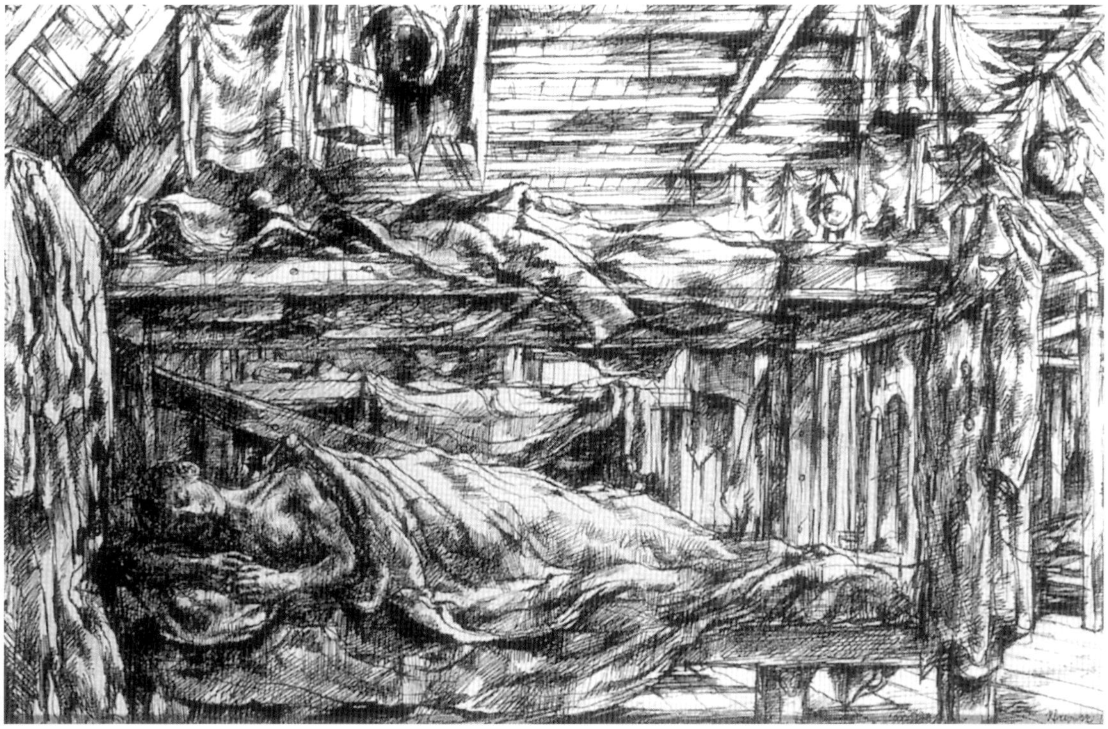

Plate 168. *Barrack Scene,* 1942. Ink

manifestation of English art's devotion to its own land and lights. In the depths of war, Mortimer found his English Neo-Romantics 'in revolt against the European tradition of humanism':

> All these artists avert their eyes from and thus condemn the civilization we now see in the apparent process of collapse. The appeal of their art… is to mystics and particularly to pantheists who feel a fraternity, or even a unity, with all living things, to those with the 'sense sublime of something far more deeply interfused'.[7]

Mortimer's term was quickly taken up, as it served a need. The painter and critic Robin Ironside, in a survey of 'Painting Since 1939' published immediately after the War, saw the Neo-Romantic impulse pushing French doctrines out of England.[8] So it seemed to wishful thinking then.

* * *

Against the squalor of Army life, Minton felt the immanence of landscape. It had nothing to do with the Parisian *émigrés*, as he wrote to Michael Middleton in September 1942: 'Pavel, Eugene and all the boys, Ayrton too cannot give me any line on this.'

Tired of Pioneer Corps tedium, and with his brother Richard soon to enlist in an Infantry battalion, Minton decided to join the Infantry himself. When his selection for officer training took him to the west coast of Wales, north of Sutherland's Pembrokeshire, the raw materials of a landscape vision showed themselves. In January 1943 he wrote to Ayrton of mountains near Harlech

> … mottled and serrated like Sutherland with intricate lines of stone walls like netting spread unevenly and swept by winds one can almost see roaring in whirlpools and eddies round the peaks and out to writhing grey sea.

Here was something he found 'more straightforward and direct' than any hints from Paris. Minton concluded 'I feel happier finally in the English tradition'.

Then the mountain vision was overlaid with an opposite experience, but as powerful. On a week's leave in London, he fell violently in love with a soldier about to be posted to India: 'I felt my guts being torn out piece by piece by this boy just by the way he looked at me.' Minton confessed his homosexuality to Ayrton, and added that he had been secretly in love with Ayrton when they were in Paris. Ayrton, invalided out of the RAF and teaching at Camberwell School of Arts and Crafts, was living with a woman. Minton's letter looked his own homosexuality full in the face: 'By this world's standards I am a monster, vain, selfish perverted.'[9]

6. 21 March 1943 to Ayrton (quoted in Spalding, 51).
7. *New Statesman*, 28 March 1942 (quoted in Yorke, *The Spirit of Place*, 22-23). Mortimer's quoted words are from Wordsworth's 'Tintern Abbey'.
8. Robin Ironside, 'Painting Since 1939' (Longmans Green for the British Council, 1947).
9. 21 March 1943 (Spalding, 52).

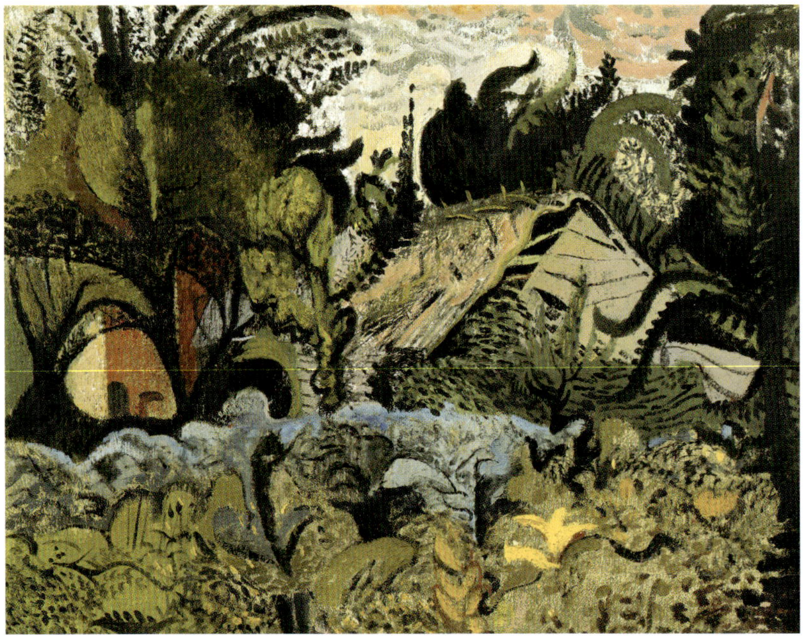

Plate 169. Robert Colquhoun: *Marrowfield, Worcestershire,* 1941. Oil

Glasgow City Council (Museums)/ The Bridgeman Art Library

Assigned to the Oxfordshire and Buckinghamshire Light Infantry, Minton proved unequal to officer duties and broke down. From hospital, he was interviewed by psychiatrists: homosexuality was recognised, and he was discharged. 'I have saved my soul at the expense of the community,' he wrote to Michael Middleton, 'and climbed back into the ivory tower'.

Where was Minton's ivory tower now? The magnet for every proscribed and persecuted minority in wartime England was inevitably the welter of London and the relative invisibility it conferred. Homosexuals gathered from every corner of Britain in certain pubs and clubs round Fitzroy Square and Soho. Many artists were there.

Several of Minton's friends in London were already beginning to give a form to Neo-Romanticism for their generation. Two were founding patrons of little magazines – John Lehmann (*Penguin New Writing*) and Peter Watson (*Horizon*). Both were well placed to introduce like-minded artists, and Watson actually supported several young painters: two Scots who had come to London together, Robert Colquhoun (1914-62) and Robert MacBryde (1915-66), were known as 'the Roberts'.

Colquhoun had painted some tumbled Neo-Romantic landscapes soon after they came to England in 1941 (Plate 169). At their Kensington flat, the Roberts had thrown a party for Minton while he was still in the Army. Minton had also visited them in company with the youngest of their generation, Lucian Freud and John Craxton. They were barely twenty, both from distinguished families and attracting attention from Piper, Moore, Sutherland and Kenneth Clark. Watson paid the rent of their studio.

Craxton (exempted from military service for pleurisy) had drawn outstanding Neo-Romantic images. His ink and wash *Poet in a Landscape* revivified the 'stump-work' technique

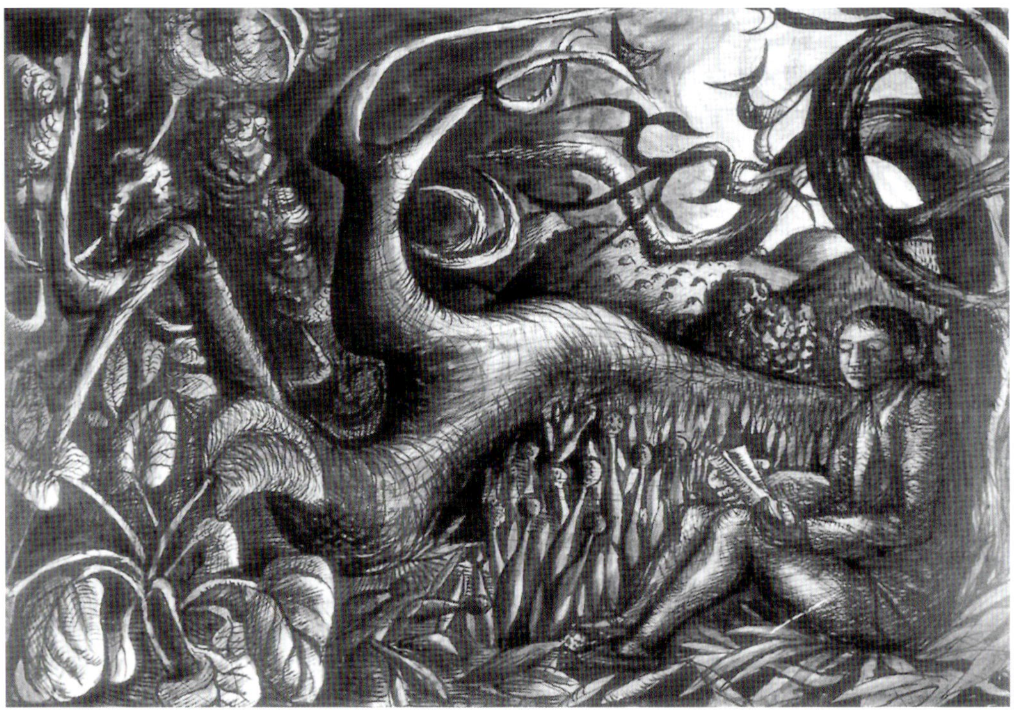

Plate 170. John Craxton: Poet in a Landscape, 1941. Ink and wash

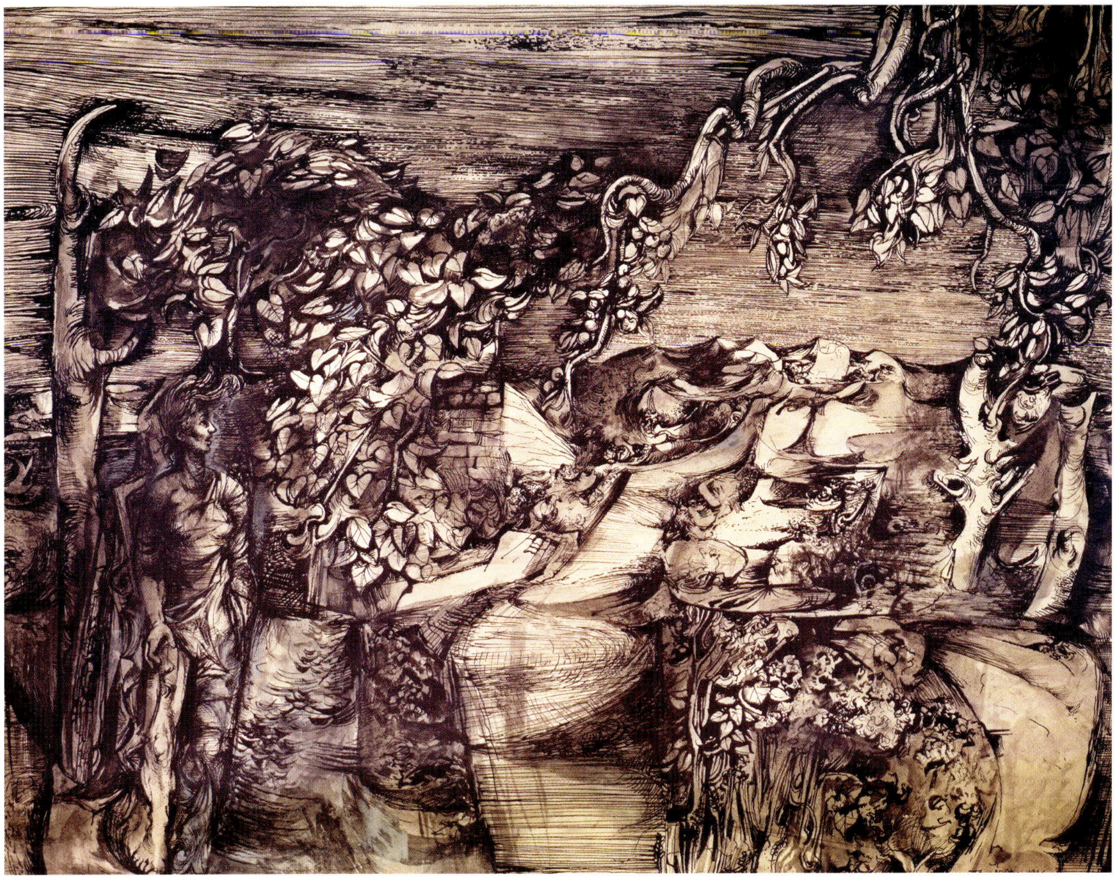

Plate 171. *Recollections of Wales,* 1944. Ink and wash
The British Council Collection

of Palmer's *Valley Thick with Corn.* But Craxton's reader (an admitted self-portrait) finds himself amid nature less refulgent than menacing (Plate 170). In the summer of 1943 Craxton joined Graham Sutherland and his wife for drawing in Pembrokeshire.

When Minton left the Army, he was invited by the Roberts to share their flat in Kensington. They were happy for him to occupy a back bedroom, use a side-table in the big studio, and pay rent. Before arriving in London, the Roberts had been practically teetotal. Two years of Soho pubs and clubs had set them both on the road to alcoholism. Minton, as a sort of junior partner, quickly found himself there too.

He taught three days a week at Camberwell School of Arts and Crafts, a post secured for him by Ayrton. Minton disliked teaching, he said, almost as a violation of secrets: 'I believe too much in the idea of painting to make public property of it'. Yet he confided to one of the youngest girls at Camberwell:

> I alternate between two moods about drawing – despair and utter despair: Bach, beer and sex are the only comforts… How can one be alive and not feel some sort of wonder, some sort of disquiet and heartbreak?

Such naked revelations of private anxieties, side by side with Minton's quick wit at the expense of every institution, made him an unforgettable teacher.

Teaching might be 'a necessary compromise'. But the compromise for Minton was not about finance: he shared his money with profligate generosity. It was teaching's contact with the young that galvanised him. And his fascination with innocent youth now came together with landscape dreams to produce his best work.

His technique is the ink and wash of early Palmer. But Minton's line keeps the distress of his Army *Barrack Scene, 1942,* as it moves out into woods and the occasional harvest. He began in some sense with *Recollections of Wales* (finished in 1944) (Plate 171). The witness is androgynous; and refulgence is edged with Sutherland's Pembrokeshire hardness. The barely controlled energy of Minton's vegetation suggests alarming mutability – approaching mineral on one hand, bird or animal on the other: the *Book of Durrow* vision persisting yet.

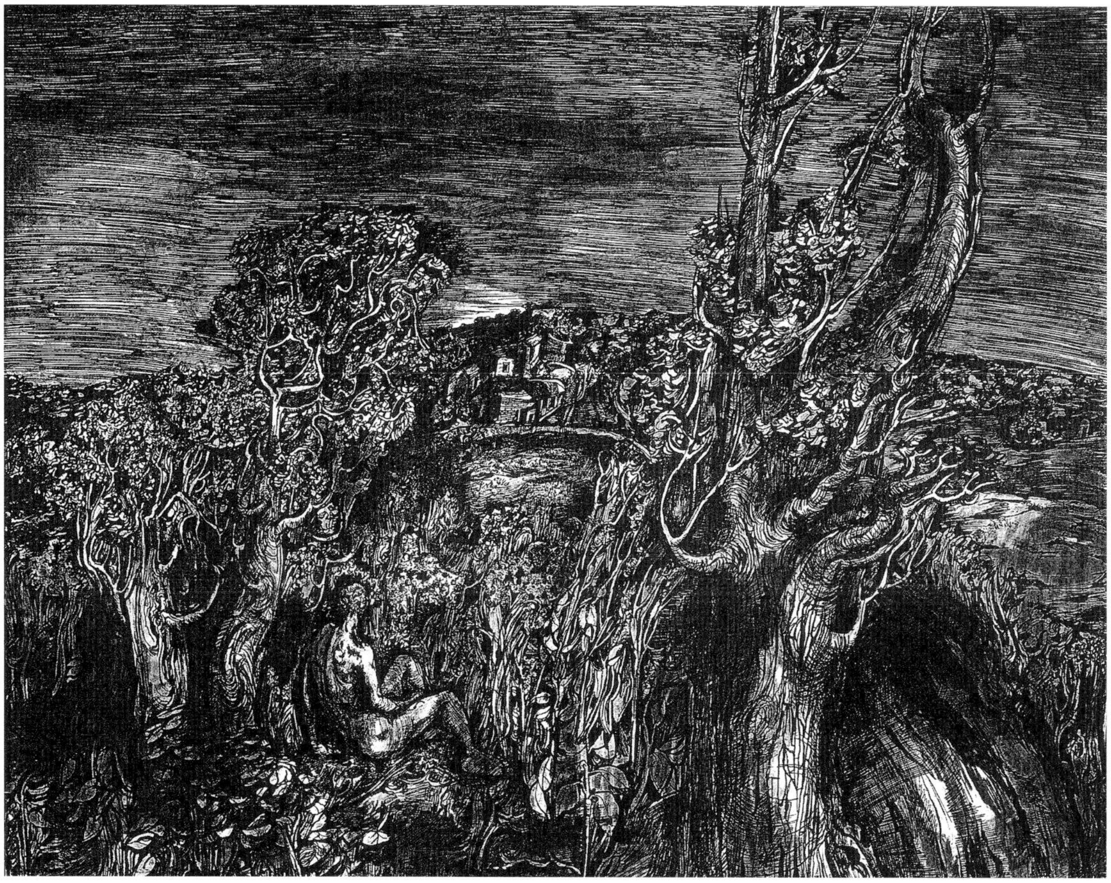

Plate 172. *English landscape,* 1943. Ink

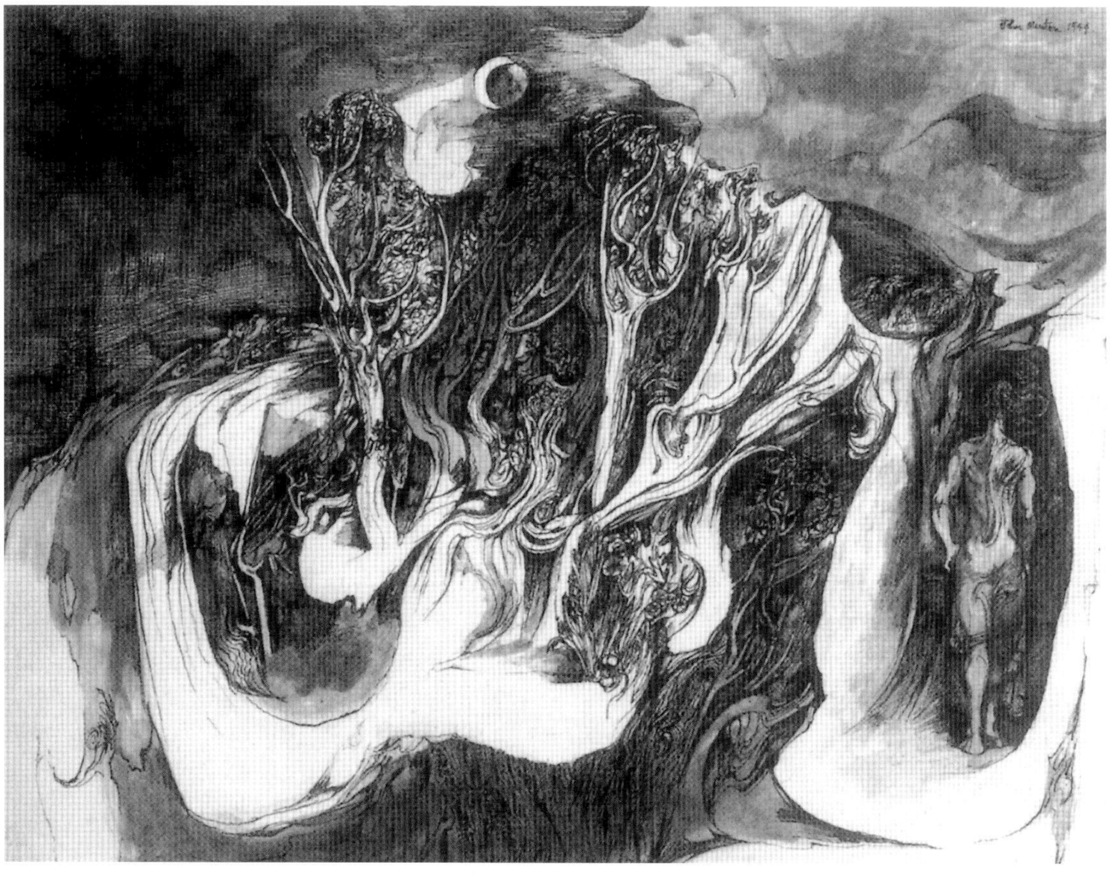

Plate 173. *Landscape with figure,* 1944. Ink and wash

From late 1943 for the next two years, Minton's ink and wash drawings opened the heart of his Neo-Romanticism. Not all are dated, but they show a secrecy gradually relaxing. In *English Landscape* (1943), a dark-lined sky and thick woods run harshly back towards a small patch of light at the horizon over a distant hamlet (Plate 172). Most of this is within the purview of a young nude, seated as if waking to the scene. Vegetable growth generates threatening vigour. At the lower right a steep road disappears in a tunnel of foliage.

In *Landscape with Figure* (1944) under a distant Palmerish moon, the tunnelled road has become a covert which the nude has risen to enter with purpose (Plate 173). Minton's tortured penwork is counterpointed now with broad areas of light wash – comparable to work being done then by Michael Ayrton. In Minton's picture the white shapes suggest less bone than flesh.

Yet sexual aggression was not really the way Minton wanted to take his art. The most Palmerish of his Neo-Romantic drawings is *Harvester Resting* (Plate 174) – a hatted and loosely clad youth asleep against a stook, with others filling the hillside guarded by a hoary tree. In the sky above this latest 'Sleeping Shepherd' a new moon edges the ghostly orb.

Coloured washes embroider a figureless *Harvest Moon* (1944). This landscape of shore, sea, and sky in broad areas is set with resilient leaves and grasses almost hiding a huge rock (Plate 175). Yet the lyric is gentle, as in much of Minton's best work: his atmosphere moves away from Sutherland, back through Nash, to touch hands with Palmer's young excursions along the English south coast.

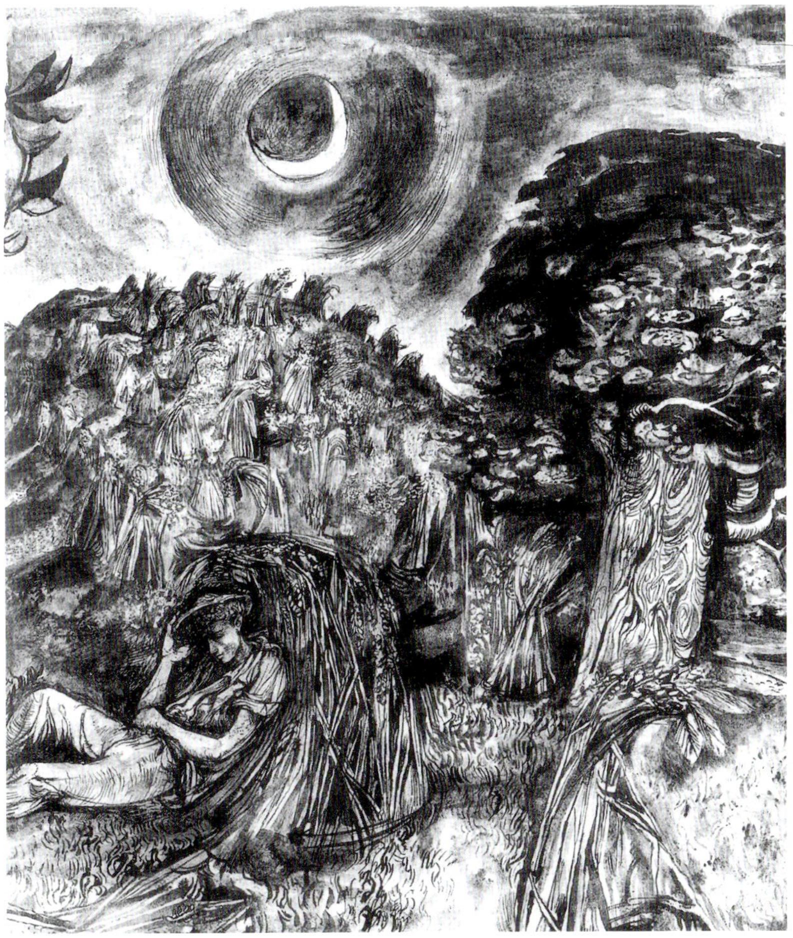

Plate 174. *Landscape with Harvester Resting*, *c.*1944. Ink and wash with body colour

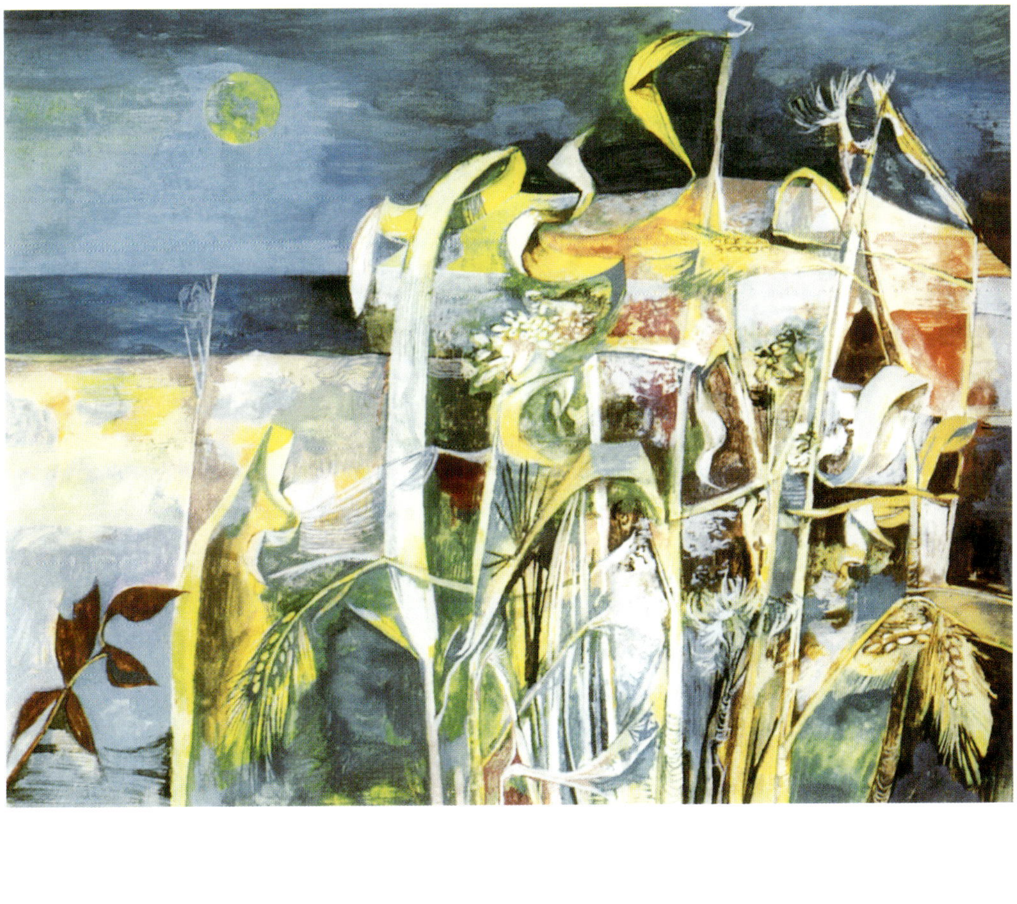

Plate 175. *Harvest Moon*, 1944. Ink and wash

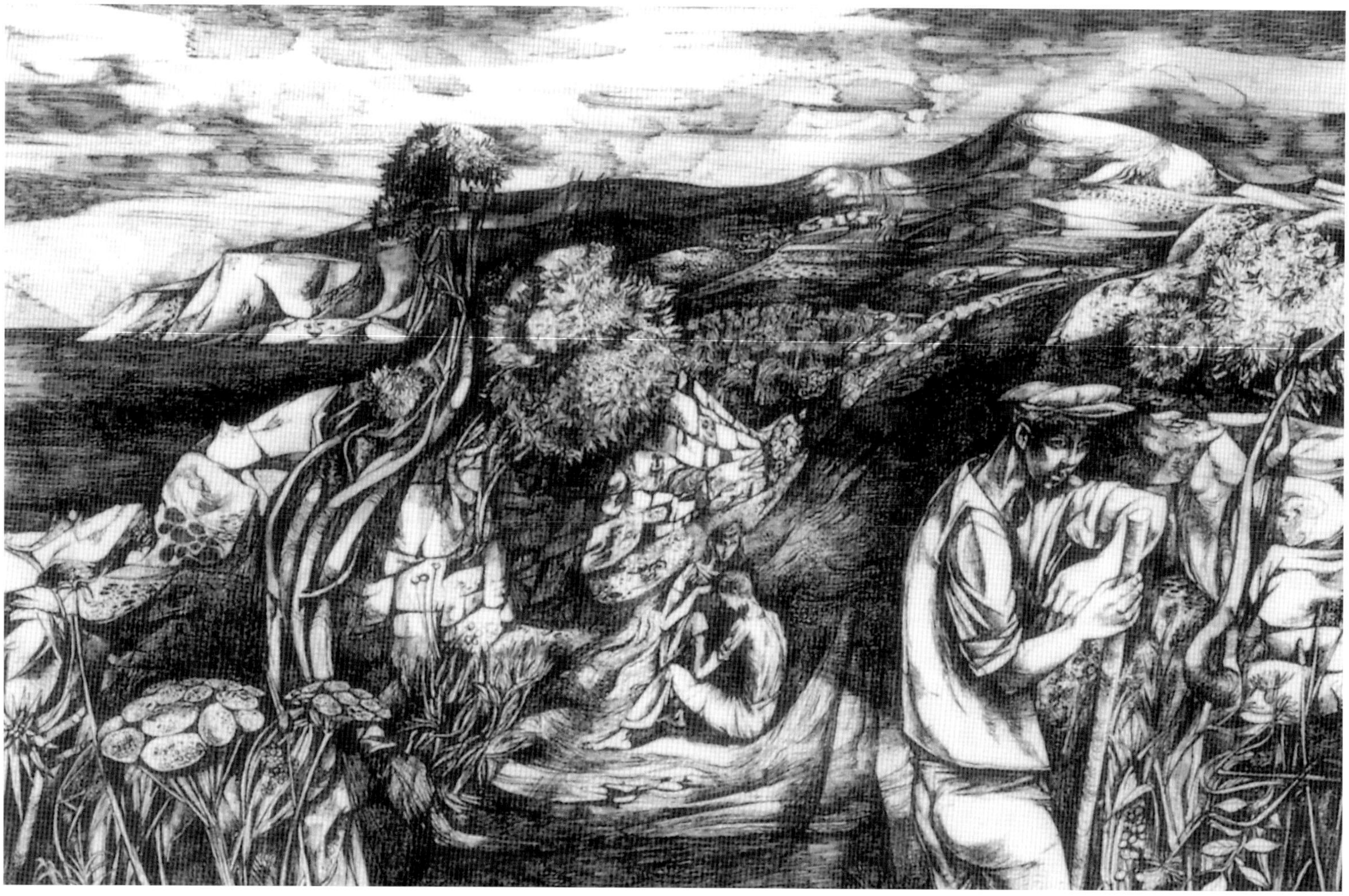

Plate 176. *Summer landscape,* 1945. Ink

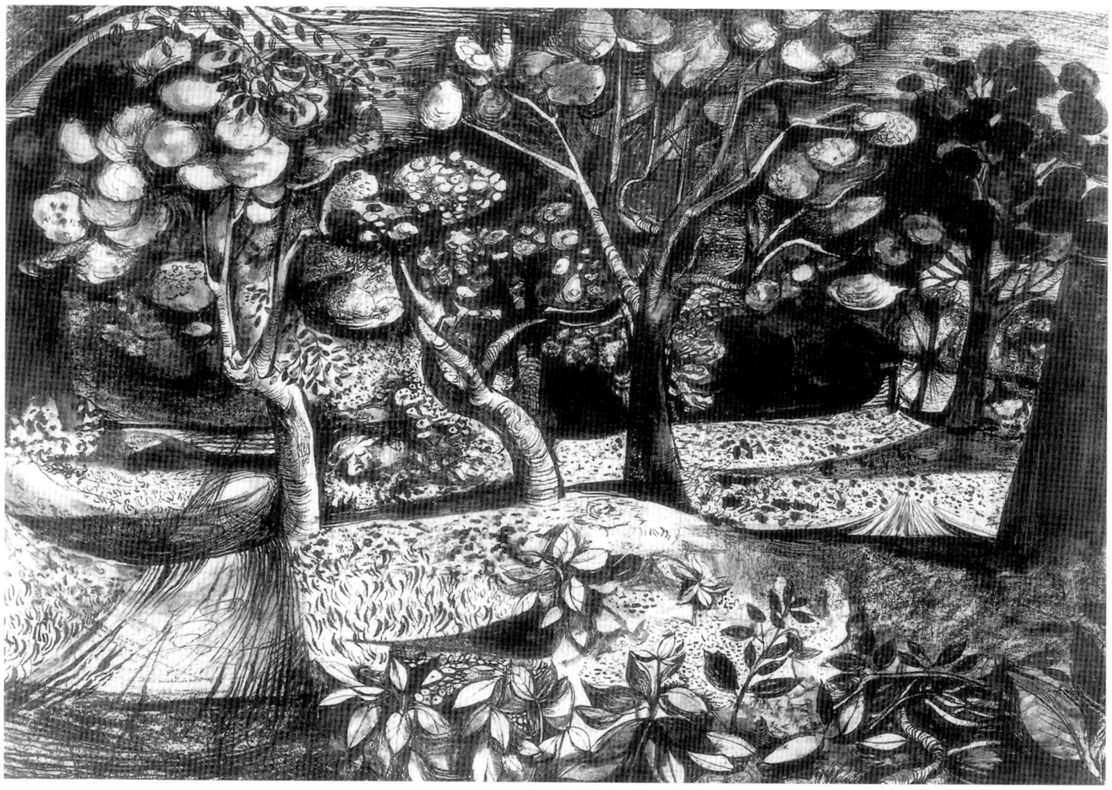

Plate 177. *Dark Wood, Evening,* *c.*1947. Ink and wash

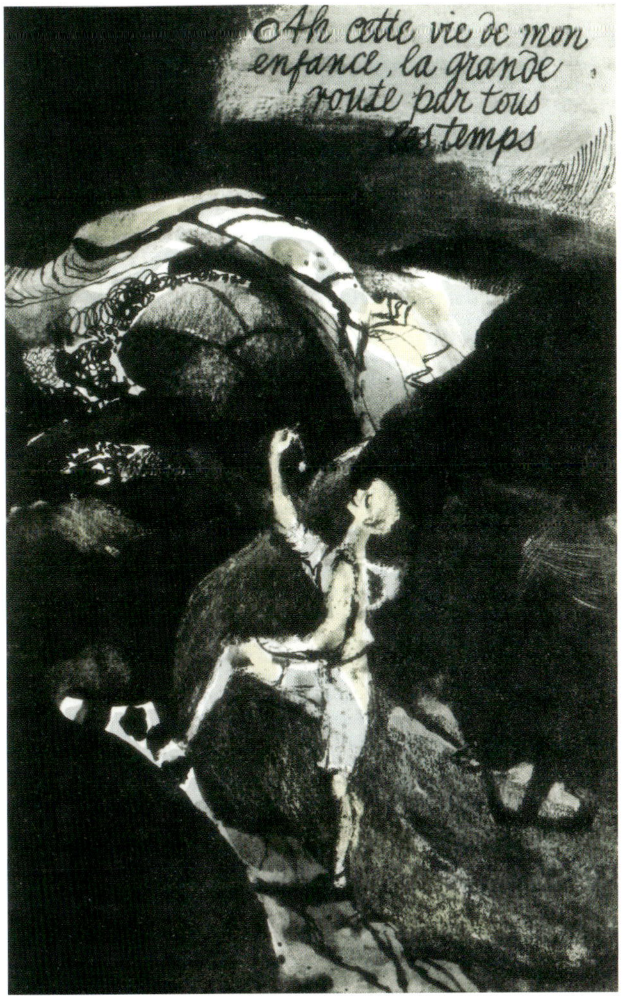

Plate 178. Keith Vaughan: *'The Impossible'*, for *A Season in Hell,* 1949. Lithograph

Monochrome returns with Minton's human figures. Two young men share the centre of *Surrey Landscape* (1944), with their surrounding woodland palpably opening and brightening. Yet almost with the end of the War in 1945, Minton's balance of contemplative figure in enhanced landscape begins to shiver. *Summer Landscape* (1945) draws a complex counterpoint of seacoast rocks with inland vegetation sheltering a boy and girl mutually absorbed – while in the right foreground a capped man holds a wooden staff as he stares emptily away (Plate 176). The brilliant light picks out a large protuberance of hillside above his head, while anthropomorphic rocks before him sprout twisted saplings. It is an image of exclusion from paradise.

From this point Minton's drawings divide – between fine landscapes dominated by illustrative human activity (*Hop-Pickers*, 1945), and lonely scenes with leaves larger and shapes loosening. A sunlit *Path through the Woods* is enlarged to become *Dark Wood, Evening* (Plate 177). These images are haunted as by the ghost of Palmer in the process of self-banishment from Shoreham. By 1946-7 Minton is drawing *Withered Plants and Landscape.*

The War's end had brought new troubles. Its final year had taken the twenty-year-old life of Richard Minton, killed in Belgium. With Richard went John's last deep affection within his family. In 1945 Churchill, who had played a vital part in the Allied victory, was thrown out by the British electorate. They installed a Labour government – which started a National Health Service but turned further the screws of rationing shortages. Victorious nation and crumbling Empire raised a kind of desperate hysteria that was new in British life.

Minton and the Roberts felt it all. They had taught him much about oil painting. But now the Roberts separated themselves from any English influence, making gritty remarks about Minton's Neo-Romantic drawings. Minton returned his oils to city subjects, with stylised figures such as Colquhoun had evolved (via their older friend the 'displaced' Polish artist Jankl Adler) out of Picasso. When two exhibitions in 1945 seemed to show Minton a success equal to Colquhoun's, the Roberts grew jealous. Minton's physical attraction to Colquhoun then became a destabilising factor.

After a summer holiday to Cornwall in 1946 with another Neo-Romantic artist, Keith Vaughan (1912-1977), Minton and Vaughan decided to take a floor each of a house in Hamilton Terrace, Maida Vale. They shared similar backgrounds. Vaughan was himself homosexual. He too had lost his father early, and had had a younger only brother killed in the War. He too had begun the War as a conscientious objector, and had then joined the Pioneer Corps – before being posted as orderly to a prisoner-of-war camp in Yorkshire. There he had found opportunities of sketching fellow soldiers to develop his own fascination for the male body. Vaughan was also a draughtsman, but he had to work at it.

Vaughan had been taken up by Peter Watson in 1942. Then John Lehmann had made Vaughan art editor of *Penguin New Writing*. There he met all the younger Neo-Romantic artists and many others. He found, as Minton had, a resonance in the menace of Sutherland's landscapes.

While Vaughan was living below Minton, he was commissioned by Lehmann to illustrate a new translation of Rimbaud's *Season in Hell.* It proved an ideal vehicle for Vaughan's tortured privacy (Plate 178). From its appearance in 1949, the little book took an instant place among the masterpieces of Neo-Romantic illustration.

Neo-Romanticism found sweeter renewal in Minton's postwar illustration. Commissioned by Lehmann to make four seasonal cover designs for *Penguin New Writing*, Minton deftly simplified his drawing to print in black with two colours (one that of the overall cover) for economy that compromised no vital quality (Plate 179).

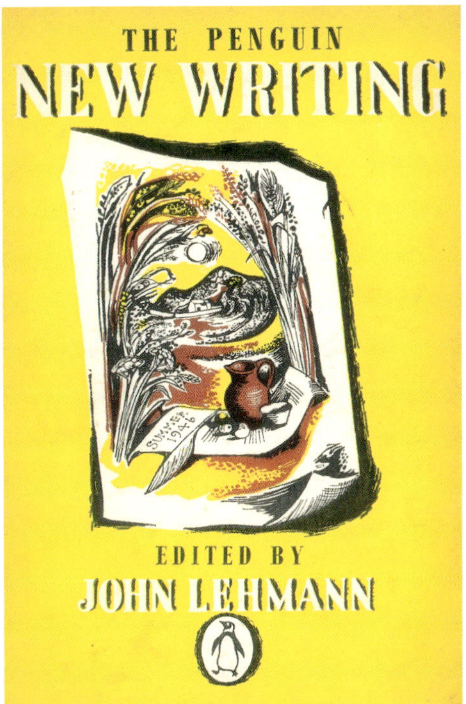

Plate 179. Cover for *Penguin New Writing*. Lithograph

Other commissions came fast. For the Hungarian *émigré* publisher Paul Elek, Minton illustrated a book which suited him as Rimbaud had suited Vaughan. Minton's was another

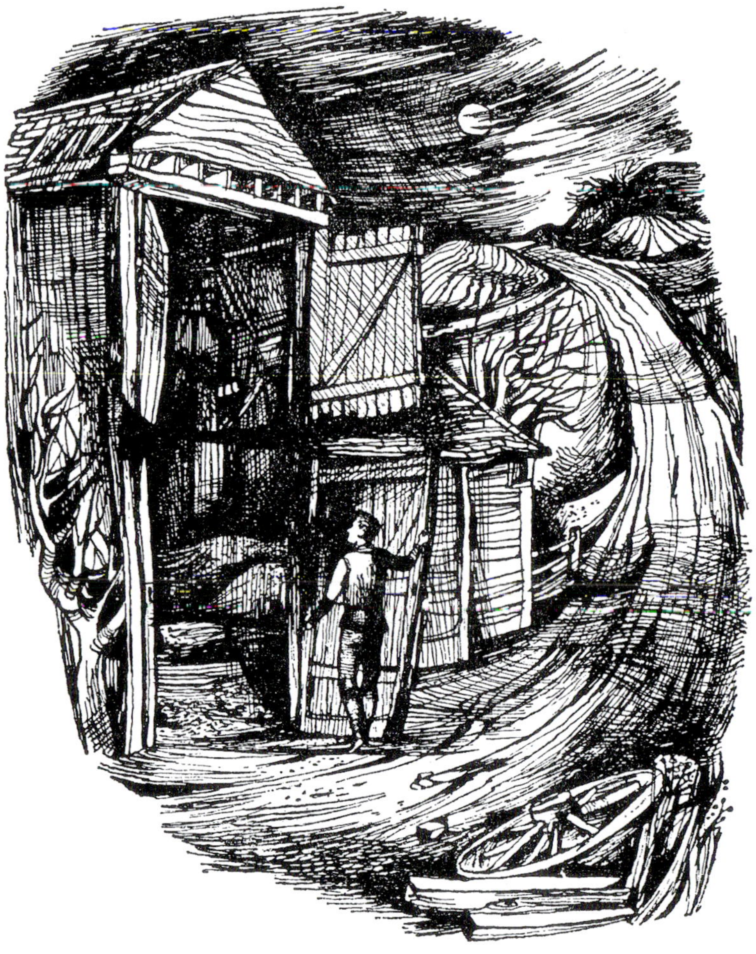

Plate 180. Le grand Meaulnes, illustration for *The Wanderer,* 1947. Ink

French masterpiece, Alain Fournier's *Le grand Meaulnes*. Once translated as *The Lost Domain*, it reappeared in 1947 as *The Wanderer* with Minton's illustrations evoking young love soiled and betrayed by the loss of innocence (Plate 180).

Minton found the innocence annealed in Blake, about whom he broadcast in May 1947:

> Blake... saw the universe with a mixture of tremendous awe and tenderness, and still had the capability of wonder and delight: seeing the microcosm and the macrocosm – the minute complex landscape of the hedgerows, the single flower...
>
> Blake lived at a time when already the clouds of an industrial misery were descending... a voice that still speaks of some sort of joy and wonder...
>
> Take the train to Kent, and there in the warm honey-coloured days of late summer, the glowing amber sun casting pointed shadows across the evening landscape, the moon a pallid disc, the evening star chill and bright, one is reminded again of Blake...

More still of Palmer. So Minton sought to renew his own vision – within a London commuting journey reversed.

Reviewing an exhibition of Minton's new work a year later, his friend Michael Middleton was able to find some promise in the loosening textures. Yet 'the restlessness with which he is still casting about for fresh novelties of manner suggests a certain instability.'[10] Minton was approaching his thirtieth birthday.

In the summer of 1947 John Lehmann sent Minton with the young writer Alan Ross (who lodged for a time in the boiler room at Hamilton Terrace) to do a book on Corsica. Travelling together, Ross wrote of corruption and decay while Minton sketched exotic beauties both landscape and human. Their book took its title from a line by Louis MacNeice: 'Time was away and somewhere else'. When it appeared, *Time was Away* appealed to numbers of English people longing for a holiday of sun and warmth abroad – and forbidden by their government's 'exchange control' designed to keep at home what little money England had at the end of the War.

Minton sketched compulsively wherever he went. At Edie Lamont's home in Kent, he made drawings for the publisher Michael Joseph to illustrate *The Country Heart* by H.E. Bates (Plate 181). Here is a ghost of Palmer's line secularised for a modern printer's dark green ink.

Plate 181. Headpiece for *The Country Heart,* 1949. Ink

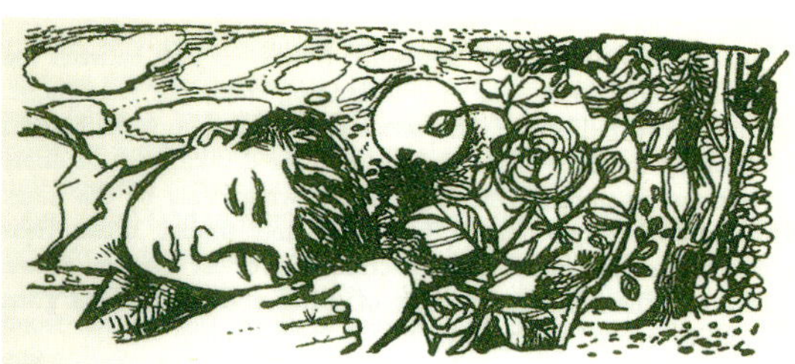

One of his favourite students at Camberwell, Bobby Hunt, began to help draw some of Minton's numerous dust-jacket commissions. (Minton still signed them: Bobby, he said, was his 'ghost'.) He painted Bobby's portrait – alone beside a window looking on to a garden of darkening shapes, and then as one in a trio of young friends. He painted another young man, Eric Verrico, against an autumnal background, which proved a true forecast when the boy's parents forbade him to see Minton any more.

He continued to teach at Camberwell until December 1947. When he left, the students gave him Geoffrey Grigson's newly published *Samuel Palmer: The Visionary Years*. Its thesis was that once Palmer turned thirty, left Shoreham and married, it was all up with his art. Minton (who turned thirty himself at Christmas) wrote to Edie Lamont of Palmer:

> It's an awfully sad and depressing business seeing how he was gradually devoured by circumstances, and how a sensitive person is finally destroyed by other people. ...
>
> The very weakness which was Palmer's makes his brief period of illumination so potentially touching and personal like a first awakening, a sense of first wonder.[11]

The words were a closer character of Minton himself.

After Camberwell he taught two terms at the Central School of Arts and Crafts, and then from the autumn of 1948 at the Royal College of Art. Minton always condemned Abstraction, and usually tried to push his students out of it. Once he painted a parody abstract, successfully passed it off under a pseudonym, and advertised the fraud to them all. 'Painting is made out of love for the subject,' he told them. And again: 'A man who paints puts his heart on the wall.' Yet if a student earned independence, Minton respected that. When Frank Auerbach came to the College in 1952, Minton said: 'You know what you want to do. I shall leave you alone.' Auerbach recalled: 'He had an incorruptible conscience about art.'[12]

But Minton was seeing his own defence against Palmer's supposed fate more and more in the youth of his students. He infused his teaching with still greater energy to make them all his friends. Every party drew him. Friends and students spilled through his flat at all hours with hangers-on drawn in by his manic generosity. They became known as 'Johnny's Circus' (Plate 182). It so disturbed the introverted Keith Vaughan that he moved out from under Minton in 1952.

Minton moved to a small Victorian house off Kensington High Street – close to Palmer's *rus in urbe* cottage a century earlier. Minton had already said in his broadcast: 'Blake reminds us of something we have lost, perhaps forever.' Now the Lefevre Gallery owner advised him: 'Moons are out.' Minton retailed it to all his friends. Critics took account of his shift in outlook with the phrase 'urban romantic'. It was not quite a contradiction in terms.

His drawing took on new spikiness. Figures came farther forward, filling formulas to express the ways he saw those drawn to 'Johnny's Circus'. Yet the sight of Minton dancing all by himself in an underground London club haunted one recollection of him:

> … his long, sad clown's face, lashed by breakers of dark hair as he danced a frenetic solo on an otherwise unoccupied dance-floor. His arms and legs were flying this way and that – the limbs of a loosely-strung puppet, each of which was being worked by a different person…
>
> Clapping and encouraging him was a ringside audience of the faceless nonentities whom he had gathered as an entourage as a magnet does rusty filings.[13]

In 1953 a new Police Commissioner and the Home Secretary announced a campaign against 'male vice' to 'rip the covers off all London's filth spots'. Minton moved house again – farther

10. *Spectator*, 18 Feb 1949.
11. 16 Dec 1947 (Spalding, 129).
12. Spalding, 177.
13. Ruthven Todd, 'Fitzrovia and the Road to the York Minster, or Down Dean Street' (Michael Parkin Fine Art, 1973).

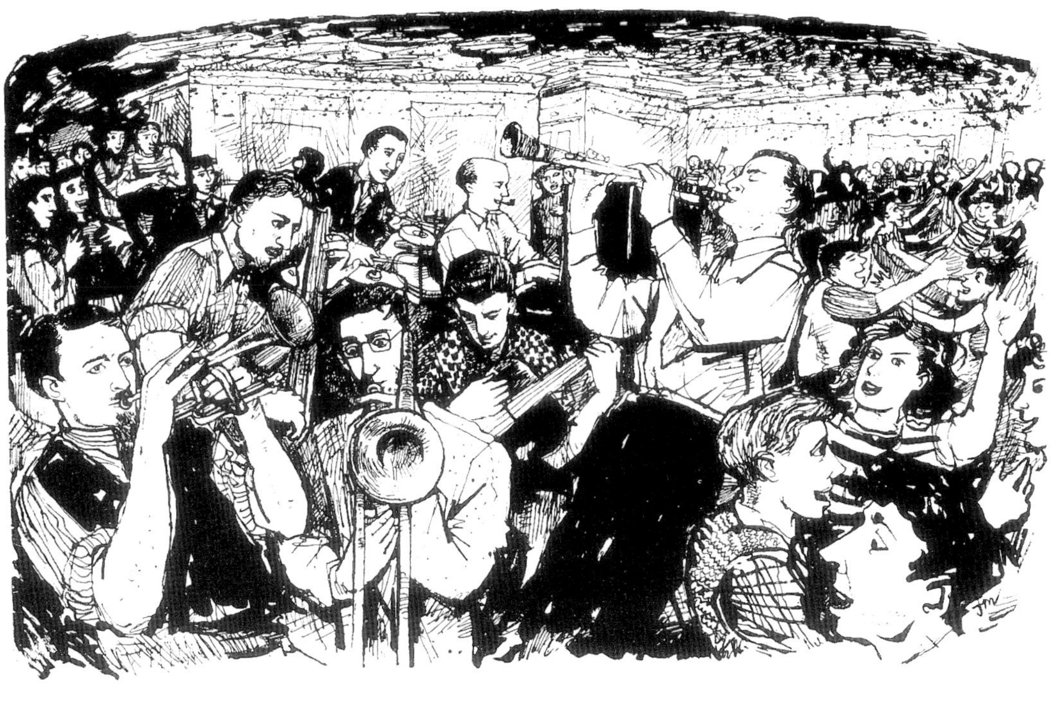

Plate 182. Cover illustration for *Our Time*, August 1949 (with Minton's self-portrait lower right). Ink

from Soho, to Allen Street behind Cheyne Walk in Chelsea. The house had seen a recent suicide. Minton celebrated it when the Roberts came to visit: 'I love the presence of death.'[14]

With the erosion of Neo-Romanticism, Minton tried vainly to extend his art. His drawing, sullied by advertising commissions, too often descended into pastiche. So had his life, as he searched with less and less success for friends who could help him. When the pressure grew too great, on 26 November 1955 he attempted suicide. One of his young men found him in time.

He raked together thirty 'recent paintings' for a show at the Lefevre Gallery in February and March 1956. Critics pointed to dull painting and repetitious poses in the portraits of young men. One of his friends estimated that Minton was getting through a bottle and a half of whisky every day.

He was absent from his Royal College tutorials more often than he attended them. Realising he was losing effectiveness, he asked for a year's unpaid leave. The College Rector praised a 'typically disinterested act', and granted the leave. He hoped his Senior Common Room might still enjoy Minton's company whenever he was nearby, but added: 'How sad the Painting School will be.'[15]

They were indeed. One first-year student who had Minton as his tutor was twenty-three year-old Graham Arnold. He had deeply valued Minton's sympathy with his own promptings for landscape. Successor tutors only growled questions about why Arnold did this or that. The young man's memory brightened at the contrast of Minton 'jumping up and down exclaiming "More of it! More of it!"'.

Minton went, along with everyone else in 1956, to see a loan exhibition of American painting at the Tate Gallery. It had been heralded by every device of advertising – ubiquitous posters and flyers, glossy catalogue, constant 'plugs' on radio and television. It was said that the American Central Intelligence Agency was behind the transparent attempt to hijack the centre of art across the Atlantic.

The exhibition's final room held paintings of 'Abstract Expressionism'. Minton saw them as utterly corrupt – self-indulgent and publicity-seeking. Yet students everywhere began to imitate them. One young man at the College poured bitumen over a large board and went over it with a bicycle wheel. It traduced everything Minton understood as art.

Still the College students asked for Minton's presence at their Sketch Club on 3 December 1956. He arrived in wild despair, laying about him with biting condemnations of every Abstraction and crudity. Suddenly he spun round and flung out his arm towards a large brown and grey canvas by Graham Arnold of *Rhubarb Sheds* in Yorkshire (recalled by the artist himself as 'a forlorn landscape with a forlorn sky'): 'That's the only real painting here!', Minton shouted.

Some of the students retaliated with a news-sheet claiming every generation's right to revolutionise its ideals. Minton's, it implied, were *passé*. Even Graham Arnold had been astonished at the extremity of Minton's despair: it went beyond the most passionate teaching.[16]

Yet everyone was appalled, little over a month later in January 1957, when news came of Minton's suicide. He was just thirty-nine. Friends recalled his vow never to touch forty – and a recent party he had thrown to give away everything in his studio: 'Have a drink!', he had cried; 'Have a picture!'

* * *

Minton's funeral on 24 January 1957 seemed a belated farewell to a vision already past. Neo-Romanticism had failed to sustain every one of its younger adherents. Michael Ayrton, after a brief flirtation in the 1940s, had found a fascination with figures in violent motion that would take him into sculptures of the Minotaur. Colquhoun and MacBryde had left Neo-Romanticism behind for renewed French influence; but they painted less and less as alcohol and poverty overcame them. John Craxton at the War's end had found his way to Greece: there through a long career he added to the classical inheritance of idealised young male figures.

Young male figures equally obsessed the eldest of the English Neo-Romantics, Keith Vaughan. He had remained in London, to breast the full force of the abstract movement. With supreme effort, he managed to synthesise his male bodies with Cubism. Yet his achievement seemed nullified as soon as the wheel of fashion turned again.

In the early 1960s another new mode seized the young. 'Pop Art' brought back subject matter – but used cynically as the language of advertising. An advertisement in fact had given one celebrated 'Pop Art' collage its title: *Just what is it that makes today's homes so different, so appealing?* The artist, Richard Hamilton, defined Pop Art with a list of attributes:

> Popular (designed for mass audience)
> Transient (short-term solution)
> Expendable (easily forgotten)
> Low cost – Mass produced
> Young – Witty – Sexy – Gimmicky – Glamorous – Big Business.[17]

It was Vaughan's turn to feel traduced. Returning from an exhibition of Pop Art in 1964 when he himself was fifty-one, Vaughan wrote in his diary:

> After all one's thought and search and effort to make some sort of image which would embody the life of our time, it turns out that all that was really significant were toffee wrappers, liquorice allsorts and ton-up motor bikes. ... I understand how the stranded dinosaurs felt...
>
> One hoped, I suppose, in the end to hand on to someone who saw further, had more talent, more youth, energy, more time before him, to complete what one had started, or relayed from the past. But not this. Perhaps it is the iron curtain between the generations...
>
> What is disappointing in the work of so many of the more talented young painters is... the bland, positive, hard-edged assurance which leaves out of account the one thing which seems to me most characteristic of this age – namely its basic contradictions and dialectical quality.[18]

To live with contradictions and dialectics needs patience and distancing. Pop Art overrode all that with its novelty attack. So it seemed the newest fascism. French absolutism was familiar enough, but here from across the Atlantic – from the supposedly demotic United States – was another such challenge. Pop Art struck Vaughan as the *reductio* of Abstract Expressionism:

> Its main sources were anarchy and a sense of decoration. Its achievement was to show how much could be done with so little. ... Such fantasies can appeal only to a society deeply frustrated by having had its spiritual problems transposed into economic ones.[19]

A dozen years later, in 1977, mortally ill with cancer, Vaughan himself committed suicide.

The persistent advertising of values essentially foreign to English inheritance in the years after the Second War had one new result. It combined with increasing pressures of commerce and communication everywhere to produce a succession of panaceas never seen before. Now a fashion could rise, gain its noisy following, and disintegrate – all in less than the lifetime of a single career. Each ebb left its *soi-disant* adherents stranded earlier in life – and farther than ever from the newest novelty.

The axles of these antagonisms were all fixed in the great cities. That in itself was nothing new. Most of the pastoral visionaries back to Samuel Palmer had their beginnings close to London: Griggs, thirty miles north at Hitchin, had been the most distanced. Each of them had felt a creative need to escape the city, and each had made his own way to do it.

Now the two artists who had found fullest youthful focus in Neo-Romanticism had lived their lives in London: and both had ended in suicide. Colquhoun and MacBryde, also remaining in London, had been virtual suicides. The fact that all were homosexual could suggest an inheritance played out – or merely persecuted for its difference.

The younger Neo-Romantics had translated Stanley Spencer's 'field full of folk' through their own sexual orientation to the city. But Minton above all had set it within a powerful counterpoint of pastoral vision. It broadened and deepened his art. Many of his pupils such as Graham Arnold, leading normal lives, treasure the memory of his inspiration to this day.

14. Spalding, 194.
15. Robin Darwin to Minton, 7 April 1956 (Spalding, 216).
16. Graham Arnold, conversation with the writer, May 2002.
17. Quoted in Yorke, *The Spirit of Place*, 280.
18. Keith Vaughan, *Journals 1939-1977* (Murray, 1989): 7 April 1964 (p 140).
19. Quoted in Yorke, 280: vividly illustrated in a tag from *Colours Magazine*: 'For every doubt there is a product.'

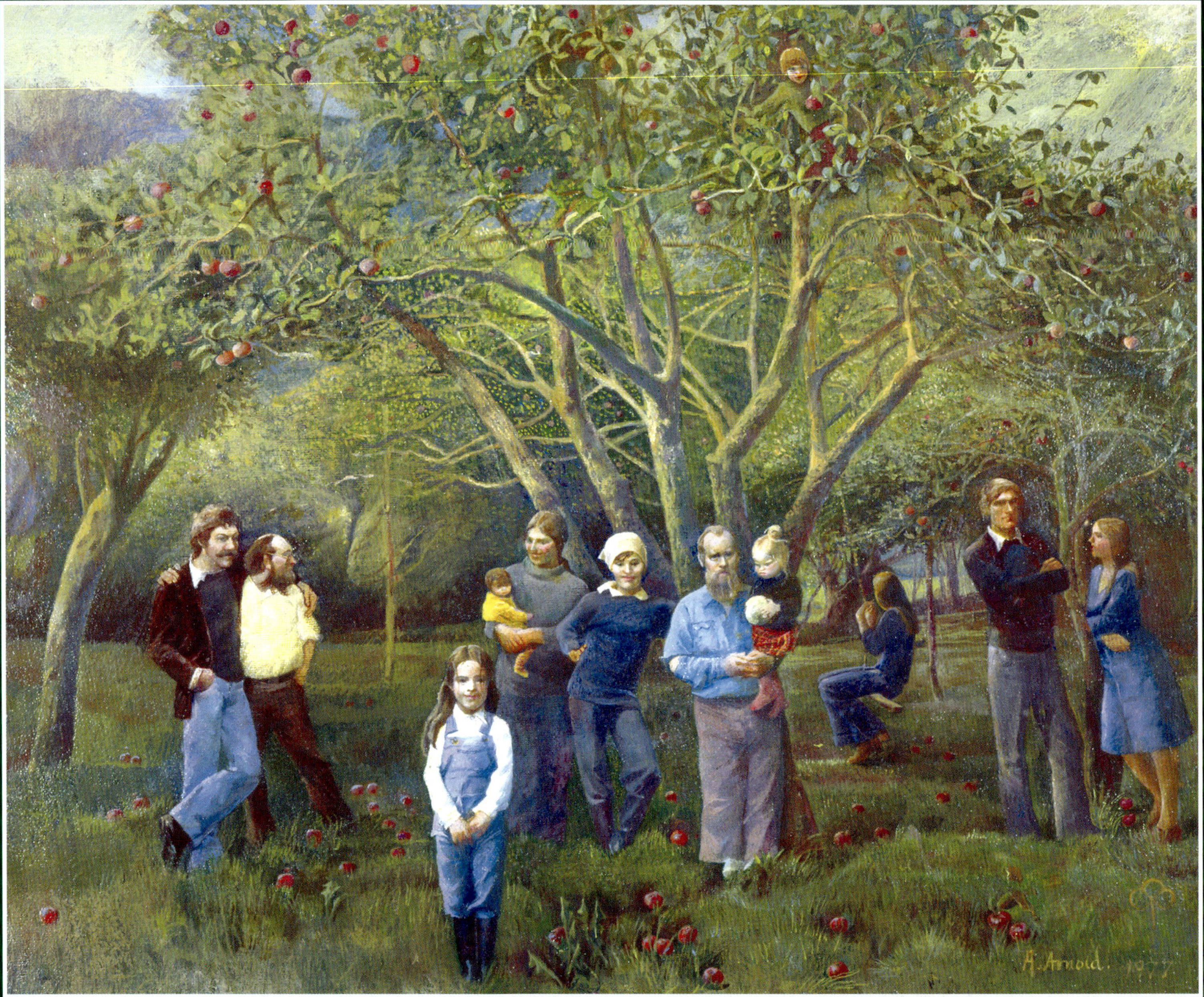
A. Arnold.

CHAPTER 9

The Ruralists

Harvest Home

The French had long purveyed their own Classicism. They were less given than the Germans to definings of national ideals. Instead they gradually asserted style and technique over all subject matter. There was an echo of that absolutism in the way French art had been advertised in England. The Roger Fry doctrine had been thought by many to resemble Fascist politics. Thus old Henry Tonks at the Slade had met the news of Fry's death in 1934 by saying 'that from the point of view of British painting he felt as though Hitler and Mussolini had passed away'.[1]

Yet when the Second War ended in 1945, Fry's followers set about the renewal of French influence in England. They attacked the latest Neo-Romanticism. And to their attack they now added a new condemnation of all subject matter as a Fascist tool. Their political goal was a socialist Europe.

Many had thought they saw a mighty opposite to Fascism in Soviet Communism. Yet in the end Communism and Fascism were both recognised in England as totalitarian. The Second War had imposed more abridgments of English freedoms than at any time since the Cromwell dictatorship, and the nation wanted no more of it. Still the art-totalitarians persisted.

Here were the lines of a dispute that was to rake British art for much of the remaining century. It was, in its essence, an immanence of geographic tradition challenged by a mind-set bent on destroying localism to pursue an internationalist grail.

To carry pastoral vision through the later twentieth century thus posed challenges. Against an internationalist market increasingly driven by American fashion and money, the young Ruralists formed their group for mutual support. The group's core has maintained the Ruralist presence over thirty years. The hardy perennial of Ruralism has outlasted by decades comparable groups in English art – the Pre-Raphaelites, the Neo-Romantics, all the later popular and unpopular fronts.

One secret of the Ruralist success lies in its members' separate and combined abilities to develop his or her creative individuality, while keeping close friendship with the others. So their paradox reaffirms their vision, reflecting as from a prism an essential luminosity of local lands and climates.

* * *

A first sighting of this group-ideal came in the spring of 1958, when John Minton's pupil Graham Arnold (b.1932) visited Digswell House to meet its founder. Henry Morris (1889–1961) saw the practice and the enjoyment of arts as twin integers of civilisation. He had secured Digswell, a small country house in Hertfordshire, as a residence for artists. He invited Arnold to be one of them.

At Digswell, Arnold saw serious artists and craftsmen of every kind from sculptors to weavers, all working in ideal surroundings. Each was provided with an apartment in the house or a purpose-built studio in the park, at low rent. So there was creative privacy with the stimulating proximity of others. Just outside the gates lay the larger community of Welwyn, to be invited in for regular exhibitions and sales of work.

When Graham Arnold went to Digswell he was an intensely private young man, and private he remains. But for the experience of Digswell, he is certain, it would never have occurred to him to join – let alone help to conceive – any group.

One of Arnold's great grandfathers came from the Kentish village of Eynsford, close to Palmer's Shoreham. The rest of his forebears on both sides had lived about Beckenham, a suburb

Opposite:
Plate 183. Ann Arnold: *The Ruralists at Coombe, 1976.* Oil, 1977. Left to right: David Inshaw, Graham Ovenden, Juliette Blake, Annie Ovenden holding Emily, Jann Blake, Peter Blake holding Daisy, Ned Ovenden (in the tree), a friend of David Inshaw, Graham and Ann Arnold

1. Recalled by Paul Nash (quoted in Yorke, *The Spirit of Place*, 55n.).

being overtaken by the spread of south London. Even a century earlier, William Cobbett had written in his *Rural Rides*: 'When you get to Beckenham, which is the last parish in Kent, the country begins to assume a cockney-like appearance.' Yet as with Samuel Palmer's childhood five miles to the north, a century and a quarter earlier, real country still beckoned almost over the next hill.

Arnold's father was on his way to becoming publishing manager for the Religious Tract Society in London. Charles Arnold was a devoted amateur painter, self-taught. 'His books', his son remembers, 'were all on Renaissance techniques – mostly Italian, always in oils'. Graham, his fourth child, was the only one to show real interest in art. It made a bond between them.

On a family holiday in 1936 near the Essex coast, Arnold senior heard of a large oil painting coming up at a local auction. It was very probably by the seventeenth century Dutch master of light in landscape Aelbert Cuyp. Cuyp was valued by older collectors next to Claude Lorrain. The painting showed cows in a gentle place of transcendent light. Mr Arnold went to the auction and bought the painting for £36 – most of the family's holiday money. They returned early to Beckenham, with the painting strapped to the car's luggage rack.

In their house the painting was hung in a locked parlour, to which special visitors might be admitted. When Graham, aged six, asked to see the treasure, he was taken into its luminous presence and received an unforgettable vision. To see and compare famous Cuyp paintings, father and son visited public collections including the Dulwich Gallery.

The Second World War broke almost over their heads, as Beckenham was under the German flight path. Graham's father took the painting to his London office for safekeeping in an iron vault. The vault survived a direct hit on the building, but the intense heat turned its contents to ash. The loss of the painting surrounded its memory with a very spirit of light.

Graham Arnold recalls no doubt from early childhood that he must be a painter. Both parents supported the idea. Even before the Cuyp's destruction, 'my father used to take a tremendous interest in making sure that I would paint. Each weekend he would set up a still life for me to paint':

> He had a large box in which he kept various objects and reproductions: one was *Hope*, by Watts, in its frame. This would be at the back of a still life, with other objects arranged in front of it.
>
> First, he insisted on me making a drawing of it in pencil. He felt that drawing is the basis of all painting. Once you had worked it out – found out how it operated – in pencil, you moved on to the painting: either enlarging it by squaring it up, or drawing it directly on to the canvas: a complete drawing, with all details, before painting.
>
> Then, using just the basic colour of raw umber, white, and ivory black, you painted on the drawing a monochrome in oils. While that dried, you put it aside for two or three days, and went on with something else. When the oil paint was bone dry, you would then start the local colour. It was thus an exposition over time.
>
> My father's method involved an elimination of self. It wasn't your intention to impose any kind of brilliant brush-stroke or virtuoso painting on the canvas. All you were trying to do was to reproduce what you could see in front of you with great accuracy.
>
> He said over and over: 'Don't *paint* a picture. You must *make* a picture – like a kitchen table.' Ever since then I've wanted to cut things up.[2]

To cut things up is to diversify shapes through altered contexts – like Griggs's 'ruins', to open a way towards some new synthesis.

One of the objects in Arnold senior's box for assemblages was a prism. Its division of light into spectral components revealed another way to cut things up. Spectrums and the prism itself (inherited from his father) figure repeatedly in Graham Arnold's mature paintings. He still acknowledges his father as 'my greatest inspiration and helpmate in art'.

Their house at Beckenham was made uninhabitable by bomb blast in 1940. Mother and children were evacuated to the Welsh border town of Hay-on-Wye. There they went into a cottage in a narrow street at the southern edge of the town. Looking left from the cottage door, fields and steep hills seemed almost on top of them.

The wealth of scents and colours, natural shapes and prospects through the clean air led Graham to play truant from school again and again to explore: 'I had no idea of the vastness of it'. When after two years it was time for the family to return to London, the boy felt 'a sense of loss' which the mature artist never forgot.

Back in the repaired house at Beckenham in 1944, he discovered music. His mother played the family piano. Lessons were arranged for his elder sisters, but neither really grasped the chance. So Graham's urgent request for lessons was denied. Undaunted, he identified printed notes with keys of the piano, and taught his fingers to find the chords of Rachmaninov's C sharp minor Prelude.

He took his performance to his sisters' teacher, and secured more than lessons. The teacher gave him gramophone records of Beethoven's Fifth Symphony, with instructions to play only the first four-minute side until he had learnt its every figure and device. For there were the roots of all the Symphony to follow.

Notions of keyboard virtuosity came with a boyfriend of Graham's eldest sister. He could play solo parts in the Schumann and Grieg Concertos, and he played them on an exhibition Broadwood owned by his father, a piano dealer. The instrument, when opened, showed abstract painted decorations – which offered to link its music back to prism and spectrum.

Books were always in the Arnold house. Literature rose to urgency for Graham when his father brought home books by the Victorian novelist and nature writer Richard Jefferies. They were being reprinted one by one for the Religious Tract Society. Jefferies's books centred on Wiltshire, but they showed the boy with his own memories of Hay-on-Wye how a sense of particular place could focus the lights and shadows of nature elsewhere.

The new Jefferies editions were illustrated by modern English wood engravings. Those by Agnes Miller Parker carried the principle of his father's still life arrangements a stage farther. Arnold remembers: 'She was inclined towards a loose surrealism' of sharply rendered objects. The images 'had a profound effect' on him.

His father planned his education with care. From 1944 Graham went to Beckenham Technical College. Next door was the senior Art School, where beginning College students were allowed to attend on Saturday mornings. In 1947 Graham transferred to the Art School.

Many of the Art School students were returning War veterans, four and five years older than himself. Every one of them showed a skill at drawing the human figure that astonished him, as he had no prior experience of that. The School's assistant drawing master, Tom Freeth, set Graham to life drawing many hours early and late.

Teachers of painting at the School raised a sharp contrast. When young Arnold showed them pictures he had painted in the vein of the Parker engravings and his father's arrangements, the painting teachers 'almost laughed themselves silly looking at these "ancient works" as they called them'. They condemned them as 'absolutely the wrong way to go about oil painting'. Arnold recalls:

> Instruction at the School was based almost exclusively on the Impressionistic method of painting – where you simply looked at what you were painting and mixed up the colour and tone simultaneously – *drawing* with the brush.
>
> Compared to the solemnity of the Flemish and Italian Renaissance painters, the subject for them played almost no part. They would take three herrings and an onion for three weeks' painting, and say: 'You are here to study tones. The objects are simply an excuse to make a painting.' It all came from Cézanne – everything reduced to cube and circle.

The teachers insisted on a severely limited palette to concentrate their 'immediate painting': 'thick, tactile, very dark paint'. It suited well enough the granites of coastal Cornwall near Land's End, where Graham had spent some weeks in the summer of 1947 (between Technical

2. Taped statement at a Ruralist exhibition, Bath, 1977; taped conversation with the writer, 2002. Later quotations in this section are taken from these sources.

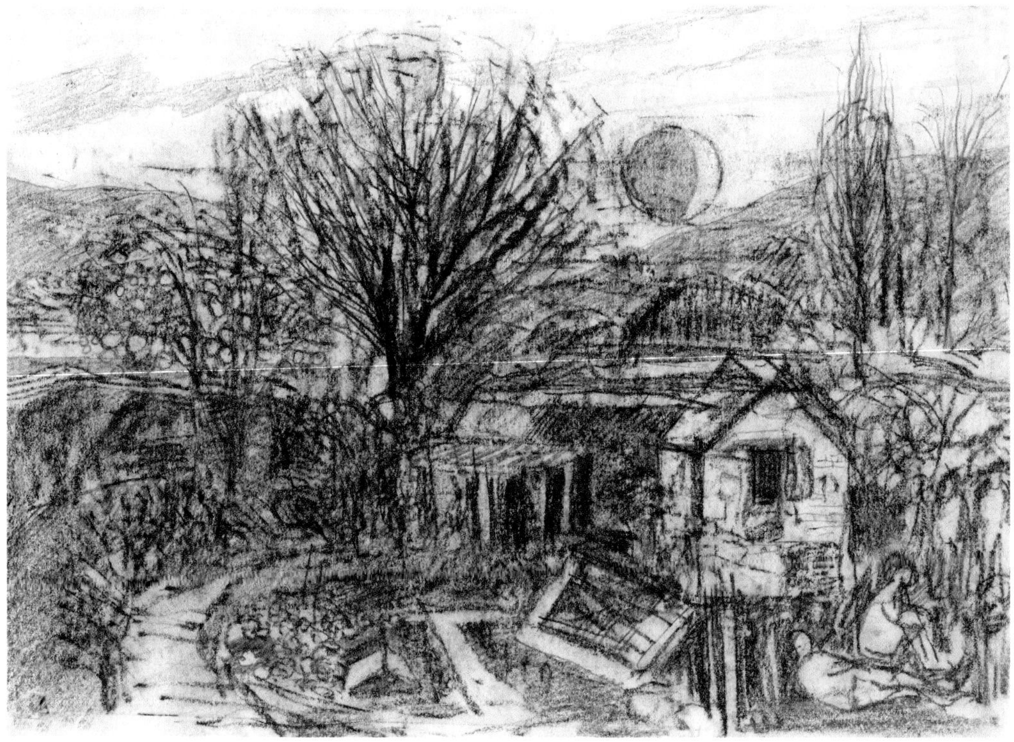

Plate 184. Graham Arnold: *Shoreham landscape, c.*1950–52. Conté crayon. The earliest known proto-Ruralist work

College and the Art School) staying with his godmother and making sketches to work up later.

A summer expedition in 1948 brought him to Palmer's Shoreham, fifteen miles south-east of Beckenham (Plate 184). Grigson's book about Palmer's 'Visionary Years' had recently appeared, and one of his teachers had suggested the little pilgrimage. The sixteen-year-old artist allowed dusk and darkness to fall, and spent the night in Shoreham Church.

That summer he also cycled up the coast of East Anglia. Following in the footsteps of Griggs and Piper, he drew ruined churches and deserted villages; he returned for further sketching there two summers later. He went to Romney Marsh with John Piper's recently published little book of images in his bag. The summers of 1949 and 1951 found Arnold cycling westward: first through Paul Nash's Dorset and Wiltshire to draw Maiden Castle and Stonehenge, later over Exmoor and Dartmoor to the gates of Cornwall.

Two years of National Service followed – mostly teaching in Malaya. The time there added nothing to his painting: 'The whole experience of the jungle was totally alien.' Instead he had taken out a portable gramophone and twelve 78 rpm records (all he could carry): favourite sections of larger works from Elgar to Stravinsky.

Back in England in the autumn of 1954, beginning to paint again 'was like taking the cork off the bottle – lots of still lives and landscapes about Beckenham'. The drawing master Freeth 'cycled over every day to see how I was getting on'. That encouragement remains a grateful memory amid the arid fields of his formal painting instruction.

His goal was admission to the Royal College of Art, and he attained it. Beginning in the autumn of 1955, his College tutor assigned for the year was John Minton. Already deep in private troubles, Minton was often absent. But when he came, his teaching proved unique for Arnold:

> Minton taught by encouragement. He did not try to impose any form of seeing on me – which they most certainly had done at Beckenham. Even at the College he was a lone force.
>
> A lot of tutors there – Robert Buhler and Ruskin Spear and Roger de Gray and Carel Weight – were all against what I was painting. What they disliked most was my subject matter, which for me was very important.
>
> Minton particularly liked paintings I had done of Cornwall. But he advised me to avoid getting in a rut by deliberately seeking new places. I had a large map of England up on the wall – threw a dart at it, and where the dart landed that's where I went.

His new expedition took him to Yorkshire.

At the College a student's tutor changed each year. In any case Minton requested leave in the Spring of 1956. He returned for the Sketch Club that December: and amid the multiplying student Abstractions, Minton praised a large grey Arnold painting of Yorkshire farm sheds as 'the only painting here'. It was the last sight of Minton: a few weeks later he committed suicide.

Arnold never found any other tutor so good. His second year had brought Buhler. Third and worst came Ruskin Spear with an aesthetic harking back to the world of Sickert fifty years earlier. Yet now the West End galleries were filled with 'kitchen sink' social realism. Arnold's paintings followed neither:

> Ruskin Spear in particular used to hate my work, and we had stand-up rows. He condemned my painting as 'too picturesque'.
>
> I can remember saying to him, 'Yes, but I love the Picturesque.'
>
> He used to shout back: 'Well, you shouldn't!'

Each summer Arnold took himself back to Cornwall for recuperative drawing.

Still the Royal College staff recognised talent. Arnold won prizes and travelling scholarships to go to Rome – for two years, if he was careful with the money. Nearly half went on the purchase of a motor scooter to take him there. The trip out filled several weeks, with stops at Van Gogh's Arles, and at Vence, where Gordon Craig still lived in octogenarian seclusion.

At Rome Arnold occupied an expensive studio at the British School for a few weeks. Exploring the surrounding country, ninety miles east he found the hill town of Anticoli Corrado. There was a studio to rent for £5 a month, 'and be on my own'. From early 1959 he settled down for his remaining eighteen months – 'lived like a hermit and painted fourteen hours a day'.

He encountered Samuel Palmer's trouble with the new lights and colours. But he fought them through, as he described it to me more than forty years later:

> At first I had great difficulty in 'translating' the Italian landscape. Seeing Italian painting made me realise that my painting [dulled by Beckenham Art School and not brightened at the Royal College] was denying a large percentage of life.
>
> My palette brightened in Italy – moving away from raw umbers and blacks and greys towards much warmer tones – burnt siennas, yellow ochres: the colours of Italy are very rough.

He made motor-scooter excursions south to Naples, Pompeii, and Sicily; north to Florence and Arezzo, there to look at the frescos of Piero della Francesca:

> All the work I had done at Beckenham appeared as nothing but sketches, compared to the *Resurrection* of Piero. It gave me a different idea of composition – of geometry and large-scaled form linked to the human figure.

'Italy rekindled the feeling of the Cuyp – and my father's idea of painting – as very much a part of life, to be taken seriously.' He saw it again in the work of Masaccio: 'the key in which the whole work is conceived'.

> Minton had been very keen on Renaissance composition – flat planes and structure – producing the painting *within* the frame. Especially when I saw Piero's *Flagellation* – where the whole thing is constructed three-dimensionally in a box which fits into that oblong – I made the connection.

But then there was something else. Coming out of the church at Arezzo one day, looking at the surrounding landscape, Arnold realised that Piero della Francesca had painted the land of Italy because it was his own:

> Piero's landscapes *are* Tuscany, especially the clouds. Clouds are different in each place.
>
> This made me ask: Were my own landscapes sufficiently tied to their place, or were they generalisations? When you think of Palmer, the clouds are of a particular locality brought to a sharp focus.

> It was during this time on my own, forced to reconsider *where* I was painting, that I began to realise that landscapes of Italy were not the real subject matter of my own inner world of poetry – of music – of emotions springing from deep within.[3]

Returning from Italy in the summer of 1960 with forty paintings, the motor scooter's main spring broke under the weight. He had just enough money left for petrol, none for repairs. The journey through the Alps and France, restricted to twenty miles an hour, took seven weeks. He slept under the stars and lived off summer fields.

Arnold's residence at Digswell House, Hertfordshire, had been arranged before his trip to Italy. Arriving there now in the late summer of 1960, he settled into a studio on the ground floor of the big house. The founder Henry Morris had begun a slow physical decline, but the younger man became his particular friend. Arnold recalled:

> That summer of 1960 seemed to have an unlimited number of fine tranquil evenings and we would often drive out into nearby countryside... There was one particular stretch of field with a stream meandering across lined with willow trees, behind which rose a small rounded hill where cattle would be grazing. This meadow seemed to Henry to contain the essence of the English countryside, and we returned to it on countless evenings. Its beauty was almost more than he could bear. ... He would lift his hand and say 'Look, the cattle are still in the meadow.'
>
> One luminous still evening, while we were visiting this field, he told me how before the First World War he had sat in an orchard with friends, on such an evening, and how they had talked of eternity. He had then thought that his life was like eternity, and that the quality of that single evening would last forever. The War had come, and he had never seen his friends again. He paused and said to me: 'Death has the smell of new mown hay.' ...
>
> Death was always near at hand, having an almost visible presence. He continually believed that there were three of us... He would refer to the passage in 'The Waste Land':
>
> Who is the third
Walking beside you?[4]

The lesson of nature's fragility was driven home by Morris's death fifteen months later. Arnold has never interested himself in conventional politics. But 'green' issues have been at the forefront of his consciousness since Digswell (and behind it since the wartime years at Hay-on-Wye).

One of Henry Morris's last acts had been to commission Arnold to paint a large mural for the Digswell Arts Trust. Its subject was 'England': and Morris 'had very strong ideas about what he wanted this picture to convey. He wanted it to be the essence of England.' The twenty-eight year-old Arnold spent much time on it:

> It was almost a portrait of the country round Digswell then. There was a farm nearby, and a little hill just behind us – which became a housing estate four years later.

From Digswell he had begun going back one day a week to Beckenham, to teach at his old Art School. So he came to know the teacher and students of another small art school close by at Epsom. Arnold recalls:

> Ron Benham had a little school of English painting of his own there. I took an instant liking to him when I discovered that we had the same attractions for the countryside – authors – everything. He lived incredibly simply over a stable with an outside staircase, and there he kept a sort of open studio.

One of Benham's students was twenty-four-year-old Ann Telfer. Quick understanding sprang up, and in the spring of 1961 Arnold asked her to marry him. They were engaged before Ann went for a short trip to Italy, visiting places Graham had visited. They celebrated her return with a Midsummer Day party at Digswell, and five weeks later they were married.

* * *

Ann's ancestry was in western and northern England. She was born at Newcastle in 1936, by some years the youngest of three children. When she was two, the family moved to Surrey. Their large house at Ewell bordered Epsom Downs – close to where John Piper had grown up thirty years earlier. 'We were right at the edge of farm land,' she recalls. It was still a good place for childhood.

Her father, Dr Edmund Telfer, had come from a family background of craftsmanship and scarce money. Through talent and scholarships and hard work he had earned two doctorates and an international reputation as a naval architect. He had designed propellers for the *Queen Mary*, which made its record maiden voyage in the year of Ann's birth.

Before and during the Second World War, Dr Telfer designed secret vessels at his London office. At home he took over the children's nursery as a drawing office. He had 'a very good eye', his daughter remembers. 'He could draw beautifully: if he were here, he'd have done a fine pencil drawing of you.'

'My mother was artistic in quite a different way. She was more intuitive, and loved literature rather than painting. She taught us to imagine how other people might feel – and how one's behaviour could be modified.' Ann's elder sister and brother were interested in the arts, but both pursued successful scientific careers.

It was a family of individualities – 'a loving family', Ann recalls, but a family where every victory had to be won:

> My father had especially strong views on education. In him I could see somebody who worked incredibly hard. Like all of us, he was really *into* what he was doing. He was *the* concentrated person in the family. My sister and brother not quite so much so: still pretty good. My mother didn't rule, but organised, the roost.
>
> It involved a lot of entertaining – because my father was very good at his job. He was always going to conferences abroad. And then we had everybody to our house – a lot of different kinds of people, all intelligent and sophisticated and high-powered and self-driven.[5]

Among the guests were artists and writers from a London arts club to which the elder Telfers belonged. 'So I knew what artists were like,' Ann concluded early: 'I'd met them and talked to them, and thought them normal people. Mistakenly I believed this.' (She laughs heartily as she confides this.)

> I started to draw as soon as I could hold a pencil – before I could write. I was very keen from the word 'go'. I used to do anything – landscapes, animals, people.

Her focus was the Surrey country of her home. 'I just loved being out. I was out *all* the time – just being outside and playing as imaginative children do (*did*, I should say: they don't do it so much now).'

> The town was dangerous when I was a little child. It was dangerous to go to London. There were bombs everywhere – it wasn't a normal time. (I was nine when the War ended.)
>
> I recognised that the country was my place. I always wanted to go *deeper* into the countryside – it was never quite deep enough. The colours – the silence – the fact that nobody was going to disturb me. Being able to be contemplative is very important to me. I need dream-time. I get very disturbed if I am not able to have this time.
>
> Both parents encouraged us. My father made comments from time to time. He didn't ever say, 'That's good.' But occasionally he used to frame my things; and I would think, 'Oh! he must like that.'

She did not enjoy formal schooling:

> I'd loved it as a tiny child. But they put me up three classes; I was completely out of my depth – and switched off into a dream world. My public school was a ghetto for middle-class girls. The teachers were all Oxbridge graduates. I was always reprimanded for being dreamy. My interest was art.

3. Letter to the writer, July 2002.
4. Written for and printed in Harry Rée, *Educator Extraordinary: The Life and Achievement of Henry Morris (1889-1961)* (Longman, 1973), 130.
5. Taped interview, August 2002, with Ann Arnold's subsequent comments added. Later quotations in this section are taken from these sources.

At twelve she was given three months' leave to visit her father, who had gone out to Istanbul to inaugurate a university chair of naval architecture.

A year later she was diagnosed with tuberculosis. It was virulent in post-war Europe, and highly contagious. No drugs were yet available. The only treatment was bed rest. When several months at home brought no improvement, she was ordered into hospital in London. It was dark and fog-ridden. But a programme of art therapy there drew her interest.

At sixteen she seemed cured and went home. Country air buoyed the exuberance of escape:

> I had always had the idea that it was a perfectly normal thing to do to be a painter. My father wasn't there to dictate what I should do – which he would have done. So I went along to Epsom Art School and enrolled: my own doing.
>
> My father was annoyed when he heard of it: he felt his influence overtaken. He said that I should continue my general education. So in the evenings I went and did general education, as well as being at Art School. I worked very hard at both, and I overdid it.

After a year she suffered a relapse. This time ten months of hospital were followed by six months in a sanatorium near Aldershot. It was different country from Epsom – closer to William Hyde's old haunts: 'more woodland and weald'. Again at the sanatorium there was art therapy. 'I painted continually.'

When at last Ann could return to Epsom Art School, her painting teacher Ron Benham helped her to compress the normal three years into two, with a major scholarship. She remembers:

> It was a good school, and small – seven to fifteen painting students in a year. It had an architectural department (Richard Rogers was a student) – a great variety of departments but only a small number in each, and you knew them all.
>
> So you had cross-referencing all the time, on an informal basis – waiting in the tea-queue. You'd notice what other students were doing, not necessarily to talk about except to other painters: and we talked all the time.

Benham was younger than most teachers there – a fine painter, trying to recover from War-service horrors, with literary interests to share with Ann: 'He introduced me to Hardy, Richard Jefferies, Edward Thomas, and Samuel Palmer. Most of all he loved the country itself.' That love infused his teaching, she recalls:

> At Epsom there weren't as many promptings of contemporary fashion as at other art schools. They all had their particular look – they painted a certain way. Ours was less flamboyant – closer to the subject. We had some amazingly good students, who set a standard: there was always somebody to look up to.

She graduated in 1957 at twenty-one, wanting only to paint.

Yet what she had seen through illness prompted a wish to make some more direct social contribution. A way to combine her desires lay in art therapy. She went through the rigorous training (including a complete Freudian analysis, which she hated) to work at a remarkable place nearby. 'The Burgh Heath Centre used the arts to help troubled children and adolescents to express their damaged souls. It had good results. They devised a course of training to enable me to teach, since no formal training in art therapy was available then.'

They used music – a long-standing interest of Ann's:

> The first serious composer I liked was Elgar. I had a great uncle who was in some respects like the young Elgar: he had a music shop, was the local choirmaster and leader of the musical society in Kendal. He died when I was ten, and left his records to his nieces and nephews. Some of the records that came to me were the *'Enigma' Variations*: very accessible for someone of ten.

Her art therapy and teaching at the Burgh Heath Centre extended Ron Benham's precepts in several ways: 'The children and adolescents did wonderful things – because they were painting directly the *content*: not *how* you paint, but subjects.' She spent ten years there. She tried to keep her own art developing: 'but therapy took a lot from me.'

In her fourth year of the work she met Graham Arnold:

> I'd actually seen his work at the Royal College – these lovely great cornfields against the sky in different tones of sienna and umber, but they did have a terrific light in them.
>
> Cornish colours in those days were very different. Many of the house roofs were repaired by cementing over the slates for economy: and the reflected light was 'foreign'.

Graham saw in Ann's work a still stronger sense of place:

> Her painting in the country contained a quality which my own paintings lacked, but *shouldn't* have lacked. It was something which had been of great interest to me in literature. Richard Jefferies and Hardy were always about a particular locality, deeply seen and deeply experienced. I wanted that in my painting.

He was at work on the Digswell mural. After they married in July 1961, they went to live at Digswell. They stayed in its arcadia for three years. But Graham had taken a post as senior art lecturer at the Kingston Polytechnic, five miles from Ann's family home near Epsom. Commuting across London was awkward.

Kingston Polytechnic had been another small art school – like Epsom, like Beckenham. 'It was really an extended family, Graham remembered, 'with one man in charge of the painting group. He made all the decisions.' Such a teacher had to be good: otherwise the students would go elsewhere.

Now the Labour government had decided to involve more of the populace in higher education. They funded expansions of art schools into Polytechnics – ultimately to become universities. Arnold recalls the effects:

> With the rise of the Polytechnics, a lot of things which I held in high esteem were thrown out. The whole teaching attitude became revolutionised. Money was being poured in, and you had to justify everything you did – within a staff of twenty or thirty each trying to do the same.
>
> It had a bad effect on the students. I have always felt strongly that each person has an inherent quality individual to him. But the training they were getting in these new courses tended to steamroller over that. Modern art education was producing the same standard painting from Falmouth to Newcastle.

Behind his growing apprehension lay the remembered horror of Minton's suicide. One contributing cause had surely been the younger Neo-Romantic's inability to sink any deep rural roots. Jefferies and Hardy fifty years earlier, Arnold observed, 'were always about a particular locality and man's effect on it: a place deeply seen and experienced – locality brought to a sharp focus':

> Those people had the time to be on their own – embedded in an area of country that they could really feel in depth; and in tune with the forces of nature, which are more important than anything: the seasons, the days, the winds and clouds.

In search of these, in 1964 the Arnolds moved south to the depths of western Sussex. The village of Ashington lay ten miles east of Elgar's old country retreat at Brinkwells. It seemed to offer instant relief to Graham especially:

> Living in the country enables you to settle right down, to be far more contemplative, to allow things to come *into* you. You become aware of the rhythm of it, its mystery and charm.

Yet Ashington brought new problems. It was fifty miles from where they both worked; and farther still from a visiting tutorship at the Royal Academy Schools which Graham had added.

Some nights they spent with Ann's parents, always longing for the deep peace of Sussex.

Affairs at Kingston Polytechnic went from bad to worse. Ann recalled:

> Kingston in the end got dreadfully tense, because it was becoming competitive within the Polytechnic: more and more meetings demanding space and students, and people got horrid to one another.

Anxiety and stress made Graham so ill that his doctor advised him to give up teaching altogether.

Ann resigned her therapist's job in 1967, after two ectopic pregnancies made it impossible to have children. She had wanted them, and was much upset. 'But it is very difficult to combine painting with caring for children. I made the conscious decision to devote myself to painting.'

> I began to paint larger compositions with people and incidents in them. The landscape was the outer world: and my inner world began to coincide with it. My experiences, visions, and feelings inhabited the landscape. (I had encouraged others to do this when I was an art therapist, but was somehow inhibited from doing so myself.) Landscape painting was both a response to reality and a symbol of it.

Graham's response to their problems emerged in a series of assemblage projects. Their roots were in his father's old assemblages made for his boyhood painting. He still discussed his work in detail with his father. Arnold senior's death in 1971 seemed to set off a chain reaction in Graham's assemblages.

Their aim was always to synthesise his own experience: 'places, individuals, memories of childhood' brought together in a kind of surrealist montage. Now he began to add actual objects – diary pages, old photographs, scissors and keys – set in shallow box-frames within the painted composition.

Arnold identified 'heroes' in the arts, and associated special colours with each hero for painting. When the colours for a hero became too numerous, he reduced them by assigning a number to each colour and spinning a roulette wheel. The reduced array he wove into spectral stripes. With each spectrum he filled a large square; and below it he filled another half-square with objects – to draw all these private responses into a golden mean.

He projected a series of big compositions in this format. Taking the collective title of Liszt's ten *Harmonies poétiques et religieuses*, Arnold planned ten compositions, each devoted to a hero. Liszt was first, followed by Ruskin; Richard Jefferies, T.S. Eliot. Hardy, Wordsworth, and Elgar were among those to come. Yet as the series neared its half-way point, there was still no revelation.

Within sight of his fortieth birthday and in weakened health, practicality became more urgent. If he was not to continue teaching, nor Ann either, how were they to live? An answer appeared gradually. It emerged in a janus: half in their memory of the artist community at Digswell, the other half in the person of a former pupil now coming into very close friendship.

* * *

David Inshaw is eleven years younger than Graham Arnold, seven years younger than Ann. Inshaw's earliest life had not been in southern counties, nor had art been in his family. His immediate roots were in the soil: he was born among smallholdings that still edged the suburbs of Wolverhampton, on the first day of spring in 1943.

His father was away at the War, serving as a bomber pilot in the RAF. Mother and son (with a second son born eighteen months later) lived with her parents. David recalls vividly his grandfather and the place that defined him:

> He lived off this piece of land his whole life – five, six, seven acres – a couple of fields. Ever since before the First World War he had planted crops, and harvested, and taken them to market at Wolverhampton with his horse and cart. The horse was called Dobbin, and he used to plough behind that horse.

> Just the other side of the orchard was a farrier, who shod all the local horses. I can remember standing in the doorway watching the horses being shod, and the darkness – the cavernous feeling of the forge: big men in leather aprons, and the smell of hot shoes being put on to the horses' hooves.[6]

Looking back, he realises: 'It was extraordinary to have had this glimpse of a life that now seems almost mediaeval.'

'My grandmother's father lived next door. I remember a strange dark interior with very old furniture, and this bent little man living alone in his nineties.' Great-grandfather Aston had been born in the Worcestershire hamlet of Broadheath. Elgar had been born there in 1857, and family legend hinted that they might have gone to school together. David's great-grandfather had spent much of his life as a gardener for big houses in the district. His last job had been as superintendent of the large cemetery at Bromsgrove, as David was told:

> He laid out the cemetery the way it is today – full of topiary: vast avenues of spheres and cones that are now thirty feet high. I first saw them years later. My mother had told me about them, because she noticed that I was painting topiary.

Soon after 1950, everything about the scenes of Inshaw's early childhood changed very quickly:

> The local council compulsorily purchased my grandfather's land for council housing. It destroyed him: he didn't last very long after that. They built a great housing estate, and Grandad's land disappeared.

Going back there later, a single poplar tree remained standing at what had been the end of his grandfather's yard: 'That was a beacon. We always knew where Grandad lived by this tree: everything else had gone. And eventually the tree went.'

When the War ended, his father came home. David was between two and three: 'I didn't really meet him until then. He wasn't part of my world. We hadn't bonded at the beginning, and the gap remained.' Many fathers and sons at the end of the War had the same experience, as David Inshaw realises now:

> I'm sure my father felt it. He had been living on the edge for four or five years as a bomber pilot. Not many of them survived. He did: and when it was over he found himself with a family, and the need to find a job.
>
> He carried on flying in the Auxiliary Air Force. In the evenings he would come and do aerobatics over the house. And the last thing he'd do was to fly across the cornfield straight at the house – and straight at us in the upstairs window. Then he'd just pull out right over the house guttering.
>
> I was five, and it was visually exciting. He was a mad sod – young with energy.

Bernard Inshaw found a job in London, in the new field of Industrial Safety. He bought a house in Kent near the RAF aerodrome at Biggin Hill, and moved his wife and sons there when David was seven.

> To us children Biggin Hill was amazing. It had grown up at the turn of the twentieth century, when people had bought £5 plots in this valley and built shanties of corrugated iron and matchboarding. Over fifty years the gardens had become so overgrown that the shacks were then mysterious places behind their verdant facades.

With Kent came different freedoms. 'The whole valley was a playground for us children. We were out every day to wander in nature, bird-watching, birdsnesting, building camps.'

> Weekends I went with my mother, my brother, and a couple of friends on family picnics along the River Darent. At Shoreham my mother mentioned that an artist had lived in the big white house by the bridge. So Samuel Palmer was the first artist I ever heard of.

6. Quotations in this section are taken from a taped interview in July 2002 and subsequent conversations.

His father took the boys camping and fishing in Cornwall: 'When you're seven and camping in Cornwall, you're very close to the earth – close to the coast. At that age experience becomes fixed forever in the memory.' But the distance between father and son remained.

David had a trouble which was sharpened by school:

> I used to stutter really badly. School friends waited for me to say certain words, and burst out laughing. So I kept very quiet.
>
> When it came to reading, I was quite dyslexic. I spelled very badly, and used to jumble up words. It wasn't known as dyslexia in those days – it was just 'thick'.
>
> I knew I was bright. I was quick-witted, I could think quickly. But this reading and writing was a problem.

Drawing offered a way out. From the age of five or six he had been drawing 'all the time'. 'That was my way of putting down what I saw and thought and felt.' Art was his best subject at school.

'Then by a miracle I got into Grammar School.' Stresses there made his stuttering worse. 'The art room was a sanctuary, where you could go and spend a quiet hour drawing.' The art teacher was an old man, accommodating enough. When he retired in David's fourth year, his place was taken by a young teacher, Ron Drury. He saw the boy's potential, and convinced his parents to let him go to Art School.

The nearest Art School was at Beckenham, a mile down the road. It was where Graham Arnold had studied. Methods there were still traditional enough to include the use of a Claude-glass. Inshaw remembers:

> It sorted out tonal values. When you look at something, it's quite difficult to work out the tones and set them down. But the Claude-glass pulled it all together, and gave you an idea of the darkest and lightest colours. I remember using it in Knole Park, where I used to go painting quite a lot.

After two years' general art study, he had started painting. Graham Arnold returned to teach at Beckenham, but the painting style there remained much what Arnold had encountered a decade earlier: 'quite vigorous, thick paint', Inshaw recalls: 'very emotional, very physical, energetic kind of painting'. Arnold concentrated on a few students, Inshaw and his friend John Morley among them.

In 1963 Inshaw and Morley went up to the Royal Academy Schools in London. Influence in the next few years came less from formal teaching at the Schools than from the metropolitan art world itself. Inshaw remembers:

> When I went to London I was totally bombarded by American Pop Art. It was in all the Galleries. You just had to confront it, and find some way of dealing with it. I was young, innocent, and I thought: if that's what art is about, perhaps I should be doing that.

His fellow-students felt the same. Inshaw and a few others took to having silk screens made, to impose on their canvases while painting parts of them: the idea was to give their own work a commercial, printed look.

They asked for Graham Arnold's teaching again at the Academy Schools, and he came. But Arnold's full-time teaching was now at Kingston. He asked Inshaw to do a couple of days' teaching there – 'to get a student's perspective on other students: and I was cocky enough to do it'.

Arnold brought his wife Ann to visit the Inshaw home at Biggin Hill. But 'the paradise of Biggin Hill was coming to an end,' Inshaw remembers. 'They were going to develop the valley – to knock down all those shanty houses.' So another formative scene was set to disappear.

David's father bought a building plot on a private estate at Dormansland over the Sussex border. There he asked his sons to help him build a house for the family. They agreed dubiously, lacking any experience. Then Mr Inshaw turned to organising a World Congress of Industrial Safety: he worked himself to illness, and a long stay in hospital followed. His sons were left to build the house by themselves. David went down from the Academy Schools at weekends to work on it. It took two years to build the four-bedroomed house of wood, but the results were excellent. It still stands today in good repair.

Yet their father never lived in it. Bernard Inshaw's insistence on his own ideas became in the end too much for his employers, the Royal Society for the Prevention of Accidents. So Inshaw senior 'turned his back on England' (in his son's words) and went to Canada. There he took a post with the Canadian Government.

His wife, after some hesitation, made up her mind to join him. The sons pleaded with them to keep the house and let it. But the parents needed money for a house in Canada, and sold the house their sons had built for them all. When the younger son Nigel later went out to join them in Canada, it left David (since his father had been an only child) the last of the family in England.

At the end of his time at the Academy Schools in 1966, he found a teaching post at the West of England College of Art in Bristol. His brother was still there to drive him to the interview, David recalls: 'On the way back we stopped at Avebury. I'd never been there. It wasn't a tourist attraction in those days. The huge stones were just there, and nobody about.'

At Bristol he made a real friend when Alfred Stockham joined the College staff in 1968. Stockham was ten years Inshaw's senior – halfway towards a surrogate fathership, still close enough for intimacy. Inshaw recalls: 'Alf was special: he was relaxed – calm and reassuring.' They found a flat to share: the ground floor of a grand house overlooking the Avon Gorge. Its disadvantage emerged slowly. It was close enough to the Art School that students dropped in on the young teachers at every hour of day or night. Painting time contracted.

David had fallen in love with a literature student named Christine Butler. When he went out to Canada to visit his parents, she put into his hands his first Hardy novel, *Tess of the D'Urbervilles*. Hardy's evocations of the heart of rural England made a deep impression. On his return from Canada, Inshaw plunged into Hardy's novels and poems.

The experience touched his painting. One of his first pictures on returning kept an influence of Pop Art. A huge drive-in movie screen (encountered in Canada) showed Christine's face across it 'as a great dream'. In the sky above he set an airplane. But below the giant screen he painted the green grass of England. The picture was bought by a young man whose sister worked for the Tate Gallery administration in London.

When Christine Butler went away to Algeria, David fell in love with a gifted art student doing a preliminary year at Bristol, Corinne Shefford. When it came time for her to apply for further study, he recommended Graham Arnold's course at Kingston, and she went there. Inshaw bought a car and learned to drive. It opened possibilities in every direction.

He drove often to the Arnolds in Sussex. Closer friendship blossomed with this other senior by a decade and his wife. Inshaw recalls: 'We would talk about our thoughts and feelings, and the art we wanted to do.' Graham Arnold had added collage to his spectral stripes and prisms. But he was as frustrated as David with his own art. 'We'd got off on tangents,' Inshaw recalls: 'I'd gone down a wrong path.'

> We were looking for something that was closer to what we saw in front of us. We talked about finding a way of communicating our feelings through subject matter.
>
> It was to do with nature. The Arnolds were living in the country – I'd grown up in the country. We loved where we lived, and knew we were a part of it. We felt its legacy in Elgar's music, in Hardy's writing: and we wanted to develop that in our art.

Graham and Ann recalled the artist group at Digswell. With David they sat late into the night listening to every Elgar record at high volume – as if to force some defining insight. From the legend of David's great-grandfather, Ann grasped the place-name 'Broadheath'. They could form a 'Broadheath Brotherhood'.

Since it was for mutual encouragement in exploring a country of the spirit still on their horizons, they kept it semi-secret. Inshaw recalls:

> The secrecy was because we were all searching for a particular way of working. It related to Elgar and Palmer certainly. These things were still in us, but we had been totally distracted by what was going on in the art world. So we were trying to find a way back.

The assemblages in Graham Arnold's paintings began to include large old keys, as to some forgotten lock.

Three seemed a small number for a Brotherhood, so they sought to recruit friends. John Morley and his wife Diana Howard had just bought a cottage in Suffolk, and he wanted to keep his independence. Ann Arnold's friend Peter Nott and his wife were interested, but did not feel sufficient dissatisfaction with his teaching at Epsom. So the membership remained at three.

At Bristol Inshaw was asked to add the teaching of print-making – etching and silk-screening. The aim of asking a painter to teach graphics was to prevent the students from becoming enmeshed in process. For Inshaw himself, it had an opposite result. From the late 1960s his own painting began to pursue 'intensity of feeling' through 'a meticulous, precise, obsessive' technique.

It was brought to focus by a chance visit to Montacute House near Yeovil. There he found himself fascinated by the topiary: 'You didn't know what was going on behind it.' Behind the experience at Montacute lay his memories of the overgrowth hiding shanties at Biggin Hill. But the Montacute topiary combined mystery with grand history: nature with Hardy's 'hand of man' upon it. Inshaw made topiary excursions to see gardens as far away as Levens Hall in Westmorland.

The fascination of topiary lay in its clipped surfaces. Seen at any distance, topiary shows textures as tight as the dots of a screened print, or a screened painting: yet its roots are in growing nature. So it could touch back to Palmer's early 'stump-work' drawings, and the textured resiliences of Griggs etchings.

But topiary textures celebrate nature more vividly than any monochrome, because the vision is green. Inshaw's painting found a minuscule articulation of topiary and lawns through finest points and strokes of brushes dipped in bright colours. So it could be made to illuminate its textures as from within. Here the Pre-Raphaelites had gone before him.

Those young painters had felt the thralldom of love for beautiful women, as Inshaw felt it now. The intensities came together in his love for Jill Pollard. He painted her first in 1971 – dressed in red, seated in brilliant light from a low sun beyond the picture. Light and shadows pattern a wide lawn of greenest hues backed by fine-textured topiary bushes, with further lawns and bushes rising under heavy clouds. On the grass close to the girl's feet stands a raven matching his smaller shadow to her own. *The Raven* became the picture's title.

The painting technique of print-like dotting evolved into something of Inshaw's own: 'I was trying to make paintings that fulfilled a sense of the moment – which then grows and develops and spreads – and becomes something else.' All this was rendered with intense detail: 'Every ounce I had went into each one – nothing to spare on anything else. Ten years I painted pictures with that sort of intensity.'

He painted Jill again as one of two girls playing *The Badminton Game* (1972-73) – a silent ballet counterpointed across a net of cobweb reticulation, before towering topiary bushes and trees beside a tall old red brick house (Plate 185). The luminous *Game* is played below a ghostly moon, as the light of another distant low sun strikes shadows across a lawn now slightly roughened.

He completed the trilogy in a painting titled after a Hardy poem, *She Did Not Turn* (1974). At the bottom centre of a bare, steeply rising harvested landscape touched by a rainbow, the girl shows only her blue-caped back overlaid with a sensuous long twist of golden hair as she moves away – up a shadowed track through rough, still luminous grass.

The right-hand horizon holds a mammary hill-shape surmounted by a small clump of trees – as if to recall Nash's Wittenham Clumps in the finely drawn textures of Griggs, with Inshaw's

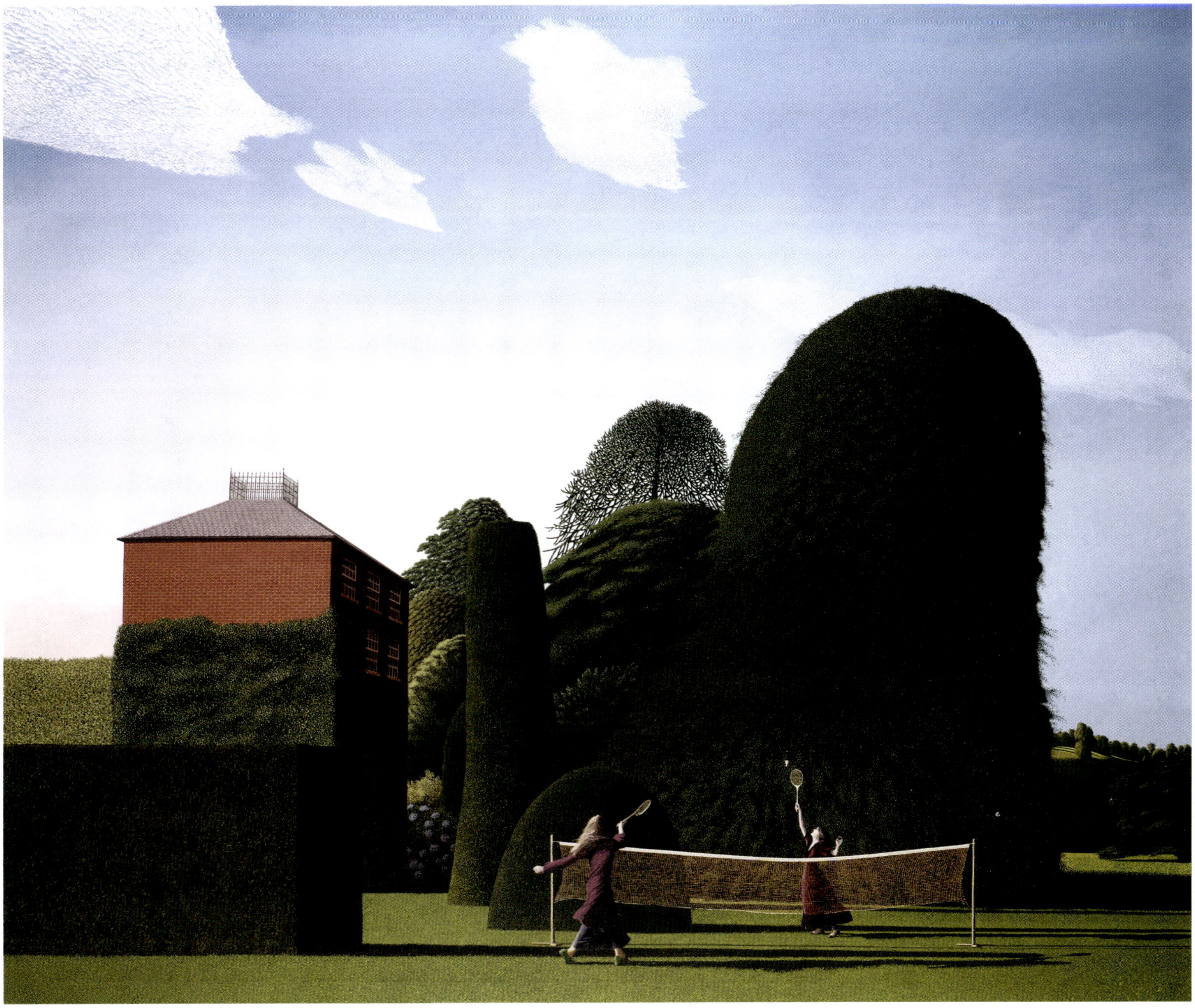

own intensity of colour. His inspiring place was now Furze Hill in Wiltshire, near Devizes, where he had moved in the midst of painting the Jill trilogy.

When the lease on the Bristol flat ran out in 1971, Inshaw had felt the need to put distance between himself and the College. He drew a circle with a forty-mile radius round Bristol: on that circle was Devizes, an old market town high up on the North Wiltshire Downs.

> Alf and I used to come out to Marlborough of an evening and go for a walk on the downs. So I knew the area. And I'd got to know Avebury and Silbury. It was a chalk landscape. I had grown up in a chalk landscape on the Kentish Downs. So I seemed to know it: plants – flowers – grass – sky – shapes.

In Devizes he found a studio, and the whole arrangement suited him:

> I'd do my three-and-a-half days a week teaching, and stay with Alf in Bristol. And three-and-a-half days I'd be in Devizes. I knew nobody, and had no distractions at all. I painted twelve hours a day. Nobody ever came. It was great.

Plate 185. David Inshaw: *The Badminton Game,* 1972-73. Oil

> The town has a circular shape. There's the castle, and all roads go round the castle. And the hills have a circular feeling. You feel rather kept within this place by the shape of it. The landscape has a feminine feel in its soft undulating hills.

On the doorstep was Salisbury Plain and Stonehenge. The South Coast was within easy driving, and London just over an hour away.

Hardy wrote that beauty of association means more even than beauty of aspect. Inshaw says:

> It took me a while to build up associations about Devizes. But associations really are strong keys to what a landscape has to hold.
>
> You can see the processes of time on the landscape round Devizes. My own associations grew as I recognised man's influences on it. The more time you spend there, you go back layer by layer into time. The associations gave me the impetus to paint about it.

The Broadheath Brotherhood took a step forward over New Year in 1972. Inshaw was preparing a one-man show for the Arnolfini Gallery in Bristol: he planned an elaborate launch, with a montage of slides, readings, and music. To make an Elgar tape, he was staying overnight with the Arnolds in Sussex.

Thinking of his lonely progress in Wiltshire, and of his friends' problems of illness and teaching, David proposed what Graham recorded in his diary as 'a well thought-out plan'. They could pool resources to buy and share a large house, and economise outgoings: 'There would in this large house be room for a studio for each. It would be a mini-Digswell – in the Wiltshire area.' Soon the plan envisaged Graham Arnold giving up teaching altogether. At the end of February 1972 Graham wrote:

> Suddenly Dave said we could go and live in his house at Devizes: Ann and I buying half of Dave's house, selling our own house at Ashington.
>
> All seemed possible. So simple we could hardly believe it. We were overjoyed, put on Beethoven's 5th, and all three of us were all smiles.

The Arnolds' home in Sussex took more than two years to sell. When at last the time came to move, the prospect of leaving caused Ann to ask Graham to paint the beautiful old church at nearby Warminghurst – a favourite place, often visited. Graham wished to include a great oak standing by the churchyard. But church and tree demanded separate pictures. His painting of the church, revised over nearly a decade, set out to capture in light the spirituality of the place.

The oak tree dominated a pencil drawing dated May 1974 (a month before their move west). The oak appears amid a procession of middle-ground foliage to recall Paul Nash's 'Bird Garden' drawings sixty years earlier: but Arnold's draughtsmanship is his own.

The foreground lawn showed a large table tomb at first undecorated. When he was given a facsimile fifteenth century illuminated manuscript of King René of Anjou's *Book of the Heart Captured by Love*, Arnold set that knight's helmet on his drawing's tomb. To his signature Arnold added, for the first time, the secret Broadheath Brotherhood initials 'B·H·B' (Plate 186).

A succession of titles for this drawing over the years builds up a palimpsest of reflections: 'Oak Tree and Grave' (1975), 'Merlin's Tomb by the Oak Grove' (1978), 'Oak Tree and Helmet' (1981), 'The Sacred Oak' (1992), and later still 'Knight's Tomb'. He kept it many years, and noted: 'This drawing has always been for me a very special one, for it showed me the way I must take.'

That way was to 'personalise and intensify' the subject matter of particular place. So it began to suggest a more subtle Surrealism than his father's arrangements of objects, or his own developments from them so far. Graham Arnold was forty-two.

David Inshaw at thirty-one, by contrast, was just finishing an achievement of considerable integrity and impact in his Jill trilogy. The counterpoints hinted at complexities the former teacher and former pupil might find living their lives in close parallel.

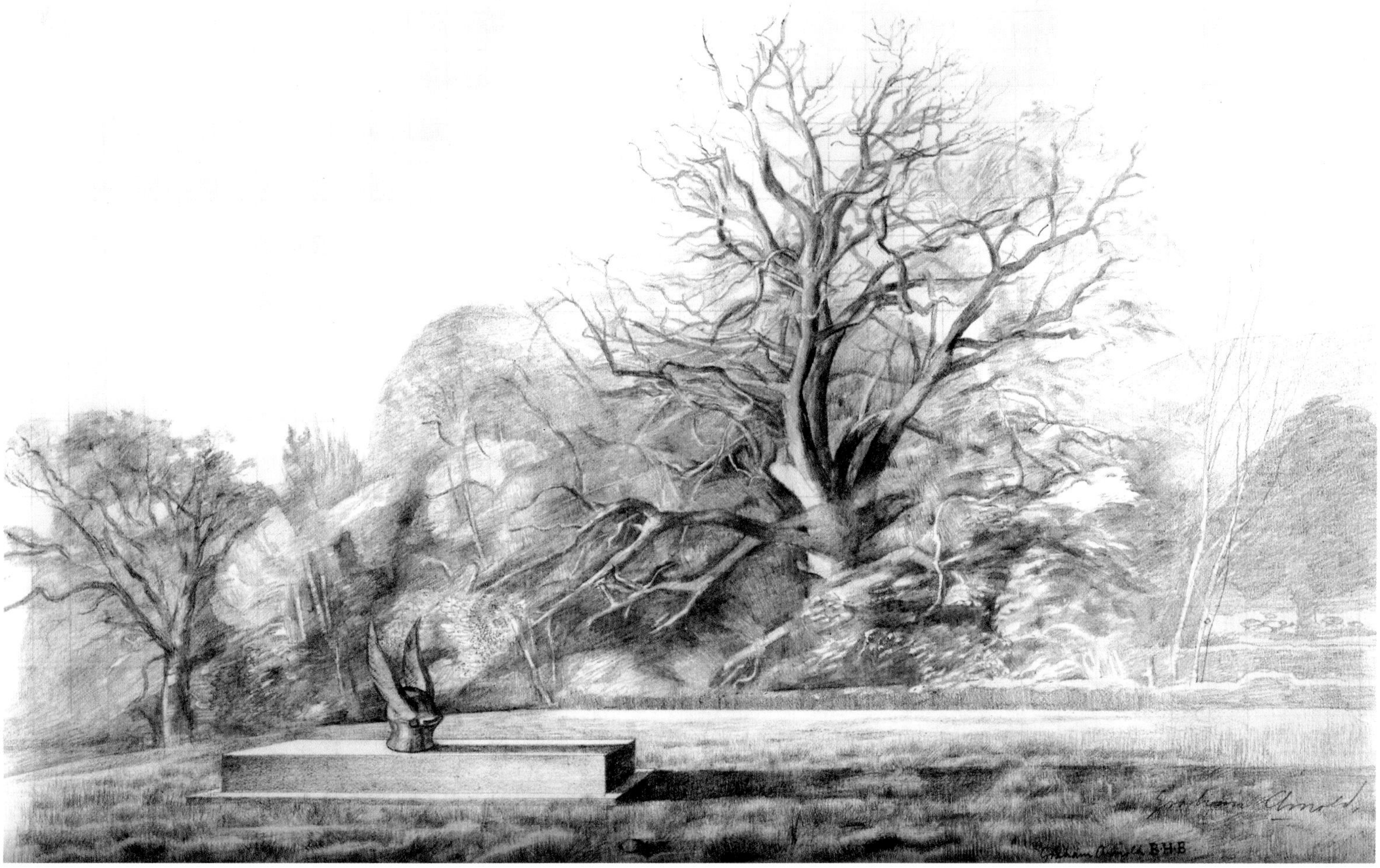

Plate 186. Graham Arnold: *Knight's Tomb*, 1974. Pencil

The summer of 1974 brought the Arnolds to Devizes. Almost as soon as they came, David Inshaw received an invitation to contribute a picture to an exhibition being organised for the Bath Festival by Peter Blake. Inshaw had met him at a recent dinner party. Blake at forty was a rising star, soon to touch international fame. Yet he too had come to live in the west country near Bath. His deep-voiced gentleness of speech impressed Inshaw as a memorable strength.

When Peter Blake came to Devizes to collect his choice of an Inshaw picture, he met the Arnolds. David recalls:

> Graham and Ann had just arrived. They had all their work there. It turned out that Peter and Graham had been at the Royal College together. And Peter said: 'We'll have one of each for the show.' So he included Graham and Ann.
>
> We had tea together that day. And we told him about our little group, and our ideas and aims.

Peter said he knew other young artists with similar feelings. The little Brotherhood might expand at last.

* * *

Peter Blake sees himself now as 'a cuckoo in the Ruralist nest'.[7] Yet for four years he thought of himself as a Ruralist; and throughout the years since then he has remained the Ruralists' close friend. The paradox roots back to patterns in Blake's earliest experience.

He was, more than the others, a child of the city. His parents had married and lived at Dartford, downriver from London. At nearby Grayford, Kenneth Blake worked as an electrician for the armaments firm Vickers. Peter was the first child, born 25 July 1932 (a month after Graham Arnold's birth fifteen miles to the west). His earliest memories are of rooms and flats – before his parents bought their semi-detached house when he was five. It made a secure little household. Peter recalls:

7. Information not otherwise attributed in this section is taken from a conversation with the writer, 17 Oct 2002.

My Mum and Dad used to go out shopping on a Friday night and bring back presents. I remember them buying me little boxes of lead soldiers, so if the War hadn't intervened I think I might have started to collect them.[8]

He went to an infant school, named for a memory of pastoral heritage surviving amid Thames-side industry: The Maypole School. His sister Sylvia was two-and-a-half years younger. Their mother was expecting a third child when War was declared in September 1939. So Peter (aged seven) and Sylvia (less than five) were evacuated to some neighbours' friends who were farming fifty miles north in rural Essex.

At Helion's Bumpstead, near the Suffolk and Cambridgeshire borders, Mr and Mrs Loft had a young family of their own. Peter's time, when not attending the village school, was taken up with helping on the farm. At nine he was 'riding and guiding' the big Suffolk farm-horses, and soon drove the tractor.

His rural life was punctuated by visits home to Dartford: he keeps vivid glimpses of the Battle of Britain and the Blitz. The last year of the War brought rocket attacks. Peter was sent to his grandmother in Worcester. There he attended 'a tough Modern Secondary School' set between railway lines and the gentle residences of Rainbow Hill (in one of which Elgar had lived until his death a decade earlier).

In Worcester Peter heard the announcement of VE Day in May 1945. At thirteen he returned to Dartford to take up life with his own family, now including a younger brother – after the loss of nearly half that life.

Vocation began to show itself in 1946 when he was sent to the Technical College and School of Art at Gravesend (a short railway journey towards the mouth of the Thames). Amid extensive war damage here, he found a 'wonderful junkyard' beside the station. 'It was a long thin yard,' he remembers, 'and the farther you went along it, the more undisturbed it was. You'd always find something.'

A set of Shakespeare appealed to him for its leather bindings. A papier-maché tray was inlaid with mother-of-pearl. And then there were humble paintings – 'Sunday paintings' Blake calls them now, by people with weekday jobs. All these junkyard finds were relics from lives past, only to be imagined now. They caught the interest of the boy recently returned from a half-lost childhood.

How to resolve these shards of things once loved into some renewing life? His parents, feeling that their son must now be allowed some chance to find himself, accepted his idea that he should study art. At first it was graphic design. Slowly he gravitated to painting.

He did well enough at the Gravesend Junior Art School to go on to the Senior School in 1949. Two years there led a teacher to suggest he apply to the Royal College of Art in London. He was accepted – pending two years' National Service (which took him up and down the west of England from Blackpool to the Cotswolds, and to Northern Ireland).

Young Blake came to the Royal College in 1953, two years before Graham Arnold. Their tutors were the same men. But Blake at twenty-one had learned pragmatism. There was no question of him offering 'ancient works' against prevailing fashions. He took his tutors' varied teachings as ready contributions to finding an expression for himself. Many of his paintings then showed urban children, sometimes bearing marks of injury, wearing or holding advertisements promising post-war profusion.

Two techniques marked frontiers during Blake's years at the Royal College, and each held something for him. The first was collage – defined by Blake as 'something attached to something else'. Those things had had prior existences separately. So they could express his experience of fragmentation. Collage became a permanent part of him – often as 'work in progress':

I am always working on various groups of independent collages. For example, I am working on a series of collages called *Memories of Place*, one of which is made from objects that I found at the seaside with my daughters, Liberty and Daisy, when they were small. Also in progress is the ongoing series *In Homage to Collagists* where I work in the style of my main influences, Joseph Cornell and Kurt Schwitters.[9]

The goal at every level is synthesis, but synthesis ongoing. His object-filled studio is itself, he says, 'a big collage' of work in progress.

Then came the second novelty. The outlook of collage appeared to expand, during Blake's years at the Royal College, with the arrival of Pop Art from postwar America. Pop Art offered the brashness of ubiquitous commerce, spiced by the trouble it gave many elders. (It was an exhibition by Pop Art's importer, Richard Hamilton, that caused Keith Vaughan secretly to doubt the achievement of his entire life's work.) Blake added its emblems to his images of young people compromised.

Both Pop Art and collage redefined the roles of artist and audience. Collage appeared on one level to render individual skill and technique irrelevant. Pop Art appeared to replace the artist's taste with what the audience wanted. Peter Blake looks back over his own Pop Art thus:

> My work... aimed to have the directness and distribution of pop music. This was my main aim as a Pop artist, but unfortunately it totally failed. Most Pop art simply became big business.
>
> Oddly enough, it has worked since, when I have produced multiples. By the time of the cover for The Beatles' *Sgt. Pepper's Lonely Hearts Club Band* (1967) it worked totally. If you bought the record you also bought a piece of art on exactly the level that I was aiming for.

For the record cover Blake and his wife Jann had staged an elaborate colour photograph of the four Beatles dressed brightly as old-fashioned bandsmen in a municipal flower garden, backed up by dozens of life-sized figures of creative 'lonely hearts'. Neither Samuel Palmer nor Elgar was there; nor Hardy. (Peter Blake's idea of an iconic novel was Scott Fitzgerald's *The Great Gatsby*.) The cover 'lonely hearts' heroes, chosen with help from the Beatles themselves, included the author of *Alice in Wonderland*, Oscar Wilde, Karl Marx, and Marilyn Monroe.

In the light of The Beatles cover's huge success world-wide, Peter Blake looks back to it to understand why his earlier efforts had not won such acclaim:

> It didn't work with my early Pop constructions... because the language and the content were not right. It would only have worked had I used formats of the kind of things given away in *Boyfriend* magazine. I would have been extremely sophisticated to have picked up on the fact that that was what was needed.[10]

Needed, he felt, to return art to some vital involvement with the great mass of people living with the results of nearly half a century's organised violence. So a young revolutionary could argue, with backing from every Marxist critic.

Peter Blake's achievements in Pop Art and collage, coupled to his skill with pencil and brush, have won him very wide recognition throughout Britain and abroad. He has enjoyed extraordinary media coverage, international exhibitions, membership in the Royal Academy, a CBE and in 2002 knighthood. His soft-spoken personal influence has been powerful from the beginning. As early as 1965, as a young teacher at the Royal College of Art, he was able to turn the entire teaching staff round – on the question of admitting a student whose work could both worry and embarrass them: Graham Ovenden.

Pop Art's reversal of roles for artist and audience, however, offers flat contradiction to every tradition of pastoral vision. So it seemed a paradox when in 1969 Blake decided to leave the London suburb of Chiswick (where he had lived most of his time since graduating from the Royal College in 1956) for the country.

The idea of rusticating may have come from his wife, the American draughtsman and sculptor Jann Haworth. Born the daughter of a Hollywood film director in 1942, with a degree from the University of California and study at the Slade School in London, she had married Peter Blake in 1963. The birth of their first child in 1968 made them both think about a child's environment. Some photographs taken then by a cynical London press pitchforked a decision already half taken to leave London.

8. *A Cabinet of Curiosities from the collection of Peter Blake* (Morley Gallery, 1999), 9.
9. Peter Blake, *About Collage* (Tate Gallery Publishing, 2000), 19, 21.
10. *About Collage*, 21.

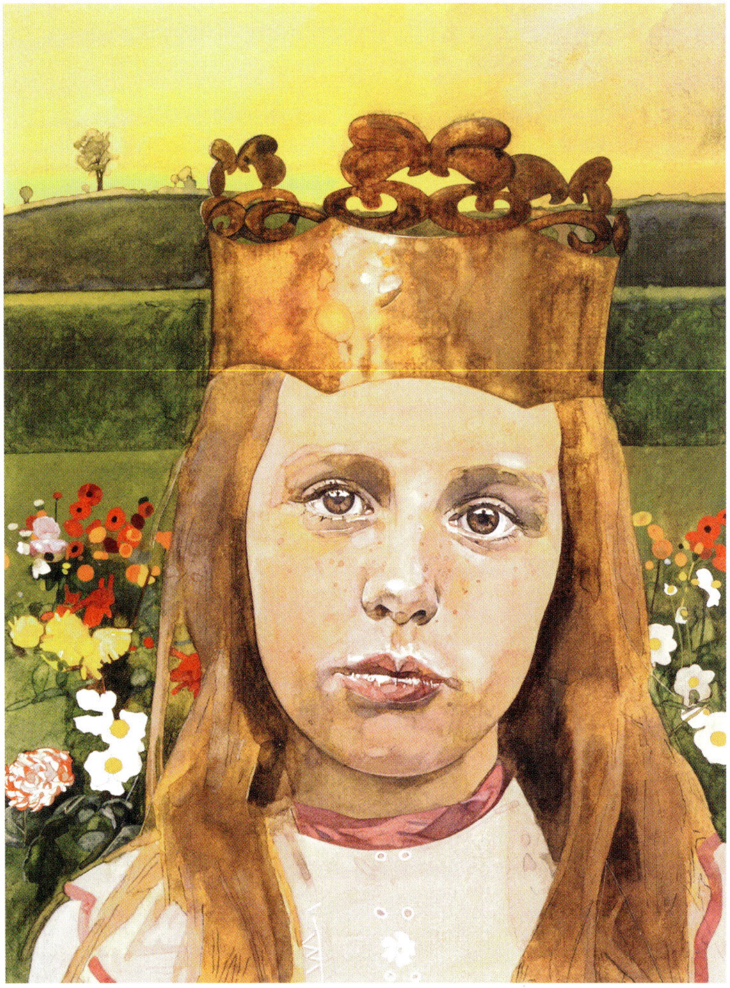

Plate 187. Peter Blake: *Queen Alice* in a Somerset landscape, 1970, illustration for *Through the Looking Glass.* Watercolour

In Somerset country south of Bath, they bought and renovated a former railway station at Wellow. Their new life in this ancient monument of Pop Art would itself make a collage. A broader collage opened on the prospect of these urban artists translated to the green shades. Blake's art found a compromised innocence in images of fairies. He felt little impulse to paint 'the cow shit and flies'.[11] He painted instead a series of pictures for Lewis Carroll's *Through the Looking Glass* (Plate 187).

Bath and its metropolitan neighbour Bristol took the Blakes to their hearts. Exhibitions in London hardly diminished as West-country galleries beckoned. It was for a show to be called 'Peter Blake's Choice' at the Bath Festival in 1974 that Blake asked to include a picture by David Inshaw. And thus he had met the Arnolds.

Hearing of their semi-secret little 'Broadheath Brotherhood', Peter's mind went instantly to his former pupil and friend Graham Ovenden and his wife Annie. The Ovendens were living and painting in Cornwall as they built their dream house at the edge of Bodmin Moor.

With the 'Broadheath' three, Blake himself and Jann, the Ovendens could bring an extended 'Brotherhood' up to seven. That number, Blake's experience told him, would wield a force that London critics, like it or not, could not ignore. The Ovendens signalled their keen interest.

* * *

Graham Ovenden was born in February 1943 (a month earlier than David Inshaw) in Alresford, Hampshire – twenty miles inland from the South Coast cities of Portsmouth and Southampton. His family home was a two-down, two-up dwelling at the end of a terrace. Beyond lay a farm and stable, with the road running down to 'rather wonderful water meadows and the bottom reaches of the river,' Graham Ovenden remembers. 'But opposite our cottage was the Gasworks, still operative.'

> It was a strange combination of pastoral with the relics of nineteenth-century industrial engineering. Think of Blake's lines about building in England's green and pleasant land. I remember as a child harebells – those most exquisite blues, and the delicacy of them.[12]

The coupling of pastoral with industrial presence found a kind of echo in his parents' marriage. His mother was a devoted pianist, in moments rescued from child-bearing and child-rearing. Five of her six survived, and she shared her music with them all. Graham recalls: 'We were the sort of family where everybody was set to play the piano. It was a necessary part of one's childhood.'

The husband and father was an aeronautical test-engineer working with Barnes Wallis for the RAF. Mr Ovenden was often away at a factory in Hertfordshire, but never for long enough to mystify his place in the family home. Graham had none of David Inshaw's trouble in bonding with his father. Yet there was a mystery:

> My father always said he was of Grammar School quality but didn't have the opportunities, coming from a very poor environment. We don't know who his father was. We had this amazing grandmother who seems to have dropped children and families all over the place, not telling anybody else that they existed.
>
> He was brought up by the Cornish side of the family, the Tremeeres. They also lived in Alresford, about a hundred yards away.

They were his father's aunt and uncle, but Graham was encouraged to think of them as grandparents. Their house became a second home during his mother's frequent pregnancies. Like his own home, it was gas-lit. The Tremeeres took him farther into a Victorian past.

11. Quoted in Natalie Rudd, *Peter Blake* (Tate Publishing, 2003), 64.
12. Quotations in this section are taken from a taped conversation with the writer in July 2002.

There were magic images in that house. One was a chromolithograph depicting the hymn 'Rock of Ages': a rock in the sea with shipwrecked people clinging to it.

Then my 'grandmother' had an elaborate musical box. As I was a careful child, I was allowed to wind it and play the tinkling tunes. One was a selection from *The Pirates of Penzance*. And there was a large model of the Taj Mahal, brought back by an uncle from the War. It was finely carved in an ivory-like material, and it glowed from its corner in their rather gloomy sitting room.

The Tremeeres themselves were anything but gloomy. 'Grandmother Tremeere was as sweet a lady as ever lived.' Her husband took Graham for long country walks:

At the end of our road was a semi-ford and shallows, where the river branches round in a large arc. If we walked to the right, there was a fulling mill – a black-and-white structure built on a bridge over the river. One always wondered at flood time whether you'd see it floating down the river.

If we walked to the left – the adventurous route, up to the Downs (Plate 188) and then right around to where the gypsies camped with their wooden caravans and horses – we would go past watercress beds and come to the Eel house (another building on brick arches over the river) where they trapped eels in season.

My grandfather pointed out everything. He was a baker by trade, and had a very good nose. He could always tell whether a loaf was well baked by sniffing the air. And he was rather like that with plants. He was very knowledgeable in country matters and country products – how country economies worked.

Listening to this 'grandfather' talk about rural commerce, 'it was brought home to me very early. A child of that age doesn't understand the aesthetics: one accepts things for what they are – their beauty. At Alresford I was totally the child in grace.'

The grace extended, in those immediate post-war years, to childhood freedoms which he feels have no parallel today:

In the wake of the War, the freedoms one had as a child were a great opening up. We went everywhere at will, mostly without supervision. No traffic on the roads, so you cycled. I was a great cyclist from the age of six. So one got around and saw far more than the average television child sees now.

You could just walk into the Gasworks – even to where they were stoking the great hell-fire glowing retorts, and actually help pull them out with the rakers – which to a young man of six was excitement indeed.

Looking back on it, I see the beginnings of my interest in the art of John Martin: because there was no internal lighting in those buildings – just the incredibly vivid reds and oranges.

The remembered edge of industry and pastoral gradually showed him something else:

I've always thought the happiest state for a man to be in is to have a balance between practical abilities and intellectual abilities, and bring the two together.

If you think of it, the great works of art *are that*. Unless you know something of engineering, your whole gothic cathedral falls down (and on occasion they did).

Graham discovered his first artist on holiday some years after the War. Rummaging with his father in a bombed-out rectory, they saw

Plate 188. Graham Ovenden: *The Haunted Grove*, Fobdown near Alresford, 1955. Pencil. His earliest surviving drawing, aged twelve

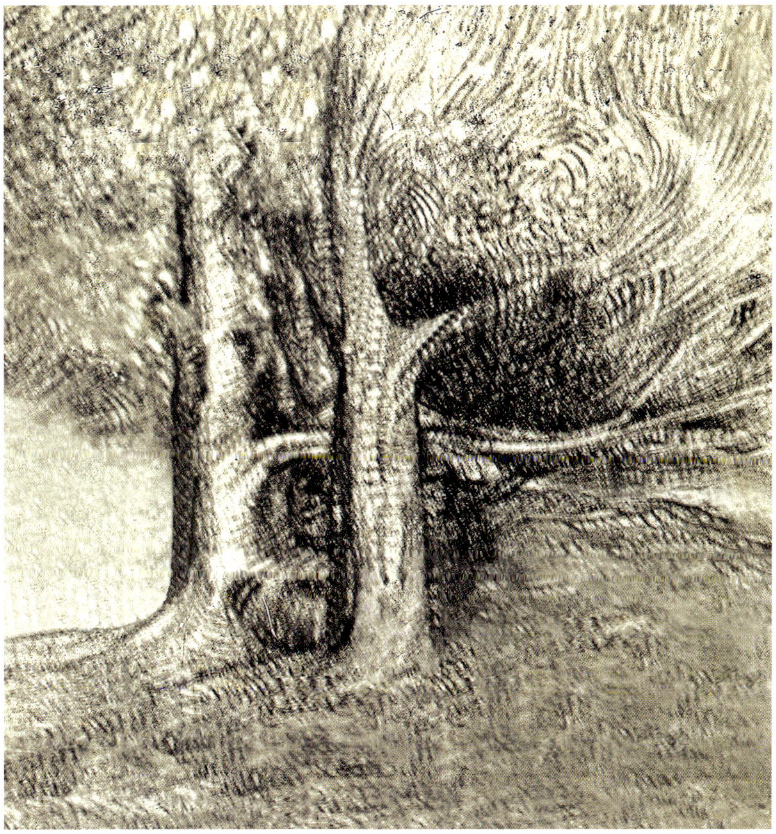

under a staircase a shelf of books still undamaged. All were in German, one of them devoted to German Romantic art. It contained several reproductions of paintings by Caspar David Friedrich (1774-1842). They proved 'seminal':

> That book came into my life before Claude and Constable, Turner and Palmer. Friedrich is the great master of mountain landscapes. To this day I draw inspiration from them, in the same way as when I look at Palmer's Valley of Vision. It's a different vision, but they open comparable insights.
>
> Friedrich still has an identification with that time in my life: the great mysteries – seeing beyond the horizon – the edge of the sea. All his landscapes have that quality.

Friedrich had once observed of painters: 'The noble person sees God in everything; the common fellow sees only the form, not the spirit.'

Graham's own painting started when an aunt gave him a set of oil paints in little round drums:

> I can remember the joy of being able to manipulate colours – to do things which you couldn't do in any other medium. It was a revelation to me. I remember being told to go to bed about nine o'clock in the evening, having sat there the whole afternoon and evening painting away in a state of real excitement.
>
> I painted landscapes, romantic scenes – the things children will do; and I grew quite accomplished.

Another favourite book in those years also looked backwards. Mrs Barbauld's *Hymns in Prose for Children* had been handed down in the Ovenden family as a natural extension of their faithful church attendance (still twice a Sunday in Graham's childhood). Mrs Barbauld's was an earlier world than the Tremeeres', yet her book addressed children. So its retrospect pointed back to a phase of his own experience from which he might just begin to feel a hint of distancing.

Distance was marked in the death from pneumonia of Graham's younger sister Lesley. Her baby-image remains with him:

> As a very young child, one doesn't understand the nature of death. Children appear, and then they go away.
>
> As I did not see her die, it was not traumatic in that sense. But in retrospect, it does leave a hole.

Asked if this loss might have planted a seed of his mature art's fascination with little girls, he answered:

> It's not something I've ever analysed. But I think, with the sense of loss, and the growing away from the state of grace – and after all, death is an absolute – it could well be.

There remained his elder sister Julia, and another sister and two brothers below him. With Julia he went to a little Dame School run by two sisters who were gifted teachers, loved by their pupils. It set a standard of school happiness never equalled afterwards.

As War industries wound down, his father spent more time at home. Graham remembers shared radio listening to the whole gamut of music – and more walks. His father had his own sense of time passing. 'He was intrigued with the remains of great gardens round a house burnt out during the War and abandoned: you can imagine the effect this had on me.' Another discovery was the mausoleum of a family once grand in the neighbourhood:

> I knew what nostalgia was early. Think of an environment surrounded by these great estates in decay. From a very early age I loved graveyards. Here was this family tomb in Old Alresford churchyard: the gate was always slightly ajar, where you could walk down steps into the mausoleum.

'Living in country areas', Ovenden says of his childhood, 'the time-perspective almost ceased to exist. Events that happened centuries ago were talked about almost as if they had happened yesterday. That's a wonderful situation to be in, because it does give a vividness.' Like other Ruralists to be, Graham Ovenden grew up without the experience of television, with its levelling of all sights, all places.

One day his father took him to Southampton docks to see the last of the four-stack liners, the *Aquitania*, in her final call prior to the breakers' yard: 'I was awestruck at the sheer size... It touched memories of the Gasworks.' There was a family tradition of an 'uncle' who had gone down in the *Titanic*.

In 1951, when Graham was eight, the family moved to the outskirts of Southampton. Mr Ovenden needed to find post-war work. Now their family filled a larger house. Its setting was in Graham's eyes 'still quite pastoral':

> The road in front was unmade, so it was full of puddles and potholes – lovely for kids. And we were surrounded by woods and heathland, with a few bungalows here and there.
>
> But just down the road was the huge factory site of an abandoned brickworks. It must have been the largest in Southampton, with enormous stacks and pottery kilns – as they had made pottery as well as bricks.
>
> This was our roaming ground, and it was vast. We would play under high beams overhead, and climb down the underground tunnels where they used to do the firing. There were also 'the cliffs' (as we called them) where they had mined the clay on the spot. To us they were mountains, about forty feet high: we had wonderful slides down them.

Yet this juxtaposing of industry and nature held a difference. 'The gasworks at Alresford was in a field with nature very close. But about the Southampton brickyard, nature was taking over again. So I began to be aware of man's works encroached on by nature: it really was the regeneration of nature on man's despoiling.'

He found it hard at first to cope with the large and crowded Junior School at Southampton. 'Fortunately as a child one adapted fast.' The School authorities began to hang Graham's pictures on the walls: 'they showed enthusiasm and real interest.'

There were still no lessons in art. But music lessons continued without a pause. To follow his mother's piano tutelage, his parents found an accomplished teacher in Mrs George, a graduate of the Guildhall School in London. She took Graham through his Associated Board grades while constantly stimulating his love for music.

At twelve he began a series of extraordinary 'lessons' with the elderly Albert Ketelby. Ketelby was the composer of much descriptive music: 'In a Persian Market' and others had once enjoyed vast popularity in England. Ketelby's name had special resonance in the Ovenden household: quantities of his music there hinted at the composer's affection for Mrs Ovenden's mother (a fine pianist who had died young). Graham's mother played 'Bells across the Meadow' and other Ketelby favourites until her children knew them by heart. The vivid pictorial covers started Graham on his first collecting.

Ketelby was living his old age on the Isle of Wight. However it began, Graham would take the paddle-wheel steamer across to Ryde, often staying over the Friday night. The old man was still a fine pianist: and the 'lessons' were mostly illustrated reminiscences of composers and eminent musicians he had known. Another vanished era came up before Graham: 'He taught me that nostalgia can reach the edge of anguish. And when it does, it becomes art – sometimes great art.'

The old musician's reminiscences started the boy on a new collecting interest: 78 rpm records. Back in Southampton, he was delivering newspapers on his bicycle for pocket money. Along the paper-route and beyond, he haunted second-hand shops for records of music written or played by the figures Mr Ketelby talked about. Sometimes composer and performer came together, as when Graham found his first Elgar record: Sir Edward himself conducting *Salut d'amour*.

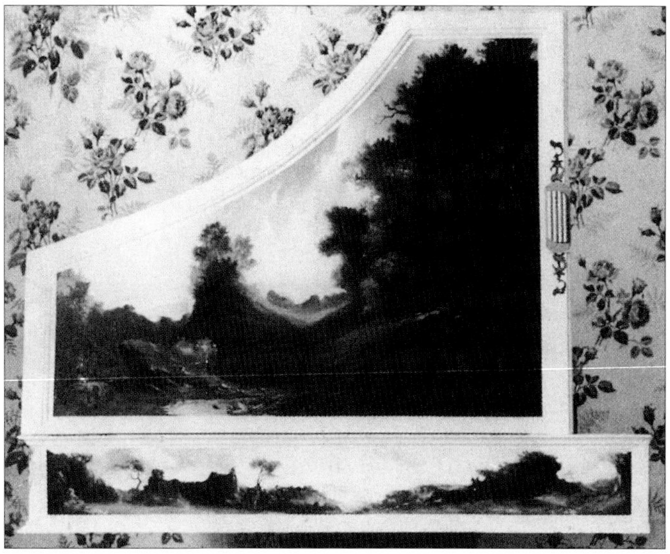

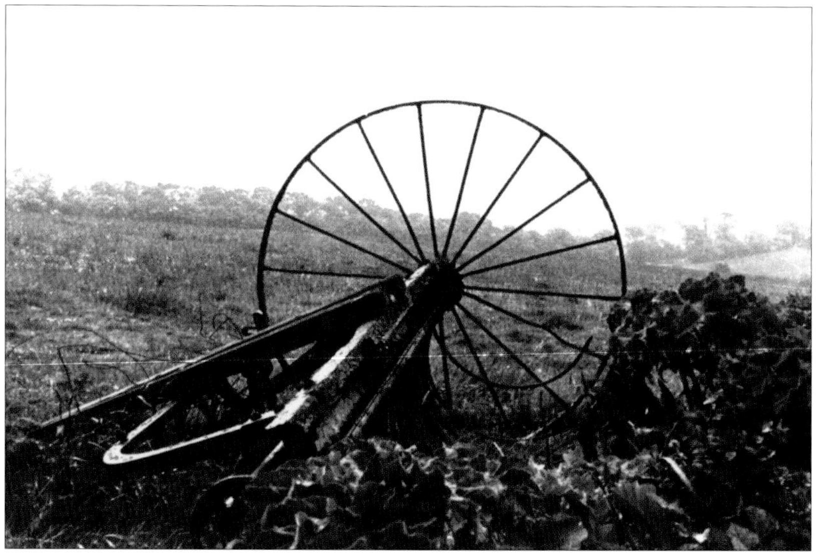

Above:
Plate 189. Graham Ovenden: Harpsichord case, 1955. Photograph

Above right:
Plate 190. Graham Ovenden: Harrow in a Hampshire field, 1955. Photograph by Graham Ovenden, aged twelve

Through recordings Graham discovered the harpsichord, in the magisterial Bach performances of Wanda Landowska. They inspired him at twelve to build his own harpsichord from scratch – and decorate its case and lid with painted pastoral visions combining Claude Lorrain with Rembrandt (Plate 189).

Amid such discoveries, Grammar School seemed irrelevant. Ovenden remembers one or two sympathetic teachers, and a headmaster who took his time coming to terms with such a pupil. He concludes:

> Nothing of any value was taught me at Grammar School – mainly because the subjects were academic subjects, which any intelligent child will absorb and know about in any case. All the things you *wished* to know were not taught there: the nature of the world, the mysteries of the world.

Ever since his father had given him a Kodak Brownie camera at nine, Graham had been taking photographs. Thus he recorded his impressions of the derelict brickyard from many angles. Cycling took him farther: a surviving print from 1955 (when he was twelve) shows a huge oak bole in the New Forest, taken from an angle in a light to suggest a male torso. Another photo from that year renews the counterpoint of nature with country industry (Plate 190). The juxtaposition is enhanced by skills of focus, use of natural light, and his own printing.

The next year he took his camera to London:

> I'd visited London once or twice, because some distant relative lived in the East End. But at the age of thirteen I suddenly felt a need to pack myself and my camera up, start walking the streets of East End London and photograph them. They offered a vastly extended version of the Southampton brickyard site.
>
> I was earning enough to pay a friend to do my weekend paper rounds. I used to catch the early train up on a Saturday, sleep rough overnight and come back by the last train on Sunday. I went at all seasons – probably twenty to twenty-five weekends a year.

This ground showed a new centre of interest: girls about the East End streets, from toddlers to those only younger than himself with knowledge beyond their years (Plate 191). Balancing on the edge of his own maturing, young Ovenden learned to make his shutter-timing just anticipate a composing form or gesture in ways that mark the gifted photographer. The constantly renewed theme was innocence and its loss. Looking back on that time, he says:

> The passion for little girls – let's spell it out – begins very early. And I can assure you that it's not solely by any means a sexual one. I understand Dickens's imagery of the angel-child. Somehow they seemed to be the logical foil for those vast and monumental [building] works of man. The child fleetingly passes in front of it – a melodic line against the great architectural structure of the music.

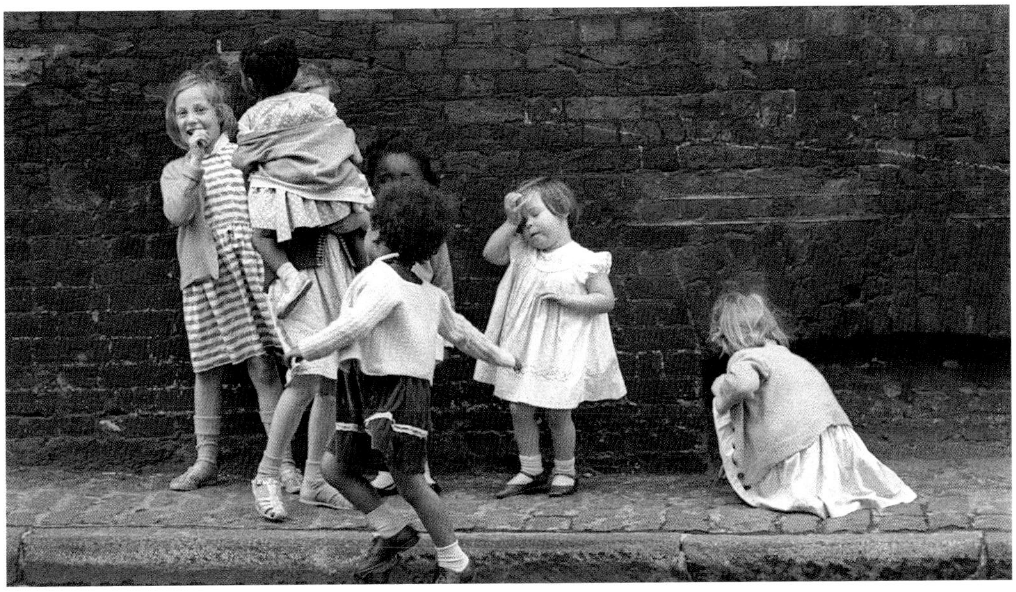

Plate 191. Graham Ovenden: *Stepney Street Kids,* 1959. Photograph

It was the beginning of what would become, with landscape, a central subject in his art:

> From the earliest age I had been partly aware of ghosts – not in the sense of gothic horror-haunt, but in the fact that life was a passing, fleeting moment. Every landscape and environment in which I find myself is haunted in that sense: I am aware of the presence of past individuals – not specifically, but as a whole. One is aware not only of the physical perspective, but the perspective of time. And also the timelessness.

He saw, at thirteen, that this was a special moment in the East End – with survivals whose poignancy was sharpened by the destructions of war all around:

> I couldn't have been less interested in the great buildings of the *West* End. It was the back streets, the perspectives of long-terraced houses intermingled with factories and strange derelict back yards. There was a lot of bomb damage as well, where nature had taken over.

Here were Sutherland's and Minton's war-time London subjects in retrospect.

Everywhere there was talk of rebuilding. The places in young Ovenden's camera – like the little girls passing through them, like the child-feelings surviving in himself – were doomed to be overwhelmed by unknowable replacements. Record their moments, then: capture these gossamers, even as the old gramophone records captured the music of Mr Ketelby's vanished friends.

Back at home, the developing of his photographs led Graham to start drawing the girls:

> I suddenly realised it was possible to expand the instant of time into something other. My figure-draughtsmanship was appalling, and I had to work very hard on it. I still had no formal instruction in art: I simply sat down and worked away at it, throwing away acres of paper in the process.

In 1959, when Graham was sixteen, his parents accepted their son's destiny as an artist, and allowed him to enrol in the Southampton College of Art. There at last he met his first formal instruction in art – and was lucky enough to find an inspired teacher in the artist James Sellars:

> He taught me the *process* of looking. He always did his own work with us – so you became part and parcel. Quite stern: he had a sharp tongue if he thought you were messing about. This was something I thrived on, because I too was always a hard worker. The great pleasure of life is working hard on the projects one wishes to work at. Then the small amount of leisure you give yourself you enjoy to a far greater extent.
>
> Jim instilled in me the absolute discipline of taking sketchbooks with me when I walked out. Sometimes I took the camera. One develops one's own particular *way* of looking, and adds to one's visual vocabulary – not 'changes' it. But with Jim I was always prepared to wear the mask of the student. He was a man passionate about art and the pastoral nature of art.

Sellars's great enthusiasm was for the visionary art of Samuel Palmer, and he opened its inspiration to Graham Ovenden.[13] Sellars took his best students on drawing expeditions as far west as Swanage. There Paul Nash had lived and painted for a time. But young Ovenden was honing his own draughtsmanship while he pursued one of Nash's goals: Ovenden's hill and rock formations began to explore shapes shared with the maturing human body.

In summer holidays alone, the boy put his bicycle in the train to Plymouth. Making a centre at an uncle's house on the edge of Dartmoor, he explored with sketchbook and camera as far as Cornwall. The results, when translated into oils at home, combined textures of Palmer's Shoreham drawings with concentrations of luminous colour (Plate 192) which had been Ovenden's own from his first childhood paintings at Alresford.

Looking back over his four years at Southampton Art College ending in 1963, Ovenden concludes: 'Jim Sellars was the only one who taught me anything there.' The School made no recommendation for a student's further career. Sellars, who had studied at the Royal College of Art, suggested Ovenden apply there. But the date for applications had passed, and Graham had to wait nearly a year to win a needed scholarship.

In the interval of waiting, he held down the only regular job of his life, at a local builder's merchants. Sellars and his wife (a fine botanical illustrator) watched over him 'for that very dangerous year without the structure of school'.

During this year he took his last East End photographs. 'The thought of living in London to attend the Royal College negated the mystery of photographing it.' Rebuilding and new building had begun everywhere. At Southampton the brickyard was cleared for a new school. At Alresford the green fields of his childhood were disappearing under housing estates.

In retrospect, Ovenden thinks now that the best thing of all that Sellars taught him was how to draw a professional's line under innocence. Yet the maturing student retained a secret corner of innocence in himself – 'not intending to be secret, but retrospectively: me going off and doing my things, and doing them in total naïvety in as much as – I just felt the huge need to do it.' It was not a formula for deft pupillage at the Royal College of Art.

For his College entrance in 1965 he submitted paintings of ideal landscapes and girls: 'One differentiates formally, but not emotionally – the emotive reason behind them all is identical.' He owed his Royal College scholarship to Peter Blake, who told Graham later: 'We were very bemused, but I was enthralled by your subject matter.' Ovenden specifies: 'He meant the girl pictures. I think they rather perturbed the others.'

He hated student London. He wandered through Kensington Gardens, where Palmer had once sought to rekindle the lights of Shoreham. Ovenden recalls:

> I got very lonely, and used to walk round Hyde Park at night (it was before they locked it) to keep my thoughts off – the environment. I would walk there sometimes the whole night through. (One used to see interesting night life there.)
>
> It's a very good way of getting anguish out of the soul, coming to terms with the total organic entity of nature. You suddenly realise that one's span is limited – that you are a part of this organic growth and evolution.
>
> You get that sense in Friedrich's painting, and in Palmer's. I think that's terribly important for a painter of nature, and particularly for a pastoralist. If you eventually *don't* know that relationship with nature – when you are really just an extension of it all – you're never really going to succeed.

He found little enough of that search at the Royal College in the 1960s:

> I was still quite a bit of a loner. And I have to say that with one or two exceptions I rather despised my fellow students because they were lazy layabouts – and very unaccomplished artists.

Except for Peter Blake, he had comparable feelings about his College tutors. A few were kind but ineffectual. Others showed real hostility to his deepest desires and goals. When Ovenden

13. Sellars wrote the first modern evaluation of Palmer's entire career: *Samuel Palmer* (Academy Editions, 1974).

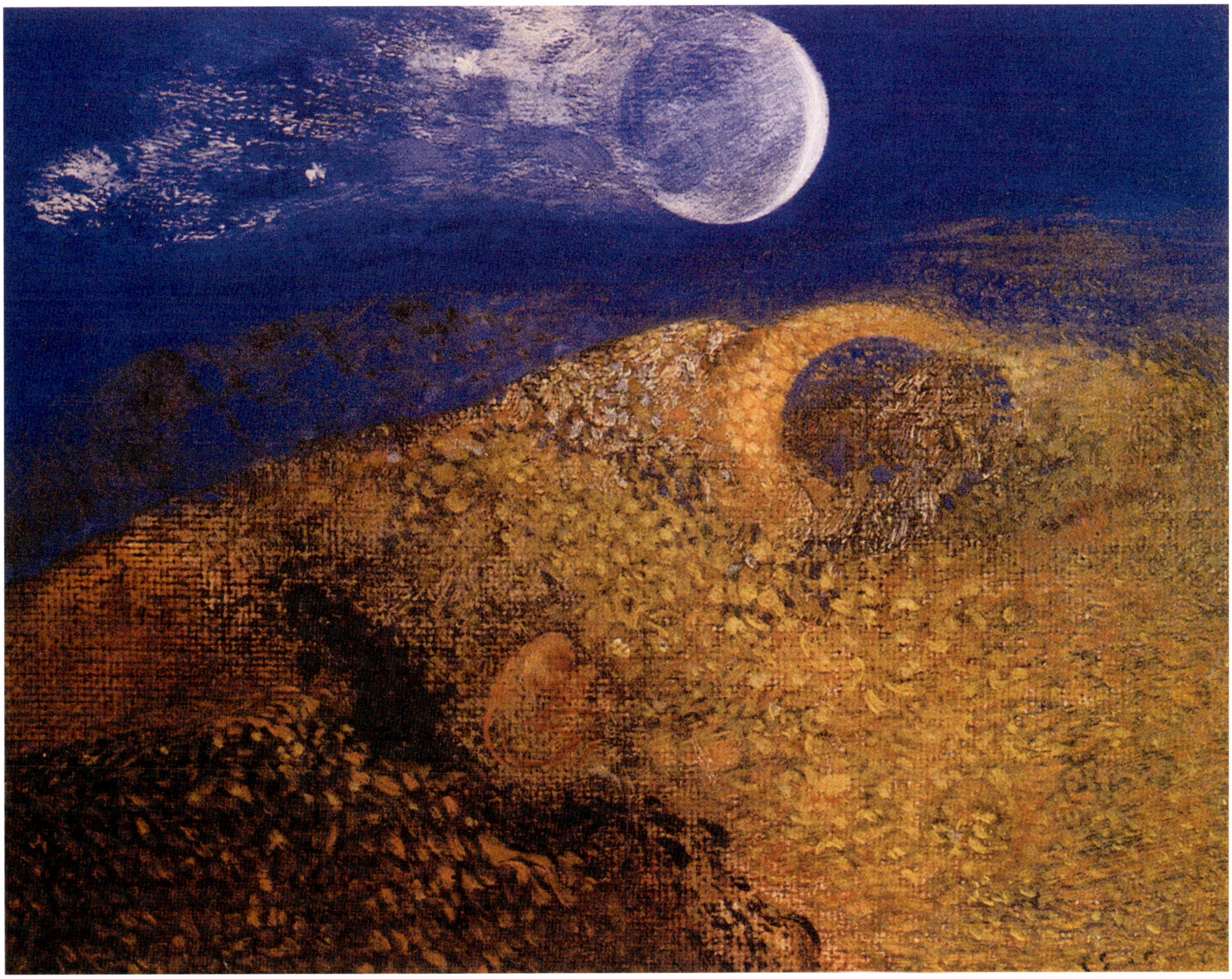

Plate 192. Graham Ovenden: *Landscape with Moon,* 1963. Oil

was offered an outside show of his work in his last year, the College principal Darwin forbade it. No explanation was made.

Through it all, the friendship of Peter Blake shone as a beacon. Ovenden remembers:

> Though you had your official tutor, he was *still my* tutor. The only pleasure for me at the Royal College was the fact that Peter was there. He's another Jim Sellars to me – not only in the wisdom he brought to his teaching, but at a deeper level of friendship.

When he lost his rented student room in his last year, Peter and Jann Blake took him to live in their flat at Chiswick.

* * *

He had already met the girl he was to marry. Ann Gilmore was two years younger than Graham. She had been born just as the Second World War ended, in May 1945, in rural Buckinghamshire. Her father at the time was a farm labourer, and the family lived in a cottage on the end of a cowshed – an arrangement for sharing warmth that reached back to before history was written.

When Ann was two, her family moved into a new council house up the road. They were still surrounded by country. But from the new front windows you could see, across two-and-a-half miles of fields and orchards, a palace. It was Waddesdon Manor, one of the Rothschilds' houses. The Rothschilds also owned all the farms. But the tenant farmers did not mind children walking through their fields, she remembers, 'as long as you closed the gates':

> There was a big field at the back of our house, and a hundred or two hundred yards away was an avenue of horse-chestnut trees leading down to another farm. The field was ploughed, and I can remember going one day with a couple of bigger children, and we walked to the end of that ploughed field. I was scared because it was such a long way from home. I remember that feeling of walking *all the way* to those trees.[14]

At seven she was given her first job – to look after three younger children from a neighbouring house where both parents were away at work:

> We used to play all the time – just roaming across fields. The upper reaches of the Thame River were a few fields away.
>
> Then there was the Rothschilds' orchard just down the road. There was the poultry running around their pens. But we kids knew how to get in, and up the trees to get the plums and apples. It was a paradise.

Trees were the centre of this paradise. Annie (as she began to be called) had one brother, a year older: 'but he was a bit timid – he couldn't climb trees'. She found other children who could: 'We spent our life climbing trees. There's quite a few in the area with my initials engraved in the bark.' The reward of climbing was the view from the top, 'and the wind blowing – the swinging. There was a row of beech trees where the branches came down, and we would swing on them. We also had bicycles, and used to ride round the villages.'

At the Council School she was handed a palette of paints:

> It was a piece of wood, and nailed to it were the little crinkly tops of beer bottles. In each of these beer-tops was a tiny bit of water-based powder paint. That was the first palette I ever came across. I can remember it quite clearly, so it must have impressed me.

But when she was eight her mother was diagnosed with cancer and given a year to live. It brought life at home to a sudden end.

Through the interest of her godfather, she and her brother were given scholarships to a boarding school set up by the Saddlers' Company for orphans and prospective orphans. The Junior School was mixed girls and boys. Annie excelled at art lessons. The best sketches were shown in frames on the School dining room walls. One day she found all the frames filled with her work.

Her mother seemed to make progress towards recovery, but doctors remained dubious. So Annie went on to the Senior Girls' school at Sawbridgeworth, Herts. – 'in a very nice old manor house with big grounds and gardens'. She did well at sports, cookery, and art:

> I was pretty average at everything else. But the thing about being good at art was the Headmistress: her obsession was the School play. She liked me because I always painted sets for the play. I used to get out of lots of lessons I didn't particularly like by saying: 'Oh, I've got to go and do that set.' And off I'd go.

At senior school she met her only teacher of art to make a deep impression. Mr Hunt had studied at the Slade. 'To my mind, he could paint anything. I thought he was brilliant.' He allowed the girls to paint subjects of their own choice in powder paints. It was always painting for Annie, never drawing. One of Mr Hunt's precepts remains with her, 'and I still paint every picture to this':

> It's light against darkness, and it's dark against light. I was in his class three years. He was the one who said I should go to Art School.

She graduated in 1961, and went home for the summer. Her mother, despite every prognosis, was confirmed in her recovery. She asked what Annie proposed to do. 'Oh, I'm going to Art School.' Her parents 'didn't really approve, because there was no money, and the uncertainty of it all.' Yet she was allowed to telephone the High Wycombe College of Art. Term was to start the following week, but she was asked to bring in her portfolio:

> They looked at my folder of work, and said: 'OK, you start on Monday.'
>
> My father would drive me to Aylesbury, where he was working then as a spot-welder. I used to catch the bus on to High Wycombe – an hour and a half each way – and he'd meet me in the evening.

She spent the journeys reading books from the College library – Arnold Bennett and all the Thomas Hardy novels:

> I suppose I related to them – old country stories. I thought of my life as being in the country: you couldn't get out and go anywhere. I saw myself as a Hardy heroine – Tess of the D'Urbervilles. And of course Gabriel Oak in *Far From the Madding Crowd* – I rather fancied him. I read lots of things, but those stood out.

The Art College was a four-year course. The first two provided general introductions: 'We did painting, life drawing, print-making, illustration; and book-binding in the evening.' No stipend was available for the first two years, so she worked weekends and holidays at a coffee bar in Aylesbury.

For the last two years she wanted to begin the painter's course. But just then her father had a stroke, and a week later he died. 'That turned my world upside down.' With a view to practicality, she changed her course to graphic design and illustration. She took her diploma in both in 1965.

After several months working as an orderly at Stoke Mandeville Hospital, Annie and a friend from College decided they must get to London. There Annie found employment in a series of design posts. Her only illustrated book was a catalogue of cookers for the Gas Board.

Then at a party she met Graham Ovenden, in his final year at the Royal College of Art. 'He was quite a shy little thing, and I think my maternal instincts were triggered. We started going out.' But when the Royal College gave him Second-class honours, a new Graham rose up:

> He refused to accept it, and created quite a fuss – on the grounds, I think, that he worked very hard and none of the other students did: he was always there from nine in the morning till nine at night. I think the Second was just politics.

He saw before she did that it was a match. When Graham's sister Julia vacated her flat in suburban Richmond (to buy a house in Hounslow), Graham and Annie took over the Richmond flat to live together until their marriage on 1 March 1969. 'We had a lot in common,' Annie recognises, 'and that's always kept us together. I think if I hadn't married Graham, I probably wouldn't be painting now.'

During the first year or two, Annie's graphic design work paid the bills while Graham established himself with two West End galleries. When his income from them seemed secure enough, they started a family. May 1971 brought a son whom they named Edmund Dante, and called Ned.

House prices were rising and a friend urged them to make a purchase while they could. Both wanted to return to the country, but judged they needed a little longer to make Graham's reputation secure in London. Julia now decided to sell her semi-detached house in Hounslow, and agreed to wait while Graham and Annie found a mortgage. Annie was staggered at the £7,500 purchase price: 'It backed on to a cemetery, so it was quiet at the back. We had a little garden, a quiet road in front, and we thought: This will do us to get started.'

14. Quotations in this section from taped conversation, July 2002.

It did not do. Hounslow lay under the flight-path in and out of Heathrow Airport. Graham remembers:

> The amount of racket and noise was almost unbelievable. We had known before we moved that airplanes flew over, but not that they were enormous, at roof-height, and on occasions every three minutes.

Peter and Jann Blake had moved to Wellow in Wiltshire and urged the Ovendens to follow. Near them was an area of great Elizabethan and Jacobean houses, one of which was for sale. Graham and Annie went down to confront 'grand oak-panelled hallways and about forty-eight rooms'. Then they learned that William Beckford's Lansdowne Tower in Bath was for sale. Graham still enthuses:

> It was absolutely wonderful. But having a 160-foot tower as part of your house is quite a responsibility. Imagine the scaffolding bill if you had to repair the top of it. Eventually we learned that it sold for £15,000.

Back in Hounslow Annie read *Dalton's Weekly*, listing houses for sale all over the country. One evening, finding nothing under 'Cottages for Sale', she looked at the 'Business' section and saw:

> 'Barley Splatt, near Bodmin, Cornwall. Secluded cottage, 22 acres, own trout stream. Possible pony-trekking establishment. Mortgage available.'
>
> I thought, that sounds nice. We laughed about it a bit. A little while later I picked it up again, and said: 'You know, this *does* sound nice.' Graham said: 'Go and look at it if you want to.' He didn't want to come. If I liked it, we'd buy it. It was £25,000, and I thought: We have no money like that.

But she set off next day in their Beetle car with Ned and a friend. It took so long to get there that they put up at a bed-and-breakfast. Next morning she found their way to Barley Splatt:

> It was completely idyllic: small cottage, fairly derelict, with a cowshed under a huge oak tree, and other little sheds. We walked in the woods and down by the river. It was winter, and I saw this lichen hanging down from the trees: it had a fairy quality.
>
> So I phoned Graham and said: 'Well, it is absolutely amazing. I can't believe that you can *buy* something like this. But you'll have to come down – because you'll hate the house.'
>
> Graham said: 'Well, don't worry about the house. We'll build something.'
>
> If only I'd known. I should have known. Graham always goes for the top. He doesn't cut corners.

Next day Graham came:

> I approached it from the top of the lane looking down on it. I took one look and thought: 'Oh, my God, we've got to have it. Because this is where I can build the house which I've always known at the back of my mind for at least fifteen years had to be done.' It was an old dream: I had Ludwig-of-Bavaria syndrome – Lord Bute of Castell Coch.

His fascination for these ultimates of Victorian Gothic might have started in the Tremeeres' gas-lit sitting room with its model of the Taj Mahal. Fed with boyhood sights of the great liners off Southampton, it came to early focus in the huge backgrounds of his East End photographs. From them had sprung a new collection: Victorian photographs – many of grand buildings afterwards destroyed.

Most recently, with Annie, he had added the collecting of children's books – like Gordon Craig before him – with their cloud-capped towers of never-never lands. Now Graham, like Craig, had the repeated experience of turning such dreams into his own art. That art could find literally a new dimension in architecture.

The house-agent found a bank manager willing to give the large mortgage they needed, and

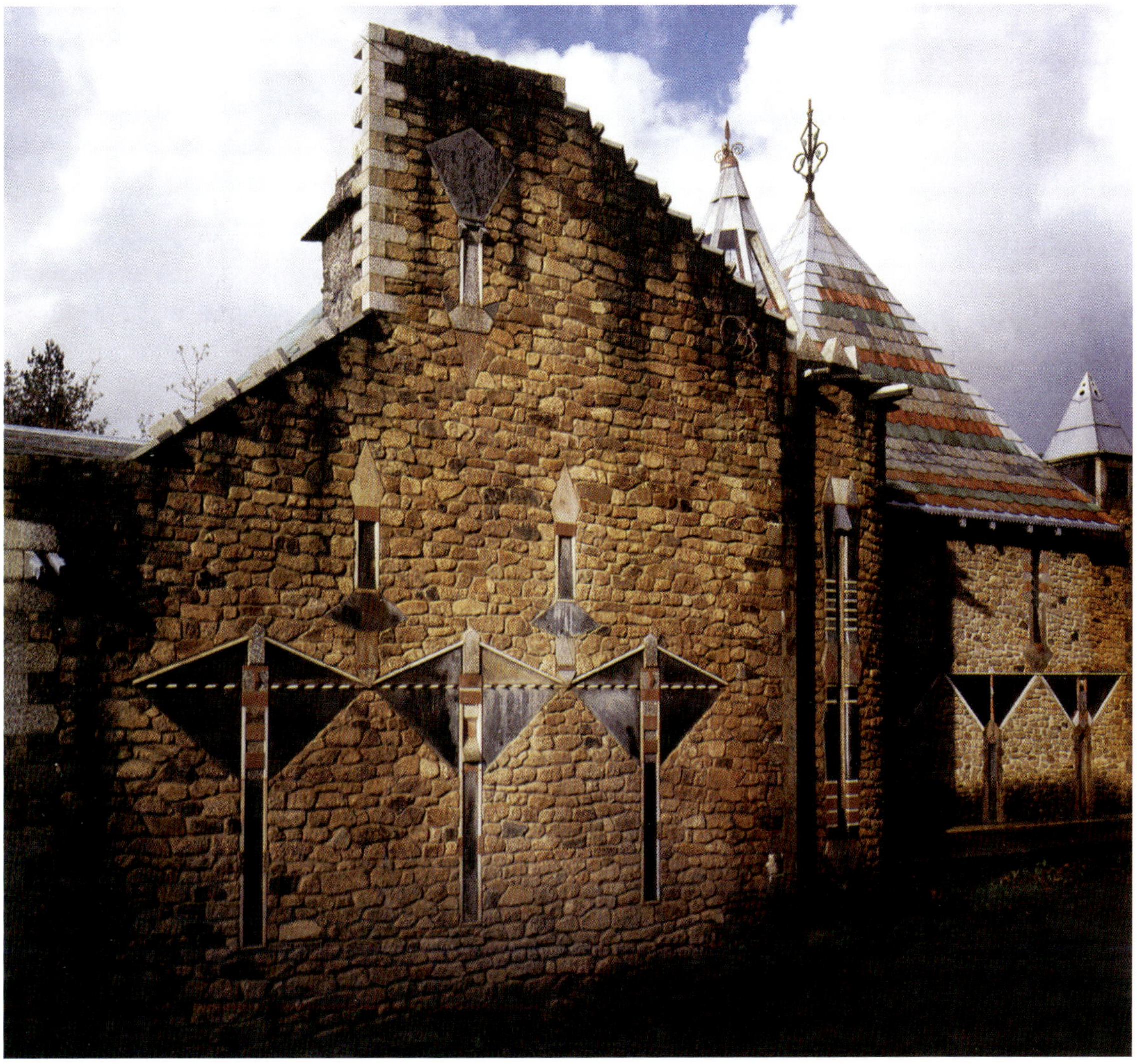

Plate 193. Graham Ovenden, with Martin Johnson: Barley Splatt, near Bodmin, Cornwall. Photograph, *c.*1985

the Hounslow house when it sold fetched double its purchase price. So there was a respectable deposit. Graham started drawing plans with their architect friend Martin Johnson. The vision was Graham's: the choice of materials, the unique decorations for the house outside and in.

They moved down in June 1973, to squash into the cottage. Graham himself did much of the building labour over the next dozen years. He had occasional hired help by ones and twos. But Annie recalls him cutting all the granite – 'spending hours on that machine we bought, sawing away'.

They lived a partitioned existence. Once a septic tank was built in a lower field, a temporary kitchen and bathroom could be made at the cowshed. Another shed was adapted for Graham's temporary studio. And they slept in the old cottage; that was repaired sufficiently to be taken into Graham's plans for the only Gothic Revival house to be built in England since the Second World War. The ghost of Griggs stirred then.

The plan centred on a fifty-foot banqueting hall of double height with minstrel gallery and organ at one end. To the cottage core, a new and spacious kitchen was added first. Along the lane beside the cottage, a decorated outer wall would guard the whole domain (Plate 193).

* * *

In March 1975 Peter Blake invited them to Wellow to meet the others who might form the new group he talked of. Meeting the Arnolds and David Inshaw made a real success all round. The Blakes' little daughters were there, and the Ovendens' Ned. Excitement held the day as they sat round the Blakes' eight-sided table designed by Pugin to enjoy a substantial meal.

The shared goal emerging that day is encapsulated by David Inshaw: 'We were looking for a way of identifying our inner feelings about our environment in a direct way.'

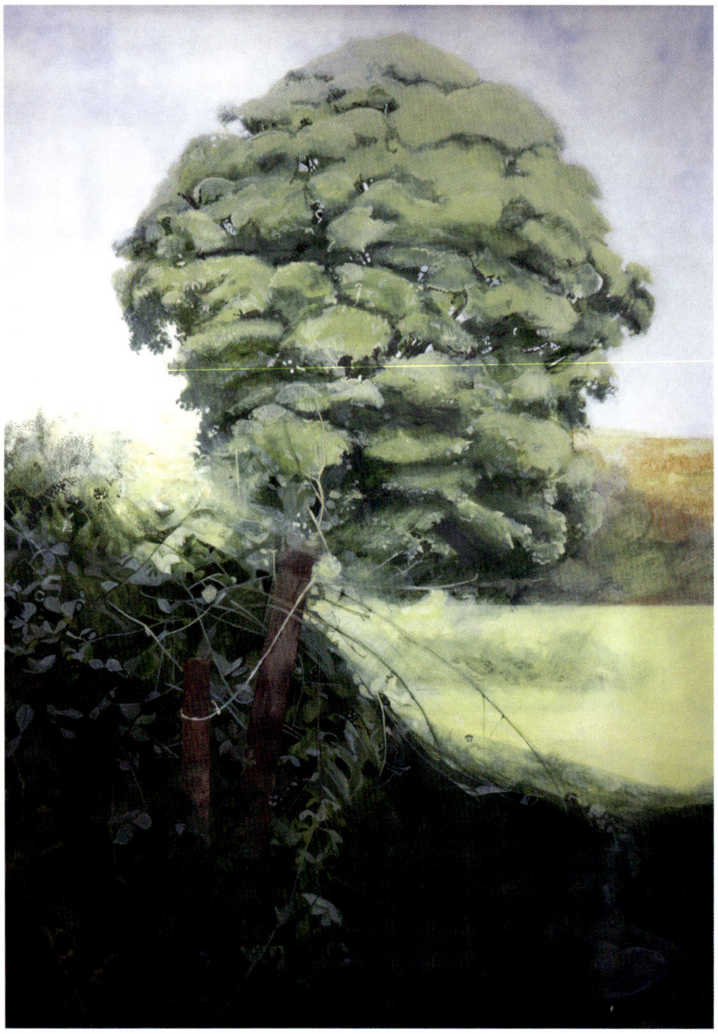

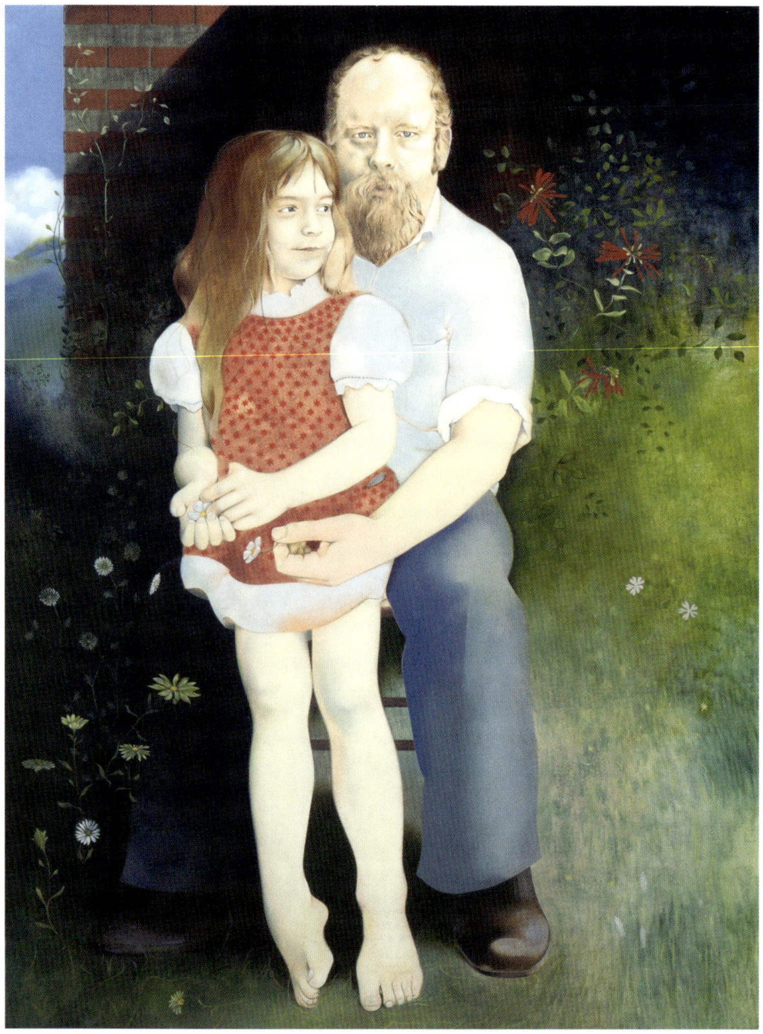

Above:
Plate 194. Annie Ovenden: *Tree at Panter's Bridge,* 1976. Wash

Above right:
Plate 195. Graham Ovenden: *Peter Blake with Juliette,* 1976–78. Oil

> We decided to meet four times a year, on each Quarter Day; each taking it in turns to be host to all the others. We were going to have a holiday in Cornwall for two weeks every October. And we were going to have exhibitions up and down the country wherever we could.

Then a strong immediate plan emerged:

> We were going to go away for a year, and each do a painting that we felt would show our feelings about the group and about what we were searching for. Peter had just been made a Royal Academician. He was in charge of hanging the Summer show in 1976, and he said he would try to have all our pictures hung together.

Annie Ovenden had felt on the sidelines at first. Since art college, she had painted only occasional pictures for her mother's birthday. Now she had Ned, and another child on the way.

> I was known just as a jobbing designer. When Peter said, 'Annie, we'd like you to be in on it,' I thought they wanted me to do all the posters – which I did.
>
> But I remember as he said that, I thought: I know what I'm going to do. I'm going to *paint*. I always thought I would get back to it.

So Annie's first serious painting would carry the half-promise of a place in the Royal Academy Summer Exhibition.

What should they call themselves? A canvass of writer friends drew several ideas. 'Pastoralists' was rejected as too specific to literature. Then Graham Ovenden's patron and friend Laurie Lee put forward the old word 'ruralist' – someone who goes from city life into the country. No one took it up until Ann Arnold's father, Dr Telfer, pointed out that it exactly described their case. So the new 'Brotherhood' would be 'of Ruralists'.

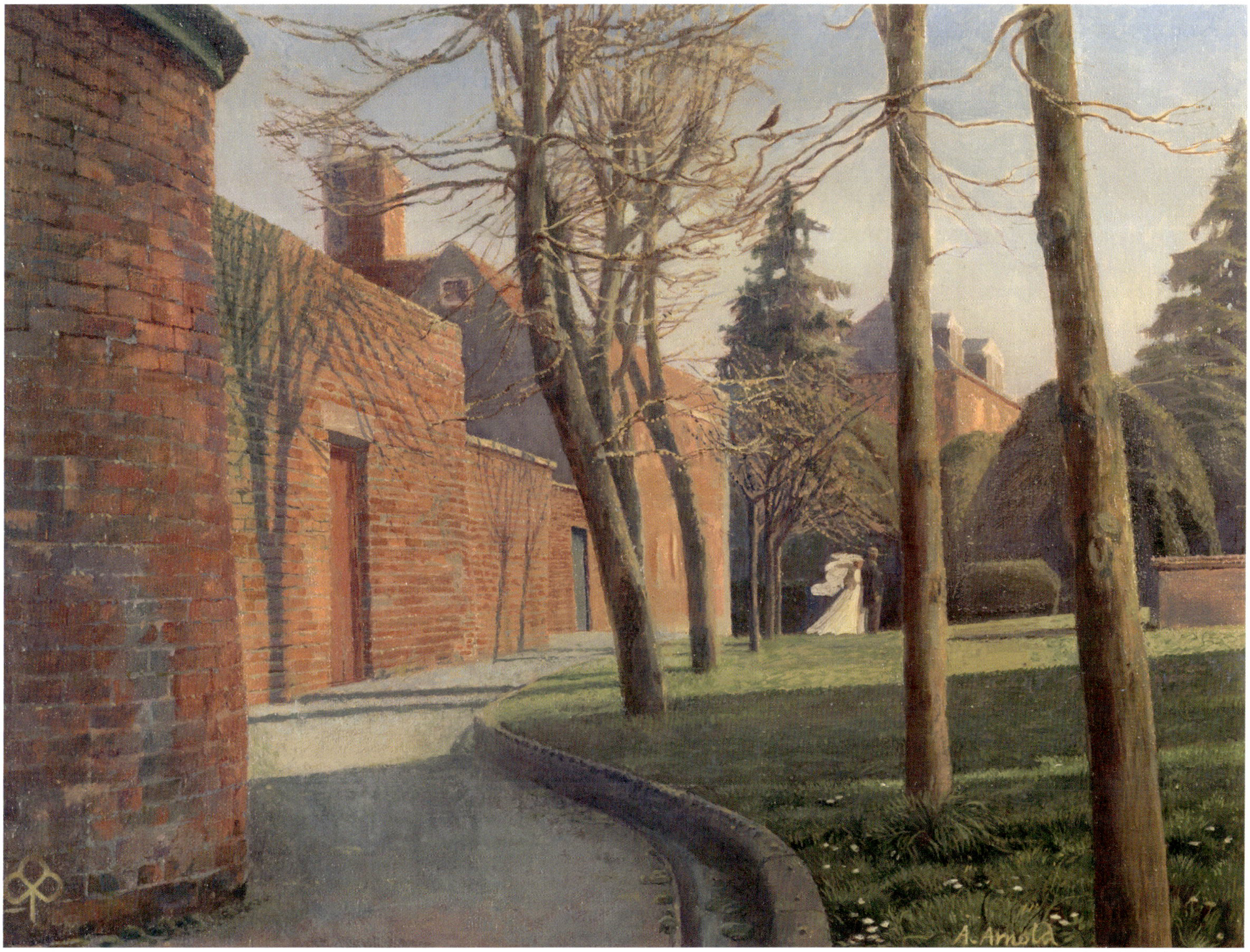

Plate 196. Ann Arnold: *Wiltshire Wedding*, 1975–76. Oil

They all went away to paint their pictures for the 1976 Academy. Annie Ovenden found her subject in a tree near Panters Bridge, at the entrance to their lane in Cornwall (Plate 194). The excitement of real painting even in snatched time gave her tree on the canvas a quality of explosion, as she says: 'a hydrogen bomb, which at the time I suppose was in the air politically. It wasn't intentionally done, but it sort of has that feel about it now.' Yet her central precept remained there too:

> It was the light. The tree is full of light, and there's a lot of darkness in the foreground leaves and fence. It's a contest between the two. I like to think of trees as uplifting: something coming out of the dark into light. It's this feeling of surge, well-being.

Graham Ovenden's old gratitude to Peter Blake flowed into a big informal portrait of Peter with his eldest daughter, finely drawn in light colours on a richly rendered lawn with flowers (Plate 195). The portrait's background divides in a way that would prove prescient. A small glimpse at the left opens an airy Ovenden prospect of distant hillsides with clouds in a blue sky: but that is cut off by a wall of Victorian brick rising to the top of the picture, and running into deep shadow.

Ann Arnold's *Wiltshire Wedding* (Plate 196) was her first painting since moving to Devizes. The setting is the churchyard next to their house. Here brick walls and buildings appear in sunlit balance with sky and lawn, trees and topiary. Down the benign prospect, a white-clothed bride pauses with her father on their way to the crowning day of her life – as Ann 'saw it one day' from their new window.

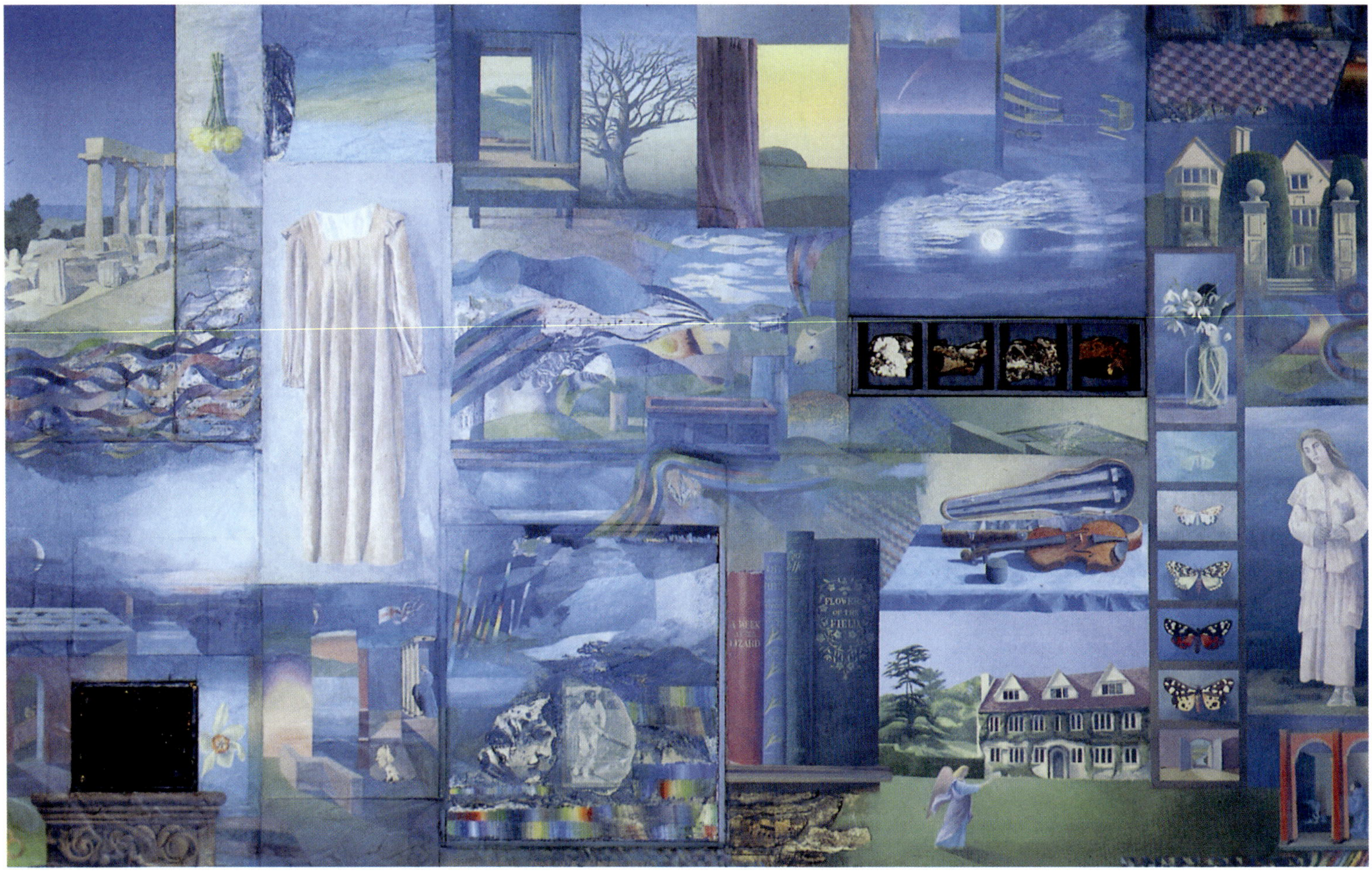

Plate 197. Graham Arnold: *Memorials of a Quiet Life,* 1975-76. Oil with collage and assemblage

Graham Arnold painted *Memorials of a Quiet Life* as a dream-collage of his own country experience now newly enfranchised. His picture brought together classical ruins from Sicily, English country houses, comet and rising moon, a violin for music, favourite books, dresses hung as for use a century ago, his own drawing of the *Knight's Tomb* now half-realised in painted miniature – and through curtained windows, prospects of Silbury Hill and the Salisbury Plain (Plate 197). This too was a first painting from Devizes. The multifarious images are combined on what the artist described as 'symphonic' scale.

Peter Blake's *Titania* would be shown in 1976 as still 'in progress' (Plate 198). It was to go through many later changes. For Blake was seeking (as he said) to set himself in an adolescent girl's mind, while continuing to look steadily with his own adult male sexuality. 'I was trying to invent a novelty': not to cover parts of the body according to convention, but to show his teen-aged Titania with those parts decorated, even pierced. It took Graham Ovenden's fascination with girlhood innocence down a different path.

Childhood innocence in its earliest phase filled Jann Haworth's beautiful terracotta bust of their baby daughter Daisy – garlanded with daisies, attended by a toy butterfly, and set within a frame of fabric and glass and wood.

A different innocence haunts David Inshaw's *Cricket Game* (Plate 199). Here an overwhelmingly quiet landscape begins to engulf players dwarfed in distances of lengthening shadows. The sheer power of the landscape presence recalls Samuel Palmer. On Inshaw's horizon stands such a clump of trees as had repeatedly drawn Paul Nash – rendered now with an atmospheric softness that sacrifices nothing to fine draughtsmanship.

All these works appeared together in the 1976 Academy Summer exhibition under a large banner devised by Peter Blake reading 'The Brotherhood of Ruralists'. It caused David Inshaw some misgiving. He remembers hoping that they might have continued the low-key, semi-private atmosphere of the little 'Broadheath' group:

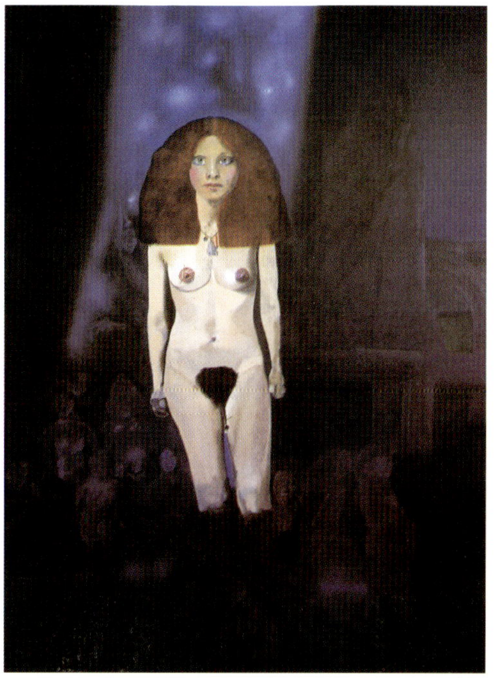

Plate 198. Peter Blake: *Titania*. Oil as it was shown in 1976, specified 'unfinished'; later extensively repainted.

> But it quickly became apparent that it was going to be a much more public enterprise. We were going to Go Public. The banner at the RA was obviously a public statement.

Inshaw found himself wishing not to have definitions forced.

The media picked them up instantly. There was a big article in the *Sunday Times* Colour Supplement. The critics all set out their own definitions – some as straw men to knock over as irrelevant to the twentieth century: unprogressive, reactionary, sentimental, 'harking back'.

Against that, a segment of the public took to the Ruralists warmly – occasionally hotly. After one of the exhibition openings, the Ruralists went off to have a meal in a nearby pub. The door opened on Ruralist protagonists and antagonists in pitched battle, Annie Ovenden remembers: 'they were actually throwing things across the room.' Another day she found David particularly upset by one critic's comparison of a Ruralist exhibition with the popular film *The Sound of Music* starring Julie Andrews. When Annie tried to brush it away, David said: 'But you don't understand: Julie Andrews wants to buy one of my pictures.'

A year later John Read made an affectionate film of them all on holiday and called it 'Summer with the Brotherhood'. Inshaw recalls:

> It was totally idyllic. The summer was beautiful, and we were filmed in rather beautiful situations. Afterwards we got a lot of enquiries about how people could join: where could they get forms to fill in?

* * *

Jann Haworth wanted to make her own extension. After the Ruralists were established, she tried to draw on them to teach at an infant school she had started at Wellow. 'The Looking-Glass' she called it, after the sequel to *Alice in Wonderland*. She invited the schoolchildren and their parents on Ruralist sketching holidays – which looked suddenly like becoming public events. At least one Ruralist showed resentment.

Then Jann found herself in love with another man. Without much warning, she abandoned Peter. Peter, left alone at Wellow – bought and decorated and lived in at Jann's wish – descended into nervous breakdown. David Inshaw and Graham Ovenden tried to help him through the

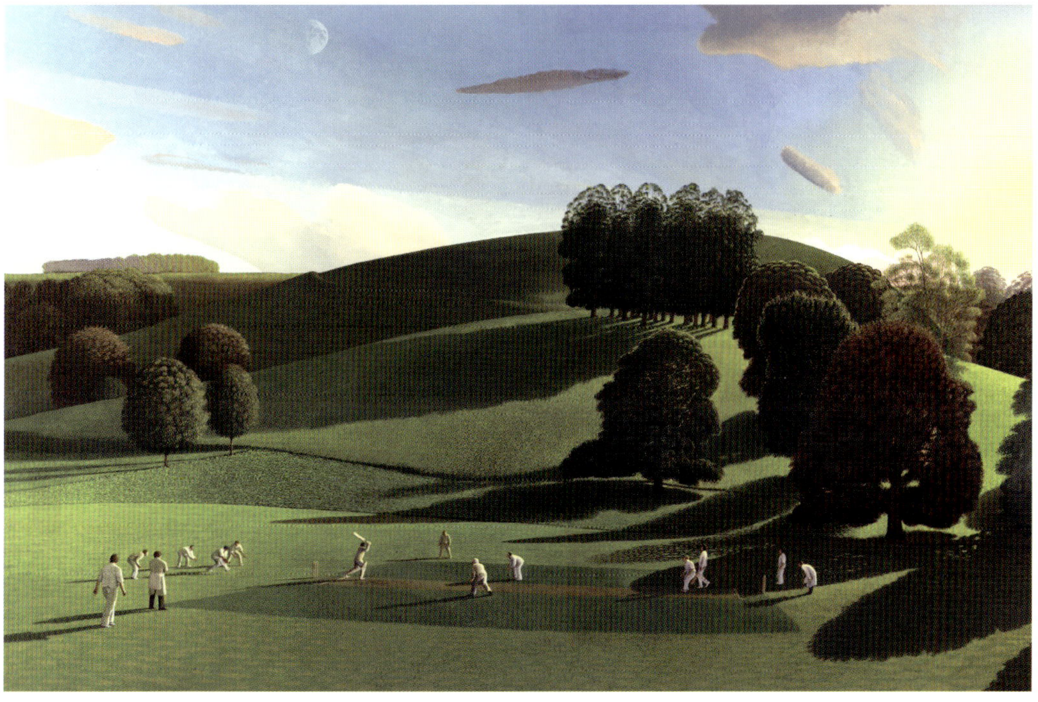

Plate 199. David Inshaw: *The Cricket Game,* 1976. Oil

hours and weeks. They had little success. By the end of 1979 there appeared no alternative to Peter's return to London.

The whole group continued in shared projects. The first, devised on what proved to be the final full Ruralist holiday in 1979, was 'Ophelia': innocence in an enhanced landscape, with Millais' famous Pre-Raphaelite painting one inspiration. At the Bristol Museum in July 1980 the Ruralists together showed eighteen images of Ophelia.

Jann Haworth exhibited a terracotta mask – open-eyed, open-mouthed, decorated with ribbons. Ann Arnold and Annie Ovenden each contributed a lyrical oil. David Inshaw showed a painting and six drawings of Ophelia in different situations. Graham Arnold showed only four pencil drawings, large and fine. His planned oil painting had been interrupted by a heart attack: he was not yet fifty. Graham Ovenden's *Ophelia* was a buxom teenager with blossoms falling off her dishevelled dress, as she pulls luxuriant long hair away from a too-knowing face under a waxing moon. But Peter Blake's *Ophelia* brought his own agony to another 'work in progress'. His semi-nude entered the water with her left forearm amputated.

Blake's *Ophelia* was to go through many evolutions over many years. None of them was painted in the country. Turning away from the shell of his life in Somerset, Peter would never live in the country again. And thus he felt he could no longer be a Ruralist. Despite that, he has remained the Ruralists' firm friend and advocate throughout a career whose popularity with the public has outstripped all the others. Jann Haworth left in a more definitive way, taking her new man back to California and leaving her friends' letters unanswered.

All this deeply affected David Inshaw, who had himself recently married. He still lived side by side with the Arnolds in Devizes, but the old dynamics seemed to assert themselves less comfortably now. Looking away to broaden both outlook and technique, Inshaw could not avoid the immanence of Peter Blake's growing public success. Peter was also David's senior by a decade.

Two events of the next years increased Inshaw's unease. In October and November 1980, Graham Ovenden was hauled into the Old Bailey to defend himself against a charge of fraud arising from a prank. As Victorian photography had risen in popular interest, Ovenden felt the qualifications of some newly risen pundits inferior to his own.

To cheer a photographer friend down on his luck, Ovenden suggested the lark of photographing a modern child, with face appropriately dirtied, against an old chimney – to see whether it would pass muster among the 'experts'. Then came a refinement: Ovenden made careful drawings after his friend's photographs, which the photographer in turn re-photographed in softer focus. These too passed. Thus the unaccountably forgotten Victorian photographer 'Francis Hetling' was 'discovered'. The National Portrait Gallery mounted an exhibition of his work with Arts Council funding.

Then someone tried to sell 'Hetling' prints as coming from the collection of Graham Ovenden, and the fat was in the fire. Ovenden proved a redoubtable witness over three days in the box. When the judge appeared incredulous that the origin of such photographs could be in drawings, Ovenden dashed off another such drawing on the spot. Graham Arnold testified to having heard Ovenden propose it simply as a hoax – 'pastiche' without any financial motive.

Ovenden's QC, John Mortimer, defended his client by observing that the mock photographs were worth more than had been paid for them when it could be shown that they were in fact works by Ovenden.[15] Mortimer summed up the wrong-headed prosecution by asking: 'Since when has it been a crime to tweak the nose of the Arts Council?' After a fortnight the prosecution was withdrawn. Peter Blake had attended the trial every day, and made himself Ovenden's sympathetic host throughout the ordeal. But David Inshaw saw the whole affair as 'quite traumatic' for the Ruralists.

The next year, when a large travelling exhibition of work by the Ruralists and their friends (again with Arts Council support) registered a national success, Inshaw saw the moment as unrepeatable. Their best work as a group was here. Their point was made and accepted. So it might follow that the Ruralist day was done. Years later Inshaw analysed his own thinking:

15. John Mortimer, *Murderers and Other Friends* (Viking, 1994), 113-116.

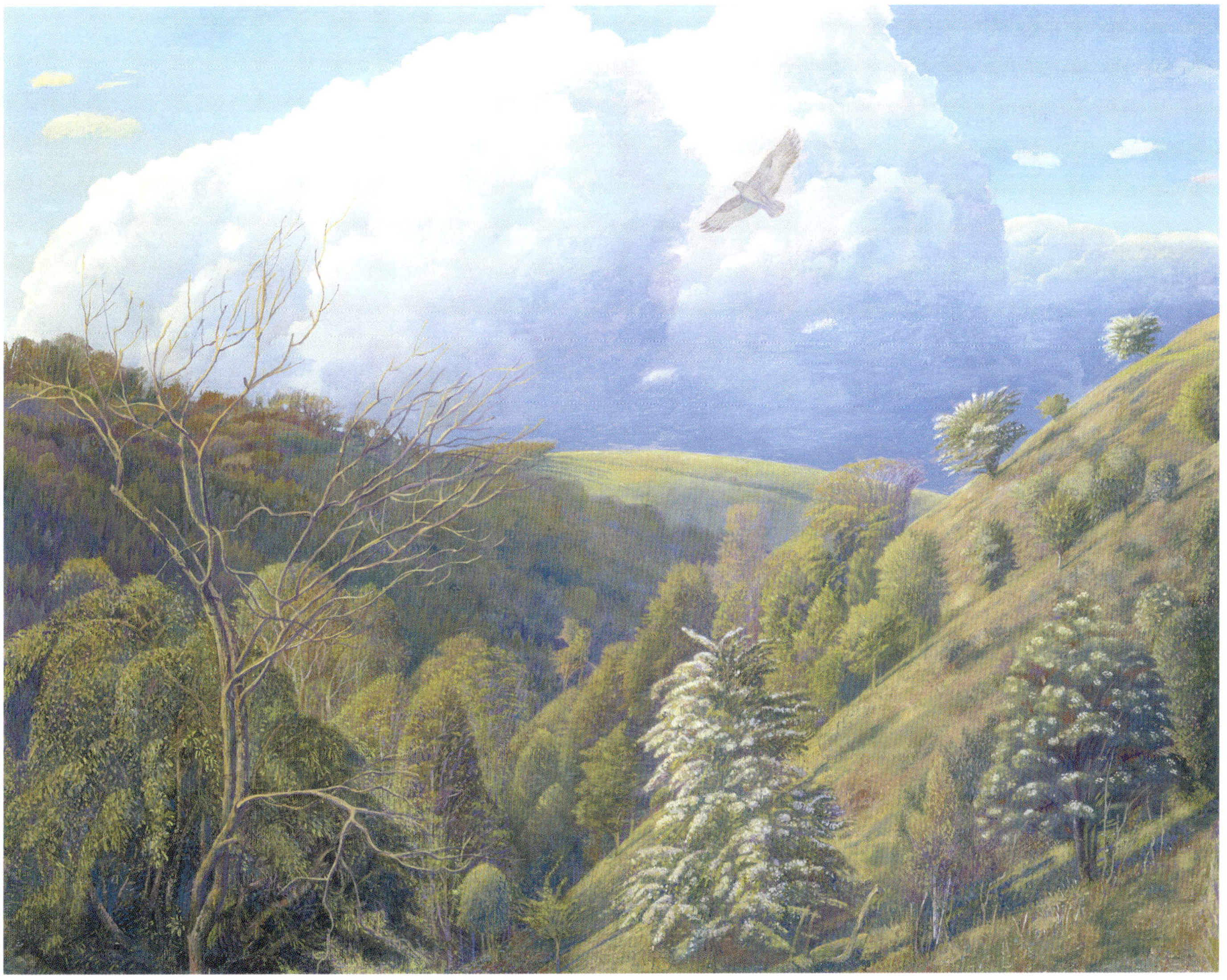

Plate 200. Ann Arnold: *The Hill in Spring*, 1987. Oil

Life always seems to go in phases – in hindsight anyway. …

For me change is important, not destructive – but change in the context of development through time. I felt that, to gain strength – to move on – the thing was to go off your own way with what you'd got [from the group] and develop in your own way.

I felt that the group had become rather inward-looking, and I was looking for a way out.

The way seemed to open in 1983. That year in London the Tate Gallery mounted a big retrospective show of Peter Blake's work. Applause was general, and a CBE followed. Ruralism appeared as only one strand in Blake's synthesis of private impulse with a Pop-art 'take' on modern advertising. Pop Art was not really David Inshaw's vehicle, yet Peter Blake's success on such a scale showed a new template. Inshaw announced his resignation from the Ruralists.

He had been a moving force in founding the Broadheath Brotherhood and, with Peter Blake, he had brought the Ruralists together. Friendship remains. In the late 1980s Inshaw left Devizes with a new partner – not for London, but the borders of Wales. Six years later he was back in Devizes. There he still paints nature – birds, trees and lawns, man and woman, coasts and bonfires.

Arnolds and Ovendens – the introduced rather than the introducers – had less regard for public events and fashions. As the organising centre fell away, the Grahams and Anns drew quietly together in their pursuit of private inspirations. The continuing group provided the intimate support of close friendship with the contrasts that define.

Ann Arnold has kept her counterpoints of close and distant textures within rich atmospheric watercolours and oils. Her work still sings its clearest lyric of country vision in privacy (Plate 200). Graham Arnold has led his collage-painting to repeated syntheses in single subjects, both

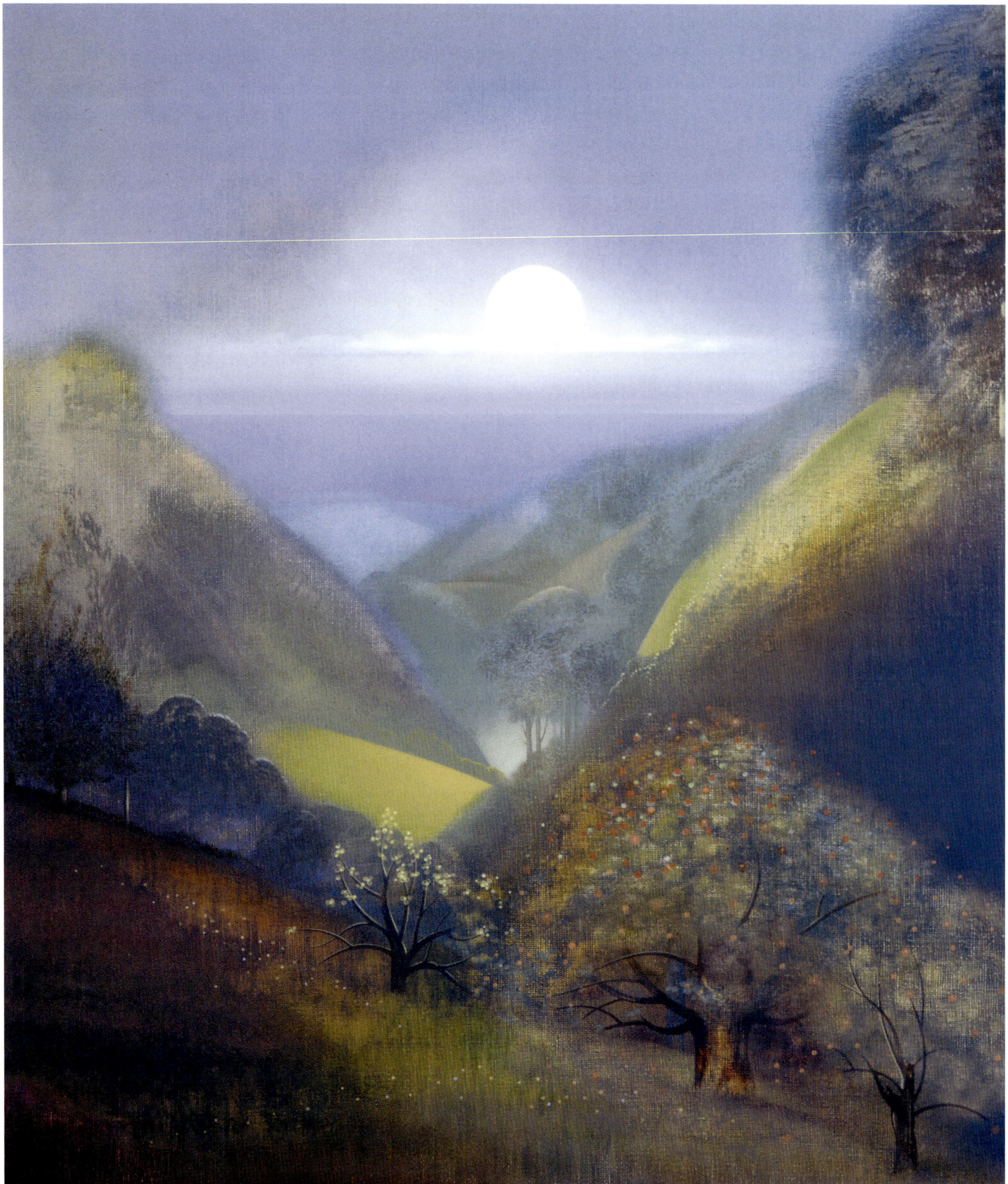

Plate 201. Graham Ovenden: *Orchard Moon*, *c.*1995. Oil

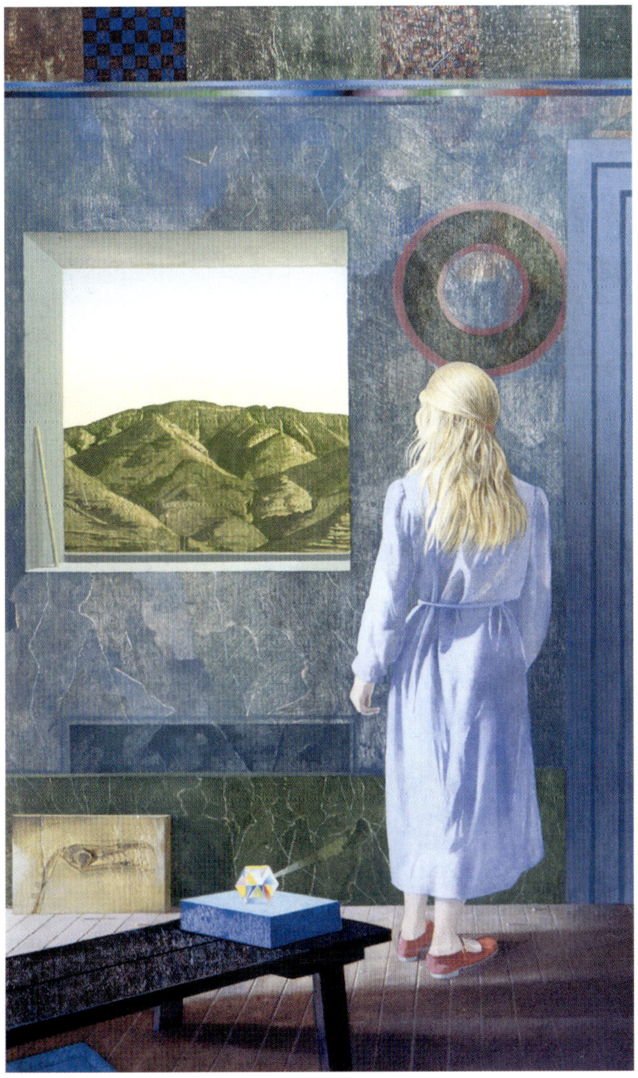

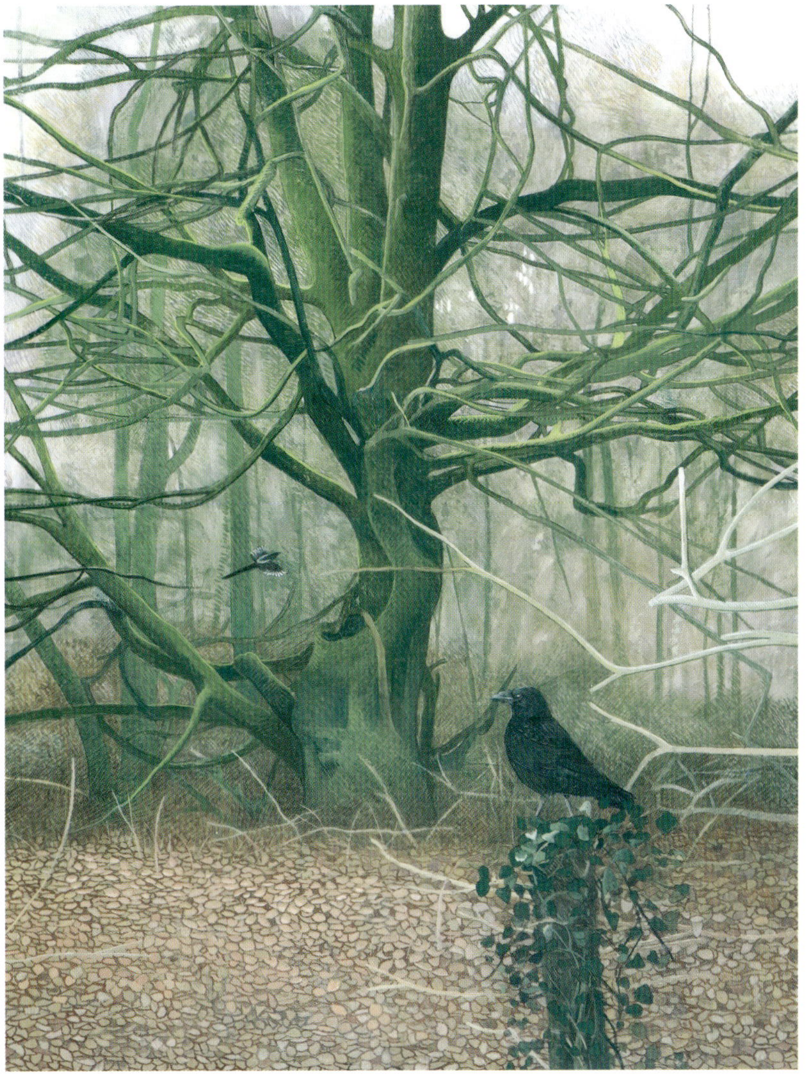

Above left:
Plate 202. Graham Arnold: *The Anteroom*, 1997-99. Oil

Above right:
Plate 203. Annie Ovenden: *The Eye of the Bird*, 2005. Oil

complex and plenary (Plate 202). His syntheses are fed through large and masterly pencil drawings – some used quickly for painting, others waiting: some exhibited, others kept back.

Graham Ovenden has maintained his parallel evocations of innocence at the edge of vision – through incandescent landscapes of the mind (Plate 201), through girl children at every stage of insight. The girl images have continued to foment suspicion and anger in some quarters. Ovenden sees the real guilt 'not in him who takes the fig-leaf off to reveal nature's truth, but in him who puts the fig-leaf on to conceal it'.

The youngest of the four, Annie Ovenden, continues to evolve her vision (Plate 203). A significant extension of her tree theme appeared in 1999, in a series of twelve paintings of a single great beech tree month by month through the year, in changing lights and leafage.[16] This suite was followed by a further innovation in her work: a group of large, highly finished pencil studies, followed by different pen and ink drawings, of huge and ancient trees. She has recently expanded her painting vision again in a series of luminous nocturnes – sightings and half-sightings about houses and churches, churchyards and gardens and lawns, from Cornwall to the Cotswolds.

The Ruralist friendship was paradoxically deepened by the Arnolds' move north in 1986 to the Welsh borders of Shropshire. The Ovendens reaffirmed the friendship again when in 1999 they began to hang annual Ruralist exhibitions in the great hall of their house at Barley Splatt. The big house has arrived at its final stage of building, much through the interest of their son Ned, who has made himself a successful craftsman-builder. Ned bends equally keen eyes on a growing collection of paintings – many purchased 'at source'. The Ovendens' daughter, Emily, has made her own mark with a Ruralist story. With illustrations by her mother, this story has taken its place in an ongoing series of privately printed Ruralist books.

* * *

16. Published in reproduction as *The Beech Tree: Paintings January 1999 to December 1999*, with Poems by Daniel Nanavati and Shänne Sands (Barley Splatt, Cornwall: Footsteps Press, 2000).

Not all the Ruralist pictures have yet been drawn and painted. As this chapter is thus incomplete, so the book as a whole may be incomplete. Yet here an opposite question rises: is the history of English pastoral vision itself now approaching an end?

The Ruralists are of the last generation to grow up virtually without television. Only to *hear about* other places and people is to be encouraged to form private pictures out of your own experience – as in the reading of books. (I know this, since I too am of the Ruralist generation, and had no formative television.)

But to *see* every foreign thing served up, with only a degree less vividness than your own primary experience, is to feel shrinkage at the roots of identity itself. In the universalising purview of television, the demotic 'learning' of visual travel can match (or overmatch) private knowing. Are the roots of local, and even private, experience now washing away in a flood of what Henry James described (at the very beginning of the 'communications century') as the sense of 'rounding the extravagant curve of the globe'?

Is that curve any longer so extravagant? Is a halved sheep's carcass in formaldehyde exhibited now as new sensationalism? Or does it raise a silent cry after innocence lost? Does the halved sheep extend pastoral vision, or merely cut it down to newer urban notions of its proper size?

The sum of David Inshaw's disengagement, as he looks at the more constant Ruralist careers now, is that his friends' art has not changed with the years. Subject matters, and to an extent styles, have remained for the Ruralists as steady ideals.

The fact worries others as well. The continued Ruralist presence has raised oppositions of an intensity and persistence that seem surprising responses to celebrations of quietness. Clearly the opposers feel a threat in the Ruralists' refusal to engage the day-to-day fashions which pursue each other across the world stage. Are such fashions embraced as so many attempts to unify world culture against further wars? Or are they merely so many advertisements for consumption?

What separates the Ruralists from many currencies in London and Europe and New York may be less any special subject matter, or technique, than just the long-lined quietness in their separate lyrics. Their pictures dismiss any facile charge of sentimentality and escapism, through the profound identifications they exude with perhaps a single valley and its hillscapes.

The French Impressionist Monet found his later inspiration in an elaborate private garden made for that purpose. But English pastoral visionaries have all found their ideals less in gardened ordering than in more relaxed dialogues of broader nature with its inherited millennia of human habitation.

Palmer found his vision first at Dulwich and Shoreham. Through his later years he sought to broaden its times and places. Griggs came to see a threat of the vision's total loss through a Great War whose final influence was to internationalise. Paul Nash proposed English vision's engagement to continental Surrealism – before Sutherland reduced it back to elemental rocks and shards of wood on one of Britain's loneliest seacoasts. John Piper regenerated the vision through the length of Britain – but darkened under a Second internationalising War.

The achievement of the Ruralists, against all the odds, has been to restore to pastoral vision a light of innocence. So they have raised a paradox sharper perhaps than any other challenge to the spread of communications and its levelling effect. The Ruralists' art returns yet again to the vitality of interior experience in dialogue with other private places of nature.

For the Ruralists and their creative forebears, the garden is not wholly made by men and women, even if they are artists. It lies rather in the Eden of private experience and memory to be uncovered and shared. Such gardens of the spirit, the Ruralists' art suggests, still hold real hope for our planet.

EPILOGUE

The turn of another century saw ever-increasing concentrations of multiplying populations in large towns and cities. The preponderance in every form of 'democracy' could give the government itself an appearance of moving against all that remains of country life. The nostalgia never far below the surface of English romance and British pragmatism began then to face in two opposite directions. One side embraced a 'look your last' despair that could become self-fulfilling. Another side forced the protest into organisations whose collectivising power could threaten to nullify any privacy of vision.

Can the traditional English combination of pragmatism with romance find a saving solution? The character of 'our island' has endured less by revolution than evolution. Already there are younger artists than the Ruralists seeking their ways to take up the challenge of continuing. It would be worse than folly for any government to try to stop them.

A stoppage of the country voice would mean stoppage of the voice of Eden itself – of innocence, with its hope in personal discovery and private illumination. That hope has defined western civilisation since its beginnings. No generation will willingly accept that all its achievement – its past – is writ on water.

Better to accept the past, to honour it as our first parent, and to seek in its genes a key to the only future which can hold true fulfilment.

Select Bibliography

Alexander, J.J.G., *Insular Manuscripts 6th to the 9th Century* (Harvey Miller, 1978)

Arnold, Graham: A Retrospective (Machynlleth: Tabernacle Cultural Centre, 1992)

Blake, Peter, *About Collage* (Tate Gallery Publishing, 2000)

Blake, Peter, Retrospective Exhibition catalogue, with the artist's 'Explanations & Thoughts toward my art exhibition', 'A selection of work in progress', etc. (Tate Gallery, 1983)

Blake's Engravings, William, with an introduction by Geoffrey Keynes (Faber, 1950)

Blake, Life of William, by Alexander Gilchrist (Dent: 'Everyman' revised ed, 1945)

Clark, Kenneth, *Landscape into Art* (Murray, 1949)

Craig, Edward Gordon, *The Mask. A [Monthly] Journal of the Art of the Theatre,* 1908-1929. Reprinted with an Introduction and Index by Lorelei Guidry (New York: Benjamin Blum, 1966-68)

Craig, Edward Gordon, *Woodcuts and Some Words* (Dent, 1924)

Craig, Edward Gordon, Index to the Story of My Days: Some Memoirs of, 1872-1907 (Hulton Press, 1957)

Craig, Edward Gordon, by Denis Bablet, trans Daphne Woodward (Heinemann, 1966)

Craig, Gordon: the Story of his Life, by Edward Anthony Craig (Gollancz, 1968)

Craxton, John: Paintings and Drawings, with text by Geoffrey Grigson (Horizon, 1948)

Gilpin, William, *Observations, relative to Picturesque Beauty... in... the Mountains, and Lakes of Cumberland and Westmoreland* (3rd ed: R. Blamire, 1792)

Griggs, F.L., 'An Artist Looks at Hitchin' (Hitchin: Reginald L. Hine, 1946). Originally published as 'Hitchin and Neighbourhood in the Nineties' (Hitchin & District Regional Survey Association, 1936)

[Griggs], *A Gothic Vision: F.L. Griggs and his Work,* by Francis Adams Comstock (Oxford: Ashmolean Museum, with Boston [U.S.A.] Public Library, 1966)

Griggs, F.L.: The Architecture of Dreams by Jerrold Northrop Moore (Oxford University Press, 1999)

Hussey, Christopher, *The Picturesque* (Putnam, 1927, reprinted Frank Cass, 1967)

Hyde, William, Articles in *Pall Mall Magazine:*
'A Sussex Valley in Spring' (XXIX, no 120: April 1903)
'Autumn near London' (XXXI, no 127: Nov 1903)
'The Thames at Night' (XXXIV, no 136: Oct 1904)
'Dover and Calais' (XXXVI, no 148: Aug 1905)
'An April Day on the Surrey Hills' (XXXIX, no 168: April 1907)

Inshaw, David, with text by Nicholas Usherwood (Academy Editions, 1978)

Linnell, David, *Blake, Palmer, Linnell and Co.* (Lewes, Sussex: Book Guild, 1994)

Mellor, David, *A Paradise Lost: The Neo-Romantic Imagination in Britain 1935-55* (Lund Humphries, 1987)

Minton, John, 'Speculations on Contemporary Painting', a Lecture delivered at the City of Birmingham College of Arts and Crafts on 25 June (City of Birmingham School of Printing, 1952)

Minton, John: 1917-1957. A Selective Retrospective, with essays by Frances Spalding and Rigby Graham Newtown (Davies Memorial Gallery, 1993)

[Minton] *Dance Till the Stars Come Down: A Biography of John Minton* by Frances Spalding (Hodder & Stoughton, 1991)

Nash, Paul, *Outline* (Faber, 1949)

[Nash] *Poet and Painter: Letters between Gordon Bottomley and Paul Nash 1910-1946,* ed Andrew Causey (Bristol: Redcliffe Press, 1990)

Nash, Paul: The Portrait of an Artist, by Anthony Bertram (Faber, 1955)

Nash, Paul, by Andrew Causey (Oxford University Press, 1980)

Nash, Paul: Modern Artist, Ancient Landscape, ed Jemima Montagu (Tate Publishing, 2003)

Neve, Christopher, *Unquiet Landscape: Places and Ideas in Twentieth-Century Painting* (Faber, 1990)

Oakeshott, Walter, *The Sequence of English Medieval Art* (Faber, 1950)

Ovenden, Graham, with essays by Victor Arwas, Clive Aslet, Laurie Lee, Robert Melville, & Clive Wainwright (Academy Editions, 1987)

Palmer's Sketch-book 1824, Samuel, facsimile, with introduction and commentary by Martin Butlin (Trianon Press, 1962). Another facsimile, also with introduction and commentary by Martin Butlin, was produced under the title *Samuel Palmer: The Sketchbook of 1824* (Thames & Hudson, in association with the William Blake Trust, 2005)

Palmer, Samuel, *An English Version of the Eclogues of Virgil, with illustrations by the Author;* with his essay 'Some Observations on the Country and on Rural Poetry' (Seeley, 1883)

Palmer, The Letters of Samuel, ed Raymond Lister (2 vols, Oxford University Press, 1974)

Palmer, Catalogue raisonné of the Works of Samuel, by Raymond Lister (Cambridge University Press, 1988)

Palmer, Samuel, A Catalogue of the Etchings of, with Introduction, Notes, Etc. by R.G. Alexander [with the help of F.L. Griggs] (Print Collectors' Club, 1937)

Palmer, Samuel: A Memoir by A.H. Palmer (Fine Art Society, 1882)

Palmer, The Life and Letters of Samuel, by A.H. Palmer (Seeley, 1892)

Palmer, Samuel, and other Disciples of William Blake. Catalogue of an Exhibition of Drawings, Etchings & Woodcuts [at the] Victoria and Albert Museum, with an Introduction and Notes by A.H. Palmer (London Board of Education, 1926)

Palmer, Samuel: The Visionary Years, by Geoffrey Grigson (Kegan Paul, 1947)

Palmer, Samuel, by Colin Harrison (Oxford: Ashmolean Museum, 1997)

Palmer, Samuel, 1805-1881: Vision and Landscape. Exhibition catalogue with essays by William Vaughan, Elizabeth E. Barker, Colin Harrison *et al* (British Museum Press, 2005)

Piper, John, *British Romantic Artists,* later incorporated in *Aspects of British Art,* with an Introduction by Michael Ayrton (Collins, 1947)

Piper, John, *Stained Glass: Art or Anti-Art* (Studio Vista, 1968)

Piper's Places: John Piper in England and Wales, by Richard Ingrams and John Piper (Chatto & Windus: The Hogarth Press, 1983)

Piper, John. Retrospective Exhibition catalogue (Tate Gallery, 1983)

[Piper,] Myfanwy Evans, ed, *The Painter's Object* (Gerald Howe, 1937)

Ruralists, The Brotherhood of, with text by Nicholas Usherwood (Lund Humphries, 1981)

'Ruralists, The Brotherhood of, and their friends in the Secret Garden', by Jane Brown, in *Hortus* 9 (Spring 1988)

Ruralists, The, ed Christopher Martin (Academy Editions, 1991)

Ruralists, The Brotherhood of: A Celebration, with essays by Peter Nahum, Jerrold Northrop Moore, and Laurie Lee (Bodmin, Cornwall: Ruralist Fine Art, 2003)

See also under individual artists' names: Arnold, Blake, Inshaw, Ovenden

Soby, James Thrall, *After Picasso* (New York: Dodd, Mead, 1935)

Sutherland, Graham, 'A Trend in English Draughtsmanship', in *Signature* 3 (July 1936)

Sutherland, Graham, 'Welsh Sketch-Book', in *Horizon* V no 28 (April 1942)

Sutherland, Graham, 'Thoughts on Painting', in *The Listener* 46 (6 Sept 1951)

Sutherland's Sketchbook, Graham, with an introduction and letters by the artist, and a List of Sketches (Marlborough Fine Art, 1973)

Sutherland, The Work of Graham, by Douglas Cooper (Lund Humphries, 1961)

Sutherland, Graham: A Biography, by Roger Berthoud (Faber 1982)

Sutherland, Graham, Inspirations, by Rosalind Thuillier (Guildford: Lutterworth Press, 1982)

Sutherland, Graham. Retrospective Exhibition catalogue, with text by Ronald Alley (Tate Gallery, 1982)

Vaughan, Keith, 'A View of English Painting', in *New Writing and Daylight* (Winter, 1943-44); reprinted in *Penguin New Writing* 31 (1947)

Vaughan, Keith, *Journals 1939-1977* (Murray, 1989)

Yorke, Malcolm, *The Spirit of Place: Nine Neo-Romantic artists and their times* (Constable, 1988)

INDEX

Page numbers in bold type refer to illustrations and captions

Abstraction, 87, 90, 136, 141, 151, 153, 158, 168, 173, 179, 183-187, 192, 193, 197, 207, 208
Adams, Gilbert, **167**
Adler, Jankl, 205
Alexander, Russell, 107, 109-110, 113, 115, 116
American Central Intelligence Agency, 208
'Ancients, The', 47, 64, 104, 146
Anderson, Stanley, 162
Anjou, King René of, 226
Arnold, Ann, **210-211,** 216, 217-220, 226-227, 230, 241, 243, **243,** 246-247, **247,** 249
Arnold, Charles, 212-213, 220
Arnold, Graham, 208, 209, **210-211,** 211-216, **214,** 219-220, 222, 226-227, **227,** 230, 242, 244, **244,** 246-249, **249**
Arnolfini Gallery, Bristol, 226
Ashbee, Charles Robert, 104
Ashton, Frederick, 187
Auden, W.H., 187, 195
Auerbach, Frank, 207
Ayrton, Michael, 195, 196-197, 199, 201, 203, 208

Bach, J.S., 132, 234
Bacon, Francis, 24
Balfour, Arthur, 90
Bamfylde, J.C., 63
Barbauld, Mrs, 232
Barley Splatt, 240-241, **241,** 249
Barret, George, 26
Barrie, J.M., *Peter Pan,* 95, 142
Barry, Kathleen – *see* Sutherland
Bates, H.E., 206
Bayes, Walter, 108
Beardsley, Aubrey, 82, 102-103, 127, 128, 162
Beatles, The, 229
Beaverbrook, Lord, 175
Beckenham Art School, 213, 216, 222
Beckford, William, 240
Beerbohm, Max, 133
Beethoven, Ludwig van, 30, 226
'Beggarstaff Brothers' – *see* William Nicholson and James Pryde
Bell, Clive, 144, 182, 198
Bell, Vanessa, 196
Belloc, Hilaire, 92, 96, 179
Benham, Ron, 216, 218
Bennett, Arnold, 150, 239
Beowulf, 11
Berman, Eugène, 197, **197**
Bertram, Anthony, 153
Betjeman, John, 153, 188, 192
Bewick, Thomas, 190
Bible, King James, 24
Binyon, Laurence, 163
Blackwood, William, 90-91
Blake, Jann – *see* Haworth
Blake, Daisy, **210-211,** 244
Blake, Juliette, **210-211, 242,** 243
Blake, Peter, **210-211,** 227-230, **230,** 236-237, 240, 241-246, **245**
Blake, William, 7, 13, **28, 35,** 130, **166, 171,** 230
influence on:
Craig, 125, 135
Griggs, 104, 108, 115
Hyde, 77, 81, 92, 94
Minton, 206, 207
Nash, 145, 155, 156
Palmer, 27-39, 42, 43, 44, 45, 46-48, 51, 59, 71
Piper, 186, 187, 188
Sutherland, 167-168, 170, 171
Bloomsbury, 15, 144, 151, 171, 182, 186, 196
Blunt, Anthony, 144
Britten, Benjamin, 187
Broadheath Brotherhood, 223, 226, 230, 244
Brown 'Capability', 18
Browne, Gordon, 126
Browne, Sir Thomas, 152
Browne, Theresa, 109, 110
Buhler, Robert, 214, 215
Bunyan, John, *Pilgrim's Progress,* 13, 16, 18, 21, 24, 30, 36, 56, 59, 143, 152
Burges, William, 100
Burke, Edmund, 16

Calvert, Edward, 46-48, **48,** 55, 60, 190
Camberwell School of Arts and Crafts, 199, 201, 206, 207
Cambridge 'Apostles', 144
Carfax Gallery, London, 147
Carroll, Lewis, *Through the Looking Glass,* 230, **230**
Cathach of St Columba, 10, **10**
Central School of Arts and Crafts, 207
Cézanne, Paul, 162, 174, 213
Chagall, Marc, 192
Chamberlain, Neville, 197
Chaucer, Geoffrey, *Canterbury Tales,* 14, 76
Chelsea College of Art, 166
Childe, Wilfred Rowland, 107, 110
Churchill, Winston, 148, 192, 205
Clark, Kenneth, 166, 171, **171,** 173, 174, 188, 189, 195, 200
Clark, Ruth, 153
Claude Lorrain, 16, **16,** 19, 23, 36-38, 42, 57, 59, 72, 78, 96, 139, 212, 232, 234
Claude-glass, 16, 17, 222
Cobbett, William, *Rural Rides,* 212
Cockerell, Sydney, 103
Coleridge, Samuel Taylor, 'Kubla Khan', 18-19, 26, 103
Collage, 156, 183, 185, 209, 223, 228-230, 244, **244**
Colquhoun, Robert, 200-201, **200,** 205, 208, 209
Communism, 186
Soviet, 211
Constable, Archibald, publishers, 86, 88, 90, 91-93, 96
Constable, John, 9, 12, 26, 72, 186, 190, 232
Cooke, George, 24, **25**
Cooper, Douglas, 170
Cope, Charles West, **62,** 63
Cornell, Joseph, 228
Cotman, John Sell, 189
Cowper, William, 24
Cox, David, 26
Craig, Edward Gordon, **2-3,** 7, **Chapter 4** and 144, 162, 170, 190, 215, 240
influence on:
Minton, 197
Nash, 141-142, 143, 145, 146, 147, 150-151
Piper, 184, 187
Crane, Walter, 129
Cranko, John, 187
Craxton, John, 174, 200-201, **200,** 208
Creswick, Thomas, 63, 68
Cubism, 15, 136, 141, 147, 168, 170, 174-175, 181, 182, 183, 186, 209
Curtis, A.C., **74-75,** 94
Cuyp, Aelbert, 212, 215

Danby, Francis, 88
Darwin, Charles, 11, 87
David, Gérard, 16
Defoe, Daniel, *Robinson Crusoe,* 60, **60,** 129, **129,** 131, 132, 138-139, **139**
Dent, J.M., publisher, 82-83, 128
Dickens, Charles, 24, 234
Digswell House and Arts Trust, 211, 216, 219, 220, 223
Doré, Gustave, 88
Dorynne, Jess, 129, 130-131, 184
Dowdeswell Gallery, London, 90
Drury, Alfred, 162, 164
Drury, Paul, 162, 164, 165
Drury, Ron, 222
Dulwich, 24, 30-33, 36, 39, 40, 44, 53, 55, 167, 250
Gallery, 26, 27, 30, 40, 212
Dumas, Alexandre, 131
Duncan, Isadora, 135
Durrow, Book of, **8,** 10-11, 12, 201
Dürer, Albrecht, 26, 29, 32, 35, 100, 108, 126
Duse, Eleanore, 135

Earlom, Richard, 22-23, 42
Eastop, Geoffrey, 193
Elek, Paul, publisher, 205
Elgar, Sir Edward, 7, 115, 120, 214, 218, 219, 220, 221, 223, 224, 226, 228, 233
Eliot, T.S., 220
Elizabeth II, Queen, Golden Jubilee, 14
Elizabeth, Queen (the Queen Mother), 14, 191
England, Church of, 12, 13-14, 22, 46, 99
Epsom College of Art, 162, 179, 218
Epstein, Jacob, 141
Etching Club, The, 62-64, 70, 86
Evans, D.H., stores, 196
Evans, Frederick H., 82, 86, 88, 96
Evans, Myfanwy – *see* Piper

Fantin-Latour, Henri, 96
Fascism, 196, 211
Festival of Britain, 1951, 175
Finberg, A.J., 111-112
Fitzgerald, F. Scott, 229
Forster, Edward Morgan, 144
Fournier, Alain, 206
Francesca, Piero della, 215
Freeth, Tom, 213
Freud, Lucian, 174, 200
Friedrich, Caspar David, 195, 232, 236
Fry, Roger, 15, 144, 182, 187, 198, 211
Futurism, 141

Gad & Keningale, etching printers, 64
Garnett, Constance, 82
Garnett, Edward, 82-86
Garnett, Olive, 84-85
Garnett, Richard, 82
George VI, King, 191
Gibson, May, 128
Gielgud, John, 197
Giles, Martha, 21
Gilmore, Ann – *see* Annie Ovenden
Gilpin, Rev William, 16-18, **17,** 19, 22, 24, 30, 42, 103, 188
Gimson, Ernest, 111, 117
Giraudoux, Jean, 197
Girtin, Thomas, 190
Godwin, Edward, 124, 126-127
Goethe, J.W. von, 126, 132

INDEX

Goldsmiths' College, 162-164, 174
'Gothick Revival', 12
Goulding, Frederick, 70, 108
Grafton Galleries, London, 144
Graham-Dixon, Andrew, 171
Grand Tour, 9
Granville-Barker, 138
Gravesend Art School, 228
Gray, Roger de, 214
Gray, Thomas, 107, 190
Greenwich, 24,75, 96
Gregory, Pope, 10
Grey, Sir Edward, 99
Griggs, Frederick Landseer, 19, **Chapter 3** and 123, 131, 139, 145, **146**, 149, 153, 168, 170, **180**, 190, 192, 195, 212, 241, 250
influence on:
Graham Arnold, 214
Inshaw, 224
Nash, 141, 146
Piper, 179-181, 184, 186, 188-189
Sutherland, 161, 162, 164-165
Griggs, Nina, 113, 115, 116, 120
Grigson, Geoffrey, 206, 214
Gross, Anthony, 196, **196**
Guild of Handicraft, 104

Haden, Seymour, 70, 77, 163
Hamerton, Philip Gilbert, 66, 70-71
Hamilton, Richard, 209, 229
Handel, George Frederick, *Acis and Galatea,* 133, **133**
Hardy, Thomas, 175, 218, 219, 220, 223, 224, 226, 239
Harrison, Colin, 42
Hartley, Eustace, 83, 84
Haworth, Jann, **210-211**, 229-230, 244-246
Haydn, Franz Joseph, 30, 190
Heine, Heinrich, 129
Henry VIII, King, 12, 58
Hepworth, Barbara, 153, 154, 184
Herkomer, Hubert von, 127-128, **127**, 132
Hewlett, Maurice, 95, 180
High Wycombe College of Art, 239
Highways and Byways County guides, 93, 102-108, **103, 105**, 110, 113, 146, **146**, 162, 179, 185
Hitchens, Ivon, 184
Hitler, Adolf, 195, 197, 211
Hofmannsthal, Hugo von, 135
Holding, Eileen – *see* Piper
Housman, A.E., 95, 120
Housman, Laurence, 77, 90
Howard, Diana, 224
Hueffer, Ford Madox, 79, 83, 85, 88, 90-93
Hunt, Bobby, 206
Hutchinson, publishers, 95
Hyde, Lydia, 93, 96
Hyde, William, **Chapter 2** and 99, 101, 131, 138, 141, 142, 149, 179, 192, 218

Ibsen, Henrik, 134
Peer Gynt, 132, **132**
Rosmersholm, 135
Impressionism, 55, 61, 82, 213
French, 15, 90, 250
Industrial Revolution, 13, 14, 28, 55, 57
Inshaw, David, **Frontispiece**, 29, **210-211**, 220-227, **225**, 230, 241, 244-247, **245**, 250
interlace illumination, **8**, 10-12, **10-12**, 185
Ironside, Robin, 199
Irving, Sir Henry, 125, 126-128, 129, 130
Isherwood, Christopher, 187

James, Henry, 115, 250
Jefferies, Richard, 213, 218, 219, 220
Jewson, Norman, 117, 120
Job, Book of, 21, 35, **35**, 36, 47, 187, **187**, 188
John, Augustus, 141
Johnson, Martin, 241, **241**
Joseph, Michael, publisher, 206

Keats, John, 32, 101
Kells, Book of, 12, **12**
Kennington, Eric, 143
Kensington Gardens, 88, **89**, 95, 142, 161, 236
Kessler, Count Harry, 134-135, 138
Kestleman, Maurice, 182
Ketelby, Albert, 233, 235
Kingston Polytechnic, 219, 220, 222, 223
Kipling, Rudyard, 83

Lambeth Bible, **45**
Lambeth School of Art, 77, 84, 94
Lamont, Edith, 196, 206
Landowska, Wanda, 234
Lane, John, 82
Lee, Laurie, 242
Lefevre Gallery, London, 207, 208
Lehmann, John, 200, 205, **205**, 206
Leyden, Lucas van, 30
Lindisfarne Gospels, 11-12, **11**
Linnell, Hannah – *see* Palmer
Linnell, John, 25-32, **26, 27**, 35, **35**, 36, 44, 46, 48, 51-53, 56-59, 61-62
Liszt, Franz, 220
London
County Council School, Bolt Lane, Fleet Street, 143
East End, 234-235, 240
Lorrain, Claude – *see* Claude
Lucas, E.V., 82
MacBryde, Robert, 200-201, 205, 208, 209
Macmillan & Co, publishers, 93, 102, 104, 161, 162
MacNeice, Louis, 206
Mallows, C.E., 101
Malory, Sir Thomas, *Le Morte d'Arthur,* 82, 100, 115, 120, 128
Manet, Edouard, 186
Mantegna, Andrea, 29
Margate, Kent, 21, 22, 24, 64, 71
Marlborough Galleries, London, 175
Marriott, Frederick, 162
Marsh, Edward, 148
Martin, John, 88, 231
Marvell, Andrew, 177
Masaccio, 215
Matisse, Henri, 162, 174, 192
Maugham, Somerset, 175
Melville, Robert, 174
Meredith, George, 82, 86-87, 90, 93
Meryon, Charles, 100, 107
Meynell, Alice, 90
Michelangelo, 27, 29, 41, 51
Middleton, Michael, 197-200, 205
Millais, John Everett, 246
Millard, Patrick, 196
Millard, Walter, 100, 101
Milton, John, 18, 19, 24, 45, 50, 62-64, 67-72, 80, 83-84, 94, 189
Minton, John, 174, **Chapter 8** and 211, 235
influence on Graham Arnold, 214-215, 219
Minton, Richard, 196, 198, 199, 205
Mondrian, Piet, 184
Monet, Claude, 250
Moore, G.E., 144
Moore, Henry, 153, 154, 166, 174, 184, 198, 200
Morley College, 184
Morley, John, 222, 224
Morris, Henry, 211, 216
Morris, William, 100, 103, 104
Mortimer, John, 246
Mortimer, Raymond, 174, 198-199
Muir, Nina – *see* Griggs
Mulready, William, 25, 26, 27
Murray, John, publisher, 93
Mussolini, Benito, 211

Nash, John, 142, 148, 150
Nash, Margaret, 147, 148, 149-151, 153, 155
Nash, Paul, 7, **Chapter 5** and 161, 170, 173, 179, 184, 187, 192, 250
influence on:
Graham Arnold, 214, 226
Graham Ovenden, 236
Inshaw, 224, 244
Minton, 203
Piper, 181, 182, 189
Sutherland, 165-169, 177
Neo-Romanticism, 174, **Chapter 8** and 211
Nevinson, Christopher Richard, 148-149, **149**
Newton, Sir Isaac, 24, **166**, 167-168
Nicholson, Ben, 153, 154, 183, 184, 187
Nicholson, William, 128-130, **129**, 133
Nietzsche, Friedrich, 132
Nott, Peter, 224

Odeh, Margaret – *see* Nash
'Orwell, George', 186
Osborne, Malcolm, 162
Ovenden, Annie, **210-211**, 230, 237-243, **242**, 245, 246-247, 249, **249**
Ovenden, Emily, **210-211**, 249
Ovenden, Graham, 44, **210-211**, 229, 230-244, **231, 234, 235, 237, 241, 242**, 245, 246-247, **248**, 249
Ovenden, Ned, **210-211**, 239, 241, 242, 249

Pall Mall Magazine, 93-94
Palmer, Alfred Herbert, 45, 58, 62, 70-72, 99, 120
Palmer, Hannah, 56-59, 61-62, 66, 69, 71-72
Palmer, Samuel, 7, 12, 19, **Chapter 1** and 75, 78, 81, 83, 97, 123, 127, 131, 132, 137, 139, 162, **163**, 179, 190, 218, 250
influence on:
Graham Arnold, 214, 215
Graham Ovenden, 232, 236
Griggs, 99, 100, 102, 103, 104, 106, 107, 108, 120
Inshaw, 221, 223, 224, 244
Minton, 196, 198, 201, 203, 205, 206, 207
Nash, 142, 147, 150, 154, 156, 158
Piper, 181, 182, 183, 184, 187, 189, 193
Sutherland, 163-171, 174, 175
Palmer, Thomas More, 58, 66
Parker, Agnes Miller, 213
Pascal, Blaise, 24
Payne, Richard Knight, 24
Pelagius, 10, 13
Pellew, Claughton, 144, 147
Penguin New Writing, 200, 205, **205**
Pennell, Joseph, 102, 180
photogravure, **76, 78, 79**, 82, **82-90**, 94
Picasso, Pablo, 136, 174, 184, 185, 197, 205
Guernica, 155, 168, 171, 172, 198
'Picturesque', 13, 16-19, 24, 189, 192, 215
Pilgrim's Progress – *see* Bunyan
Piper, Eileen, 182, 184

Piper, John, 57, 155, 159, 162, 174, **Chapter 7** and 195, 196, 198, 200, 217, 250
influence on Graham Arnold, 214
Piper, Myfanwy Evans, 155, 184-185, 186, 187
Piranesi, Giovanni Battista, 107
Plato, 50
Pop Art, 131, 209, 222, 223, 229, 247
Post-Impressionism, 144, 190, 198
Pre-Raphaelites, 9, 26, 61, 190, 211, 224, 245
Price, Uvedale, 24
Pryde, James, 128-130, **129**
Pugin, Augustus N.W., 241
Purcell Operatic Society, 132-134
Pyle, Howard, 126

Rachmaninov, Sergei, 213
Rackham, Arthur, 94, 95, 162, 174
Raphael, 27, 41
Read, Herbert, 150, 182, 198
Read, John, 245
Redgrave, Richard, 63
Reinhardt, Max, 137
Rembrandt, 100, 234
Repton, Humphrey, 18
Reynolds, Sir Joshua, 195
Reyntiens, Patrick, 192
Richmond College, 182
Richmond, George, 26, 47-48, **48,** 52, 56, 63, 64, 69, 146
Richmond, Sir William Blake, 146
Rimbaud, Arthur, 205
Rogers, Kate, 84
Rogers, Richard, 218
Romney Marsh, 78-79, 83-86, 141, 151, 153, 179, 183
Ross, Alan, 206
Rothenstein, William, 144, 147
Rothschild family, 238
Rouault, Georges, 192
Royal Academy, 78, 96, 120
Schools, 25, 222, 223
Summer Exhibitions, 44, 101, 242, 244
Varnishing Day, 164
Royal College of Art, 182, 207, 208, 214-215, 219, 227, 228, 229, 236-237, 239
Royal Society of Painter-Etchers, 163, 165
Royal Society of Painters in Water Colours, 59
Ruralists, The Brotherhood of, **Chapter 9**
definition, 242
see also individual members: Arnold, Ann; Arnold, Graham; Blake, Peter; Haworth, Jann; Inshaw, David; Ovenden, Annie; Ovenden, Graham
Ruskin, John, 61, 180, 182, 196, 220
Ruysdael, Jacob, 51, 87
Ryder, Albert, 96

St John's Wood Art School, 196
Sambourne, Linley, 127, **127**
Santayana, George, 7, 13-14, 15, 190
Sardou, Victorien, 129
Schwitters, Kurt, 228
Sellars, James, 235-237
Serlio, Sebastiano, 134, 135, **135**
7 & 5 Society, 183, 185, 186-187
Shakespeare, William, 7, 14, 40, 63-64, 123, **123,** 126, 128-129, **129,** 134, **134,** 137-138, 189
Shaw, Martin, 132
Shell Guides, 153, 166, **166,** 169, 188
Shelley, Percy Bysshe, 95
Shoreham, Kent, 40, 44-48, 51-59, 62, 64, 163, 167, 174, 190, 196, 211, 214, 221, 236, 250
Sickert, Walter Richard, 196
Sitwell family, 187, 192
Slade School of Art, 104, 144, 146, 162, 211, 229
Smetham, James, 190
Smith, Mrs Bernhard, 163
Soby, James Thrall, 197
Society for the Protection of Ancient Buildings, 100, 103
Society of Wood Engravers, 138
Southampton College of Art, 235, 236
Sparkes, John C.L., 77, 84
Spear, Ruskin, 214, 215
Spencer, Stanley, 196, 209
Spender, Stephen, 187
Spenser, Edmund, *Faerie Queene,* 59
Stanislavski, Constantine, 124, 137
'Stepniak', 82
Stevenson, Robert Louis, 82, 131
Stockham, Alfred, 223, 225
Stravinsky, Igor, 214
Street, George Edmund, 100
Studio, The, 111
Stump-work embroidery, 22, **22,** 32, 34, 42, 44, 46, 49, 51, 53, 55, 56, 61, 62, 66, 170, 175, 224
Sullivan, E.J., 162
Surrealism, 124, 131, 141, 151, 153, 158, 166, 173, 183, 186, 197, 226, 250
Sutherland, Graham, 19, **Chapter 6** and 179, 181, 189, 192, 195, 198, 200, 235, 250
influence on Minton, 201, 203
Sutherland, Kathleen, 162, 165, 166, 174

Tate Gallery, 163, 208, 247
Tatham, Frederick, 45, 47
Tchelitchew, Pavel, 197
Telfer, Ann – *see* Arnold
Telfer, Dr Edmund, 217, 242
Terry, Ellen, 124, 125-129, 132, 134
Thomas, Dylan, 3, 172
Thomas, Edward, 218
Thompson, Lawson, 100
Thomson, James, 19, 30
Thornton, Dr Robert, 28
Tonks, Henry, 104, 144, 146, 162, 211
Toulouse-Lautrec, Henri de, 129
Townsend, H.J., 63
Tree, Herbert Beerbohm, 137
Trevelyan, G.M., 116
Turner, Charles, **23**
Turner, J.M.W., 9, 12, 15, 23, **23,** 24, **25,** 26, 32, 42, 62, 72, 78, 87, 171, 186, 190, 232

'Unit One', 153
Valpy, Leonard Rowe, 67-68, 71
Varley, John, 25
Van Gogh, Vincent, 174, 215
Vaughan, Henry, 14-15, 168
Vaughan, Keith, 205, **205,** 207, 208-209, 229
Vaughan Williams, Ralph, 187
Verrico, Eric, 206
Virgil, 19, 28-29, 31, 32, 34, 35, 38, 45, 170, 171, **171**
Eclogues, 28, 47, 71-72, 99, 100
Georgics, 42, 43, 66
Vorticism, 141, 147, 148, 149, 151

Wagner, Richard, 126, 132
Walker, Emery, 103
Wallis, Barnes, 230
Wars, world
First, 9, 87, 96, 99, 107, 109, 113, 141, 148-150, 168, 173, 183, 186, 250
Second, 155-156, 161, 172, 173-174, 179, 195, 197-200, 205, 211, 212, 217, 228, 250
Wate, William, 23
Watson, Peter, 200, 205
Watts, George Frederick, 212
Waugh, Evelyn, 192
Webb, Philip, 103, 131
Weight, Carel, 214
Wellington, Robert, 166-167, 187
West, Anthony, 187
West of England College of Art, 223
Whistler, James McNeill, 70, 90, 100, 163
Whitman, Walt, 49, 130, 131
Wilde, Oscar, 82, 128, 147
Wilenski, R.H., 198
Wittenham Clumps, 146-147, **146-147,** 148, 153, 156-159, 167, 179, 187, 224, 244
Wordsworth, William, 7, 14, 26, 28, 103, 220
Wrightson, Hay, **98-99**

Yeats, William Butler, 136
Yellow Book, The, 82, 128
Young, Edward, 21
Young, G.M., 55

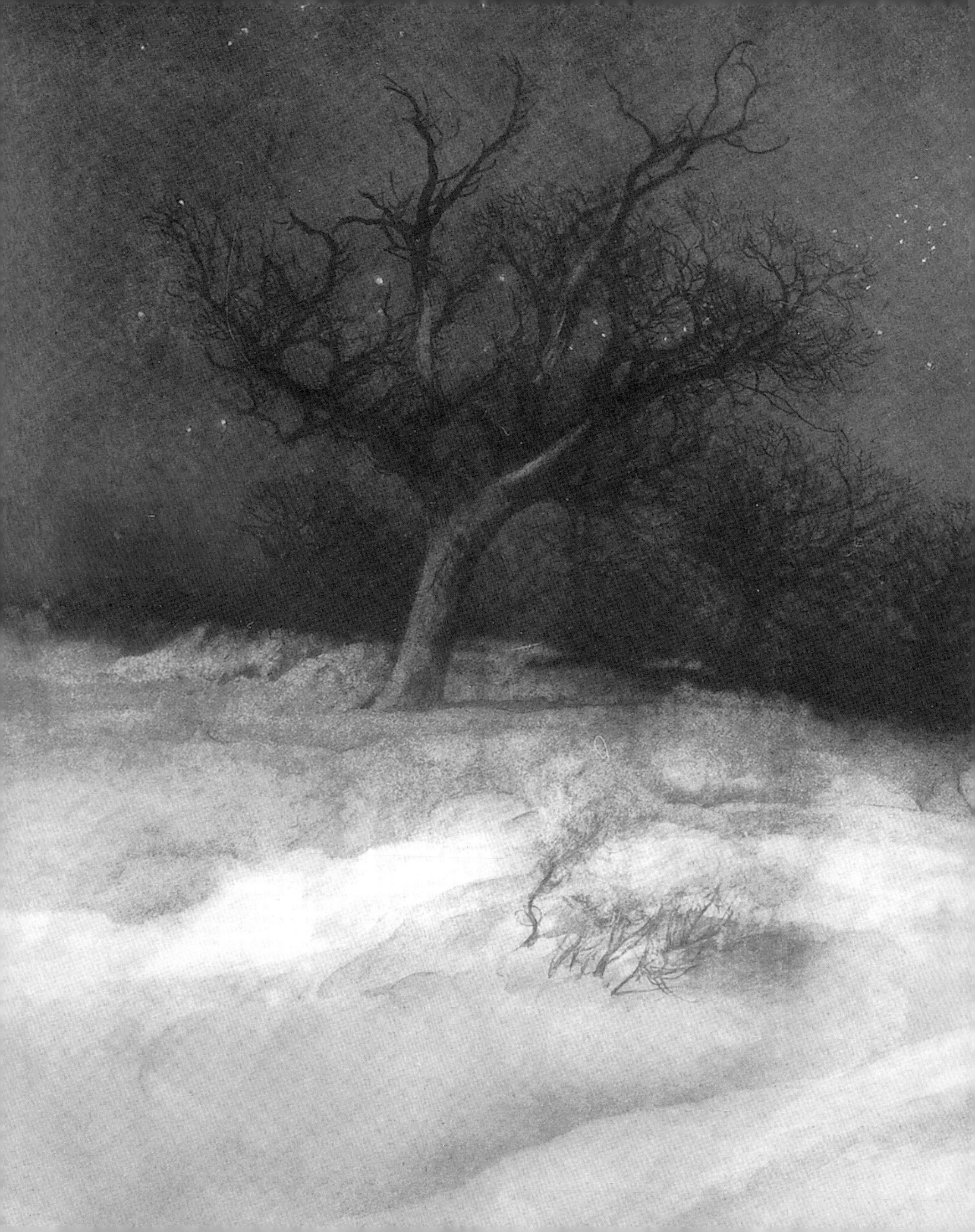